£3·50

CW00495158

THE PERILOUS CROWN

MUNRO PRICE was born in London, and was educated there and in Cambridge, where he took his PhD. He specializes in eighteenth and early nineteenth-century France, and has lived and taught in Lyon and Paris. He is currently Professor of Modern European in History at the University of Bradford. His previous, critically acclaimed book, *The Fall of the French Monarchy*, won the Franco-British Society's Literary Prize and was shortlisted for the Longman-*History Today* Prize.

ALSO BY MUNRO PRICE

Preserving the Monarchy:
The Comte de Vergennes, 1774–1787

Louis XVI and the Comte de Vergennes:
Correspondence 1774–1787
(Edited with John Hardman)

The Fall of the French Monarchy

MUNRO PRICE

THE PERILOUS CROWN

France Between Revolutions

PAN BOOKS

For Simon and Antonia Cox

First published 2007 by Macmillan

First published in paperback 2008 by Pan Books
an imprint of Pan Macmillan Ltd
Pan Macmillan, 20 New Wharf Road, London N1 9RR
Basingstoke and Oxford
Associated companies throughout the world
www.panmacmillan.com

ISBN 978-0-330-42638-1

1 3 5 7 9 8 6 4 2

A CIP catalogue record for this book is available from
the British Library.

Typeset by SetSystems Ltd, Saffron Walden, Essex
Printed and bound in the UK by
CPI Mackays, Chatham ME5 8TD

Visit *www.panmacmillan.com* to read more about all our books
and to buy them. You will also find features, author interviews and
news of any author events, and you can sign up for e-newsletters
so that you're always first to hear about our new releases.

'You need perils. They are titles to the crown.'

Adolphe Thiers to Adélaïde d'Orléans,
30 July 1830

PHOTOGRAPHIC ACKNOWLEDGEMENTS

Archives de France, Paris — 28, 29.
Bibliothèque Nationale de France (Cabinet des Estampes) — 7, 19, 21, 22, 23, 26, 27.
Bridgeman Art Library — 1 (Wolverhampton Art Gallery), 2 (Château de Versailles),
    3 (Musée Condé, Chantilly), 4 (Château de Versailles), 5 (Hôtel de Beauharnais,
    Paris), 6 (Musée des Beaux-Arts, Dunkirk), 8 (Bibliothèque Nationale de France),
    10 (Musée Carnavalet, Paris), 11 (Private Collection), 12 (Château de Versailles),
    15 (Musée Condé, Chantilly), 18 (Château de Versailles), 20 (Musée Condé,
    Chantilly), 24 (Private Collection), 32 & 33 (Musée Carnavalet, Paris).
The Metropolitan Museum of Art — 16 (purchase, Rogers and Fletcher Funds, and
    Mary Wetmore Shively Bequest, in memory of her husband, Henry L. Shively
    M.D., 1965 (65.14.5), photograph © 1980 The Metropolitan Museum of Art).
RMN — 13 & 14 (photos © RMN / all rights reserved).
Roger-Viollet — 25, 30, 31.
The Royal Collection — 17 (© 2005 Her Majesty Queen Elizabeth II).

CONTENTS

ACKNOWLEDGEMENTS

In researching and writing this book I have incurred substantial debts of gratitude to individuals and institutions both in France and England. I must first thank Mgr le comte de Paris for his permission to consult the Archives de la Maison de France held in the Archives Nationales, which have formed my most important source. I am also very grateful to the British Academy for the award of a Research Readership for 2004–06, without which the book could not have been written.

Two further archival sources have been very important to my work. The comte de Bryas very kindly allowed me to consult the remarkable correspondence between his ancestor Marshal Gérard on the one hand, and Louis-Philippe, his son the duc d'Orléans, and his sister Adélaïde on the other. The duc d'Ayen generously gave me access to the immensely rich papers of his ancestor comte Molé. I owe both these introductions to the marquis de Breteuil, and once again find myself much in his debt. I was also given much helpful guidance to the Molé papers by their archivist, Florence de Peyronnet.

At the Archives Nationales, M. Bruno Galland, Director of the CHAN, was always a source of friendly advice and assistance. I am also grateful to M. Jean Pouessel of the Archives Privées for help with consulting the Archives de la Maison de France, and to M. Luc Requier of the Communications Department for photographs of objects in the Musée de l'Histoire de France. The staff of the Cabinet de Estampes at the Bibliothèque Nationale also kindly provided important photographs at short notice.

On a practical level, it would have been impossible to spend so much time in Paris researching for the book without a roof over my head. For help in providing this I am very grateful to Bertrand Rosenthal and Laure de Gramont.

In London, I owe much to the helpfulness and efficiency of the staff of the British Library, and especially the London Library.

For comments on drafts of chapters I thank Dr Philip Mansel,

Professor Pamela Pilbeam, Lady Antonia Fraser and Stanley Price. For other advice on points of research I am indebted to Dr Robert Tombs, Professor Hugh Brogan, Doña Gerarda de Orléans, Lord Thomas of Swynnerton, Ricardo Mateos, Steven Clay, Thibaut Trétout, Dr Emma Barker and Philippe Godoy. As ever, Andrew Lownie was an excellent friend and agent. I am also grateful to the staff of the Chapelle Royale at Dreux for a fascinating tour, to Howard Farrar, Development Director of Claremont Fan Court School, for kindly taking an afternoon to show me round Louis-Philippe's last place of exile, and to Anthony Klugman, who shared the driving on these trips.

At Macmillan my editor, Georgina Morley, has provided encouragement and good advice throughout. Finally, the patience and eye for detail of the book's production team – Georgina Difford, Sue Phillpott for the copyediting, and Josine Meijer for the illustrations – have added considerable polish to the original.

Dramatis Personae

LOUIS-ANTOINE, DUC D'ANGOULÊME (1775–1844). Eldest son of the comte d'Artois, later Charles X. Heir to the French throne from 1824 to 1830.

MARIE-THÉRÈSE, DUCHESSE D'ANGOULÊME (1778–1851). The only child of Louis XVI and Marie Antoinette to survive the French Revolution. Married her cousin the duc d'Angoulême in 1799.

HENRI, DUC D'AUMALE (1822–97). Ninth child of Louis-Philippe and Marie-Amélie; a capable soldier and a considerable collector. Married *Maria Carolina of Naples* in 1844.

ODILON BARROT (1791–1873). Lawyer, deputy, and Prefect of the Seine from 1830 to 1831. Throughout the July monarchy, leader of the loyal opposition, the 'dynastic left', in the Chamber of Deputies.

CHARLES-FERDINAND, DUC DE BERRY (1778–1820). Second son of the comte d'Artois, later Charles X. The only offspring of the elder Bourbon branch to have children.

MARIA CAROLINA, DUCHESSE DE BERRY (1798–1870). Daughter of Ferdinand I of the Naples; married the duc de Berry in 1816.

ADÈLE, COMTESSE DE BOIGNE (1781–1866). Close to the court under the Bourbon restoration and especially the July monarchy; mistress (and possibly the secret wife) of Chancellor Pasquier, and one of the greatest memoir-writers of the nineteenth century.

PRINCE LOUIS-NAPOLEON BONAPARTE (1808–73). Napoleon's nephew, and his heir after the Duke of Reichstadt's death. In December 1848 elected President of the French Second Republic, which he overthrew in a coup d'état in December 1851, proclaiming himself the Emperor Napoleon III the following year.

HENRI, DUC DE BORDEAUX; after the mid-1830s known as the COMTE DE CHAMBORD (1820–83). Posthumous son of the duc de Berry. From the 1830 revolution to his death in 1883, the rightful King of France – 'Henri V' – to supporters of the elder Bourbon branch.

ACHILLE-LÉON-VICTOR, DUC DE BROGLIE (1785–1870). Scion of a famous noble family; father guillotined during the Reign of Terror. A member of the liberal opposition under the Bourbon restoration, and like his friend Guizot a leader of the *doctrinaire* group. Under the July monarchy, prime minister from 1835 to 1836, and a supporter of the policy of *résistance*.

THOMAS-ROBERT BUGEAUD, MARSHAL OF FRANCE (1784–1849). Rose through the ranks in the Napoleonic wars; a firm supporter of the July monarchy, and Governor-General of Algeria from 1840 to 1847.

ELIE, DUC DECAZES (1788–1860). Centrist politician under the Bourbon restoration, and favourite of Louis XVIII. Minister of police from 1815 to 1818, and prime minister from 1819 to 1820.

ANDRÉ-MARIE DUPIN (1783–1865). Lawyer and liberal deputy under the Bourbon restoration, and a leading figure in the 1830 revolution. A close friend of Louis-Philippe and Adélaïde, and their legal adviser. President of the Chamber of Deputies from 1832 to 1840.

FÉLICITÉ, COMTESSE DE GENLIS (1746–1830). Author, educationalist and disciple of Rousseau; tutor to Louis-Philippe, Adélaïde and their two brothers, and their father's mistress. Louis-Philippe later claimed she had been his only love.

ETIENNE-MAURICE, COMTE GÉRARD, MARSHAL OF FRANCE (1773–1852). Napoleonic general, prominent in the Waterloo campaign; liberal opposition deputy under the Bourbon restoration. Close to both Louis-Philippe and Adélaïde; prime minister under the July monarchy in 1834, and commander of the Paris National Guard from 1838 to 1842.

FRANÇOIS GUIZOT (1787–1874). Historian, deputy and one of the dominant political figures of the July monarchy. Foreign minister from 1840 to 1847, and prime minister from 1847 to 1848.

FRANÇOIS, PRINCE DE JOINVILLE (1818–1900). Seventh child of Louis-Philippe and Marie-Amélie, who made his career in the navy until 1848. Married *Francisca of Bragança*, daughter of the Emperor of Brazil, in 1843.

AUGUSTE-FRÉDÉRIC VIESSE DE MARMONT, MARSHAL OF FRANCE (1774–1852). One of Napoleon's youngest marshals, whose defection to the Emperor's enemies in 1814 led directly to his abdication. Rallied to the restored Bourbons, but his reputation never recovered.

LOUIS-MATHIEU, COMTE MOLÉ (1781–1855). From a prominent family of magistrates; father guillotined during the Reign of Terror. Minister of justice under Napoleon from 1813 to 1814. Minister of the marine in the duc de Richelieu's government from 1817 to 1818. Prime minister under the July monarchy from 1836 to 1839, pursuing a moderate centrist policy.

CAMILLE BACHASSON, COMTE DE MONTALIVET (1801–80). Son of Napoleon's minister of the interior, a close friend and confidant of Louis-Philippe, and later his executor. Himself minister of the interior under the July monarchy in 1830–1831, 1832, 1836, and 1837–39. Also intendant-general of the civil list in 1830, 1832–36, 1836–37 and 1839–48.

MÉLANIE, COMTESSE DE MONTJOIE (d.1848). Adélaïde's closest friend, and her lady-in-waiting since 1808.

ANTOINE, DUC DE MONTPENSIER (1824–90). Tenth child of Louis-Philippe and Marie-Amélie; married the sister of the Queen of Spain, the *Infanta Luisa*, in 1846.

ADOLPHE-EDOUARD MORTIER, MARSHAL OF FRANCE (1768–1835). A competent rather than brilliant soldier in the Revolutionary and Napoleonic wars, but honourable and universally liked. A good friend of Louis-Philippe, and his prime minister in 1834–35.

GEORGES MOUTON, COMTE DE LOBAU, MARSHAL OF FRANCE (1770–1838). A talented Napoleonic general, and later a pillar of the July monarchy. Commander of the Paris National Guard from 1830 until his death in 1838.

LOUIS, DUC DE NEMOURS (1814–96). Fourth child of Louis-Philippe and Marie-Amélie; married *Victoria of Saxe-Coburg* in 1840.

FERDINAND-PHILIPPE, DUC D'ORLÉANS (1810–42). Eldest son of Louis-Philippe and Marie-Amélie, and the hope of the Orléans dynasty.

HÉLÈNE, DUCHESSE D'ORLÉANS (1814–58). Daughter of the Prince of Mecklenburg-Schwerin; married the duc d'Orléans in 1837.

LOUISE D'ORLÉANS (1812–50). Second child of Louis-Philippe and Marie-Amélie; married *King Leopold I of the Belgians* in 1832, founding the present Belgian royal family.

MARIE D'ORLÉANS (1813–39). Third child of Louis-Philippe and Marie-Amélie and a talented artist and sculptor. Married *Duke Alexander of Württemberg* in 1837.

CLÉMENTINE D'ORLÉANS (1817–1907). Sixth child of Louis-Philippe and Marie-Amélie. Highly intelligent and highly political; married *Prince Augustus of Saxe-Coburg* in 1843. Their son Ferdinand became the first King of Bulgaria.

ETIENNE DENIS, DUC PASQUIER, CHANCELLOR OF FRANCE (1767–1862). From a famous family of magistrates; father guillotined during the Reign of Terror. Prefect of Police under Napoleon and foreign minister under the Bourbon restoration from 1819 to 1822. President of the Chamber of Peers throughout the July monarchy, and created Chancellor of France in 1837.

CASIMIR PÉRIER (1777–1832). Prominent banker and liberal deputy under the Bourbon restoration, playing a key role in the 1830 revolution. As prime minister under the July monarchy from 1831 to 1832, a champion of the policy of *résistance* against further concessions to the left.

JULES, PRINCE DE POLIGNAC (1780–1847). Leading ultra-royalist and close friend of Charles X. French ambassador to London from 1823 to 1829, and prime minister from 1829 to 1830.

NAPOLEON FRANCIS CHARLES, DUKE OF REICHSTADT (1811–32). The only legitimate child of Napoleon I, by his second wife Marie-Louise of Austria. Napoleon II to Bonapartists but never reigned; died in Vienna aged twenty-one.

ARMAND-EMMANUEL DU PLESSIS, DUC DE RICHELIEU (1766–1822). Leader of the political centre-right during the Bourbon restoration; prime minister from 1815 to 1818, and again from 1820 to 1821.

HORACE, COMTE SÉBASTIANI, MARSHAL OF FRANCE (1772–1851). Talented Napoleonic general and diplomat, and liberal opposition deputy under the Bourbon restoration. Close friend and confidant of Louis-Philippe and Adélaïde; foreign minister under the July monarchy from 1830 to 1832, and French ambassador to London from 1835 to 1840.

NICOLAS JEAN-DE-DIEU SOULT, MARSHAL OF FRANCE (1769–1852). One of Napoleon's most famous commanders, and his chief of staff at the battle of Waterloo. A shrewd politician as well as soldier, and Louis-Philippe's prime minister from 1840 to 1847.

CHARLES-MAURICE, PRINCE DE TALLEYRAND (1754–1838). Veteran diplomat and statesman; bishop under the old régime, politician during the Revolution, and foreign minister from 1797 to 1807. A friend of Louis-Philippe's, he played an important role in the 1830 revolution, subsequently filling the key post of French ambassador to London from 1830 to 1834.

ADOLPHE THIERS (1797–1877). Journalist, historian, and after Talleyrand France's greatest political survivor of the period. One of Louis-Philippe's most influential supporters during the 1830 revolution. Prime minister under the July monarchy in 1836 and 1840, he ended as the founder of the Third Republic.

JOSEPH, COMTE DE VILLÈLE (1773–1854). Wily ultra-royalist politician under the Bourbon restoration; prime minister from 1822 to 1828.

HOUSE OF
BOURBON

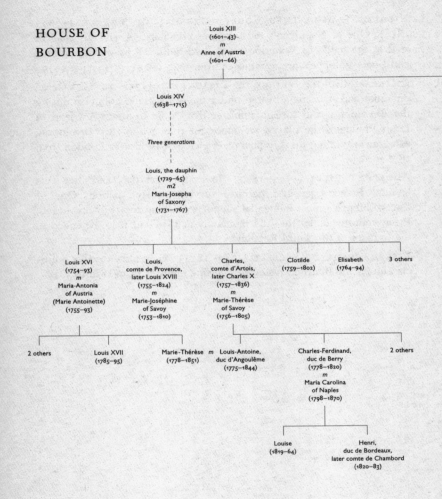

Louis XIII
(1601–43)
m
Anne of Austria
(1601–66)

Louis XIV
(1638–1715)

Three generations

Louis, the dauphin
(1729–65)
m2
Maria-Josepha
of Saxony
(1731–1767)

Louis XVI
(1754–93)
m
Maria-Antonia
of Austria
(Marie Antoinette)
(1755–93)

Louis,
comte de Provence,
later Louis XVIII
(1755–1824)
m
Marie-Joséphine
of Savoy
(1753–1810)

Charles,
comte d'Artois,
later Charles X
(1757–1836)
m
Marie-Thérèse
of Savoy
(1756–1805)

Clotilde
(1759–1802)

Elisabeth
(1764–94)

3 others

2 others

Louis XVII
(1785–95)

Marie-Thérèse
(1778–1851)

m   Louis-Antoine,
duc d'Angoulême
(1775–1844)

Charles-Ferdinand,
duc de Berry
(1778–1820)
m
Maria Carolina
of Naples
(1798–1870)

2 others

Louise
(1819–64)

Henri,
duc de Bordeaux,
later comte de Chambord
(1820–83)

HOUSE OF
BOURBON
(ORLÉANS)

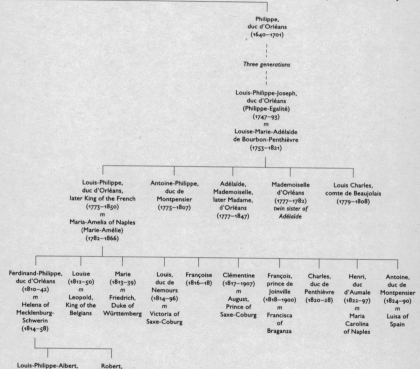

Philippe,
duc d'Orléans
(1640–1701)

Three generations

Louis-Philippe-Joseph,
duc d'Orléans
(Philippe-Egalité)
(1747–93)
m
Louise-Marie-Adélaïde
de Bourbon-Penthièvre
(1753–1821)

Louis-Philippe,
duc d'Orléans,
later King of the French
(1773–1850)
m
Maria-Amelia of Naples
(Marie-Amélie)
(1782–1866)

Antoine-Philippe,
duc de
Montpensier
(1775–1807)

Adélaïde,
Mademoiselle,
later Madame,
d'Orléans
(1777–1847)

Mademoiselle
d'Orléans
(1777–1782)
twin sister of
Adélaïde

Louis Charles,
comte de Beaujolais
(1779–1808)

Ferdinand-Philippe,
duc d'Orléans
(1810–42)
m
Helena of
Mecklenburg-
Schwerin
(1814–58)

Louise
(1812–50)
m
Leopold,
King of the
Belgians

Marie
(1813–39)
m
Friedrich,
Duke of
Württemberg

Louis,
duc de
Nemours
(1814–96)
m
Victoria of
Saxe-Coburg

Françoise
(1816–18)

Clémentine
(1817–1907)
m
August,
Prince of
Saxe-Coburg

François,
prince de
Joinville
(1818–1900)
m
Francisca
of
Braganza

Charles,
duc de
Penthièvre
(1820–28)

Henri,
duc
d'Aumale
(1822–97)
m
Maria
Carolina
of Naples

Antoine,
duc de
Montpensier
(1824–90)
m
Luisa of
Spain

Louis-Philippe-Albert,
comte de Paris
(1838–94)

Robert,
duc de Chartres
(1840–1910)

INTRODUCTION

> We are not savages who have arrived naked on the banks of
> the Orinoco to found a society. We are an old nation, per-
> haps too old for this era. We have an established govern-
> ment, an established king, established prejudices. We must,
> as far as possible, blend all these things with the Revolution,
> to ease the shock of the transition.[1]

THESE WORDS OF the great orator Mirabeau to the National
Assembly in the first year of the French Revolution were not
only profound, but prophetic. Throughout the nineteenth century
– and even, it could be argued, up to the present day – France's
history has been defined by the struggle to reconcile the traditional values of which Mirabeau spoke, and the legacy of the
Revolution. Of these traditional values, the most central was monarchy. For almost half a century after the Revolution, France
struggled to forge a compromise between this ancient principle
and the ideals of 1789, and create a formula for political stability.
Even so, the period was punctuated by a further dramatic revolution, in July 1830, making this search all the more urgent. It is
no coincidence that just after that upheaval, Victor Hugo reread
Mirabeau's speech, and quoted it with approval in his journal.[2]
   Although crucial to the formation of modern France, this era
is very little known on this side of the Channel. Between the
twin peaks of Napoleon and the *belle époque*, even the well
informed sense only a confusing age of shifting regimes, revolutions and the occasional coup d'état. Yet the period between 1814
and 1848 has both coherence and considerable relevance to British
history and politics. From the restoration of Louis XVIII to the
French throne, to the overthrow of Louis-Philippe in the revolution of February 1848, France's political system drew closer to
that of Britain than at any moment before or since – indeed, in

many ways was explicitly modelled on it. Her written constitution, the Charter, embodied the essential features of Britain's
unwritten one. The head of state was a constitutional monarch,
ruling in conjunction with a two-chamber legislature – the
Chamber of Deputies, the equivalent of the House of Commons,
and the Chamber of Peers, corresponding to the House of Lords.
Like the Church of England, Catholicism was the official faith
within a framework of religious toleration, though it was disestab-
lished after 1830.

On the surface, little of this political system remains in France
today. Louis-Philippe was the last French king, and despite several subsequent attempts, the monarchy has never been restored.
While the hereditary principle survives – just – in the British
House of Lords, it was abolished for the Chamber of Peers in
December 1831, and the Chamber of Peers itself has long since
given way to a Senate. Yet in a more profound sense, the French
constitutional monarchy has some substantial achievements to its
credit. It laid the foundations both of parliamentary government
and of press freedom in France. Most French history books recognize, rather grudgingly, that the constitution of the Third
Republic, France's longest-lasting regime since 1789, was largely
framed by former partisans of Louis-Philippe.

Given the importance of this era, its neglect remains perplex-
ing. One reason may be that it is rarely studied as a whole. The
1830 revolution, when the elder branch of the Bourbon dynasty
was deposed, and replaced by the younger Orléans branch under
Louis-Philippe, has led most historians to divide it into two.[3] This
gives the impression of two short-lived regimes, the restoration and
the July monarchies, each overthrown violently and thus easily
dismissed as pre-ordained failures. This picture is unfair. France's
basic form of government, constitutional monarchy, continued after
1830, and its framework, the Charter, was not abolished but simply
modified. 1830 proved not the system's weakness, but its resilience; it
emerged from the revolution on firmer foundations, to reach its
apogee under Louis-Philippe.

Behind the standard view that the French constitutional monarchy could never have succeeded lie deeper reticences – even a
sense that the whole concept was somehow unFrench. The great

French historian François Furet wrote recently of Louis-Philippe's regime: 'This bastard monarchy ... never really found its national footing: it was too monarchic to be republican, and too republican to be monarchic.'[4] In this perspective, there seems little choice between absolute monarchy and absolute republicanism; Louis-Philippe's policy of compromise and reconciliation appears not wise or statesmanlike, but illegitimate.

This argument has been taken to a further level. It has been claimed that in discarding the constitutional monarchy, the French cast off not just its trappings, but the fundamental principle on which it was based. The most effective supporters and practitioners of the French constitutional monarchy were all passionate believers in liberalism − above all individual liberty, the separation of powers, and freedom of speech and conscience. Not coincidentally, they saw the British political system as a model of these virtues, though they were not always correct in this view. In his revealingly titled book *The Impossible Monarchy* another eminent French historian, Pierre Rosanvallon, concludes that in repudiating the constitutional monarchy, France also rejected liberalism. 'The failure of the constitutional monarchy,' he writes, 'reflects the fundamental illiberalism of French political culture.'[5]

Is this pessimistic verdict justified? It is certainly striking that when liberalism is discussed in France today, it is generally its economic, rather than its political, form that is invoked. Significantly, this is usually in a pejorative sense − as in *le libéralisme sauvage*, the unfettered free market − and associated with the Anglo-Saxon countries: *le libéralisme anglo-saxon*. Yet it is too sweeping to claim that political liberalism has failed to find any place in French political culture. Modern France has all the basic attributes of a constitutional system: a representative government, freedom of speech and religion, an independent judiciary. Granted, these values have often had difficulty in establishing themselves during the many periods of bitter strife opened by the 1789 Revolution, of which Mirabeau warned and which Louis-Philippe spent his life trying to close.

The judgement that the constitutional monarchy was a short-term failure is harder to refute. Louis-Philippe had no successors on the throne of France. But it is much less obvious that the regime's failure was pre-ordained – that it was, in Rosanvallon's words, an 'impossible monarchy'. It was in serious difficulties by the 1820s, but the storm of 1830 actually left it on a firmer constitutional basis, with many of the Charter's original ambiguities resolved. It had re-established its authority by 1835, and over the next thirteen years appeared finally to have given France political stability. Far from being inevitable, its collapse in February 1848 was the product of short-term blunders and miscalculations. The obstinacy of an ageing king, and his prime minister's refusal to concede modest parliamentary reform, allowed a movement for limited change to spiral out of control.

In the writing of history, the losers often get a raw deal. By the end of the nineteenth century, the republic had gained the support of the majority of French people, even if only, in Adolphe Thiers' words, as 'the government which divides us the least'. Yet the republic's eventual victory does not mean that other outcomes were not possible, or not even, at certain junctures, probable. Of these, the constitutional monarchy, and the political tradition it represents, deserve particular respect and recognition.

One of the strongest criticisms of the constitutional monarchy is that it wilfully ignored the social effects of the industrialization that gathered pace in France in the 1830s and 1840s, and that this contributed significantly to its overthrow in 1848. It is certainly true that the French economy expanded dramatically in this period: in 1841 industrial production grew by 16 per cent more than the annual average for the nineteenth century. The mushrooming of great manufacturing cities in northern France often had grim human consequences – one contemporary estimated that of the 70,000 inhabitants of Lille, 22,000 were paupers. If Louis-Philippe's ministers stuck broadly to a policy of laissez-faire in confronting this suffering, they were by no means unique in this; their British counterparts did exactly the same. Yet, as in Britain, these economic principles were often tempered in practice by doses of interventionism. In March 1841 a bill was passed limiting child labour in factories, and a second, more stringent, one was being prepared when the July monarchy fell.[6]

In reality, the problems of emerging industrial society had little effect on the regime's fate. Throughout the July monarchy, only

10 per cent of all strikes took place in the newly developing manufacturing sector. Probably the factory workers were too downtrodden and apolitical to take radical steps to better their condition. Louis-Philippe was overthrown not by an industrial proletariat, but by one of the most economically traditional sections of the French population, the Parisian artisans. Ironically, this was one of the few groups that did benefit from government aid in times of distress. Well aware of the link between high bread prices and political discontent in the capital, in the economic crisis that preceded the 1848 revolution the king and his ministers spent nine million francs on subsidizing Parisian bakeries. Faced with an acute slump and hardship at this juncture, the monarchy did what it could within the limits of its understanding. Its decisive failure was not economic or social, but political: the refusal to concede electoral reform, followed by overconfidence and then panic during the revolution itself.[7]

*

THE YEARS 1814 TO 1848 in France form a vast subject – the old nineteenth-century histories of the restoration and the July monarchies run to eight and nine volumes respectively. My aim has been to tell their story by focusing on two people who not only played a leading role in shaping them, but who were themselves defined by the revolutionary era that opened in 1789. They are Louis-Philippe, King of the French from 1830 until his fall in 1848, and his devoted sister Adélaïde. Brave, witty, highly intelligent and incredibly garrulous, Louis-Philippe was condemned by the 1789 Revolution, which he initially supported, to wanderings that led Heine to compare him to Ulysses.[8] Like Ulysses, he preferred to vanquish his enemies by cunning. Returning to France at the Bourbon restoration, he spent much of the next sixteen years in despair at the conservatism of his cousins Louis XVIII and Charles X. Called upon to replace the latter in July 1830, he became one of the most effective – and underrated – kings in the history of France, and certainly her most successful constitutional monarch.

This achievement, however, would have been impossible without Adélaïde. Quite as courageous and intelligent as her brother, and equally well educated thanks to an avant-garde governess, after fifteen years of separation during the revolutionary years she spent the rest of her life by his side. Louis-Philippe's highly visible style of kingship, and the fact that he married and had a large family, have consigned his sister to the shadows – her only biography was written in 1908.[9] This has obscured the truth that Louis-Philippe's reign was in fact a political partnership with Adélaïde. In 1830, she played a decisive part in gaining him the throne. Thereafter, the two met in his study for two hours every evening to formulate policy, and she handled much of his diplomacy, particularly relations with Britain. A remarkable person in her own right, Adélaïde became the most powerful Frenchwoman of the nineteenth century. One of the aims of this book is to restore her to her rightful place in the history of these years.

Apart from its political importance, the relationship between Louis-Philippe and Adélaïde is also, in its way, a love story. Certainly not incestuous, it was based on a profound affection and deep similarities of outlook and temperament. These sprang from shared early traumas – the execution of a father during the 1789 Revolution, and the death of two younger brothers from tuberculosis contracted in prison at the same time. Adélaïde never married. Partly this was because her own years of wandering as a penniless exile drastically reduced her chances of finding a suitable husband, but her passionate attachment to her elder brother left little room for any other man.

The scholarly neglect of the French constitutional monarchy, to which there are only a few exceptions,[10] means that many important archival sources have remained unexploited. This is especially true of Louis-Philippe's and Adélaïde's correspondence with each other and with their inner circle, held in the Orléans family papers in the Archives Nationales in Paris. After their return to France in 1814, whenever the two were apart they wrote to each other daily. By no means all of these letters survive, but enough remain to give a vivid sense of the personal and political closeness of brother and sister. Louis-Philippe's actions as king can be traced in detail in his voluminous correspondence with his ministers, some, but by no means all, of which has been studied. For Adélaïde, there is an important political correspondence with the great statesman and diplomat Talleyrand during his period as Louis-Philippe's ambassador to London between 1830 and 1834. Even more significant are the hundreds of Adélaïde's letters and instructions to General Horace Sébastiani, her friend and confidant, and Talleyrand's successor in London from 1835 to 1840. These reveal the full extent of the power her brother delegated to her, as well as her exceptional grasp of foreign policy. Adélaïde's correspondence with Talleyrand was published in 1890; her letters to Sébastiani are used here for the first time.

Other valuable sources for the history of the July monarchy remain in private hands. The Archives Bryas at the Château de Mauvières contain a revealing series of letters from Louis-Philippe, his son and heir the duc d'Orléans and Adélaïde to Marshal Gérard, a trusted ally, and prime minister in 1834. These letters too have remained unconsulted until now. Count Molé, veteran politician and another of Louis-Philippe's prime ministers, left extremely rich archives at the Château de Champlâtreux, which shed much light on the politics of the period in general and on Molé's relations with Louis-Philippe in particular.

Focusing on Louis-Philippe and Adélaïde in this study of the constitutional monarchy confers important advantages. Both wrote an enormous amount, and with considerable style, especially Louis-Philippe. Naturally they were not always objective, but where their statements may have been biased they are balanced here by being put into context. As far as possible, however, I have tried to let Louis-Philippe and Adélaïde recount their own experiences in their own words. In this way, I hope to do justice to this remarkable brother and sister, to the political system they helped to shape, and to their contribution to the making of modern France.

Prologue: Spring 1814

On 24 April 1814, King Louis XVIII landed on French soil at Calais after an absence of twenty-three years. He had fled the country in June 1791, in the midst of the French Revolution, as a royal prince, the comte de Provence. The following turbulent years had cut a swathe through his family; his elder brother King Louis XVI, his sister-in-law Marie Antoinette, his nephew Louis-Charles and his younger sister Elisabeth had all died either on the guillotine or in prison.

The sight that greeted the newly arrived monarch was impressive. Packed on to the pier was a shouting, cheering crowd, headed by the local and municipal authorities and, rather bizarrely, a group of virgins in white.[1] After a series of effusive loyal speeches, the king climbed into a carriage and was drawn to a thanksgiving service in the cathedral not by horses but by the citizens themselves – no mean feat, since Louis at a conservative estimate weighed over seventeen stone.

This spontaneous enthusiasm was a great surprise. The Bourbon dynasty to which Louis XVIII belonged had not ruled France since 1792 and was widely assumed to have been forgotten. It was not even known whether Louis' political preference was for a constitutional monarchy or for a return to the absolute monarchy as it was before 1789. Indeed, until he had actually reached Paris the king had every interest in keeping his views on this crucial subject as secret as possible. Yet what the crowds that cheered Louis were hailing was not a particular political position, but an end to over twenty years of almost continuous warfare. The military glories of the Revolution and then Napoleon had come at a cost of 1.4 million dead Frenchmen.[2] What Louis XVIII represented above all as he docked at Calais was a promise of peace.

The monarch presented to his people in the spring of 1814 hardly embodied the traditional idea of a French king. For a start, he had been living in exile in England for the past six years. A childless widower of fifty-nine, short and white-haired, his most striking physical feature was his girth: the English diarist Greville likened his movements to 'the heavings of a ship', while the prince regent, after investing him with the Order of the Garter three days before his departure for Calais, remarked that fastening the Garter around Louis' leg had been like buckling it around the waist of an ordinary man. His health was also alarmingly poor. Since 1800 he had been a martyr to gout, which often forced him to use a wheelchair.[3]

Louis' greatest strength was his intellect. He was highly educated, excelling in literature and the classics, and fluent in English and Italian. He had a capacious memory, particularly for the works of Horace, his favourite author, whom he constantly quoted.[4] He was also a noted bibliophile. Above all, during his long exile, spanning both the Revolution and the fifteen-year rule of Napoleon, he had shown a realism and a pragmatism that had, often against all the odds, ensured that he remained a player in international politics until his chance finally came in 1814.

If these qualities made the king a formidable character, they did not necessarily make him an attractive one.[5] He was fundamentally cold, and the dictates of necessity since 1789 had accentuated an aspect of his personality that was probably latent before – a some-times nauseating hypocrisy. The one thing that remained constant throughout the insincere performances he often gave was the shrewd expression in his beady brown eyes, the 'penetrating, lynx-like gaze' memorably described by Marshal Macdonald in his memoirs.[6]

Louis XVIII's single failure in the spring of 1814 sprang not from his head, but from his feet. In late March, just as the future of France was being decided, he was suddenly incapacitated by a severe attack of gout. The political consequences of this illness were extremely significant. The regime of Napoleon that had succeeded the Revolu-tion was on the point of collapse. After twenty-two years of almost continual warfare between France and the major European Powers, the latter were now on French soil; the allied armies of Russia, Prussia and Austria were advancing on Paris from the east, while the Duke of Wellington's Anglo-Portuguese force had thrust across the Pyrenees and was menacing Toulouse. On 12 March, Bordeaux became the first major French town to declare openly for Louis and a restoration of the Bourbon dynasty. At 3 a.m. on the 31st, Paris capitulated, and a few hours later the Czar of Russia and the King of Prussia made a triumphal entry into the capital. On 6 April, with his last armies melting away, Napoleon abdicated as Emperor of the French at Fontainebleau. Yet as France plunged into a political vacuum, with the seat of power vacant and up for the taking, Louis remained at Hartwell House in Buckinghamshire, his home for the previous five years, literally unable to move.

One senior member of Louis' family, however, had the full use of both legs, and had already used them to transport himself to the scene of the action. This was Charles-Philippe, comte d'Artois, Louis' younger brother, heir and, as Charles X, his eventual successor.[7] In early January 1814, with his elder brother's blessing, Artois secretly left England for the continent and joined the Allied armies at Vésoul in eastern France. With the fall of Paris, his presence in the capital became vital, since even now the restoration of the Bourbons was not a fait accompli, and other options, the most obvious of which was a regency for Napoleon's three-year-old son the King of Rome, still remained open. Hastily armed by Louis with letters patent creating him Lieutenant-General of the Kingdom, it was Artois who received the overtures of those Parisian politicians who were now working for a restoration, above all Napoleon's former foreign minister Talleyrand.[8] On 6 April, the same day that Napoleon abdicated, these intrigues bore fruit when the Senate, the senior constitutional body he had created, recalled the Bourbons to the throne. The road to Paris lay open.

On 12 April 1814, the comte d'Artois entered the capital. The Parisians were delighted with what they saw. Unlike his obese sibling, Artois was slim, handsome and wore his fifty-seven years lightly. Mounted on a white horse, and so moved he could barely speak, he acknowledged the explosion of joy that greeted him as he rode into the centre of Paris with perfect dignity. After attending a *Te Deum* in a packed Notre Dame, he then moved on to the Tuileries palace where he took up residence.

Lieutenant-General of the Kingdom until his ailing brother's arrival, for a fortnight Artois was de facto ruler of France. That fortnight was to weigh heavily not only on the immediate, but on the long-term future of the Bourbon restoration. Charming and

generous to the point where even his enemies liked him, Artois was
also incurably impulsive, intellectually challenged, and inflexibly
conservative in a way that his pragmatic brother never was. Notably
promiscuous in his youth, after the death of his long-term mistress
Mme de Polastron in 1804 he had abandoned his former ways and
turned to religion. However, the ostentatious piety of his later years
left his fundamental character unchanged. As Sir Denis Brogan puts
it: 'From being a frivolous and dissolute young man, he had become
a frivolous and pious old man.'[9] Allowing Artois on to French soil
without the restraining influence of the king left him free to do
serious damage to his family's cause, and this he swiftly proceeded
to do.

Determined to impose his own reactionary vision on the restored
monarchy that was taking shape, Artois threw all his undoubted
energies into creating 'facts on the ground' that Louis would be
unable to ignore once he finally did arrive in France. In his fifteen
days of power, from 16 April to 2 May 1814, he managed to set up
a network of agents and collaborators all over France devoted to
his own brand of ultra-royalism, and which functioned virtually as
a parallel government to that of his brother once the latter was
eventually installed. The so-called 'green cabinet' headed by Terrier
de Montciel, a former minister of Louis XVI, controlled an entire
royalist secret police system that reported directly back to Artois
himself.[10]

This shadow government continued to function, with deeply
divisive effects, right up until 1820. As baron Pasquier, former
Napoleonic state councillor who rallied to the Bourbons and was to
end as chancellor of France, put it succinctly in his memoirs: 'Almost
all the mistakes made during this first year [1814] . . . were the logical
consequence of the measures taken by Monsieur [Artois' courtesy
title] during his lieutenant-generalcy. By the time Louis XVIII
arrived, it was less a question of taking action than of repairing the
harm done.'[11]

Even after his lieutenant-generalcy lapsed, Artois remained in a
powerful position. Not only was he the king's younger brother and
heir, he himself had sons who could eventually succeed him: the duc
d'Angoulême and the duc de Berry. Yet under the surface problems
lurked. Angoulême, the eldest, had married Louis XVI's and Marie

Antoinette's sole surviving child Marie-Thérèse in 1799, but the union had produced no offspring and by 1814 was no longer expected to. Berry was certainly fertile, as a string of illegitimate children testified, but his reputation for debauchery had damaged his chances of finding a suitable wife, and when his uncle was restored to the throne he was still unmarried. If the crown seemed guaranteed to Artois and his line until the next generation, their prospects thereafter looked distinctly fragile.

On 3 May 1814, after leisurely stops at Boulogne, Abbeville, Amiens and Compiègne, Louis XVIII and the duchesse d'Angoulême finally arrived in Paris and were reunited with Artois and his family. Louis' welcome was more muted than his brother's three weeks earlier. He was no fairytale prince, and the contrast between his vast form, seated in a carriage drawn by eight necessarily strong horses, and the dashing air of Artois and his sons riding beside him on horseback, was painful. Matters were not helped by the fact that the duc d'Angoulême, fresh from Wellington's army in south-west France, was wearing the uniform of a British general.[12]

Finally the cortège reached the Tuileries palace, linking the Pavillon de Marsan and the Pavillon de Flore of the present-day Louvre and facing the Tuileries gardens. It was a highly charged moment. The last time Louis had seen it was the night of 20 June 1791, when he had fled revolutionary Paris for the safety of the border. The last time the duchesse d'Angoulême had seen it was 10 August 1792, when the Paris crowd had stormed it, massacring the royal bodyguard of Swiss Guards, overthrowing the monarchy and paving the way for her parents' execution. Not surprisingly, as she alighted in front of the building she fainted. This weakness came a poor second to *raison d'état*, and once recovered she was swiftly hustled on to the balcony with her uncles and cousins to salute the crowd. A gruesomely contrived scene was then played out, in which, as the pre-eminent living symbol of royal suffering during the Revolution, she was crowned with a garland of flowers by the king. Louis XVIII's hypocrisy was on full display that day; according to one source, while smiling and waving to his subjects below, he constantly muttered to himself: 'The villains, the Jacobins, the monsters!'[13] It was not a promising beginning.

Chapter One

THE ORLÉANS:
FATHER AND SON

WHATEVER THEIR PRIVATE EMOTIONS, the family gathered on the Tuileries balcony had put on an outward show of benevolence and unity. The Parisians massed below would, however, have registered one notable absentee – Louis-Philippe, duc d'Orléans, the king's first cousin and the senior prince of the blood. Since 1808 Louis-Philippe had lived in Sicily, where he had married a Neapolitan Bourbon princess. He had heard only on 24 April of Napoleon's abdication and the proclamation of Louis XVIII when the British ship *Aboukir* arrived in Palermo.[1]

A prudent man, Louis-Philippe had decided against a public return to France at this stage. He was unsure of the reception he would get from his newly restored cousins, and feared that the policies they would pursue in power would prove too reactionary for his taste. In particular, he was determined not to uproot his family until he had first scouted out the terrain. On 1 May, therefore, he embarked incognito on the *Aboukir* and set sail for Genoa as a first stop on the way to Paris, disguised as the secretary of a British officer, Major Gordon. He left behind his wife Marie-Amélie, his son Ferdinand-Philippe, his daughters Louise and Marie, and his sister

Adélaïde. Somewhere between Palermo and Genoa, the *Aboukir* passed another British ship, the *Undaunted*, carrying Napoleon to Elba.[2]

As Louis-Philippe began his journey to Paris, he had every reason to be concerned about how Louis XVIII would receive him. For over twenty years, his family had been deeply estranged from the elder branch of the Bourbons. Louis-Philippe's father had embraced the French Revolution wholeheartedly, and in 1793, as a deputy to the National Convention at Louis XVI's trial, had actually voted for his cousin's death before in turn facing the guillotine that November. Though he himself had never gone to such extremes, Louis-Philippe had served the Revolution enthusiastically as a general before emigrating when its slide towards Terror became clear. Throughout the years of exile he had carefully kept his distance from Louis and Artois. With his cousin now restored to the throne, it was by no means certain that the actions of the Orléans family would be forgiven.

Louis-Philippe d'Orléans was born in the early morning of 6 October 1773, into one of the greatest princely houses of Europe. The Orléans' eminence was bolstered by a colossal fortune, the greatest in France after the king's, and a network of prestigious international marriages. Above all, as descendants of a younger brother of Louis XIV, they were the senior princes of the blood royal, and of all the interlocking branches of the Bourbon dynasty, the one closest to the throne.[3]

Louis-Philippe's life was to be defined by the deeply ambivalent relationship between his own family and their reigning cousins. Since the Orléans were next in the line of succession should the elder branch fail, things could hardly have been otherwise. The lives of all the ducs d'Orléans were conditioned by this fact, but it had proved most pernicious to Louis-Philippe's own father, Louis-Philippe-Joseph. Appropriately for a man whose secretary for a time was Laclos, the author of *Les Liaisons Dangereuses*, Louis-Philippe-Joseph was remarkably debauched even by the tolerant standards of the day. Yet, although often weak, inconsistent and easily influenced, he was also a man of some imagination and talent. Admittedly so as to find a way of paying off his debts, he transformed the arcades and gardens of the Orléans' Paris residence, the Palais-royal, into a major commercial centre, dominated by boutiques, cafés and pleasure-grounds.[4]

As with all his line, the key to Louis-Philippe-Joseph's personality and actions was a bitter frustration at being denied a political role by the elder branch. In his case, this soon blossomed into a venomous feud with his cousin Louis XVI, and Marie Antoinette. Desperate to prove himself in the military field, in 1776 he was finally given the naval command he coveted. But two years later, in his first action at sea, against the British in the American war of independence, he was widely accused of incompetence if not cowardice, and felt that the king and queen had not sufficiently taken his side in the subsequent controversy.[5] Humiliated and furious, Louis-Philippe-Joseph withdrew from the inner circle of the court, and spent the next decade striking a series of those symbolic attitudes that were the only form of political opposition permitted to princes of the blood.

The first of these, which would durably shape his son's outlook and politics as well as his own, was Anglophilia, or 'Anglomania' as it was more unkindly known in late-eighteenth-century France. This cult of Britain ranged from imitating her manners, fashions and lifestyle to admiration of her political system and religious tolerance.[6] It was in these last aspects that the oppositional subtext was most obvious. To show approval of a constitutional monarchy in which the royal authority was tempered by a two-chamber legislature, and religious minorities left relatively undisturbed, was at the very least implicitly to criticize France's absolute monarchy, where the king was in theory answerable to God alone, where there was no central representative body, and where persecution of non-Catholics was still a fact of life. As if this was not provocative enough, for the last century Britain had been France's great national enemy in a series of global wars of which the war of American independence was only the latest.

If Anglomania had a founder, it was probably Voltaire, with his famous *English Letters* of 1734 praising Britain's political liberty, religious toleration and flourishing intellectual life. Montesquieu followed, writing approvingly of the British constitution in *The Spirit of the Laws* of 1748. Significantly, by the mid-eighteenth century

Anglophilia had already become something of an Orléans family tradition, probably in reaction to Louis XIV's exhausting and unsuccessful wars with Britain.[7]

French Anglophilia reached new heights in the 1770s, and the most high-profile pioneer of this revival was Louis-Philippe-Joseph. As befitted a prince of pleasure, his first – and durable – contribution was sporting. Fascinated by the British aristocratic obsession with betting on horses, along with Louis XVI's younger brother the comte d'Artois he organized in 1775 the first ever English-style horse race in France on the Sablons plain west of Paris. He also patronized English artists. The most famous portrait of him, in the splendid uniform of colonel-general of hussars, is by Sir Joshua Reynolds.[8]

Most important of all, Louis-Philippe-Joseph made three visits to England as soon as the American war of independence had ended, in the spring and summer of 1783 and 1784. His initial motivation was sporting and social; he rented a palatial London town house at 35 Portland Place, became a boon companion of the equally extravagant George, Prince of Wales, and immediately on arrival rushed off to Epsom for the Derby. Yet he also showed considerable interest in, and approval of, the British system of government. In May 1783, he attended a debate in the House of Commons in which Pitt the younger made a celebrated speech. According to one source, as he was leaving, Louis-Philippe-Joseph remarked to a group of MPs that 'he would be most happy to sit among them if he were an Englishman, and that he admired a government in which political authority derived from the will of the people'. The rejection of his own country's political system could not have been clearer.[9]

Admiration for Britain, and British liberties, formed a legacy Louis-Philippe-Joseph left not only to his son Louis-Philippe, but to a whole section of the French political class down to the present day. His other bequest to Louis-Philippe, which again had a strong subtext of opposition to the elder branch of his family, was even more formative. This was the radical new system of education that he approved for his children.

This remarkable programme was conceived and executed by one of the most extraordinary women of her day. Félicité, comtesse de Genlis, was highly intelligent, manipulative and ambitious, as well as stunningly beautiful. Married to the captain of Louis-Philippe-

Joseph's guards and herself lady-in-waiting to the latter's wife
Marie-Adélaïde, by the summer of 1772 Mme de Genlis was Louis-
Philippe-Joseph's mistress, although his wife remained unaware of
the fact until fifteen years later.[10]

Yet Mme de Genlis, remarkably for her time and sex, aspired less
to be the companion of a prince of the blood than to form his
children according to her own ideas. Linked to the Enlightenment,
though always opposed to its attacks on religion, she was determined
to make a name as a public figure in her own right rather than in the
wake of a powerful man. Education, she decided, was the best field
in which to accomplish this. Her aim, revolutionary in an era when
male children of the aristocracy were taken from their governesses at
the age of seven and entrusted to tutors of their own sex, was to
draw up and supervise the education of all her lover's children, both
male and female, from beginning to end. By early 1782, she had
achieved her goal.[11]

By this time Louis-Philippe-Joseph had five children: Louis-
Philippe, the eldest, born in 1773 and known from 1785 by his
courtesy title of duc de Chartres, his younger brothers the ducs de
Montpensier and Beaujolais, and the twin girls Adélaïde, known as
Mlle de Chartres, and her sister Mlle d'Orléans. Mme de Genlis
brought them all under her wing in a pavilion built specially for her
purpose in the gardens of the convent of Bellechasse, on the site
of the present-day no. 11 Rue St Dominique. Almost immediately
tragedy struck, when the five-year-old Mlle d'Orléans caught measles
and died, leaving the entire family, and especially her twin Adélaïde,
distraught. But Mme de Genlis was not to be deflected, and for the
next nine years Bellechasse was to be her laboratory.

Mme de Genlis drew her educational ideas from two sources: the
prelate and philosopher the abbé Fénelon, who had died in 1715, and
Jean-Jacques Rousseau. On the surface, Fénelon was a conventional
choice. Yet his masterpiece *Télémaque*, a didactic fable derived from
the *Odyssey*, did implicitly criticize the absolute monarchy, arguing
that the king was subject to the laws of his country as they had
evolved over time, and also that his subjects, especially the elites,
had some right of participation in his decisions.[12]

More obviously avant-garde was Mme de Genlis' reliance on
Rousseau. She had known the philosopher in the 1760s, and been

deeply influenced by his ideas, especially his insistence, clearly
relevant to the upbringing of children, that personality could be
shaped by environment. She also absorbed many of the precepts of
Emile, Rousseau's famous treatise on education, with its focus on
developing the child's emotions as well as reason, the importance
of exposure to nature and the open air, of physical exercise, and of
manual as well as intellectual work.[13]

Armed with these authorities, Mme de Genlis drew up a programme for her charges that was at once remarkable and rather
terrifying. From 6 a.m. to 10 p.m. daily, the Orléans boys were
pummelled into intellectual and physical shape. Their syllabus consisted of literature, history, natural science and modern languages
(taught all or in part by Mme de Genlis herself), and mathematics,
physics, Latin and Greek, which were entrusted to tutors. Most
remarkable was Mme de Genlis' method of teaching modern
languages as an applied rather than as an academic discipline. Instead
of tutors, three valets, one English and one German and one Italian,
were employed to talk only these languages to the princes. Thanks
to this, for the rest of his life Louis-Philippe spoke fluent English and
Italian and good German, to which he later added Spanish.[14]

Mme de Genlis' ideas on physical formation and exercise were
even more ferocious. What little sleep the princes were allotted took
place on wooden boards covered only by a straw mat, with just one
blanket during winter and a sheet in summer. Exercise consisted of
training in a primitive gymnasium, and a peculiar form of torture
designed to increase endurance – the constant wearing of clogs with
special lead soles. Already weighed down with this burden, the
princes were also sometimes made to carry loaded builders' hods up
and down the staircase at Bellechasse for fifteen minutes in the middle
of their art lesson.

Apart from one communal lesson at which a set book was read,
the princes' one sister, Adélaïde, was not educated with them. This
was ironic, since next to Louis-Philippe she was to prove the most
remarkable family member of her generation. Instead, Adélaïde was
placed under the supervision of a sub-governess, Mlle Rime. Mme
de Genlis did, however, personally give her lessons in playing
an instrument at which she herself was a virtuoso, the harp. She

successfully transmitted her talent to Adélaïde, who was to remain an excellent harpist her whole life.[15]

Years later, in 1807, Louis-Philippe commented caustically on how inferior Adélaïde's education had been to his own and his brothers'. Yet, taken as a whole, this verdict is unfair. It may be true for the years at Bellechasse, where Louis-Philippe was present. It is not for those of the Revolution, in which he was absent and Adélaïde was Mme de Genlis' principal and sometimes only pupil.[16] In fact, Adélaïde was probably fortunate not to have undergone a full-scale Genlis education. She may have missed out on some natural science, but at least she was spared the leaden-soled clogs.

Mme de Genlis' programme had one final feature, and it was perhaps the most revolutionary of all. In another decisive break with tradition, the Orléans offspring were not tutored alone, but together with several other children from different ranks of society. Perhaps predictably, four were relatives of Mme de Genlis, and three more were from the high nobility.

Most extraordinary was one further addition to the schoolroom at Bellechasse. This was a young English girl of mysterious origin, known as Pamela Syms. The fact that a foreigner of completely obscure background should find herself being educated with French princes of the blood led many contemporaries to assume that Pamela's outward identity was merely a convenient fiction, and that she was in fact Mme de Genlis' illegitimate child by the duc d'Orléans. Many subsequent historians have tended to the same conclusion. It is more likely that Pamela was genuinely an abandoned child, the illegitimate daughter of an English naval captain and a washerwoman, born in Newfoundland in 1774 and secured for the Orléans household in 1780 by Louis-Philippe-Joseph's confidential agent in London, the diplomat and spy Nathaniel Parker Forth. Five years later, Pamela was joined by a second English girl, again supplied by Forth: Hermine Crompton, the product of another illicit romance, this time between an English army officer and a parson's daughter.[17]

The inspiration for these benevolent kidnappings stemmed, once again, from Mme de Genlis' twin admiration for Rousseau and for Britain. With Pamela and Hermine, children without a past, she could apply the method of *Emile* in a way she never could with the Orléans children and mould them exactly in accordance with her pedagogical principles. The presence of Pamela and Hermine also reinforced her charges' familiarity with England and its language.[18]

Mme de Genlis was easily the most formative influence on the Orléans children, and above all on Louis-Philippe and Adélaïde. To the end of his life, Louis-Philippe regarded himself as Mme de Genlis' creation. In 1847, in an intimate conversation with Victor Hugo, he remarked:

> She brought us up quite ferociously, my sister and I . . . It was she who accustomed me to sleep on wooden planks. She ensured that I was taught all sorts of manual trades; today, thanks to her, I can turn my hand to any of them . . . She was systematic and severe. When I was small, I was scared of her; I was a weak, lazy, cowardly boy; I was scared of mice. She made me into a pretty tough but decent man.

Mme de Genlis made one further indelible mark on Louis-Philippe. In the course of the same interview with Victor Hugo, he admitted with startling frankness:

> I have only ever been in love once in my life . . . with Mme de Genlis . . . As I got older, I began to realize that she was very pretty. I had no idea what was the matter with me when I was with her. I was in love, but I didn't know it. But she, who knew all about those matters, saw it straight away. She treated me very badly . . . She kept saying to me: 'But Monsieur de Chartres, why are you always hanging around my skirts?' She was thirty-six, I was seventeen.[19]

This testimony, and the delicacy of Mme de Genlis' position, make it unlikely that this early – and apparently unique – love was ever consummated. Yet Louis-Philippe's confession, made nearly sixty years later to a great writer who was also a personal friend, underlines the indelible impression she made on him.

*

AFTER SEVEN GENERALLY HAPPY and successful years, outside events began to close in on the charmed circle of Bellechasse. In September 1788, faced with impending national bankruptcy, Louis

XVI summoned the Estates General, France's traditional representative body, which had not met for 175 years.

The duc d'Orléans could hardly wait to take the opportunity the Estates General offered to transfer his personal opposition to Louis XVI on to a wider stage. Already, two years previously, he had openly declared that the new loans demanded by the government to tackle the financial crisis were illegal, and had been exiled to his estates for his pains. Now, he quickly moved to ensure that he would have a part in shaping the dawning new era, by becoming a deputy to the Estates General.[20]

The first move of the duc d'Orléans' campaign could not have been more public, and Louis-Philippe was involved in it from the start. When the Estates General opened on 5 May 1789 in the *salle des menus plaisirs* at Versailles, Orléans refused to sit with the rest of the royal family on its raised dais, despite Louis XVI's express request. Instead, he sat with his fellow-deputies in the body of the hall, and deputed Louis-Philippe to take his place among his cousins, sitting at the right hand of the king. The symbolism of Orléans' gesture, translating into spatial terms the political gulf between himself and the king, was lost on nobody.[21]

No sooner had it begun meeting than the Estates General became paralysed by a struggle over the fiscal and social privileges of the nobility and clergy, which the deputies representing the common people, the third estate, wished to see abolished. When, on 17 June, the third estate took the revolutionary step of declaring itself alone the National Assembly, the duc d'Orléans led over the liberal minority of forty-seven noble deputies to join it. On 2 July, the Assembly showed its gratitude by electing him its president by a crushing majority, but he felt it best to decline the honour.

On 11 July, Louis XVI tried to regain the initiative by dismissing the popular minister Necker, and rumours spread that his next step would be to crush the National Assembly by force. Two days later, determined to forestall this possibility and pushed beyond breaking point by unprecedentedly high bread prices, the Parisians rose in revolt. On the 13th, huge crowds took control of the capital, acquiring muskets from the Invalides military hospital and gunpowder by storming the Bastille fortress the next day. Although the duc d'Orléans took no direct part in the rising, his name and liberal reputation served as a symbol for the insurgent people of Paris; his bust, looted from a waxworks museum, was carried along with Necker's at the head of the demonstrations.

On 14 July, Louis XVI lost control of Paris. On 5 October, Paris took control of him. Stirred by further rumours of royal plots against the National Assembly, an unruly crowd seven thousand strong set out that morning for Versailles to bring the royal family back to the capital. Behind them marched twenty thousand men of the Paris citizens' militia, the National Guard, formed the previous July to keep order in the revolutionary capital, and commanded by the popular hero Lafayette.[22] On arrival the crowd swiftly got out of control, the queen was almost assassinated, and several of the Royal Bodyguard were killed. The next day, surrounded by a disorderly mob and followed by the deputies of the National Assembly, the king and his family were escorted back to the capital. At the head of the procession, held aloft on pikes, were the heads of two of the butchered Bodyguards.

By pure chance, the sixteen-year-old Louis-Philippe was afforded a grandstand view of the Parisians' return from Versailles with the royal family, and he never forgot the spectacle. Two months previously Mme de Genlis, already seriously alarmed by the violence in the capital, had moved the Orléans children from Bellechasse out to a house at Passy, which overlooked the road from Paris to Versailles. Standing on its terrace on the afternoon of 6 October surveying the exulting homeward-bound crowd, he caught sight of a blur in its midst he could not distinguish. Years later, in his memoirs, he recalled what happened in precise detail:

> I raised my eyeglass to see what this was, and it dropped from my hand when I saw two bloody heads being carried on pikes! . . . And, difficult though it is to believe, I was witness to an even greater horror! These monsters, seeing that a curl of hair on one of the heads had come undone, forced a wigmaker they found to re-curl and powder it, before tranquilly continuing on their way! I saw this with my own eyes.[23]

The October days raise in its starkest form the question of whether during the French Revolution there was ever an 'Orléanist plot' to seize the throne. The authorities were sufficiently shocked by the events of October to institute a judicial inquiry into whether they constituted a criminal conspiracy, whose aim presumably had been to place the duc d'Orléans on the throne either by murdering the royal family or, more likely, by frightening them into fleeing from Versailles. Although the inquiry initially concluded that there was enough evidence to indict Orléans, in October 1790, after frantic political manoeuvring by the duke's supporters, all charges were dropped.[24]

Orléans himself may not actively have intrigued to depose his cousin in October 1789. It is, however, likely that, in the event of the royal family's flight from Versailles, leading members of his circle were planning to have a form of regency conferred on him with the title of Lieutenant-General of the Kingdom. From that high office, of course, it was but a short step to the throne itself. The same plan, and the same title, were proposed almost two years later in June 1791, when Louis XVI destroyed his political credibility by the flight from Paris that was foiled at Varennes.[25] On neither occasion did the lieutenant-generalcy of the kingdom fall at Orléans' feet. Forty years on, things would turn out very differently for his son Louis-Philippe.

The strongest argument against any sustained Orléanist plot lies in the personality of Orléans himself, who seems to have been constitutionally incapable of any consistent course of action. At the core of his character was a settled weakness, which became more glaring every time he failed to rise to the circumstances the Revolution thrust upon him. By 1790, this trait had become complicated by a further factor. As diplomatic reports on his behaviour from this year make clear, he had become a confirmed alcoholic, with a suitably princely predilection for champagne.[26]

Meanwhile, as the prospects for a regency approached and receded, Orléans' private life was coming apart. His long-suffering wife had finally decided that Mme de Genlis' presence in her household was intolerable. The duchesse d'Orléans did not resent the fact that Mme de Genlis had been her husband's mistress. In fact, she got on extremely well with Mme de Buffon, who had now replaced Mme de Genlis in that capacity. What she could not stomach, as a pious Catholic conservative, was Mme de Genlis' increasingly radical political stance and the fact that she was transmitting this to the Orléans children. Reports towards the end of 1790 that Louis-Philippe

had danced to the notorious revolutionary song, the 'Ça Ira', at a
ball given by the Parisian branch of Coutts Bank, of all places, did
little to reassure her.[27]

The duchesse d'Orléans' revolt was thus no simple tussle with
her husband's mistress, but a battle for her children and for her
political beliefs. The final straw was the news, in early November
1790, that Louis-Philippe had joined the left-wing Jacobin club. On
2 April 1791, the duchesse went to Bellechasse, confronted Mme de
Genlis, and demanded that she leave her official post as Adélaïde's
governess and sever her connections with the other Orléans children.
Mme de Genlis agreed, but the battle was only just beginning. The
duke was incensed when he heard of his wife's ultimatum, and the
couple had a furious row in which they may even have come to
blows. On 9 April, the duchesse left the Palais-royal for good, and
began proceedings for a legal separation from the duke.

Unsurprisingly, in the duchesse's absence Mme de Genlis swiftly
reneged on her promise of resignation. She made a theatrical
departure for the Auvergne, but the fourteen-year-old Adélaïde was
so distraught by this separation that she fell first into hysterics and
then into a deep depression. This so alarmed the duke and his sons
that they begged the governess to return; on 12 May she returned
triumphantly to Paris.

The progress of the Revolution ensured that Mme de Genlis'
victory was short-lived. When the king unsuccessfully fled Paris in
June 1791, it was widely assumed that his aim had been to mount a
counter-revolution with the help of his fellow European monarchs,
in particular his brother-in-law the Emperor of Austria. From the
moment of his recapture, the left wing of the National Assembly,
including many friends of Mme de Genlis, embarked on a drive for
war with Austria. This, they reasoned, would finally force Louis XVI
to make a choice: either sincerely to embrace the Revolution, or face
exposure as the friend of a hostile power.[28]

The increasingly extreme and violent atmosphere both inside and
outside the Assembly terrified Mme de Genlis and, like Louis XVI,
all she could think of was flight. She had no intention, however,
of giving up the prize she had just successfully wrested from the
duchesse d'Orléans, the possession of Adélaïde. Therefore she artfully

convinced the duc d'Orléans that Adélaïde's fragile health required a trip to take the waters at Bath. In October 1791 she embarked from Calais for England, accompanied by Adélaïde, Pamela, and her own niece Henriette de Sercey. The cure at Bath completed, the little group were soon comfortably ensconced in a rented house at Bury St Edmunds.

While providing short-term safety, Mme de Genlis' actions carried considerable long-term risks. Emigration from France by those who opposed the Revolution was assuming significant proportions, and was now a burning political issue. It became especially acute when, in the six months following Louis XVI's botched flight, over half the army's officer corps joined the counter-revolutionary émigrés gathering along the Rhine. In Paris, the Assembly's response was a ferocious decree of 9 November 1791 requiring anyone deemed to be an émigré to return to France by 1 January 1792 or be declared suspect of conspiring against the state.[29] The king refused to sanction the decree, but it was an ominous foretaste of things to come. The longer Mme de Genlis and Adélaïde stayed abroad, the likelier it was that their names would find their way on to the official list of émigrés, with consequences that were all the more alarming for being unknown.

Despite this menace, Mme de Genlis showed no signs of wishing to return to France with her charges. She turned a deaf ear to the increasingly desperate pleas of the duc d'Orléans, who if nothing else was a devoted father, to return his daughter. In fact it was concern for Adélaïde, quite as much as the less altruistic factors usually cited, that prompted Orléans' most notorious political action at this time, his public change of name in September 1792 to Philippe-Egalité.

It is generally held that Orléans did so simply to preserve his voting rights, and thus his place in a revolution becoming steadily more extreme. Having presented himself for re-inscription on the electoral roll, so the story goes, he was abruptly told that his 'feudal' surname of d'Orléans was no longer valid, and tamely accepted the humiliating and provocative alternative offered, Egalité. Yet this is only part of the truth. Orléans agreed to the change for a further, crucial, reason: he was already preparing legal steps to ensure that Adélaïde was not placed on the list of émigrés, which of necessity required that he have a recognized name and civil status.[30] The final transformation of the duc d'Orléans into Philippe-Egalité stemmed at least partly from a father's love for his daughter.

Between Adélaïde's departure for England and Orléans' revolutionary rebaptism, however, the Revolution had entered its most decisive phase. On 20 April, the campaign to resolve France's problems by foreign aggression triumphed, and war on Austria was declared. The results, however, were unexpected and unwelcome. Austria and Prussia quickly formed an alliance, and by the summer of 1792 their combined armies had entered eastern France and were advancing on Paris. Panic gripped the capital, and its first victim was what was left of the monarchy. Convinced that Louis XVI and Marie Antoinette were in league with the enemy, the extreme radical leaders Danton, Marat and Robespierre, backed by the Paris crowd, planned an assault on the Tuileries palace to dethrone the king.

The attack, on the morning of 10 August, began in confusion and ended in a bloodbath. The king and his family took refuge with the National Assembly next door, but Louis XVI inexplicably neglected to order the Swiss Guards not to open fire if the Tuileries were invaded. The arrival of the crowd thus provoked a bloody battle, and when the Swiss finally laid down their arms, they were butchered on the spot or as they fled to safety through the Tuileries gardens.[31] The memory of this horror would echo down the years and, exactly twenty-eight years later, play a crucial role in the fall of another Bourbon king.

While the monarchy was being immolated, Louis-Philippe was at the front, facing the oncoming Austrians and Prussians. As a member of the royal family, he had already become colonel of his own regiment in 1785 at the tender age of twelve, and was itching to display his military prowess. He was aided in this ambition by the fact that by the time war was declared so many officers had emigrated that he was now the most senior colonel on active service in the French army. His next promotion, to lieutenant-general, followed almost automatically, and entirely by the book, on 11 September 1792. It is a rich irony that one of the chief military beneficiaries of the 'career open to talent' so loudly proclaimed by the Revolution should have been an eighteen-year-old former prince of the blood with no previous combat experience.

In fact, General Egalité, as he was now officially known, proved to be an excellent soldier. He stood firm under the cannonade of Valmy, where the French army turned back the Prussians advancing on Paris and so saved the Revolution. At the battle of Jemmapes of 6 November 1792, in command of the centre of the army, he broke through a strongly held Austrian position and played a decisive part in a victory that opened the whole of Belgium to the French forces.[32] These feats of arms shaped Louis-Philippe's whole future. Not only did he always remember them as the high point of his life, after the restoration of the monarchy in 1814 they would secure him precious popularity as the one surviving French prince who had not rejected the Revolution, but actually fought for it on the battlefield.

Yet even as the war hung in the balance, Paris and its political turmoil were never far away. Elections for a new representative body, the National Convention, had been held, the republic declared on 21 September, and preparations begun to try Louis XVI for treason. In the midst of all these upheavals, finally yielding to Philippe-Egalité's pleas and threats, Mme de Genlis arrived back in France on 20 November with Adélaïde, Pamela and Henriette de Sercey.

The returning prodigals could not have chosen a worse moment. Just a few days before, the authorities had placed their names on the list of émigrés. Almost immediately on arrival in Paris, the little group was arrested and taken to the Hôtel de Ville for interrogation. There, it was decided that Mme de Genlis and Adélaïde should be imprisoned until their case could be more fully examined. Rushing to the Hotel de Ville on hearing the news, Philippe-Egalité stormed and pleaded until it was agreed that the two women could provisionally be released, on condition that they left Paris within twenty-four hours and French soil within five days. Increasingly dependent on his son, Philippe-Egalité now summoned him back from the front to help resolve the crisis. It was decided that Louis-Philippe would take Adélaïde, Mme de Genlis and their party back with him into Belgium, where they would both be beyond the French frontier and under the protection of the French army.

The family gathered back at Bellechasse, Adélaïde weeping and traumatized by her ordeal, and then moved to the Orléans country estate at Le Raincy, north-east of Paris. There, Philippe-Egalité had a furious, definitive row with Mme de Genlis. Already incensed that she had imperilled his daughter by her long stay abroad, he hotly rebutted her charges of political extremism. From that moment on all communication between the two ceased, and the only way the forthcoming journey could be arranged was by Louis-Philippe shuttling back and forth between their respective rooms.

Fittingly for a family whose private and public lives were so inextricably intertwined, there was another matter of national, indeed international importance to be discussed during those last days at Le Raincy. This was the question of what attitude Philippe-Egalité should adopt towards the imminent trial of Louis XVI. It had been decided that the former king would be tried by the National Convention, to which Philippe-Egalité had just been elected as a deputy, thus casting him in the invidious role of sitting in judgement on his own cousin.

Despite his dislike of Louis XVI, it seems likely that Philippe-Egalité had little desire to see him tried for his life, and made several efforts to avoid taking part in the trial. Louis-Philippe was particularly adamant that his father should stay away, and when he arrived back from the front the two had a long conversation on the subject stretching into the night. They came up with two stratagems. The first was that Philippe-Egalité ask to be excused because of his blood relationship with the accused; the second, that he plead that the notorious enmity between himself and his cousin precluded him from serving as a judge. It swiftly became clear that neither was feasible. Desperate, Louis-Philippe then put a final plan to his father: the whole family should take refuge in the United States. Yet Philippe-Egalité replied that the thought of leaving France, particularly for somewhere as far away as America, 'was odious to him'.[33]

These crucial issues were still unresolved when, early on the morning of 4 December, Louis-Philippe, Adélaïde, Mme de Genlis, Henriette de Sercey and Pamela left Le Raincy for Belgium. At the moment of departure, Mme de Genlis, who was still not speaking to her former lover, made him a deep curtsey, to which he returned a bow but not a single word. Turning away, Philippe-Egalité tenderly said farewell to his son and daughter. Then, as Louis-Philippe prepared to descend the main staircase, he called him back with the words: '... if you can find some way of getting me out of this unhappy trial, that would be a great relief'.[34] He stayed at the top of the stairs as the little party climbed into their travelling carriage and drove off. Louis-Philippe and Adélaïde never saw their father again.

Chapter Two

THE ORLÉANS:
BROTHER AND SISTER

AS THEY HEADED FOR the frontier with their calculating governess, neither brother nor sister could have imagined that twenty years of exile now stretched before them. Although their long emigration would leave an indelible mark on each, their essential attributes, both physical and intellectual, were already in place. Just turned nineteen, Louis-Philippe was a handsome young man, with regular, slightly heavy features, an aquiline nose, brown eyes and chestnut hair. Highly intelligent and the main focus of Mme de Genlis' educational efforts, he had initially embraced the Revolution with late-adolescent enthusiasm. Over the last few months, however, he had been revolted by its deepening descent into violence, and in particular was horrified by the increasingly likely prospect that the king might be executed.

Adélaïde, now fifteen, was strikingly similar to her brother in appearance and outlook, to the extent that she would later be described as his 'female version'. Unfortunately, while she shared many of Louis-Philippe's features, these did not confer on her his good looks. Her face was strong but hardly beautiful, with a beaky nose and heavy-lidded eyes. Worst of all, she had inherited her father's ruddy complexion and bad skin, which would later allow her political enemies to insinuate that she also shared his weakness for drink. There is no evidence to support this assertion. Extremely intelligent like her brother, she never possessed his stoical and equable temperament. Deeply affected by the death of her twin sister at the age of five, she was emotionally frail, and physically both delicate and restless. Throughout her life she found it difficult to keep still, and her face easily betrayed her feelings. It was to take the hard school of the emigration to channel her intellect and nervous energy and create a formidable woman.[1]

On the road to Belgium, a mature relationship began to form between Louis-Philippe and Adélaïde that would shape the rest of their lives. It became increasingly clear to Adélaïde that her elder brother was her only resource. She was separated from her father and her two other brothers, who faced an uncertain future in Paris. Her mother, estranged from the rest of the family, had been forced to abandon her to the care of her governess. Now her governess, whom she had previously adored, had begun to reveal herself as both unreliable and manipulative. In this confusing and frightening situation, her brother, with his dependability, sound judgement and genuine affection for her, was the only person on whom she could rely.

For Louis-Philippe, Adélaïde was not only a person in her own right, but the embodiment of his family duty. At what would prove their final meeting, his father had solemnly entrusted her to his care, and he was determined to fulfil this trust.[2] As the Revolution took its toll of their family, brother and sister eventually developed a more equal relationship, with Louis-Philippe coming to rely on Adélaïde's advice in many vital areas. Yet on Adélaïde's side its core would always remain rooted in the terrifying revolutionary years, in the boundless devotion of a frightened young girl for her protective older brother.

The family party's destination was Tournai, just over the Belgian frontier and only a short distance from Louis-Philippe's military headquarters at Liège. There, a few weeks later, Pamela married the radical Irish aristocrat Lord Edward Fitzgerald, after one of the most bizarre — and shortest — courtships of the period. Lord Edward had caught sight of her just the previous month at the theatre in Paris and immediately fallen in love with her because of her resemblance to his dead mistress Elizabeth, the wife of the playwright Richard Brinsley Sheridan. He followed her to Tournai, where the wedding took place on 27 December, with Louis-Philippe, Adélaïde and Mme de Genlis signing the marriage contract. The newly-weds then left for Dublin, where Lord Edward would meet his tragic end, leading the United Irishmen in rebellion against England, six years later. Although Pamela lived on until 1831, Louis-Philippe and Adélaïde did not see her again for over twenty years.[3]

On 23 January 1793, a shattering piece of news arrived at Tournai: Louis XVI had been executed two days before, with Philippe-Egalité voting in the Convention for his cousin's death. Despite all his son's entreaties at their last meeting, Philippe-Egalité had finally decided to take part in the former king's trial. His own explanation of his vote for the death penalty merely underlined the basic weakness of his character. To his younger son Montpensier, who had begged him the previous day to stay away, he admitted that he had left for the Convention on the morning of the verdict determined to vote against the death penalty. 'Once in his place on the [deputies'] benches', however, 'he had been so surrounded, beset, assailed and menaced that he no longer had any idea what he was doing'.[4] Philippe-Egalité's vote was a disaster, both for himself and for his house. It may have regained him a little temporary credit among his republican friends in Paris, but throughout Europe as a whole, where Louis XVI's execution had been greeted with horror, it branded his entire family with the indelible mark of regicide.

But Philippe-Egalité's own nemesis was now close at hand, and in the best traditions of Greek tragedy its instrument was to be his own son. At the end of March 1793, alarmed by the increasingly dictatorial powers the Convention was arrogating to itself, and fearful for his own future after a stinging defeat by the Austrians at Neerwinden, Louis-Philippe's commander-in-chief, General Dumouriez, decided to organize a military coup. While some of its aspects remain mysterious, its main aim was to march on Paris, liberate the surviving members of the royal family and restore a constitutional monarchy under Louis XVI's seven-year-old son, who, to his supporters, had automatically become Louis XVII on his father's death. As a close confidant of Dumouriez, Louis-Philippe clearly knew of the plan and lent it his tacit, if not active, support.[5]

Unfortunately for the plotters, the government had long been suspicious of Dumouriez, and had its eye on them. It was given further ammunition by Louis-Philippe himself, in an extremely imprudent letter he wrote to his father on 30 March, denouncing the Convention and all its works, which was intercepted by the authorities. On 4 April, the news came that Dumouriez had definitively gone into rebellion, arresting the commissioners sent to call him to order and handing them over to the Austrian army; Louis-Philippe's letter was then read aloud in the Convention to a Chamber packed with shocked deputies including his father. Automatically suspected of complicity with Louis-Philippe, Philippe-Egalité and his whole family were placed under house arrest the same day.

Meanwhile, on the Belgian border, Dumouriez' coup had got off to a bad start. Already the Convention had issued a warrant for Louis-Philippe's arrest, which Dumouriez intercepted. Louis-Philippe's first thought was for Adélaïde, who would be left defenceless if he were taken. Although she was laid low with a fever, on 3 April he hauled her out of bed, bundled her into a travelling-carriage with Mme de Genlis and Henriette de Sercey, and sent her over to the Austrian lines with a cavalry escort provided by Dumouriez. After several alarms and excursions, the party eventually reached the Austrian headquarters at Mons. There, exhausted but safe, Adélaïde promptly collapsed with measles.[6]

Having done his duty to his sister, Louis-Philippe returned to help Dumouriez convince his army to march on Paris. It soon became clear that the task was impossible: at one point the conspirators were even fired on by their indignant troops. The choice was now between flight and capture. On the evening of 5 April, just two days after his sister, Louis-Philippe in turn crossed the Austrian lines with his commander and a handful of officers and men.

The son's defection sealed the father's fate. Still fearing Philippe-Egalité's influence in the capital, the Convention decided to imprison him and his two younger sons, Beaujolais and Montpensier, in Marseille. There the three of them were kept in harsh conditions in a dark, airless cell in the tower of Fort St Jean. Montpensier was seventeen, Beaujolais thirteen.[7] Then in October 1793, as the Terror gathered pace, Philippe-Egalité was transferred back to Paris for trial. On 3 and 4 November he underwent a long series of interrogations, whose main aim was to link him to Dumouriez' plot through Louis-Philippe. On the 6th he went before the Revolutionary Tribunal, and was sentenced to death.

Philippe-Egalité met his end with immense, insouciant courage. If anything, he viewed the prospect of death with relief; his only request after hearing his sentence was that it should not be delayed. This was granted, and at five o'clock that evening, perfectly dressed, he mounted into the tumbril. As the convoy passed slowly through the streets, he surveyed the crowd with a mixture of disdain and bravado. The only time he showed emotion was when, for some unexplained reason, the cart halted for several minutes in front of his old home, the Palais-royal, now expropriated and its façade painted with the words 'National Property'.

One suspects that this unscheduled stop was less an accident than a deliberate act of cruelty designed to break the condemned man's nerve. Whatever the case, it failed. On arrival at the foot of the guillotine in the Place de la Révolution, Philippe Egalité marched firmly up the steps of the scaffold. He was wearing an excellent pair of boots, and the executioner's assistants, who traditionally received their victims' clothes as perquisites, tried to take them off before tying him to the plank. 'Leave that for now,' said Philippe-Egalité impatiently, 'they'll come off more easily when I'm dead.'[8]

*

HIS FATHER'S LAST MONTHS, and the manner of his death, left a double burden that Louis-Philippe was to carry for the rest of his life. As the son of a regicide, he knew he would face deep hostility everywhere in the monarchical Europe through which he was now travelling. His political, and even his economic, future was extremely uncertain. After November 1793, these external handicaps were compounded by a deep personal guilt. By his own involvement in Dumouriez' plot, he had directly brought about the death of a father whose actions he had often deplored, but whom he unquestionably loved. The remorse Louis-Philippe must have felt can only be imagined, and would have broken a lesser man. Yet he not only surmounted it, but went on to gain the crown that his father had been unable, or unwilling, to grasp.

The first burden, the hatred he engendered as the son of a

regicide, was the most obvious and immediate. He swiftly encountered it in Switzerland, which he chose as his first place of refuge
after his flight from France. From the moment of their arrival in
Basel at the end of April 1793, he, Adélaïde, Mme de Genlis and
Henriette de Sercey were driven from town to town both by angry
Swiss and, above all, by French royalist émigrés. On the main square
in Zurich, an émigré ripped off part of Adélaïde's dress with his
spur, reducing her to tears.[9] At Zug, she came close to death, or at
least serious injury, when a rock was hurled through the open
window of the room in which she was sitting, only narrowly missing
her. Throughout these ordeals, the fugitives could count on only two
friends: the marquis de Montesquiou, another refugee French general
but one who was well regarded by the Swiss authorities, and the
comte de Montjoie, who had commanded the escort that had conducted Adélaïde across the frontier.

Neither Louis-Philippe nor Adélaïde ever forgot this searing
experience. It left the normally equable Louis-Philippe with an
abiding hatred of the émigrés and their politics, which only intensified
when he and they returned to France with the restored monarchy.
Adélaïde's loathing of them, rooted in the assaults at Zurich and at
Zug, was even greater, and she took less trouble to conceal it. Its full
fruits, however, were not to ripen until 1830.

The flight through Switzerland also destroyed any last illusions
brother and sister may still have retained about the true character of
their governess. Thoroughly rattled by the hostile scenes en route,
she blamed not the émigrés, but her two companions for provoking
them, and made it clear that she would take the first available opportunity to abandon them. Throughout the journey to Zug, she railed
at Louis-Philippe and Adélaïde, calling the one 'a monster' and the
other 'a sullen little fool'. Her pièce de résistance, however, was only
revealed once Zug was reached. She announced that she was leaving
for Lausanne, where she had hopes of another position as governess.
Yet in her eyes this in no way deprived her of the right to determine
Adélaïde's future, which she had decided should be not with her
elder brother, but with her Italian cousin the Duke of Modena.
Devastated, Adélaïde begged not to be sent away, and, in the course
of a furious row with Mme de Genlis, Louis-Philippe scotched the
plan in terms that revealed the depth of his bond to Adélaïde: 'As

long as one drop of blood rests in my veins, you will not dispose of my sister as you please.'[10]

It was becoming urgent to move on, since the party had been recognized, putting its safety once again in jeopardy. At this point the marquis de Montesquiou came to the rescue. He lived near Zurich at Bremgarten, where there was a convent, and he suggested that Adélaïde and Henriette could be installed there under suitable incognitos. In an act of incredible opportunism, Mme de Genlis, whose position at Lausanne had failed to materialize, now performed a complete volte-face and insisted on staying with her charges. At the end of June 1793, Adélaïde and Henriette arrived at the convent of St Claire at Bremgarten posing as two Irish sisters, the Misses Stuart, with Mme de Genlis in the role of their aunt, Mrs Lennox.[11] Having escorted them safely there, Louis-Philippe then discreetly left to avoid arousing suspicion. Adélaïde did not see him again for fifteen years.

Adélaïde's first sustained surviving writings date from Bremgarten, and give important insights into her developing intellect and character. They take the form of notes on her lessons with her governess, and prove that whether or not her education had been neglected beforehand, she was now being subjected to the full Genlisian programme. One exercise book is crammed with the histories of France, Spain and Portugal, the lives of the saints and, more curiously, of the wives of the Roman emperors.[12] Most striking, however, and a further indication of the Orléans family's traditional Anglophilia, is a whole notebook devoted to British history and literature. Adélaïde was clearly most interested in the latter, in which she rather arbitrarily also included science and philosophy; there are pages of detailed résumés of the lives and works of Richardson, Fielding, Garrick, Pope, Locke and Newton. Her views on some British playwrights seem slightly prudish by today's standards. She considered that the Restoration playwrights 'dishonoured the English stage by their abominable licentiousness', while *The Alchemist* was 'a very boring comedy about a charlatan who dupes idiots'.[13]

Occasionally across these pages, Adélaïde's developing political views can be glimpsed. Criticizing the works of Mrs Macaulay, a popular contemporary British historian with radical leanings, she revealed an equal dislike of arbitrary government and revolutionary anarchy. 'Mrs Macaulay,' she wrote, 'has been reproached for some exaggerated views in her historical works. She loved liberty and she was right to do so; all generous souls must detest despotism, but she is said to have praised the murder of Charles I; if that is so, reason and justice denounce such a judgement.'[14] One suspects that Adélaïde had another example of regicide in mind as she penned this condemnation.

Yet Bremgarten too proved only a temporary refuge. In May 1794, Mme de Genlis revived her project of trying her luck elsewhere. She wrote to Louis-Philippe, now duc d'Orléans and head of the family after his father's death, and he jumped at the opportunity. Adélaïde's situation was resolved by sending her to another relative, not the Duke of Modena but his sister Fortunée, princesse de Conti, who was separated from her husband and lived at Freiburg. On 11 May, Adélaïde set out for Freiburg; a week later, Mme de Genlis departed for Hamburg.

For the next fourteen years, Adélaïde's life was defined, as it had been for the previous two, by the need to keep one step ahead of the advancing French armies. After two years at Freiburg, again secluded in a remote convent, she had to flee east with Mme de Conti to Landshut in Bavaria. Two years after that, the war spread to Germany, and Adélaïde had to pack her bags again. This time she and Mme de Conti found refuge in Hungary, at Pressburg (now Bratislava). Here, with a long stretch of the Danube between them and the front line, they lived in relative tranquillity until 1802.[15]

For once, this sojourn was not interrupted by a French invasion, but by changed family circumstances. After eleven years of separation from her children, Adélaïde's mother reappeared on the scene. Throughout the Reign of Terror, the duchesse d'Orléans had lived in the shadow of the guillotine, and had emerged from it only through a combination of good connections and luck. Initially incarcerated in the grim prison of the Luxembourg, she had managed to get herself transferred to the notorious *pension* of Dr Belhomme, a private house of arrest which offered – to paying guests only – shelter from the speedier aspects of revolutionary justice. There, she had met a fellow-prisoner, a deputy to the Convention named Rouzet who had been accused of excessive 'moderation'. Rouzet swiftly conceived a profound attachment to the duchesse, and after the fall of Robespierre and his own release had left no stone unturned until she too was set free in September 1795.[16]

Convinced that she owed him her liberty if not her life, the duchesse d'Orléans became Rouzet's devoted companion for the rest of her life. Whether or not the two were actually lovers remains a moot point, but from 1795 until his death Rouzet lived with the duchesse as master of her house. When two years later the government, alarmed by signs of a royalist revival, expelled her from France, Rouzet followed her. The couple installed themselves at Figueras, north of Barcelona. Five years later, having finally accepted that she could not hope to return to France, the duchesse decided that Adélaïde should join her there. On 29 November 1802, Adélaïde arrived at Figueras and was reunited with her mother.[17]

During these years, Louis-Philippe had been wandering not just the continent, but the globe. For eight months after leaving Adélaïde, he worked as a schoolmaster at Reichenau in southern Switzerland, but had to leave after making the school cook pregnant, the only recorded time in his life that he had a casual affair. (Soon after its birth, the child was placed in an orphanage in Milan, and its subsequent fate remains unknown.)[18] He spent the next year and a half travelling through northern Europe, including three months exploring Lapland and the Arctic Circle. On his return, he settled in Friedrichstadt, a small town in Denmark.

It was here, in early 1796, that Louis-Philippe received an offer he was unable to refuse. Still anxious to remove from the scene as many members of the royal family as possible, the French republican government proposed a bargain: if Louis-Philippe left Europe for America, his two brothers Montpensier and Beaujolais, still held in prison, would be released and allowed to join him.[19] Louis-Philippe immediately agreed and embarked for Philadelphia, where he landed on 21 October. There, on 7 February 1797, Montpensier and Beaujolais arrived on the Swedish ship *Jupiter*.

The brothers' American sojourn lasted three full years. With Philadelphia as their base, they made expeditions south to Virginia, where they stayed several days with George Washington, west to Kentucky and Tennessee, and north to the Niagara Falls. During these travels, Louis-Philippe became friendly with an Indian chief, and was accorded the highest honour his tribe could bestow –

sleeping in the chief's wigwam between his grandmother and his aunt.[20] At the end of 1797, however, the brothers' last remaining reason for sticking to their bargain with the French government was removed when their mother's expulsion released her from its clutches. They soon began making preparations to return to Europe, and settled on England as the most promising refuge. Having received assurances that they would be well received, they set sail from New York, and landed at Falmouth on 27 January 1800.

Like his father, Louis-Philippe immediately took to England; unlike his father, he made it his second home. In the eight years he lived there between 1800 and 1808, he absorbed its culture, its politics, and especially its language: in all his later correspondence, whenever he needed a phrase to express his true feelings he used an English one.[21] Already an admirer of England's constitutional government, Louis-Philippe was deeply grateful for the shelter she had given him and his brothers, and heartened by her implacable stand against their common enemy, the French Revolution. Over the years, these sentiments if anything grew stronger, and were to make him the most Anglophile ruler France has ever had.

In June 1800, the three Orléans princes moved into a substantial rented property at Twickenham, then a small village on the south-western outskirts of London, where Louis-Philippe would live for the rest of his sojourn. There he led an agreeable semi-rural existence, similar to that of a country squire, and on which to the end of his life he was to look back with affection. His letters are sprinkled with references to 'old Twick', 'the peace of Twick' and even (in English) to 'my peaceful retreat in old Twick on the banks of the Thames'.[22] He made close friends among the English aristocracy and royal family; from Lord and Lady Holland, pillars of the Whig party and hosts of its greatest London salon, to George III's daughter Princess Elizabeth, whom for a time he considered marrying, and her brother the Duke of Kent, the future father of Queen Victoria.[23]

In one area in particular, the stay in England brought positive developments. Almost immediately after their arrival, Louis-Philippe and his brothers were reconciled with the elder branch of the Bourbon dynasty through the good offices of the comte d'Artois, who was then living in London. On 15 February 1800, they paid a formal visit to Artois at his house at 46 Baker Street, bringing with them a common declaration that passed over the family splits during the Revolution as 'forever regrettable circumstances', and declared their undying fidelity to Louis XVIII. The following July, a gracious letter arrived from Louis, who was currently residing in Latvia, accepting their submission.[24]

On the surface, the bitter divisions of the 1790s — Louis-Philippe's espousal of the Revolution, his service in its armies, above all his father's vote for Louis XVI's death — were forgiven and forgotten. In reality, however, they were not so easily expunged. This was hardly surprising, since the issue that had caused them in the first place, that of whether the Bourbons should accept the principle of a constitutional monarchy or stick to the old regime, remained unresolved. At various points after 1800 Louis-Philippe made clear his preference for the former, but it was by no means clear whether his cousins had abandoned their commitment to the latter. As late as January 1814 Louis-Philippe wrote a forthright letter urging Louis XVIII to promise the French people both the maintenance of the key reforms of the Revolution, and 'a constitutional system capable of guaranteeing the rights of all', but received no response.[25] It is significant that Louis-Philippe decided to return to France only after hearing that his cousin, at the last possible moment before entering Paris, had agreed to the drawing up of a constitution.

In the midst of these improved circumstances came tragedies. Both Montpensier and Beaujolais had contracted tuberculosis during their long imprisonment in Marseille, and slowly began to succumb to its effects. Montpensier died in May 1807, and Beaujolais a year later during a stay in Malta, where Louis-Philippe had taken him in search of a drier climate. With his father and two brothers dead and his mother and sister far away, Louis-Philippe was more alone than ever before.

Yet even as Beaujolais was dying, a chain of circumstances was in motion that would restore to Louis-Philippe his one surviving sibling. In February 1808 Napoleon Bonaparte, who four years earlier had crowned himself Emperor of the French, invaded Spain. Figueras, just over the border, was swiftly overrun, and the duchesse d'Orléans and Adélaïde found themselves facing the perils of an occupation. Worse was to follow. In June, Barcelona rose against the French forces, who replied by bombarding the city and its surroundings.

After the first shell fired fell on their house, the duchesse and her daughter decided to flee. In the early morning of 15 June, having waded across a torrential river in water up to their breasts, they reached sanctuary at the convent of Villasacra.[26]

Having shaken off the French, Adélaïde now decided it was time to do the same with her mother. Until her arrival at Figueras, she had been unaware of the extent to which Rouzet dominated the household there, and she quickly found the duchesse's blind devotion to him unbearable. At Villasacra she took the decision to strike out on her own – a remarkably brave and adventurous one for a single woman in the middle of a war zone. Three weeks later, she took ship for Malta to find Louis-Philippe, with whom she had kept up a correspondence despite the vicissitudes of wartime, and who was now the only remaining family member able and willing to help her.

Unfortunately, the journey was to be longer and more tortuous than Adélaïde expected. On landing in Malta, she discovered that her elder brother had left for Sicily to visit his cousins the Neapolitan Bourbons. Malta, where her younger brother had just died, held few charms for her, so she decided to sail for England and wait there. She finally disembarked at Portsmouth on 23 November 1808, to find that Louis-Philippe had preceded her by a month.

After fifteen years of wanderings, brother and sister were reunited. From now on, they resolved, they would never be separated again. In practical terms, this would not always prove possible, but from November 1808 to the end of their lives Louis-Philippe and Adélaïde would never be apart for more than a few months. The basis of this relationship was an irreplaceable bond. With their father and two brothers dead, and their mother and governess estranged from them, each had only the other with whom to share the memory of their youth. To all intents and purposes, they were the only survivors of their family.

Being the last of the family also imposed the duty of continuing it. The only way the Orléans name could be preserved was through Louis-Philippe, so it was clear that he would have to find a wife. He summed up the problem himself in a letter to Adélaïde of 1806:

A number of people have got it into their heads that . . . they should marry me off, but I replied that there was a time for everything, and that before thinking of getting married, I needed to find a woman whom I could marry and who wanted to be married to me, that *unfortunately* you were my sister, and that since there was no way that I could . . . marry you, it could not be thought of for the moment . . . but that if I wasn't your brother, I would get on with it straight away.[27]

In fact, even before Adélaïde landed at Portsmouth, Louis-Philippe had begun the search for a suitable wife who was not his sister. The aim of his excursion to Sicily from Malta was to explore the possibilities offered by the twenty-six-year-old Princess Maria Amelia, the last unmarried daughter of Ferdinand IV of Naples and the Two Sicilies. In every way, the journey proved fruitful. Tall and angular, with blonde hair, blue eyes but bad teeth, Maria Amelia was not a conventional beauty. But she was intelligent and well educated, even if her deep piety was foreign to Louis-Philippe. Above all, she possessed innate decency, allied to an immense dignity that later prompted Talleyrand to remark that she was the last remaining great lady in Europe.[28]

Louis-Philippe swiftly recognized Maria Amelia's qualities, and she his. Yet it still took over a year for the marriage negotiations to be completed. Since Sicily would now be his home, Louis-Philippe used the time to relocate his surviving family there. Adélaïde arrived in September 1809. However, it took a special voyage to retrieve his mother, along with the inevitable encumbrance of Rouzet, from Minorca. They all gathered in the royal palace in Palermo for the wedding on 25 November. Louis-Philippe emerged from the ceremony as a Sicilian prince, and Maria Amelia as Marie-Amélie, duchesse d'Orléans.

Well before the wedding, Louis-Philippe had made one thing quite clear to his future wife. Adélaïde's presence in their lives, and under their roof, was non-negotiable. The response did not disappoint him. Already deeply in love with her prospective husband, Marie-Amélie immediately welcomed her future sister-in-law with remarkable generosity, helped by the fact that she genuinely liked her. By September 1810, Louis-Philippe could write to Adélaïde that all their futures were 'inseparable'.[29] Whenever he was away from home, Adélaïde kept Marie-Amélie company, and he would write to only one of them, knowing they would read his letters together.[30] In every sense but the sexual, there were always three people in the marriage.

Louis-Philippe's great strength, and the secret of much of his success, is that from 1809 on he was buttressed by two remarkable women, both of whom were devoted to him. Yet within this arrangement there was a clear division of labour. Marie-Amélie's role was the traditional one of wife and mother: she idolized her husband, looked up to him and never doubted his judgement. Louis-Philippe, for his part, repaid this devotion with undoubted love and tenderness. Above all, Marie-Amélie performed the primordial duty of assuring the Orléans line in exemplary fashion: within ten months of her marriage she had produced a male heir, Ferdinand-Philippe, duc de Chartres, followed over the next decade by five more sons and four daughters. Yet while Marie-Amélie had both good judgement and good sense, clearly displayed in the detailed journal she kept for most of her life,[31] her preoccupations were essentially domestic and familial. Though she certainly had political opinions, these were generally conventional and, where they touched on France, markedly conservative. She was, after all, the niece of Marie Antoinette.

If Marie-Amélie's chief concern was Louis-Philippe's private contentment, that of Adélaïde was his public success and glory. Unlike her sister-in-law, politics was her meat and drink. It was also soon clear that she had a remarkable aptitude for it. This stemmed from two sources. In contrast to the vast majority of her female contemporaries, Adélaïde had received from Mme de Genlis an extremely avant-garde education that emphasized history, philosophy and political thought. In addition, the vicissitudes of emigration had transformed her out of all recognition from the delicate, neurasthenic girl of 1794. As her daring journey to England had proved, she now possessed qualities of boldness and decision that even her brother, for all his toughness and resilience, sometimes lacked.

In the early nineteenth century, it became common to dub women who wielded political influence over powerful men 'Egerias', after the nymph who is said to have advised Numa Pompilius, the second king of Rome.[32] Adélaïde was unquestionably Louis-Philippe's Egeria. From 1808 on, he listened constantly to her advice, never took a political decision without consulting her, and at the most crucial moment of his life let her views determine his actions.

Yet in two significant ways Adélaïde's position was unique. Unlike the other great Egerias of her age — Guizot's princesse de Lieven, Chateaubriand's duchesse de Duras, Molé's comtesse de Castellane[33] — she was not the mistress of a powerful man, but his sister. This conferred on her the immense advantage of a recognized position at the heart of his family, and the sort of permanence that could rarely be gained from a liaison. And whereas her rivals received the confidences of writers and politicians, Adélaïde became the Egeria of a king.

Her political role was also shaped by the fact that she remained single. There was no husband, children or acknowledged lover to dilute her attachment to her brother. A number of factors account for this. The most obvious was the French Revolution. Before its outbreak, Adélaïde was a sought-after match: young, intelligent, and heiress to one of the great fortunes of Europe. Her family's plan at this time was to betroth her to the comte d'Artois' eldest son, the duc d'Angoulême.[34] The Revolution made her a fugitive, sequestrated her dowry and, to ensure she got the worst of both worlds, transformed her into the daughter of a regicide from whom any suitable prospective husband would recoil in horror. By 1814, when she had recovered her position, she was thirty-seven, an old maid by the standards of the day, whose chances of marriage were effectively ruined.

Another major reason for Adélaïde's failure to marry was her passionate devotion to Louis-Philippe. Her fervent love for him, so palpable in all her mature writings and correspondence, left little room for any other man.[35] Yet occasionally there are hints that this might not have been the whole story. At several points in the intermittent journal she kept from 1817 to 1841, and which up until now has remained unused by historians, Adélaïde tacitly acknowledged that her feelings for her brother alone could not make her happy. In her lowest moments, she even sought religious consolation for this lack of fulfilment. It was, she concluded, an act of God's mercy 'to make me worthy of Heaven, since alas if my heart had found satisfaction in this world it would have attached me too much to earthly things!'[36]

It is difficult to tell whether these intimate passages in Adélaïde's journal concern emotional frustration in general, or specific unhappy experiences of love. On the evidence currently available, no judgement is possible.

As a highly intelligent single woman of substantial means, Adélaïde could also have chosen to lead an independent life. An increasing number of her contemporaries were taking this path, of whom Mme de Staël was only the most famous, and George Sand and Marie d'Agoult would continue the trend into the next generation.[37] Yet Adélaïde rejected this option, and on the role of women at least, her views remained conventional. For her, the family remained the wellspring of both the private and the public good: the only valid way for a woman to live outside it was in a convent.[38]

Although Adélaïde remained deeply religious to the end of her life, there is no record of her ever having considered taking the veil. By 1814, it was also reasonably certain that she would not marry and have children of her own. Living with them as she did, it was thus inevitable that her brother's children should become her substitute family. She helped bring them up, and remained a constant presence in their lives. As a contemporary biographical note on her in the Orléans papers rather cloyingly puts it: 'Her brother's family is her own; and in this sweet and unalterable union she no longer has any unhappy moments except those when she is unable to do good.'[39]

This was the household whose prospects were so dramatically changed when the *Aboukir* landed at Palermo with the news of Napoleon's fall. Adélaïde's journal records Louis-Philippe's reaction: 'He threw his arms around my neck and burst into tears, saying "My dear friend, the Allies are in Paris; Buonaparte is overthrown; Louis XVIII is proclaimed; I have to go!"' A week later, on 1 May, Adélaïde and Marie-Amélie accompanied Louis-Philippe on board the *Aboukir* to say goodbye: 'We sat on the sofa in his cabin, with him between the two of us, and we stayed there right up until the cruel moment when . . . it was time to leave. He embraced Amélie, then me, and pressed me to his heart, this good and beloved brother, in a way that I shall never forget as long as I live.'[40]

*

HAVING LANDED AT Genoa on 6 May, Louis-Philippe immediately took the road to Paris. A little before midnight on the 16th, he entered the city of his birth, which he had not seen for twenty-one years.

Once installed in his hotel, chosen because its owner was his father's former tailor, Louis-Philippe wrote that same night to his cousin the king. The response was more than he could have desired. Louis XVIII received him the next day at the Tuileries, embraced him, confirmed him in his military rank of lieutenant-general and, in a particularly gracious gesture, added to this Philippe-Egalité's old title of colonel-general of hussars. Most important of all, he immediately restored all the Orléans properties that had not been sold during the Revolution and empire. The majority of these, miraculously, had not been broken up and sold because of their very size and importance, but had been retained by the state.[41]

Two days later, Louis-Philippe took formal possession of the Palais-royal. Since he wished to avoid a commotion, he walked there incognito, and entered the building through the garden. He described what followed in a letter to Marie-Amélie whose laconic tone only heightens the sense of the emotion he must have felt:

> I began to climb [the great staircase], when the nasal voice of an old Parisienne shouted down to us: 'You can't come up here!' I went over to the next staircase ... and asked the way to the estate office with equal lack of success, and so I had to steel myself to mount the third staircase, which was particularly painful for me, since it was the one leading to my father's apartment. Another old woman yelled at us: 'The estate office is right at the top!' I almost burst into tears seeing all this again, and especially the upper floors, but finding that the corridor I used to take from my own apartment to my father's was open, I went along it and met the concierge, who accompanied me to the main apartments.[42]

That evening Louis-Philippe went to reclaim another of his family's Parisian properties: the folly and English gardens of Monceau laid out by Philippe-Egalité in 1778. Monceau was now a public park, and at its entrance its returning owner had a strange and moving meeting:

> The old gatekeeper who had been there for forty-two years, and who had seen me in swaddling-clothes, fixed his eyes on

me as I went in, and then intercepted me on one of the paths and stood in my way without saying a word. I recognized him straight away, in spite of his wrinkles and grey hair, and said to him: 'Is it you, Fraud?' – 'Yes, it is Fraud, and it really is you, and not just you, but your father to the life.' There were many people strolling in the garden, and everywhere that gaiety one only finds in France; some of them were singing and dancing in a ring, others were singing as they walked. What a change of scene for me; quite unbelievable.[43]

Louis-Philippe had come into his own again; but everywhere he looked the ghosts were palpable. Over the next decades, he would do his best to lay them to rest. Like the rest of the country, however, he would always remain haunted by the Revolution and its consequences.

Chapter Three

TEN MONTHS AND
A HUNDRED DAYS

BY THE TIME LOUIS-PHILIPPE arrived in Paris to claim his inheritance, Louis XVIII and his immediate family had settled back into the Tuileries palace. The ageing king installed himself in the royal apartments along the central façade, while the comte d'Artois took up quarters overlooking the Rue de Rivoli, in the Pavillon de Marsan, whose name swiftly came to designate the ultra-royalist party that paid court to him there. Artois' second son Berry lived on the ground floor of the Pavillon de Marsan, while the duc and duchesse d'Angoulême occupied the other end of the palace, the Pavillon de Flore overlooking the Seine.[1]

The Tuileries, however, had had many occupants since 1789. Dragged to Paris from Versailles during the October days, Louis XVI and Marie Antoinette had lived there as phantom constitutional monarchs until the bloody storming of the palace on 10 August 1792 had ended their reign and, within eighteen months, their lives. During the Terror, the Tuileries had housed the Committee of Public Safety. Napoleon had had a longer tenancy, of fourteen years, but had in turn been evicted the previous month. If the restored Bourbons were to make their residence permanent, they would have to show they understood post-revolutionary France better than their predecessors.

Yet as Louis XVIII returned from his quarter-century of exile, the country he found was in many ways unrecognizable. The France of his youth had been an absolute monarchy, in which the king had been, in theory at least, accountable to God alone. Below the crown, in carefully graded tiers, had stretched a society of orders, each of which was legally defined. The first estate, the clergy, owing ultimate allegiance to the Pope, had enjoyed substantial administrative autonomy, significant tax exemptions and vast lands. The second estate, the nobility, had been clearly subject to the king, but had also been granted tax exemptions as well as important seigneurial rights in the countryside and a monopoly of public and military offices. The third estate had comprised the rest of the population, from the urban and rural bourgeoisie to the working class of the towns and the peasantry. Although it had grown in prosperity in the course of the eighteenth century, in 1789 it still shouldered most of the burden of taxation and had none of the privileges of the nobility and clergy.

Undermined by financial crisis, the absolute monarchy had already abdicated much of its authority when it was overtaken by the revolutionary flood. From 1789 to 10 August 1792, Louis XVI's authority had been drastically curtailed by a constitution that transferred most of his powers, most crucially that of the initiative in legislation, to a single-chamber National Assembly. The republic that had succeeded the constitutional monarchy had oscillated between parliamentary anarchy and temporary repression in moments of crisis. Finally, Napoleon had succeeded in imposing order on France at the price of full-scale dictatorship. Although in theory he had been restrained by a Senate and a Legislative Body, in practice these had almost no effective power and barely disguised the authoritarian nature of his rule.[2]

The changes to French society between 1789 and 1814 had been just as dramatic and far more permanent. The society of orders had been swept away and replaced by a more flexible one of classes. Above all, a significant amount of land had been transferred from the privileged orders, the nobility and clergy, to the middle classes and, to a lesser extent, the peasantry. Perhaps a tenth of all French land changed hands, two-thirds of which had previously belonged to the church, and one-third to the Crown and the émigré nobility. The church came off worst: its lands, comprising between 6 and 10 per cent of the whole of France, were confiscated as early as November 1789, many of its priests were victims of the Terror, and the Concordat of 1801 that finally settled its status subjected it to careful control by the state. The nobility held its position better, but still suffered appreciable losses. One study estimates that a typical provincial noble may have lost one-third of his income and one-fifth of his land during the Revolution.[3]

The *biens nationaux*, as this transferred property was known, were a powerful symbol of the Revolution, and created its most important vested interest – they had been bought by over half a million people. Other major reforms were now firmly established. The breaking of the nobility's stranglehold on justice, administration and the officer ranks of the army had opened the way to that most trumpeted achievement of the Revolution, the 'career open to talent'. Freedom of religion, though more contentious, had emancipated France's Protestants and Jews and attached most of them to the new order.[4] To attempt to reverse any of these changes in a return to the old regime would have been not only unwise, but probably impossible.

The king whose success depended on coming to terms with this new France had little, if any, real sympathy for it. The first proclamation he had issued on becoming king in exile, the declaration of Verona of 1795, had been a ringing endorsement of the old regime, apart from certain unspecified 'abuses'. Since then he had moved with the times, but neither far nor fast enough. By 1805, he had accepted that in the event of a restoration France's post-revolutionary administrative and judicial structure should stay in place. He also recognized that the antiquated Estates General could no longer be revived as the country's representative body, only excluding as a substitute a permanent single-chamber legislature of the sort that had dominated the early 1790s.[5] Yet given the upheavals of the Revolution, these were minimal concessions, and they left a great deal unspecified.

In reality, Louis never had a free hand to design his own restoration. On the international level, the Allied Powers whose armies surrounded him had decided that France needed a liberal constitution, not as a matter of principle but simply to ensure her future stability and thus the peace of Europe. The domestic situation was also extremely delicate. On 3 April 1814, in a manoeuvre carefully orchestrated by Talleyrand, Napoleon's own Senate had proclaimed his deposition. Three days later, the Senate had published a draft constitution of its own for the new monarchy, intended to make absolutely sure there was no return to the old regime. Avoiding all mention of divine right, it merely noted that the French people had 'freely' recalled Louis XVIII to the throne. It stipulated that the existing Senate and Legislative Body should counterbalance the royal authority, and participate in lawmaking, and that no new taxation should be legal without their consent. There would be no return to the tax exemptions of the absolute monarchy, the current judicial system would be preserved, and freedom of religion and conscience, as well as substantial liberty of the press, would be guaranteed.[6]

This so-called senatorial constitution deeply dismayed Louis XVIII. At the core of his objections was a profound point of principle. Unlike Talleyrand and the Senate, he still viewed the royal authority as derived not from a contract between king and people, but ultimately from God himself. This was not simply a moral question; as subsequent events would show, it cut to the heart of the restoration settlement. As it was, Louis waited until just a few hours before his entry into Paris before publishing his riposte to the senatorial constitution, which itself reveals much about his state of mind. This document, the declaration of St Ouen, reasserted his own control over the negotiations in hand. Like the Senate's draft, it provided for a two-chamber legislature, complete religious freedom and a wide measure of liberty of the press, and guaranteed that taxation would be freely voted, not imposed. Crucially, it also promised that the *biens nationaux* would remain in the hands of their current owners. But in contrast to the senatorial constitution, the declaration of St Ouen was presented not by the people to their king, but to the people by their king — or, to be more precise, by 'Louis, par la grâce de Dieu roi de France et de Navarre'. In Louis' eyes at least, he had kept his freedom of action.[7]

Once in possession of the capital, the king and his advisers next faced the task of working up the extremely brief declaration of St Ouen into a full-scale constitution. This was entrusted to a commission whose leading members were the chancellor Dambray, comtes Beugnot and Ferrand, and the abbé de Montesquiou. Working at breakneck speed, within a fortnight they had produced the required document.

The constitutional Charter, as it was christened, was to define the nineteenth-century French monarchy. Its provisions, contained in seventy-six articles, confirmed and expanded upon those of the declaration of St Ouen.[8] The king was the sole source of executive authority, and exercised legislative power in conjunction with a Chamber of Peers and a Chamber of Deputies. The right to initiate legislation, which Louis XVIII himself regarded as the 'greatest ornament of his crown' and whose abolition had done more than almost anything else to turn his elder brother Louis XVI against the Revolution, was the prerogative of the king alone. No taxation could be raised without the consent of both Chambers. Freedom of religion was guaranteed, but Catholicism was formally recognized as the state religion. Article 8 provided for freedom of the press, 'in conformity with the laws that correct abuses of this liberty'. The *biens nationaux* were included in a general confirmation of existing property rights.

The composition of the two Chambers was spelled out in considerable detail. The king had the right to nominate an unlimited number of peers to the upper Chamber, on either a hereditary or a lifetime basis. The Chamber of Deputies was elected by Frenchmen over thirty who paid 300 francs or more in tax per annum. The deputies themselves had to be over forty and pay tax of 1,000 francs or above. They were elected for five years, with a fifth of their number being renewed by partial elections each year.

The most important result of these provisions, which was undoubtedly intentional, was to create an extremely small electorate. Of a total French population of thirty million, just over 90,000 were given the vote.[9] Convinced that the horrors of the Revolution had largely been caused by turbulent assemblies elected on wide franchises, the Charter's framers were determined that their successor should represent only the most reliable and conservative members of society. Yet this decision risked dangerously narrowing the new regime's basis of support. Under the British monarchy to which so many restoration politicians looked for inspiration, 440,000 of a population of approximately twenty million had the vote even before the 1832 reform bill, by which a further 216,000 were added to their number.[10] The nineteenth-century French monarchy never had the confidence to follow suit.

If the letter of the Charter was contained in its seventy-six articles, its spirit lay in its preamble. Its ultimate aim was to reaffirm the continuity of French history across the traumatic divide of the Revolution; or, in its more poetic words, to 're-forge the chain of time'. Expanding on the declaration of St Ouen, it stated firmly that the sole source of sovereignty lay in the monarch. Yet this tradition-alist stance was reconciled with present needs by an appeal to history: 'We have borne in mind that, although authority rests entirely in the person of the king, his predecessors have never hesitated to modify its exercise in accordance with changing times.' On the other hand, it was made absolutely clear that the liberties the French would hence-forth enjoy were in no sense natural rights, but simply the product of the king's unforced generosity. As the preamble concluded: 'We have, voluntarily and by the free exercise of our royal authority, accorded and do accord, concede and grant to our subjects ... the following constitutional Charter.'[11]

The true nature of the Charter, and thus of the monarchy it created, remains ambiguous and difficult to define. It certainly did not inaugurate fully fledged parliamentary government, but still less did it mark a return to the old regime. Yet if its shape seems unfamiliar today, it becomes more intelligible in the context of its time. Since 1789 there had in fact been not one, but three, forms of monarchy available to France. None of them had managed to establish themselves during the Revolution, but each had partisans, and was to continue to do so until well into the nineteenth century. The Charter was a hastily concocted blend of two of these strands.

The first prototype had been sketched out by Louis XVI himself in 1789, when by recalling France's ancient representative body, the Estates General, for the first time in almost two centuries, he had recognized that the absolute monarchy had come to an end. In a royal declaration on 23 June that year, after much hesitation, he had outlined to the Estates the sort of political and social system he wished to see emerge from their deliberations. The declaration had granted many generally desired reforms: significant liberty of the press, a virtual end to arbitrary imprisonment, and administrative decentralization. Above all, by conceding that all new taxation, substantial loans and the royal budget would henceforth be subject to the consent of the Estates, it had transformed France into a form of constitutional monarchy. Yet by insisting that the Estates General continue to be divided into the traditional three orders, thus entrenching the privileged position of the nobility and clergy, the declaration aroused the passionate hostility of the third estate and its supporters and ensured that it was never applied.[12]

Nonetheless, Louis XVI and his declaration continued to hover over French royalism until the promulgation of the Charter and even beyond. Partly this was because of its status as the last reform programme freely granted by a reigning French monarch between 1789 and 1814. Louis XVI had certainly regarded it as his last valid public act, before the fall of the Bastille and the October days had made him a virtual prisoner of Paris. Without ever mentioning the dead king or the declaration of 23 June, the Charter's preamble drew a clear moral from their fate: '. . . when the wisdom of kings accords freely with the wishes of the people, a constitutional charter may be long-lasting; but . . . when violence forces concessions from a weak government, public liberty is in no less danger than the throne'.[13]

In his wish to 're-forge the chain of time', Louis XVIII saw the Charter as merely the latest in a long line of reforming edicts issued by his illustrious ancestors, from Louis the Fat (an unfortunate choice given his own dimensions) to Louis XIV. But although this was never openly stated, the most recent link in the chain was undoubtedly the declaration of 23 June. In one other crucial way, the declaration had a continuing influence. In discussing the ideas of conservative (or ultra-), royalists during the restoration, historians have tended to emphasize their predilection, if not for the old absolute monarchy, then at least for a strong royal authority closely linked to the Catholic church – the so-called alliance of throne and altar.[14] Yet the ultras were just as, if not more, attached to that other essential component of the pre-revolutionary monarchy, the society of orders. This principle the declaration of 23 June had attempted, albeit unsuccessfully, to prolong into the modern age. The declaration thus provided inspiration for those who, if they realized that it was no longer feasible to resurrect a society based on three legally defined orders, nonetheless strove after 1814 to revive as much of it as possible by consistently strengthening the nobility and the clergy. Unsurprisingly, the greatest exponent of this strategy was the comte d'Artois, the future Charles X.[15]

Preference for a society of orders rather than for one of classes had always divided the ultras from more moderate royalists, both during and after the Revolution. The latter, by contrast, had put their faith in an assembly divided not into three estates reflecting the traditional division of the country at large, but in a two-chamber legislature on the English model. In the Estates General, and later the constituent assembly, they had been known as the *monarchiens* or, significantly, 'anglomaniacs', and led by substantial figures like Mounier, Malouet, and Lally-Tollendal. Unlike the ultras, they had firmly supported the end of noble social privilege, the career open to talent, and significant church reform. Genuine constitutional monarchists, they had nonetheless championed the royal prerogative, and fought for the king's right to an absolute veto on legislative proposals from the Assembly. By the end of 1789 they had ceased to be an effective political force, and when their ideas were revived in the summer of 1791 in a desperate attempt to slow the pace of the Revolution, they had no more success.[16] Yet in form at least, the Charter of 1814 owed more to the *monarchiens* than to any other royalist group.

In contrast to the previous two, the final form of monarchy elaborated during the Revolution had actually been implemented, if only for three years. This was the type of kingship that Louis XVI had exercised from the fall of the Bastille until the storming of the Tuileries on 10 August 1792, and which had been codified by the constitution of 1791. It has since been termed 'republican monarchy', and the epithet seems justified. Under its terms, effective power lay not with the Crown, but with a single-chamber National Assembly, which had the sole power to initiate legislation, the right to impeach ministers and ratify declarations of war and treaties of peace, and substantial powers over the church. The king, by contrast, had only a suspensive veto that could block legislation he opposed for two sessions of the legislature only.[17]

By so drastically attenuating the royal power, this system did indeed present many of the features of a republic. Despite its dismal failure in practice, it still retained adherents during the restoration,

particularly among those politicians who would form the left wing
of the liberal opposition. Their doyen was that hero of the early
period of the Revolution, and one of the actual framers of the 1791
constitution, Lafayette.[18] Well past middle age in 1814, but buoyed
up by excellent health and inexhaustible vanity, Lafayette was to the
left what Artois was to the right. It was unfortunate for the stability
of the restoration that from the outset these two baleful survivors of
the Revolution were plotting at its extremes.

The Charter was an uneasy compromise between the monarchy
outlined on 23 June 1789 and the version elaborated later that year
by the *monarchiens*. From the latter it borrowed its 'English-style'
two-chamber legislature, and its acceptance of the most important
moderate reforms of the Revolution. To the former it owed its strong
emphasis on the royal authority, and its insistence that the initiative
in undertaking fundamental political change had to come from the
king and not the nation. Traces of the 'republican monarchy' of 1791
were, unsurprisingly, nowhere to be seen.

Whether or not the Charter created a constitutional monarchy is
a difficult question. In some ways it did, most obviously by installing
a parliament that met regularly at prescribed intervals and without
whose consent no legislation was legal. On the other hand, it reserved
to Louis XVIII powers that his present-day counterparts would
barely recognize. He alone had the right to declare war and conclude
peace. His ministers were responsible, but whether to him or to the
Chambers was not specified, adding to his already wide powers in
forming and dismissing ministries. He could also dissolve the
Chamber of Deputies and call new elections if he saw fit.[19] Above
all, the premise that sovereignty was not shared between king and
people, but rested undivided in the hands of the Crown, finds little
echo in the constitutional monarchies of today. Given these strictures,
it seems best to adopt Stéphane Rials' definition and conclude that
the Charter inaugurated a 'limited monarchy'. The royal authority,
although superior to that of a legislature, was nonetheless restrained
by one, as opposed to a 'parliamentary monarchy', where power was
formally shared between crown and parliament.[20]

Since it failed to prevent a revolution in 1830, historians have
been divided over the long-term viability of the 'limited monarchy'
of 1814. Some have argued that it began with every chance of success,

and that its failure was essentially the product of avoidable circumstances. Others have regarded it as virtually doomed from the start.[21] As far as the Charter is concerned, the latter group have emphasized two significant flaws that, they claim, ensured that from the start it would never enjoy the confidence of the majority of the French.

According to this view, the first mistake lay in the form of promulgation of the Charter, as a grant accorded 'by the free exercise of our royal authority'. This raised an alarming question: if the king could bestow the Charter at his pleasure, could he not, if he tired of it, also revoke it at his pleasure? This prospect certainly worried some contemporaries, especially those in the liberal opposition. Yet other phrases in the preamble belied this interpretation. While insisting that the Charter was a voluntary concession, the king undertook to uphold it not only on his own part, but also on behalf of his successors, 'and for ever'. It is difficult to see how this oath could have been more binding.

The debate over the origin of power raised by the Charter was a genuine one, but given time and stability it could have become academic. To make a comparison with Britain, the seventeenth-century Stuart monarchy experienced many major crises, yet between 1688 and the mid-eighteenth century a consensus was reached, based on custom and practice, over the respective rights of crown and parliament.[22] If the French governing class (not to mention the people) had had the same confidence in Louis XVIII and Charles X that the majority of their British counterparts had earlier had in William III or George I, the results might have been similar. That they did not reflected more on Louis and Charles than on the Charter.

The second flaw was far more serious. This was the famous article 14. Outwardly it seemed uncontroversial – 'The king is the supreme head of state, he commands all military and naval forces, declares war, concludes treaties of peace, alliance and commerce, makes nominations to all posts in the public administration, and frames the regulations and ordinances necessary for the execution of the laws and the safety of the state.' It is very unlikely that the Charter's authors had any sinister intention in mind in drafting these words.[23] The last phrase, however, was later taken by the ultras to justify the king suspending, or even repealing, the Charter at a

moment of national emergency. As such, it was invoked by Charles
X in the royal coup d'état of 25 July 1830 that led to revolution two
days later.

At that point, Charles X's opponents lost no time in accusing him
of acting illegally and of tearing up the Charter. In fact, article 14
could indeed be stretched to include the drastic actions he took. Yet
the fact that it could be interpreted this way, so contrary to the
intention of the other articles, created a surreal situation in which
the Charter contained its own negation. It raised the possibility
that the king could, while protesting complete fidelity to the Charter,
comprehensively violate its spirit, which is precisely what Charles X
did in 1830. His arguments may have been specious, but article 14
allowed him to make them.

The historical debate about the Charter, its nature and its
prospects shows no sign of ending. Yet this has made surprisingly
little use of a remarkable analysis set down by the man who, more
than any other, enabled the monarchy to survive the crisis of July
1830. In November 1849, at the end of his life, Louis-Philippe penned
a substantial set of manuscript recollections – entitled 'Souvenirs' –
of his experiences in 1814. Mostly they are a personal narrative, but
they contain a long digression on the Charter which is striking in its
force and acuity.[24]

Interestingly, throughout his account Louis-Philippe makes little
distinction between the political views of Louis XVIII and Charles
X. Historians have tended to see the former as significantly more
attached to the Charter than the latter, but Louis-Philippe presents
both men's commitment to it as equally tepid. One must make allowance for bias here: Louis-Philippe disliked Louis XVIII intensely,
and was not about to do anything to show him in an attractive or
a liberal light. He had been motivated to write this part of his
'Souvenirs', he claimed meaningfully, 'to reveal the political system
of Louis XVIII, and the true spirit of his actions'.[25] But Louis-
Philippe was an extremely privileged observer of the events he
described, and his testimony has to be taken seriously.

For Louis-Philippe, the two great errors of the Charter were
precisely those identified by its later critics. The first was its character as a purely voluntary concession by the king. As the 'Souvenirs'
put it:

Louis XVIII wished that to the common people the Charter should have the appearance of a fundamental law of the kingdom, but he did not wish it to be one in reality, and it is important to grasp the fact that this act emanating from the royal authority and no other source only became a law of the kingdom through the tacit acceptance of the two Chambers, which it created or constituted, without any discussion, any preliminary vote, and even without any subsequent vote expressing, or confirming, their acceptance.[26]

This is, of course, an excellent description of a 'limited monarchy' as defined by Stéphane Rials. Louis-Philippe accepted that Louis XVIII's oath on his part and that of his successors to observe the Charter for ever did calm fears that it might be revoked at a later date. Yet he put his finger on one of its major weaknesses, the insecure and subordinate position to which it relegated the legislature. As his disapproval at the way the Chambers were treated in 1814 makes clear, in his eyes they had a perfect right to collaborate in framing the constitution, even if this meant dividing the source of sovereignty. In adopting this stance, Louis-Philippe showed that he was far more prepared to contemplate genuine parliamentary monarchy, again according to Rials' definition, than his cousins.

The central purpose of Louis-Philippe's analysis, however, was to underline just how disastrous article 14 was, and to assign to it the principal blame for the revolution of July 1830. 'It has . . . been only too clearly demonstrated,' he wrote, 'that . . . the last words of article 14, so fatally inserted into the Charter, proved sufficient for a king, even a conscientious one like Charles X, to consider himself authorized to annul the Charter without breaking his oath. It was thus precisely this article 14, which both Louis XVIII and Charles X equally considered to be the palladium of the royal authority and the antidote to everything that they regarded as dangerous in the Charter, that contained the germ of the repeal of the Charter and the destruction of their throne.'[27]

Again, account must be taken of Louis-Philippe's enmity towards Louis XVIII, but these words raise a disturbing possibility. This is that, while concealing their motivation from the commission drafting the Charter, Louis XVIII and his younger brother themselves inserted the fateful last phrase into article 14 to give themselves the freedom to suspend the constitution if they saw fit. Alternatively, if they did not personally add the phrase, they may early on have spotted its potential and had identical views on how it could be used in the event of a crisis. Louis-Philippe clearly believed that one of these explanations was correct, and that Louis XVIII was thus quite as responsible as Charles X for undermining the restoration settlement.

In the summer of 1814, however, this storm was just a tiny speck on the horizon. On 4 June, magnificently attired in his royal robes, Louis XVIII made his way to the Palais-Bourbon, then as now the seat of the Chamber of Deputies. He was greeted by the members of the new Chamber of Peers, made up mostly from former senators of Napoleon. These were joined by the Chamber of Deputies, into which the previous regime's Legislative Body had been transformed until new elections could be held. The king made a short and gracious speech, followed by a longer one from chancellor Dambray outlining the main principles underlying the Charter. Comte Ferrand then read out the preamble and the seventy-six articles of the act itself.[28] Up until this moment, the audience had not known what to expect, after the rejection of the senatorial constitution and its replacement by the vaguely worded declaration of St Ouen. They were mightily relieved by the Charter's generally liberal provisions, and gave it an enthusiastic reception. The Bourbon restoration was now formally accomplished.

*

THROUGHOUT THESE MONTHS, Louis-Philippe had been observing his cousins' manoeuvres with concern and not a little suspicion. This was accentuated by the fact that Louis XVIII carefully avoided consulting him on his first moves. From the moment his ship arrived off Genoa on 6 May 1814, Louis-Philippe was writing to Adélaïde (in English): 'As for me, I am always in the dark, and certainly not in so great a hurry.'[29] The news from France he did receive made him even gloomier. In particular, he saw that the ultra-royalists were already experimenting with a technique that they would put to much greater use over the next few years: to condemn publicly the excesses of their grassroots followers, while turning a blind eye to them in practice. Louis-Philippe wrote to Adélaïde three days later:

> If the leaders are sensible, the party as a whole is not; it's the same old tactic, to disavow from the top what is encouraged down below. At least they say that Louis XVIII will accept the senatorial constitution with minor changes. Please God he will! It is simply crazy to start all that up, even before getting established, and to throw everybody into the arms of the large Buonapartist and anti-royal party in the army. I tell you this, my dear sister, in all confidence, as this is perhaps the last time I will be able to write to you frankly before my return ... I fear you may not be seeing Paris again, as none of this may last long.[30]

Travelling up through France to Paris was an unsettling experience for Louis-Philippe, and brought back painful reminders of death and exile. His reaction to one formality in particular, noted in his 'Souvenirs', reveals just how shaken he still was by his personal tragedies during the Terror. Whenever gendarmes came to check his passport, he found it difficult to remain composed. 'I admit,' he wrote, 'that with the memories I had, these visits, although entirely silent and completely inoffensive, were always difficult for me, because they brought back to me the many dreams, in which so many times I had seen them gathered around me, to escort me to the scaffold!'[31]

The past twenty-five years had left their mark on Louis-Philippe's politics as well as his personality. He had begun the Revolution as a convinced constitutional monarchist, and at its height had dabbled in republicanism. By 1814, however, he had reverted firmly to his original stance. Above all, from the beginning of the restoration he preached moderation. He made his views clear in a letter to Louis XVIII written from Palermo that January, but to which he received no reply. In it, he insisted on the need for 'a constitutional system capable of guaranteeing the rights of all', the maintenance of the revolutionary abolition of privileges, and especially the sanctity of the *biens nationaux*.[32]

This letter, and the profound issues it raised, formed the crux of Louis-Philippe's first conversation with Louis XVIII on his return to

Paris. As Louis-Philippe recounts in his 'Souvenirs', Louis could not have been more cordial, confirming and raising his cousin's military rank and immediately returning to him the Palais-royal.

> Then, after a moment of silence, the king looked at me meaningfully and said: 'Extraordinary as this may seem to you, it was only on arrival here that I received the letter you wrote me last winter from Palermo. I found it very sensible, and in any case you see that I have done everything you recommended, only,' he added with an ironic laugh, 'I did not wish to become king by the grace of the Senate.' 'That is understandable, sire,' I replied, 'and I was happy to read of the intentions that your majesty has manifested to the French nation, in his declaration of St Ouen.' 'Yes, I think that they are satisfactory.'[33]

Whatever Louis-Philippe may have said in this interview, it is unlikely that he found the declaration of St Ouen as satisfactory as his cousin did. He was probably simply relieved that at least some of the attributes of a constitutional monarchy had been conceded. There is no contemporary record of how he greeted the Charter when it was promulgated a fortnight later, but his state of mind can be deduced from what he wrote about it years later in his 'Souvenirs'.

These concerns, however, were for the future; for the moment, Louis-Philippe's reception in Paris had been friendly, and he had no reason to fear for his personal position. It was now safe, he decided, for his family to join him. On 3 July, he left Paris for Palermo to escort them back himself. He arrived in Sicily eleven days later, and preparations for the return journey began.

The voyagers who set sail for France on 27 July made up a diverse group. At its core were Louis-Philippe, a heavily pregnant Marie-Amélie, their four-year-old son the duc de Chartres and their daughters Louise and Marie, aged two and one respectively, and Adélaïde. A nucleus of retainers had already formed around them, many of whom would dominate their household for the next thirty years or more. Louis-Philippe had brought two aides-de-camp from Paris, the comte de Ste Aldegonde and baron Atthalin. Demonstrating Louis-Philippe's determination to appear at ease in post-revolutionary France, both men had served Napoleon. Ste Aldegonde, although a member of the old-regime nobility, had been an aide-de-camp of the very plebeian Marshal Augereau, while Atthalin, 'the handsomest man in the French army', had been on the staff of the emperor himself.[34]

These military men were complemented by a remarkable woman. Mélanie, comtesse de Montjoie, was the daughter of Colonel de Montjoie, who had accompanied Adélaïde and Mme de Genlis into exile back in 1793, had rejoined the French army, and been killed at the battle of Friedland in 1807. She had known Adélaïde since childhood. After the first tribulations of the emigration the two had been reunited in Barcelona, and from then on she had been Adélaïde's lady-in-waiting. She was memorably described by a contemporary memoirist who disliked her as 'a conceited woman with the body of a grenadier'.[35] Other sources, though, portray her as both upright and intelligent. Whatever her qualities and faults, apart from Louis-Philippe she was Adélaïde's closest friend and confidante.

Throughout the voyage and her journey up to Paris Adélaïde kept a journal which reveals much about her state of mind as she prepared to return home after a quarter-century's exile. Unlike Louis-Philippe, she had an intermittent habit of recording her experiences in a diary. She thus left accounts of some of the most important moments of her life, both public and private, in vivid prose as she saw them at the time. While Louis-Philippe was an indefatigable correspondent and wrote recollections of various phases of his life after the event, none of the impressions he left have the immediacy of those of his sister. In her journal, unused until now, Adélaïde revealed her personality and feelings in a way her brother never did.

To begin with, the journey was uneventful. For part of the time on board ship, Atthalin kept Adélaïde amused with his personal reminiscences of Napoleon, with whom he had remained right up to the departure for Elba. Significantly, in view of what was later alleged about their relationship, Adélaïde was immediately taken with Atthalin: 'M. Atthalin,' her entry for 29 July reads, 'has a very noble and excellent spirit, he spoke to me this morning in a way that gave me great pleasure and which gives me a very high opinion of him.'[36]

More intellectual activities, however, were not neglected. By 1 August Adélaïde had finished the six volumes of Mme de Staël's *Delphine*, though her verdict was not favourable. 'It is interesting,' she noted, 'there are charming things in it, but the substance is worthless, and reading it made me ill.' Even so, Adélaïde refused to give up yet on Europe's most famous female writer and intellectual. A month later, travelling up the Rhône to Lyon, she was struggling with *De l'Allemagne*.[37]

On 13 August the ship dropped anchor outside Marseille and five days later, after a period of quarantine, the Orléans family entered the city. They received a rapturous reception: 'Both sides of the street were lined with troops as well as an immense crowd crying blessings on the king and on our family.' On arrival at the Préfecture they found that, not to be outdone by the welcome Calais had given Louis XVIII, thirty virgins in white were waiting in the first reception room to greet them. These young ladies, however, had gone one better than their Calais counterparts: they were wearing large fleurs-de-lys on their heads.[38]

Marseille, however, had a much grimmer sight for Louis-Philippe and Adélaïde – Fort St Jean, where their brothers Montpensier and Beaujolais had been imprisoned during the Terror, and from where their father had been taken to his death. On 20 August they steeled themselves to visit the castle. It was all too much for Adélaïde. 'I could hardly hold back my tears,' she wrote, 'the nearer I approached the more my heart shrivelled inside me; when I found myself on the drawbridge of that terrible place, I cannot describe my feelings! . . . Alas! I was walking on the same path by which they had taken my unfortunate and beloved father to . . . !'[39]

Adélaïde's grief was complicated by a feeling common to many returning exiles: that the crowds now welcoming her back would a few years ago have been baying for her destruction. She noted bitterly the comment of the guide, Mangin, who had shared her father's and brothers' captivity, that during that time 'the thing that upset my poor Montpensier the most was the insults that were hurled at them! [As I was being told this] I could hear these same people crying: "Long live the king, the duc d'Orléans and all his family", what a world this is! . . . and what a horrible and harrowing contrast! . . . At that moment I almost hated the crowd for its cries of goodwill, which seemed to me a profanation!'[40]

On 22 August the party moved on from Marseille, to pursue the next stage of their journey by boat up the Rhône. Some painful memories had been left behind, but along their route they could also

see ominous portents for the future. At Valence they attended a
review, which Adélaïde found 'a fine spectacle'. But beneath the
surface, all was not well. Many of the troops, she noted, 'had been
in Buonaparte's Guard; the officers cried: "Long live the king",
but very few of the soldiers took it up; they were cold and silent'.
A similar scene was enacted further along the Rhône, when the
group passed a boat 'filled with soldiers, who all shouted: "Vive
l'empereur." M. de Ste Aldegonde was furious.'[41]

These incidents formed part of a wider, and unsettling, picture.
Historians remain divided over the returning Bourbons' treatment of
the ex-Napoleonic army; to some, it was both vindictive and foolhardy, to others it was simply an attempt to make the best of an
almost impossible situation. Either way, it played a crucial part in
determining the immediate fate of the restoration. On the one hand,
with the collapse of Napoleon's empire his vast army had to be scaled
down to a reasonable size. On the other, many returning émigrés
were demanding military positions as rewards for their loyalty over
the past quarter-century, and could not be too openly alienated.[42]

Some mistakes in handling this extremely delicate situation were
inevitable, but others were eminently avoidable. In the course of June
1814, well before the Orléans family arrived in Marseille, the army
had been reduced from 500,000 to 223,000 men.[43] For the peace of
Europe and the national finances, this was a necessary step, but it still
created a reservoir of almost 300,000 demobilized, often unemployed
and therefore often discontented ex-soldiers. Most dangerous were
the ten to twelve thousand Napoleonic officers retired on half-pay, of
whom Conan Doyle's fictional Brigadier Gérard is the most famous
example. Fervently Bonapartist, and with their careers abruptly
brought to an end by the new regime, if Napoleon ever returned
they could be relied upon, like Gérard, to rally to his colours.

It was unfortunate that, while dismissing so many soldiers
associated with a period of unparalleled national glory, the government also handed out military posts to returning émigrés who, if
they had fought at all since 1789, had fought on the Allied side
against France. To be fair, appearances were sometimes deceptive. It
is true that 387 new generals were created, but most of these titles
were purely honorific. A more serious mistake was the revival of the
king's household troops – the whole panoply of Gardes du Corps,

Cent-Suisses, Gardes de la Porte du Roi, Mousquetaires Gris and
Mousquetaires Noirs of the old regime. A particularly stupid error,
which revived all the memories of the ghastly confrontation and massacre of 10 August 1792, was the raising in September 1814 of five
Swiss regiments. These measures created a privileged army-within-
an-army of 6,024 men, all of whose soldiers had the rank and pay of
officers — a royal equivalent of Napoleon's Imperial Guard but,
unlike the latter, militarily almost useless. Inevitably, it was hated.[44]

Worst of all were the decisions taken regarding the Imperial
Guard itself. This was the veteran elite of the revolutionary and
Napoleonic army, a formidable fighting force of over one hundred
thousand men fanatically devoted to the fallen emperor. The most
sensible course would have been to disband it entirely, retiring some
Guardsmen and dispersing the remainder among the rest of the army
in small enough numbers so as not to become a focus of sedition.
Instead the regiments were kept intact, but simply renamed, and
reassigned to different provincial garrisons.[45] No doubt the discontented soldiers Adélaïde passed on the Rhône were on their way to
just such a destination. The threat they posed to the restored
monarchy was obvious from the start.

It is significant that as she journeyed up to Paris Adélaïde should
have paid such particular attention to these military matters. No
doubt schooled by her brother, a revolutionary general as well as a
royal prince, she quickly grasped the crucial importance of the army
to the new regime's fortunes. Her political eye was developing fast.

At last, on 22 September, the travellers reached the capital, and
settled into the Palais-royal. There, on 25 October, Marie-Amélie
gave birth to a second son, Louis-Charles, duc de Nemours. Though
the event could hardly have been planned, the timing could not have
been more pointed. At the opening of the new reign, the contrast
between the appearance of a second male Orléans heir and the
childless state of the elder branch was blatant. Was Louis-Philippe's
decision to name his latest son after the king and his brother a
deferential gesture, or a twist of the knife?

For the first time since 1791, the Orléans and their cousins were
back in Paris together. Whether they would achieve a happier
coexistence this time was a very moot point. Louis XVIII deeply
distrusted Louis-Philippe, and watched his every move. His daughter-

in-law the duchesse d'Angoulême, Louis XVI's and Marie Antoinette's last surviving child, made her feelings even plainer. When
Louis-Philippe had visited her for the first time since the Revolution, in England in 1808, she had fainted. 'Her ostensible aversion to
M. le duc d'Orléans faded with time,' commented the contemporary
memoirist the comtesse de Boigne, 'but she was never able to surmount or to hide the repugnance' she felt for Adélaïde. In contrast,
she conceived a great liking for Marie-Amélie, whose mother had
been her own aunt, always referring to her, in terms that deliberately
invited comparison, as 'my real cousin'.[46] Oddly, it was the most
reactionary Bourbon of all, Artois, who got on best with Louis-
Philippe and Adélaïde. Although his politics were alien to them, he
had genuine warmth and charm, and seems sincerely to have wished
for family reconciliation.[47]

If all was not well between the Tuileries and the Palais-royal,
outside their walls the atmosphere was unstable. Some developments,
however, were positive. The Treaty of Paris of 30 May ended
twenty-five years of European war on terms remarkably generous
to France; her borders were re-established as they had been on
1 January 1792, with some minor rectifications in her favour, the
Allied forces immediately evacuated her soil, and no war indemnity
was levied.[48] The contrast between this settlement and the brutal
treatment most of the victorious Powers had themselves at various
points experienced at Napoleon's hands is remarkable. As the French
historian Bertier de Sauvigny puts it: 'Having too easily surrendered
to the intoxication of military power, France now had the chance of
regaining her prestige and rank as a great nation, if she could
transform herself from a force for upheaval and war into one for
stability and peace.'[49] It was with this aim in mind that Talleyrand,
now Louis XVIII's foreign minister, left in September for the
congress being called in Vienna to determine the shape of post-
Napoleonic Europe.

The domestic situation, however, was more intractable, and
almost every decision the government took was bound to alienate
some sections of the population. In late July the finance minister,
baron Louis, presented to the Chamber a draft budget for 1814 and
1815. Its aim was to achieve a balance of revenue and expenditure
for 1815, but this entailed maintaining and even increasing the heavy

tax burden inherited from Napoleon. Particularly unpopular was the decision to retain the hated *droits réunis*, the indirect tax on wine, tobacco and salt that fell disproportionately on the poor, and which Artois had rashly promised to abolish on his entry into France. Baron Louis' policy of fiscal prudence certainly benefited the national finances, but it cost the new regime significant grassroots support.[50]

Besides the future of the army, the most difficult problems the restored monarchy faced concerned the church and the *biens nationaux*. These in turn raised the spectre of the issue that had done so much to cause the Revolution in the first place – the position of the nobility and clergy. Despite the Charter's guarantee of freedom of conscience, its recognition of Catholicism as the state religion marked the beginning of a drive to recover for the church at least some of its pre-revolutionary status. A mission was sent to Rome with the aim of annulling the Concordat of 1801 by which Napoleon had brought religious peace to France, and returning to that of 1516 which had previously regulated ecclesiastical relations with the state. Catholic schools were given much more freedom from government control, while an order forbidding cafés to open on Sunday mornings met a predictably hostile response.[51]

More worrying was the fact that, despite the promises contained in the Charter, the public remained deeply suspicious of the returning monarchy's intentions regarding the *biens nationaux*. Matters were not helped by the government's proposal in September to return all of these properties that remained unsold – comprising perhaps 350,000 hectares – to their original owners. Inevitably, this raised fears that the next step might be to restitute the rest. The bill was passed, but only after fierce opposition. The same tensions were visible at local level. Against this background, for several months from late 1814, rumours swept through parts of the country that the seigneurial system and the ecclesiastical tithe were about to be restored, creating something of a rural panic.[52]

All the indications were that almost a year after the king's return, stability in France remained fragile. The blame for this did not lie entirely with the new regime. The transition from Napoleon's vast defeated empire to a middle-ranking European power was never going to be easy. But the government compounded its problems by a series of fundamental mistakes. By the spring of 1815, it was clear that the restored monarchy was in difficulties. Nowhere were its setbacks more keenly followed than on the island of Elba.

*

AT 11 P.M. ON 5 MARCH 1815, an unexpected visitor arrived at the Palais-royal — the comte de Blacas, minister of the king's household and close confidant of Louis XVIII. Louis-Philippe's presence, he explained, was required urgently at the Tuileries. In the course of the short journey, Blacas imparted the explosive news. Napoleon had escaped from Elba, landed in France at Golfe-Juan, and with a thousand loyal soldiers was advancing on Grenoble.[53]

On arrival at the Tuileries, Louis-Philippe was immediately ushered into the king's study. Proving that troubles never arrive singly, Louis XVIII was in the middle of a severe attack of gout that had left him unable to move. Nonetheless, he was not unduly worried by the news of Napoleon's return. To disembark in France with only a thousand men seemed a lunatic enterprise that could only end in the dispersal by the first available government troops of the tiny army and the capture or death of its leader. Louis XVIII could not know that less than forty-eight hours later the troops sent to confront Napoleon, and then the garrison of Grenoble itself, would go over to their old chief without firing a shot. The Bourbons' mismanagement of the army over the previous year was bearing poisonous fruit.

In the meantime, the king outlined his strategy to his cousin. Napoleon's progress would be contained by concentrating forces under the comte d'Artois at Lyon, the duc de Berry at Besançon, and the duc d'Angoulême at Nîmes. Louis-Philippe himself would join Artois at Lyon. An extremely loaded conversation ensued. Louis-Philippe disagreed strongly with these dispositions, arguing that before dispersing the royal princes to various corners of France, it would be more sensible first to operate the troop concentration nearer Paris, and bolster the morale and loyalty of the soldiers. To this end, he offered to station a corps himself between Paris and Lyon. Louis, however, 'pretty sharply' rejected these ideas.[54]

With one line of attack blocked, Louis-Philippe now tried another. ' "Is your majesty not worried," he inquired, "about staying here alone in Paris, because in the state you are in, unable to budge from your armchair, it seems to me highly desirable that you should keep one of the princes with you, and I would be very glad if your majesty would assign this post to me." "I am very grateful to you," the king replied, "but I have no need of anyone, and it is best that you go to Lyon, not necessarily this evening, but get your boots greased, and come back to see me tomorrow morning." '[55]

This exchange, carefully recorded by Louis-Philippe in a further series of recollections – or 'Relation' – of his actions during the Hundred Days of Napoleon's return to power, leaves a decidedly odd impression. It provides the first of a series of indications that in early 1815 he was pursuing some sort of plan that he kept hidden from his cousins, and which may even have aimed at the throne. At no other point in his life does his conduct give off such a whiff of conspiracy against the elder branch of his family.

Ever since his return to France, Louis-Philippe had enjoyed several political advantages over his relatives. He had supported the Revolution, without being associated with its excesses; he had fought for France rather than against her, with some glory, in 1792 and 1793; and he was now known to be firmly in favour of a liberal constitution. He was certainly not above advertising these facts, and had done so with most effect on 29 May 1814, when he had gone to mass at the Tuileries in his old lieutenant-general's uniform of the post-1789 army, which his cousins had pointedly refused to wear. Immediately a gaggle of Napoleonic marshals rushed up to him, exclaiming with joy and 'making delighted bows'.[56] Over the next few weeks, they vied with each other to pay their court at the Palais-royal. Most prominent were those who had fought with Louis-Philippe in those first revolutionary campaigns – Mortier, Macdonald, Berthier, Ney.

The homage of these legendary figures highlighted the trump card Louis-Philippe held over the elder branch – he was popular with the army. As Louis XVIII's government multiplied its errors, it is scarcely conceivable that it did not occur to him to play it. The possibility certainly seems to have occurred to others, particularly Napoleon's sinister ex-chief of police, the former Terrorist Joseph Fouché, who had retired to his estates as early as September 1814, declaring that the regime had at most six months left.[57] Fouché's prophecy was precisely – and uncannily – correct.

Most significant of all, Fouché's old master also had his eye on

Louis-Philippe. On Elba, Napoleon was kept well informed of events on the French mainland, and of how rapidly the restored monarchy was discrediting itself. If, as seemed quite possible, Louis XVIII could be overthrown and replaced with a ruler fully prepared to accept post-revolutionary France, then the two leading candidates were himself and Louis-Philippe. But Louis-Philippe had the advantage of actually being in France, and rumours may even have reached Elba of a possible military coup to propel him to power. This would certainly explain Napoleon's cryptic comment, made shortly after his return to power: 'It wasn't Louis XVIII I dethroned, it was the duc d'Orléans.'[58]

Napoleon's motivation in launching the Hundred Days remains controversial. Was it fear that he was about to be sent further into exile, to the Azores or even St Helena, amplified by Louis XVIII's failure to pay the annual pension of two million francs promised to him at his abdication? Or was it a final opportunistic gamble, betting on the Bourbons' weakness and the power of his own legend?[59] Amid these arguments, however, the possibility that the escape from Elba was a pre-emptive strike against Louis-Philippe has been neglected. It would certainly make more sense of its timing, unless Napoleon really was convinced that he was about to be moved immediately to an Atlantic island. That he made his attempt while the Congress of Vienna was still sitting and able to coordinate action against him seems foolhardy, unless he was having to act fast to forestall a rival.

This interpretation also helps explain one part of the Hundred Days that has never properly been integrated into the received version – the so-called 'conspiracy of the North'. On 7 March, before the news of Napoleon's first success had reached Paris, General Jean-Baptiste Drouet d'Erlon, commanding the 16th military division at Lille, marched his troops out of barracks and towards Paris. D'Erlon did not openly declare his purpose to his troops, but such a movement, undertaken without orders, could only have been a prelude to some sort of coup d'état. His advance, however, was halted by the arrival of Marshal Mortier, who recalled the division's officers to their allegiance. D'Erlon and his co-conspirators were forced to flee. Whatever his original motivation, d'Erlon swiftly reappeared in Napoleon's army, commanding the 1st Corps in the first great infantry attack at Waterloo.[60]

One could conclude from this that the 'conspiracy of the North' was simply a rather far-flung outpost of a wider Bonapartist plot culminating in the Hundred Days. Yet Fouché was closely connected to it, and Fouché seems actively at this point to have been considering an Orléanist solution to France's problems.[61] It is perhaps significant that in his 'Relation' of the Hundred Days Louis-Philippe himself felt it necessary to deny any involvement in the 'conspiracy of the North'. He even asserted that in France, at least, there were no conspiracies preceding the overthrow of the Bourbons, only to add, rather lamely, 'or at least it is possible that there were none'.[62] Yet if he did contemplate replacing Louis XVIII himself, Louis-Philippe had no need to participate in these intrigues, but merely to keep himself informed of their progress. It may be, as the great writer and politician Chateaubriand concisely put it, that 'M. le duc d'Orléans did not conspire in fact, but by consent.'[63]

Or perhaps Louis-Philippe did do more. It is slightly chilling to find him suggesting to Louis XVIII, just two days before d'Erlon marched his division out from Lille, that he himself should be given command of a corps just south of Paris. If he had indeed been in league with the northern conspirators, this would have enabled him to seal off the capital completely from the rest of France, while taking the wind out of Napoleon's sails by the timely proclamation of a truly liberal monarchy. The scheme may seem far-fetched, but was Napoleon's successful descent on the French coast with only a thousand men any less so?

Also suspicious is Louis-Philippe's smooth change of tack, once his demand for a corps was rejected, to a request to stay in Paris by the king's side. One can imagine how uneasy the thought of sitting immobile in his chair with his Orléans cousin looming over him must have made Louis XVIII. Nothing could have been better suited to a swift end to his reign had d'Erlon's division actually reached Paris.

Despite the king's refusal of both his proposals, Louis-Philippe returned to the charge the next day in an interview with Blacas. His primary purpose was still to avoid at all costs being sent to Lyon. When Blacas held firm, he brought up his second suggestion again, but in terms considerably more graphic than he had used with the king: 'Seeing that I was getting nowhere by this series of arguments however convincing they appeared to me, I tried another, and spoke to him of the position of the king, who was unable to move from his armchair, and could be suffocated from one moment to the next by an access of gout or a stroke.'[64] One wonders if he was hoping to accelerate the process.

Once again, the point of this was a plea to be allowed to remain in Paris. However, in a new twist, Louis-Philippe dressed this up in altruistic language: 'I told [Blacas] that if [the king] did not judge me worthy of this position of confidence, he should at least keep [his nephew] M. le duc de Berry with him.'[65] Though this is unlikely ever to be proved, Louis-Philippe's insistence over two days that he remain in or close to Paris, and its consistent refusal, does leave a sense that he had been conspiring in some fashion, and that his cousins had smelt a rat. This impression is heightened by Blacas' admission at the end of the interview that before leaving for Lyon Artois had made Louis XVIII give him his word of honour to send Louis-Philippe to join him there. Insultingly, the only part of Louis-Philippe's advice the king did take was to keep Berry in Paris.

Whatever dreams he may have cherished, Louis-Philippe's only option now was to grease his boots. At least his sojourn in Lyon was short. On arrival there on the afternoon of 9 March, he learned that Napoleon had entered Grenoble, and that all the troops he had encountered had gone over to his cause. It also swiftly became clear that their comrades at Lyon were on the point of following suit. At a tense review of the garrison on the Place Bellecour, Artois could raise not a single cry of 'Long live the king!' 'Red with anger', the prince dismissed the troops, and shortly afterwards took the road to Paris.[66] At nine in the evening, Napoleon arrived in the city.

Foreseeing what would happen, Louis-Philippe had left Lyon even before Artois. Shortly afterwards, an incident took place that must have given him some satisfaction at his cousins' expense. En route to Paris he encountered the 72nd regiment of the line, on its way to Lyon under the command of General Simmer. Since there was clearly no point in it continuing there, Louis-Philippe ordered Simmer instead to fall back on Roanne. It became perfectly clear that Simmer, a Napoleonic veteran, intended to stay where he was as a prelude to joining his old master. Yet every cloud has a silver lining. Just as Louis-Philippe's carriage was preparing to depart, Simmer wrenched open the door and blurted out a short speech:

> Monseigneur, I don't know if I will ever see you again, but I want to assure you that my comrades and I, we remember the welcome you gave us at the Palais-royal, and that never, under any circumstances, will we ever confuse you with those buggers of émigrés who have ruined your cousins the princes.[67]

Fortified by General Simmer's homely words, Louis-Philippe arrived back in Paris on 12 March. It was now perfectly clear to him that the restored monarchy was about to fall, and his first thought was to save his immediate family. That very night, he packed off his wife and children to London via Calais, without asking Louis XVIII's permission for fear it might be refused. Over the next few days, he had two further meetings with Louis, conducted with that strange frankness that moments of crisis can bring even between settled enemies. The king confided his fears for his future if he was forced to leave France again, and in particular that even if they were victorious the Allies would not give him a second chance.

All this raised the central question: what was Louis XVIII to do as Napoleon neared Paris with most of the army enthusiastically following? Some royal advisers, such as Blacas, Chateaubriand and Marshal Marmont, actually argued that the old king should stay in Paris and, flanked by the Chambers of Peers and Deputies, simply shame the usurper into withdrawing. This proposal has since generally been dismissed as an absurd product of desperation, with not a moment's chance of practical application.[68] Yet Louis-Philippe's 'Relation' provides some evidence that Louis XVIII did seriously consider it. During their second conversation, on 15 March, Louis-Philippe told his cousin that the monarchy was now close to collapse. '"Yes," replied the king, "you've always seen the blackest side of things, but if it happens, it happens – I'm sixty years old, and at my age one makes one's decision and one waits." '[69]

The implication of these words, that Louis XVIII was indeed inclining to stay put and wait for Napoleon, horrified Louis-Philippe, who was well aware of his cousin's likely fate if he did. Rather oddly, given his enmity for Louis XVIII, he desperately tried to talk him out of doing so. One can only speculate on his reasons, but perhaps, with his own plans ruined by the rapidity of events, he genuinely felt some concern for the sick old man's well-being. He therefore decided to shock him out of this course of inaction:

> 'But sire,' I continued, 'I hope that your majesty is not telling me that he will stay here if Buonaparte arrives?' 'Why not?' replied the king. 'Well, sire,' I said, 'I have heard a very grim joke, based on a rumour that you told somebody that you would not move from your armchair in the Tuileries whatever happens, but I cannot believe that your majesty would actually do this.' 'And what is this joke?' asked the king. 'Sire, it is that in that case the victim would be too big for the executioner.'[70]

One suspects that Louis-Philippe rather enjoyed conjuring up this ghastly image in front of his obese cousin. Since the king did in fact leave the Tuileries four days later, it may have had the desired effect.

By this time, Louis-Philippe had finally been offered an independent command, that of the Army of the North between Paris and the Belgian border. On the evening of 16 March he left Paris for Péronne, where he made his headquarters. He quickly coordinated his strategy with Marshal Mortier, who had fought with him at Jemmapes, and was now in command at Lille. A large, affable and thoroughly honourable man, Mortier had been one of the first marshals to attend the Palais-royal receptions in 1814, and was to become a close friend of Louis-Philippe.[71] Nonetheless, it was only at this juncture that the two men had their first long conversation. 'The Bishop of Cambrai gave me a grand dinner,' Louis-Philippe recalled, 'after which I got into a carriage with the Marshal, and we swapped war stories along the whole journey, because he had fought the first campaigns in the same army as me, and had often been in my division when Dumouriez was our general.'[72]

Before leaving Paris, Louis-Philippe had put one important arrangement in place. Adélaïde had not accompanied Marie-Amélie and the children to London, and now agreed to stay on in the capital for as long as possible and manage her brother's affairs in his absence. In his 'Relation', Louis-Philippe is keen to stress that these were purely domestic:

As for my sister, she decided to remain at the Palais-royal for as long as possible, and this she did courageously up until the last moment, for she left only three or four hours before the king himself. It was a real comfort for me to keep my sister by my side, when circumstances, and the well-being of my children, had forced me to send my wife away, and it had the twofold advantage of making my wife's departure less obvious, and of enabling my sister, should I be called away suddenly, to stay long enough after my departure to finish all my business at the Palais-royal.[73]

One somehow doubts that this pact was quite so innocent. While Louis-Philippe was establishing himself at Péronne, the fate of France was being decided in Paris. It was therefore essential for him to have a completely reliable ally in the capital, able to act as his eyes and ears – and perhaps more. In such moments of crisis, only members of his immediate family could be trusted with the task, and none more so than his tough and devoted sister. If Louis-Philippe was still intriguing against his cousins, then messages could be passed through Adélaïde without directly compromising him. He may have hoped even now that she might transmit a call from prominent politicians to take the throne as the monarchy's last hope. During the Hundred Days, Adélaïde was not able to fulfil this role. Fifteen years later, however, she was.

On the surface at least, life in Paris remained normal. To keep up appearances, Adélaïde went to court once, but the king did not speak a word to her. Unlike her sister-in-law, she felt it best not to quit the capital without Louis XVIII's permission, but when on 19 March she heard that the last army between Paris and Napoleon had changed sides, she decided it was time to go. At eight that evening she left. Three hours later Blacas, who must by now have been heartily sick of his nocturnal missions to the Palais-royal, arrived with the news that the king was about to depart. Blacas also brought a bankers' draft for 100,000 francs, which was forwarded to Adélaïde, but proved impossible to cash.[74]

By now, Louis-Philippe had made Lille his main base of operations. Returning there on the evening of 21 March after a tour of inspection, he found Adélaïde and Mélanie de Montjoie waiting for him. Their journey, fortunately, had proved uneventful. But an even more august figure was on the road behind them. The next day Louis XVIII himself arrived in the city, accompanied only by a very small escort including Blacas and Marshals Macdonald and Berthier.

A final political battle was now joined. Blacas proposed that the king's household troops, currently bogged down in mud near Beauvais, should join him at Lille, take possession of the citadel, and defend him there. Yet the troops of the line were already showing signs of disaffection, and it was well known that they hated the household troops. In a striking illustration of how deeply the latter were loathed, Louis-Philippe even claimed that the regular soldiers would have fired on them had they appeared in the city.[75]

If Lille could not be held, the king would have to retreat once more. This raised the momentous question of crossing the Belgian frontier. Louis-Philippe was convinced that if his cousin did this, his cause was lost. In doing so, Louis XVIII would become the first King of France to flee his country. Even Louis XVI, escaping from Paris back in 1791, had not intended to do so, but the mere assumption that he had done had wrecked his reputation and tainted him with treason.[76] Louis XVIII and Artois had indeed fled France during the Revolution, but neither had been wearing the crown at the time. Louis-Philippe, echoed by Mortier and Macdonald, sensed that for the king to step on to foreign soil, perhaps to return with foreign troops, would be fatal to the monarchy. National feeling, honed by hatred for the émigrés and vastly inflated by the military glories of republic and empire, would be permanently alienated.

Instead, Louis-Philippe argued, Louis XVIII should stay within France and make for Dunkirk, whose sympathies were strongly royalist. If his situation on land should prove untenable, he should even board a ship – anything rather than associate himself with the Allied Powers.[77] Again, it may seem surprising that Louis-Philippe was so keen to give good advice to his cousin and rival. But since whatever ambitions he may have harboured had now been so thoroughly ruined by Napoleon, he probably felt that his best course was one of honest independence rather than open disloyalty. After all, he was now giving his advice not in a private conversation, but in a public discussion in front of witnesses.

At first, Louis XVIII accepted the proposal. It was now midnight; he announced that he would leave in one hour. Then half an hour

later, just as everyone was going to bed, he sent word that he had
changed his mind, and would leave France after all. Quite what
motivated this about-turn remains obscure, but deep-seated suspicion
of any action suggested by Louis-Philippe must have played a part.
On 23 March, at midday, Louis-Philippe, Macdonald, Mortier and
Blacas gathered in the king's study. Louis told them that he would
leave Lille at 3 p.m. and head into Belgium. If necessary, he added
airily, he could then travel to Dunkirk from there. Louis-Philippe,
however, was determined to stress the gravity of this decision. 'Your
majesty should not delude himself in this way,' he warned. 'The
frontier is a Rubicon which, once crossed, is not so easily re-crossed.'
His point was emphasized when at the end of the meeting Macdonald
and Mortier respectfully resigned their posts, saying that they would
escort the king as far as the border, but no further. Louis XVIII may
have been disconcerted by this, for when Louis-Philippe asked for
instructions he was greeted by a rare outburst of petulance. 'By my
faith,' the king snapped, 'you can do whatever you want.'[78]

A few hours later, Louis XVIII crossed his Rubicon into
Belgium, stopping first at Ostend before installing himself in some
style in Ghent. By this time Artois and what remained of the
household troops had also taken shelter over the border, at Ypres.
Louis-Philippe, however, remained a little while longer in France.
During this time he took a controversial action which earned him the
renewed hatred of the ultra-royalists and which finally doomed his
relations with the king. He issued a circular letter to the generals
under his command, informing them that Louis XVIII's departure
from France annulled the effect of his previous orders, and recommending that their future conduct be guided by their 'judgement and
patriotism'.[79] This was, after all, only recognizing the reality of the
situation, and Louis-Philippe's main desire seems to have been to
spare his officers confusion and agonizing questions of loyalty. Yet
his emphasis on the king leaving France could not have failed to
touch a raw nerve at Ghent. In addition, it was a fine distinction
between dispensing soldiers from observing specific orders of the
king, and actually releasing them from their oath of obedience. It
was a distinction his enemies were not inclined to make.

At 3 a.m. on 24 March, Louis-Philippe and Adélaïde left Lille.
Mortier accompanied them as far as the city gates. Brother and sister

then crossed the border, heading for Mons and Tournai. Eerily, it was exactly the same road they had taken, almost nineteen years ago to the day, after Dumouriez' bid to end the Revolution had failed. The route into exile is always the same.

*

ON 3 APRIL 1815, Louis-Philippe and Adélaïde arrived in London, and established themselves in Twickenham. For Louis-Philippe, it was a return to the scene of the happiest days of his emigration, but the pleasant riverside village must also have held sad memories of his dead brothers Montpensier and Beaujolais.

Across the Channel the continent was in turmoil, and the future unknowable. Napoleon was again master of France, but he would still have to fight for his crown. As early as 13 March, the representatives of the Powers gathered at Vienna had declared him an outlaw, and made it clear that the only response to his return would be war. Over the next few weeks both Napoleon in Paris, and Wellington and Blücher's Anglo-Prussian army in Belgium, prepared to take to the field.

In all the Allies' declarations, however, there was one significant omission. No mention was made of who, or what, would replace Napoleon in France once he had been overthrown. It was a clear sign that, after the catastrophic collapse of the restored monarchy, the Allies now had major doubts about whether the elder Bourbons were really capable of bringing peace and stability to France. Louis XVIII himself had foreseen this development; in a remarkable moment of frankness during their interview of 13 March, he had confided to Louis-Philippe: '. . . if I was unfortunately forced to leave France, I'm not really sure what would become of us, because it won't be like the last time. Then, they thought it wasn't our fault. But now, I fear it will be very different, and they will say to us, 'You went back, and you weren't able to cope.'[80]

This new twist, of course, breathed new life into Louis-Philippe's candidacy for the throne, which now began to receive support in some very high circles indeed. The most powerful monarch at the Congress of Vienna, Czar Alexander I of Russia, who had grave reservations about Louis XVIII, now openly argued that Louis-Philippe should replace his cousin once Napoleon was defeated. In

Paris that virtuoso of betrayal, Fouché, also seems to have continued to work for the Orléanist cause, even though Napoleon had just reinstated him as chief of police. Rumours of this intrigue even seem to have reached Wellington in Brussels, since in the course of April he wrote twice to the British foreign minister Lord Castlereagh that the 'Jacobin party' (presumably Fouché) and the army within France were conspiring on behalf of Louis-Philippe.[81]

Naturally, these hints were more than enough to alarm Louis XVIII. Deciding that the safest place for Louis-Philippe would be under his own eye, he wrote to him on 10 May summoning him to Ghent. A week later Louis-Philippe replied with a refusal. Neatly avoiding the trap, he pointed out that since he did not yet know what policy the king would follow if restored, he did not wish to be tied to it in advance by appearing at his court in exile. On a more personal level, he added a long list of instances in which Louis XVIII's personal conduct towards him had been unsatisfactory, from showing insufficient regard for his rank to consistently ignoring his political advice.[82] Apart from giving Louis-Philippe an opportunity to vent all his accumulated resentment at the way his cousin had treated him, not joining him in Belgium was also excellent politics. In France, Ghent was swiftly to become a symbol of reaction, and even thirty years later the accusation of having been there in 1815 remained one of the worst that could be made against a public figure.[83]

The fate of Louis-Philippe, Louis XVIII, and of France itself, however, would be decided not by intrigue and diplomacy, but by military force. On 15 June Napoleon launched himself against Wellington and Blücher. His aim was to win a swift and stunning victory that might shake the unity of the Allied coalition against him, and enable him to play off its members against each other. For the first two days his offensive succeeded brilliantly. In London, the tension mounted. On 20 June Louis-Philippe drove his carriage from Twickenham into London to get the latest reports from Belgium. Passing through Hammersmith, by an extraordinary coincidence he spotted his old commander Dumouriez, who had been living in England for twelve years, standing 'gibbering' on the pavement.[84] He stopped, and learned from the victor of Valmy the news of Waterloo.

Two days later, Napoleon signed his second, and final, abdication.

This left two contenders for the throne in the lists – Louis XVIII and Louis-Philippe. Within a week, it became clear that it was Louis XVIII who would be preferred. He was, after all, clearly king by right of succession, and this chimed well with the principle of legitimacy as the basis of political authority, recently proclaimed by the Allies as the best answer to republicanism or Bonapartism. Ironically, it was Britain, which had in the past taken considerable liberties with her royal succession, that now proved the staunchest defender of the elder Bourbon. When asked about Louis-Philippe's candidacy, Wellington replied: 'He would simply be a usurper of good family.' [85]

Despite this crucial support, however, Louis XVIII was taking no chances. Determined to get back on to French soil as soon as possible, on 24 June he crossed the frontier behind Wellington's army. It is clear that he was also acting according to Wellington's wishes, since after the slaughter of Waterloo the Iron Duke wanted as few casualties as possible on his advance, and hoped that the presence of the king would help lessen resistance. Yet it was at least partly through his haste in forestalling Louis-Philippe that Louis XVIII committed his greatest mistake during the second restoration – returning to France in 'the baggage train of the enemy'.

As ever, Louis-Philippe took this blow philosophically. For now, he was quite happy to stay in his 'dear Twick'. His cousins, however, were not about to let him off so lightly. As with all the other members of the royal family, his property in France had been confiscated by Napoleon. By the simple expedient of omitting his name from the list of those whose assets had been restored, Louis XVIII compelled Louis-Philippe to return to Paris to resolve the matter, and thus extracted what small homage could be gained by his presence. On 28 July, Louis-Philippe arrived in the capital.

The prevailing atmosphere was ghastly. The Hundred Days had created something close to a civil war. Everywhere those who had remained true to the Bourbons were turning on those who had rallied to Napoleon. Sometimes the effects were comic. Fouché, who had switched his allegiance to Louis XVIII the moment he saw which way the wind was blowing, and as a result had kept the ministry of police, was now in charge of drawing up the proscription lists of his former colleagues. One of these was Lazare Carnot, an eminent ex-revolutionary who had served as Napoleon's minister

of the interior. On being assigned to internal exile, he wrote one
sentence to Fouché: 'Where do you want me to go, traitor?' The
reply was equally pithy: 'Wherever you like, imbecile.'[86]

Yet in general the White Terror, as it came to be known, was a
murderous affair, and Louis-Philippe's letters from Paris to Adélaïde
and Marie-Amélie show vividly how appalling he found it. In the
south, where the situation was further poisoned by religious hatred
between Catholic and Protestant, roughly three hundred people were
assassinated or massacred in the 'illegal White Terror'.[87] The most
illustrious victim was Marshal Brune, Napoleon's governor of Provence, who on 2 August was butchered, thrown into the Rhône and
used as target practice by a royalist gang. In letters to his wife and
sister a week later, Louis-Philippe expressed his shock at this atrocity.
Interestingly, he showed no compunction in relating to Adélaïde the
grisly details he spared Marie-Amélie: 'I am still utterly horrified by
the information being received about the death of Marshal Brune,
part of which you will find in *Le Messager* of this evening. Everyone
is saying, but it is not being printed, that he was cut into pieces while
he was still alive.'[88]

The 'legal' White Terror was less barbaric, but more extensive.
Over the next few months, four senior officers were tried and shot,
including Marshal Ney, 'the bravest of the brave', who had defected
to Napoleon after promising to bring him back to Paris 'in an iron
cage'. By the end of 1815 roughly five thousand people had been
brought before the courts for political crimes, of whom over half
were convicted. Most sweeping of all, between 50,000 and 80,000
public officials, or over a quarter of the total, were purged on
suspicion of disloyalty during the Hundred Days. Although Louis
XVIII was repelled by the 'illegal' White Terror, he strongly
supported its 'legal' incarnation. Significantly, in view of Louis-
Philippe's claim in the 'Relation' that the king was fully aware of the
potential of article 14 from the beginning, there is clear evidence that
he considered punishing the Bonapartist leaders using the emergency
powers it granted him.[89]

If the king repudiated the brutalities in the south, his brother
had no such inhibitions. Indeed, Artois' comments at this time as
reported by Louis-Philippe make one's hair stand on end. Given his
feelings about the elder branch of his family, it is of course possible

that Louis-Philippe may have distorted or exaggerated Artois' words. If Louis-Philippe's account had, like his Memoirs, been intended for publication, this argument could be made, but it is difficult to see what he would have gained by twisting the truth in private letters to his wife and sister. His description of Artois' reaction to Marshal Brune's murder and the massacre of thirty-seven Protestants at Nîmes should therefore probably be taken at face value:

> Monsieur [Artois' courtesy title] tells me that in the south the reaction is under way, and that Marshal Brune has been assassinated at Avignon, his body dragged through the streets and finally thrown into the Rhône. Monsieur added that [Brune] had been a great rogue, but that he was annoyed that he had been got rid of in that way, although he was delighted that he was no longer in this world. There has also been some work of this nature at Nîmes, but we can also be satisfied that its only victims have been directed at known rogues, added Monsieur.[90]

Conversation then turned to the alarming number of Bonapartists who had been sneaking up to the Tuileries and shouting 'Vive l'empereur!' This had been curtailed by preventing the public from stopping as they passed in front of the palace. 'It is true,' commented Louis-Philippe wryly, 'that this also prevents anybody from shouting "Long live the King!", but it means that public order is no longer disturbed, and that's the main thing.' According to him, Artois favoured much bolder measures:

> Monsieur thinks that the matter would have been much more speedily resolved if from the first day the first two people who had shouted had been tried for sedition and immediately shot on the Plain of Grenelle [just outside Paris]. But as for me, I prefer [the measures actually taken], because I recall that terrible phrase of Shakespeare: Blood will have blood.[91]

Artois' words were particularly disastrous and divisive since he was not just the king's brother, but the heir to the throne. Yet such sentiments, which were also common throughout the court, did not alarm Louis-Philippe alone. They also caused consternation among the Allied monarchs who had just returned the Bourbons to the throne, and were now in Paris to negotiate the new peace treaty that would close the Hundred Days. One of these was the Austrian Emperor Francis I. In a remarkable unpublished letter to Marie-Amélie of 10 August, Louis-Philippe recounted a long conversation with Francis, who was aghast at the situation he found. Francis had begun by expressing the hope that Marie-Amélie, who was his cousin and of whom he was very fond, would visit him in Paris, then checked himself, saying: 'It's no place for ladies at the moment.' The most Marie-Amélie should do, he thought, was to come over for three or four days only, 'leaving the children where they are; because I wouldn't want to see your children here for anything in the world'. After all, Francis added significantly, 'they're the only ones of the family'.[92]

It was only when Louis-Philippe mentioned the general political situation that Francis revealed the full extent of his exasperation with the elder Bourbons:

— 'Ah, please God [matters will soon be arranged]. Finally, we'll be able to breathe again, but with things going on this way, ah, my God, we really don't know what to do; me, I want things to be sorted out, but we need a government here, because without that, no, no, it's useless.'

— 'Your majesty has put his finger on it, we need a government here, but now that the king is here, he must be strengthened by all possible means.'

— 'Yes, "possible", well said, but, I don't know how to put it, they are not liked; me, I know all about people, and I'm telling you; everyone likes [you] perfectly well, ah, I see that very clearly; as for the king, if it was just him, it wouldn't be so bad, but *the others*, ah, my God, people talk about them like that, between clenched teeth, yes, I hear it all the time . . . Tell me now, what has the duc de Berry done that everybody should hate him so? You have no idea how they detest him; me, I see it, no, no, it's true; me, I'm telling you, they detest him.'

— 'Eh, oh well, sire, it's simply that he sometimes has little moments of impatience, of anger, because at bottom he's a good soul.'

— 'Yes, yes, I believe you, he's a good soul, but he tears people's epaulettes off, what's all that about? That's pretty stupid.'

– 'Your majesty is quite right, he sometimes gets agitated, he's never quite learned to control it. It's a pity.'[93]

The sheer fragility of the second restoration is sometimes passed over. But Francis I's words underline just how precarious it was, and how sceptical even leading European monarchs were about its chances of survival.

Incidentally, this letter also displays one more of Louis-Philippe's personal qualities, his not inconsiderable talent as a mimic. The artful repetition of Francis' verbal tics – 'me, I know all about people', 'me, I'm telling you', 'no, no, it's useless' – conjures up to the life the down-to-earth, inarticulate, but commonsensical and often underestimated emperor. In fact, Louis-Philippe's gift for imitation was so ingrained that it sometimes landed him in deeply embarrassing situations. He once walked into a reception at the Palais-royal absentmindedly aping Talleyrand's club-footed gait, unaware that his subject was walking directly behind him.[94]

Once the restitution of his sequestered property was resolved, Louis-Philippe saw no reason to remain in Paris. He left the capital on 18 August, pointedly on the day before the first major victim of the 'legal' White Terror, General de La Bédoyère, was due to be shot. A few days later, he was back in Twickenham.

Eighteen months of self-imposed exile now began. Since Louis-Philippe was determined not to appear openly disloyal to his cousins, this was the best way of showing silent disapproval of the White Terror and the government's policy of reaction. During this period he made only a few short trips to Paris, when absolutely necessary. But otherwise it was a happy interlude. For the first and only time, Louis-Philippe lived with his wife and sister in the country he so much admired. His love of England, however, did not blind him to how very different it was from France. Years later, as King of the French, he evoked these differences to Victor Hugo. The latter, no mean mimic himself, set down Louis-Philippe's words in his journal:

It was in this conversation that the king said to me: – 'Have you ever been to England?'
   – 'No, sire.'
   – 'Ah well! When you do go – because you will – you'll see; it's strange, it doesn't resemble France in any way; there

you have order, everything's in its place, there's symmetry, cleanliness, boredom, pruned trees, pretty cottages, mown lawns, and in the streets a profound silence. The passers-by as serious and silent as ghosts. The moment you start to talk in the street, being French and lively, you see these ghosts turn around and murmur with an inexpressible mixture of gravity and disdain:- *French people!* When I was in London, I used to go for walks, giving my arm to my wife and my sister, and we would chat, not very loudly you know, we're well brought up people, and all the passers-by would turn around, middle-class as well as common folk, and we would hear them grumbling behind us: — *French people! French people!*'[95]

Chapter Four

CROWN AND PARLIAMENT, 1815–29

IN JULY 1815, EVEN BEFORE he had left France for England, Louis-Philippe had written to a confidant: 'The future does not look rosy.'[1] At the time, his pessimism seemed justified. Quite apart from the horrors of the White Terror, it was clear that the victorious Allies would extract a heavy price for the Hundred Days. The second Treaty of Paris of November 1815 had none of the generosity of that of the previous year. France's borders were rolled back from those of 1792 to those of 1 January 1790, amputating significant territory on her northern and eastern frontiers. An army of occupation was imposed, to remain in place for three to five years, and the cost to be defrayed by its hosts to the tune of 150 million francs per annum. To this was added a heavy war indemnity of 700 million francs.[2]

The second Treaty of Paris became to patriotic Frenchmen what the Treaty of Versailles was to Germans after the First World War: a hated symbol of defeat and humiliation to be expunged at the first available opportunity. The French foreign minister, the duc de Richelieu, signed it in much the same spirit as did the German delegation at Versailles: 'After what I've consented to,' he remarked, 'I deserve to go to the scaffold.'[3] Even the pacific Louis-Philippe commented that he was tempted to copy Voltaire and end all his letters with the exhortation 'Crush this infamy', not in reference to religious bigotry as Voltaire had done, but to the Treaty of Paris.[4]

Unable or unwilling to curb its own adherents, tainted by collaboration with the enemy and forced to sign a hated peace treaty, the second restoration seemed set for the same fate as the first. Yet in fact it was to last not ten months, but fifteen years. Despite constant buffeting by partisan passions and domestic crises, during this time it gave France what no regime since 1789 had been able to offer – a measure of political continuity and peace with Europe. This may have been purchased at the expense of glory, but then glory, as the whole continent had learned over the past quarter-century, has its price.

The Charter defined both restorations; its successes were theirs, and so were its failures. Unlike France's previous constitutions, despite its faults it did prove workable in practice. The most striking feature of politics was the strength of the royal prerogative. The king had the sole initiative in legislation, and on a day-to-day basis the ministers were generally responsible to him rather than to the Chambers. The political complexion of the Chamber of Deputies, coupled with the royal power of dissolving the Assembly and calling new elections, ensured that virtually until the end of the restoration there was never any serious possibility that the king might have to choose ministers from a grouping unacceptable to him. When this possibility became reality, as it did from November 1827, it precipitated the end of the regime.

If the king framed legislation and the ministers were simply his agents charged with translating it on to the statute book, then the role of parliament, in theory at least, was consultative and passive. It did of course have the power of refusing the budget, but this was a weapon of absolute last resort and was in fact never used. Within parliament, opposition as we understand it today, as an active and organized body in combat with the sitting ministry and its almost automatic replacement if the latter falls, was never a reality. In the view of many contemporaries, it was not even desirable in theory. As a *Guide for Electors*, inspired by Louis XVIII's favourite minister Elie Decazes, stated baldly: 'The opposition should be numerous enough to give its opinion weight and to oblige the Chamber to discuss its views scrupulously; but not so numerous as to actually defeat the ministry. In a word, it must never have a majority; if it did, the government would be forced off course, the authority that proposes the law lured beyond its objectives, and the power of initiative warped.'[5]

Yet for all these powerful restrictions, the restoration political system did have one major achievement to its name. It introduced France to modern parliamentary government, and for long enough for it to take root. These roots have never been torn up since, despite two serious subsequent attempts to do so, first by Napoleon III and then by Vichy. But Napoleon III had virtually given up his effort by the end of his reign,[6] while Vichy was simply the short-lived consequence of a catastrophic military collapse. The restoration may have lacked the gaudy plumage of other post-revolutionary French regimes, but it left a more lasting constitutional legacy.

Despite the curbs placed on the opposition, the period did also witness the first glimpses of that other essential characteristic of parliamentary government, a party system. This remained embryonic; the political parties of the restoration did not survive it, though the public careers of many of their leaders did. Most parties in the Chamber of Deputies relied heavily for their unity on a mixture of royal favour and loyalty to individual leaders. National organization, though developing, remained patchy. Yet though many of their edges were blurred, one can discern three main political groupings.

The best-organized, at least until the restoration's final years, were the ultra-royalists, or ultras. Their party discipline was formidable, both in debates and in votes in the Chamber. Much of this was the work of the royalist secret societies that had formed to resist Napoleon, and now moved from clandestinity into the open political arena. The ultras also had the advantage of recognized and effective leaders: the wily operator comte Joseph de Villèle in the Chamber of Deputies, and in the Chamber of Peers the famous writer and thinker Chateaubriand, and the veteran royalist conspirators Jules de Polignac and Mathieu de Montmorency. Over them all, of course, hovered the benevolent patronage of the comte d'Artois.[7]

The ultras' ideology was not entirely consistent; while they were generally nostalgic for the old regime, they sometimes differed on which of its aspects should be stressed. Some, inspired by the counter-revolutionary philosophers Bonald and de Maistre, inclined towards theocracy, while for others the supremacy of the royal authority was paramount. Many also subscribed to a strain of 'decentralizing' thought that sought to maintain and extend the local liberties that had existed before the Revolution. The ultras also faced the tactical problem of whether, if at all, they should accept the Charter. Chateaubriand did so sincerely, Villèle as a regrettable necessity, but Polignac publicly refused to for some time, ostensibly because he could not stomach its concessions to non-Catholics.[8] Yet despite these divergences, in practical terms the ultras generally maintained a common front in the face of their numerous opponents.

The sincerest defenders of the Charter in both Chambers were the moderate royalists. It is tempting to dub them 'the centre', except that they consistently tended to divide into two – the 'centre-right' and the 'centre-left'. In the former group, the dominant figure was the duc de Richelieu, twice prime minister and a man of considerable intelligence and great integrity. Richelieu believed in moderation as a virtue in itself, and was pragmatically prepared to accept post-revolutionary French society. Yet he had no sympathy for the Revolution per se, which had caused him to emigrate to Russia for twenty-five years, and when the governments he led came under pressure, as they frequently did, his instinct was to form a pact with the ultras.[9]

The centre-left, on the other hand, accepted the changes brought about by the Revolution on principle rather than through necessity. It was no coincidence that its leaders were either nobles who had accepted office under Napoleon, or new men who had made their careers in his service. The most prominent of them was the minister of police, Elie Decazes, the son of a bourgeois notary from Libourne near Bordeaux.[10] But the real core of the centre-left was a group of brilliant intellectuals whom Decazes used as his 'brains trust', although he did not always take their advice. Its principal figures were the philosopher Pierre-Paul Royer-Collard, the historians and councillors of state François Guizot and Prosper de Barante, the comte de Serre, justice minister from 1818 to 1821, and the publicist Charles de Rémusat. By the autumn of 1816 they had been dubbed the *doctrinaires*, and the label stuck for the rest of their political careers. The *doctrinaires* did indeed possess a clear doctrine: free of nostalgia for the old regime, they aimed to establish a new political order based on reason, and to 'end the Revolution' by reconciling it with France's previous history. The *doctrinaires* were a significant force during the restoration, but their influence would reach its height under Louis-Philippe.[11]

The last important party in the Chamber and the country was the liberals. Although for form's sake it professed loyalty to Louis XVIII, its members were fundamentally hostile to the Bourbons, or at least to its elder branch. It emphasized national rather than royal sovereignty, opposed all formal social privilege, and was strongly anti-clerical. Its most eminent intellectual was Benjamin Constant, the philosopher, writer and former lover of Mme de Staël, and its most potent symbol Lafayette.[12] On a more practical level, it was given much support and direction by two powerful bankers turned politicians, Casimir Périer and Jacques Laffitte.[13] Within the Chamber, the liberals advocated strictly constitutional opposition; outside it, however, there is considerable evidence that they did not. They had close links with the Bonapartists, and through them with the army and the possibilities that it offered for a coup d'état. Their membership also overlapped with that of several republican secret societies such as the Carbonari, whose aim was a popular insurrection. The most notable example of this overlap was Lafayette, one of the leaders of the Carbonari, and after October 1818, also a deputy.[14]

Despite the danger posed by the extremes, the centre held for five years. Much of the credit for this achievement belonged to Louis XVIII himself. From a truly horrendous situation in the summer of 1815, the ailing king stubbornly set about recovering his position. Most important, he chose the moderate royalists as his partners in this enterprise. Partly this was simple pragmatism; he knew that the policies of the ultras risked a repeat of the Hundred Days, or, worse, a full-scale revolution. Yet at the end of a life whose actions had sometimes proved divisive, Louis does seem genuinely to have wished for national reconciliation. When in early 1818 Artois threatened to emigrate once more, this time to Spain, if his brother did not dismiss his centrist ministry, the king replied with a ringing profession of faith: 'The system I have adopted and which my ministers are faithfully following is founded on the maxim that I must not be the king of two peoples, and the chief goal of my government is that these two peoples, who are so much in evidence today, should eventually become one.' It was the finest sentiment Louis XVIII ever expressed.[15]

These years revealed most clearly the king's greatest political quality, his tenacity. His health was failing, yet the course he chose subjected him to exhausting opposition not only from the ultras in the Chambers, but also from most of his own family. He had no children of his own, and knew that when he died his heir, Artois, would almost certainly abandon the current course and embark on one that risked disaster. Louis sometimes expressed the hope that he might outlive his brother, but barring a miraculous hunting accident this seemed most unlikely. As the king put it bluntly in the same letter of 1818 to Artois: 'I cannot envisage without trembling the moment when my eyes will close.'[16]

Louis XVIII's embrace of the political centre was unquestionably his own decision. Yet it was helped by the fact that at this juncture, rather alarmingly, he found love. The object of his affections was his minister of police, Elie Decazes. The precise nature of the relationship is very difficult to fathom, since Louis' own sexuality remains a grey area. Outwardly he appeared to be heterosexual: he had managed to impregnate his wife, Marie-Joséphine of Savoy, twice, though on each occasion Marie-Joséphine miscarried, and further efforts were hampered by growing evidence that she was alcoholic and lesbian. Louis had then turned to another woman, the witty and imperious Mme de Balbi, who became his mistress for fourteen years.[17] On the other hand, Louis' emotional life was also marked by a series of extremely close friendships with younger men – the duc de Lévis, the comte d'Avaray, Blacas, and finally Decazes. There is no evidence that any of these were sexual, although one of Louis' letters to Lévis, written in English in the style of Smollett, is both obscene and slightly voyeuristic.[18]

Louis was fond of stressing the paternal element in his relations with these younger men, and it is significant that they began only after he had given up hope of having children with Marie-Joséphine. In the case of Decazes, this was carried to extremes. Sometimes Louis would set down his feelings in full: 'My Elie, I love you, I bless you with all my soul, I press you against my heart. Come to it and receive the tenderest embraces of your friend, your father, your Louis!' At other times he would express them in acronyms, of which he was very fond. A message of 11 April 1816 ends 'm.e.j.t.p.s.m.c.e.j.t.b.m.e.m.f.' (*Mon Elie, je te presse sur mon coeur et je te bénis, mon Elie, mon fils* – 'My Elie, I press you to my heart and I bless you, my Elie, my son'.)[19]

The king's friendship with Decazes added a powerful emotional buttress to his determination to pursue a middle way in politics. When his moderate prime minister, the duc de Richelieu, found that he could no longer work with the ultra-dominated Chamber of Deputies, the king dissolved it, in September 1816. The general election of the following month returned a substantial majority on which the ministry could rely, and ushered in the four-year 'liberal restoration'. The period witnessed important legislation, some of it short-term and partisan, but much of it durable. The electoral law of February 1817 was clearly designed to favour the centre at the expense of the ultras, and lasted for only three years. The military law of 1818, however, was to become one of the foundation stones of the modern French army, increasing its size from 150,000 to 240,000, reintroducing a degree of conscription, and professionalizing the officer corps. In fact the chief architects of the ministry's programme, working furiously behind the scenes, were the *doctrinaires*. Barante played a key role in shaping the army law and sat with Guizot and Royer-Collard on the commission that prepared the electoral law. The *doctrinaires'* influence was never greater than on 26 January 1818, when the minister of war, Marshal Gouvion St Cyr, rose in the Chamber of Deputies to present the army law. An actor in his youth, he gave a brilliant performance, but his speech had actually been written by Guizot. As the veteran politician Count Molé commented cattily: 'Gouvion . . . shone with all the eloquence of Guizot.'[20]

The other great achievement of these years belonged to Richelieu. This was the *libération du territoire*, the removal of the occupying forces within the minimum period, three years, stipulated by the second Treaty of Paris. It was coupled with France's readmission into the European states system. In the autumn of 1818, Richelieu journeyed to Aix-la-Chapelle, where the Allied Powers had gathered for one of the periodic congresses they had agreed to hold on the model provided by Vienna. On 9 October, it was agreed that in exchange for a final hefty indemnity payment of 265 million francs,

the foreign troops would leave French soil by 30 November. At the
same time, as a precautionary measure the Allies — England, Austria,
Russia and Prussia — renewed the Quadruple Alliance of 1815, but
softened the impression that it was directed against France by inviting
her informally to join its deliberations.[21] Richelieu had good reason
to be satisfied; if his country had fallen a long way from her
Napoleonic pinnacle, at least her relations with the rest of Europe
were returning to normal. France had lost an empire, but was
beginning to find a role.

On his return to Paris, however, Richelieu found his ministry
deeply divided. The cause was the yearly elections to replace one-
fifth of the Chamber of Deputies that had taken place in October
1818. The new electoral law, as intended, had hit the ultras hard. Yet
the chief beneficiaries had been not the moderate royalists, but the
liberal opposition, which had gained approximately twenty new
deputies, including Lafayette. This menace from the left faced the
moderates with what was to become their perennial dilemma. If their
hold on power weakened, in which direction should they look for
allies? From the differing answers given, the 'two centres' could be
clearly discerned: the centre-right, led by Richelieu, which instinc-
tively looked to the ultras, and the 'centre-left', led by Decazes,
which inclined towards the liberals.

It is a measure of the power wielded by the crown during the
restoration that in his struggle to shift the ministry to the right,
Richelieu soon lost to the king's favourite. He resigned on 26
December 1818, and was replaced by General Dessolles as prime
minister and foreign minister, but the real leader of the government
was Decazes, who was now minister of the interior as well as of
police. The most significant addition to the ministry was comte
Hercule de Serre as keeper of the seals. Highly intelligent and an
excellent orator, de Serre was closely linked to the *doctrinaires*.
With their help, he pioneered in 1819 an important relaxation of the
press laws.[22] Finally, a cabinet reshuffle in November 1819 saw the
departure of General Dessolles, who was replaced as prime minister,
unsurprisingly, by the minister of the interior. Decazes had reached
the zenith of his power.

*

NATURALLY, THE 'LIBERAL RESTORATION' was followed with great interest in Twickenham. After the sanguinary reaction of the White Terror, it seemed that Louis XVIII was finally adopting the course that Louis-Philippe had recommended to him in 1814. After eighteen months of voluntary exile, the Orléans family began to think of return. A further factor may also have influenced them. They did not know whether the political thaw would last long, but they were sure that Louis XVIII would not. From his long knowledge of Artois, Louis-Philippe was convinced that he would not be able to keep his throne for long. In that case, his own candidacy stood its strongest chance if he himself was back in France. One cannot be sure that this was Louis-Philippe's reasoning, but it does make sense of his actions. On 12 February 1817, as he had done in April 1814, he travelled to France for a preliminary reconnaissance. Satisfied with what he found, he returned to England. A few weeks later, he left Twickenham for the last time, and by mid-April was back in the Palais-royal with his family.

If the policy direction of the ministry was now more to his taste, Louis-Philippe's relations with his cousins remained as grim as ever. In particular, the mutual dislike between himself and Louis XVIII soon plumbed new depths. The main reason for this was probably his and Marie-Amélie's remarkable and continuing fertility; in June 1817, just after their return to Paris, they produced another girl, Clémentine, then two more boys, François, prince de Joinville, and Henri, duc d'Aumale, in 1818 and 1822 respectively. The elder branch, on the other hand, still remained childless, making an eventual Orléans succession highly likely, and this no doubt explains the old king's increasing malice towards Louis-Philippe. No occasion was too petty for him to display it; having a dislike of gloves, he once publicly tore out of his hands a pair that Louis-Philippe was holding, on the pretext that this was contrary to etiquette.[23] On all major public occasions, the Orléans were relegated to an inferior position, on the extreme fringes of the royal family.

As could have been expected, this vendetta reached its peak when the elder Bourbons did finally manage to produce a child. In June 1816, during Louis-Philippe's absence in England, Artois' son Berry had married his Neapolitan Bourbon cousin Caroline. The Orléans were not invited to the wedding, an insult made even more cutting by the fact that Caroline was Marie-Amélie's niece. After two miscarriages, on 21 September 1819 Caroline gave birth to a healthy daughter. Although this was not the hoped-for son, it did at least hold out the prospect of one. Above all, the baptism of Mademoiselle, as she was known, presented Louis XVIII with another splendid occasion to humiliate Louis-Philippe. After the ceremony, the Grand Almoner presented the pen successively to the king, Artois, the duchesse and the duc d'Angoulême and the duc de Berry to sign the act as witnesses. Just as he was about to give it to Louis-Philippe, however, Louis XVIII burst out in the high falsetto he sometimes used to dominate proceedings: 'Leave the pen, and have it handed over by one of the chapel clerks.' Louis-Philippe had to wait, silent and furious, while a sufficiently minor functionary was found to perform the task.[24]

While not as spectacular as Louis-Philippe's tussles with the king, this pattern of rivalry and distrust was repeated elsewhere in both families. In particular, the mutual loathing between Adélaïde and the duchesse d'Angoulême remained very evident. Interestingly, Adélaïde seems to have transmitted this dislike to the younger generation. When she was away from Paris her niece Louise, to whom she seems to have been especially close, wrote her letters peppered with unflattering references to the elder branch in general and the duchesse d'Angoulême in particular. A typical one, undated, announces the latter's arrival for lunch:

> Today we've got [the duchesse d'Angoulême] coming for lunch, and the prospect gives me very little pleasure; she will arrive at 10.30, then after lunch there will be a carriage ride in the park, and then we'll send her back by boat to St Cloud. I would be very happy to get out of this, as you can easily imagine.[25]

Things were no better by the end of the restoration, as Louise made clear to her aunt in 1827:

> I am sure you won't envy us our Sunday at St Cloud [with the elder Bourbons] because it will be a real chore . . . such tedium from 2 p.m. right up to 11, as I don't suppose [the duchesse de Berry's] ball will finish any earlier, is quite frightening.[26]

Yet away from the pinpricks of the court, Louis-Philippe was able to construct what in his own case the Revolution had so brutally interrupted, a happy family life. In 1824 his last offspring, a son, Antoine, duc de Montpensier, was born, giving him a total of eight children who survived into adulthood. They were healthy, intelligent and boisterous, and many of their surviving letters reveal a pleasing sense of humour. It was no doubt Mme de Genlis' legacy that the girls received quite as good an education as the boys; when Clémentine began to show an aptitude for history, the famous historian Michelet was engaged as her tutor.

In bringing up his children, Louis-Philippe applied faithfully to them the principles on which Mme de Genlis had raised himself and Adélaïde. A 'modern' curriculum emphasizing literature, history, the sciences and modern languages was established. Following Mme de Genlis' method, the latter were taught by giving the Orléans boys foreign valets who spoke only in their native tongue. However, Louis-Philippe also employed an elderly German professor, who in his youth had taught Metternich. Again following Mme de Genlis' example, every evening he examined his children's exercise books, signing them off and sometimes adding corrections of his own. Above all, Louis-Philippe considered history important; so important, indeed, that he decided to teach it himself. From 1824, he began giving history lessons to his older children which took place every Saturday and lasted the whole morning.[27]

Louis-Philippe's most important pedagogical decision, every bit as radical in its way as his own father's decision to entrust his children's education to Mme de Genlis, was to educate his sons not at home, but at school. Beginning with the eldest, the duc de Chartres, all were sent to the prestigious Lycée Henri-IV in central Paris. The first three, Chartres, Nemours and Joinville, were day boys only, but the two youngest, Aumale and Montpensier, were boarders. The arrangement was not as democratic as it might at first appear; in addition to the regular school staff, the princes had their own tutors, with whom they lunched separately in the common dining-room and who gave them extra private lessons in the course of the day.[28] The results were impressive. All the princes ended as excellent students, especially Aumale and Montpensier. The tutors also benefited, since after their educational duties had ended they generally stayed on as their former pupils' private secretaries. Auguste Trognon, a historian and Guizot's assistant when the latter lectured at the Collège de France, and the writer and journalist Alfred Cuvillier-Fleury, who respectively taught Joinville and Aumale, remained attached to the family for the rest of their lives.[29]

Beyond its educational purpose, sending the Orléans boys to school was also a political and cultural statement, and as such could not fail to escape the sharp eyes of Louis XVIII. The old king was appalled by this initiative and its democratic overtones. On 1 November 1819, he summoned Louis-Philippe to the Tuileries and attempted to dissuade him from enrolling Chartres at Henri-IV. The subtext of the ensuing exchange was entirely political. The king's first objection was less to communal lessons than to communal recreation: 'Everyone will call each other *tu* and *toi*; they will play silly games together.' He then revealed his true concern by citing the precedent of a long-dead family member, the prince de Conti, who had also been sent to school and had ended up as a leading opponent of Louis XV. Louis-Philippe's answer showed the extent of the divide, on every level, between himself and his cousin. It was essential, he stated, that his eldest son's ideas 'should be in harmony with those of the nation and of his generation'.[30] The king could insist no further.

Orléans family life had two settings. The winter was spent in the Palais-royal, but the summer months were passed at the Château de Neuilly on the western fringes of Paris, which was the favourite residence of adults and children alike. The château itself was a large nondescript eighteenth-century building, but its great glory was a huge park of over five hundred acres sweeping down to the Seine. It also included the island of La Grande Jatte, later to become the public pleasure-ground immortalized in Seurat's painting. Nothing remains today of either the chateau or its grounds.[31]

This easy lifestyle was lubricated by the vast income that Louis-Philippe had recovered in 1814, and which increased substantially in the course of the restoration. The death of his mother in June 1821 added to his paternal inheritance the vast Penthièvre fortune, which had again remained intact because the state had not sold it during the Revolution. A contemporary estimate put this at 23,770,000 francs, of which the duchesse bequeathed two-thirds to Louis-Philippe and one-third to Adélaïde. Six months later, Louis-Philippe and Adélaïde's aunt the duchesse de Bourbon also died. The duchesse de Bourbon had been Philippe-Egalité's sister, and had shared his radical views if not quite his enormous wealth. Still, she left her nephew and niece four million francs to divide between them.[32]

After years of dependence, Adélaïde was now an immensely wealthy woman in her own right. In no way, however, did this tempt her to separate from her brother's family. Her principal residences continued to be the Palais-royal and Neuilly, and her role in both households actually expanded. To her primary relationship with Louis-Philippe and her subsequent one with Marie-Amélie was now added a major part in the upbringing of their children, to whom she was devoted and who were clearly substitutes for those she had never had. Her love for her nephews and nieces was unquestionably reciprocated, as an undated and anonymous early poem from one of them makes clear:

> When God receives my prayers and sighs,
> You rise at once before my eyes,
> Only my parents, and no other,
> Are as dear as you, my second mother.[33]

By the 1820s, however, Adélaïde had begun to feel the need for a home of her own where she could spend at least part of the summer. In September 1821, just three months after her mother's death, she travelled into the Auvergne (with Louis-Philippe) to inspect the château and estate of Randan near Vichy, which had come up for sale. Adélaïde liked the property, bought it, and set about rebuilding it from top to bottom. The result was not a great success; the original medieval castle was torn down and replaced by a mock-Gothic one, bristling with heavy brick towers and pointed roofs. On the other hand, the new château did have an imposing terrace, with splendid views over the surrounding mountains.[34]

Adélaïde also intended Randan as a further contribution to Orléans family life, by having her brother and his family come to stay with her for several weeks each summer. Yet this kind thought presented the practical problem of how in the pre-railway age to transport a family with eight children by often difficult roads all the way to the Auvergne. Louis-Philippe's latent eccentricity is most

clearly revealed in the solution he devised — an immense twelve-
seater charabanc resembling, as his son Joinville recalled in his
memoirs, 'a travelling menagerie'. Noisy, unwieldy, and drawn by
six savage horses, it must have terrorized the roads of central France
each summer. This is certainly the impression given by Joinville:

> If we met oncoming carriages or carts, it was a question of
> whether our horses would swerve too much or not enough.
> These encounters were announced by the postilions starting to
> shout; if the horses didn't swerve enough, there would be a
> terrible collision, with torrents of oaths and a tinkle of broken
> glass from carriage lamps and windows. If on the other hand
> they swerved too much, [the charabanc] would tip gently on
> one side, often finishing in the ditch. A clamour would then rise
> from all the family, with everyone checking themselves for
> bruises and then starting to laugh, as the contraption was set
> right. Further on, another accident; going through a village the
> postilions, for the sake of effect, would start using their whips:
> the horses would get excited and the charabanc would speed up.
> This was fine if the village street was straight, but if there was
> a turning the horses would take it too fast and we would crash
> violently into the corner. Immediately the wheelwrights and
> hotel-keepers, always on the lookout for accidents, would come
> running up. Four hours for repairs! The grown-ups would
> fulminate, but the children would be delighted.[35]

The road also had perils of a different sort. One such was posed by
the village of Magny, which appears to have become a byword
among the family for its dirty inn and eccentric inhabitants, headed
by the parish priest. Louise related with great glee to Adélaïde a
particularly embarrassing encounter there:

> . . . towards the end of our lunch [the landlord of the inn] came
> into the dining-room, and with an extraordinary grimace
> announced that the parish priest had arrived and was asking to
> see us, but that he had told him to wait a moment. When lunch
> was over I quickly ran into the next room to take my precau-
> tions [i.e. use the chamber-pot], but, dear aunt, guess what I
> saw when I opened the door! The priest had got there before
> me; I shut the door again pretty quick as you can imagine.

The priest was clearly not the only sight of Magny. 'As for the fat woman,' Louise ended her letter, 'I looked for her everywhere, but in vain; I think we must have gone past her inn.'[36]

Adélaïde's attention was not exclusively centred on her family. During these years she also became close to one of her brother's aides-de-camp, baron Raoul de Montmorency. Thirteen years younger than Adélaïde and the scion of France's oldest noble family, Raoul was, like all Louis-Philippe's aides-de-camp, a close friend as well as servant of the Orléans. He was also something of a self-taught cook, as a letter of Marie-Amélie to Adélaïde reveals: 'Raoul came to dinner and brought with him his famous cheese soup, which I am sure must be excellent but which was burnt so no one could eat it, which really upset poor Raoul.'[37]

Raoul, however, meant more to Adélaïde than his cheese soup. It is probable that she fell in love with him, though how far, if at all, he reciprocated her affection is unclear. The only direct evidence of an attachment is a letter of 25 February 1817 of Louis-Philippe to Adélaïde, then taking the waters at Cheltenham, warning her of rumours circulating in Paris linking her and Raoul.[38] But there are other possible indications. Adélaïde's journal starts up again at this point, but its first pages, covering the period 12 February to 20 March 1817 – exactly when Louis-Philippe was writing to her about Raoul – have been torn out.[39] Over the next three years, the tone of the diary entries is that of a woman in deep emotional distress, which could at least in part have been caused by an unhappy experience in love. It may also be significant that in late May 1820, while the Orléans family was at Neuilly, Raoul felt obliged to resign as Louis-Philippe's aide-de-camp, citing unspecified but powerful reasons with which the latter reluctantly felt obliged to concur.[40] An entry in Adélaïde's journal, headed simply 'May 1820', could be read as reflecting sad recognition of the end of a relationship:

We arrived at Neuilly this year on Saturday 7 May; I have had much heartbreak since having left, but by God's grace I am now more resigned; I know that I cannot be happy in this world, and I no longer seek to be, I live from day to day, I thank God when I have some consolations and satisfactions; whenever the pain of my heart revives more piercingly, I offer it up to God, and tell myself that it is a mercy on His part to make me worthy of Heaven ... I offer up my sufferings to God for myself, and for my friends! ... Those who have once had a place in my heart shall have it always! ... Oh yes, always![41]

*

OUTSIDE THE WORLD OF NEUILLY, Randan and the Lycée Henri-IV, by late 1819 the 'liberal restoration' was running into difficulties. In fact, Decazes' appointment as prime minister, which at first sight seemed its apogee, was really a symptom of its decline. The root of the problem was the partial elections to the Chamber of Deputies of September 1819. After its recent legislative achievements, Decazes was looking to this vote as proof of the electorate's support of the ministry's policies. The result was a rude shock: instead of showing their gratitude to the government, the voters instead swung massively behind the left. Of the fifty-five seats up for election, the liberal opposition won thirty-five, while the ministry lost fifteen. The effect was magnified by the poor showing of the ultras, resentful and demoralized by the new electoral law. Worst of all, the electors of Grenoble chose as their deputy the veteran revolutionary politician and 'regicide', the abbé Grégoire. In fact, Grégoire was not strictly speaking a regicide; he had indeed been a deputy to the Convention in 1793, but had been absent when it had voted to execute Louis XVI. He had, however, written to the Convention expressing complete support for its decision and comparing monarchy to leprosy, so the effect of his 1819 election on the Tuileries can well be imagined.[42]

Decazes' response to the crisis – a new electoral law to muzzle the left – reveals the limits of his constitutional principles. It also provoked a split in the ministry. General Dessolles, Marshal Gouvion St Cyr and baron Louis refused to countenance this tack to the right, and resigned. It was against this background that Decazes was obliged to assume the prime ministership himself, while de Serre remained as keeper of the seals and baron Pasquier, an experienced survivor who had been successively a judge under the old regime, a prisoner under the Terror, a councillor of state under Napoleon and was now a deputy under the restoration, was brought in as foreign minister.[43]

The elections of September 1819 exposed the central dilemma of the 'liberal restoration'. The moment it began to dismantle the more repressive aspects of the 1814 settlement, the result was not an increase in its popular support, but a rush to the left. The issues raised by this fact go well beyond the events of 1819, and raise the most central question of all: how far was the restoration as a whole ever viable? In order to have any chance of survival, it had to create a consensus, and to do this it had to win over former enemies, especially those who had supported the Revolution and Napoleon. Yet all its advances were stubbornly resisted. As has recently been argued, this may have owed much to memories of the White Terror; the liberal opposition seem to have suspected that the role of leading ultras in the atrocities of 1815 had been covered up by successive governments, and it is noticeable that its electoral advance in September 1819 was swiftly followed by demands for these cases to be reopened. This in turn provoked a counter-mobilization by the ultras, alarmed that if the liberals ever gained control of the Chamber of Deputies some very uncomfortable investigations indeed would be launched.[44] Thus attempts at national reconciliation, far from bolstering the political centre, ended by strengthening the extremes.

Perhaps the only way to resolve this conundrum would have been for the king to take an exceptionally bold step, and bring some leaders of the liberal opposition into the ministry. It is, however, highly unlikely that Louis XVIII ever considered this. He would no doubt have felt, as his brother did a decade later, that this would have been seen as a sign of weakness and led only, as it had for Louis XVI, to the overthrow of the monarchy. If the liberal advance had continued unchecked under Louis XVIII, this would simply have brought forward the moment when the crucial question that always haunted the restoration was posed: what would happen if the crown ever faced a hostile liberal majority in the Chamber? Assuming that Louis XVIII would have refused to choose his ministers from this majority, he would, like his brother in 1830, have faced the grim alternative of extra-constitutional action.

If the regime could not be saved from the left, it would have to be rescued by the right, and this change of policy was Decazes' first act as prime minister. The means he chose to accomplish this was the new electoral law, which immediately aroused the fury of the framers of the previous one, his allies the *doctrinaires*.[45] As his majority dwindled yet further in the Chamber, Decazes was forced to rely on right-wing votes for survival while the law was prepared. Thus the swing to reaction that eventually brought the restoration down was initiated by its most famous politician of the centre-left. This irony exposed both the continuity, and the fragility, of the edifice.

As Decazes was making his short-term calculations, fate intervened. On Sunday 13 February 1820, the Paris Opera, then in the Rue de Richelieu, was staging an opera, *Le Rossignol*, followed by two ballets, *Le Carnaval de Venise* and *Les Noces de Gamache*, as part of the carnival season before Lent.[46] Louis-Philippe decided to attend with Marie-Amélie, who was making her first outing after another pregnancy, and Adélaïde. As the peformance was about to begin, the duc and duchesse de Berry arrived and took their seats in the box opposite, and Louis-Philippe, Marie-Amélie and Adélaïde went over to greet them. During the interval of the second ballet, the duchesse de Berry, who felt ill, decided to leave.[47]

The duc accompanied his wife to their carriage, which was parked in the adjoining Rue Rameau, and handed her in. Since his current mistress, the dancer Virginie Oreille, was performing that evening and he wanted to see her afterwards, he then turned to go back into the Opera. The time was just before 11 p.m. Suddenly a stranger in a long overcoat rushed towards Berry, evaded a sentry, a footman and the two noblemen in attendance, and plunged a seven-inch dagger up to the hilt into his right breast. Berry realized immediately that the wound was mortal; he exclaimed: 'I am murdered! This man has killed me!', then pulled out the dagger himself and was helped back into the opera house. Several doctors were swiftly called. Berry was taken first to the withdrawing-room behind the royal box, then to the manager's office, where there was enough room to put a mattress on the floor. Stretched out in this cramped room, Berry entered his death agony, by turns tossing feverishly and vomiting blood.[48]

Outside, in the first moments of shock the assassin had managed to break away and get a head start on his pursuers. He was finally brought to bay by a waiter in the nearby Arcade Colbert, securely tied, and taken to the guard post at the Opera.[49] He turned out to be Louis-Pierre Louvel, a thirty-seven-year-old saddler. Short, dark, balding and solitary, Louvel was a fervent Bonapartist who had followed Napoleon to Elba, where he had worked in the ex-emperor's stables. He had taken part in the Hundred Days and been present at Waterloo, and ever since had been perfecting a plan to kill all the Bourbons, preferably one by one. Berry was first on his list, because he was clearly the only member of the family capable of fathering an heir. Louvel hoped, with undeniable logic, that killing the duc would doom the whole line to extinction.[50]

While Berry was being carried bleeding from withdrawing-room to manager's office, the performance was still going on and no one had the faintest idea of the drama being enacted at their backs. However, one of the usherettes had seen what was happening and thought she should alert Louis-Philippe and his family. She knocked on the door of their box and spoke to Atthalin, who was accompanying them that evening. On hearing the news, Louis-Philippe, Marie-Amélie and Adélaïde stood up and rushed to their dying cousin's bedside.[51] The scene was ghastly; the duchesse de Berry had thrown herself shrieking on her husband's body, and her dress was covered in blood. As the news spread, shocked family members, courtiers and ministers, some still dressed in their carnival costumes, began to arrive and pressed into the stifling room – Artois, the duc and duchesse d'Angoulême, Decazes, Richelieu, Chateaubriand, even Berry's two children by a previous English mistress, to whom he said his farewells in English.[52]

At 5 a.m. the king arrived. With great nobility, Berry pleaded passionately with him to spare the life of the assassin. Louis, who had no intention of doing so, merely replied: 'Nephew, you are not as badly hurt as you think, we will talk about it.' At 6.35 a.m., Berry finally stopped breathing, and the king himself closed his eyes. Yet even in the midst of his grief, Louis did not forget to fire one more shot at the Orléans. On the pretext that they should get some rest, he ordered them to go home just before Berry died. Adélaïde had already fainted and been carried out, but Louis-Philippe and Marie-Amélie had stayed, and were surely right to see their dismissal as a symbolic exclusion from a family that should have been united in sorrow.[53]

The wider political backlash against Berry's murder was savage, and its principal target was Decazes and the opening he had given to the left. 'I have seen Decazes' dagger, and it was a liberal idea,' trumpeted Charles Nodier in the influential *Journal des Débats*.

Chateaubriand went one step further, and assigned the moral blame for Berry's murder to Decazes with a famously vicious phrase: 'His foot slipped in blood.' The pressure on the king to dismiss Decazes, not only from the ultra politicians and press but from his own family, became intense. The duchesse d'Angoulême went down on her knees to beg Louis to part from his favourite, brandishing the outrageous threat that otherwise the royal bodyguard might kill Decazes: 'Sire, it is to avoid another victim.'[54] After a week of this, Louis finally gave way, but not before he had made Decazes a duke and peer, and found him a prestigious new post as ambassador to London. The new prime minister, for a second time, was a reluctant Richelieu.

The great irony, of course, was that Decazes had already begun moving to the right before Berry's assassination. Yet although it did not cause this development, the murder did greatly accelerate it. Over the next four months, Richelieu's ministry passed a battery of conservative legislation. The 'exceptional laws' empowered the government to detain anybody suspected of conspiracy against the king or the safety of the state for up to three months, while all periodicals were subjected to review by the censor before publication. Finally, and most significant, the electoral law first conceived by Decazes was voted on 12 June 1820. Its key feature was an increase in the number of deputies from 258 to 430, with the 172 new deputies being selected by special electoral colleges composed of the wealthiest 25 per cent of voters in each Department of France. Since the latter also retained their vote in the original 258 seats, they therefore had in effect a double vote. The aim, of course, was to skew the franchise as far as possible in favour of the wealthiest section of the electorate, who would also, it was assumed, be the most conservative.[55]

In the short term, the 'law of the double vote', as it was dubbed, amply fulfilled these expectations. In the elections of November 1820, in which not only the usual fifth of seats but also the 172 newly created ones were to be filled, the left lost heavily, sinking to 80 deputies, while the ministry and the ultras rose to 190 and 160 respectively. Yet in the longer term the law set a dangerous precedent. Weighting the electoral system so heavily towards the elite widened the gap between the monarchy and the nation, and encouraged ministers to further steps along this path, which would culminate in the disastrous four ordinances of July 1830.

By the time of the elections, royalist morale had already been boosted by a crucial development that seemed almost miraculous – the birth on 29 September of a posthumous son to the duc de Berry. Immediately given the name and title of Henri, duc de Bordeaux, the baby finally guaranteed the elder branch a future. The duchesse de Berry took extraordinary precautions to prove that the child was really her own, even demanding that Marshal Suchet, one of the official witnesses, should give the umbilical cord a tug to ensure it was attached to her. The grizzled marshal had stood on the battlefields of Germany and Spain without flinching, but this was too much for him, and he only did so after considerable persuasion.[56]

Naturally, Louis-Philippe remained unconvinced. In his view, the birth had taken place suspiciously quickly. Rushing over to the Tuileries, he repeatedly interrogated poor Suchet as to whether the umbilical cord really had been attached. When Suchet affirmed that that had indeed been the case, Louis-Philippe for once let the mask drop. In front of the duchesse de Gontaut, who was holding the baby in her arms, he barked: 'So we will never count for anything in this country!' At a stroke the prospects of his own son, who the day before had been third in line to the throne after the elderly Artois and the sterile Angoulême, had receded dramatically. Adélaïde underlined the point to the duchesse de Gontaut in making her excuses for her brother: 'One never gives up a crown without regret.'[57]

Electoral success and the birth of the duc de Bordeaux secured the political dominance of the centre-right and the ultras. It did not, however, improve Richelieu's position. The Chamber's centre of gravity had moved firmly to the right, making his policy of governing with ultra votes while keeping the ultra leaders out of the cabinet ultimately untenable. His position was further undermined by developments at the Tuileries. With Decazes banished to London, the versatile king had switched to a female favourite, Zoé, comtesse du Cayla. A witty, intelligent brunette of thirty-five, Mme du Cayla first became intimate with Louis XVIII in the summer of 1820. She was soon making regular visits to him every Wednesday afternoon, during which, he instructed his servants, he was never to be disturbed. Whether this implies that Louis' relationship with Mme du Cayla was sexual remains unclear, though a rumour has always persisted that he would take snuff from her breasts.[58]

Yet Mme du Cayla was far more than merely the 'royal snuff-box', as malevolent courtiers dubbed her.[59] She was also closely connected with the ultras through her friend Sosthènes de la Roche-foucauld, an aide-de-camp of Artois, and was happy to use her new position to advance their policies.[60] Thus the ground was well prepared when in November 1821 the ultras, in a completely oppor-tunistic alliance with the left, voted a condemnation of Richelieu's foreign policy. Disgusted, Richelieu resigned on 12 December, and was replaced as prime minister by the ultra Villèle.

Villèle was to govern, with some success, for seven years, the longest tenure of any restoration prime minister. This fact gives weight to the argument made by some recent historians that the restoration monarchy remained workable until well into the 1820s, and certainly was not inevitably doomed as early as 1819.[61] There is much cogency to this interpretation, and evidence to back it up. Villèle's ministry scored a major foreign policy coup in Spain, with a victorious military intervention in 1823 to save King Ferdinand VII from a domestic revolution. It then won an important general election victory the same year, and skilfully managed the delicate transition from the reign of Louis XVIII to that of Charles X.

Yet these achievements, though significant, were not durable. Villèle's strategy was to deploy a whole range of corrupt and repressive methods – heightened press censorship, administrative purges, last-minute revision of electoral rolls and redrawing of constituency boundaries – to ensure the subservience of parliament and the political nation to the ministry's will. This was not the first time such tactics had been used, and it would certainly not be the last; Decazes had been an adept in these black arts, and so would successive governments until well into the Third Republic. Until 1827, they served Villèle well. However, Villèle's problem was not means, but ends. Once his ascendancy was in place, he used it to force through measures that were clearly intended to benefit the nobility and clergy, and which proved so unpopular that even the tightly controlled electorate he had created eventually rebelled. Villèle's 'system' was highly effective, but within seven years it had buckled under the strain of delivering unacceptable policies.[62]

In ultra terms Villèle was a moderate, in that he wished to introduce right-wing measures gradually rather than suddenly and brutally, as did some of his colleagues. It is probable that towards the end of his ministry he was rushed into some controversial legislation that he would have preferred to delay, and it could be argued that he would have achieved his aims had he been allowed to proceed at his own pace. Yet the rising tide of opposition from 1827 shows clearly how unpalatable the ultra programme was to almost all sections of society, however it was implemented. Villèle's methods, if continued, would no doubt have postponed a confrontation, but they would not have avoided it.

While endorsing Villèle's approach, Louis XVIII was well aware that it raised problems which had to be handled with great care. He had no confidence, however, that Artois shared his views. As he grew older and more ill, he feared increasingly for the future. Above all, he knew that the chief beneficiary of Artois' mistakes as king would be Louis-Philippe, whose remaining bonds of loyalty had been seriously weakened by the birth of the duc de Bordeaux, and whose actions – or lack of them – smacked strongly of a waiting game. In April 1821 he confided his forebodings to the future minister baron d'Haussez. The king's words stand as a tribute both to his own subtlety, and to that of Louis-Philippe: 'The duc d'Orléans ... remains quite still, but nevertheless I notice that he is moving forward. This activity without movement worries me. What does one do to stop a man who does not move? It's a problem I shall have to solve. I certainly wouldn't care to leave it to my successor.'[63]

By the autumn of 1824, however, it became clear that Louis XVIII was going to have to do just that. His health was entering its final decline: he now had wet gangrene in his right foot, and dry gangrene at the base of his spine, probably caused by hardening of the arteries linked in turn to diabetes. The king's neck could no longer support the weight of his head, but he insisted on going on working. The result was that his head would constantly fall forward on to his desk, leaving it bruised and bloody. Villèle, horrified by this sight, eventually persuaded him to rest his head on a cushion placed on the desk, and it was in this grotesque and tragic position that Louis XVIII gave his last audiences.[64]

On 13 September 1824, Louis-Philippe and his family were staying at their property of Eu near Dieppe when a messenger arrived

from Artois asking them to return to Paris immediately, as the king
was dying. They set off immediately, and arrived back at Neuilly at
3.45 a.m.[65]

Adélaïde kept a detailed diary of the events of the next few days,
which has never been published, and which casts revealing light
both on Louis XVIII's last moments and on her own reaction to
them. For example, she repeats the well known fact that the king
was reluctant to take the last sacraments, and that it was only on
the insistence of Mme du Cayla, during his last meeting with her
on 11 September, that he did so. Adélaïde, however, adds the telling
detail that immediately afterwards Mme du Cayla left for her country
home at St Ouen. This implies strongly that she had indeed had
some form of physical relationship with Louis, since it had always
been a custom of the French monarchy that as soon as the king
agreed to take the sacraments his mistress should leave court, to
enable him to die in a state of grace.[66]

Arriving at the Tuileries at around midday on the 14th, Louis-
Philippe, Marie-Amélie and Adélaïde forced their way through a vast
crowd in the courtyard, past the courtiers massed in the Galerie de
Diane, and then into the king's study adjoining his bedroom where
they found his closest relatives. The comte d'Artois embraced them,
weeping, while the duchesse d'Angoulême told them that the king
was still reluctant to have the prayers for the dying said. Adélaïde's
comment on this makes clear, with remarkable honesty, the mixture
of dislike and compassion for Louis XVIII this aroused in her:

> I admit that this detail upset me. Although I had no affection or
> indeed any particular feelings for the king, far from it, I pitied
> him. Why, once he had received the sacraments, made his peace
> with God and set an example, go on tormenting him with these
> prayers? They could have been said very quietly, and would
> certainly have done his soul just as much good.[67]

Having decided not to enter the king's bedroom for the moment,
the Orléans were about to leave when Artois invited them back for
dinner that evening. At 5.45 p.m. they returned to the king's
apartments, and sat down to eat. Adélaïde did not, however, find it a
comfortable experience:

The king's place was laid, his whole dinner-service was laid out, as if he was about to come and dine, except that it was covered with a veil ... everything was set out and proceeded as if the king was there. I cannot convey the impression this service set out around this empty place made on me, coupled with the thought that the unfortunate monarch was dying in the room next door.[68]

The Orléans cannot have got much sleep that night, because at 5 a.m. another messenger was sent to fetch them back to the Tuileries. However, it was a false alarm; Louis XVIII, having appeared to be on the point of death, had rallied again. A few hours previously, the dressings on his foot had been changed, an excruciating process that took three-quarters of an hour. One of the courtiers present gave Adélaïde an account of the operation that amply confirms all the well known stories about the effects of the king's gangrene:

M. de Boisgelin told me that he had witnessed the dressings being changed, and that the state of [the king's] body and above all that of his foot and of his leg was beyond description, that he was missing three toes from one foot and that one could see the bones protruding from this foot and from the base of the leg ...[69]

With her customary frankness, Adélaïde noted that Louis XVIII's death-agony had now gone on so long that it had bred a sort of indifference in those around him. This led her in turn to a devastating reflection on the poverty of the old man's emotional life:

One is now so used to the idea of [the king's] death, that one sees clearly that everybody is just waiting for this moment, without regret or emotion and even with a sort of impatience. Alas! Poor humanity, and this is the result of having no friends, of having never known how to love and therefore how to be loved ... It is a sad and disgusting spectacle![70]

In fact, the long wait was drawing to a close. At 1 a.m. on 16 September, the Orléans were woken once more and summoned to a final vigil at the Tuileries. Again they battled past the crowds in the Galerie de Diane, and this time went into the king's bedroom. It was packed with family members, courtiers and clerics: Artois, the duc and duchesse d'Angoulême, the duchesse de Berry, the duc de Bourbon, the Archbishop of Paris, the Grand Almoner, the Bishop of Hermopolis, the comte d'Avaray, Blacas and Boisgelin. Louis-Philippe found a chair to sit in, while Adélaïde and Marie-Amélie contented themselves with folding stools. Yet even at this solemn moment, there was a touch of black comedy:

> The silence was only interrupted by the king's breathing, which from time to time stopped, and by the prayers of the Grand Almoner and the priests, but suddenly we heard a louder sound; I thought that it was the king's death-rattle, but it was nothing of the sort; it was poor M. d'Avaray, who had fallen asleep, and was snoring with terrific force . . .

A little while later, the end came:

> The breathing became less and less audible, the confessor, the doctors, the gentlemen-in-waiting approached the king's bed, there was a general movement, and we *all* stood up. A candle was brought to the doctors who held it before the king's face, which I saw perfectly; it was black and yellow, the mouth was open and its expression was dreadful. M. le duc d'Angoulême repeated two or three times to [Artois]: 'Father, it's over.'

In the next emotion-filled moments, Adélaïde made her first two political gestures of the new reign. They blatantly revealed her lack of loyalty to her cousins, and served notice of her actions six years later:

> M. le comte Charles de Damas went up to [Artois], and said in a solemn and broken voice: 'Sire, the king is dead.' Everybody then rushed to kiss the new king's hand, but I wasn't able to . . . The new king then said, 'I wish to kiss the [old] king's hand', so the duc de Duras took the dead king's arm from out of the bed, and the king went down on his knees and kissed his hand. Madame [la duchesse d'Angoulême], M. le duc d'Angoulême, Mme la duchesse de Berry, my brother and sister [in-law] and M. le duc de Bourbon all did the same. However, I admit that I only pretended to do so; it could do [the dead king] no good and my feelings did not incline me to it, so I

thought it best to abstain. The smell from the bed was enough
to knock you over.[71]

*

THE NEXT FEW DAYS brought a significant improvement in Louis-
Philippe's position. On 17 September the new king received the
whole royal family at St Cloud (where Adélaïde once again refused
to kiss his hand),[72] and then summoned Louis-Philippe for a private
interview four days later. During this meeting he announced that
Louis-Philippe would be granted the exalted title of Royal Highness,
which he had always coveted, in place of his current one of Serene
Highness. In this family matter Charles X, who has always been
excoriated for his thoughtlessness and stupidity, showed far more
intelligence than had his dead brother. By refusing to grant Louis-
Philippe and other Bourbon cousins like the Condé the title of Royal
Highness, Louis XVIII had sought to establish a distinction between
his immediate family and the princes of the blood to the former's
advantage. In fact, this policy had created considerable ill-will and
done some damage to the unity of the regime. In contrast, Charles
X's reversal of this stance overjoyed Louis-Philippe and reattached
him to the dynasty at an important transitional moment.[73]

In the course of this long conversation, every word of which
was later retailed by Louis-Philippe to Adélaïde and recorded in
her journal, Charles made it clear to his cousin that his days of
humiliation and exclusion were at an end. He freely admitted that his
brother's attitude towards the Orléans had been unfair, and claimed
that he had disapproved of it at the time: 'I often said it to the late
king, pinpricks never do any good, but he had some ideas in his
head that could never be overcome.' Charles' wider goal, which he
outlined with considerable honesty and good sense, was family unity.
To this end, he was quite prepared to raise the subject, so rigidly
taboo under Louis XVIII, of the succession. Shrewdly, he appealed
to Louis-Philippe's self-interest by reminding him how close he still
stood to the throne, despite the birth of the duc de Bordeaux:

> It is very important both for you and for us that we should be
> firmly united, because finally, my dear fellow, look here, you
> must be aware of your position, it is delicate and important;

after all, between you and the throne there is only a four-year-
old child, and at the least a four-year-old child is a very small
thing . . . it is essential for us and even more so for you, that if
he should die, you or your offspring should succeed without
difficulties or embarrassments.[74]

Charles X emerges from this account as a more sympathetic
figure than he is usually painted: frank, generous, and capable of
sound initiatives. It is ironic that Louis-Philippe, who detested his
principles, always felt far more affection for him than for Louis
XVIII, whose views were often closer to his own. It added an extra,
painful dimension to the clash that would later take place.

If Charles showed a sure touch in dealing with his family, it soon
became clear that this did not extend to politics. Over the next few
months, his government introduced a series of deeply unpopular
measures that would soon engender a formidable backlash. Much of
this legislation originated not with Charles, but with Louis XVIII
and Villèle – further evidence of the essential continuity of restoration politics. Yet Charles' accession certainly accelerated its pace. At
the beginning of each parliamentary session the king would present
Villèle with a list of proposals that he wanted to become law, which
both cut across the latter's gradualist approach and made his task
much more difficult.[75]

The content of these proposals was deeply divisive. What Villèle
was being forced to introduce more and more rapidly was the ultra
programme, with all its destabilizing implications for French society
and politics. While this recognized the impossibility of returning to
the old regime in its entirety, it was absolutely determined to restore
as far as possible one of its central aspects – the society of orders.
To this end, a whole battery of bills was prepared to reinforce the
social and economic power of the nobility and clergy.

The most important was the indemnity law in favour of the
former émigrés. This had been conceived by Louis XVIII as a way
of healing one of the most gaping wounds of the Revolution, the
issue of the *biens nationaux*. The old king had had a conscience about
those nobles who for twenty-five years had sacrificed everything for
him and then returned to France to find their ancestral properties in
the hands of others. As well as righting this wrong, in his view, an

indemnity would also bolster the position of the nobility in post-revolutionary France. Above all, the indemnity would finally dispel the insecurity that still hung over the *biens nationaux*, whose sale was in many cases still being disputed by their former owners.

In the long term, the indemnity bill did fulfil the objectives Louis XVIII set for it, and ensured that in time the revolutionary land sales were no longer questioned. In the short term, however, it created a great political storm. The financial means proposed to fund the bill, a conversion of the rates on government bonds from 5 to 3 per cent, were rejected by the Chamber of Peers, which argued that small bondholders should not have to finance compensation for émigrés. Instead, Villèle was forced to resort to a complicated combination of a voluntary conversion and revenue from certain taxes and a sinking fund to save the project. In April 1825 a bill was finally passed authorizing the payment of an indemnity of 988 million francs in 3 per cent bonds. Of this, 630 million francs were eventually paid out to approximately 700,000 claimants.[76] Ironically, by far the largest payment – 17 million francs – was made to Louis-Philippe for those parts of the Orléans estate that the revolutionaries had sold off.[77] Once again, Charles X had been good to him.

Strengthening the nobility was also the aim of a further piece of legislation that Villèle's ministry introduced in March 1826. This was a bill to reverse at least partially one of the major social changes of the Revolution – the abolition of primogeniture. In families paying at least 300 francs in direct tax, the measure laid down that the eldest son would henceforth be entitled to a disproportionate share of the father's estate unless the latter specifically requested otherwise. This was an obvious attempt to build up once more that essential prerequisite of noble power, a substantial landholding base. As such, it was furiously attacked by the liberal press and by pamphlets as a blatant effort to reverse the Revolution and restore the old regime. After a passionate debate, the Chamber of Peers, at this time a far more moderate body than the Chamber of Deputies, rejected the bill. There was no doubt of the popularity of the decision: Paris celebrated with illuminations and fireworks for five days.[78]

The second plank of the ultra programme, rebuilding the status of the clergy, met if anything with greater hostility. Even before 1789, anticlericalism had been a significant force in French society, and the religious upheavals of the Revolution had entrenched it still further. Anticlericals formed a broad coalition ranging from disciples of the Enlightenment to Catholic Gallicans suspicious of papal pretensions, peasants fearful that a resurgent clergy might reimpose the tithe in the countryside, and sections of the urban working classes, particularly in Paris. Their particular *bête noire* was the Catholic religious orders, above all the Jesuits, whom they saw as the shocktroops of papal and royal despotism, exercising a particularly insidious influence on the young through their traditional role in education. It was thus unfortunate that the first religious bill of the new reign was expressly designed to favour these orders. For the first time since the Revolution, they were to be allowed a legal status, permitting them to acquire property and receive donations. It mattered little that, to assuage public opinion, this applied only to female orders; it was generally assumed to be but a first step towards extending the same rights to their male equivalents. The bill did eventually pass the Chambers, but only with severe restrictions.[79]

This trial balloon, however, was as nothing to the restoration's most notorious piece of religious legislation – the law of sacrilege. This proposed an ascending order of penalties for sacrilegious acts, culminating, in the case of profanation of the Host itself, in the punishment for parricide – amputation of the right hand before decapitation. The bill's ostensible purpose was to address the rising number of recent incidents of desecration in churches. Its real aim, however, was to symbolize, in a particularly brutal form, expiation for the sins of the Revolution, and to place the apparatus of the state at the disposal of the church in a highly charged area. Most insidiously of all, by criminalizing impious acts solely against the Catholic church and no other, it undermined the equal toleration of faiths promised by the Charter.[80]

In reality, the law's bark was worse than its bite. Its definition of sacrilege was so restrictive that the possibility of conviction became virtually nil – to qualify as such, the offending act had to be committed 'voluntarily, publicly, and through hate or contempt for religion'. Then as now, public profanation of the Host has never posed a major problem of law and order in France. Even the grislier refinements of the penalty for parricide were soon dropped from the bill. In fact, after its passage through the Chambers in April 1825 amid furious debate, the sacrilege law was never once applied, leaving one wondering about the point of the whole exercise. Yet its effect on public opinion was disastrous, reviving memories of that old-regime bigotry so famously denounced in the previous century by Voltaire.

Nostalgia for the old regime was on full view on 29 May 1825, at Charles X's coronation. Whereas Notre-Dame in Paris had sufficed for Napoleon, and would have done so for Louis XVIII had illness not intervened, Charles deliberately returned to the traditional site where French kings were crowned, Reims cathedral. Admittedly, some aspects of the ceremony were updated – the emblems of royal authority were presented by four of Napoleon's marshals, and the coronation oath was revised to omit the commitment to extirpate heresy and to include a promise to uphold the Charter – though revealingly not in place of, but in addition to, the kingdom's ancient 'fundamental laws'. Yet the overriding symbolism was that of the pre-1789 monarchy, with pride of place being given to the clergy and nobility or, as one hostile observer put it, to 'clerical and feudal mummery'. Before being crowned, Charles prostrated himself in front of the Archbishop of Reims to be anointed, a gesture that further alarmed contemporaries already fearful of the new reign's theocratic tendencies. The crown was then placed on Charles' head by the archbishop and the two senior princes of the blood. One of these, naturally, was Louis-Philippe. Just five years later, he would take it off.[81]

The mistakes of 1825 and 1826 could not fail to provoke a backlash. The first major sign of this came at Charles X's review of the Paris National Guard at the Champ de Mars on 29 April 1827. The National Guard had always been a volatile body. Formed in July 1789 as a citizens' militia to keep order in Paris and commanded by Lafayette, it had proved an unreliable instrument of authority during the Revolution. It had split between conservative and radical elements, and the latter had played a major part in the overthrow of the monarchy on 10 August 1792. Napoleon had shrewdly put the National Guard into mothballs, but had been forced to mobilize it in 1814 in the face of the Allied invasion of France, and Louis XVIII had thought it politic not to stand it down. Although the criteria for entry ensured that its composition was predominantly bourgeois, as

an institutional legacy of the Revolution it was bound to be hostile
to anything recalling the old regime.[82] When Charles X, having
firmly associated himself with everything the National Guard most
disliked, then decided to review it, trouble could have been expected.

Louis-Philippe was present, next to Charles, at the review, and
left a detailed account of what happened. Twenty thousand National
Guardsmen were drawn up on the Champ de Mars, and as the royal
party approached cries of 'Down with Villèle!' and especially 'Down
with the Jesuits!' began to be heard. As the king passed the 5th legion
of the Guard, the situation teetered on the edge of farce. A man in
the front rank shouted 'Down with the Jesuits!', whereupon the
colonel, Sosthènes de la Rochefoucauld, jumped down from his horse
and punched him. A nearby Guardsman hit back at La Rochefoucauld, and the two had to be separated. Worse was to follow. When
Charles came to the 7th legion, another man in the front rank stared
him full in the face and again shouted 'Down with the Jesuits!'
Turning to Marshal Oudinot, commander of the National Guard, the
king ordered him to arrest the offender, and then addressed a general
rebuke to the whole legion: 'I came here to receive homage from my
people, not insults.' The effect was spoiled, however, by the Guardsman who had insulted him obstinately refusing to leave his rank just
a few paces away. The king became more and more angry: 'Marshal,
get that man to leave the ranks.' The man spoke up again: 'I've only
demanded what's legal' (that is, that the Jesuits should be denied
formal status). 'Leave the ranks!' repeated the king, now furious, and
pushing his horse up against him. 'You are not fit to parade in front
of me – get out, obey, obey!' The man finally stepped backwards
and left the ranks with considerable sang-froid.[83]

In fact, only a small minority of the National Guards on review
had been insubordinate, but the government overreacted. The next
day, an ordinance appeared dissolving the entire National Guard of
Paris. The decision was certainly the work of Villèle, and a sign that
after seven years in power he was beginning to lose his grip. It was
also harshly executed, with some National Guards being chased out
of their barracks by regular troops. At a stroke, the monarchy had
earned itself the bitter hostility of a dangerous section of able-bodied
Parisian males with military training. In an egregiously stupid
oversight, the Guards were not even disarmed before disbandment,

and were allowed to take their uniforms and muskets home. The uniforms vanished for the time being, but the muskets reappeared in July 1830.[84]

Further evidence of Villèle's decline was not slow in coming. In early 1827, the ministry prepared a relatively minor bill stipulating that henceforth only voters could serve on juries. The aim was probably to dissuade liberal voters from registering as electors, since jury service could be demanding and they were felt to have less leisure time to spare than their wealthy, often landed counterparts on the right. However, this routine attempt at gerrymandering backfired spectacularly. It meant that from now on the voter and jury lists would have to be compiled together, which provided a powerful weapon against electoral fraud. Peers favourable to the opposition first spotted the potential of the bill, and passed a series of amendments clearly directed at breaking Villèle's grip on the electoral process. In contrast to previous practice, voter lists now had to be published well before election day and made easily available to the public, and a workable system of appeals against exclusion from the list was set up. The results of the bill, passed on 2 May 1827, were striking: having decreased, mostly through government fraud, from 110,000 in 1820 to 70,000 in August 1827, by the time of the next election the following November the electorate had increased sharply to 88,000, a rise of approximately a quarter.[85]

On the opposition side, the law of 2 May 1827 sparked a chain reaction. The liberal press immediately publicized its implications, and campaigning organizations were swiftly set up to spread the message. The two most famous, and effective, were the Society of Friends of Freedom of the Press, inspired by Chateaubriand, and the Aide-Toi, le Ciel t'Aidera (God Helps Those Who Help Themselves) Society, headed by François Guizot. Despite its clumsy name, the Society of Friends of Freedom of the Press specialized in often brilliantly written and witty pamphlets attacking the government, while the Aide-Toi concentrated on establishing local electoral registration committees directed from its Paris headquarters. The latter's efforts were particularly successful; local committees were set up in thirty-five departments, and played a major role in the dramatic electoral expansion of the following months.[86]

Against this darkening background, in October that year Charles and Villèle took the surprising decision to call a general election. The prime mover seems to have been Villèle, but his motivation remains obscure. Reports from around the country revealed strong public opposition to the ultra programme of the previous two years, so he may well have decided on an election before this developed too far. There was also dissension among his own followers, and he probably saw a modest liberal electoral advance as a good way of frightening them back into obedience. But the outcome was disastrous. Galvanized by their new national and grassroots organizations, the opposition mounted a sustained and passionate campaign. In two rounds of voting on 17 and 24 November, the government lost its majority. In an age when party divisions were so fluid, it is difficult to give precise figures, but the new Chamber of Deputies comprised roughly 195 supporters of the government, and for the opposition 199 of the left and 31 of a breakaway ultra grouping inspired by Chateaubriand, as well as 5 of uncertain allegiance. The situation was made even worse by the fact that in 1824 Villèle had replaced the old system of renewing the Chamber by fifths every year by a single general election every seven years. The new dispensation was not about to disappear.[87]

Had Charles X cared to listen, the lessons of the 1827 election were very clear. The shift to the right, evident from 1819 and culminating in the ultra legislation of 1825 and 1826, had come to a dead end. The policies of Charles and Villèle simply were not acceptable even to the tiny proportion of the French people who had the vote. The wave of sympathy provoked by the duc de Berry's murder had been squandered, and Villèle's artful fixing of the electoral system had come apart. A tack to the centre was the only sensible course. It was unclear, however, if Charles had the sense to see this.

The upheaval of November 1827 underlines a wider truth about the restoration. However much power the Charter gave to the Crown, the nature and rhythm of politics were now predominantly determined by the voters. The great turning-points of the period – the 'liberal restoration' of 1816–19, the swing to the ultras in 1820 and 1823, and now the opposition victory of 1827 – had all been the result of elections. At crucial moments, especially in 1819 and 1827, the ministry, far from shaping events, had simply reacted to them.

The restoration political system, although still very much a 'limited monarchy', was slowly evolving into a parliamentary one. In a country where free and meaningful voting had previously flourished only at the beginning of the Revolution before withering under Napoleon, the importance of this development should not be underestimated.

For the moment, Charles X bowed to the will of the parliamentary majority. After a series of complicated intrigues, Villèle left power and a new ministry was announced on 5 January 1828. Broadly centrist, its leading figure was Jean-Baptiste, vicomte de Martignac, a handsome, womanizing ex-lawyer from Bordeaux of considerable oratorical skills and moderate principles, who became minister of the interior. Realistically, given the circumstances, Martignac embarked on a policy of conciliation with the opposition. He introduced a bill to combat electoral abuses, followed by a liberalization of the press laws. In June 1828 he pandered to the left's obsession by severely restricting the teaching activities of unofficial religious orders, headed by the Jesuits.[88]

The problem was that Martignac never had the confidence of the king, who accepted him only as a temporary necessity while a riposte from the right was prepared. Above all, faced with a hostile Chamber, Charles was determined to reinforce the ministry with someone he could trust. Louis XVI had done much the same thing when confronted with an increasingly turbulent Estates General in the summer of 1789, and since Charles himself had been one of the principal supporters of this move at the time, the analogy may well have been in his mind. The parallel was hardly comforting.

Memories of 1789 were made even more acute by Charles' choice of minister-confidant. Tall, red-haired and horse-faced, prince Jules de Polignac was the son of Marie Antoinette's hated favourite the duchesse de Polignac, who had fled France at the fall of the Bastille and never returned. As a royalist conspirator against Napoleon, prince Jules had been captured and imprisoned for ten years, during which he had become profoundly religious. His long incarceration probably accounts for the impression he often gave of abstraction, even of living in another world. Yet there were persistent rumours that this attitude stemmed from a less tangible source. 'When I'm tired, I lie down on my sofa, and the Virgin Mary appears to me, encourages me, advises me. I wake up, and I march ahead, proud that all my doubts have been resolved,' he once allegedly confided to the duc de FitzJames.[89]

If Polignac's religious ideals came from an extreme wing of French Catholicism, his political ones, rather surprisingly, came from Britain. In his own eccentric way, he was yet another of those early-nineteenth-century Frenchmen profoundly influenced by their neighbours across the Channel. In 1816 he had married a Scottish heiress, Barbara Campbell, and since 1823 had been French ambassador in London. He was an admirer of the British constitution, and in particular of the status and power it accorded to the nobility, which he dreamed of importing into France.[90] This distorted gloss on British institutions, however, was not likely to go down well in post-revolutionary France, where it looked suspiciously like a recipe for a return to the old regime.

Charles first tried to insert Polignac into the ministry as early as the summer of 1828, but the attempt was unsuccessful. A new opportunity presented itself the following January when the foreign minister, La Ferronays, had a stroke in the king's study and had to take leave to recuperate. The ministry, however, held together and limped on. The fatal blow came not from the Tuileries, but from the Chamber of Deputies, which in April 1829 rejected a government bill to make some municipal and local offices elective. From then on, Martignac and his colleagues were doomed.

Over the next few months, with the support of Charles X, Polignac set about trying to form a ministry. To his credit, his preference was for a broad-based coalition, and to this end he sounded out many politicians of the centre-left. He claimed to be prepared to serve simply as minister without portfolio, so even at this stage he may still have been following his original plan of reinforcing the king's government rather than leading it. Yet none of the moderates he contacted were prepared to serve with him, so he was forced ever rightwards in his search for colleagues.

On 5 August, Martignac was unceremoniously dismissed, and three days later the new ministry was announced. If it had been designed to shock public opinion, it could not have been more successful. Polignac, as foreign minister, was unpopular as a former émigré, conspirator against Napoleon and extreme Catholic. The new minister of the interior, the comte de la Bourdonnaye, was the leader of the most hard-line ultras in the Chamber of Deputies, and was notorious for having demanded, in the wake of the Hundred Days, 'fetters, executioners and tortures' for captured Bonapartists. The comte de Bourmont, minister of war, had not contented himself with mere words in 1815; on the eve of Waterloo, he had deserted Napoleon's army and joined the Allies, and had gone on to appear as the main witness for the prosecution at the trial of Marshal Ney.[91] The comtes de Chabrol and de Montbel, at the ministries of finance and of education and religious affairs respectively, were more moderate but secondary figures. Finally, Jean-Joseph de Courvoisier was appointed as keeper of the seals. Courvoisier was respected as a long-serving judge and deputy of the centre-left, but his reputation was undermined by a slightly disturbing obsession with the Apocalypse.[92] If his detractors had known what was coming, they might have taken him more seriously.

Chapter Five

CRISIS AND
CONFRONTATION

VISITORS TO PARIS TODAY who see the July Column rising above
the Place de la Bastille, where the first French Revolution began,
often assume that it commemorates the events of July 1789. In fact,
the fifty-two-metre-high monument, topped by its golden effigy of
the Spirit of Liberty, celebrates the no less tumultuous days of July
1830. Yet this symbolic overlap between the two revolutions is
appropriate. The upheaval of 1830 strikingly echoed that of 1789;
many of its leading protagonists were the same, their thoughts and
actions often conditioned by their experiences forty-one years earlier.
The decisive moments of July 1830 eerily echoed, sometimes to the
smallest details, those of that earlier summer.

There was, however, one essential difference between the two
revolutions. The revolution of 1830 did not end in a republic, but in
a change of dynasty. Where his father had failed – or been unwilling
– to seize his chance in 1789, Louis-Philippe ended by mounting his
cousin's throne. The broad outlines of the story are familiar. Far less
well known is the decisive part played in this process by Adélaïde. In
fact, through a remarkable combination of opportunism and courage,
it was she who gained the crown for her brother.

Both the Revolution of 1789 and that of 1830 began as a defensive reaction against a perceived coup d'état by the king and his ministry. What the government's intentions actually were in both cases, and the extent to which, if at all, it was acting illegally, remain controversial. Far more is known of the aims of Charles X and his advisers, mostly through the diaries and memoirs of key participants, than of those of Louis XVI and his ministers, where several gaps remain. On the other hand, the exact means the government intended to use to impose its plan in the event of resistance, including the use of force, are much clearer in the first revolution than in the second. The most baffling aspect of the 1830 revolution is the crown's lack of preparedness for the possibility of its measures triggering a Parisian uprising.[1]

The Polignac ministry appointed on 8 August 1829 certainly did not enter office with the intention of mounting a coup d'état. Initially it hoped to muster a majority in the Chamber of Deputies, but this hope was dashed at the end of the month by the defection of Chateaubriand and the group of dissident ultras he headed to the opposition.[2] The parliamentary session had already ended on 31 July, and, with the prospect of a minority government now inevitable, Polignac was in no hurry to recall the Chamber. In fact, by various devices he managed to prevent it assembling until the beginning of March 1830.[3]

During the intervening seven months, the government took no initiatives, with one exception – the planning of a military expedition to Algiers. France had a series of grievances against Algiers and its ruler, the Dey Hussein. Like the other European Powers, she was concerned to end the menace of Algerian pirates in the Mediterranean. She was also at loggerheads with the Dey over the price of trading concessions in his territories, and a debt owed to him for supplies to Napoleon during the Egyptian campaign of 1798. It was in the course of an interview about the last matter with the French consul, on 30 April 1827, that Hussein had escalated the dispute into a diplomatic crisis, by striking the consul three times on the sleeve with his fly-whisk.[4]

After the failure of a punitive blockade, it was left to the Polignac ministry to avenge outraged French honour. On 31 January 1830, the council of ministers decided to launch a direct military expedition to capture Algiers and dethrone the Dey. Yet the government was not solely motivated by diplomatic considerations. It is highly probable that it saw the Algiers expedition as a means of countering its domestic unpopularity by a bold foreign adventure that would, it hoped, bring it a much needed transfusion of military glory.[5] For all these motives, the Polignac ministry had the dubious honour of beginning the French conquest of Algeria.

The only other major political event during this period was the departure from the ministry, after only three months in office, of the hard-line minister of the interior La Bourdonnaye, who had made himself so obnoxious to his colleagues that they took the first available opportunity to rid themselves of him. To fill the gap, Montbel moved to the interior ministry from education and religious affairs. Montbel was replaced at his former post by the public prosecutor of Lyon, the comte de Guernon-Ranville, who deserves to be remembered for his Christian name alone – Martial-Côme-Annibal-Perpétue-Magloire. But posterity owes Guernon-Ranville a greater debt, since he kept a detailed diary during his ministry that forms the most valuable surviving guide to the motivation of Charles X and his government on the eve of the July revolution.[6]

As winter passed into spring, the trial of strength with the Chambers could no longer be postponed. The opening of the parliamentary session was fixed for 2 March 1830, when the king would make his speech from the throne outlining his ministry's programme. The fact that this contained two major items, the budget and a series of projected public works, alone gives the lie to claims that Polignac entered office intending to carry out a coup d'état.[7] On the other hand, the government was resolved to brook no challenges to its authority. In this it had the full support of Charles X. The king knew from the press and public reaction to its appointment that his new ministry was violently unpopular. However, it reflected his own views and enjoyed his confidence, and he was determined to sustain it. For him, the dramatic electoral shift to the left since 1827 was not a simple warning that France would no longer accept ultra policies, but evidence of a sinister liberal, crypto-republican conspiracy aimed at the throne itself.

Charles did not appoint Polignac in August 1829 with the aim of taking emergency powers and suspending the Charter. However, his obstinate defence of Polignac against growing parliamentary and public opposition eventually forced him into a position in which this became the only option. For the king to defend unpopular ministers was perfectly legal. As the sole source of executive power, he alone appointed them, and while the Charter stipulated that they were 'responsible', it did not specify whether this was to him, the Chambers, or both. The Chambers certainly had no formal means of forcing the resignation or dismissal of ministers of whom they disapproved. On the other hand, for the king to keep in office indefinitely a ministry unable to command a parliamentary majority was at best a recipe for political stalemate and paralysis of government.[8] Charles X was entirely within his rights to support Polignac as he did. Whether he was wise to do so is a very different matter.

The reasons why Charles clung on to the Polignac ministry were hardly complex, but they were deeply rooted. The right to appoint and dismiss ministers was the most personal, as well as the most central, attribute of the royal prerogative. In countries where the power of the crown was limited by a representative body, monarchs fiercely resented attempts by parliament to force them to part from ministers they liked or to work with ministers they did not – the British examples of George III with Bute and Fox, and of Queen Victoria with Melbourne and Peel, are only the best-known.[9] For Charles X, however, this issue had an even more profound significance. As a young man in July 1789, he had played a key role in the formation of the last ministry his elder brother Louis XVI had freely appointed. Headed by the conservative baron de Breteuil, its aim had been to break the challenge to the royal authority posed by the increasing demands of the Estates General, and its overthrow by the Parisian rising of 14 July had marked the king's first major defeat at the hands of the French Revolution.[10]

It is clear that Charles was obsessed with the thought that the horrors of the Revolution might repeat themselves under the restored monarchy. He was constantly drawing parallels between the events of 1789 and those of contemporary France. Convinced that his elder brother had destroyed himself by concessions to the revolutionaries, his one fixed thought was not to make the same mistake with the left-wing opposition in the Chamber of Deputies, which he regarded as their heirs. Above all, he saw Louis XVI's forced dismissal of the

Breteuil ministry in 1789 as the first step in his downfall, and was
inflexibly determined not to repeat the mistake with Polignac. As
the crisis of 1830 gathered pace, he made the point explicitly to his
assembled ministers:

> The spirit of the Revolution remains completely unchanged in
> the leaders of the left; in attacking the ministry, it is at the
> monarchy that they are really aiming, it is the monarchical
> system that they wish to overthrow.
>
> I have, unfortunately, more experience in this matter than
> you, Messieurs, who are not old enough to have witnessed the
> Revolution; I remember what happened then; the first concession
> that my unhappy brother made was the signal for his fall ...
> [his opponents] also made protestations of love and fidelity, all
> they asked for was the dismissal of his ministers, he gave in,
> and all was lost.[11]

In this frame of mind, on 2 March, the king made his speech
from the throne to the peers and deputies assembled in the great
gallery of the Louvre. Resolved as he was to reassert his authority,
he must surely have recalled another critical moment in 1789, the
royal session of 23 June, when Louis XVI had appeared in person
before the Estates General to break its challenge to his power and
outline a vision of the monarchy of which traces still remained in the
Charter. The actual programme Charles announced, however, contained no great surprises – the expedition against Algiers, and his
ministry's uncontroversial domestic measures.

The inflammatory part of the speech came at the end. In words
of carefully weighed menace, Charles warned his audience that he
would not tolerate attempts to wreck his ministry: 'If culpable
intrigues set obstacles in the path of my government that I do not
wish to foresee, I will find the strength to overcome them in my
resolve to uphold public order, in the justified confidence of the
French people, and in the love that they have always shown for their
king.' Significantly, these words uncannily echoed those with which
Louis XVI had closed the royal session of 23 June 1789: 'Gentlemen,
you have just heard a statement of my provisions and my objectives;
they conform to my lively desire to act for the good of all. If, by a

remote mischance, you were to abandon me in such a fine enterprise, I should effect the good of my peoples alone; alone I should consider myself their true representative.'[12]

To Louis-Philippe, from his seat close to the throne, the parallel would have been very obvious, since like Charles X he too had been present at the royal session of 23 June 1789. Indeed, the occasion was seared on his memory. Since his father was sitting with the deputies, he had been required to accompany Louis XVI with the other princes of the blood to the hall of the Estates General. As the son of a prince who had very publicly gone over to the opposition, his reception by the rest of the royal family had been glacial; he was not offered a seat, and for the five hours it took to arrange the seating arrangements for the session he had been forced to stand, with nobody addressing a word to him. One can only speculate on Louis-Philippe's thoughts as he sat, forty-one years later, listening to one of those who had snubbed him then repeating exactly the sentiments of the doomed Louis XVI.[13]

Whatever Louis-Philippe's musings may have been they were interrupted by an unscripted, and slightly uncanny, event. At the moment when he was most precisely echoing his dead brother's words in 1789, with the phrase 'that I do not wish to foresee', Charles put added emphasis into his voice and gestures, knocking from his head the jewelled hat he was wearing. It rolled to the feet of Louis-Philippe, who rose, picked it up, and handed it back to Charles with a deep bow. The symbolism of the king's hat at Louis-Philippe's feet was lost on nobody present.[14]

The threatening tone of Charles X's speech was unmistakeable. What it meant in practice was less clear. Some deputies saw it as proof that the king was preparing to invoke article 14 of the Charter to take emergency powers and govern by ordinance; but it is clear from the surviving diaries of the ministers that this course was not at that moment contemplated.[15] Yet the deputies felt that Charles had deliberately thrown down the gauntlet, and were determined to respond. Over the next few weeks, they drew up an address in reply to the speech from the throne that clearly set out the doctrine that the king should only choose ministers who enjoyed the confidence of parliament. Since Charles had flouted this principle in appointing Polignac, the address concluded, on a note of rhetorical regret, that the accord between government and people necessary for normal politics to function no longer existed.

On 18 March, the address was voted by 221 deputies, a majority of thirty. These men would soon become famous as 'the 221' who had defied the king and brought on a revolution. Charles was furious, with some justification; he had been foolish to choose a ministry unable to command a parliamentary majority, and in doing so had shown ignorance of one of the central principles of successful constitutional government, but he had a point in claiming that the Chamber of Deputies had rejected his ministers without giving them a chance to be judged by their actions. At a meeting of the council of ministers on 17 March, when the basic terms of the address were already known, it was agreed, with only Guernon-Ranville dissenting, that the Chamber should be dissolved to make way for new elections. First, however, it should be prorogued until 1 September, to give the government as much time as possible to manipulate the electoral process. It was also hoped that by then the Algerian expedition would have been brought to a successful conclusion, allowing some of its glory to reflect on the ministry.[16]

The Chamber was suspended on 19 March, leaving Charles and his ministers free to pursue their strategy unhindered. Within a few weeks, however, they had changed their minds about the timing of the planned election. To wait until September, they now decided, was too risky; after all, the attack on Algiers might fail, which would have a disastrous effect on public opinion, and they were alarmed by the prospect of carrying on for so long with no budget voted. On 17 April, they decided that the elections should be held at the end of June.[17]

This decision inevitably led to a far more fateful one. If, despite the government's best efforts, the elections returned an even more hostile majority, what action should be taken? It was at this point that drastic measures were first raised as a serious possibility. There is evidence that Polignac had already decided to take this path, regardless of the verdict of the voters. When Guernon-Ranville walked with him to the Chamber just before the prorogation, and attempted to persuade him to keep it in session in the hope of building a working majority, he simply replied: 'A majority! That would really cause me problems; I wouldn't know what to do with it.'[18] Yet at the council meeting of 20 April, when the question of the king invoking article 14 and taking emergency powers in the event of the elections going badly was first openly raised, it became clear that several of Polignac's colleagues were not so sanguine. Bourmont and d'Haussez were prepared to use article 14, but Montbel was deeply reluctant, Chabrol and Guernon-Ranville would only do so as an absolute last resort, and Courvoisier was adamant that its terms did not cover the sort of actions being contemplated.[19]

If a hard-line course were to have any chance of success, a homogenous ministry was an absolute necessity, so a further reshuffle was the logical consequence. It took place on 20 May. Courvoisier and Chabrol resigned; the former was replaced at the justice ministry by the comte de Chantelauze, a senior magistrate from Grenoble, Montbel moved from the interior to take Chabrol's post as finance minister, and the interior ministry was split in two, with responsibility for public works going to a career civil servant, baron Capelle, and the rest to Villèle's former justice minister, the uncompromisingly conservative comte de Peyronnet. It was made clear to the new ministers that they would be expected to endorse emergency measures if necessary. At the first meeting of the council they attended, the king read them a short statement, concluding that if a hostile majority were the result of the elections, without acting unconstitutionally he would 'make [his] prerogative respected'.[20] The ministry thus formed was essentially one of combat.

Over the next few weeks, the king and Polignac set about perfecting a further weapon for use in the coming electoral battle. They decided that Charles should issue a personal proclamation, exhorting the voters to reject the arguments of the opposition and rally to the government. It was presented to the other ministers as a fait accompli, and they were extremely dubious about its wisdom. It meant that the king was stepping down from his position as arbiter into the political fray; it would be divisive even if the ministry won the election, but if it did not the crown would be seriously compromised. Admittedly, Charles X's appeal spoke of maintaining the Charter and made no mention of any emergency measures, but it was still a foolhardy gamble.

The proclamation appeared on 13 June. The next day, Charles' daughter-in-law the duchesse de Berry invited the royal family and the Orléans for a visit to her château at Rosny, on the Seine north-west of Paris. As soon as Louis-Philippe arrived, the king asked him what he thought of his declaration. With consummate diplomacy, Louis-Philippe answered by praising the only aspect of it he felt able to endorse, Charles' promise to uphold the Charter. This paved the way for a remarkable conversation, which Louis-Philippe later transcribed. It is a crucial eyewitness account (though not necessarily from an unbiased source) of Charles X's motivation and aims in the unfolding political crisis. The dialogue begins with Louis-Philippe congratulating the king on his intention to stay within the constitution:

— 'Your majesty has done very well to insist on his willingness and resolution to maintain the Charter in its integrity, because it is only the fear that this might not be the case that has produced everything that has displeased your majesty, and, if the king may permit me to say it, <u>outside the charter there is only disaster and perdition.</u>'
— 'Yes, disaster and perdition, well said, you're absolutely right, I'm completely convinced of it − <u>outside the Charter, no salvation,</u> there's no doubt about that. And I say to you that they can do what they like, they will never be able to make me go beyond the bounds of legality, and I shall stay firmly within the legal order.'
— 'Your majesty could take no better course, a return to the old regime is impossible.'
— 'Impossible, utterly impossible. No, no, as for that, our only haven is the Charter, and I'd go further; look, I'm older than you and I saw more of the old regime than you, and I tell you that even if a return to it were possible it wouldn't be desirable. On the other hand, in the same way that I wish to and should uphold the Charter, everybody must stick to it, and I must find a way of bringing people back within it if they go beyond it − because, by my faith! it's too much to demand the right to appoint ministers.'
— 'But sire, I don't believe anybody's thinking of that.'
— 'Ah, you're mistaken.'[21]

How can this exchange, in which Charles X protests his determination to maintain the Charter apparently in all sincerity, be reconciled with the explicit evidence from his ministers that at exactly the same time he was contemplating suspending it? It is of course quite possible that he was simply lying about his intentions to a cousin whom he knew disagreed with his political views and whose links to the opposition he distrusted. But there is an alternative explanation, which fits better with the surviving sources and makes more sense of the king's thoughts and actions.

Charles may have been profoundly unwise to take the course he did, but there is a powerful argument that the real fault lay with the Charter itself. The presence of article 14, allowing the monarch to suspend the Charter at a moment of national emergency, ensured that it contained its own negation. It is thus perfectly possible, even probable, that Charles saw no contradiction in assuring Louis-Philippe that he would rigidly respect the Charter, at the same time making plans to set it aside. It was a surreal situation, but no less real for all that. As Louis-Philippe put it so pithily in the recollections written during his own final exile: 'It has been only too clearly proved ... that ... the last words of article 14, so fatally inserted into the Charter, sufficed for even a conscientious monarch like Charles X to feel himself authorized to annul the Charter without breaking his oath to uphold it.'[22]

A further piece of evidence exists which also strongly supports this interpretation of Charles' reasoning. Once again, its source is Louis-Philippe, though this time indirectly. It comes in the diary of his librarian and close confidant, Jean Vatout. On 19 June, five days after the conversation at Rosny, Vatout set down a detailed account of it as related to him by Louis-Philippe. The overall sense is exactly the same as Louis-Philippe's own transcription, though Charles' tone appears more combative and emphatic. Vatout's version, however, attributes to the king a significant phrase that does not appear in Louis-Philippe's: 'In any case, entrenched behind article 14, I'll see what happens, and if [the opposition] persists in going outside the Charter, I'll know what measures to take.'[23] Vatout's account is second-hand, and Louis-Philippe may have embroidered the conversation in retelling it; but if so, it is odd that he did not repeat it in his own memoir. Vatout's memory of the occasion, written just five days afterwards, is also more likely to have been accurate than that of Louis-Philippe, writing eighteen years later.

Events now gathered pace. On 13 June the expeditionary force dropped anchor off Algiers, and ten days later won its first victory. The news of this reached Paris on the 23rd, on the same day that the general election began. The ministry had grounds to hope that its original gamble would pay off, and that it would reap the reward of military success at the polls. The electorate, however, was unimpressed. The opposition was well organized; it had a rallying-cry in the address of the 221, and the local committees of the Aide-Toi, le Ciel t'Aidera, so successful in the 1827 election, embarked on another voter-registration drive. When the election results were finally announced in the third week of July, it was clear that the government had sustained a decisive defeat – 270 opposition deputies were returned, including 201 of the 221, and only 145 for the ministry.[24]

The scenario first considered by the ministers two months earlier – that the general election would return a majority as hostile, if not more so, than the previous Chamber – had come to pass. At a council meeting on 29 June, when the broad outline of the results was already known, a detailed discussion began on what action to take. The possibility of working with the new Chamber was barely raised. Instead, attention immediately focused on whether or not in the present circumstances the terms of article 14 justified suspending the Charter. After a long debate, it was unanimously agreed that 'by virtue of article 14, the crown is empowered to take all extra-legal measures that appear necessary in order to save the state if it is menaced by an imminent danger, to a point where existing legislation is clearly insufficient to maintain public order; that in this case it is permitted to apply that highest political law: *Salus Populi Suprema Lex*.' Admittedly this was a very right-wing ministry, but its complete agreement on this point underlines just how open article 14 was to a hard-line interpretation.[25]

Over the next fortnight the consequences of this decision moved inexorably forward. On 6 July the council agreed a plan to use article 14 'to dissolve the new Chamber as soon as the elections are over, to form another Chamber by modifying various aspects of the current electoral law, and at the same time to suspend the liberty of the press'. The only dissenting voice, by his own account, was Guernon-Ranville's: while accepting in principle that article 14 could be used in the present situation, in practice he thought it would be wiser only to do so if the new Chamber rejected the budget and could thus itself be accused of acting unconstitutionally. The next day, the ministers assembled in the king's presence, and each reported his opinion to Charles that the circumstances did justify recourse to article 14, with Guernon-Ranville again giving his qualified dissent. Summing up all views with some acuity, the king remarked that 'he saw with great satisfaction that we were *all* agreed on the right that article 14 of the Charter reserved to us; and that as for the rest, the only disagreement between us was over *timing*.'[26]

Between 10 and 24 July, the council meetings were almost entirely devoted to the business of embodying its strategy in four royal ordinances. Those concerned with elections and the electoral system were drafted by Peyronnet, and that suspending the freedom of the press by Chantelauze. The first ordinance, subject to renewal every three months, imposed pre-publication censorship on all newspapers, periodicals and pamphlets of less than twenty pages. The second dissolved the newly elected Chamber of Deputies, the third remodelled the electoral system in a highly restrictive sense, and the fourth announced that fresh elections would be held under the new regulations in two stages, on 6 and 13 September.[27]

The most substantial ordinance was the third. As in the first years of the restoration, the Chamber of Deputies would now be elected for five years, with a fifth of its members being renewed every year. The overall number of deputies was reduced to 258. The main thrust of the ordinance, however, was directed against the urban middle classes, whom the government felt were the mainstay of the opposition. The *patente*, a business tax, was excluded from the criteria to be used for calculating eligibility to vote, with the aim of disenfranchising bourgeois voters in the towns. Henceforth the actual duty of choosing deputies would be given to electoral colleges composed of the most highly taxed voters in each Department of France. The aim, reflecting Polignac's obsession with building an aristocratic system, was clearly to base the monarchy's support on a small elite of conservative landowners. It is not entirely clear what the ordinance's effect on the franchise would have been, but some estimates conclude that the electorate would have been cut by 75 per cent.[28]

A brief ray of sunshine lit up the gathering gloom of these days. On 9 July, news reached Paris that Algiers had fallen and that the

Dey had surrendered. Bourmont, the minister of war, had retrieved
the reputation he had lost at Waterloo, but at a price: he himself
was wounded and one of his sons was killed at his side during
the assault.[29] On Sunday 11 July Charles X attended a *Te Deum* at
Notre-Dame to give thanks for the victory. The crowds outside,
however, were pointedly silent, to the extent that the king himself
was disconcerted. It was an ominous sign.

On the 24th, the council met to put the finishing touches to the
ordinances before presenting them to the king the next day. It was
now d'Haussez' turn to get cold feet; as a career administrator, he
felt that the electoral ordinance was gravely flawed and the one
dealing with the press 'unworkable'. He also feared that insufficient
measures had been taken to contain any resistance that might break
out. D'Haussez ended by giving his approval to the ordinances
because he felt that it would be cowardly to withhold his support at
this late stage. As he did so, however, he made a gesture that reveals
how haunted he and his colleagues were not only by the French
Revolution, but by the English civil war. He gazed ostentatiously
around all the walls of the room while speaking, so that Polignac
asked him: 'What are you looking for?' 'The portrait of Strafford,'
he replied.[30]

The next day, Sunday 25 July, the ministers travelled to St Cloud,
where the court was currently installed. After hearing mass, the king
then held a council. The scene is described by Guernon-Ranville:

> The four ordinances were . . . read. The ordinances on the press
> and on the elections were presented to the king by the president
> of the council [Polignac]. Before signing them, the king
> appeared absorbed in deep reflection; for several minutes he sat
> with his head resting on his hand and his pen two inches from
> the paper; then he said: 'The more I think about it, the more
> convinced I am that it is impossible to do otherwise', and he
> signed . . . We all then countersigned in the most profound
> silence.[31]

The provisions of the four ordinances are very clear, but their
actual political aims have been remarkably little analysed since.
Their opponents at the time claimed, as have many subsequent
historians, that their goal was to reimpose the absolute monarchy

and the old regime. This is not the case. Had the ordinances remained in force, France would have remained just within the confines of a limited monarchy according to Stéphane Rials' definition. The royal power would still have been restrained by a representative body, albeit one chosen by only a tiny elite, and no doubt reduced to subservience much of the time by the usual methods of political and electoral manipulation. The principle that the crown rather than the nation was the ultimate source of sovereignty would thus have been ferociously reasserted. This is unsurprising given that the ordinances were the product of a confrontation between Charles X and the Chamber of Deputies over one of the central aspects of the royal prerogative, the king's unfettered right to choose his own ministers.

Even under the harsh provisions of the ordinances, however, the Chamber would have remained more than a mere figleaf designed to cover the nakedness of absolutism. It would have retained several key powers – above all that of consent to taxation. With the electorate slashed and the press muzzled, France under the ordinances would have been a very repressive place; but all avenues for future opposition would not have been entirely cut off.

If Charles and Polignac did not contemplate restoring the absolute monarchy, did they wish to return to the old regime, with its hierarchy of legally defined orders stretching from clergy to nobility down to third estate? Although in their conversation of 14 June 1830 Charles was disingenuous with Louis-Philippe about his views on the limits of the Charter, he went out of his way to deny any intention of reimposing the old regime. 'Even if it were possible, it would not be desirable' were his words, and there is no reason to doubt them.

Yet even if they knew that reverting formally to the society of orders was a pipedream, one can certainly argue that Charles X and Polignac wished to preserve, and even reinforce, its characteristics in the France they ruled. In his heart, Charles probably never abandoned the conception of monarchy that Louis XVI had proclaimed to the Estates General on 23 June 1789, and which had haunted his successors ever since. In April 1791, having fled the Revolution, Charles had written to his beleaguered sister-in-law Marie Antoinette in Paris: 'The declaration of 23 June and the broad sense of the *cahiers* [the lists of grievances presented to the Estates General] are bases from which I shall never stray.'[32] Making due allowance for changing circumstances, he never did.

Louis XVI's declaration had outlined a limited monarchy, buttressed by a strong royal authority, and resting on the traditional three orders. Charles X and Polignac remained faithful to the spirit, if not the letter, of its provisions. To restore the formal privileges and status of the nobility and clergy was clearly unthinkable. On the other hand, to extend their position and power to the point where they could dominate the post-revolutionary society of classes certainly was not. Both Polignac and Charles were devout to the point of mysticism, and determined to extend the moral and educational influence of the Catholic church. Polignac's great aim was to make the Chamber of Peers the bastion of a revived aristocracy consolidated by the restoration of primogeniture.[33] The third of the four ordinances was a significant step along this path, and would have ensured the election of a Chamber of Deputies composed entirely of wealthy landowners and no doubt containing a high proportion of nobles. It was also aimed against the same enemies the crown had faced in 1789 – excluding the *patente* and the door and window tax from the criteria for eligibility to vote was designed to exclude precisely those urban bourgeois whom Charles and Polignac saw as the heirs of the third estate. The king and his ministers may have balked at restoring society as it was before 1789, but they did aim to preserve as much of it as possible into the modern age.

Invoking article 14 to claim emergency powers was probably legal, and the four ordinances had a coherent political goal which nonetheless fell short of formally restoring the absolute monarchy and the old regime. But these initiatives hardly constituted a realistic political plan. To put them in a comparative perspective, at exactly the same moment as the British political system, under pressure from social and economic change and a growing popular movement, was about to extend its base beyond the nobility and the landed interest with the 1832 reform bill, Charles X and his ministers were moving in precisely the opposite direction. Polignac, in his enthusiasm for the British aristocracy, wished to transform the Chamber of Peers into a French House of Lords and make it the cornerstone of the monarchy, when across the Channel its equivalent was entering a process that led to its irreversible decline. To make a further parallel, more distant in time but nearer home, it was as if Louis XVI had attempted to resolve the crisis of 1789 by disenfranchising the third estate.

*

THE FOUR ORDINANCES were printed in the official government newspaper, the *Moniteur*, early in the morning of 26 July, and began circulating in Paris a few hours later. As the news spread, there was a general rush to cafés that stocked copies of the *Moniteur* for their clients, and in the garden of the Palais-royal, where the 1789 revolution had started, those with copies of the paper stood and read the ordinances aloud to silent groups that gathered round them. Yet although there was shock and disapproval, there was also no immediate resistance. Partly this was because Monday was still often regarded as a holiday, the workers' traditional 'Saint Monday', so that many Parisians were taking their leisure in the inns and cabarets on the city's outskirts.[34]

The first moves towards outright defiance came, unsurprisingly, from those whose livelihoods were most directly threatened by the ordinances – the journalists, newspaper proprietors and printing workers.[35] The owners of the opposition paper the *Constitutionnel* went swiftly to the office near the Place des Victoires of their lawyer, the deputy André Dupin, to consult him about their legal situation, and invited several colleagues from other titles to join them. The meeting agreed that the ordinances were illegal, but broke up without agreeing any plan of action.

It was another liberal newspaper, the *National*, based a short distance away on the Rue Neuve-St-Marc, that first raised the standard of revolt. Monarchical but strongly anti-dynastic, it had only been publishing for six months, since January 1830. Its principal editor was a remarkable young man who, over an exceptionally long political career, was to become one of the dominant figures of nineteenth-century France – Louis-Adolphe Thiers. Short, gnome-like, bespectacled, the illegitimate son of a genteel ne'er-do-well, Thiers had been born in Marseille in 1797, had qualified as a lawyer, and had arrived in Paris to seek his fortune in 1821.[36] He had soon gravitated towards journalism, and his sharp, cynical intelligence, immense energy, wit and eloquence had two years later secured him

the most important introduction of his life, to Talleyrand. Deeply
disillusioned with Louis XVIII and then with Charles X, exiled from
power in a form of semi-disgrace, the ageing prince saw in Thiers
both a spiritual son and a useful instrument. If Thiers was the
National's begetter, Talleyrand was its godfather; it was first planned
at his country house, and its principal financial backer was his banker,
Jacques Laffitte.[37] It might have been created for just such an
opportunity as the crisis of July 1830.

By late morning on 26 July, the *National* had already published
a special edition calling for a tax strike to combat the ordinances.
Thiers now set to work drafting a second proclamation. Surrounded
by an agitated crowd including many journalists, two deputies and a
senior judge, he swiftly produced a call for a more general mobilization against the government: 'The legal regime is now interrupted;
that of force has begun. In this situation obedience ceases to be a
duty.' But Thiers cannily stopped short of endorsing outright revolution: 'France,' he concluded, 'must judge how far it ought to carry
its resistance.' The protest was then signed by forty-eight journalists,
from eleven newspapers, for publication as soon as possible.[38]

In all that happened on 26 July, the memory of 1789 was
omnipresent. It is no coincidence that Thiers, the journalist, was
also a historian, and had written a multi–volume history of the Revolution, as had also his friend, fellow-editor of the *National* and
co-signatory of the protest, François-Auguste Mignet.[39] On a wider
scale, there is a pervasive sense that the reactions of Parisians were
conforming to a script set down by the first revolution. The Palais-
royal, where Camille Desmoulins had first called on the people to
rise on 13 July 1789, also saw the first violence of 26 July 1830. Just
after 8 p.m. that evening, police arrived to close an opposition
printing-press in one of its arcades. A crowd gathered, shouting
'Long live the Charter!' and, more ominously, 'Down with the
Bourbons!' By 10.30 p.m. it had grown so large that the authorities
felt it necessary to close the gardens. The demonstrators re-formed
outside in the Place du Palais-royal, and proceeded in two groups up
the Rue de Rivoli and the Rue de Castiglione, shouting slogans and
smashing street-lamps. As chance would have it, this second party
ran into Polignac and d'Haussez, returning by carriage to the foreign
ministry from a council meeting in the justice ministry on the Place

Vendôme. The ministers were recognized and pelted with a volley of stones, which broke the carriage windows and hit d'Haussez. The coach sped the final hundred feet into the courtyard of the foreign ministry, where the gates were swiftly closed behind it.[40]

The man on whom the government relied to disperse resistance should it become serious was Auguste-Frédéric Marmont, Duke of Ragusa. One of Napoleon's marshals and now fifty-six, he had had a distinguished combat record in Italy, Egypt and central Europe, though during the Peninsular War he had been soundly beaten by Wellington at Salamanca. Though polished, handsome and well educated, Marmont had major character flaws which had severely damaged his reputation. In his youth he had been excessively indulged by his father, a Burgundian country gentleman who had retired early from the army to devote himself exclusively to hunting and his son's upbringing. Perhaps because of this, Marmont grew up vain, extravagant and volatile, with a distinct tendency, once off the battlefield, to flee responsibility. Above all, though his physical bravery was unquestionable, he had no political courage.[41]

Marmont's failings had been most famously revealed in April 1814. In the last stages of Napoleon's campaign of France, he had helped defend Paris, and on the city's surrender on 31 March had marched his corps of twelve thousand men to Essonne to cover the emperor's last remaining army at Fontainebleau. However, the previous night he had been visited by the ubiquitous Talleyrand, working for the restoration of Louis XVIII, and had a long conversation with him whose content remains mysterious. Three days later, Marmont signed an agreement with the Austrian commander Schwarzenberg to pull his troops out of the front line and bring them over to the Allied side. This action did not in itself cause Napoleon's downfall, since the emperor had already agreed to abdicate before he knew of Marmont's defection. What it did do, by destroying Napoleon's bargaining power, was to ruin any chance of him securing the succession for his son under the regency of the empress Marie Louise.[42] This was quite enough to earn for Marmont a lasting place in France's pantheon of traitors; his title was swiftly adapted into a new verb, *raguser*, to betray.

Unpopularity was not the only cross Marmont had to bear by 1830. In the course of the 1820s, he had invested heavily in a model farm near his home town of Châtillon-sur-Seine, whose centrepiece – which he was convinced would make him a fortune – was a flock of 'sheep in coats'. The marshal was convinced that sewing sheep into overcoats would improve their fleeces and protect them from disease. He immediately put this visionary scheme into effect, and constructed for this purpose a three-storey-high sheepfold on his farm. Unfortunately, the overcoats were expensive, made the sheep unbearably hot, were ineffective against disease and failed to produce the high-quality fleeces desired. By 1826, Marmont's sheep had ruined him, and he was only able to salvage his finances with the aid of a substantial loan from the king.[43]

The appointment of Marmont, Napoleon's great betrayer, to the command of the troops in Paris in July 1830 has often been viewed as a deliberate flouting of popular opinion in the capital. This is not the case. The period 1 May to 1 September 1830 was simply Marmont's term of duty as major-general of the Royal Guard, and this automatically gave him charge of the 1st military division garrisoned in Paris in the event of an emergency.[44] In view of Marmont's reputation, it would have been wiser to make an alternative arrangement. Giving him command in the capital was dangerously unimaginative, but was not a deliberately provocative decision.

This development was displeasing not only to the Parisians, but to Marmont himself. Acutely conscious of the cloud hanging over him, he had been desperate to lead the expedition to Algiers to recover his tarnished glory. When the post was given instead to Bourmont, he was so furious that he considered resigning his major-generalship, and only decided not to because he needed the money to pay his debts. A moderate liberal in politics, he disapproved of the direction the Polignac ministry was taking. Now, instead of replenishing his laurels in Africa, he was being given a task for which he had no appetite and which threatened to make him more hated than ever.[45]

The secret of the ordinances had been so well kept that, like everybody else, Marmont only knew something was afoot on the morning of 26 July. Bizarrely, there was no copy of the *Moniteur* available, so he went into Paris to find one. Meanwhile Charles X, like Louis XVI on 14 July 1789, had gone hunting for the day, and did not return until 10.45 p.m. Stepping down from his carriage, he asked Marmont if he had been in Paris, and what the situation was. Marmont replied that the capital was gripped by fear and despondency, and that the stock exchange had tumbled, but the king did not seem unduly concerned.[46]

Estimates vary of the number of troops available to Marmont in the event of a Parisian rising. This has usually been reckoned at between 11,500 and 13,000 men of all arms. However, the most detailed surviving table, in the archives of the war ministry, gives a rather higher figure, of 17,093 – though this does need some adjustment downwards since it records only the total of men available rather than of those actually present, 'which it is impossible to determine exactly'. Of these, 13,700 were infantry, 2,200 cavalry, and 1,100 artillery. Over half belonged to the Royal Guard, and perhaps half of these were Swiss troops. It was enough to contain an insurrection, but not a revolution.[47]

The great mystery of July 1830 is why, having launched extraordinary political measures, the government failed to back them with the most elementary military precautions. Paris was a turbulent city, and the birthplace of the greatest revolution of modern times. At the very least some resistance might have been expected. Once again, the comparison with July 1789 becomes inescapable. Then, in a similar situation, the baron de Breteuil had felt it necessary to have 100,000 men at his disposal in the event of a revolt in the capital, and the 30,000 who had been gathered by the time the Parisians rose had been insufficient to put down the rebellion.[48]

Yet despite this ominous precedent, Charles and Polignac seem genuinely to have believed that Paris would remain quiet. Otherwise, it is inconceivable that they would have deprived themselves of 40,000 of their best soldiers by sending them on the Algerian expedition just two months before. Unlike in 1789, no reinforcements were ordered to the capital. An incredible lack of preparedness in those troops on the spot was also permitted. All four lieutenant-generals of the Royal Guard were absent from their posts, many of the other officers had departed for their constituencies to vote in the elections, and General Coutard, who had day-to-day command of the Paris garrison, was away taking the waters. Marmont claimed that when the crisis struck over half of his senior officers were on leave.[49]

The reasons for the imperturbable confidence of the king and his

prime minister are very difficult to fathom. They may have been
comforted by the fact that the last serious disturbances in Paris, a
small rising in the Rue St Denis after the 1827 election, had been
swiftly crushed. They were also bolstered in their view by the Prefect
of Police, Jean-Henri Mangin, an impetuous and volatile character.
When Guernon-Ranville, increasingly concerned about the potential
effect of the ordinances on public order, questioned him on 25 July
about the situation in Paris, Mangin replied impatiently: 'Whatever
you do, Paris will not stir; act boldly, I will answer for Paris – on
my head, I will answer for it.'[50]

In addition, Charles X's personality, breezy and optimistic,
inclined him to act without considering the obstacles in his way.
Throughout his life he had consistently mistaken his desires for
realities. Had July 1830 been the first revolutionary situation in which
he had found himself, his confidence might have been understandable.
Yet he had been intimately involved in the confrontation of July
1789, not least in helping to bring the baron de Breteuil's ministry to
power. He thus had plenty of warning of the kind of reaction the
ordinances might provoke, but chose to ignore it. In particular,
despite being obsessed with the events of 1789, he seems entirely to
have passed over their military aspect, and this is baffling.

The case of Polignac is more controversial. This is because of
persistent claims that his inaction during the crisis was the result not
of natural, but of supernatural, factors – to be precise, his conviction
that the Virgin Mary was appearing to him and reassuring him that
all would be well. The main source for this is a damning passage in
the memoirs of baron Pasquier, who spent the July revolution
desperately trying to persuade the king and his ministers to compromise with the Chamber. According to Pasquier, on the evening of
28 July the commander of the military academy of St Cyr, the comte
de Broglie, himself a devout Catholic, went to St Cloud to warn the
king that the situation in Paris was worsening. In Pasquier's words,
Charles then replied:

> 'My dear count, I see I must tell you everything. Well, Polignac
> has had another of his apparitions this evening; he has been
> promised help, ordered to persevere, and assured of a complete
> victory.'

The comte de Broglie, despite his piety, could not accept such a confidence without being astounded; stupefaction reduced him to silence. A second person met him coming away from this interview in deep distress, with his head in his hands; and when he asked what was wrong [Broglie] replied: 'What can one do? All is lost, there's nothing more to hope for.' He then recounted what had just passed between himself and the king. I have the story from this very person.[51]

Polignac's biographer has cast doubt on Pasquier's account, pointing out that it is third-hand, and in the first case from an anonymous source. He also stresses that in all Polignac's private correspondence and voluminous religious writings, there is no mention of the Virgin ever appearing to him.[52] On this reading, while Polignac's deep religious faith is unquestionable, he was far from the mystic visionary of so many subsequent accounts.

However, this interpretation leaves out one piece of evidence which, though not conclusive, is first-hand. As early as 20 April 1830, Guernon-Ranville confided to his diary that he was tempted to believe that Polignac 'was guided by influences quite beyond the ministerial sphere'.[53] Admittedly, he often found Polignac exasperating, but his journal is an eyewitness account, and based on regular personal contact with the prime minister. The received picture of Polignac in July 1830, praising Our Lady and neglecting the ammunition, may be exaggerated, but it cannot be discounted.

The last major player in the impending explosion had as little notice of it as anyone else. Louis-Philippe was having breakfast at Neuilly on the morning of 26 July when he saw the four ordinances printed in the *Moniteur*. He rushed to find Marie-Amélie, who was doing her hair, waved the paper at her, and exclaimed: 'Well, my dear, they've done it, they've mounted a coup d'état!'[54] Marie-Amélie was horrified. For the rest of the day everybody crowded into the salon, where Louis-Philippe sat on a large divan, 'sad, saying little, but listening to and approving [what was being said]'. At one point he burst out: 'They're mad! They'll get themselves exiled again! Oh! It's already happened to me twice!' Come what may, this time he was clearly determined to stay in France.[55]

In this shocked household, the one person who immediately

thrust aside all doubt and hesitation was Adélaïde. While her brother sat pensively on the divan and her sister-in-law busied herself with her correspondence, she 'expressed herself with vehemence and indignation'. Significantly, she also warned everybody in the room to remain on their guard in public.[56] She had clearly calculated that the situation might well turn to her brother's advantage, and was determined that the opportunity should not be squandered. She was less discreet, however, a few hours later, when the former minister comte Molé came to dinner. Warmly supported by her confidante Mme de Montjoie, she urged Louis-Philippe to go to Paris and put himself at the head of the opposition. Her nieces also rallied to her; Louise argued that resistance could no longer remain within the bounds of legality, and Marie openly spoke of insurrection.[57]

These words have important implications. In a further parallel with 1789, they raise the question of whether or not there was a pre-existing Orléanist conspiracy in July 1830. In fact, there is considerably less evidence that Louis-Philippe was plotting to seize the throne than in the case of his father forty-one years earlier. It is more likely that the thought actively repelled him. When Vatout, having heard his account of his conversation with Charles X in June 1830, suggested that Louis-Philippe might soon have an opportunity to take the crown, he refused to hear of it. If a revolution broke out, he insisted, he would simply retire to Randan and sit the crisis out there.[58] It is true that as the revolution gathered pace, several of the political figures among Louis-Philippe's friends urged him to intervene, but this was not an unnatural reaction, and there is no evidence that they had concerted their actions with him beforehand.

The only whiff of conspiracy, unsurprisingly, emanates from Talleyrand. The great survivor may have been on the margins of politics since 1815, but he was still a force to be reckoned with. Tall, club-footed, completely self-possessed, he imposed himself as much by his presence as by his words. With his carefully powdered white hair surrounding an immobile, mask-like face, he resembled, as Guizot memorably put it, 'a dead lion'.[59] However, at the age of seventy-six, his intelligence was still very much alive. Talleyrand has often been maligned as an unprincipled opportunist. He was certainly a formidable intriguer, but he was also a genuine constitutional monarchist. He had been the principal architect of the Bourbon restoration, but knowing the conservatism of the elder branch, he had always seen the Orléans as a sort of reserve option should the former prove incompatible with post-revolutionary France. If that were to prove the case, the work of 1814 could be completed, as he saw it, by recourse to Louis-Philippe: 'What we have been unable to do in one step, we shall do in two.'[60]

By the summer of 1830, Talleyrand had decided that it was time to take the second step. That June, he paid Louis-Philippe a visit to give him some advice. Vatout recounts what happened in his diary:

> I was playing billiards one evening with the duc d'Orléans at Neuilly. The prince de Talleyrand came in; the duc, the duchesse and Mademoiselle [Adélaïde] went [with him] into the duchesse's room. Nothing was revealed of the conversation; but in 1830 I learnt what he had come to say: 'The elder branch is finished; be careful not to give your son to Mademoiselle de Berry [there had been talk of a marriage between the duc de Chartres and the daughter of the duc de Berry]; alone, you may succeed; linked to them, you'll be chased out as well.' Old fox! What a nose![61]

No doubt, as he did when Vatout raised the prospect of the crown, Louis-Philippe listened to Talleyrand's advice, but did no more. Adélaïde, however, may have gone further. By this time she had become a close friend of Talleyrand; she shared his political views, and he appreciated her forceful intelligence. The two corresponded, and had a mutual go-between in the princesse de Vaudémont.[62] As in 1815, there is a sense that Adélaïde may have been playing a subtle – and entirely deniable – game on her brother's behalf.

Thus right up until the 1830 revolution the crucial distinction had been preserved: there were many people working for the duc d'Orléans, but none actually with him. Yet the mere fact that he had listened to their proposals, amplified perhaps by carefully chosen words from his sister, had created the impression that were the crown to be offered, he would not disdain it. The best summary of the situation is given by Thiers, whose manuscript 'Notes on the events of 1830' is a crucial source for the history of the period, and which no evidence has yet emerged to contradict:

One of the questions most often addressed to the house of
Orléans was whether it would accept the crown ... The
partisans of the Orléans family, even the most active of whom
never conspired with them, and some of whom had never even
seen them, affirmed that they would accept, and felt that in such
a circumstance, it was best to seem assured even if nobody was
entirely sure, since an air of certainty attracts followers.[63]

Above all, Louis-Philippe did nothing because Charles X was doing
his work for him. If he wanted the crown, the unpopularity of the
king's policies might very soon give him his opportunity. If he did
not, silence and discretion were still the wisest course. Put most
simply, Louis-Philippe did not conspire because he did not need to.

As 26 July drew to a close, the general atmosphere was one of
deep foreboding. Nobody, from the court at St Cloud, to Louis-
Philippe and Adélaïde at Neuilly, to the Parisians returning to their
homes, knew what the next day would bring. Although none of
them could have guessed it that evening, the 'three glorious days'
were about to dawn.

Chapter Six

THE JULY REVOLUTION

THE FIRST DAY OF what was to prove to be a revolution did not begin auspiciously for its leaders. Despite the fact that journalists from eleven newspapers had signed the protests against the ordinances the previous day, only four carried Thiers' call for resistance on the morning of 27 July – the *National*, the *Globe*, the *Temps* and the *Journal du Commerce*. Soon afterwards police arrived to close their offices; the editors of the *National* locked their doors and the gendarmes had to break them down.[1]

The press having been silenced, those opposition deputies currently in the capital, with extreme hesitation, took the stage. At 3 p.m., about forty gathered at the house of one of their leading colleagues, the tough, eloquent deputy for Paris, Casimir Périer. Today, however, Périer was far from pugnacious; he was convinced that the government had massed troops to break any revolt once and for all, and argued forcefully that resistance should be kept strictly within legal boundaries. In the end, the only agreement reached was to nominate three of those present, including Guizot, to draft an address of protest to the authorities, and to meet the next day at noon at the residence of another of the group, Pierre Audry de Puyraveau, to discuss it.[2]

Deeds, rather than words, were only to be found on the streets.

Since the early morning groups of Parisians headed, once again, for the gardens of the Palais-royal. Significantly, they were led by the printing workers, whose existence was most obviously threatened by the ordinances. Initially the crowd was peaceful, but just after midday the news of the closure of the protesting newspapers acted as a catalyst to action. Anti-government cries were heard and, sure sign of impending trouble, the shops along the arcades began putting up their shutters. At 1 p.m. the police cleared the gardens, but the people simply streamed outside on to the Place du Palais-royal. At 3 p.m. a squadron of mounted gendarmes charged the gathering and cleared the square, which was then occupied by two detachments of the 3rd regiment of the Royal Guard. About an hour later, provoked by showers of stones thrown from the crowds on the fringes of the square, a few soldiers, probably without orders, opened fire. This was the signal for their comrades to move into the Rue St Honoré and to fire indiscriminately into the surrounding streets. The first deaths of the July revolution occurred here, and gave the resistance the martyrs it needed; the corpses were loaded on to stretchers and paraded around, to fuel popular anger.[3]

Meanwhile, at St Cloud, after attending mass, at 11.30 a.m. Charles X sent for Marmont and ordered him to Paris. At this stage, he clearly regarded the trouble there as nothing more than a passing disturbance. 'It appears,' he told Marmont airily, 'that there are concerns for the tranquillity of Paris. Go there, take command, and first go and see the prince de Polignac. If everything is in order by the evening, you can return to St Cloud.'[4]

By 1 p.m. Marmont was established in the headquarters of the 1st military division in the Tuileries. His first measures were energetic; almost all of the Paris garrison were deployed to guard the key points commanding the city, such as the Place de la Madeleine and the Place de la Bastille. The only serious violence of the afternoon occurred in the Rue St Honoré and the narrow Rue St Nicaise running off it, where the Royal Guard charged and dismantled several barricades that had been erected. The crowds, however, continued to grow, especially around the Place de Grève in front of the Hôtel de Ville and the Place de la Bastille in the working-class district of the Faubourg St Antoine, famous for its turbulence during the 1789 Revolution. In an ominous development, arms shops also started to be attacked and looted in the course of the evening. Yet Marmont still felt the situation was sufficiently under control to send his troops back to barracks, at around eleven o'clock.[5]

By early next morning, Wednesday 28 July, the marshal's mood had changed. It became clear that the crowds of the previous day were not dispersing, but increasing and beginning to build barricades. At this point Marmont revealed exactly the same flaws that had earned him notoriety in 1814 – he allowed a political situation to turn his head, and to distract him fatally from his military duty. Going far beyond his brief, at 9 a.m. he wrote a stark letter to Charles X. Its echo of the duc de la Rochefoucauld-Liancourt's famous words to Louis XVI bringing news of the fall of the Bastille was so striking that it may even have been deliberate. 'This is no longer a riot,' Marmont warned, 'this is a revolution. It is urgent that your majesty take measures to pacify the situation. The honour of the Crown can still be saved; tomorrow perhaps it will be too late. I am taking measures to combat the revolt. The troops will be ready at noon, but I await with impatience your majesty's orders.'[6]

Beneath the coded phrases, the message was clear: the king should calm the Parisians by adopting a conciliatory policy, which would presumably involve revoking the four ordinances. It showed that virtually from the start Marmont was pessimistic about his chances of defeating the rising – hardly an ideal frame of mind for a commander whose orders were to do just that. However, none of these doubts showed in his first orders of the day. The 1st regiment of the Royal Guard was placed on the Boulevard des Capucines along with two cannon and a hundred lancers, the 2nd in reserve at the Place de la Madeleine, the 3rd with two hundred lancers on the Place du Carrousel, one line regiment on the Pont Neuf, two more on the Place Vendôme, and another, supported by a detachment of cuirassiers, on the Place de la Bastille. The garrisons of Orléans, Beauvais, Compiègne, Melun, Provins and Fontainebleau were also summoned, and the 4th regiment of the Guard, already on its way to Paris from Caen, was urged to arrive as quickly as possible. Finally, Marmont sent for four batteries of artillery from Vincennes.[7]

In 1830, urban warfare was still in its infancy. The subjugation of cities whose populations were in insurrection remained a relatively rare phenomenon. For the French military, the only well known recent example was the siege of Saragossa during the Peninsular War twenty-two years before, an atrociously bloody and protracted affair. In 1812, the Russians had burned Moscow soon after Napoleon entered it, but there had been no mass resistance. Still, Marmont felt that these precedents had taught him enough to be confident of his strategy. As he observed in his memoirs: 'The occupation of the public squares is the first prerequisite for mastery of a town; and, since almost all the communications converge on them, it is indispensable.'[8] His aim was therefore to garrison these squares with large detachments of troops, which would ensure their own communications by sending out regular linking patrols along the boulevards, and from this position of strength move inwards, tightening their net around the rebellious quarters.

There was, inevitably, one major problem in using troops against their own civilian compatriots. Soldiers, particularly those from line regiments, detested being involved in civil conflicts, and the longer they were kept inactive, in close proximity to or actually in contact with the people, the more likely this was to sap their morale. Even elite formations were not immune to this contagion: at the outbreak of the French Revolution, the French Guards regiment had mutinied, and many of its number had actually helped the Parisians storm the Bastille.[9] Ominously, by 8 a.m. on 28 July over sixty men of the 5th and 50th regiments of the line stationed on the Place Vendôme had gone over to the insurgents. When he heard this, Marmont had good reason to be concerned.

The marshal's solution was to rally his men by taking the offensive. Three columns were formed to advance east and tackle the insurrection on its home ground. The first, under General Quinsonnas and consisting of two battalions of the 3rd Guards regiment and two cannon, was to move along the Rue St Honoré and take up position in the Place des Innocents. The second, commanded by General Talon and made up of another battalion of that regiment, fifty lancers and two cannon, was to proceed along the right bank of the Seine and occupy the Place de Grève. Finally, General de St Chamans was to take three Guards battalions totalling 750 men, 150 lancers and two guns by way of the northern boulevards to the Place de la Bastille, reinforce the line regiment and the detachment of cuirassiers already there, and open communications with Talon on the Place de Grève.[10]

Against this impending assault by regular troops, the Parisians had resources of their own. They had no overall leadership of the kind exercised by Marmont, but within their own districts they had considerable knowledge of street warfare.[11] Their principal weapon, which was to become the symbol of July 1830 and indeed of all the nineteenth-century French revolutions, was the barricade. Made principally from cobblestones ripped up from the street, but reinforced with furniture, barrels, carts and even on occasion overturned omnibuses, the biggest presented formidable obstacles, sometimes towering to a height of ten feet. Barricades had first sprung up in Paris in 1588, when the Catholic League had driven Henri III from the capital. They had been unnecessary in 1789, since the people had seized the city on 14 July and kept control of it throughout the Revolution. Now, forty-one years later, they came into their own.

Barricades were by no means the Parisians' only means of defence. If troops made a frontal assault on them, the houses on either side could be used to assail them from. From the upper floors, where the poorer citizens generally lived, musketry, cobblestones, chairs and utensils of all kinds could be unleashed on the hapless men below. Small wonder that most soldiers loathed what they called 'this war of chamber-pots'. In addition, if commanders like Marmont aimed at establishing continuous control around the rebellious quarters and then breaking up the resistance within, the Parisians fully understood the importance of isolating the forces sent against them, above all by cutting their lines of retreat. Thus in July 1830 Marmont's columns constantly found themselves threatened from the rear, as barricades were quickly thrown up and trees felled across the streets down which they had just come.[12]

After two centuries in which Paris had seen no major fighting, how was it that its citizens were so familiar with these tactics? It is unlikely that folk-memories of the 'Day of the Barricades' in 1588 still survived, but other sources of military expertise were much closer to hand. The number of Napoleonic veterans in Paris probably ran well into the hundreds, and almost by definition they hated the Bourbons. Accounts of July 1830 are full of references to these men acting as leaders at a local level. A report of the fighting in the 2nd *arrondissement* later cited, among forty-three combatants who had shown exceptional bravery, five former officers and soldiers who had automatically assumed command, while a doctor treating the wounded recalled that two-thirds of the injured he saw were ex-servicemen.[13] Even if they had little detailed knowledge of street fighting, these veterans would have been familiar with the basic principles of mounting a defence, and able to instruct civilians how to handle firearms. If the July revolution was in some senses a replay of 1789, in others it was an extension of the Napoleonic wars.

Marmont's three columns soon found out just how formidable their opponents were. Quinsonnas' troops occupied the Place des Innocents without difficulty, but swiftly found themselves hemmed in by the Parisians, who swarmed through the surrounding streets, blocked the exits from the square with barricades, and exacted a heavy toll with their musketry. Although reinforced towards the end of the afternoon by a battalion of Swiss Guards, the soldiers' position became untenable. Their only option was to break out, so they fought their way down the Rue St Denis, under furious fire from bullets and missiles of all kinds from the surrounding houses, until they reached safety on the banks of the Seine by the Pont des Arts. Further south, Talon's column met a similar fate; it was actually forced to withdraw from the Place de Grève, and only managed to get back in by deploying its cannon, firing grapeshot, against the crowd. Soon, however, it found itself virtually besieged inside the Hôtel de Ville, and did not manage to extricate itself until shortly after 10 p.m., retreating towards the Tuileries along the right bank of the Seine.[14]

St Chamans' column got into trouble early on, since it had not been issued with sufficient ammunition. It reached the Place de la Bastille, but soon found its communications with Marmont cut by numerous barricades built and trees felled behind it as it advanced. St Chamans then tried to force a passage down the Rue St Antoine to join up with Talon on the Place de Grève, but his troops were twice driven back by fire from barricades and adjoining houses. Finally, he managed to cut his way south to the Pont d'Austerlitz and, crossing the river, led his troops back via the southern boulevards.[15]

As his battered columns pulled back to the Tuileries on the evening of 28 July, it was clear that Marmont had suffered a serious reverse. Its essential cause lay beyond his control: he had simply not been given enough men to do the job. In this situation, however, one does wonder if it was prudent to take the offensive at all. Marmont might have been wiser to establish a strong defensive position in the Tuileries from the very beginning and wait for the reinforcements he had ordered to come up from the provinces, although leaving his men inactive could have sapped morale and encouraged desertion.

Other factors contributed to the defeat. There was a disastrous failure to provide the troops with adequate rations. There were no reserves of food and drink, and no transport for the columns to carry what was available. Furthermore, the portable cooking-pots tradition-ally carried by each company had recently been suppressed in the name of economy and replaced by large fixed ones in barracks. This meant that the soldiers had no way of boiling up their soup on the move. Thus for most of Marmont's troops, the only meal they had during the whole of the hot, dangerous day was breakfast in barracks before moving off. None of this can have boosted their fighting spirit.[16]

It has never been clear exactly what rules of engagement Marmont laid down. In his memoirs, the marshal claims that he instructed his column commanders to fire only if they encountered a concerted volley of fifty or more muskets. According to St Chamans, these orders were more aggressive; he recalls Marmont telling him to respond to showers of stones with musketry, and to musket-fire with cannon. St Chamans adds, however, that it was understood that he would use force only if he encountered serious resistance. Although the evidence is inconclusive, fear of excessive civilian casualties probably limited the actions of the troops, increasing their own casualties and further sapping morale. Marmont himself wrote that on one occasion, on 29 July, he forbade his men to fire on a crowd facing them because it contained women.[17] His scruples would not be shared by his successors in June 1848 and May 1871.

While the fighting raged, attempts at negotiation did not entirely cease. At their noon meeting at Audry de Puyraveau's house, the deputies agreed to send a deputation of five of their number to the

Tuileries. Périer, the banker Jacques Laffitte, the lawyer François Mauguin and two distinguished Napoleonic generals, comte Gérard and the comte de Lobau, were chosen.

Arriving at the Tuileries at about three in the afternoon, they found the marshal writing a letter to the king. They begged him to help them achieve a ceasefire, but added that the Parisians would only cooperate if the ordinances were revoked. Marmont replied that this went well beyond his powers, but he unwisely let slip a comment that betrayed his unhappiness with the policy he was having to defend: 'You are complaining about things which I am far from approving, but there are military considerations.'[18]

What Marmont did agree to do was ask Polignac, who had now moved into the Tuileries, if he would see the deputies. Polignac's reply was a curt refusal. In his letter to Charles X, however, Marmont added a sentence that did directly broach political matters: 'I think it is urgent that your majesty profit without delay from the overtures that are made to him.'[19] Marmont's conduct with the deputies may well have had important repercussions. The undertone of doubt and hesitation in his words may well have given the impression, and particularly to Périer, that from the marshal downwards the military's fighting spirit was crumbling. This had crucial consequences the following day.

By late afternoon Marmont had a reply from the king, who simply instructed him to 'concentrate his troops, hold firm, and operate in masses'. By dawn on the 29 July, he had made his dispositions. All his forces were withdrawn to defend the complex of the Tuileries and the Louvre. He placed two battalions of Swiss Guards in the Louvre, backed by a further Swiss battalion, two regiments of the Royal Guard and six cannon in the Place du Carrousel. Then, in a line stretching from east to west, came two regiments of the Royal Guard, with two cannon, in the Place Louis XVI (now Place de la Concorde) and the Boulevard de la Madeleine; two line regiments, the 15th and 50th, with two cannon, in the Tuileries gardens; and the 5th and 53rd line regiments on the Place Vendôme. At least on the surface, Marmont had great confidence in this deployment. Just before 9 a.m., as the ministers prepared to travel to St Cloud to see Charles X, he told them: 'You may assure the king that, whatever happens, without the need for reinforcements, should the whole population of Paris take up arms against me, I could hold out here for a fortnight ... Yes, this position is impregnable, and I could defend it against all Paris for a fortnight.'[20]

A defence of the Louvre and the Tuileries, however, held further traumatic memories of the French Revolution. On 10 August 1792, Louis XVI and the royal family, surrounded by a few National Guard formations and the Swiss Guard, had attempted to make a last stand against a Parisian insurrection aimed at overthrowing them. In the ensuing confusion, the Swiss had fired on the crowd before being overwhelmed. They were either massacred at their posts, or cut down by the infuriated populace as they fled westwards through the Tuileries gardens.[21]

The Swiss Guard in July 1830, standing in almost exactly the same spot as their butchered predecessors thirty-eight years before, could hardly have avoided drawing uncomfortable parallels with their present situation. For some, the associations would have been particularly eerie. Since the Swiss Guard was a close-knit body, with service ties stretching over generations, many of its officers and men in July 1830 came from the same families as the defenders of the Tuileries in August 1792. Their commander, Colonel de Salis, had two relatives who had fought on 10 August, only one of whom had survived, while Colonel de Maillardoz had lost both his father and his brother that day. They cannot have relished the possibility that they were about to share their kinsmen's fate.[22]

It took less than two hours for history to repeat itself. The sequence of events is not entirely clear, but at about 10 a.m. the 5th and 53rd regiments of the line stationed in the Place Vendôme left their posts and went over to the Parisians. There had been warning signals since the beginning of the conflict; on 27 July several soldiers of the 5th had deserted, and on the 28th men from both regiments had been seen fraternizing with the crowd. According to Marmont, the catalyst for their defection was the appearance on the Place Vendôme of Casimir Périer, who, he claimed, delivered a short, but effective harangue, urging them not to fire on the people.[23] If this is the case it is most likely that Périer, having gauged the temper of Marmont and his troops the previous day, had realized their weaknesses and decided the moment had come for a bold throw. Whatever the exact facts, the result was crucial — most of the western end of Marmont's line melted away.

A chain reaction now developed. Fearing that the two other line regiments might follow the example of the 5th and the 53rd, Marmont pulled them back to the Champs-Elysées. To plug the gap in his defences, he withdrew the Swiss battalion from the Place du Carrousel and placed it in the Tuileries gardens, then replaced the latter with one of the other Swiss battalions in the Louvre. However, in the course of this redeployment a fatal mistake occurred. In the confusion of their retreat from the Louvre, the Swiss battalion left an entrance to the building, next to the Rue du Coq, unguarded. A few intrepid Parisians spotted this, charged inside and opened fire. To the commander of the remaining battalion, Colonel de Salis, it seemed as if he was about to be cut off. According to Marmont, he lost his head and, 'convinced that he was in danger of being blockaded in the Louvre, he left his post hurriedly and in disorder'. Salis' sudden panic probably owed much to the memory of his relatives' fate, abandoned in 1792 to the fury of the people.[24]

The example of this one battalion proved contagious, and soon spread to all the Swiss. Seeing Salis' soldiers fleeing from the Louvre, their comrades on the Place du Carrousel, seized by a similar panic, bolted westwards across the courtyard of the Tuileries and into the Tuileries gardens, where they were joined by the Swiss battalion stationed there. Marmont himself was swept away by the flood, and only managed to rally his men at the Etoile. His instinct was to hold his ground there; he still had several thousand troops, backed by artillery, in sight of the Tuileries, and felt that this at least provided the king with the means to negotiate from a position of strength. Yet just as he had finished drawing up his men, a message arrived from St Cloud, where the news of his retreat had been received shortly before. It informed Marmont that the duc d'Angoulême had taken overall command, and ordered a general withdrawal to St Cloud. Disconsolately, the marshal and his men broke ranks and abandoned the Etoile. Paris had been definitively lost.

Militarily and politically, the rout at the Tuileries was the decisive moment of the 'three glorious days'. It was totally unexpected. At a stroke, it tipped the scales against the royal government, and anything was now possible. This was immediately clear to one observer. From the windows of his strategically placed house on the corner of the Rue St Florentin and the Place Louis XVI, Talleyrand watched the broken Guards regiments fleeing through the Tuileries gardens, across the square and up the Champs-Elysées. Rather theatrically, he took out his watch, looked at it, and announced to the friends standing around him: 'Twenty-ninth July, five minutes past midday, the elder branch of the house of Bourbon has ceased to reign.'[25]

The evacuation of Paris ended the serious fighting of the July revolution. According to official records, 496 Parisians were killed and 849 wounded over those three days, while roughly 150 royal troops died, 580 were injured and 137 went missing.[26] But if the military phase of the revolution was over, its political phase was just beginning. Had the elder branch of the house of Bourbon really ceased to reign? If so, who – or what – would replace it?

*

BY THE EVENING OF 29 JULY, the crown was no longer the sole source of authority in France, but was challenged by two different centres of power in Paris. The first consisted of the liberal deputies meeting at Laffitte's house, which since that morning had become the de facto headquarters of the political opposition. However, as the royal government's authority collapsed in the course of the day, the deputies were faced with successive responsibilities that they could not shoulder alone. They found themselves in exactly the same position as their revolutionary forebears on 14 July 1789. With the traditional forces of order in flight, if Paris was not to be delivered up to anarchy it needed a functioning authority with the means to impose its will if necessary. Following the precedent of 1789, a municipal commission was therefore set up. Its members were Laffitte, Périer, Audry de Puyraveau, Mauguin and another deputy, Auguste de Schonen. Laffitte stayed put, feeling that he would have more influence where he was, but the other four hurried off to the Hôtel de Ville to assume their functions. To preserve order, it was also decided to revive the National Guard, disbanded in 1827. In a highly charged gesture, this was entrusted to its original commander in 1789 and the greatest living symbol of the Revolution, the sprightly seventy-three-year-old Lafayette.[27]

At St Cloud Charles X realized, too late, that the only way he could now save his throne was by compromise. At 4 p.m. on 29 July he followed the example of his brother on 16 July 1789, did what he had sworn never to do, and dismissed his ministers. Polignac was replaced by the duc de Mortemart, a forty-seven-year-old ex-soldier who had just returned from a posting as ambassador to St Petersburg, and it was agreed to revoke the four ordinances and to offer ministerial posts to Périer and General Gérard. Mortemart, however, was extremely reluctant to accept his new role, and the reason he gave says much about Charles' priorities. 'The king thinks I'm an atheist,' he complained, 'I'm certain of it.'[28] As a result, he argued, he would never have the royal confidence. He was also suffering from a serious fever, not the best qualification for the task ahead.

Mortemart's fears were justified. It was essential that he go to Paris as soon as possible to negotiate an end to the crisis, but Charles initially refused to give him the necessary minimum for this: plenipotential powers, a written confirmation of the withdrawal of the ordinances, the dismissal of the Polignac ministry, the revival of the National Guard, and the offer of ministries to Périer and Gérard. The king gave way only at 7 a.m. on 30 July, after Mortemart forced his way into his bedroom demanding these concessions. Mortemart set off immediately for the capital with three companions including the liberal peer the comte d'Argout, but he had already lost several precious hours. This delay was the final nail in the coffin of Charles X's reign.

Meanwhile in Paris, the moment of political decision had arrived. The chance of a negotiated solution that would keep Charles on the throne was receding, but what could be put in its place? Over the last three days the streets had echoed to cries of 'Long live Napoleon!' Admittedly, the emperor had been dead for nine years and his son was currently living under Austrian surveillance in Vienna, but the popularity of Bonapartism was alarming. Republicanism, too, had significant support, and Lafayette, currently at the Hôtel de Ville with the municipal commission, was strongly suspected of favouring it. To the deputies and journalists gathered at Laffitte's house, both these prospects were deeply uncongenial. Neither a restored empire nor a republic was likely to be accepted by the other Powers, and could lead to a European war. A republic would add to this an upheaval in the domestic social order. There was, however, one other possibility, that perennial reserve option since 1814: a properly constitutional monarchy under Louis-Philippe that would finally respect the Charter.

On the evening of the 29th, three members of the gathering at Laffitte's house decided that the time had come to launch the Orléanist candidacy. They were Laffitte himself, Thiers, and the distinguished Corsican General Horace Sébastiani, who had served Napoleon as both a soldier and a diplomat, and was currently liberal deputy for Vervins. Sébastiani was a close friend of both Louis-Philippe and Adélaïde.[29] This trio now took an extraordinary leap in the dark. As Thiers underlines in his manuscript notes, they had no certainty that Louis-Philippe would accept the crown, but they thought that he would, and that was enough. On this tenuous basis Thiers, with the aid of his friend Mignet, drew up a terse and effective manifesto to be printed and distributed that night throughout Paris. It read:

> Charles X can never again enter Paris; he has caused the blood of the people to be shed.
> The republic would expose us to frightful divisions; it would embroil us with Europe.
> The duc d'Orléans is a prince devoted to the cause of the Revolution.
> The duc d'Orléans has never fought against us.
> The duc d'Orléans was at Jemmapes.
> The duc d'Orléans has carried the tricolour under fire; the duc d'Orléans alone can carry it again; we want no others.
> The duc d'Orléans has declared himself; he accepts the Charter as we have always wanted it.
> It is from the French people that he will hold his crown.[30]

This was striking prose, but it was now absolutely essential to know whether Louis-Philippe would lend himself to the plan. As Sébastiani put it, 'The friends of the Orléans family should no longer hesitate to compromise it.' It was agreed that Thiers would leave immediately on horseback for Neuilly to see Louis-Philippe, with two companions, including an officer of the National Guard with permits to get them through the militia posts around Paris. Thiers also carried a short note from Laffitte: 'I beg M. le duc d'Orléans to listen to M. Thiers in all confidence and to what he is charged to say on my behalf.'[31]

At Neuilly, the atmosphere of the past seventy-two hours had been tense and uncertain. On 27 July, Louis-Philippe had received a former neighbour from Twickenham, an elderly English lady, and taken her on a tour of the park. When Marie-Amélie asked him whether the children could make a trip to the swimming-pool on the Quai d'Orsay, he had agreed, but added ominously: 'That reminds me that my brother Montpensier also went to the swimming-pool on a day of troubles, 10 August [1792], and wasn't able to get back.' Later in the day, Mme de Boigne paid a visit and had a long talk with Adélaïde, whom she found horrified by the ordinances and the prospect of civil war, and lamenting that the family was not safely out of harm's way at their property of Eu in Normandy, where they had been planning to go in a few days' time. Not once was Louis-Philippe's political position mentioned. This display of consternation may have been genuine, but it was more likely an example of that 'reserve' that Adélaïde had so strongly recommended to her relatives the previous day.[32]

The family's anxiety had reached a peak on the 28th. Throughout the day, musketry and the rumble of cannon-fire could clearly be heard at Neuilly. It was, however, very unclear what was happening; the reports brought by a stream of visitors and messengers were hopelessly contradictory. What is clear is that the sound of fighting, far from cowing Adélaïde, brought out her martial instincts. At dinner that evening, while the gunfire sounded and Louis-Philippe sat looking sad and pensive, she whispered to Vatout sitting next to her: 'If only I carried a sword!' There is also a sense from the surviving records that the household was beginning to look to her for direction. When Vatout heard rumours from his friends that the royal government might send troops to Neuilly and put Louis-Philippe under guard, it was to Adélaïde that he confided his fears: 'I said to her: "You should persuade your brother under no circumstances to sleep at Neuilly, but at Villiers [a small château on the edge of the estate]." She did not reply *ad hoc*, but the prince slept [there] in the small pavilion known as La Magnanerie.'[33] It was in this unlikely refuge, used for rearing silkworms, that Louis-Philippe spent the nights of 28 and 29 July. Adélaïde and Marie-Amélie, the only people who knew where he was hidden, kept him informed of all the latest news from Paris.

Louis-Philippe did not have to stay long with his silkworms. Towards mid-morning on the 29th his estate manager, Badouix, arrived at Neuilly from Paris with the sensational tidings of the rout of the royal troops. The reaction was one of unrestrained joy. If at this point Adélaïde had had any remaining doubts about what she and her brother should do now, they were removed by what happened shortly afterwards. As the family was sitting down to lunch, a cannonball, fired by Marmont's gunners as they withdrew to St Cloud, whistled overhead before burying itself a little distance away in the park. Adélaïde had experienced bombardment before, when a shell had crashed into her mother's house during the struggle for Barcelona in 1808. But then it had been Napoleon's soldiers firing on her; now it was her own cousin's, and this seems to have been the last straw. According to the philanthropist Benjamin Appert, who was present, she turned to Marie-Amélie and said: ' "My dear friend, from this moment we can't remain with that crowd [Charles X and his supporters], they are massacring the people and firing on us, we must make a decision." Then', continues Appert, Adélaïde 'tearing up all the red, white and blue silk she could find in her wardrobe, made up tricolour cockades for everybody in the palace, and distributed them herself. From that instant it was obvious that the house of Orléans was lost if the king's cause should triumph.'[34]

With Marmont's troops streaming past the gates of Neuilly on their retreat west, Louis-Philippe's hideout at La Magnanerie was clearly too close for comfort, and Adélaïde decided that he should move further away. Early on the morning of 30 July, dressed very simply and accompanied only by his aide-de-camp Colonel de Berthois, he set off on horseback for his château of Le Raincy just east of Paris. On his grey hat he wore a tricolour cockade specially made for him by Adélaïde.[35] Shortly afterwards, the children were moved further away from the main road, to Villiers. With considerable courage, Adélaïde and Marie-Amélie stayed on at Neuilly.

Thus when Thiers, whose permit had not spared him a series of tedious wrangles with the National Guard posts en route, finally arrived at Neuilly towards mid-morning, he found not Louis-Philippe, but his wife and sister. Thiers was first ushered in to see Marie-Amélie, who told him that her husband had just left, but that she would listen to what he had to say, transmit it to Louis-Philippe and bring back a prompt answer. She then sent for Adélaïde, who swiftly arrived, followed by Mme de Montjoie.

Thiers was the only one of the participants to record the discussion that ensued, but his account accords with all the known facts. Although there were four people in the room, Thiers presents the conversation as almost entirely between himself and Adélaïde. He began by conveying the message from Laffitte and Sébastiani that the time had come for Louis-Philippe to claim the throne. Adélaïde's initial response was cautious. While making it absolutely clear that the Orléans family supported the Parisians in their struggle against the king, she was concerned that if the dynasty was changed too quickly, a genuine popular movement would appear to the other European Powers as simply a palace revolution, and that if they then decided to support Charles X 'the cause of liberty would be lost'.[36]

To these objections Thiers had ready answers. France, he asserted, wanted a properly representative monarchy, embodied in a new dynasty which owed its crown to the people and would keep within the limits prescribed by the constitution. Europe knew that the Orléans had not conspired to overthrow Charles X, and would be relieved that despite the upheaval the monarchical principle was still being upheld. However, there was not an instant to lose. In some quarters there was support for a continuation of the elder branch under the duc de Bordeaux reigning as Henri V, in others for Napoleon's son the Duke of Reichstadt, currently living in Vienna with his mother's Habsburg relations, while a significant group 'would go straight for the republic'. 'There is a clear field,' Thiers urged. 'Anything is possible at this moment. We must hurry.'

Thiers' trump card, however, was an appeal to Adélaïde's courage:

> To all these arguments, let me add a last one that is decisive. Thrones are obtained only at the price of difficulties and dangers ... If the duc d'Orléans comes today into the middle of Paris, declares that he is rallying to the revolution, has come to share all the dangers the French are facing, and to put

himself at their head, he will have played his part in the July revolution. I cannot hide from you that there will still perhaps be great dangers to surmount; that Charles X is at St Cloud, and that he still has forces at his disposal. But you need perils. They are titles to the crown. The duc d'Orléans must decide. The destiny of France must not be left hanging in the balance.[37]

This was the most important moment in Adélaïde's life. She rose to it memorably. Writing as a historian, in the third person, Thiers recalled her response:

Mme Adélaïde, touched above all by this last consideration, rose and said to M. Thiers: 'If you think that the adhesion of our family can be of use to the revolution, we give it gladly. A woman is nothing in a family. She can be compromised. I am ready to go to Paris. What happens to me there is in God's hands. I will share the fate of the Parisians. I demand only one thing; that M. Laffitte or General Sébastiani come in person to fetch me.'

M. Thiers, thinking that it was sufficient to have [the agreement of] one member of the family, no matter which one, for it to be compromised, felt that this first promise was enough. 'Today, Madame,' he said to Mme Adélaïde, 'you have gained the crown for your house.'[38]

Thiers' final flourish was no more than the truth. Adélaïde's intervention was absolutely decisive; it secured the throne for her brother, and decided the fate of the July revolution. Scarcely less remarkable were the terms in which it was couched. How many years of frustration lay behind the words: 'A woman is nothing in a family'! Yet however heartfelt the phrase, it was probably also part of a cunning stratagem. Though this is difficult to prove, there may well have been a traditional expectation among the royal families of Europe that, at moments of great crisis, responsibility for essential measures should be assumed by one of its women to avoid compromising the male head of the house. Marie Antoinette had done this during the Revolution, taking day-to-day charge of Louis XVI's secret diplomacy so that even if this was discovered, her husband could be shielded from blame and the crown eventually passed on intact to her son.[39] In the same way, if Charles X did manage to turn the tables on Paris, Adélaïde was offering herself up to protect her beloved brother from the king's revenge. Her recognition that in these circumstances women were expendable was brutally realistic, but it underlines all the more her extraordinary devotion.

Adélaïde's promise enabled Thiers to return immediately to Paris to report on the success of his mission to Laffitte and Sébastiani, who he found had moved to the Chamber of Deputies with about forty or fifty of their colleagues. Laffitte and Sébastiani agreed that her word was sufficient for their purposes. Their goal was the crown for Louis-Philippe, but they decided, so as not to alarm some of the more conservative deputies, to limit themselves for the moment to an interim measure. They proposed that Louis-Philippe be invited to become Lieutenant-General of the Kingdom, a procedure that had been used before when the king was absent or otherwise prevented from ruling. After a deputation sent to confer with the Chamber of Peers came back with an affirmative answer, the question was put to the vote and carried with only three dissenting voices.[40]

So far, all these crucial steps had been taken in Louis-Philippe's name, but without his formal consent. The time had now come for him to sanction them in person. In the early afternoon, Marie-Amélie and Adélaïde sent word to him that he should return from Le Raincy immediately. A further reason for haste was the news that a commission of twelve deputies, including Adélaïde's friends Sébastiani and the deputy and lawyer André Dupin, were en route bringing the offer of the lieutenant-generalcy of the kingdom, and it would not do for him to be absent a second time. A few hours later, Louis-Philippe arrived back at Neuilly, slipped into the park, and stationed himself in a glade near the bank of the Seine called the Bosquet des Tourniquets.

It was here, at about 8 p.m., that Adélaïde and Marie-Amélie joined him, and the final decision was made. Louis-Philippe agreed to accept the deputies' offer, go to Paris, and rule, for the time being, as Lieutenant-General of the Kingdom. He then sent for the commission, which now arrived in the Bosquet des Tourniquets and read him, by torchlight, the invitation to accept the lieutenant-generalcy.

Louis-Philippe accepted it, and the die was now cast. At ten o'clock, with a small escort, he set off on foot for the Palais-royal.[41]

No record exists of that evening meeting in the Bosquet des Tourniquets between Louis-Philippe, his wife and his sister. It was almost certainly Adélaïde who played the decisive part, and persuaded her brother to assume the lieutenant-generalcy. After all, she had already in effect accepted it on his behalf that morning. She had decided the previous day that a clean break should be made with the elder branch, and was determined that the rest of her family should follow suit.

In assessing Adélaïde's role in founding the July monarchy, there is one last possibility to consider – that her acceptance of the crown on her brother's behalf was not in fact spontaneous, but part of a set-piece scenario carefully choreographed by Louis-Philippe himself. This is a variation on the 'Orléanist conspiracy' theory; according to this view Louis-Philippe was waiting for the throne to be offered to him, and determined to accept it if it was, but was equally determined not to compromise himself until the success of his candidacy was certain. It was thus his idea, not Adélaïde's, that he should go into hiding, leaving his wife and sister to undertake negotiations and make promises that, from his point of view, were entirely deniable. None of this detracts from Adélaïde's courage in shouldering this responsibility, but it makes her brother, rather than herself, the principal actor in the drama.

This reinterpretation of Adélaïde's actions also has implications for those of her sister-in-law. Marie-Amélie has traditionally been portrayed as, of all her family, the one most sympathetic to the elder branch (the duchesse de Berry was, after all, her niece), and the most reluctant for her husband to supplant them. This interpretation has recently been challenged, and the argument advanced that Marie-Amélie's scruples were simply a 'comedy' designed to embellish the fiction that her family had not conspired to take the throne.[42] But on balance the most reliable contemporary evidence, above all Vatout's journal, supports the conventional view that Marie-Amélie was genuinely reluctant for her husband to become king.[43]

Did Louis-Philippe and Adélaïde plan the scenario of 30 July between them? The best evidence for this is that something

suspiciously similar had occurred before, in March 1815, when
Adélaïde had stayed behind in Paris to act as Louis-Philippe's eyes
and ears while he headed north to rally resistance to Napoleon. In
1815 as in 1830, the air had been thick with rumours of an Orléanist
candidacy. Yet there were important differences between Louis-
Philippe's position then and now. To begin with, he was significantly
older — fifty-seven as opposed to forty-two — and less inclined to face
the challenges of kingship. The poisonous legacy of the Hundred
Days, and the polarization of politics since, also meant that France
was a distinctly less inviting prospect to govern than she had been
before Waterloo. As Thiers put it to Adélaïde: 'The crown . . . is too
perilous today to be an object of ambition.'[44]

There is more evidence that Louis-Philippe took the steps leading
to the throne in a mood of resignation rather than triumph. He was
extremely resilient, but although he never flinched in the face of
obstacles he was prone to view them with a fatalism sometimes tinged
with depression. He had a tendency towards indecision in moments
of great crisis, whereas she had a remarkable capacity to make up her
mind and act on it. It is, of course, possible that Adélaïde orchestrated
their joint response to the deputies' offer, but to do this she and
Louis-Philippe would have had to know it was coming, and the
most important testimony, that of Thiers, is adamant that they did
not. It is much more likely that Adélaïde took the leading role
at Neuilly in response to developing circumstances, persuaded her
brother to go into hiding, accepted Thiers' offer on her own initiative, and finally, on the night of 30 July in the Bosquet des Tourniquets, convinced Louis-Philippe to accept the lieutenant-generalcy
of the kingdom. This view is supported by a short summary of
Adélaïde's life in the Orléans papers written after her death, probably by her nephew the duc de Nemours: 'Devoted to her brother,
under the restoration she helped to rally around him the most
distinguished men of the liberal party, and in 1830 to decide him to
accept the crown.'[45]

One final piece of evidence, unfortunately now vanished, confirms
this reading of events. In early 1831, Adélaïde had a large fountain
in bronze and white marble erected in the Bosquet des Tourniquets.
Set into it was the cannonball that had shot over her head as she and
her family were having lunch on 29 July 1830, and which she had had

carefully retrieved. Below it she had placed two inscriptions. The first read: 'On Thursday 29 July 1830 the cannonball that forms the motif of this bas-relief was fired into the park of the Château de Neuilly by the troops of the Royal Guard who, repulsed by the Parisians, were retreating to the Bois de Boulogne.' The second stated: 'On Friday 30 July 1830, on this spot Louis-Philippe d'Orléans met the first delegates of the French people who had come to offer him the lieutenant-generalcy of the kingdom.'[46]

Yet it was also in the Bosquet des Tourniquets, before the delegation arrived, that Adélaïde probably overcame Louis-Philippe's last hesitations about accepting the crown. The fountain was destroyed during the 1848 revolution, and not a trace of it remains. Is it too fanciful to see it, standing for seventeen years in the very place where she had finally gained her brother the throne, as Adélaïde's own monument to her greatest achievement?

*

MEANWHILE, AT ST CLOUD and in Paris, Charles X and his ministers were making their last desperate attempts to retain the crown for the elder branch of the Bourbons. Shortly after 7 a.m. on 30 July, the duc de Mortemart had left St Cloud for the capital with the comte d'Argout and two other emissaries. However, his journey did not go according to plan. Arriving at a National Guard post in the village of Boulogne, the party was roughly treated by the militiamen, and forced to get out and continue on foot. Mortemart and his companions tried to cut through the Bois de Boulogne, but soon found that it was full of skirmishers from both sides sniping at each other. They therefore had to retrace their steps and follow the Seine on its meandering course into Paris. In this way they came to Passy, but were unable to cross the river there, and had to go on to the Pont de Grenelle. From there they trudged along the Rue de Vaugirard to Laffitte's house, but found that most of the deputies gathered there had now departed for the Chamber. Those who remained assured Mortemart that the time for negotiations with Charles was now past, and that the only hope of saving the monarchy lay with Louis-Philippe.

By now, unsurprisingly, Mortemart's fever had worsened considerably, but he nonetheless decided to struggle on to the Chamber of Peers at the Luxembourg palace to parley with his colleagues there. He could barely walk, and had to be supported by Argout the whole way to the Luxembourg. He arrived there in a terrible state, and was immediately placed in a hot bath on the orders of a doctor who happened to be on the premises. Despite his sufferings, Mortemart did attempt to have printed the new ordinances repealing those of 25 July and installing the new ministry, but no newspaper, even the official *Moniteur*, would accept them. Ill, isolated and with no means of imposing his will on events, he had become a phantom prime minister.[47]

Even before Mortemart had departed, the situation at St Cloud had been going from bad to worse. Retreating from Paris on the 29th, Marmont had met the duc d'Angoulême on the road outside the village of Boulogne, and had been greeted 'coldly'. Having taken over command in the wake of a disaster and no doubt looking for someone to blame, it is probable that Angoulême was already harbouring dark suspicions that Marmont had just betrayed the king as he had previously betrayed Napoleon. The next day was spent reforming the troops at St Cloud, but in the early evening, concerned by a trickle of desertions, Marmont issued an order of the day to the Royal Guard, thanking them for their courage and loyalty and informing them that the four ordinances had been withdrawn and Mortemart appointed prime minister.

Unwisely, the marshal did this without consulting Angoulême. When he reported his action to Charles at nine that evening, the king told him he had made a mistake and advised him to clear the matter up immediately. Marmont went straight away to see Angoulême, but no sooner had the door shut behind him than the latter grabbed him by the throat, shouting: 'Traitor! Miserable traitor! You go ahead and issue an order of the day without my permission! Give me your sword!' A struggle then ensued for the weapon, in the course of which Angoulême cut himself on it. Eventually the luckless marshal was marched out of the room by six of the Royal Bodyguards and confined to his room under arrest.[48]

Marmont's detention did not last long. Within half an hour the captain of the Bodyguard arrived with the marshal's sword, gave it back to him, and took him to see the king. Attempting to patch things up, Charles said that there had been fault on both sides, and that his son and Marmont should now make up their quarrel. Marmont initially refused: 'Sire, my sentiments towards you are unquestionable, but your son fills me with horror!' Finally he was persuaded to make a public reconciliation with Angoulême, but the charade was complicated by the fact that he was much the taller of the two: '[Angoulême] had difficulty embracing me, because I certainly made no effort to stoop to his level. He took my hand, which I did not shake. I made a profound bow without looking at him, and went back to my quarters.'[49]

While Marmont was sulking in his rooms, reports arrived that the Parisians were planning an attack on St Cloud, and it was decided to retreat to the Trianon, in the park of Versailles. The withdrawal began at 3 a.m. in an atmosphere of funereal gloom, and the Trianon was reached four hours later. There the king called a council of his remaining ministers, and a plan was drawn up to move the government to Tours on the Loire and, backed by the loyal troops and inhabitants of the provinces, continue the struggle against Paris. Shortly afterwards, however, this decision was overturned by the arrival of the rearguard, demoralized and in disorder. Angoulême had bungled his retreat; the Royal Guards under his command had refused to fire on the advancing Parisians at the Pont de Sèvres, and six companies of Swiss had surrendered in the park of St Cloud. Swiftly concluding that the Trianon was no longer secure, the royal caravan packed up once more and set off for the royal residence of Rambouillet, where it arrived as dark was falling.[50]

The critical events of 31 July took place in Paris. Louis-Philippe began his day early; having arrived at the Palais-royal just before midnight the previous evening, he was up at 4 a.m. to receive the duc de Mortemart. He presented an extraordinary sight – wigless, sweating, his shirt undone, with a Madras handkerchief tied round his head which he then took off and twisted continually in his hands. In an emotional outburst, he assured the duke that he had come to Paris only because the revolutionaries had compelled him to, and that he would 'rather be torn in pieces' than accept the crown. He even gave Mortemart a letter for Charles X protesting his fidelity, although admittedly only in very general terms, which the duke carried away concealed in his cravat. Louis-Philippe showed a similar reluctance to assume power later in the morning, when he received a further delegation of deputies offering him the lieutenant-generalcy. To their entreaties he simply replied that he saw no urgent need to accept their invitation.[51]

Were these two scenes yet more 'comedies', designed in the one case to pull the wool over Charles X's eyes for as long as possible, and in the other to maximize his own value to the opposition? The fact that Louis-Philippe asked Mortemart to return to him his letter to Charles as soon as he heard that the king had left St Cloud tends to support this view. On the other hand, it may simply be that, momentarily deprived of Adélaïde's bold counsels, he was seized by the indecision to which he was prone in a crisis. It is significant that his first action after replying to the offer of the lieutenant-generalcy was to send a messenger to Talleyrand to ask what he should do. The prince's reply was typically laconic: 'He should accept.'[52]

Once Talleyrand's verdict had been received, matters moved fast. Louis-Philippe, Sébastiani and Dupin swiftly sat down and drafted a declaration in which Louis-Philippe accepted the lieutenant-generalcy. This was then carried to the Chamber of Deputies, who applauded it, ordered its immediate publication and appointed a committee of four, including Benjamin Constant and Guizot, to draw up a proclamation of its own. When this was done, ninety-five deputies signed it and went in procession to the Palais-royal to present it to Louis-Philippe. Laffitte then read it aloud to the assembled throng. The solemnity of the occasion was only slightly marred by the fact that, still convalescent from an attack of gout, he was balancing precariously on a crutch.[53]

One final obstacle needed to be overcome. Over in the east of the city, at the Hôtel de Ville, the municipal commission and Lafayette were acting as the government of Paris. They were surrounded by a huge crowd, whose mood was volatile. The few Bonapartist agitators who appeared had been quietly detained, but there was significant support for the republic among those who had gathered, and an obvious potential president at hand in Lafayette. It seemed from soundings taken the previous day that the old man was reluctant to assume this role, but with so many armed and radicalized citizens on the streets nothing could be taken for granted. It was therefore necessary to make a symbolic pilgrimage to the

1. *Above*. The arrival of
Louis XVIII at Calais,
24 April 1814, by Edward Bird.
Note the welcoming committee
of virgins in white.

2. *Right*. Louis-Philippe,
aged nineteen, as a
French Revolutionary
general, 1793. A portrait
painted retrospectively by
Léon Cogniet, 1834.

3. Adélaïde in 1838,
by Marie-Amélie Cogniet.

4. Adélaïde being given a
harp lesson by her governess,
Mme de Genlis, c. 1785.
Adélaïde's adopted sister,
the mysterious Pamela Syms,
is turning the pages.

5. Louis XVIII in coronation robes, by Gérard.

6. Charles X before the fall, by Horace Vernet.

7. Charles X after the fall: 'Pity a Poor Blind Man!', by Charles Philipon.

8 and 9. Repeating revolution: the Palais-royal on 12 July 1789 (*above*) and on 27 July 1830 (*below*).

10. The Parisians forcing the Swiss Guards from the Louvre, 29 July 1830, by Jean-Louis Bezard.

11. Force for order or disorder? A company of the National Guard in the Champ de Mars, 1836.

12. Louis-Philippe
as King of the French,
by Winterhalter.

13. Queen Marie-Amélie, by
Winterhalter.

14. Adélaïde, by Winterhalter.

15. The hope of the dynasty:
Ferdinand-Philippe,
duc d'Orléans,
by Ary Scheffer.

16. Napoleonic veteran, prime minister of Louis-Philippe, friend of Adélaïde: Etienne-Maurice, comte Gérard, Marshal of France, by David.

Hôtel de Ville, the traditional locus of revolutionary Paris, to draw the sting of the republicans.

At about 2 p.m., a bizarre procession formed up in the courtyard of the Palais-royal. At its head was Louis-Philippe, now in National Guard uniform, on a white horse called Clio. Behind him were the deputies, led by the gouty Laffitte and the elderly Benjamin Constant, the godfather of French liberalism, both in sedan chairs. The column then set off for the Hôtel de Ville. This took some courage on the part of all concerned, but particularly Louis-Philippe; at any moment along his route, a republican activist (or supporter of Charles X) could have ended his prospects, and his life, with a bullet. As the party advanced along the right bank of the Seine towards the Hôtel de Ville, there were extraordinary scenes; the press of people became so thick that Louis-Philippe was unable to use his reins to guide Clio, and the horse stopped walking and was literally carried along by the flood. But the crowd was not uniformly enthusiastic. As Louis-Philippe and his companions moved eastwards, shouts of 'Down with the Bourbons!' and even 'Down with the duc d'Orléans!' began to be heard.[54]

At the Hôtel de Ville, Lafayette greeted Louis-Philippe at the foot of the main staircase and escorted him into the great hall, which was packed with citizens and combatants, by no means all of whom were friendly. The deputies' proclamation was then read aloud, and Louis-Philippe promised to uphold the guarantees of public liberties it contained. This was enough to satisfy Lafayette, who shook his hand. However, through the open windows loud shouts of 'Long live the republic!' and 'Down with the duc d'Orléans!' could be heard from the Place de Grève. At that moment Lafayette revealed once again his genius for the symbolic populist gesture. He took hold of one end of a large tricolour flag lying in the hall, gave the other end to Louis-Philippe, and the two of them advanced with it on to the balcony. At first the people only cried 'Long live Lafayette!', but when he dramatically embraced Louis-Philippe they gave both men a prolonged ovation.[55]

This was the second pivotal balcony scene Lafayette had played in his career. On 6 October 1789, he had probably saved Marie Antoinette's life by appearing with her at Versailles in front of a

furious mob and disarming its hostility simply by kissing her hand.
Louis-Philippe had good reason to remember the occasion; his own
father had been watching from the crowd. Once again, the great
moments of the Revolution were being reprised, but in different
circumstances and to a different purpose.[56]

With his 'republican coronation' at the Hôtel de Ville, Louis-
Philippe had cleared the last major hurdle on his road to power. Yet
a few pockets of radical resistance remained to be mopped up. On
the evening of 31 July, the indefatigable Thiers brought a number of
the younger republican leaders to the Palais-royal to see for themselves whether Louis-Philippe would make an acceptable head of
state. One of them, the firebrand Godefroy Cavaignac, the son of a
Jacobin deputy to the Convention, had the bad taste to remind Louis-
Philippe during the conversation that both their fathers had voted for
the death of Louis XVI. Apart from this unwelcome interruption,
though, Louis-Philippe largely succeeded in bamboozling his listeners
with generalized protestations of sympathy for their point of view,
while avoiding any specific commitments. He did the same with
Lafayette the next day, when the latter came with the municipal
commission to give up their powers into his hands. It was during this
interview that Lafayette famously announced his support for 'a
popular monarchy surrounded by republican institutions'. Louis-
Philippe, seeing nothing in this that could tie his hands for the future,
readily agreed.[57]

Yet behind Lafayette's vague phrase lay a rather more tangible
goal. If the republic was impossible, then he aimed to achieve the
next-best thing, the 'republican monarchy' that had briefly been
installed by the constitution of 1791. It is hardly surprising that
Lafayette should have wished to revive this model, since he had been
one of its chief architects at the time. This republic in all but name,
along with some major democratic reforms, was the aim of the so-
called 'programme of the Hôtel de Ville' that Lafayette and his
radical associates tried to press on Louis-Philippe during the tumultuous days of 31 July and 1 August. It was never formally drafted,
allowing Louis-Philippe to claim later with some justification that it
had never been presented to him. Its main points, however, seem to
have been explicit recognition that the sole source of sovereignty was
the people, abolition of the hereditary element in the Chamber of

Peers, a complete reform of the justice system, absolute liberty of the press, and, most important, virtual universal male suffrage for local and municipal elections along with the lowering of the taxpaying qualification to vote in general elections from 300 to 50 francs.[58]

Such far-reaching demands starkly revealed the differences between the left and right wings of the July revolutionaries – between those who wanted at the very least an entirely new constitution, taking that of 1791 as its blueprint, and those who were broadly satisfied with the Charter and had only taken up arms to defend it against subversion by Charles X. There was no doubt on which of these two sides Louis-Philippe stood. He always claimed to approve of the 1791 constitution, but his praise stopped well short of reintroducing it thirty-nine years later. As for the republic, the grisly events of 1793 and 1794 had for him, along with the majority of the political nation, indissolubly associated it with the worst excesses of the Reign of Terror. Since 1814 he had firmly supported the Charter, which while granting the essential concessions necessary to reconcile the monarchy with the Revolution, still gave the king far more power, and far fewer Frenchmen the vote, than the constitution of 1791. In July 1830 'republican monarchy', let alone an actual republic, was completely unacceptable to him.[59]

By 1 August, Louis-Philippe's eloquence and cunning had seen off the immediate challenge from Lafayette and the young republicans. This did not ward off the danger they posed in the longer term. Although a minority movement, republicanism was a force to be reckoned with, with strong support in the cities and above all in Paris. Deprived of its natural leader by Lafayette's refusal to stand, it had missed its chance this time. But that still left a substantial rank and file, who distrusted Louis-Philippe from the start. As the nature of the July monarchy became apparent, this suspicion turned to fury against him for, as they saw it, cheating them of their goals. They swiftly determined to overthrow him, and their methods would not stop at constitutional ones.[60]

Meanwhile, at Neuilly, Adélaïde had spent 31 July keeping abreast of the news from all sides; her messengers had even informed her of the altercation between Marmont and the duc d'Angoulême at St Cloud. Around midday, Mme de Boigne arrived from Paris on an important mission. A strong supporter of Louis-Philippe's bid for power, she had been alarmed by a rumour that he had already formed a provisional government, with Sébastiani as foreign minister. This would be fatal to the new regime's prospects for international recognition, since the doyen of the foreign diplomats was the Russian ambassador Count Pozzo di Borgo, originally Corsican and a bitter enemy of his fellow-Corsican Sébastiani.[61]

Amazed that the Orléans family seemed unaware of this vendetta, Mme de Boigne first wrote to them at Neuilly, then decided to go there in person. No transport was available, so she walked all the way in the intense heat, on the arm of the eminent scientist François Arago, who had offered to escort her. She arrived, exhausted, to find Adélaïde very much in charge. She had already passed on Mme de Boigne's warning to Louis-Philippe, and received an assurance from him that Sébastiani would not become foreign minister. She now asked Mme de Boigne, a trusted friend of Pozzo di Borgo, to inform him of this as quickly as possible, which Mme de Boigne readily agreed to do. She then sent her off to try and comfort Marie-Amélie, who was distraught at the turn events were taking, and terrified that her husband would be branded a usurper.[62]

Mme de Boigne's final piece of advice to Adélaïde was that the Orléans family should immediately go to Paris, both as a gesture of confidence in the Parisians and to lend Louis-Philippe moral support. Adélaïde agreed, but felt that on this matter she had to wait for her brother to send for them. That evening, however, he did, dispatching his secretary Oudard from the Palais-royal as a messenger. Adélaïde and Marie-Amélie decided that the journey should be made as discreetly as possible, both for reasons of security and to avoid the appearance of a public triumph over the elder branch. Accordingly, as soon as night had fallen all the children were marshalled and led out of the park of Neuilly on to the main road. There the adults hailed a passing omnibus, and everybody climbed in. At the Place Louis XVI it was impossible to go any further because of the barricades, so the party got out and divided into three groups. Oudard gave his arm to Marie-Amélie, Adélaïde took charge of the princesses, and Louis-Philippe's aide-de-camp Anatole de Montesquiou escorted the princes. Just before midnight they all arrived safely at the Palais-royal, where Louis-Philippe greeted them with relief.[63] It is one of the few recorded occasions on which a victorious revolutionary leader's family have rejoined him by public transport.

The next morning Adélaïde swiftly moved into the arena that more than any other she was to make her own over the next eighteen years – diplomacy. Before seven o'clock she had sent for Mme de Boigne and asked her to arrange a meeting with Pozzo di Borgo. Mme de Boigne arrived at the Palais-royal to find Adélaïde in her small private gallery; her study, with its windows and mirrors smashed and its panelling riddled with bullets, was unusable. No sooner had the two women begun discussing the interview with Pozzo than two small but significant incidents occurred that underlined both Adélaïde's qualities as a politician, and the instinctive deference that her sister-in-law showed her in these matters. First, Marie-Amélie entered the room looking deeply worried. The duchesse de Berry had just sent her a messenger asking for advice, and she did not know what to say. 'Send back a few meaningless compliments,' replied Adélaïde sternly, 'but put nothing on paper.' No sooner had Marie-Amélie left than Adélaïde ran after her. 'Above all, sister,' she repeated, 'put nothing on paper.'[64]

Adélaïde decided that it would be more discreet for her to meet Pozzo di Borgo at Mme de Boigne's house than for Pozzo to come to the Palais-royal, but she first wanted to consult with Louis-Philippe, who was currently absent. At this point Marie-Amélie rushed in again: 'Sister, sister, Sébastiani is here! He's furious!' Clearly, Sébastiani had heard that he was not now to be foreign minister, and had stormed round to the Palais-royal in a rage. But Adélaïde did not bat an eyelid. 'Calm down,' she replied, 'I'll have Sébastiani brought up here. Furious or not, he'll just have to submit to necessity; I'll talk to him myself.'

While Adélaïde faced down the angry Corsican, Mme de Boigne and Marie-Amélie waited in the Salon des Batailles overlooking the main courtyard. Soon a commotion from outside announced Louis-Philippe's return, and this brought Adélaïde out to join them. She was followed by Sébastiani, still discontented but now quiescent; as he passed Mme de Boigne he shot her a poisonous look that showed he knew of her role in his discomfiture.[65]

After a swift confabulation with her brother, Adélaïde was ready to go to meet Pozzo at Mme de Boigne's house on the Rue d'Anjou, just west of the Place de la Madeleine. She and Mme de Boigne took extraordinary precautions not to be recognized. Each took an arm of Mme de Boigne's steward, who had accompanied her; to attract less attention, Adélaïde wore a heavy veil, and they talked English along the way so as not to be overheard. The most formidable obstacle, however, awaited them in the Place Louis XVI. This was Talleyrand's strategically placed window, an occupational hazard for all conspirators between the Tuileries and the Champs-Elysées during the July revolution. As soon as Adélaïde caught sight of it she tried to hide behind Mme de Boigne. 'I don't want the lame old man to spot me,' she whispered. 'He's so sharp! He's quite capable of seeing who I am from his window. I don't want him to notice me going past, and still less to reveal myself in conversation with him.'[66]

Fortunately Talleyrand's house was passed without incident, and Adélaïde was soon closeted with Pozzo di Borgo at the Rue d'Anjou. The long interview that followed, to which there were no witnesses, had two important results. Already reassured by Mme de Boigne's shuttle diplomacy, and now certain that Sébastiani would not be foreign minister, Pozzo used his influence to scotch a plan mooted by some of his fellow-ambassadors to join Charles X at Rambouillet. He also sent off two dispatches to St Petersburg recommending acceptance of Louis-Philippe's regime. Of course, Pozzo did not merely act from personal motives; he had strongly disapproved of the four ordinances. However, on 31 July he had wavered, and might well not have opposed the diplomatic corps moving to Rambouillet, or written dispatches so favourable to Louis-Philippe, had Adélaïde and Mme de Boigne not handled him so adroitly. As it was, the menace of immediate opposition from the most formidable, and conservative, continental Power had been removed.[67]

At Rambouillet, Charles X's position was disintegrating fast. His remaining troops, discouraged by repeated retreats, were becoming increasingly disorganized. Probably on the advice of the British ambassador Lord Stuart de Rothesay, he now tried a different tactic: to attempt to bring Louis-Philippe back into the fold by sanctioning his appointment as Lieutenant-General of the Kingdom. At dawn on 2 August, the king's letter to this effect was brought to the Palais-royal. Louis-Philippe's reply was eloquent by its omissions. He said nothing about the lieutenant-generalcy, implying that since he had already received it from the people it was no longer in Charles' gift. All he did promise was to do everything in his power to ensure the royal family's safety. The message was clear — Louis-Philippe no longer recognized his cousin's authority.[68]

In the course of 2 August Charles' military position worsened dramatically. That morning, the three regiments of the heavy cavalry division of the Royal Guard openly deserted, and headed for Paris. Already the previous day, the colonels of the other Guard regiments had met and discussed the best means of making their peace with the new regime. They took no action for the present, but Colonels de Salis and de Besenval, commanding the Swiss troops, had no such inhibitions. They immediately sent their colleague Colonel de Maillardoz off to Paris to ask Louis-Philippe for a safe-conduct for themselves and their men through Burgundy back to Switzerland. It was granted straight away.

Behind the Swiss colonels' dubious initiative, once again, loomed the spectre of their ancestors' treatment in the 1789 Revolution. An anecdote from Marmont's memoirs clearly illustrates this. On the afternoon of 2 August, he encountered Colonel de Besenval's 2nd Swiss regiment falling back on Rambouillet from the village of Le Perray, and instructed it to hold its ground. Although his men had just come up from Orléans and had seen no fighting as yet, Besenval showed the utmost reluctance to obey orders. It turned out that at Le Perray the regiment had been approached by a motley force of around 150 peasants and that, as Marmont drily observed, 'this redoubtable force had inspired the terror that now possessed M. de Besenval'. What Marmont neglected to add was that Colonel de Besenval was a relative of the General de Besenval who had commanded the Paris garrison on 14 July 1789, had almost been lynched after the fall of the Bastille, then tried for his life and only released six months later. It would thus be understandable if Colonel de Besenval was worried about sharing his uncle's fate.[69]

The news of Louis-Philippe's rebuff of his overture, coupled with the troop desertions, now forced Charles X to play his last card. At midday on 2 August, surrounded by his family and advisers, he sat down and wrote out his abdication. Both he and the duc d'Angoulême, who also signed it, gave up their rights to the throne in favour of Berry's posthumous son the duc de Bordeaux, whom they recognized as King Henri V. Drafted in the form of a letter to Louis-Philippe as Lieutenant-General of the Kingdom, the document ordered him immediately to proclaim the accession of Henri V and to take all necessary measures to ensure the stability of the new reign. It was brought to Louis-Philippe at the Palais-royal just before midnight. But his response was not what the old king had hoped. Louis-Philippe sent back a polite acknowledgement, adding that he had ordered the act of abdication to be deposited in the archives of the Chamber of Peers. However, he made no mention of Henri V, and took no steps to ensure that he was proclaimed king.[70]

Louis-Philippe's action – or lack of action – was never forgiven by the elder branch, and inaugurated a bitter feud between itself and the Orléans family until well after his death. In the eyes of Charles X and his descendants, their cousin had betrayed not only his family but the principle of legitimacy. For his part, Louis-Philippe later claimed that his own preference would have been to act as regent for the young Henri V, but that this was simply impossible: after three days of bloody fighting against Charles, the revolutionaries would never have accepted his grandson's succession in any form. Even if they had, Louis-Philippe reasoned, there would have been constant political clashes between himself and the young king's family and entourage that would have made his own job impossible. Finally, had the child died at any point during Louis-Philippe's regency, he himself would inevitably have been accused of poisoning him.

It is impossible to tell whether Louis-Philippe's arguments were sincere or simply excuses designed to cover his earlier decision, taken on 30 July, to seize the crown for himself. There is, however, one piece of evidence that may imply that he was genuinely hesitating between the regency and the crown as late as the first days of August. It appears from the correspondence of his superiors in London that on the evening of 2 August, as soon as the abdication was received at the Palais-royal, the British ambassador Lord Stuart de Rothesay was summoned by Louis-Philippe. He was asked to send one of his staff to Charles X with a specific offer: that the duc de Bordeaux could remain in France, presumably as king, on the express condition that no member of his family stayed with him. The mission was entrusted to the British diplomat Colonel Caradoc, who only set off from Paris on 5 August, by which time Charles and his family were retreating further westwards from Rambouillet. Caradoc caught up with Charles on the 7th and transmitted his message; it was considered but finally refused, because the duchesse de Berry refused to be separated from her son.[71]

Like all of Louis-Philippe's dealings with the elder branch during these days, this is a very ambiguous episode indeed. On the one hand, it could be taken at face value. On the other, Caradoc took a suspiciously long time to reach Charles X, so that by the time he did so Louis-Philippe was on the point of being crowned king. It is also highly plausible that Louis-Philippe knew that the duchesse de Berry would never consent to abandon her son; Caradoc could thus be allowed to depart in the certainty that his mission would fail. In this perspective, Louis-Philippe's offer was simply an artful piece of window-dressing, designed both to counter legitimist accusations of bad faith and, perhaps more important, to pacify England – in 1830 as in 1814 the staunchest supporter of the elder branch. We shall never know the truth. However, with Adélaïde by his side in the Palais-royal, whatever his internal scruples Louis-Philippe would have been under very great pressure to keep to the path that led to the crown.

A sincere overture towards Charles X is also difficult to reconcile with Louis-Philippe's sanction of a parallel initiative at the same time. On the morning of 3 August, Paris was seized by a completely untrue rumour that the royal troops had murdered emissaries sent to Rambouillet to negotiate the royal family's withdrawal. This was the catalyst for a huge crowd of between 14,000 and 20,000 Parisians to form on the Place Louis XVI, shouting: 'To Rambouillet!' The movement may have been spontaneous, but supporters of Charles later accused the authorities of engineering it so as to clear the capital of troublesome elements on the day the Chambers were scheduled to open for the new session. Far from attempting to disperse the gathering, Louis-Philippe actually ordered Lafayette to organize a force of seven thousand National Guards to escort it on its march. He also sent on ahead three commissioners, Marshal Nicolas-Joseph Maison, the deputy de Schonen and the lawyer Odilon Barrot, to convince Charles to leave Rambouillet before the Parisians arrived.[72]

In fact, the 'march on Rambouillet' was yet another replay, down to the smallest details, of a great scene from the French Revolution, in this case the Parisian crowd's 'march on Versailles' of 5 October 1789. The 'march on Versailles' had also been a response to rumours that the king was plotting counter-revolution, as well as a probable attempt to divert the crowd from venting its discontents in the capital itself. In October 1789 as in August 1830, the people had been accompanied by Lafayette's National Guard as well. The parallels are most suggestive, however, in one area in particular: the part played in both events by the Orléans family. Although conclusive evidence is lacking, Louis-Philippe's father was consistently accused at the time of having organized the 'march on Versailles', most likely with the aim of frightening Louis XVI and his family into flight so that he himself could seize the crown. But if this *was* the goal, it had been foiled by the fact that the royal family stayed put and even allowed itself to be taken to Paris next day, not least perhaps to deny Orléans possession of a vacant throne.[73]

If Philippe-Egalité really had been aiming for the crown in October 1789, then forty-one years later his son had learned carefully from his mistakes. Louis XVI had not fled because the decision to stay or to go had been left to him. Louis-Philippe took no such chances; in this light the dispatch of the commissioners ahead of the 'march on Rambouillet' was a masterstroke, designed to exert as much pressure as possible on the wavering Charles X to depart before the Parisians arrived. The stratagem worked perfectly. The commissioners played their part with ruthless efficiency, Marshal Maison assuring the king that the advancing crowd numbered between 60,000 and 80,000 — at least a tripling of their actual number. When Charles — whose personal courage was not above reproach during this episode — gave way and agreed to leave, Barrot made a theatrical announcement to the assembled courtiers on leaving the king's study that shamelessly evoked the spectre of the French Revolution: 'A hundred and fifty thousand men are on our heels, a short distance away; it is 1792, 1793 again in all their fury. Let us be thankful that the most awful horrors have been avoided.'[74]

By midnight the royal caravan had packed up and set off westward once again, this time to Maintenon. But the commisioners' work was not yet finished. They stayed with the king, ostensibly to guarantee his safety and offer him advice, but in reality to make sure that he left the country as quickly as possible. The moment of decision came on the morning of 4 August at Maintenon, the last point at which Charles could have turned southward to make a stand on the Loire. After a long and exhausting interview, Maison, Barrot and de Schonen finally broke down the old man's resistance. Instead of going south, Charles agreed to continue westwards, to Cherbourg, and there take ship for England. Over the next days, at a painfully slow pace in the vain hope that a change of fortune might still save the throne for his grandson, he led his convoy through the country-side, escorted by the commissioners and surrounded at every stop by silent or hostile crowds. The October days had given way to the return from Varennes.[75]

Eventually, on the morning of 16 August, the royal family reached Cherbourg, where an American ship, the *Great Britain*, was waiting for them in the harbour. By this time their party had dwindled to less than seventy. Charles took his leave of the commissioners and his remaining officers, and then went on board with the duc and duchesse d'Angoulême, the duchesse de Berry and the duc de Bordeaux. At 2.30 p.m. the *Great Britain* set sail, arriving at Cowes that evening. A few days later the former King of France was installed in a country house offered to him by a local Catholic gentleman, Lulworth Castle in Dorset.[76]

By the time Charles X finally left France, a new regime had been founded. On 3 August Louis-Philippe had opened the new session of the Chambers as Lieutenant-General of the Kingdom, and had recommended to their members the political reforms he considered indispensable. In keeping with his long-held analysis of the principal failure of the restoration, he drew his audience's attention 'above all, to article 14 of the Charter, which has been so odiously interpreted'.[77]

A semblance of normality had returned after the upheaval of July, but the definitive shape of France's new political system still remained to be settled. By its very nature the lieutenant-generalcy of the kingdom was a temporary post, and many deputies were already worried that it could simply lead to an interregnum which would benefit the extremes of left and right. On the very day Louis-Philippe opened the Chambers, Auguste Bérard, deputy for the Seine-et-Oise department and a prominent figure in the July revolution, proposed to his colleagues gathered at Laffitte's house that Louis-Philippe be called to the throne subject to agreeing to modifications in the Charter. This plan met with general agreement, and Bérard returned home and wrote out a first draft of a declaration to this effect.

Over the next few days Bérard, ostensibly acting independently but in fact discreetly encouraged by Louis-Philippe himself and aided by Guizot and the duc de Broglie, who had now rallied to the Orléanist cause, put together a detailed project for the revision of the Charter and Louis-Philippe's elevation to the throne. Introduced in stages to the Chambers, it passed through remarkably smoothly. The only serious opposition came from without rather than within. On the afternoon of 6 August, an angry crowd still faithful to the 'programme of the Hôtel de Ville' massed outside the Chambers threatening violence. They were incensed by the fact that the proposals under discussion contained no commitment to abolish the hereditary element in the Chamber of Peers, which seemed hardly compatible with the promise of 'a popular throne surrounded by republican institutions'. An article was inserted leaving open the possibility of abolition in the future, and the demonstrators grudgingly dispersed.

On the afternoon of 7 August, the deputies approved the modified Charter by a majority of 219 to 33. Over 150, however, mostly supporters of the elder branch, stayed away. The new text was designed to prevent any further abuse of the type that Charles X had attempted, and to combine this with a modest broadening of the monarchy's support base. The preamble to the original Charter, with its assertion that the king was the sole source of sovereignty, was simply scrapped. The replacement for article 14 stipulated that although the king was the supreme head of state, he could never 'either suspend the laws or prevent their execution'. Henceforth both Chambers as well as the king had the right to propose legislation, and ministers could be impeached by the Chamber of Deputies and brought before the Chamber of Peers for judgement. Censorship was abolished, and Catholicism would no longer be the state religion, but 'the religion of the majority of Frenchmen'.[78]

The changes to the electoral laws were hardly radical, but at least they marked a move away from the dramatic franchise reductions of previous years. The minimum age for deputies was reduced from forty to thirty, and for electors from thirty to twenty-five. The actual qualifications for the vote were not included in the revised Charter, but fixed later by a law of December 1831. To be able to stand, deputies now had to pay taxes of 500 francs rather than the 1,000 stipulated in the original Charter, and the taxpaying threshold for electors was reduced from 300 francs to 200. Overall, under the Charter of 1830 approximately 166,500 Frenchmen had the vote, as opposed to 94,000 in 1814.[79] The political nation still made up only a tiny minority of the country, but it had almost doubled in size.

*

AT 2.30 P.M. ON 9 AUGUST, Louis-Philippe arrived at the Chamber of Deputies, dressed in a general's uniform and accompanied by his two eldest sons Chartres and Nemours. A throne had been set up in the Chamber under a tricolour canopy, with three stools in front of it. The surrounding hemicycle was filled on the right with peers, and on the left and in the centre with deputies. Louis-Philippe sat down on the central stool with his sons on either side of him, placed his hat on his head, and motioned the audience to sit down also. He then listened while Casimir Périer, as president of the Chamber of Deputies, read a declaration drawn up on 7 August that invited him, on the condition of accepting the modified Charter, to accept the throne as King of the French. Louis-Philippe then stood up along with the whole assembly, took off his hat, and read out in a strong voice the oath presented to him: 'In the presence of God, I swear faithfully to observe the constitutional Charter, with the modifications expressed in the declaration; to govern according to the laws; to render fair and exact justice to all according to their right, and in all things to act solely in the interest, the well-being and the glory of the French people.'[80]

As the Chamber rang with acclamations, the second part of the ceremony began. In a conscious evocation of French military glory, four Napoleonic veterans, Marshals Macdonald, Oudinot, Mortier and Molitor, displayed to Louis-Philippe the insignia of kingship: the crown, the sceptre, the sword and the hand of justice. The new king then mounted the throne to which, in a short speech, he acknowledged that 'the will of the nation has called me'. The proceedings ended with a further burst of cheering. It was hardly a coronation in the traditional sense; God had made only a fleeting appearance, and

Louis-Philippe had not even been crowned. Nonetheless, the throne had decisively passed to the house of Orléans.[81]

To Adélaïde, sitting in the gallery with the rest of the family, the scene below must have seemed the fulfilment of all her hopes. Her dress sense, always uncertain, was particularly odd on this occasion: a plumed bonnet that tied under the chin, an enormous flowing collar and large puffed sleeves.[82] Yet this slightly ridiculous costume gave a misleading impression. As the best-informed people present in the Chamber well knew, without her Louis-Philippe would not now be enthroned as King of the French.

In all the actions she had taken over the past fortnight, Adélaïde would undoubtedly have thought of herself as fighting on the side of modern government and progress. In her view, and with considerable justification, she had battled to defend liberty and constitutional principle against a reactionary coup d'état that would have rendered both virtually meaningless. Yet her bold offensive against the elder Bourbon branch also had echoes of an earlier age, that of the Fronde of the seventeenth century, when the great nobles of France, several of them women, had taken the field against the young Louis XIV to extend their power and status.

Coincidentally, one of the principal leaders of the Fronde had been another Mademoiselle d'Orléans, Louis XIV's cousin, known as the Grande Mademoiselle. This redoubtable Amazon had commanded an army, stormed Orléans using scaling-ladders, and fired the cannon of the Bastille on the royal army attacking Paris.[83] The Grande Mademoiselle was not a direct ancestor of Adélaïde, but she did share a title with her, and much of her duchy of Montpensier was now in Adélaïde's hands. We have no way of knowing whether or not Adélaïde saw the parallels between herself and her namesake in July 1830. Admittedly, in those turbulent days she fired no cannon (though cannon were fired at her), and rode to her destiny not on a horse but in an omnibus. Yet as she accepted the crown on her brother's behalf, negotiated with foreign Powers and issued brisk instructions to the future Queen of the French, Adélaïde had become a second, and greater, Grande Mademoiselle.

Chapter Seven

THE KING AND HIS SISTER

THE NEW REGIME WAS that rare phenomenon, a monarchy born of a revolution. In the summer of 1830 its revolutionary side dominated, and it was on full display at the Palais-royal. For several nights a week the palace was thrown open to the public, and the crowds thronged under the windows, calling for the new king to appear on the balcony. Louis-Philippe generally obliged, and would often accompany his audience in a rendition of the 'Marseillaise' with such enthusiasm that his voice gave out.[1]

Louis-Philippe took to the role of 'people's king' with gusto – many thought, to excess. They viewed with distaste his walking around Paris with only one attendant, and particularly his 'democratic' habit of shaking hands with all and sundry. The writer and poet Alfred de Vigny, on duty with his battalion of the National Guard at the Palais-royal on 11 February 1831, has left a memorable description of that evening:

> We were in front of the railings and I saw a multitude of men, women and children come running, and in the middle, struggling to get through, a man in a grey hat and brown coat with a large umbrella under his arm, who was shaking hands on all sides with anyone who got close, which was necessary as a

rampart or shield to fend people off. He arrived at the foot of the great staircase in a dreadful state, with his waistcoat undone, his sleeves torn off, and his hat battered by the greetings he had exchanged in the depths of the crowd that submerged him. It was the king.[2]

If Louis-Philippe showed the way, Adélaïde was not far behind. One of the first consequences of Charles X's fall had been the replacement of the Bourbons' white standard by the revolutionary tricolour, and Adélaïde literally draped herself in the restored national flag. On the day the new royal family took up official residence in the Tuileries, she appeared in 'a sky-blue skirt, a white blouse, and a red hat'. On several occasions, she also presented tricolour standards to newly formed detachments of the National Guard.[3]

The fact that the July monarchy emerged from a revolution has led many historians to assume that it marked a complete break from its restoration predecessor, and most modern studies treat it separately from the period 1814–30. Yet its 'revolutionary' appearance, which Louis-Philippe and Adélaïde cultivated so assiduously, was deceptive. In fact, there were substantial continuities between the reigns of Louis-Philippe on the one hand, and those of Louis XVIII and Charles X. Unlike the Revolution of 1789, that of 1830 did not radically alter the structure of politics and society. Above all, despite the follies of Charles X, the institution of monarchy survived, testimony to an underlying strength that is often underestimated. For all its sound and fury, the July revolution is best seen not as a definitive rupture, but as part of a much more organic process, the development of constitutional monarchy in France.

This was certainly how the founders of the July monarchy saw events at the time, and to buttress their viewpoint they made constant use of one example in particular, that of Britain. They were obsessed by parallels between French history since 1789 and that of the British revolutions of the seventeenth century, and constantly interpreted the former in the light of the latter. As early as 1819 the writer and critic Villemain, who would later become minister of education under Louis-Philippe, had published a *History of Cromwell*. He was followed in 1827 by the journalist Armand Carrel, with a study of the British restoration of 1660 which clearly invited comparisons with its French counterpart of 1814, and unflatteringly identified Charles X with James II. François Guizot's life's work, which he did not finish until 1856, was a massive *History of the English Revolution*.[4]

What attracted these intellectuals and politicians to British history was the fact that it provided a model for the way in which they passionately wished France to develop, towards a properly constitutional monarchy and a representative political system. Thiers and Mignet both saw the French revolutionary era as 'a curve on which all the points had been fixed in advance by the English revolution'.[5] What they and their colleagues were trying to create was a French version of the 'Whig history', recounting and celebrating the unfolding of constitutional government, that Macaulay was pioneering across the Channel.

This reading of seventeenth-century British history was especially comforting to these politician–historians, since it offered a ringing vindication of their own actions in 1830. If the British revolution of the 1640s corresponded to the French one of 1789, with Louis XVI playing the part of Charles I and Napoleon that of Cromwell, then the French revolution of 1830 could only be identified with the virtually bloodless Glorious Revolution of 1688, by which James II's attempts to impose absolute monarchy had been defeated and Britain's parliamentary liberties triumphantly confirmed. In this view, Louis-Philippe became the heroic William III, saving the country from the repressive schemes of that latter-day James II, Charles X. Indeed, Laffitte had launched Louis-Philippe's candidature for the throne on 28 July 1830 with the words: 'William must replace the Stuarts.'[6]

No parallel is perfect, and this interpretation had the major flaw of consciously analysing the past from the point of view of a later era. Yet it has the merit of emphasizing the elements that united the period 1814–48 rather than those that divided it. Of these, the principal one was constitutional monarchy. Its evolution during these years was far from uniform, and it traversed many storms. Nonetheless, during the reign of Louis-Philippe it developed from the restrictive limited monarchy originally conceived by Louis XVIII, if not into a fully fledged parliamentary monarchy, at least into something very close to it. The process was a dynamic one; and its failure was not inevitable.

The most obvious symbol of continuity between the pre- and

post-1830 monarchy was the Charter. Despite the urgings of Lafayette and the radicals, it was not torn up and replaced by an entirely new constitution. It was retained, but, in a typically 'English' piece of pragmatism, simply amended to avoid a repetition of Charles X's mistakes. While the king retained the power to initiate legislation, this was now to be shared with the Chambers. Above all, article 14 was altered: the king remained the supreme head of state, with the power to make 'the statutes and ordinances necessary for the execution of the laws', but it was specifically stipulated that he could 'neither suspend the laws nor prevent them from being carried into effect'.[7] Henceforth, the king could never assume the emergency powers so disastrously invoked in July 1830.

The other major modification to the Charter, announced in the revised text, was eventually embodied in a new law of December 1831. This was the abolition of the hereditary element in the Chamber of Peers. The king could continue to nominate an unlimited number of peers, although only from certain categories of notable citizens, but henceforth this could only be for life. Rather than a French House of Lords, the Chamber of Peers now resembled a Senate. Essentially this was a concession to public opinion, whose anti-aristocratic sentiments had been reinforced by Charles X's unpopular policies. Guizot, Thiers and a handful of other deputies opposed this move as a step too far in the direction of democracy, but they were massively defeated by 324 votes to 26. Louis-Philippe himself made no effort to defend the hereditary peerage; he felt that ever since 1789 the political power of the nobility had been a lost cause, and was more a hindrance than a help to a constitutional monarchy.[8]

Elsewhere, the revised document was as eloquent by its omissions as by its additions. The preamble of 1814, with its insistence that the Charter was a purely voluntary concession from the king to his people, was simply deleted. Although no text replaced it, in the circumstances of 1830 the implication was clear: the monarch owed his powers not to 'divine Providence', but to the nation, which could in the final analysis revoke them. This was certainly Louis-Philippe's own view, as later events were to prove.

The responsibility of ministers, and their relations with the monarch, formed the core of Louis-Philippe's conception of kingship. On this crucial issue, the Charter of 1830 was almost as vague as that

of 1814. It stated that the ministers were responsible, but once again
failed to specify to whom, merely contenting itself with extending the
grounds on which they could be impeached by the Chambers. The
intention was probably to establish a workable doctrine of ministerial
responsibility, in the English manner, by precedent and practice
rather than elaborate theory.[9] Learning from Charles X's mistakes,
Louis-Philippe never attempted to sustain a government that had
clearly lost the confidence of the Chambers or of the electorate. As
Adélaïde, admittedly not an impartial witness but one who knew him
intimately, put it in 1839 when the sitting ministry lost an election:
'In accordance with the loyalty and constitutional principles of our
much-loved king, he will submit to and comply with the wishes of
the country.'[10] In this important respect, Louis-Philippe contributed
significantly to the consolidation of parliamentary government in
France.

In his relations with his ministers, however, the new king was
much less self-effacing. He chose them, they were 'his' ministers, and
where he could not shape their policy himself he was determined to
make his wishes felt. It was in this area that his views were closest
to those of Louis XVIII and Charles X, and furthest from today's
notion of the role of a constitutional monarch. He generally preferred
to act as his own prime minister, presiding over meetings of the
council of ministers himself, and took a keen, often pedantic interest
in the details of legislation. He was particularly determined to keep
foreign policy, the traditional 'business of kings', in his own hands.
He did this through direct correspondence with his fellow-monarchs,
and even by communicating with his ambassadors independently of
his foreign minister. As he himself put it, dealing with the daily
business of foreign affairs was a 'primordial satisfaction'.[11]

Unfortunately, as the reign wore on, Louis-Philippe's view of the
role of ministers, and that of the ministers themselves, increasingly
diverged. This was an inevitable consequence of the evolution of
parliamentary government; the more responsible the ministers were
to the Chambers, the more they wished to shape their own policy
and not merely reflect that of the king. Ministerial responsibility
pointed to a cohesive cabinet with its own programme, obeying the
rules of collective responsibility, and preferably headed by a prime
minister. All this Louis-Philippe resisted. The result was a series of

crises whenever he was faced by an assertive prime minister, such as Thiers, Guizot or Broglie.

The analogy Louis-Philippe used, in various forms, to describe his relations with his ministers was revealing, and hardly flattering to them. He would often liken the state to a public conveyance, with himself as the driver, and them as the horses. If the latter became exhausted, it was his job to replace them with a new team – in other words, a new ministry. Hence his regular quips: 'I'm the cab-driver!', and 'My relays are ready!'[12] In the mid-1840s he explained his reasoning in more detail to the comte de Montalivet, his intendant of the civil list and one of his most trusted servants:

> When you're travelling post-haste, I assume you would want the most willing, vigorous and solid team possible; if you keep it in harness after its strength has gone, your journey gets delayed and could suddenly be interrupted by a serious accident. If, on the contrary, after going a carefully calculated distance, you substitute a fresh team for this tired one, with fresh resources you can resume your road with the same rapidity and success.[13]

This royal viewpoint was most pithily summed up by Adélaïde. Lamenting one particular ministerial crisis, she wrote: '[The king] cannot do everything himself; he needs instruments, and that, alas, is what he lacks.'[14] This was all very well in a system where the ministers were responsible only to the king; but now that a parliament was increasingly holding them to account, it is understandable that they wished to be more than a team of horses. The heightened risks they now faced were made all too plain in September 1830, when Polignac and three other ministers who had signed the four ordinances were tried for their lives by the Chamber of Peers, and eventually sentenced to long periods of imprisonment.[15]

Of all Louis-Philippe's prime ministers, the one who was least content to be an 'instrument' was Thiers, who summed up his own view of the duties of modern monarchy in a famous formula: 'The king reigns but does not govern.' For Thiers, Louis-Philippe was a controlling busybody, holding up France's steady progress towards English-style cabinet government.[16] Louis-Philippe retorted that he was simply trying to make the existing system work; without his

active involvement the egotism and rivalries of the politicians would
ruin any chance of forming stable ministries.

On this last point, one feels some sympathy for the king. His
ministers were highly individualistic and often prickly, clashing not
only with him, but frequently with each other. These tendencies were
exacerbated by the fact that the party system was significantly less
developed in France than in England. As a result, there was rarely a
compact grouping with a clear majority in the Chamber of Deputies
from which to choose a ministry. Forming a ministry with a workable
majority could be a long-drawn-out business, as leading politicians
negotiated with each other and on behalf of their personal following.
Under these circumstances, Louis-Philippe could hardly avoid being
drawn into the fray.[17]

The consequences, however, were sometimes farcical. During
one particular ministerial crisis, in October 1830, the council, presided
over by the king, met at 9 a.m. and was still in session at 5.30 in the
afternoon. At this point, Louis-Philippe went next door to relieve
himself; the ministers, seizing the opportunity, quickly fled. Hearing
what was happening, the king rushed out of the lavatory, holding his
trousers up with one hand, and managed to grab the hindmost, the
minister of justice Dupont de l'Eure. 'Go on!' he urged his valet,
'Catch them for me!', and repeated the instruction to a nearby aide-
de-camp: 'Run, run! I need them!' The ministers, however, had
sensibly scattered, and were not rounded up again until 8 p.m.[18]

Yet what Louis-Philippe lacked in dignity he made up for in
diligence. As befitted a pupil of Mme de Genlis, he believed that
every waking moment should be filled with activity. He rose between
7.30 and 8 a.m., and generally spent the morning dealing either with
diplomatic dispatches or matters relating to the civil list. He usually
continued this through lunch, which he took alone in his audience
chamber, apart from his family. The afternoon was then devoted to
seeing his ministers, either individually or in the council, over which
he presided at least once a week.

In the late afternoon he would escape his desk to stretch his legs,
either in a private section of the Tuileries gardens, or in the galleries of the Louvre after the public had left for the day. Even dinner
was a public event, as was the family salon afterwards at which the
king held open house for ministers, deputies, ambassadors and other

notables. While Marie-Amélie, her daughters and daughters-in-law, and Adélaïde sat at a round table talking and doing embroidery, Louis-Philippe would circulate amongst the company, continuing the business of the day in a more informal setting. At ten o'clock the gathering would break up, Marie-Amélie would go to bed, and the king would retire to his study to work for another four hours, rarely joining his wife before two in the morning.[19]

This punishing schedule is all the more remarkable since by 1830 Louis-Philippe was no longer a young man. He was now fifty-seven, and his youthful good looks had long since faded. While he never attained the dimensions of Louis XVIII, he had become portly. His features had grown heavy, and his luxuriant side-whiskers framed substantial dewlaps. For at least a decade he had been bald, and concealed this with an artfully arranged *toupet*.[20] Yet his constitution was extremely robust, his energy immense and his intelligence shrewd and penetrating.

Louis-Philippe may not have been a majestic king, but he was a formidable one, and nothing was more formidable than his volubility. His preferred type of conversation was the one-and-a-half-hour monologue. While these were often fascinating, for he was a brilliant talker, they could be wearying, and their long subordinate clauses, beginning with *que* or *lorsque*, even found their way into cartoons of him. Alexis de Tocqueville summed up the king's prolixity in a famously malicious anecdote in his memoirs. After an interview at the Tuileries, he wrote:

> The king detained me, sat down in a chair, gestured to me to sit down in another, and said to me informally: 'Since you're here, M. de Tocqueville, let's have a chat; I'd like you to talk to me about America.' I knew him well enough to know what this meant: I am going to talk about America ... After three-quarters of an hour, the king rose, thanked me for the pleasure our conversation had given him (I hadn't said four words), and took his leave, clearly delighted with me in the way one generally is with someone before whom one thinks one has spoken well.[21]

If Louis-Philippe was outwardly showing signs of age, so too was Adélaïde. She was four years younger than him, but she took less exercise, and had never had good looks to lose in the first place. Alfred de Vigny, who met her in early 1831, has left a vivid description of her, although this is unquestionably coloured by his hostility to the Orléans family:

> Above a short, heavy body she carried, stiffly and with her chin in the air, a square face, with a low forehead and round, deep-set eyes whose fixed and obstinate gaze seemed made not for giving or receiving impressions, but for observing and spying. She constantly ... bit her thin and pinched lips, and her nose was coarse, too red and too thick; the high colour of her cheeks gave her a violent and Bacchic air ... If she was holding a flower or a fan in her hand, she would keep tapping her fingers on it or drum them on the table or her armchair, as if impatient at some scene that was not being played out as she wished. Her voice was not soft, but muffled, as if coming up from her feet and resonating below her stomach. Her silences were agitated and vehement.[22]

The relations between brother and sister did not change when Louis-Philippe became king; if anything, they grew closer. They lived side by side in the Tuileries, and on the rare occasions when they were separated wrote to each other daily. Their closeness is palpable in these letters; one of Adélaïde's from Randan in September 1835 begins: 'You are my first thought, dear beloved friend.' Louis-Philippe was equally upset by their separations, as a note to the absent Adélaïde sent from his study in March 1835 makes clear: 'My dear friend, I am writing to you at that moment when I had the soothing habit, which we shall shortly resume, of finding you settled in that armchair with the rose pattern on a black background which I so regret to see empty.'[23]

In one respect, however, the July revolution did alter Adélaïde's status. Previously, she had officially been known simply as Mademoiselle d'Orléans. On 14 August 1830, a royal ordinance accorded her the title traditionally given to the king's sister, Madame.[24] In this way she acquired the name by which she is known to posterity, Mme Adélaïde.

The surviving correspondence between Louis-Philippe and Adélaïde covers all subjects from politics to domestic matters, and was clearly intended as an extension of the daily conversations they had when they were together. It is also remarkably uninhibited, particularly with regard to those bodily functions that the Orléans family seemed to find so amusing. Writing to Adélaïde from Fontainebleau in March 1835, Louis-Philippe informed her that having used the lavatory on his arrival, he had been compelled to send Shepherd, his English valet, to stop 'a dreadful wind which shoots up the place that produces other winds as soon as one opens the seat'. Marie-Amélie was also included in these private jokes. Congratulating himself on his decision to install several 'Cantwells' (primitive water-closets presumably named after their English inventor) in his residences, Louis-Philippe added: '[Marie-Amélie] was furious twelve years ago, when I had a Cantwell installed next to her room at Neuilly, and now she says that she couldn't live without it! O Tempora, O Mores!'[25]

Adélaïde fulfilled several functions in her brother's family. She was companion to Marie-Amélie, intimate confidante to Louis-Philippe, and 'second mother' to her nephews and nieces as they grew up. But her most important role by far was political. More than anybody else, she helped Louis-Philippe to put his particular conception of kingship into practice.

Adélaïde's political role during the July monarchy was crucial, yet it has been almost completely neglected by historians, who have concentrated on her brother.[26] Louis-Philippe was such an active and visible king that the figure in the background who advised and sustained him has been largely ignored. This is not surprising, as even at the time the full extent of Adélaïde's influence was not generally realized. Only a few discerning commentators knew, or guessed at, how important she was to her brother. Writing just after her death, Victor Hugo put it best: 'She had shared his exile; to an extent she shared his throne.'[27]

Adélaïde exercised her power in two ways: through the private advice she gave Louis-Philippe, and through the correspondence she undertook on his behalf. By its nature, the first has left fewer traces than the second. It is, however, analysed in detail in the memoirs of Louis-Philippe's close adviser the comte de Montalivet. In a long description of the king's working day, Montalivet makes clear exactly where Adélaïde fitted into it. While Louis-Philippe knew how important it was to ensure that political figures outside the government of the day remained well disposed, receiving them publicly risked antagonizing the ministers in office. This problem was circumvented by a simple stratagem. In the afternoon, after Louis-Philippe had seen his ministers, he would go to Adélaïde's study, where any other politician he wished to meet would be waiting, on the pretext of paying her a visit. This was the method most often used by Talleyrand and Sébastiani for seeing the king. On other occasions, prominent politicians would send their Egerias to see Adélaïde: the princesse de Vaudémont or the duchesse de Dino for Talleyrand, the comtesse de Castellane for Molé, Mme de Boigne for Pasquier, the princesse de Lieven for Guizot. Louis-Philippe would then come to Adélaïde's study and give them the necessary messages.[28]

Adélaïde's key advice, however, was given at a time expressly reserved for her alone: between 10 p.m. and midnight, in Louis-Philippe's study, where he retired directly after dinner. Montalivet, one of the very few people who was occasionally present, has left an eyewitness account:

> Mme Adélaïde's hour had arrived at last; she hurried to join her brother, with some needlework in her hand, and took a seat beside him [no doubt the armchair with a rose pattern on a black background]; silent when a piece of work absorbed all her brother's attention, she was always happy when the king broke off to think out loud both before her and with her. Then she was no longer the silent witness and passive confidante that she was during those [afternoon] interviews when she gave refuge, so to speak, to Louis-Philippe's secret politics and diplomacy; at this hour of the evening, when the king belonged wholly to her, she took her turn to speak, generally addressing questions in the order the king assigned to them, but sometimes bringing up subjects of her own. In this way, through this intimate communication, mingled two streams of thought drawn from the same source, retaining, through all the events of their diverse and agitated lives, a remarkable common basis, but distinguished from each other, at this moment more than any other, by nuances imposed by the conduct of politics and governmental responsibility.[29]

This striking description of two people thinking as one, carefully considering each political problem as it arose, shows just how important a part Adélaïde played in Louis-Philippe's decisions as king. Those two-hour sessions, where policy was shaped on a daily basis, were her essential contribution to the July monarchy.

If a matter was pressing, however, Louis-Philippe would call on Adélaïde at any moment, regardless of his state of dress or undress — another example of his extreme informality. One such incident was taken down by Victor Hugo from the account of one of the king's ministers, Dumon:

> One morning, the king summoned M. Dumon. The minister went into his bedroom. The king was wearing only a nightshirt. M. Dumon was a little embarrassed and inhibited by this costume. The king discussed business simply, naturally and at length without putting on his breeches, since it was summer. M. Dumon could see that the king had white skin like a woman's. Suddenly the king grabbed hold of an old overcoat lying nearby and threw it on, saying: 'By the way, I've sent for Mme Adélaïde, she's on her way; I must be decent.' Mme Adélaïde arrived and chatted with the king without appearing either shocked or surprised. Decency was limited to an overcoat.[30]

In a world where women were excluded from public affairs, Adélaïde, like all Egerias, could exert her influence on a man only in a private setting. There was never any question of her attending meetings of the council of ministers. Yet she managed to minimize even this inconvenience. Louis-Philippe made a habit of visiting her after the meetings to tell her everything that had happened. At one point in the late 1830s, it was even claimed in an admittedly hostile newspaper that the door of the council chamber was left ajar when the ministers met so that she could listen in from an adjoining room.[31] It was small wonder that when in 1836 the veteran politician Sémonville composed an imaginary female cabinet for the amusement of Parisian society, he placed Adélaïde at its head as prime minister. (Beneath her, he assigned the foreign ministry to Mme de Dino, the interior to Mme de Boigne, religion and justice to the duchesse de Broglie, war to Mme de Flahaut, the marine to the duchesse de

Massa, finance to the duchesse de Montmorency and commerce to the marquise de Caraman.)[32]

It is easier to reconstruct Adélaïde's influence on foreign than on domestic policy, because substantial written evidence has survived. Her main political interest had always been foreign affairs. Well aware of this, Louis-Philippe made her his principal collaborator in the personal diplomacy that for him was the essential task of a king. Above all, he entrusted to her much of the day-to-day management of the diplomatic relationship he valued most, between France and Britain. Throughout the 1830s she carried on an almost daily correspondence, which Louis-Philippe's foreign ministers never saw, with the French ambassador in London.

It was no coincidence that these ambassadors were among Adélaïde's closest friends: Talleyrand from 1830 to 1834, and his protégé Sébastiani from 1834 to 1840. Some of her letters to Talleyrand were published in 1890; those to Sébastiani – 235 in all – have remained unused until now.[33] It is clear that Adélaïde wrote in the king's name, and that this was understood by all concerned. She made it explicit in a moment of anger to Sébastiani, when he failed to reply to one of her letters: 'To be frank, I cannot understand your silence towards me at such an important juncture ... and especially after my letter which warned you of this and which transmitted the firm opinion and wishes of the king; I find this painful and inconceivable.'[34]

In this correspondence, Adélaïde only very rarely differentiated her opinion from that of her brother. As a result, it is impossible to know how many of the views and instructions she imparted originated with her, and how many from him. Most probably they were indistinguishable, the product of those hours between ten and midnight in the king's study. As for the replies, it is clear that Louis-Philippe read everything that the ambassadors sent to Adélaïde. Reading her letters, with their vigorous expositions, detailed mastery of major foreign policy problems from the civil war in Spain to the Eastern question, and sometimes imperious tone, one realizes the justice of Mme de Boigne's slightly barbed tribute to her capabilities:

> Nobody in the world, I think, has a more complete grasp of politics than Mademoiselle [Adélaïde]. She goes with great

perspicacity to the heart of the difficulty, concentrates on it, cuts through all circumlocution, pins down her interlocutor, and forces him into the lists to battle on that point. One can see how this approach could seem disagreeable in circumstances where virtually nobody wished to explain and commit themselves openly.[35]

Apart from Louis-Philippe's study, Adélaïde's headquarters were her apartments on the ground floor of the Pavillon de Flore, at the end of the Tuileries overlooking the Seine. The historian Raoul Arnaud, writing in 1908, has described the austere atmosphere of her salon:

> It resembled a study or an office. The princess was often seated at her writing desk, and when she was installed in the deep armchair by the fire, she only rarely did needlework; she spent her time reading or going through the dossiers that her brother had entrusted to her. There was nothing feminine in the room, no flowers, no knick-knacks, but books and official papers. Occasionally, however, the barking of the little dog which, along with Jacquot the parrot, was the sole interruption allowed to the political conversations, reminded guests that they were visiting an old spinster and not a minister of state.[36]

The circle that gathered in Adélaïde's salon was a distinguished one. The doyen was Talleyrand; now very old and more lame than ever, he would generally have himself carried by two footmen into her antechamber. Once his presence was announced, Adélaïde would leave her other visitors and go specially to greet him, an honour reserved for him alone.[37] In Talleyrand's absence, Sébastiani usually dominated the gathering. The soldier and diplomat Charles de Flahaut, Talleyrand's illegitimate son, was also often present.[38] The other significant politicians in Adélaïde's coterie were General (after 1830, Marshal) Gérard and the Dupin brothers. A well-known Napoleonic general who had fought for the emperor during the Waterloo campaign, Gérard was a close friend and confidant of Adélaïde, and this bond was strengthened by the fact that his wife was a granddaughter of Mme de Genlis.[39] Charles Dupin was an eminent mathematician and engineer, and had been a liberal deputy since 1828. His elder brother André, also a deputy, was a highly respected lawyer and Adélaïde's legal adviser.[40]

Unwavering commitment to, and preferably participation in, the July revolution — 'our great and good revolution',[41] as Adélaïde dubbed it — was the cement that bound this group together. Gérard had been one of the leaders of the opposition to the four ordinances, and had taken over military command of the capital as soon as Charles X's troops had been forced out. André Dupin had seen Adélaïde at Neuilly on 30 July just after Thiers, and had also urged her to persuade her brother to take power.[42] Loyalty to Orléanism's first disciples was a cardinal rule for Adélaïde, as she made clear in one of her letters to Sébastiani. Mme de Flahaut, she wrote, 'declared for us in 1830 right from the start . . . and broke with all her former circle for our sake; I am grateful to her, and as I have often told you I do not forget these things.'[43] She even coined her own adjective to denote support for the 1830 revolution. Writing of the new finance minister Georges Humann in late 1832, she commented approvingly: 'He is very July.'[44]

*

THE PARTNERSHIP BETWEEN Louis-Philippe and Adélaïde provided that crucial ingredient lacking in the two previous reigns, a strong centre capable of making and enforcing decisions. This was certainly needed during the first months of the July monarchy. The new regime immediately faced two serious threats, from opposite ends of the political spectrum. From the right, loyalty to the elder branch of the Bourbons — or legitimism, as it swiftly became known — ensured that a significant section of the nobility and governing class withheld their allegiance from the new king. Most legitimists signalled their disapproval by simply withdrawing into 'interior emigration' on their estates. Others, however, began actively conspiring to restore the old monarchy.

Unlike the legitimists, attempting to reverse a defeat, the republicans aimed to build on a victory. Their ultimate goal, though they often differed on the means of achieving it, was a republic based on universal male suffrage and on implementing wide-ranging social reforms. The republican movement felt that it had borne the brunt of the fighting in July 1830, but had been persuaded by Lafayette to

accept Louis-Philippe in exchange for the adoption of the shadowy
'programme of the Hôtel de Ville'. But as the conservative nature
of the July monarchy became ever clearer during the following
months, the republicans increasingly felt betrayed. For them, in the
words of the republican socialist Etienne Cabet, 1830 was a 'stolen
revolution'.[45]

Legitimism was essentially a rural phenomenon, with its main
strength in the south and in its traditional heartland, the Vendée,
in the west. In contrast, republicanism was a primarily urban movement, with its main strongholds in Paris and Lyon. The concentration
of its supporters in the capital, a stone's throw from the seat of
government, made it particularly dangerous. In addition, it was well
organized. Its principal organs in the early 1830s were two semi-
clandestine clubs, the Friends of the People and the Society for the
Rights of Man. By their very nature it is difficult to estimate their
numbers, but at its strongest the Society for the Rights of Man
probably had three thousand members in Paris alone. The Paris club
stood at the head of a network of provincial affiliates; outside the
capital, republicanism was most powerful in eastern France, Lyon
and the Rhône Valley, and the Midi.[46]

By 1832, when the Society for the Rights of Man took over the
Friends of the People, this structure had become even tighter. At its
head was a central committee of eleven, presided over by Godefroy
Cavaignac, veteran conspirator and son of a left-wing deputy to the
National Convention in 1793. The similarities between the Society of
the Rights of Man and the Jacobin club during the 1789 revolution
were thus hardly coincidental. To evade the provisions of the penal
code, which forbade unauthorized associations of more than twenty,
the branches in each Parisian section, and in any town or city where
this was necessary, presented themselves as independent clubs. Above
all, the Society for the Rights of Man was a paramilitary organization;
it was armed, and each club was required to drill and hold target
practice.[47]

The republicans were not the only paramilitary force in France
after the July revolution. The National Guard, dissolved by Charles
X in 1827, had spontaneously re-formed during the 'three glorious
days' as a nationwide organization, with particular responsibility
for keeping order in Paris. A broadly middle-class citizens' militia,

numbering forty thousand in the capital alone, its ostensible purpose was to support the authorities. In reality, however, its position was much more ambiguous than this. While the National Guard regiments – known as legions – from the wealthy western sections of Paris were mostly conservative and monarchist, those from the poorer eastern sections were far more likely to support republicanism or at least the 'programme of the Hôtel de Ville'. Less tangibly but just as powerfully, the National Guard was heir to a potent revolutionary tradition, dating back to its foundation in the first days of the French Revolution. This continuity was embodied by Lafayette, its commander in 1789, now recalled as commander-in-chief of the National Guard of the entire kingdom in July 1830.[48]

As a result, in moments of crisis the authorities could never be sure whether the National Guard was to be relied upon. When Louis XVI was overthrown in August 1792, part of the Guard had remained loyal to him, but most had sided with the revolutionaries. It had welcomed the Bourbon restoration in 1814, but had grown increasingly disenchanted with Charles X's policies, and in 1827 had made its feelings abundantly clear at the semi-mutinous review that had led to its dissolution.[49] After 1830, the active part the National Guard had played in the July revolution led Louis-Philippe to view it as a bulwark of his regime. In this he was wrong – during and indeed after his reign, the Guard continued to be as much a threat as an asset to those in authority. It was the single greatest force for instability in nineteenth-century France.

With the momentum gained from the 'three glorious days' and the sympathy of at least part of the National Guard, for several years republicanism continued to shape the political debate. In particular, the emerging groupings in the Chamber of Deputies were defined by their views on whether the leftward tide should be resisted or followed; and if followed, up to what point. On the right, the *doctrinaires*, led by Guizot and the duc de Broglie, firmly opposed any further concessions. The most prominent advocate of this policy, however, was Casimir Périer, a non-*doctrinaire* conservative.[50] More flexible in approach was the centre-left, whose leaders ranged from the cautious Molé, through the military men Gérard and Sébastiani, to the cheerfully populist André Dupin. Finally, the 'dynastic left', led by Odilon Barrot, wished for as much as was possible of the

republic, including a major extension of the franchise and 'republican
institutions', while still remaining loyal to the July monarchy. One
major politician who resisted this classification was Thiers; although
his heart probably lay on the centre-left, his firm desire for order,
and also his personal ambition, sometimes led him to side with the
right-wing *doctrinaires*.[51]

Contemporaries, and historians since, have often subsumed these
political groupings into two main tendencies – the *mouvement* and the
résistance, the former wishing to conciliate, and the latter to combat,
the left.[52] Odilon Barrot has become the symbol of the *mouvement*,
Casimir Périer of the *résistance*. But this typology obscures the
important political groupings, often subtler and more nuanced, that
lay between the two. Most crucially, it underestimates the significance of the centre-left. Politicians like Molé, Sébastiani and Dupin
played an essential role in government and parliament under the July
monarchy, and had distinct views of their own. Conservative in their
support for the existing social and political order, they felt that this
was best preserved by a flexible approach, rather than the last-ditch
defence advocated by their colleagues on the right.[53] As a result, at
key junctures they were prepared to build bridges to the left, and
even to contemplate some extension of the franchise. Their attitude was elegantly summed up by Sébastiani – 'resistance without
rigidity'.[54]

The influence of the centre-left was magnified by the fact that
Louis-Philippe and Adélaïde preferred its politicians to any others,
although the king himself grew more conservative after 1840. This
was partly a question of personality; Louis-Philippe never found
Périer or the duc de Broglie congenial. Sébastiani, Gérard and Dupin,
on the other hand, were his friends, as well as fixtures of Adélaïde's
salon in the Pavillon de Flore. They formed the inner circle of the
Orléanist regime.

In his correspondence, Louis-Philippe rarely outlined in detail his
views on domestic policy. This may have been the discretion of a
constitutional monarch, but probably owed more to his preference
for foreign policy. With Adélaïde, however, it was a different matter.
Her letters to Sébastiani and Gérard certainly cover foreign affairs,
but also discuss at length domestic politics. Here Adélaïde was
distinctly more left-wing than her brother. As with most of her

contemporaries, her political stance was determined by her attitude to the 1789 revolution. As Montalivet put it, she had shared Louis-Philippe's 'enthusiasm in the first days of the Revolution, whose principles she supported as he did'; unlike Louis-Philippe, though, 'she went as far as to excuse a good many of its excesses'. These views were coloured by a strong emotional factor – loyalty to the memory of her father, whom she had adored.[55]

Above all, Adélaïde loathed the legitimists, and was convinced that they, not the republicans, posed the greatest danger to her brother's throne. Again, this hatred was rooted in the past, in the assaults and humiliations inflicted upon her during the emigration, and her deep dislike of Louis XVIII and his family. It was also based on a shrewd insight into post-1830 politics.[56] In Adélaïde's view, Louis-Philippe, herself, the 'dynastic left' and even the republicans at least shared one thing in common – attachment to the legacy of the French Revolution. This divided them for ever from the elder branch, who in any case would never forgive the house of Orléans for, as it saw it, usurping the throne. While alliances with the left were therefore possible, the same could never happen with 'the whites', as Adélaïde, in a reference to the Bourbon colours, dubbed them. She expressed this clearly in a letter to Gérard of November 1832:

> Tonight we are having a grand dinner for various deputies at which Laffitte and other members of the [left-wing] opposition will be present ... on Friday, we will have another which will include Odilon Barrot ... I don't need to tell you that I think this is a very good thing, and that I'm very happy about it. These will return to us, the whites never will; you know I have thought that for a long time.[57]

These views closely echoed those of the centre-left. They chimed much less well with those of *doctrinaires* like Guizot, who had served Louis XVIII and only rallied late to Orléanism. To use Adélaïde's own term, the *doctrinaires* were hardly very 'July'. In fact, she strongly disliked Guizot, and was only reconciled to him towards the end of her life.

For Adélaïde, the legitimists may have been the most sinister threat on the horizon, but the first upheaval the regime faced came from a different quarter. By the end of August 1830 four of Charles

X's ministers who had signed the July ordinances, Polignac, Peyronnet, Chantelauze and Guernon-Ranville, had been captured while
trying to flee France. Polignac had tried to pass himself off as the
valet of his friend Mme de St Fargeau, but his aristocratic bearing,
and especially the fact that he never took off his gloves, aroused suspicion. On 15 August he was arrested at the Norman port of Granville
as he prepared to take ship to England, and brought to Paris amid
furious crowds calling for his death. He and his three colleagues were
lodged in the forbidding medieval fortress of Vincennes.[58]

By this time Louis-Philippe had formed his first government, a
broad coalition ranging from Guizot at the interior ministry and
Broglie at education, through Molé at foreign affairs, Gérard at war
and Sébastiani at the marine, to Dupont de l'Eure at justice. The
king himself acted as prime minister. From the moment Charles X's
ministers arrived in Paris, there was a popular clamour for their
execution, and this was swiftly seized on by radicals who hoped to
fan it into a republican revolution. Louis-Philippe and his government
had no desire to shed further blood in an act of dubious legality that
would unquestionably alienate the other European Powers. Yet if
they did nothing they would face disturbances in the capital that
could easily turn into a general insurrection. It was also clear, as so
often before and since, that in this event the National Guard could
not be relied upon. When Lafayette reviewed its 5th legion, the ranks
broke into cries of 'Death to the ministers!'[59]

On 27 September the Chamber of Deputies voted overwhelm-
ingly to have the four ministers tried by the Chamber of Peers on a
charge of treason. A fortnight later, however, it sought to mitigate
this decision by petitioning the king to introduce legislation to
abolish the death penalty, which Louis-Philippe eagerly agreed to do.
This immediately set off a wave of popular protest. Significantly, it
was aimed as much at the authorities as at the wretched prisoners.
On 9 October a large crowd gathered outside the Palais-royal in
support of the death penalty. On the 17th, the palace was virtually
besieged by several hundred Parisians who later tried to storm the
Chamber of Peers.[60]

The situation worsened the next day. Having been cleared only
with great difficulty from around the Palais-royal in the evening, the
demonstrators set off for Vincennes to deal with the four ministers

themselves, pausing only to burn down a funeral parlour and several National Guard posts on the way. At 11 p.m. they arrived at Vincennes, demanding that Polignac and his colleagues be delivered up to them. They met their match, however, in the governor of the fortress, General Daumesnil. A Napoleonic veteran with only one leg, Daumesnil had successfully held Vincennes twice against the Allies, in both 1814 and 1815, and he was not about to surrender to a civilian mob. Meeting the crowd on the drawbridge, he reminded them that Vincennes was a munitions depot. If anyone came any further, he threatened, 'I'll blow myself up with the castle and we'll all meet in the air.' Sensibly, the Parisians dispersed.[61]

Daumesnil's courage may have saved the prisoners, but it sparked the first ministerial crisis of the new regime. The next day Odilon Barrot, appointed Prefect of the Seine, issued a proclamation aimed at pacifying the people of Paris. It blamed the previous day's disturbances not on the demonstrators, but on the 'inopportune' attempt to abolish the death penalty. This was implicitly to criticize the Chamber of Deputies and the king himself, who had both supported the move. Furious, Broglie and Guizot demanded Barrot's dismissal, were rebuffed, and resigned their posts. They were swiftly followed by Molé, by baron Louis at finance, and a few weeks later by Gérard, who was suffering from poor health. After intense negotiations over the next few weeks, a new government eventually emerged, distinctly more inclined to the 'movement' than its predecessor. To strengthen it, Louis-Philippe was persuaded to appoint Laffitte as his first prime minister. Sébastiani became foreign minister, the comte d'Argout took over the marine, and one of Napoleon's most famous marshals, Soult, replaced Gérard at war. The new minister of the interior, a protégé of the king himself, was a capable twenty-nine-year-old peer and politician, the comte de Montalivet.[62]

On 10 December Polignac and his colleagues were brought under heavy escort from Vincennes to the Luxembourg palace, where their trial opened five days later. The building where they were held was turned into a virtual fortress, and the entire Paris National Guard was put on an active footing to deal with any possible disturbances. The first three days of the trial passed without incident, but as the day of the verdict approached, menacing crowds began to gather. The danger was increased by Lafayette's negligence: as commander of the National Guard, he ensured the Luxembourg itself was well defended, but did nothing to break up the demonstrators as they approached it. By 20 December the atmosphere in the courtroom had grown uneasy, and was only broken by a comic incident. Guernon-Ranville's defender, the young lawyer Adolphe Crémieux, was just finishing an eloquent speech in support of his client when he suddenly collapsed. The reason for this was swiftly made clear when his garments were loosened to revive him. Concerned that at any moment the Parisians might invade, he had prudently put his National Guard uniform on under his judicial robes, and the heat induced by these extra layers had made him faint.[63]

By the evening, it was clear that a crisis was at hand. The verdict was due the next day, and if it was not the death penalty some form of upheaval was probable – the Luxembourg might well be attacked, which could even ignite another revolution. Yet Louis-Philippe was absolutely determined to save the prisoners. So was Adélaïde. When Gérard weakly suggested that this might prove impossible, she rounded on him: 'Marshal, if necessary we shall die in the attempt.'[64] During the night, a group of key officials, including Montalivet, Lafayette, Barrot and Sébastiani, met secretly at the Luxembourg. It was decided that the prisoners would be spirited out of the courtroom before the verdict, thus outwitting the crowd, placed in a closed carriage and driven through the Luxembourg gardens, which would be occupied by reliable troops of the line. From there a squadron of regular cavalry would escort them back to Vincennes. Lafayette initially opposed the plan. Despite almost unanimous police reports that the National Guard would join the disturbances rather than repress them if the ministers were not sentenced to death, he insisted that it be allowed to participate in the rescue, and was only with difficulty argued out of the idea.[65]

Tension ran high the next morning. Thirty thousand National Guards and regular troops were massed around the Luxembourg, on the alert for an attack. Inside the palace, after the closing speeches for the defence and the prosecution, the plan to save the ministers went into action. Almost immediately, it ran into an unforeseen obstacle. Despite his promise a few hours previously, Lafayette had allowed National Guards units from the outskirts of Paris, who were particularly hostile to the ministers, to join the troops of the line in the Luxembourg gardens. He claimed that they had demanded this post, and that he had felt unable to refuse them.[66] Yet Lafayette's decision also raises the disturbing possibility that he was actively encouraging some sort of incident, either because he felt the ministers should not escape, or because he hoped that their interception would provoke a popular movement which the radicals and republicans could exploit. Neither explanation is flattering to Lafayette. If the first is accepted, he was pusillanimous and incompetent; if the second, he was verging on treason and, in the process, cynically exposing four unarmed men to lynching.

The situation was saved by Montalivet. Remembering that there was an obscure door leading from the Petit Luxembourg next to the main palace on to the Rue de Vaugirard, he ordered his own carriage up to it. There were still some National Guardsmen in the vicinity, but they appeared better disciplined than their comrades in the gardens. Asking them for help posed a significant risk, but with some courage Montalivet did so. He appealed to them to protect the prisoners, and his words won them over. In dead silence, they formed ranks as the ministers walked out to the carriage. The four men, who must have known that at any moment the Guards' discipline might snap, climbed in and were driven away, escorted only by Montalivet and a few officers on horseback. Safety was reached at the corner of the Rue Madame, when the group was joined by a squadron of cavalry, which accompanied it all the way back to Vincennes.[67]

Meanwhile, the peers had reconvened to consider their verdict. Each vote was announced individually and in public, a process that took several hours. By an overwhelming majority, the ministers were found guilty of treason and sentenced to life imprisonment with loss of all civil rights. Although Montalivet and Barrot feared the worst, there were no huge disturbances the next day; a crowd did try to storm the Luxembourg, but was broken up. On 23 December Louis-Philippe devoted the day to rallying the National Guard behind the regime. He visited its outposts in every quarter of Paris, thanked each unit for its service during the past few days, and concluded by reviewing them that evening in front of the Tuileries. He was generally greeted with enthusiasm.[68]

On the 30th, in two carriages and surrounded by an escort of hussars, Polignac and his colleagues were taken from Vincennes to their place of detention, the fortress of Ham in Picardy. At every stop crowds gathered to shout 'Death to the ministers!' As the convoy passed over the bridge at Compiègne, the cry changed to 'In the river with Polignac!', at which Chantelauze, sitting next to the intended victim, muttered drily: 'I see you're more popular than the rest of us.'[69] In fact, the prisoners served only six years of their sentence; in November 1836 they were amnestied on condition that they went into exile. Polignac was eventually allowed to return to France in 1845.

With this first great test passed, the government could now take the offensive against opponents and false friends. Top of its list was Lafayette. Not only had he been negligent – or worse – in the trial of the ministers, as commander of the National Guard he had also in the past weeks issued several proclamations urging the new regime to make radical reforms. He was clearly far too dangerous to be left at the head of such a powerful armed force, and the reckoning was not long delayed. The Chamber of Deputies was already drawing up a law on the final shape of the National Guard, and on 24 December approved an article forbidding any Guard commander to control an area larger than a commune. At a stroke this abolished Lafayette's position as commander-in-chief of the National Guard throughout the country. As compensation, he was offered the purely courtesy title of honorary commanding general of the National Guard of the kingdom.[70]

The next few hours saw complicated negotiations. Lafayette initially announced that he would resign his current post before it was suppressed, and would refuse the honorary title proposed in exchange. Presumably he was aiming to blackmail the government with the prospect that his withdrawal would cause further trouble in the capital. He made this explicit in an interview with Louis-Philippe on 25 December, when he threatened to retire to his remote château of La Grange in central France. 'What would you do without my popularity?' he asked rhetorically. The answer was unexpected. 'If you went back to La Grange?' the king replied. 'Why, I'd leave you there!'[71]

Still hoping to avoid an open breach, the government sent Laffitte and Montalivet to Lafayette to renew the offer of the honorary post, and to ask him to stay on as commanding general of the Paris

National Guard. Seeing this as a sign of weakness, Lafayette posed three conditions for his acceptance. They were quite exorbitant — abolition of the Chamber of Peers in favour of a new body made up of 'sincere friends of the revolution', a major extension of the franchise, and the formation of a new, more left-wing, ministry. What Lafayette failed to realize was that over the past few days Louis-Philippe had been carefully strengthening his position. The trial of the ministers had been successfully concluded, the review of 23 December had reasserted control over the National Guard, and even the news that the Chamber had proposed stripping Lafayette of his national command had caused no riots or mutinies. In the early hours of 26 December, Louis-Philippe rejected Lafayette's demands and sent him a curt note accepting his resignation.[72]

To cause maximum disruption, Lafayette stepped down with immediate effect. The prospect of an angry and leaderless Paris National Guard did not bear thinking about, so a successor had to be found immediately. The king and Montalivet quickly conferred and fixed on the comte de Lobau, a distinguished Napoleonic general who had rallied to the July monarchy. Montalivet rushed over to Lobau's house on the Rue de Lille, got him out of bed, and brought him back to the Palais-royal. Meanwhile, Louis-Philippe summoned the colonels of the twelve National Guard legions. When Lobau arrived, he was sufficiently awake to receive the command, and Louis-Philippe then presented him to the colonels, who accepted him with enthusiasm. When Lafayette's resignation was announced the next day, Paris remained calm.[73]

The resignation was a major victory, both for Louis-Philippe and for the July monarchy. At a stroke, it removed a dangerous rival for power who, with the armed force at his disposal, could quite possibly have mounted a coup d'état. The episode also revealed the new king as a shrewd and formidable politician. From an initially weak position, he had subtly turned the tables on his adversary, and eventually called his bluff. Even Lafayette later acknowledged how skilfully he had been handled.[74] As a result, the new regime was considerably more secure in January 1831 than it had been six months previously.

The work of December 1830 was not finally completed until March the following year, when the overall law on the National

Guard was voted. Many of the Guard's original features were retained; in theory at least, it was composed of all Frenchmen between twenty and sixty, and its officers were elected by the men. Its competence and powers, however, were carefully circumscribed. The first article of the law forbade the Guard to deliberate on any public affairs, and its units were placed under civilian authority, from the mayors of the communes to the prefects of the departments, and ultimately to the minister of the interior. Above all, its poorer – and thus, it was assumed, more radical – elements were cynically weeded out through a distinction introduced between ordinary and reserve service. The former, the only kind of regular duty, was open only to those able to spare the time to drill, and the money to afford the arms and the rather gaudy uniform of a National Guardsman. This, it was hoped, would limit the National Guard to bourgeois committed to the defence of order.[75]

Yet this artful piece of legislation contained a dangerous flaw. Even with the strictures it imposed, the number of Guardsmen throughout the country eligible for ordinary service was still over 3.5 million. In contrast, the number of voters was only 166,500. The government was thus largely relying for its defence on a body to many of whose members it denied the vote – a body, moreover, that was armed.[76] This contradiction would return to haunt the July monarchy.

*

IF THE NEW REGIME had for the moment defeated its internal enemies, its survival also depended on acceptance abroad. Here Louis-Philippe, in close collaboration with Adélaïde, played a crucial role, laying the foundations of French foreign policy for the next eighteen years.

In the summer of 1830, the risk of the July revolution setting off a general European war was very real. To a dominant section of French public opinion, the overthrow of the Bourbons went hand in hand with the breaking of the restraints imposed by the Powers on France after Napoleon's fall. The radical leaders, newspapers like the *National* and much of the Paris crowd demanded that France resume her march towards the 'natural frontiers' of the Rhine, the Alps and the Pyrenees, even if this led to armed conflict. The militaristic traditions of the Revolution and of Napoleon, effaced after Waterloo, were revived with a vengeance. It is significant that this agitation had its origins in the *mouvement*. The fact that the early-nineteenth-century French left was egalitarian and democratic in domestic policy has often obscured the fact that it was violently nationalistic in foreign policy, and a genuine menace to international peace.[77]

Although their tone was inflammatory, these calls for patriotic revival struck an emotive chord. The chief purpose of the European settlement worked out at the Congress of Vienna in 1814–15 had been to contain any future French expansionism. A cordon sanitaire of buffer states had been carefully erected along her frontiers. Belgium, previously annexed by revolutionary France, was now added to Dutch territory to form the new kingdom of Holland. To the east, the Rhineland was annexed to Prussia to block any French drive towards her 'natural frontiers' in that direction. In the south-east, Piedmont was strengthened, and backed up by the Austrian acquisition of Lombardy and Venetia, to prevent any future French descent on northern Italy.

This territorial strategy had been underpinned since 1815 by a Quadruple Alliance of Britain, Austria, Prussia and Russia, explicitly directed against future French aggression. The alliance was also based on a more general ideological premise: that the European states were best governed by their traditional, monarchical rulers – the principle of legitimacy – and that the main threat to this ideal came from the principles of the French Revolution, wherever they might appear. However, only the three most conservative Powers, Austria, Prussia and Russia, used this argument to justify actual intervention in countries where the established order was menaced by popular rebellion.[78]

Theoretically at least, France in July 1830 constituted just such a case, and Louis-Philippe had to move quickly to reassure his fellow-monarchs. He sent envoys to all the courts of Europe, with a letter explaining that he had only taken the throne so as to save France from the dangers of a republic. General Baudrand was dispatched to London, the comte de Lobau, the future commander of the Paris National Guard, to Berlin, General Belliard to Vienna, and Atthalin to St Petersburg. All brought back diplomatic recognition; while the Powers were concerned at the outbreak of a fresh revolution in

France, they decided they had no option but to support Louis-Philippe as long as he could contain its consequences. Atthalin had the most difficult task. The authoritarian Czar Nicholas I, profoundly attached to the principle of legitimacy, scarcely bothered to hide his distaste for Louis-Philippe. Rather than beginning his reply with the accepted formula, 'Monsieur my brother', Nicholas simply addressed him as 'Sire'. As intended, Louis-Philippe took this as a profound insult, and matters did not improve thereafter. Of all the European states, Russia remained the one with which the July monarchy had the coldest relationship.[79]

Louis-Philippe's foreign policy has often been dubbed one of 'peace at any price', but this is unfair. Deeply imbued with French national pride, and a successful general who had actively contributed to France's revolutionary expansion, he shared the radicals' frustration at the quarantine to which she had been subjected since 1815. But he was above all a realist, and saw clearly that if France directly challenged the Vienna settlement, she would find herself standing alone against the whole of Europe. Against the indifference or hostility of the rest of the continent Louis-Philippe had one central strategy – the closest possible relationship with Britain. This was to form the guiding principle of his diplomacy throughout his reign.

On a purely practical level, this strategy made sound sense. As the most liberal of the Powers, Britain was the least likely to be permanently offended by France's replacement of one dynasty by another – after all, she herself had done the same thing in 1688. A rapprochement with London was France's only possible means of driving a wedge between the members of the Quadruple Alliance. Yet Louis-Philippe's motives in drawing closer to Britain were also genuinely idealistic. For him, of all the major European states Britain and France were the only openly constitutional ones, with political systems founded on liberty. Determined to prevent a recurrence of the wars that had blighted his youth, Louis-Philippe was also convinced that French cooperation with Britain, apart from Russia the only superpower, offered the best hope of achieving this aim. As he wrote to Sébastiani in 1834, 'this union of France and England' should 'of itself guarantee the continuation of the general peace'.[80]

The king's views were shared by all his principal collaborators, the most important of whom was Talleyrand. Throughout his long and tortuous career, the old prince had never ceased to believe in the need for liberty and representative institutions, of which he saw Britain as the shining contemporary example. For him, France and Britain working together could form 'the balancing-point of the whole world',[81] and a rapprochement between the two countries had been one of his principal policy goals, from his first mission to London in 1792 as an emissary of the French revolutionary government. Talleyrand had also retained from the 1790s some important English friendships, mostly with like-minded liberal aristocrats from the opposition Whig party such as the Lansdowne family and Charles James Fox's nephew Lord Holland.[82] For all these reasons, and despite his age – seventy-six – on 3 September 1830 Louis-Philippe appointed Talleyrand ambassador to London.

Ironically, though Talleyrand's old-regime air and worldly cynicism made him unpopular with French radicals, their counterparts in Britain gave him a rapturous reception. For the English left, the July revolution was not only a glorious blow for freedom, but a fillip to their own campaign for parliamentary reform. When Talleyrand landed at Dover on 24 September, his carriage was drawn by an enthusiastic crowd from the quayside to his hotel. Arriving in London, he was hailed with cheers of 'Louis-Philippe for ever! No Charles X!'[83] These cries were all the more pointed since the former king was still living in Dorset.

On 6 October, the new ambassador presented his credentials to King William IV at St James's Palace. Talleyrand has often been seen as an unprincipled opportunist and serial betrayer of his many masters – in Napoleon's famous phrase, 'a shit in a silk stocking'.[84] Yet he chose this moment to make a short speech, contrasting his current mission to Britain with his first in 1792, that was both idealistic and obviously deeply felt:

> Sire, in all the vicissitudes I have traversed in my long life, of all the diverse fortunes I have experienced in forty years so rich in great events, perhaps none has so fully fulfilled my wishes as the appointment that has brought me back to this happy country. But what a difference between then and now! The jealousies, the prejudices which divided France and England for so long have given way to sentiments of esteem and enlightened affection.

Abroad, England and France both repudiate the principle of intervention in the internal affairs of neighbouring countries, and the ambassador of a monarchy unanimously founded by a great people finds himself at home in a land of liberty, welcomed by a descendant of the illustrious house of Brunswick.[85]

As a great European statesman, called out of retirement to carry out a vital foreign mission for the new regime, Talleyrand had a unique diplomatic status. No less unique were the arrangements made for him to transmit his news and advice back to Paris, and the pivotal role played in them by Adélaïde.

Alongside Louis-Philippe and Talleyrand, Adélaïde was the principal architect of the July monarchy's English policy. She unquestionably shared their vision of Anglo-French cooperation, and her political correspondence is littered with references to it. In January 1834, she reassured Talleyrand that 'there has been no change either in the system or in the intentions which you know so well, nor in our conduct . . . nor in our keen desire continually to strengthen our union with England'. Two years later, she was writing to Talleyrand's successor in London, Sébastiani: 'I am convinced like you that England is genuinely our friend, and I welcome anything that will cement and fortify our union with her, because I think it is in our interest as well as her own.'[86]

Before he left for London, Talleyrand arranged to correspond regularly with Adélaïde, on the understanding that she would in turn show his letters to Louis-Philippe. In this way the king could keep a close eye on the crucial relationship between France and Britain while sparing himself yet more hours at his desk.[87] But Adélaïde was no mere secretary. While her views on Britain closely echoed those of her brother, her own letters reveal an independent mastery of foreign policy. Talleyrand recognized this; in one letter of 1831, he even referred to himself as *her* ambassador, implicitly giving her equal status with her brother.[88]

Apart from their shared diplomatic perspective, the essential ingredient of Adélaïde's correspondence with Talleyrand was complete trust based on a tried and tested friendship. Just how far back this went he revealed in a letter of June 1831. He had loved and respected Adélaïde, he wrote, since before the Revolution, when he had visited her at Mme de Genlis' schoolroom on the Rue de Bellechasse. On both sides, the tone of the published correspondence – fifty-three letters from Talleyrand between October 1830 and September 1832, and fifty-three from Adélaïde and five from Talleyrand between November 1833 and December 1834 – is one of mutual respect and genuine affection. Yet Talleyrand, for all his age and fame, never forgot that he was addressing a royal princess. His first letter to Adélaïde from London, of 2 October 1830, begins: 'Mademoiselle has ordered me to write to her, and I obey.'[89]

The one disadvantage of the arrangement was the subordinate position to which it relegated successive foreign ministers, who rarely if ever read the correspondence. Molé became furious with Talleyrand for putting only trifling matters into his official dispatches while reserving the important ones for his private letters to Adélaïde.[90] To work smoothly, the scheme depended on compliant foreign ministers who were prepared to allow the king substantial diplomatic freedom of action, and these were not always easy to find. Yet despite these drawbacks, Adélaïde's correspondence performed its function for a decade, ensuring that France's crucial relationship with Britain never escaped the king's control. It is testimony both to Adélaïde's vital role in the July monarchy's diplomacy, and to her brother's determination to shape foreign policy on his own terms.

No sooner had the political trio of Louis-Philippe, Adélaïde and Talleyrand been formed than it faced its first major challenge. On 25 August 1830, in honour of the birthday of William I, the Dutch monarch of the united kingdom of Holland and Belgium, the Théâtre de la Monnaie in Brussels put on an opera. The piece selected was Auber's *La Muette de Portici* (*The Mute Girl of Portici*), set during the Neapolitan rebellion of 1647 against Spain. The choice was provocative, since the Belgians were chafing under the rule of their Dutch monarch, and deeply resented having been yoked to Holland in the first place under the Vienna settlement. Even more inflammatory was the high point of the piece, a stirring hymn to liberty. With this ringing in their ears, the audience left the theatre and began to riot. The commotion soon swelled into a mass rising, leading in turn to a Belgian declaration of independence on 4 October. As Philip Mansel has observed, *La Muette de Portici* 'became the first opera to start a revolution'.[91]

The Belgian revolt had major implications for Europe as a whole. Although its root causes were domestic, it had unquestionably been encouraged by the previous month's French revolution, and the most likely beneficiary was France. One of the key buffer states by which the Congress of Vienna had sought to contain France lay in ruins. An independent Belgium, with her large French-speaking population, was poised to become a satellite of France, or even to be absorbed by her, as had happened between 1792 and 1814. Naturally, much of the French public viewed this prospect with enthusiasm. Radical and nationalist opinion, led in the Chamber by Lafayette and the ex-Napoleonic general Lamarque, and in the press by Armand Carrel at the *National*, demanded a swift 'liberation' of Belgium as the first stage in a revolutionary crusade against the Vienna settlement. Yet the Powers were determined to prevent the French revolutionary contagion from breaking out all over again, and Prussia and Russia in particular prepared for military intervention on behalf of the Dutch. In the autumn of 1830, a general European conflict was again very close.[92]

Against this stormy background, Louis-Philippe was firmly resolved to keep the peace. He knew that the stability both of Europe and of France depended on it. As he shrewdly put it to his eldest son, the French Revolution had taught him that 'in our century, war and revolutionary upheaval are inseparable and synonymous'. Above all, he remained haunted by his experience of the last time the two had come together, in 1793, immolating among others his own father. Writing to Molé, whose father had also been guillotined during the Terror, he once burst out: 'I am neither able nor willing to keep cool when people say that '93 saved France! I am sure that you feel exactly the same way.'[93] He was not about to embark on any foreign adventure that might reawaken these demons from the recent past.

In a first demonstration of his Anglophile foreign policy, Louis-Philippe proceeded to steer a middle way between the Belgian revolutionaries and the European Powers by close cooperation with Britain. The key negotiations were undertaken by Talleyrand in London, where a conference of the five Powers — Britain, France, Austria, Prussia and Russia — opened on 4 November 1830 to resolve the impasse between Holland and Belgium. With Talleyrand and the British foreign minister Lord Palmerston setting the agenda, by late

January 1831 the conference had thrashed out 'bases of separation' between Belgium and Holland. The independence of Belgium from Holland was recognized. However, since the Low Countries formed such a strategically vital European nexus, the new state would be declared for ever neutral under the guarantee of the Powers.[94]

The 'bases of separation' were a considerable success for French diplomacy. Getting the Powers to agree to Belgian independence at all was a great achievement, for which Talleyrand rightly took the credit. Without launching an almost certainly unwinnable armed intervention, France had finally broken the cordon sanitaire erected around her at Vienna. Working in concert with Britain, she had also driven the anticipated wedge between the members of the Quadruple Alliance and enhanced both her status and her freedom of action. Finally, in place of the conservative doctrine of intervention in states menaced by internal revolution, Talleyrand set out his own principle of non-intervention. In theory, this stated that the sovereignty of all states should be respected; in practice, it meant that France promised to do so as long as the other Powers did the same. Non-intervention swiftly assumed a central place in French diplomacy. It was also extended specifically to include, beyond Belgium, the rest of France's neighbours — Spain, Piedmont and the Rhine frontier. If any Power intervened in these countries, France warned, this would be regarded as a *casus belli*.[95]

There were, however, several major obstacles still to be negotiated before the Belgian crisis was definitively resolved. Since it was clearly unthinkable that the new state should become a republic, a monarch would have to be chosen. At this point the Belgians, hoping to extort more concessions from the Dutch by committing France irrevocably to their own side, offered the crown to Louis-Philippe's second son, the duc de Nemours. As intended, this initiative placed Louis-Philippe in an extremely difficult position. Refusing the Belgian crown for Nemours would expose him to furious attack from radical and nationalist opinion within France, perhaps even to another insurrection. Accepting it, however, would lead to war with the rest of Europe. With considerable courage, Louis-Philippe turned down the Belgian crown on his son's behalf, and stood firm despite the abuse heaped on him by his domestic enemies.[96]

The next priority was to find an acceptable King of the Belgians.

After various Bavarian, Neapolitan and even Dutch candidates had been ruled out, Prince Leopold of Saxe-Coburg-Saalfeld emerged as the leading contender. The forty-one-year-old Leopold was personable, intelligent and politically astute. He was, however, opposed by much of French public opinion as a creature of England. This perception had some basis; he was a widower, his first wife having been George IV's daughter Princess Charlotte, who had died in childbirth in 1817, and he was the uncle of Princess Victoria, the heir to the British throne.

Resolving this problem was not beyond the wit of the seasoned diplomats gathered at the London conference. The solution – that Leopold should marry one of Louis-Philippe's daughters – was suggested by Palmerston to Talleyrand as early as December 1830, though the latter was already ahead of him. As he commented slyly to Adélaïde: 'I showed a bit of astonishment, as though the idea had never occurred to me: but I made it look like the surprise of making a happy discovery ... It is clear that giving Belgium to Leopold and marrying him to a French princess is a deal the English would be happy to strike.'[97]

Talleyrand may have made the bargain, but it was up to the prospective bride to fulfil it. Even in a family as united and affectionate as Louis-Philippe's, arranged dynastic marriages, and the painful separation from parents and siblings they brought, were seen as an unavoidable necessity. Eventually the choice fell on the nineteen-year-old Louise, Adélaïde's lively correspondent, an intelligent and well educated girl devoted to her mother and father. On 9 August 1832, at the Château of Compiègne north-east of Paris, Louise married Leopold. He was twice her age. The ceremony was punctuated by loud sobs from the Orléans family, especially the bride and her father. Nonetheless, Louise did her duty. Her marriage to Leopold produced two sons and a daughter, and founded the present Belgian royal family.[98]

Although Louise's betrothal to Leopold did not end the Belgian affair, it did put it well on the way to a resolution. In a remarkable display of political skill and courage, Louis-Philippe and his collaborators had avoided a potentially disastrous war, significantly weakened the anti-French alliance of 1815, and laid the basis of France's future partnership with Britain. Even French nationalist opinion was partly appeased by the razing of certain Belgian fortresses along the French frontier, a further concession designed to disarm hostility to Leopold.[99]

There were, however, less positive consequences, which were to dog Louis-Philippe for the rest of his reign. If Europe was grateful to him for helping to keep the peace, much of France was not. By 1830, a new generation had grown up in France which had paid none of the costs of the revolutionary and Napoleonic epic, remembered only their glories, and saw no reason why these should not be renewed. Strongly influenced by Romanticism, it found its expression in literature through Vigny, Musset and many others, in history through Michelet, and almost daily in the Chamber of Deputies and the radical and nationalist press. Its chief criticism of Louis-Philippe was summed up in one sentence in Victor Hugo's remarkable portrait of him in *Les Misérables*: 'His great fault was this: he was modest in the name of France.'[100] Yet what seemed like a failing then may seem much more like a virtue today.

Chapter Eight

THE YEARS OF DANGER

FOR ITS FIRST FIVE YEARS, the July monarchy had to fight for survival. Born of a popular uprising, it never possessed the legitimacy conferred by divine right. On the contrary, what was left of this rested firmly with the elder Bourbon branch that had been displaced. To supporters of Charles X and his grandson on the right, and to the radicals on the left, Louis-Philippe had no title to rule. To the former, he had usurped the throne; to the latter, he had cheated them of the republic. As a result, between 1831 and 1834 the regime had to face four serious republican risings, two in Paris and two in Lyon, and one royalist rebellion, in the Vendée. The years of insurrection were over by the mid-1830s, but Louis-Philippe soon had to face an even more personal and unpredictable menace – the assassin's bullet.

If the external threats to the new reign were formidable but straightforward, its internal politics were often bewilderingly complicated. Between 1830 and 1848 there were no fewer than seventeen ministries, and twenty-five weeks of 'interregnum' across the period 1832–9 in which there was no government at all.[1] Yet these chaotic appearances are deceptive. The practice of *replâtrage*, or 'replastering', in which new ministries were often constructed with several members of the previous one, ensured a significant degree of continuity.

Replâtrage is most often associated with the politics of the Third Republic, but it was begun under the July monarchy.[2] Thus Guizot served in nine of Louis-Philippe's ministries, a total of thirteen years in government, Soult in four, Thiers in six, and Charles Duchâtel in seven.

Taking account of *replâtrage* considerably simplifies the politics of the reign. The ministry of 11 October 1832, with Soult as prime minister, Broglie as foreign minister, Thiers at the interior and Guizot at education, lasted with various changes of personnel and one short rupture until August 1836. It also pursued a policy of uncompromising *résistance* to the demands of the left. In contrast, the Molé ministry that dominated the period 1836–9, although equally suspicious of radical social and political change, was tactically more flexible and made substantial gestures of conciliation towards the regime's opponents. When Guizot returned to power in October 1840, he also returned to the policies of the ministry of 11 October 1832.

It would be an exaggeration to suggest that, across the shifting political landscape, an emerging two-party system on the English model can be discerned. There were, however, some suggestive signs of convergence. Like Sir Robert Peel, of whom he was later to write a biography, Guizot by the 1840s was dubbing his parliamentary following *le parti conservateur*, 'the conservative party'.[3] Among his opponents, Molé, André Dupin and the centre-left shared with the English Whigs an emphasis on compromise and judicious concession as means of preserving the status quo. Yet the centre-left never acquired the consistency necessary to become a permanent alternative party of government. There was also one important difference between the Chamber of Deputies and the House of Commons. The dynastic left led by Odilon Barrot had significantly greater numbers and influence than its nearest contemporary English equivalent, the radicals. It is possible that, given time, Orléanist party politics might have evolved along English lines, but this prospect was swept away, along with the monarchy itself, in 1848.

Although the Belgian crisis was on its way to resolution by the beginning of 1831, the domestic situation remained volatile. On 14 February, the annual memorial service for the duc de Berry was held at the Church of St Germain l'Auxerrois, just opposite the Louvre. Since this was the first time it had taken place since the fall of the

elder branch, it was bound to turn into something of a legitimist
rally. All went smoothly, however, until a portrait of the duc de
Bordeaux was unwisely displayed. Hearing of this, an infuriated
crowd swiftly gathered and took the offensive. The worshippers
managed to escape, but the church was wrecked. The next day, the
crowd turned its attention to the Archbishop of Paris, a notorious
legitimist who was assumed to have had a hand in the commemor-
ation service. His palace was sacked, and its priceless manuscript
library thrown into the Seine and destroyed. Neither Thiers as
minister of the interior, nor Barrot as Prefect of the Seine, made any
attempt to halt the proceedings.[4]

The destruction of St Germain l'Auxerrois showed that Laffitte's
ministry, drawn from the *mouvement*, was incapable of preserving
order and preventing dangerous disturbances. The politicians of the
résistance, especially Guizot, attacked it furiously, and were not
mollified by the dismissal of Barrot, who was never to hold office
again under the July monarchy. Deciding that Laffitte had outlived
his usefulness, Louis-Philippe manoeuvred him into resignation over
a minor matter of foreign policy – the question of what attitude
France should take to Austrian intervention in central Italy. Laffitte
resigned on 12 March, realizing only afterwards that he had been
duped. Lafayette, who had experienced the same treatment three
months before, met him a few days later. 'Admit that you've been a
great idiot!' remarked Lafayette. 'I do,' replied Laffitte, 'but if I'm
Idiot the First, you're Idiot the Second; that way we're evens!'[5]
It was a wry tribute to the skill with which, just months after his
accession, Louis-Philippe had sidelined the two leading figures of the
mouvement.

Political necessity now pointed firmly to a ministry of the
résistance, and this was duly formed on 13 March. At its head was
the formidable Casimir Périer. A wealthy banker of fifty-four, first
elected to the Chamber in 1816, Périer was widely respected for his
boldness and force of character. He had immense energy, fuelled by
an obsessive need for domination and control; exactly the right
qualities to impose order on a country many feared was sliding out
of control. Yet Périer only took power reluctantly. He was unsure
whether France was ready for the stern measures he proposed to

take, and he also had a morbid conviction that office would kill him.[6] As it turned out, he was right.

Périer was determined to master not only the country, but the king. He was convinced that the present troubles could only be surmounted by a cabinet held together by ministerial solidarity and presided over by an effective prime minister. While he did not exclude Louis-Philippe from the council of ministers, he insisted that much of the business of government should be transacted by separate cabinet meetings chaired by himself. He also ended Louis-Philippe's occasional practice of allowing his eldest son, the duc d'Orléans, to attend the council.[7]

If the new ministry was to take firm action, it had to be homogenous. For Périer, the first governments of the reign, comprising ministers of differing political hues under the loose direction of the king, had proved insufficient. In contrast, all the new ministers accepted the necessity of a policy of *résistance*. Sébastiani stayed on as foreign minister, Soult as war minister and the lawyer Félix Barthe as justice minister; Montalivet moved to education, baron Louis entered the government as finance minister along with the comte d'Argout as minister of commerce, and Périer himself took over the interior ministry as well as the premiership.

Périer's first measures were harsh and uncompromising. In place of the search for consensus of the previous months, the new government recognized only friends or foes. It carried out a major purge of the administration, removing political opponents, especially those on the left. Some prominent examples were made: Barrot was dismissed from the Council of State and the radical nationalist General Lamarque was removed from his military command. A few months later, Périer tightened his grip on the police by making a former employee of his own bank, the reliable Gisquet, Prefect of Police.[8]

The ministry also launched a major offensive against the opposition press. Almost immediately after the July revolution, a battery of republican and legitimist newspapers opened up on the new regime in print and caricature. Despite increasingly severe repression, this campaign continued, with a virulence rarely if ever equalled in French history, throughout Louis-Philippe's reign. Since the revised

Charter had abolished censorship, the authorities could only act if a newspaper actually broke the law. However, with offences such as insults to the king, attacks on his constitutional authority, defamation of ministers and incitement to rebellion already on the statute books, the government had considerable freedom of manoeuvre. Casimir Périer exploited this ruthlessly, initiating over eighty lawsuits against the press. The most prominent victim was the left-wing *Tribune*, which by the time it finally closed in 1835 had been prosecuted no less than 111 times.[9] Yet trials of newspapers were a double-edged sword. Since they were held in ordinary courts, they were heard by juries, which were often sympathetic to the defendants and acquitted them. They could also give newspapers a platform to publicize their cause.

The most famous instance of this came in June 1832, when Charles Philipon, editor of the illustrated paper *La Caricature*, was tried for printing a cartoon showing the king's head as a pear. (There was a double joke here, since in French slang *poire* also means idiot.) With calculated insolence, Philipon argued that Louis-Philippe's head, with its sloping forehead and substantial dewlaps, bore such a natural resemblance to the fruit in question that the artist could quite easily have drawn the parallel unintentionally. He then proceeded to show the delighted court how, in four sequenced sketches, the king's face could indeed be transformed into a pear. The greatest satirical image of Louis-Philippe, constantly repeated and embellished over the next sixteen years, had been born.[10]

Louis-Philippe never warmed to Périer, but accepted him as a necessary expedient in the face of disorder. Adélaïde, however, remained unconvinced. On the day Périer was appointed, she seems to have made an attempt to bring him round to her way of thinking. 'The new prime minister paid his respects to the queen and to the princesses,' noted the duc d'Aumale's tutor Cuvillier-Fleury in his diary, 'he looked worried and walked up and down for some time in the gallery; Mme Adélaïde arrived to talk to him in the greatest secrecy and had already been with him for half an hour when I left for the opera.' Whatever was said, Périer proved resistant to Adélaïde's blandishments. He struggled to exclude her from politics, and deeply resented her attempts to influence policy. His attitude was summed up after his death in an anecdote recorded by Victor Hugo:

It is said that Mme Adélaïde rules the king. Casimir Périer used to detest Mme Adélaïde. One day when he was inveighing against the Chamber of Deputies which was obstructing his policies, and saying it even made him regret the absolute monarchy, Thiers said to him: 'My dear Périer, I can tell you the difference between the absolute monarchy and constitutional government in two words – putting up with the Chamber, or putting up with Mme Adélaïde. Which do you choose?' Casimir Périer was silent for a moment, then replied: 'The devil! So that's how you put it! The Chamber!'[11]

For her part, Adélaïde swiftly reciprocated Périer's dislike. She naturally fought his efforts to limit her political role. Significantly, throughout his ministry her correspondence with Talleyrand in London continued as before. Furthermore, Périer did not come up to her exacting standards of loyalty to her brother during the July revolution; she suspected that his preferred option had been a compromise that would have kept the elder Bourbon branch on the throne. Finally, Adélaïde disagreed with Périer's exclusive reliance on *résistance*, which she feared could turn Louis-Philippe from a symbol of national unity into one of division. All these criticisms of Périer come together in a long diatribe in her diary of February 1832:

... in the present circumstances the king ... is our sheet-anchor, but self-interest, self-love and egoism have the upper hand, and a harsh, unbending person is ruining all the good he is doing in many respects, by making my dear and beloved king unpopular, and by the unreasonable demands and brutality of a character that only wishes to deal with flatterers and nobodies; whereas with just a little forbearance and generosity he could be so useful and so great given his talents, but alas he thinks he is indispensable, and this is the problem that makes us all suffer – great and powerful God, grant that it does not become too dire ... if this good and perfect king could be supported as he deserves, and as he wishes to be, he would soon overcome all difficulties, and he and our dear France would both be content ... but as <u>king he has false friends</u> who were always his enemies when he was <u>duc d'Orléans</u>, and these people can never serve him well nor sympathize with our dear country ... instead of

making him friends they are making him enemies, and this is
what grieves me.[12]

It may well be that Périer's policy exacerbated the next crisis the
government had to face. A poor harvest in 1830 and an ongoing
financial depression had caused high bread prices, unemployment
and unrest throughout many parts of France, but in Lyon a further
factor was added by disputes in the silk industry, which employed
fully a quarter of the city's working population. The merchants who
supplied the raw silk to the weavers, or *canuts*, and sold the finished
product, were attempting to squeeze wages. The local prefect,
Bouvier-Dumolard, attempted to mediate and established an arbitra-
tion committee which fixed a selling-price for silk favourable to the
canuts. The merchants protested, Périer backed them and forced
Bouvier-Dumolard to cancel his award, and the result was a demonstration on 21 November that escalated into a rising. The National
Guard of the working-class districts, especially the weavers' quarter
of the Croix-Rousse, joined the insurgents and drove the garrison
out of the city. For several days Lyon was in the hands of the
workers. The government only regained control on 3 December,
when the more moderate popular leaders, alarmed by the proposals
of their radical colleagues, readmitted the army into the city.[13]

Unquestionably there was a strong left-wing element to the Lyon
rising; its principal organ was the socialist newspaper *La Glaneuse*,
and some of its leaders seem to have aimed at a society based on
cooperative rather than capitalist principles.[14] However, it is quite
plausible that by mistaking an essentially economic protest for a
political challenge, Périer created one where none existed. Certainly
his intervention in the dispute on behalf of the silk merchants and his
rebuke to his own prefect created the impression that the July
monarchy would always exercise its justice in favour of the employers
and against the workers, which did it no good. As it was, order had
been restored in Lyon, but the victory proved only temporary.

Nonetheless, by March 1832 Périer was in a strong position. After
general elections in July 1831, he had been able to forge a substantial
majority from the deputies returned to the new Chamber. In August,
an ill-advised Dutch attempt to reconquer Belgium had led to the
dispatch there, with international approval, of a French army under

Marshal Gérard. This had swiftly forced the Dutch to withdraw, which had pleased French nationalists.[15] Finally, while the Lyon uprising may have been avoidable, its suppression showed that the government was able and willing to put down large-scale disorders.

Unlike the previous challenges Périer had faced, the next one had a natural rather than a human origin. Cholera, having first been identified in the early 1800s in the Ganges delta, had appeared in Moscow in 1830. By late March 1832 it had reached Paris. It held sway in the capital for six months, killing over eighteen thousand people, mostly in the overcrowded and insanitary poorer quarters. A highly contagious disease, new to Europe and with no known cure, it caused panic; as during the Black Death, wild rumours circulated that the wells were being poisoned, and in five cases loiterers felt to be acting suspiciously were set upon by mobs and torn to pieces.[16]

While many wealthy Parisians fled precipitately, the royal family and the government stayed to share the perils of the majority. As minister responsible for public health, the comte d'Argout went in person around the worst-hit areas, caught the disease, and almost died. Adélaïde gave a massive 500,000 francs to help the victims and their families; like d'Argout she was struck down by the illness but survived. In a remarkable display of civic courage, the duc d'Orléans and Périer visited the central Paris hospital, the Hôtel-Dieu, on 1 April, touring the cholera wards and offering encouragement to the patients. Louis-Philippe had wanted to go himself, but had been dissuaded; the consequences if he fell ill were too grim to be envisaged. It was Périer to whom the trip was fatal. Three days later, he took to his bed; after rallying, and then relapsing, he died on 16 May.[17]

Although he had respected Périer's energy and determination, Louis-Philippe was not sorry to see such a brake on his own authority removed. According to Odilon Barrot, when he was told the news of Périer's death, he mused aloud: 'Is it a good thing? Is it a bad thing? . . .' Two days after Périer's demise, Rudolf Apponyi, the nephew of the Austrian ambassador, attributed rather more forthright words to the king: 'Whatever I did, all the successful initiatives were credited to Casimir Périer, and the unsuccessful ones to me; now at least everyone will see that it is I, I alone, who reign.' To this sweeping statement Apponyi added a sly qualification – 'Except for Mme Adélaïde.'[18]

The last legacy the cholera left to Paris was political. On 1 June the radical nationalist deputy, General Lamarque, succumbed to the disease. Since Périer had been given an imposing state funeral, the left-wing opposition decided to mount a similarly impressive farewell for Lamarque. Some elements, especially the republican Society for Friends of the People, had more ambitious aims: they hoped that the funeral might spark a revolution, and armed themselves in preparation. On the morning of 5 June, large crowds gathered as the procession followed its well advertised route through the popular quarters of central and eastern Paris.

The tension rose in mid-afternoon, when the convoy reached the right bank opposite the Pont d'Austerlitz, where eulogies to the dead man were pronounced from a speakers' platform. Lafayette was called on to speak, and as he began word flew round that he was about to proclaim the republic. At least some of those present must have been planning a coup, since an attempt was made to place Lafayette in a carriage and drive him to the Hôtel de Ville, the traditional starting-point of Parisian insurrection. Yet the nimble seventy-five-year-old, realizing the moment was ill-chosen, managed to evade his escort and make himself scarce. At about the same time a spectral horseman, dressed in black and carrying a red flag with the words 'Liberty or death!' inscribed upon it, rode slowly through the crowd and then disappeared. In the subsequent confusion, a nearby detachment of dragoons was fired on, six troopers were killed, and the remainder spurred into the crowd. The funeral had become a rising.[19]

The events of 5 and 6 June 1832 have been immortalized by Victor Hugo as the climax of *Les Misérables*. In this way they have provided probably the definitive image of nineteenth-century Parisian revolution, with its banners, barricades and furious battles between government troops and shirtsleeved workers. In fact, Hugo was an eyewitness of the scenes he described in his novel – and at one point an unwilling participant. On the evening of 5 June, he was sitting in the Tuileries gardens working on a play when he heard the sound of gunfire towards the east. Curious about what was going on, he walked in that direction and found the streets bristling with barricades, so he headed north up the Rue Montmartre. He then turned right into a covered arcade, the Passage du Saumon. He was barely halfway up it when he found himself hemmed in by a party of soldiers at one end, and a group of revolutionaries at the other. They immediately opened fire on each other, and Hugo hid between the shop-fronts as the bullets whistled past him. Eventually, he was able to make his escape.[20]

Aged only thirty in 1832, Hugo was already a major literary figure. The product of a deeply unhappy marriage between a Napoleonic general and the daughter of a Breton merchant, his first great success had been as a playwright. His drama *Hernani*, which opened at the Comédie Française in February 1830 and was set in sixteenth-century Spain, had flown in the face of the classical traditions of French theatre and made him the hero of the Romantic movement. A year later, his first full-length novel, *Notre-Dame de Paris*, translated into English as *The Hunchback of Notre-Dame*, appeared and was a runaway success. His experience in June 1832, however, did not find its way into his work until thirty years later, when *Les Misérables* was published. The result of this long gestation was the most vivid portrayal of a Parisian uprising ever written. While Louis-Philippe is generally remembered only by historians, millions of readers across the world are familiar with the death of Gavroche on the barricades and the flight through the sewers of Marius and Jean Valjean.[21]

As Hugo discovered, the insurgents had some early successes; they swiftly overran much of central Paris and captured over four thousand muskets from gunshops and barracks. Unlike July 1830, however, with eighteen thousand troops at their disposal the authorities were well prepared. Most crucial of all, although a few units of the National Guard went over to the rebels, the rest remained loyal. By the evening the whole of the left bank of the Seine, and the Châtelet and the Ile de la Cité on the right, were back under government control.[22]

Louis-Philippe was at St Cloud with his family when, at 8 p.m., his aide-de-camp General Heymès rushed into the château with the news of the rising. He immediately ordered his carriages, went over to the round table where the queen and the women of the household were doing their needlework, and said simply: 'Amélie, there is

trouble in Paris, I'm going there; do you want to come?' 'Certainly,'
replied Marie-Amélie, and a few moments later she, the king,
Adélaïde, Princess Louise and the duc de Nemours were heading for
the capital. Louis-Philippe was sometimes indecisive in a crisis, but
in June 1832 he rose impressively to the occasion. Immediately on
arrival at the Tuileries he reviewed the line regiments and National
Guard legions gathered on the Place du Carrousel, and gave them a
fighting speech. This action was decisive, since it definitively rallied
the National Guard to the regime. As Mme de Boigne, an eyewitness,
recalled: 'The news of [the king's] return spread rapidly, and at dawn
armed men issued from every house, ready to defend public order
and the society they believed in with their bodies and their blood.'[23]

By the next morning, the insurrection had retreated to the central
area of the right bank, between the Rue St Denis, the Marché des
Innocents and the cloister of St Merri. The republicans turned its
tortuous narrow streets into a redoubt by means of formidable
barricades, like the one described by Hugo in *Les Misérables* on
which Père Mabeuf and Gavroche are killed:

> The journals of the time which said that the barricade of the
> Rue de la Chanvrerie, that *almost inexpugnable construction*, as
> they call it, attained the level of a second storey, were mistaken.
> The fact is that it did not exceed an average height of six or
> seven feet. It was built in such a manner that the combatants
> could, at will, either disappear behind the wall, or look over it,
> and even scale the crest of it by means of a quadruple range of
> paving-stones superposed and arranged like steps on the inner
> side. The front of the barricade on the outside, composed of
> piles of paving-stones and barrels and bound together by timbers
> and boards which were interlocked in the wheels of [a] cart and
> [an] overturned omnibus, had a bristling and inextricable
> aspect.[24]

During this time Louis-Philippe was not idle, either. He reviewed
the troops stationed on the Champs-Elysées and the Place de la
Concorde, and then toured the other main areas of the capital on
horseback. Wherever he went he was greeted with enthusiasm.[25] The
courage he had shown at Jemmapes had not faded with time; several

times he rode uncomfortably close to the front line and his retinue had to beg him to turn back. This was an object lesson not only in physical bravery, but also in political skill. Louis-Philippe had learned an essential lesson from Charles X's failure in July 1830: in the militaristic post-revolutionary age, at moments of armed conflict and crisis, a leader had to encourage his forces in person.

At midday the troops, commanded by Sébastiani's brother Tiburce, made their final offensive. Barricades were stormed and the adjoining houses cleared of their defenders. The insurgents made their last stand in the cloisters of St Merri, and were finished off with artillery. While not as high as during the July revolution, casualties on all sides were significant. The army counted 32 dead and 170 wounded, the National Guard 18 dead and 104 wounded, and the republicans perhaps 100 dead and 300 wounded. The judicial repression that followed was sometimes haphazard, but hardly brutal by the standards of the time: eighty-two of those charged were convicted, and seven of them condemned to death, but these last sentences were all commuted to imprisonment.[26]

While Paris was rising, the July monarchy was being challenged elsewhere in France. Charles X's daughter-in-law the duchesse de Berry, chafing at the inaction of exile, had for some time been in contact with legitimists inside France. Calculating that Louis-Philippe's government had been weakened by the Belgian crisis and the death of Périer, and buoyed up by vague assurances of a Dutch offensive in the Low Countries, she hatched a wild scheme to land on the French coast. From there she would lead the traditionally royalist areas of the Midi and the Vendée in a revolt aimed at gaining the throne for her son 'Henri V', the duc de Bordeaux. On 29 April 1832, she landed with a few followers near Marseille, where the first rising was to take place. This was duly launched on 3 May, but only sixty people turned up, and these were easily dispersed by troops at the Hôtel de Ville. Brave beyond the point of foolhardiness, the duchesse decided not to cut her losses and re-embark, but to make her way secretly to the Vendée and try again there. Having arrived safely, she disguised herself as a male peasant and travelled round the countryside organizing insurrection.[27]

Meanwhile, the legitimist leaders in Paris, including Chateau-briand, sent desperate messages to the duchesse warning her that the regime was stronger than she thought and that the rising should be postponed. The authorities, thinking that they were promoting rather than discouraging revolt, swiftly arrested them. The sixty-four-year-old Chateaubriand was incarcerated for a fortnight in the Préfecture de Police. The duchesse's plans went forward, and on 6 June, the same day that the republicans were manning the barricades in Paris, the Vendéans took the field against the government troops and were routed. Resistance was soon at an end, and the duchesse went into hiding in Nantes.[28]

The duchesse de Berry was no longer a threat, but she had become a considerable embarrassment. The longer she remained at large, the more incompetent the regime looked, but her capture followed by a trial at which all the grievances of the elder Bourbon branch against the younger would be publicly rehearsed was hardly an appetizing prospect. The best solution was clearly for the duchesse to make a successful escape from France, and it is even possible that the king secretly worked for this outcome. The impasse was finally resolved through the equivocal figure of Simon Deutz. The son of a rabbi but a convert to Catholicism, Deutz had worked for the legitimists and knew where the duchesse was hiding. He contacted the government and offered to sell his information for 500,000 francs, a proposition that was eagerly accepted, and on 7 November the duchesse was arrested in Nantes. There was widespread public revulsion when the sordid details of her betrayal leaked out. Adélaïde did not share this view. At the grand ball given on 30 January 1833 to inaugurate the new gallery at the Tuileries, she danced the first quadrille with Deutz.[29]

If in June 1832 the republicans had mounted a tragedy, the legitimists now put on a farce. Imprisoned in the fortress of Blaye on the west coast, the duchesse provided excellent material for her supporters to portray her as the romantic victim of a usurping tyranny. This campaign was suddenly blown apart by the revelation that she was pregnant. The father was one of her co-conspirators, a lawyer named Achille Guibourg who had shared her hiding-place in Nantes, but the government considerately kept this devastating detail from the public. Instead, to save her honour the duchesse was allowed to fabricate a secret marriage that had allegedly taken place in Italy before she left for France. A frantic search within the legitimist ranks produced a chivalrous young Neapolitan nobleman, Count Hector Lucchesi-Palli, who agreed to back up the story. On 10 May, the duchesse gave birth to a baby girl. Soon afterwards, her political credibility destroyed, she was deported to Naples.[30]

The fact that republicans and legitimists had risen on the same day naturally aroused suspicions that they were in league. Although they later made informal alliances against Orléanist candidates at elections, there is no firm evidence that they plotted insurrection together.[31] It is hardly surprising that Louis-Philippe and Adélaïde thought otherwise. For them, the collaboration of legitimists and republicans against the July monarchy was a fact. Yet they differed on which was the senior partner. Louis-Philippe decided early on that the republicans were the chief menace. In June 1831, he wrote to Adélaïde: 'I don't think [the legitimists] pose much of a danger; they only amount to anything when they get behind the republicans who want to destroy me, and who form the only party that dares and is able to take pride in its opinions. No doubt France does not want a republic; but the views of republicans are not rejected like the . . . others.'[32]

Adélaïde did not agree. All her experiences and prejudices, dating back to the traumas of the emigration, predisposed her to see the legitimists as the principal enemy. In his memoirs, the duc de la Rochefoucauld notes an exchange with Adélaïde from the first days of the July monarchy, probably passed on to him by Sébastiani. To the warning that 'the throne of July has some very dangerous enemies in the revolutionaries', Adélaïde simply replied: 'Oh! . . . our enemies are not the liberals, but the Carlists [supporters of Charles X].'[33] When the first assassination attempt, whose author or authors remain unclear, was made on Louis-Philippe in November 1832, she was convinced that even if the republicans were involved, it was the legitimists who were pulling the strings. On 28 November, she wrote to Marshal Gérard that the authorities seemed to be close to unmasking 'this execrable plot. I hope this is so with all my heart,' she added, 'for I shall have no peace until all is made clear, and I remain certain that *the white* [the legitimists] is behind *the red* [the republicans], since in my eyes the two have always worked together, and every day I'm more convinced of this.'[34]

The differing views of Louis-Philippe and Adélaïde on their

enemies are revealing, since they underline a subtle yet significant divergence in their political positions. Essentially, Louis-Philippe was more conservative than Adélaïde, and he became more conservative as he grew older. At bottom he feared and distrusted the masses: 'the people are a ferocious beast,' he once remarked. Adélaïde, in contrast, grew agitated whenever the July monarchy appeared to turn its back on them, as during the ministry of Casimir Périer. Her chief political friends were on the centre-left, and she even had good relations with the more radical Odilon Barrot.[35]

Inevitably, these disparities between brother and sister went back to their experience of the French Revolution. Although both had witnessed it, fled from it and lost their father to it, Louis-Philippe had been four years older and had seen much more of its dark side — if he is to be believed, he had heard Danton boast of organizing the September massacres. Adélaïde, on the other hand, more sheltered from this as a fifteen-year-old girl, was always more inclined to stress the Revolution's generous and idealistic aspects.[36] Although she opposed both republicans and Carlists, this perspective placed her closer to the former than to the latter.

These disagreements were never able to shake the profound bond between brother and sister, but they did mean that their relationship was not always as harmonious as Montalivet portrays it. Adélaïde's journal during the July monarchy is punctuated by lamentations that she is losing her brother's confidence. It can hardly be coincidence that these generally occur when Louis-Philippe was pursuing the policies of the *résistance*, and governing with right-wing ministers rather than with Adélaïde's friends of the centre-left. On 26 April 1833 she wrote:

> My heart and soul are distraught, especially since I can no longer confide in my beloved excellent brother! Alas, my constant repetition of what I believe to be the truth has made him impatient! and something has happened that for a long time I thought impossible: I have lost his confidence. He will always completely have mine, but he will no longer listen to me! . . . Alas, to my great distress I see in what is happening at the moment and in his cruel difficulties the result . . . of the distance he has put between himself and all his old friends. God grant

that I may be wrong, and that the measures taken will turn out well, but what problems I foresee for the future![37]

Adélaïde undoubtedly exaggerated in her distress, and these disagreements were always patched up. However, in the early 1830s Louis-Philippe's ministerial choices were on balance more conservative than she would have wished. After a period following Périer's death when the king acted as his own prime minister, a new ministry was formed on 11 October 1832. Marshal Soult became prime minister and war minister, Georges Humann became finance minister, and the *doctrinaires* were given strong representation with the duc de Broglie at the foreign ministry and Guizot at education.[38] Thiers, as ever difficult to classify politically, was minister of the interior. With considerable *replâtrage*, and two short breaks when other ministries tried and failed to replace it, this government lasted almost four years. It was also solidly committed to *résistance*.

If the ministry's policies were controversial, nobody could deny the talents of its members. Broglie and Guizot were major intellects; Thiers, if less cerebral, was a formidable politician and orator. Soult, too, was an important figure, whose political career is ripe for reassessment. One of Napoleon's most distinguished marshals, he had played a crucial part in the great victory of Austerlitz, though he had subsequently been worsted by Wellington in Spain. He may have been distracted at the time by a plan to make himself King of Portugal. He had rallied to the emperor during the Hundred Days, serving as chief of staff at Waterloo, and had then retired from public life until the 1830 revolution. Prime minister for a total of nine years under the July monarchy, he is usually seen as simply a decorative figurehead, an 'illustrious sword' picked to reflect some military glory on his civilian colleagues. This is unfair. Soult was caustic, arrogant and thoroughly opportunistic, but he was also an active and effective politician.[39]

An excellent tactician, Soult can rarely have felt so cornered as when Louis-Philippe once asked him at a reception whether he recalled besieging Cadiz in 1810. Louis-Philippe had been inside the city at the time, supporting the Spanish resistance to the French. One day, he received a message from Soult asking him to a secret meeting outside the walls. He was about to go, when a warning reached him that this was a ruse to have him captured and executed. Louis-Philippe had never inquired before whether this was true or not, but now, in front of the gathering, he asked Soult with an 'enigmatic' smile: 'Hand on heart, were you going to have me shot?' One can only imagine Soult's discomfort, but he recovered well. As Hugo, who had the story from a witness, wrote:

> The marshal remained silent for a moment, then replied, with a smile as enigmatic as the king's: 'No, sire, I wanted to compromise you.'
>
> The subject of the conversation changed. A few moments afterwards, the marshal took his leave of the king, and the king, watching him walk away, said jovially to the person who had heard this exchange: 'Compromise! Compromise! That's what they call it these days – compromise! The truth is, he'd have had me shot!'[40]

*

THE MINISTRY OF II OCTOBER swiftly embarked on a major legislative programme. In June 1833 an important law presented by Guizot was passed, providing for free primary education, and this was accompanied by other measures including state funding for public works and the reform of colonial government. But the repressive aspects of *résistance* were also in evidence. In the spring of 1834 there was a significant clamp-down on opposition to the government. The activities of public criers, who often sold seditious material, were restricted. Since the republicans had often managed to circumvent the ban on forming non-authorized associations of over twenty people by splitting them up into smaller units, these groups were now made illegal even if subdivided. Prosecutions under this new law were also to be heard not by juries, but by either the Chamber of Peers or a tribunal of judges.[41]

Within a month of coming to power, the ministry of II October also scored a major foreign policy success. The Dutch were still refusing to accept the settlement with Belgium drawn up by Britain and France the previous autumn, and though their army had been forced to withdraw it still garrisoned the Belgian fortress and city of Antwerp. This was unacceptable to Britain and France, so they agreed that a French force should be sent to expel the Dutch. Russia, Prussia and Austria protested, but took no military action. On 19 November 1832, Marshal Gérard's troops began the siege of Antwerp. The dispatch of the expedition was a major diplomatic success for Louis-Philippe: just seventeen years after Waterloo, a French army was again on the offensive in Europe, this time not as a rogue state, but to bring another one to heel — and with the support of her most powerful neighbour.[42]

Unsurprisingly, Gérard's campaign caused a flood of Napoleonic nostalgia; in particular, taking place as it did in Belgium, it offered an ideal opportunity to efface the stain of the emperor's last defeat.[43] Adélaïde shared this patriotic bellicosity, but with one large reservation. Itching to prove themselves in the field, her nephews Orléans and Nemours had attached themselves to the expedition, and Orléans, who was notoriously impetuous, insisted on making several visits to the forward trench closest to the Dutch positions. The thought of the heir to the throne risking himself in this way filled Adélaïde with alarm, and she took the extremely unusual step of going behind Louis-Philippe's back. On 20 December, she wrote secretly to her friend Gérard:

> . . . now between you and me, and without our dear king knowing this, I ask you in confidence if you could not give [the duc d'Orléans] some errands or orders to carry out which would get him away from that trench, for I admit that [I am experiencing] an anxiety I am unable to express but which your heart must feel as ours do . . . and I know it is a general sentiment. Everybody is worried; yesterday evening the king held a reception and we had almost all the Chamber of Deputies, and everyone was saying now that the prince royal has proved himself he owes it to us not to expose himself to danger.[44]

It is not clear whether Gérard acted on Adélaïde's request, but Orléans and Nemours emerged unscathed. On 23 December Antwerp capitulated, the French handed the citadel over to the Belgians and, as planned, withdrew immediately. The July monarchy had gained the glory it sought, and a solution to the Dutch-Belgian confrontation could now be left to the diplomats.

Talleyrand had played a crucial role in defusing the crisis, but he

did not stay to see its resolution. In November 1834, increasingly
crippled by his lameness and exasperated by the difficult English
foreign secretary Lord Palmerston, he resigned as ambassador to
London and returned to France.[45] At just over eighty, he had earned
his retirement. His successor was his old protégé and Adélaïde's
friend Sébastiani. When the news was announced, the great caricatur-
ist Honoré Daumier published a cruel cartoon entitled *Apoplexy
Replacing Paralysis at London*. It showed an invalid carriage carrying
Sébastiani, who had suffered a mild stroke, heading for England
and passing Talleyrand in another invalid carriage coming from the
other direction. This was unfair not only to Talleyrand but also to
Sébastiani, who over six years proved himself an effective ambassador. Unsurprisingly, Adélaïde continued with Sébastiani the private
correspondence she had conducted with Talleyrand, ensuring that
France's most important diplomatic relationship remained firmly
under her – and hence her brother's – control.

Though no longer acute, the Belgian question dragged on for
five more years, until the Dutch finally agreed to accept separation
from Belgium and the last Belgian demands were settled. On 19 April
1839 the Treaty of London, by which the Great Powers guaranteed Belgian independence and neutrality, was signed. It lasted until
4 August 1914, when its violation by Germany unleashed the First
World War.[46]

At home, March 1834 saw the first *replâtrage* of the ministry of
11 October. Broglie put before the Chamber a bill to pay the USA
an indemnity of 25 million francs for American shipping seized by
France during the Napoleonic wars. The measure was narrowly
defeated, and Broglie resigned. That the government's dominant
figure should fall over such a relatively minor matter may seem odd,
but Broglie had fallen foul of the deputies' deep distrust of state
spending. His cold, haughty manner also made him ill-suited to
parliamentary politics, and it is even possible that Louis-Philippe,
whom he tried to exclude from foreign policy, encouraged those
who voted against him.[47] Certainly the king gained personally from
Broglie's resignation; the duke's replacement was the much more
pliable Admiral de Rigny. Otherwise there was little change, except
that a modest accompanying reshuffle strengthened the *doctrinaire*
ministers.

Hardly was the government re-formed than Lyon exploded again. The prime cause once more was local economic conflict. In February 1834, in an impressive display of solidarity, over twenty thousand textile workers went on strike against pay cuts. A crucial factor in their action was also fear that the government's new law on associations would dismantle existing mutual aid societies. Hardship soon forced the protesters back to work, and since strikes had formally been banned since 1791, the organizers were arrested. Their trial was the focus of large demonstrations; on 9 April missiles were thrown at the troops stationed outside the Palais de Justice, who opened fire on the crowd, and the result was another rising. Between 3,000 and 6,000 people took up arms, but they failed to extend their control beyond the Croix-Rousse and the adjoining areas. The fighting raged for four days, but by 13 April the army, showing no compunction about using cannon, was master of the city. A hundred and thirty soldiers, 170 insurgents and about 20 civilians died.[48]

The main republican paramilitary organization, the Society of the Rights of Man, was only marginally involved in the Lyon rising. In Paris, things were very different. Hearing of the events in Lyon, the leadership of the Society for the Rights of Man in the capital decided to commit its forces, a maximum of two thousand fighting men, to a supporting insurrection of their own. This duly broke out on the afternoon of 13 April, but the barricades that went up on the left bank were overrun by the army the same evening. By the next morning, the rebellion was isolated in the same quarter around the Rue St Denis and the Rue St Martin that had been its stronghold in June 1832. This time the authorities had even more troops – 35,000 of the line and 5,000 of the National Guard – poised to act against it.[49]

With odds like these, the result was pre-ordained, and within a few hours all resistance was over, at a loss to the government side of only sixteen dead. Louis-Philippe did not tour the front lines on this occasion, but the duc d'Orléans and the duc de Nemours, fresh from the more conventional fighting at Antwerp, did. The day was tarnished, however, by the 'massacre of the Rue Transnonain', in which a detachment of soldiers, thinking that they had been fired on from a house in this street, forced their way into it and shot or bayoneted twelve civilians. Daumier's famous lithograph of the atrocity, showing a family clad only in nightgowns sprawled dead in a bedroom, ensured that it was never forgotten, and a major propaganda coup was handed to the regime's opponents.[50]

Minor risings had also taken place elsewhere in France, especially Grenoble and St Etienne, and because of this, the ministry was convinced that all the April insurrections had been linked and premeditated. It therefore decided to try the leading figures arrested – forty-two from Paris, fifty-nine from Lyon and twenty from seven other cities – together before the Chamber of Peers as part of a single nationwide conspiracy. However, the crimes of 'high treason and attempts on the security of the state' of which the defendants were accused, while mentioned in the revised Charter, had still not been defined four years later, and there was no precedent for such a large political trial.[51] How to try this mammoth case, and whether it should be tried at all, remained a deeply divisive political issue for over a year.

As the republicans waited in prison for the judgement of the Peers, their most famous leader was called before an even higher tribunal. On 20 May, Lafayette died at his home in Paris, aged seventy-seven. There were fears that his funeral two days later, like Lamarque's, might provide a focus for an insurrection attempt, but in the event it passed off peacefully. At the last, the great republican returned to his aristocratic roots. He chose to be buried in the Picpus cemetery next to his wife amid the tombs of her family and many other nobles who had been guillotined on the nearby Place de la Nation during the Revolution. On a personal level, it was an understandable decision, but it outraged many of his followers.[52]

In the meantime, Louis-Philippe decided to exploit his government's victories in Lyon and Paris by calling a general election in June. The result was a comfortable government majority, but one whose lack of discipline augured ill for the future. The ministry now felt secure enough to indulge in a little internal bloodletting. Guizot and Thiers had been chafing under the dominance of Soult, and sought a pretext to remove him. They therefore picked a quarrel with him over whether France's expanding possessions in Algeria should be ruled by a military or a civilian governor. Soult unsurprisingly insisted on the former, and threatened to resign if he did not get his way. Seeing their strategy working, his two colleagues refused to be browbeaten, and called his bluff. Outmanoeuvred, the marshal was forced to resign on 18 July, whereupon Guizot and Thiers swiftly decided that Algeria was best governed by a military man after all.[53]

Soult's replacement as prime minister and minister for war was Louis-Philippe's and Adélaïde's old favourite Marshal Gérard. His appointment, following Soult's, began a tradition of reserving the premiership for an 'illustrious sword', who would both lend the regime some Napoleonic prestige and be agreeable to the king. Otherwise the ministry remained unchanged. The major issue Gérard faced on taking office was the great trial of the republican insurgents. As a man of the centre-left, sceptical about the policy of *résistance*, Gérard felt strongly that the proceedings should not go ahead, and that an amnesty for the accused should be issued instead. This immediately pitted him against Guizot and Thiers, and plunged his ministry into crisis. On 29 October, after only three months in power, Gérard resigned.[54]

A hectic game of ministerial musical chairs now began. Some of the sitting ministers made an intriguing proposal to the king: Gérard would return as prime minister, Broglie would take the foreign ministry and Admiral de Rigny the marine, Thiers and most of the others would stay where they were, but Guizot would be dropped. The most novel suggestion was that a law proposing the amnesty should be introduced, to widen the responsibility for the measure from the government to the Chamber. This was backed even by Thiers, who had reluctantly concluded that a mass trial of the republicans would be unworkable. It is unclear why this plan failed. Some sources claim that Louis-Philippe rejected it, probably because he was unwilling to work with Broglie as foreign minister. He may also have opposed the idea of an amnesty law, although Adélaïde subsequently wrote that he had supported its introduction.[55]

With the existing ministry at a loss, the only option was to try an entirely new one. Since the June elections, a significant semi-independent grouping within the parliamentary majority had come to prominence, which was soon dubbed the 'third party'. Distrustful of the *doctrinaires* and inclined to soften the policy of *résistance*, it had increasingly diverged from the government. However, it was quite unready for power; its principal backer in the Chamber, Dupin, refused to take office. A cabinet was assembled, but it was doomed from the start by the appointment of the discredited Hugues Maret, duc de Bassano, an ex-foreign minister of Napoleon, as prime minister. 'The only person in France more stupid than M. Maret is M. de Bassano,' Talleyrand once said unkindly. Faced with a barrage of incredulity and ridicule, the ministry resigned after only three days.[56]

After this disaster, the king and the politicians swiftly retraced their steps. The Gérard ministry was reconstituted, with only two exceptions – Admiral Duperré replaced Admiral Jacob at the marine, and another 'illustrious sword', in the form of Louis-Philippe's old friend Marshal Mortier, became prime minister. The new government's programme was clear from the beginning – as Thiers announced in a confidence debate, which it won convincingly, 'We are ministers of the *résistance*.' However, on the central issue of the day its support was shaky. In late December, the ministers demanded credits from the Chamber to mount the trial of the republicans, which amounted to a vote on whether this should go ahead or not. They won, but only by twenty-eight votes, which was hardly a convincing mandate.[57]

By this time Mortier had had quite enough of being prime minister. Straightforward and honourable, he was no politician; he was terrified of public speaking and had difficulty imposing his will on his ministerial colleagues. On the verge of nervous collapse, on 20 February 1835 he went to Louis-Philippe and resigned.[58]

The departure of the fourth prime minister in seven months stirred public opinion and sparked considerable polemic. Much of this centred on Louis-Philippe, and what his enemies saw as his taste for personal government. The opposition press loudly accused him either of acting as his own prime minister, or of imposing his will through old cronies like Gérard and Mortier. To combat this it repeated Thiers' formula, 'The king reigns but does not govern', and defended the practice, begun by Casimir Périer, of a united cabinet headed by an effective prime minister receiving a mandate at the beginning of its term by a vote of confidence in the Chamber.

Louis-Philippe, however, had his supporters. Perhaps the most lucid was one of the last eminent survivors of the Revolution, the eighty-one-year-old comte Roederer. Elected to the Estates General in August 1789, as attorney-general of the department of the Seine in 1792 Roederer had played an equivocal role in the downfall of the monarchy, before re-emerging as a close collaborator of Napoleon. In February 1835, just ten months before his death, he published a pamphlet entitled *Address of a Constitutionalist to the Constitutionalists*, dealing with the relations between the king and his ministers.[59] It may well have been inspired by Louis-Philippe himself, or the members of his circle. Taking the Charter as his basis, Roederer argued that since it recognized the king as the supreme head of state, the latter was free to organize his council as he wished, and in particular that a prime minister was unnecessary.

Although hardly a blueprint for what today would be regarded as modern constitutional government, Roederer's pamphlet was an eloquent defence of 'limited monarchy'.[60] Significantly, it insisted at length on the king's right to direct foreign policy himself, and even to dispense with a foreign minister. In particular, it specified that the monarch should be able to use whatever agents he pleased, whether official or not, in his negotiations: 'Nothing should prevent a constitutional king from using means that his skills can render so useful to the country. What he can do by personal meetings or by personal correspondence he can also do by means of a formal or informal agent, a regular or a secret mission, according to his choice.'[61] Almost certainly this was a subtle attempt to justify Adélaïde's political role.

Roederer's was the minority opinion. The press campaign swung the Chamber to the view that the cabinet needed a prime minister, and emboldened the other ministers to demand this too. Finally, on 12 March, Louis-Philippe had to swallow the bitter pill of accepting the duc de Broglie as prime minister and foreign minister. Thiers stayed at the interior, Guizot returned to education, and Humann to finance. After eight months of resignations and upheavals, the ministry of 11 October had in effect been reconstituted.

This time Broglie behaved with tact, treating Louis-Philippe with careful respect, and the two men began a wary collaboration. Their great test came on 5 May, when the mass trial of the republicans opened before the Chamber of Peers. It was a chaotic spectacle. The defendants refused to recognize the court, which they claimed was 'founded on bayonets', and reduced the proceedings to uproar.

However, over the next few days baron Pasquier, as president of the Chamber, managed to restore some order, helped by the cooperation of a number of the Lyon republicans. Then, on 12 July, there was a sensational development. Twenty-eight of the accused, including the president of the Society of the Rights of Man, Godefroy Cavaignac, and several other leading figures held in the Ste Pélagie prison, escaped through a tunnel they had dug into an adjoining cellar. It was a considerable blow to the authorities, and the fugitives were not recaptured, but the trial continued.[62]

Eventually, the defendants were sentenced in two batches: the Lyonnais, who had accepted the authority of the Chamber, on 13 August, and the Parisians, who had not, six months later. Nobody was condemned to death, but eighteen were 'deported' to state fortresses for life, and many more were given prison terms of up to twenty years. In a remarkable gesture of good faith the aristocratic republican, the comte de Kersausie, was put on his honour to make his own way to the prison assigned to him near Brest. Even more remarkably, he did so.[63]

The results of the trial were mixed. The republicans had hoped that it would rally support for their cause, and make martyrs of the accused. In fact, while some of the defendants showed great bravery and dignity, the violent behaviour of others created a backlash against them, and the division over whether to recognize the court was very damaging. The escape of the twenty-eight, while spectacular, had the appearance of desertion, and this impression was heightened by the fact that these numbered several of the leaders. In addition, it scarcely made the authorities look efficient. Above all, the trial was deeply divisive. It inflamed passions, creating an atmosphere in which yet more extreme acts could be contemplated and committed.

While Louis-Philippe's views are more difficult to assess, Adélaïde had had grave misgivings about the trial from the beginning. She saw clearly that it was unlikely to advance the national reconciliation she so much desired. Her hand may well have been behind Gérard's two initiatives in the autumn of 1834 to draw a line under the April insurrections by means of an amnesty. When these failed, Adélaïde watched events unfold with increasing gloom and anxiety. On 20 May 1835, she described her feelings to Sébastiani in London:

I can understand that all eyes are fixed on the result of the trial, I desire rather than hope that it will be good, but in the meantime it's making me fret and fume a good deal, and there are many things that distress me. One consolation, which I mentioned to you the last time you were here, is that our dear king, having wished to form a ministry that would have proposed an amnesty by law, is well clear of this affair; it's not his fault if he couldn't create [such a ministry] and was then compelled to go along with the only one he could get together at the time; he is letting the ministers do as they wish, and there are few council meetings in his apartments at the moment. I shall be very relieved when all the judgements are over.[64]

On 28 July, just a fortnight after the escape of the republican prisoners from Ste Pélagie, Louis-Philippe prepared to review the National Guard on the fifth anniversary of the 'three glorious days'. The atmosphere was thick with rumours of an assassination attempt on the king. On 12 July, Adélaïde had written to Sébastiani: 'You will judge from your own feelings the distress and shock that the idea of a conspiracy against the life of him who is a thousand times dearer to me than myself causes me; it seems certain that execrable plans have been laid which have been discovered in time, thank Heaven.' Yet the police did not relax their vigilance. The evening before the review they received a tip-off that there was a plot to kill the king with some sort of explosive device as he passed by the Théâtre de l'Ambigu. The theatre, however, had recently moved; officers searched the new premises, on the Boulevard St Martin, very thoroughly, but not the old ones on the Boulevard du Temple.[65]

At 9 a.m. Louis-Philippe rode out from the Tuileries, with his sons Orléans on his right and Nemours and Joinville on his left. Behind came Marshals Mortier and Maison; then three of the ministers, Broglie, Thiers and Rigny; then the general staff and other senior officers. At first the crowds seemed indifferent or even hostile, but gradually the reception improved. No doubt to Thiers' relief, the Boulevard St Martin was passed without incident. The procession then continued into the Boulevard du Temple, with a row of houses and shops on its left, and the 8th legion of the National Guard drawn up in front of the Turkish Garden on its right. What happened next is described by Joinville in his memoirs:

... right next to the Ambigu, not the current one whose surrounding area had been thoroughly searched, but the old abandoned one facing the café of the Turkish Garden, what sounded like a volley from a squad of infantry broke out ... and looking up at the sound, I saw smoke rising from a window half-closed by a blind ... I had no time to notice anything else, and didn't even see that the man on my left, Colonel Rieussec, had been killed, that [General] Heymès, whose uniform was riddled with bullets, had had his nose shot off, nor that my horse was wounded ... Our first thought was that there would be another volley: I spurred my horse forward, and grabbing the bridle of my father's horse while my two brothers struck it on the rump with their swords, we hurried [my father] through the disorder all around: horses whose riders had disappeared or were swaying wounded in their saddles, soldiers breaking ranks, men in workmen's shirts rushing towards my father to touch him or his horse, frantically shouting 'Long live the king!'[66]

With great courage and presence of mind, Louis-Philippe waved his hat in the air, cried 'Here I am!', and continued with the review. Apart from a graze where a bullet had creased his forehead, he was unharmed, but there was carnage all around him. Thiers' white trousers were covered in blood where Marshal Mortier, shot through the left ear, had fallen dead across him. The duc de Broglie was hit full in the chest by another bullet and was only saved by his Legion of Honour star, which deadened the impact. Many spectators, including a fourteen-year-old girl who collapsed dead into her father's arms, were also killed or injured. In all, eighteen people died, and twenty-two were wounded. An improvised morgue was set up in the Café Turc, and the body of Mortier, the conqueror of Hanover and victor of Dürrenstein, was dumped on the billiard table.[67]

In the meantime, the National Guards had broken down the door of the house with the smoking window, no. 50 Boulevard du Temple. In a scene with fictional echoes in Frederick Forsyth's *The Day of the Jackal*, they rushed upstairs, and discovered the instrument of the destruction. It was an 'infernal machine' — twenty-five musket-barrels mounted on a wooden frame. The man who had set it off had fled. However, he was arrested a few minutes later trying to make his escape. He was Joseph Fieschi, a thirty-five-year-old Corsican drifter, who had served in Napoleon's armies in Italy and Russia, and in September 1815 had rallied to the emperor's brother-in-law, Joachim Murat, in his desperate expedition to regain the throne of Naples. He was even found to have Murat's coat-of-arms tattooed on his chest. If he had a political motivation, it was presumably Bonapartist or republican. Fieschi had been badly wounded by his own invention: four of the musket-barrels had simultaneously blown up as he fired them, destroying three fingers of his left hand, lacerating his face, fracturing his skull and exposing the brain. Amazingly, he swiftly recovered.[68]

As soon as she heard what had happened, Adélaïde ordered her carriage and rushed with Marie-Amélie to the Chancellery on the Place Vendôme, where the review was due to end. Louis-Philippe finally arrived two hours later, having continued along the boulevards. He dismounted to thunderous applause, and burst into tears as he embraced his wife and sister. Others were not so fortunate. The wives and families of those in the reviewing party had also gathered at the Chancellery, and while word had been received that the king and the princes were safe, nobody knew who had been killed or wounded. As Joinville recalled: 'When we climbed the main staircase, some of us spattered with blood, all the women, whose festive dresses contrasted starkly with their anguish-filled eyes, rushed down to search for their loved ones. Some would never see them again.'[69]

Adélaïde was shaken to the core, but comforted herself with the conviction that her brother must have been saved by God. In a long letter to Sébastiani three days later she poured out her emotions, and admitted what a narrow escape Louis-Philippe had had:

I am not yet recovered from the terrible shock, my thoughts are so sad and dark! ... but we must put our faith in that divine Providence which has so specially watched over those who are so dear [to us], and in a more miraculous fashion than you know, because our dear beloved king had a contusion caused by a projectile going from the left side of his forehead to his right eyebrow; in the first moments he didn't notice it, it was only later that day going into dinner that I realized he had a long black smudge across his forehead – he said to me 'I don't

know what it is', I washed it and it didn't come off. That
evening he had a bad headache, and a little fever in the night;
the next morning I saw this black mark which was [peppered
with ingrained powder] and it was inflamed, everybody noticed
it, and the doctors and surgeons who examined it said there
could be no doubt that it was a contusion from some sort of
projectile or bullet, and in the most dangerous place![70]

Although Fieschi insisted that he had acted alone, in the next two
months the police tracked down and arrested two accomplices, Pierre
Morey and Théodore Pépin. With these men, the republican connection became clear. Morey was a sixty-one-year-old saddler, Pépin a
prosperous grocer aged thirty-five. Both were active members of
the Society of the Rights of Man. Indeed, when Fieschi first spoke
of his idea for a machine, which he had thought of in a purely
military connection, it was Morey who had suggested that it would
be better used on Louis-Philippe. He convinced the other man that
killing the king would infallibly bring down the entire July monarchy,
and that he would reap the glory (and the material rewards) of
restoring the republic. Pépin financed the operation, and later claimed
that he had even hinted broadly at the project to Godefroy Cavaignac
on a visit to the prisoners in Ste Pélagie.[71]

Despite this growing evidence that the plot was a republican one,
Adélaïde remained convinced, as before, that the real culprits were
the legitimists. Shortly after Fieschi's attempt, the philanthropist
Benjamin Appert, her friend and the administrator of her charities,
paid her a visit. In his memoirs, he gives a long verbatim account of
her words to him, which he may have embellished but which in its
essentials rings true:

Do you know, M. Appert, that I'm withering away on my feet!
This horrible attack on the king, for whom I'd give a thousand
lives, is giving us no peace; as I've said to you before, since the
1830 revolution the Carlists [supporters of Charles X], by their
intrigues and by their alliance with the republicans, are endan-
gering at every opportunity the prosperity of France; the
Carlists, too cowardly to act for themselves, are paying and
inciting the republicans, who show more courage and good faith

in their criminal enterprises, but who are the dupes of these wretches![72]

While the case against Fieschi and his accomplices was being prepared, the government embarked on the most severe legislative repression of the July monarchy. The assassination attempt horrified public opinion, and convinced many of the need for a clamp-down on subversion. The ministry's particular targets were the opposition press – whose savage attacks on Louis-Philippe had, it was felt, created an atmosphere favourable to assassination – and the courts, which frequently acquitted in political trials. To remedy this, it proposed a series of harsh measures. In the case of the courts, the most important were a reduction in the number of jurymen needed to gain a conviction from eight to seven out of twelve, secrecy of jury voting so as to reduce intimidation, and greater ease of retrial if the verdict was unsatisfactory.[73]

For the press, preliminary censorship was not reimposed, but a large number of new offences were outlined. Incitement to insurrection, or attacks on the king or his authority, should henceforth be tried by the Peers and not before a jury, and it would be illegal to call for a change of dynasty or a republic, to glorify the elder branch of the Bourbons or to undermine property rights or the law. Newspapers should no longer be able to publish engravings. The penalties envisaged for these infractions included imprisonment, heavy fines and eventual suspension of publication. Passed by convincing majorities in the Chambers in the autumn, the 'September laws' offered striking proof of the government's determination to crush its enemies.[74]

Fieschi's machine backfired on the republicans just as much as it had on its creator. The assassination attempt, coupled with the 1834 risings and the subsequent chaotic trial, created an image of violence and fanaticism that deeply discredited them. The September laws aimed at their complete destruction. In fact, the results of the legislation were mixed. It did not deter further assassins, and alienated those who found it illiberal and repressive. Yet it did end the more extreme attacks on the king and the monarchy in the press and ensured more convictions in political trials, and there were no more major insurrections. For over a decade, republicanism would cease to pose a serious threat to the regime.

The trial of Fieschi, Morey and Pépin opened in the Chamber of Peers on 30 January 1836. Morey was taciturn, Pépin clearly terrified. Fieschi, however, enjoyed every moment of his fame. Boastful and confident, he dominated the proceedings. Seeing that Talleyrand, who had turned up for the first day, was absent on the second, he remarked in his Corsican accent: 'I was sure that the prince wouldn't come back: he has been too upset by my voice, which is exactly the same as the emperor's.' The verdict, however, was inevitable. The three conspirators were condemned to death and guillotined on 19 February at the Barrière St Jacques in front of a vast crowd. Fieschi's head was sent to be studied by a brain specialist at the Bicêtre hospital. There the artist Brascasset painted a gruesome picture of it, which now hangs in the Musée Carnavalet in Paris.[75]

*

AS THE FIESCHI TRIAL reached its climax, the ministry of 11 October 1832, now on its fourth *replâtrage*, finally came to an end. The cause was a relatively minor matter, the reduction of the interest rate on government securities. The finance minister Humann was convinced that this was necessary, but bizarrely, instead of discussing the question with his colleagues in the ministry, on 14 January 1836 he simply announced the policy to the Chamber. The other ministers were livid and he was forced to resign. The opposition had scented an opportunity, and returned to the issue persistently over the next few days. Under this provocation, Broglie lost his temper and addressed his opponents so rudely that, seething with anger, they immediately tabled a bill demanding the interest rate reduction. The debate began on 4 February, the government was defeated by two votes on the 5th, and the ministers resigned the same day. For the second time, Broglie's personal unpopularity had been his downfall.[76]

After sixteen days of negotiations, Louis-Philippe settled on Thiers as Broglie's successor. In many ways, it was a shrewd choice, breaking up Thiers' alliance with Guizot, whom the king had not yet learned to like. With the republicans in retreat and the September laws passed, it also marked a move towards conciliating former foes. The ministry was broadly of the centre-left. Besides Thiers who became prime minister and foreign minister, Hippolyte Passy and Jean Sauzet, both of the 'third party', took the ministries of commerce and justice respectively, the comte d'Argout, essentially an independent, moved to finance, and Montalivet, whose loyalty was above all to the king, returned to the ministry of the interior.

At the age of only thirty-nine, Thiers had reached the political summit. He enjoyed a formidable reputation as a politician, orator and historian. Louis-Philippe, who in some ways resembled him, found him personally congenial and enjoyed his conversation, while Talleyrand, his greatest patron, congratulated him on his premiership with words hardly calculated to induce modesty: 'Monsieur, Europe awaits you.'

Yet Thiers also had many enemies. His political conduct was open to criticism as unprincipled, ruthless and opportunist. A contrast could be drawn between his sordid political intriguing and his lofty admiration for Napoleon: one contemporary once likened him to a sparrow nesting in the Arc de Triomphe.[77] He was also despised by many as a parvenu, an impression hardly effaced by the Grandvaux affair of autumn 1834. This was an extremely drunken house-party at the country home of a wealthy deputy, in the course of which Thiers mooned at the gathering. For the royalist newspaper *La Quotidienne*, the event was a symbol of the steady rise of the vulgar bourgeoisie since 1789 – the Revolution had overturned the social order and inflicted decades of disaster on France 'just so that M. Thiers could come, after drinking, to show France his backside by candle-light'.[78]

In domestic policy, Thiers aimed to reassure the *résistance* that order would be preserved, while holding out to the left the prospect of a gradual easing of repressive measures. This was a difficult path to follow, and Thiers' promises of liberalization were belied by his role only two years before in crushing the risings of Lyon and Paris. In the event, no conciliatory gestures such as a political amnesty were made, and apart from some laws on trade and transport little important legislation was passed. Even reduction of interest on government securities, the issue that had brought Thiers to power in the first place, was postponed.[79]

In this situation, Thiers' interest began to shift to foreign policy. He first set himself to achieve what was so vital for the future of the July monarchy, a prestigious marriage for Louis-Philippe's eldest

son the duc d'Orléans. He and the king decided that the best choice
would be a Habsburg archduchess. This would both confer unquestionable international legitimacy on the new dynasty, and also give
France another diplomatic partner as well as England. In May 1836
Orléans and his younger brother Nemours set off to visit Vienna
and Berlin, where they won golden opinions. However, in August
the Austrian government, still concerned about France's long-term
stability, refused the proposed match.[80]

Faced with this rebuff, Thiers switched to a new diplomatic
stance, which reflected his deepest preferences far more than his
previous one. Instead of making overtures to the conservative
Powers, France would return to her revolutionary heritage and seek
practical advantage and national glory in support of liberalism abroad.
This would also have the advantage of pleasing the left, and
distracting it from the government's essentially right-wing domestic
policy. Even more convenient, a suitable cause lay close at hand,
beyond the Pyrenees.

By a remarkable coincidence, both Spain and Portugal in the
1830s were in precisely similar predicaments. In each country, the
Salic law excluding women from the succession, in force in Spain
since 1713 as well as in Portugal, had been set aside. This allowed
the three-year-old Queen Isabella to ascend the Spanish throne and
the seven-year-old Queen Maria that of Portugal. However, their
respective uncles, Don Carlos in Spain and Dom Miguel in Portugal, who would otherwise have succeeded, claimed this was illegal,
and the result was civil war. Since Don Carlos and Dom Miguel
were strong believers in absolute monarchy, Spanish and Portu-
guese liberals and constitutionalists defended their nieces, making the
conflict ideological as well as dynastic. Similarly, on the international
stage the conservative Powers, Austria, Prussia and Russia, supported
Don Carlos and Dom Miguel, while France and Britain sided with
Queen Isabella and Queen Maria. In April 1834, the British and
French governments signed a quadruple alliance with the embattled
Isabella and Maria to come to Maria's aid in Portugal. Within a few
months, an Anglo-Spanish expedition had defeated Dom Miguel and
driven him out of the country.[81]

France and Britain were now faced with the problem of whether
or not to intervene in Spain, a dilemma which would be repeated

with uncanny precision during another Spanish civil war exactly a century later. On the surface, the Quadruple Alliance had laid the basis for a joint approach – and as such was a major achievement for the policy of close Franco-British relations so close to the hearts of Louis-Philippe and Adélaïde. Yet in reality there were significant differences between Britain and France. Lord Palmerston, the English foreign minister, combined enthusiasm for intervention with a basic distrust of Louis-Philippe's France, which he unfairly suspected of expansionist designs on her neighbours, including Spain.[82] In fact, majority opinion in France was against direct military involvement in Spain. Louis XVIII's successful expedition there in 1823 to aid the Spanish Bourbons had not effaced the memory of Napoleon's disastrous Peninsular War of 1808–13, with its atrocities, bloody defeats and guerrilla insurgency, and there was little desire to repeat the experience. Louis-Philippe and Adélaïde wholeheartedly shared these sentiments. In May 1835 Adélaïde wrote to Sébastiani in London:

> The news from Spain is unfortunately very bad, and adds more than ever to the pressure to intervene, which would be a very bad thing and which must be resisted, because it would only do harm; this is how [the guerrilla chief] Mina speaks of the prospect of intervention, he says that it would not be the war of 1823, but that of 1808, and I think he's right and that it would be fatal for us and one more misfortune for Spain.[83]

Unfortunately, this cautious policy risked imposing major strains on relations with the enthusiastically interventionist Palmerston, which Louis-Philippe and his sister sought desperately to avert with protestations of friendship. As Adélaïde put it to Sébastiani in March 1836, in a letter transmitting and strongly endorsing her brother's views:

> ... the king wishes above all to avoid anything that could lead to intervention, which he increasingly regards as contrary to the interests of everybody, and as most dangerous and liable to bring Spain yet more misfortunes. For the rest he wishes to aid and support the Queen of Spain by all other possible means, to collaborate with England over this, and to maintain between our two countries that good and perfect union that is so essential and precious to us as for her; you know the value that our dear

king with good reason attaches to it, a sentiment that I share
with all my heart, since I regard this union as the basis of
everything, and as the source of our strength in dealing with
the other Powers.[84]

In August 1836, however, Thiers decided to throw caution to the
winds and support an intervention that he hoped would revive
France's military glory and burnish her liberal credentials abroad.
This had the advantage of bringing France closer to England again
but, apart from the inherent difficulties of the enterprise, put him on
a collision course both with a substantial section of public opinion,
and with Louis-Philippe himself.

After heated exchanges, Thiers and the king reached a compromise. In March 1831, Louis-Philippe had founded the French Foreign
Legion as a means of siphoning off those radicals from abroad who
had flooded into France after the July revolution. In June 1835,
Thiers had persuaded him to subcontract it to the Spanish government for service against the Carlists. Now Louis-Philippe and Thiers
agreed to raise a second Foreign Legion corps at Pau in the Pyrenees
to reinforce the one fighting in Spain, and to put the whole force
under the command of a French general.[85] However, behind the
king's back Thiers continued to build up the Foreign Legion at Pau
beyond the numbers agreed. As relations with his prime minister
grew increasingly tense, in late August Louis-Philippe demanded that
these units be disbanded. Rather than accept this, Thiers resigned on
26 August.[86]

Thiers' downfall, however, was the making of the Foreign
Legion. While the 1st corps was frittered away in Spain and
eventually dissolved in 1839, the 2nd was dispatched from Pau to the
newly conquered French enclave in Algeria. Its legendary association
with North Africa was about to begin.[87]

Apart from creating yet another short-term political crisis, the
clash over intervention in Spain reveals much about Louis-Philippe's
conception of kingship. At the height of the confrontation Thiers, in
order to give his personal stand an aura of constitutional principle,
resurrected his old maxim that 'the king should reign but not govern'.
Instead, as in England, he should 'leave the daily direction of policy
to the head of a ministry enjoying a majority in both Chambers,

enabling the king to stay above the parliamentary struggle . . . so that in serious circumstances, when disagreements arise between the ministry and the Chamber of Deputies, he can act as an arbiter'.[88]

As minister of the interior and a close confidant, Montalivet was called by Louis-Philippe as a witness to a meeting where the king outlined to Thiers his own sharply different view of constitutional monarchy. What emerges from the account Montalivet later set down is that for Louis-Philippe, like all his royal ancestors, control of foreign policy and military affairs was the central attribute of kingship. He was prepared to give up the direction of domestic affairs, and indeed claimed that he had effectively done so already —

> But to want to remove me from the daily conduct of diplomacy, to force me to accept that this is not my chief responsibility, that's impossible! This includes questions of war and peace, and in this respect you know, my dear Thiers, . . . how much I value peace, and how much I am the enemy of war, though without fearing it; and with what meticulous care I ensure that this prime interest of France is not compromised by my ministers and my envoys.
>
> And the army! Am I not its commander-in-chief? And don't I daily have to see that it is always united like a family along with my sons who have all joined its ranks and try to give an example? Really, I think you are being very difficult! Have I gone beyond my rights in those matters of surveillance and direction that my conscience does not permit me to neglect? Recently on a subject of this kind [intervention in Spain] we could not agree. Eh well, what will happen? We have the Chambers: they will decide between my prudence and your rather reckless plans. What could be more constitutional![89]

For the moment, Louis-Philippe was victorious, and his vision of a monarch actively involved in government — so active, indeed, that he was able to force the resignation of a prime minister with whom he disagreed — was vindicated. This still left the question of who could succeed Thiers. The new ministry, announced on 6 September, was based on an alliance of circumstance between Guizot, from whom Thiers had separated when he formed his own ministry and who was now his enemy, and the veteran politician comte Molé and his followers. It was an uneasy partnership from the start. Molé, who became prime minister, had the support of the ministers of war, the marine and commerce in pursuing a policy of conciliation towards the parliamentary and extra-parliamentary opposition. However, Guizot and his *doctrinaire* colleagues in the ministry remained committed to *résistance*. From this point on, Molé and Guizot would be the dominant politicians of Louis-Philippe's reign, first as allies, then as bitter foes.

The summer of 1836 saw one incident that put these ministerial wranglings starkly into perspective. In the late afternoon of 25 June, Louis-Philippe left the Tuileries in his carriage to drive to Neuilly. Marie-Amélie and Adélaïde sat facing the direction of travel, while the king was opposite them. What happened next was described by Adélaïde, in noticeably shaky handwriting, in a letter to Sébastiani the following day:

> . . . at the moment the carriage was passing through the gate on the courtyard side, a monster shot at our dearest king . . . there was a noise like a pistol-shot; the king with his wonderful calm and coolness immediately said to us: 'I'm fine.' The wadding from the gun was scattered over the cushions in front of me, and the king also had some in his hair. We stopped the carriage immediately on the other side of the gate facing the bridge, and the king leaned out of the window and said: 'Someone's taken a shot at me but I'm fine'; from all sides came cries of 'Long live the king!', and at the same instant we heard that the wretch had been arrested, and we immediately turned round and came back here. The carriage was examined as soon as we had got out, and the bullet was found embedded in the panelling three inches above the head of our beloved king! Ah! my dear general, what monsters, what anxieties, you will understand how I feel; only our admirable king is completely himself and perfectly calm, but God has been good to us; we cannot acknowledge this and give thanks to Him enough. He is my trust and my consolation.[90]

The would-be assassin was a twenty-six-year-old clerk and fanatical republican called Louis Alibaud. In a further parallel with *The Day of the Jackal*, his weapon was a musket disguised as a walking-stick. If Louis-Philippe had not been inclining his head forward to acknowledge the guards presenting arms when the shot was fired, he would have been killed.

Unlike Fieschi, Alibaud was tall, personable and educated, and thus a better advertisement for his cause than the latter. His fate, however, was no different. Since he had acted alone and there were no accomplices to track down, he was quickly tried and convicted. He was guillotined at 4.55 a.m. on 11 July 1836. Meanwhile, Adélaïde took to her bed and did not make a full recovery until the autumn. Her illness, as she admitted to Sébastiani in October, was 'the result of all last summer's torments'.[91]

Chapter Nine

VICTORY AND DEFEAT

THE SUMMER AND AUTUMN of 1836 marked a turning-point in the history of the July monarchy. The personal dangers facing Louis-Philippe did not diminish. There would be four more serious attempts on his life over the next twelve years, making a total of seven, a record for a modern head of state. Yet French politics in general became more stable. Governments had an appreciably longer lifespan, with less *replâtrage* and fewer ruptures; Molé's second ministry lasted two years, from 1837 to 1839, and that of Soult and Guizot seven, from 1840 to 1847 – the longest administration of the century.

Molé and Guizot, who together succeeded Thiers until their paths diverged, were both remarkable figures. It is Guizot who has gone down in history as Louis-Philippe's favourite minister. Yet this verdict does not do justice to Molé. Louis-Philippe had backed him in several abortive attempts to form a government before he finally succeeded in 1836, and over the next three years the two men established a close and effective working partnership. Its basis was disclosed by Molé in a letter to Louis-Philippe of July 1837: 'The king told me the other day that I was the most monarchical of his ministers.' On Louis-Philippe's side, his letters to Molé reveal both trust and esteem – 'I badly need to pick your shrewd brains in which I have so much confidence'; 'I really need to see you for a talk'; 'you have all my confidence and all my affection'. Forced from office by a coalition led by Guizot, it was Molé whom Louis-Philippe called on to replace Guizot when the latter in his turn fell.[1]

Molé[2] and Guizot[3] had very different characters and backgrounds. Born in 1781, Molé was six years older than his rival. He came from a distinguished line of noble magistrates, at ease in the high society of pre-revolutionary Paris and Versailles. Guizot, by contrast, was born into a family of bourgeois lawyers, from Nîmes in the Midi. The Guizots' defining feature, however, was that they were Protestants, of a faith proscribed and persecuted in France since the late seventeenth century and only accorded civil status in 1788. Molé had made a brilliant early career serving Napoleon, becoming both a councillor of state and a count at twenty-eight, then minister of justice in 1813. He had rallied to the Bourbons in 1814, kept a low profile during the Hundred Days, and re-entered government as minister of the marine in 1817.

Simply by virtue of being younger than Molé, Guizot was able to avoid the taint of association with Napoleon. He had gained his first major post, as professor of modern history at the Sorbonne, at the end of the empire, which he had discreetly opposed. His royalism was thus unquestioned – during the Hundred Days he had even followed Louis XVIII into exile at Ghent. Molé, on the other hand, having switched from one regime to another, was already acquiring a reputation for lack of political principle. Both men supported the liberal opposition to the ultras after 1820, but this did not bring them closer – Molé never joined the *doctrinaire* group of which Guizot was such a prominent member.[4]

The two men did have one formative experience in common. It was one they shared with Louis-Philippe. Their fathers had both been guillotined during the Terror; Guizot's at Nîmes on 8 April 1794, Molé's in Paris twelve days later. Guizot never forgot his last visit, aged six, to his father in prison. This grim encounter with the Revolution, Molé once recalled bleakly, 'decided my life . . . it made me into a very different person from the one I would have been without it'.[5] Significantly, two of their colleagues had been similarly bereaved – the duc de Broglie, and the elder statesman and president of the Chamber of Peers, Pasquier. It is striking how many of the July monarchy's prominent politicians lost a parent to the Revolution,

and then devoted their public careers to ensuring that it would never
be repeated.

Molé and Guizot, however, reached different conclusions on how
this should be achieved. Guizot developed a profound distrust of
democracy, which he associated with the radical phase of the French
Revolution. For him, a major attraction of the *doctrinaires* was their
determination to build a political system based on reason,[6] rather than
on the terrifying passions of the masses that had claimed his father's
life. These factors predisposed Guizot, after 1830, to become an
inflexible champion of *résistance*.

Both Guizot and Molé wished to 'end the French Revolution' and
its legacy of division and instability. Guizot wished to do so by rigid
adherence to a set of highly conservative principles. Molé was just as
resolved to defend the political and social order if it was openly
attacked, but for him, healing the wounds of the Revolution also
entailed pragmatism and compromise: 'stretching out one's hand,' as
he once said, 'to all those who, having learned from the past, return
sincerely to the fold, without demanding that they account for their
past actions, or that they humiliate themselves'. The 'flexible resistance' espoused by Sébastiani exactly described Molé's policy. Or, as
Molé once put it in the Chamber, attacking Guizot's claim that the
doctrinaires alone were committed to upholding order: 'Resistance is
a tool of every government, but so also is conciliation.'[7]

With his high forehead, pale face and piercing black eyes, Guizot
was a forbidding but also a charismatic figure. He was a riveting
parliamentary orator, with a powerful dramatic presence: after hearing
him speak once in the Chamber, the great actress Rachel observed:
'I would like to play tragedy with that man.'[8] Molé, on the other
hand, polished, handsome and elegant, was more at home in his
ministerial study and the salons of Paris. Again, this stemmed from
the fact that he was older than Guizot; he had entered public life at a
time when parliamentary politics was in abeyance, and power was
achieved instead by serving a dominant ruler like Napoleon. In a
sense, by the 1830s Molé was a politician of a different age, while his
touchy and hypersensitive temperament was not ideally suited to the
often raucous atmosphere of the Chamber. Yet during the crisis of
his ministry, in January 1839, he more than rose to the occasion,

defending himself against the attacks of Guizot and his allies with skill and passion.

Apart from their fathers' violent ends, Molé and Guizot had one other similarity, and this too they shared with Louis-Philippe. Both men had Egerias, though in each case she was a mistress rather than a sister. The beautiful and sophisticated Cordélia, comtesse de Castellane, whose previous lover had been Chateaubriand, was Molé's partner and confidante from the early 1830s to her death in 1847. The princesse de Lieven, estranged wife of a Russian diplomat and one of the most influential political women of her age, began an affair with Guizot in 1837 and swiftly became indispensable to him. Both women ran famous salons which were centred on their respective lovers and which acted to a large extent as their political headquarters. When necessary they would themselves pass messages from Molé and Guizot to Louis-Philippe, predictably through Adélaïde as intermediary.[9]

These common points in Molé's and Guizot's backgrounds and experience did not compensate for the differences. They began by distrusting one another, and the experience of governing together turned this into deep dislike. From the beginning, the main source of tension was the question of whether the policy of *résistance* should be maintained or relaxed. Molé showed his preference immediately by issuing a royal pardon to fifty-two political prisoners, carefully balancing legitimists with republicans. The most eminent were Charles X's former ministers; Peyronnet, Chantelauze and Guernon-Ranville were allowed to return home under police surveillance, while Polignac's sentence of life imprisonment was commuted to banishment from France for twenty years.[10]

A week after the release of Peyronnet and Chantelauze, another skilful gesture of pacification was made. On 25 October 1836 the great obelisk of Luxor, a gift from the Pasha of Egypt Mehmet Ali, was erected in the middle of the Place de la Concorde at a ceremony which marked Louis-Philippe's first public appearance since Fieschi's assassination attempt. The Place de la Concorde was the most politically contested site in France. As the Place de la Révolution between 1792 and 1795, it had seen the executions of Louis XVI, Marie Antoinette, and Louis-Philippe's own father Philippe-Egalité, as well as the principal revolutionary leaders: Robespierre, Danton, Desmoulins, St Just. Between 1826 and 1830, it had been renamed the Place Louis XVI to commemorate the dead king, and work had even begun on a monument to him. Louis-Philippe, however, was determined that the Place de la Concorde should not become a symbolic focus for the continuing battle between the Revolution and the counter-revolution. The obelisk of Luxor, foreign in every sense to France and her recent history, provided the ideal means for achieving this. The monument fulfilled Louis-Philippe's hopes, and did so durably. It still stands imposingly in place today, having outlived five regimes since its inauguration.

Just five days after the installation of the obelisk, the July monarchy was briefly challenged by a new opponent. Since the death of Napoleon's son the Duke of Reichstadt in Vienna in 1832, the Bonapartist claim to the French throne had passed to the emperor's nephew, Prince Louis-Napoleon. At this stage in his life, the new Bonapartist pretender cut an unimpressive figure. Short, bandy-legged, with heavy-lidded eyes and an impassive face, he had little public presence. His appeal was not enhanced by the fact that he spoke French with a German accent, having been brought up in exile in Bavaria and Switzerland. But he had inherited his uncle's fatalistic belief in his 'star', which bolstered his most remarkable quality — resilience.[11]

In the autumn of 1835, Louis-Napoleon began preparing a plan to topple the July monarchy. As befitted a Bonaparte, he aimed to seize power not through a popular uprising, but through a coup d'état based on the army. The model was his uncle's return from Elba at the beginning of the Hundred Days.[12] Since Louis-Napoleon was based in Switzerland, the most obvious point of entry into France was Strasbourg, which he hoped would be to him what Grenoble had been to Napoleon in 1815. The colonel of one of the regiments stationed in Strasbourg was won over, and promised to rally the garrison to Louis-Napoleon and then march on Paris.

The putsch was a disaster. It began at 6 a.m. on 30 October, with the troops initially acclaiming Louis-Napoleon. However, a fatal mistake was made in allowing the garrison's commanding general to escape and recall his soldiers to their allegiance. Within two hours, Louis-Napoleon and most of his followers had been arrested. The episode showed that although some Bonapartist sentiment still remained in the army, there was far less disaffection with the July monarchy than there had been in 1815 with the restoration.[13] The circumstances that had created the Hundred Days no longer existed.

Louis-Napoleon was far more of a danger to the government as a prisoner than he had been as a conspirator, presenting exactly the same problem as the duchesse de Berry four years earlier – a trial and sentence would make a martyr of him and give publicity to his cause. After a week's deliberation it was decided simply to exile Louis-Napoleon to America, and on 21 November the would-be emperor embarked at Lorient – Louis-Philippe even giving him a remittance to ease his passage.[14] Banishment rather than retribution was an extremely astute move. Sparing Louis-Napoleon prison or the guillotine made the king look both confident and magnanimous. In fact, the attempted coup had played into Louis-Philippe's hands. While posing no serious threat, it had acted as a sufficient reminder of the dangers of upheaval to create a loyalist backlash in favour of the regime. Showing her usual shrewd grasp of public opinion, Adélaïde expressed her satisfaction to her friend Mme de Ste Aldegonde:

> I think this measure [of clemency] a good one for the past, the present and the future, and that any similar criminal enterprises which have these results will produce only a good effect, and I have confidence and the conviction that if any others arise they will have no more success than this one for the madmen who undertake them, and they don't worry me in the slightest.[15]

While the king was pondering Louis-Napoleon's future, another opponent had been removed permanently from the scene. On 6 November 1836, Charles X died of cholera at Gorizia near Trieste, where he and his family had been given asylum by the Habsburgs. This still left Charles' sixteen-year-old grandson, the duc de Bordeaux, as the focus of legitimist hopes, but it did eliminate the man who could with most reason call Louis-Philippe a usurper. Charles' death, however, raised a tricky point of protocol: should official mourning be decreed for him at the French court? On the one hand, it looked churlish not to do so, but on the other, such an act would infuriate not only the left, but many of the July monarchy's supporters.

Louis-Philippe considered whether the Orléans should go into private rather than official mourning, but eventually rejected this as too confusing, so that neither he nor his court went into black for his cousin. These subtleties were lost on Adélaïde. As she put it succinctly to Sébastiani: 'One does not wear mourning for people with whom one is at war.'[16]

The weakening of opposition to Louis-Philippe was reflected even in the calibre of his assassins. On 27 December 1836 the king, accompanied by Orléans, Nemours and Joinville, drove in his carriage to open the new session of the Chamber of Deputies. As the convoy left the Tuileries, Louis-Philippe leaned out to wave to the National Guard lining the route. At that moment a shot was fired, missing him but shattering the glass of one of the carriage windows. An onlooker had seized the attacker's arm as he fired, making the bullet go wide. Arrested on the spot, the culprit turned out to be a young republican named François Meunier. Like Alibaud, he was an unsuccessful clerk; unlike Alibaud, he was overweight, flat-footed, and simple-minded, without any of his predecessor's charisma and style. Whereas Alibaud had remained unrepentant to the end, Meunier swiftly threw himself on the king's mercy. Like Louis-Napoleon, Meunier was pardoned, and instead of being imprisoned, sent to America. Louis-Philippe had accomplished a splendid propaganda coup. The Bonapartist pretender had been reduced to the level of a dim-witted errand boy.[17]

While Louis-Philippe displayed his flair for public relations, his ministry was struggling. Whereas Louis-Napoleon had simply been deported to America, those of his followers who had been arrested were put on trial. Since these included civilians as well as soldiers, all were tried in the local court at Strasbourg rather than by court-martial. On 18 January 1837, the Strasbourg jury, more Bonapartist than its garrison, acquitted them. The government immediately introduced a bill providing for *disjonction* – ensuring that in any future case of insurrection, the military and civilian participants would be tried by different courts. Championed by the *doctrinaires* but regarded by many in the Chamber as an infringement of civil liberties, the bill was defeated by just two votes on 7 March.[18]

This setback only increased the existing tensions between the ministers. Almost immediately Gasparin, the minister of the interior and an ally of Guizot's, proved himself such a poor speaker that it was clear he would have to be replaced. Molé had no desire to appoint another *doctrinaire*, so he and Guizot remained at loggerheads while Gasparin reluctantly struggled on. Further difficulties arose when the government proposed bills to vote an independent establishment to Louis-Philippe's second son Nemours and a dowry to his daughter Louise, now Queen of the Belgians. Nemours was to be given an annual income of 500,000 francs, derived from the château and estate of Rambouillet, and Louise a million francs. However, the initial reception of these proposals by the Chamber was so tepid that it was felt best to postpone a debate. Unable to pass its legislation and immobilized by internal dissension, the administration was clearly doomed.[19]

If the impasse were to be resolved, either Molé or Guizot would have to go. Faced with this choice, Louis-Philippe much preferred to keep Molé. On 15 April a new ministry was formed under Molé that dispensed with Guizot and the *doctrinaires*. They were replaced either by politicians of the centre-left or by those personally loyal to the king. Montalivet, Louis-Philippe's trusted confidant, returned to the ministry of the interior. Of all the governments of the July monarchy, this was the one that most reflected the political outlook of the king – and his sister. As such, it was immediately attacked by the opposition press as the 'ministry of the château [in reference to the Tuileries]', or the 'ministry of lackeys'.[20] Since it contained none of the major figures in the Chamber, it was assumed that it would soon go the way of its predecessor. In fact, it lasted for two years, and developed a distinctive and often successful policy.

Formerly an indifferent parliamentary performer, Molé now began to show considerable originality and flair. This was first displayed in his speech presenting the new government to the Chamber on 18 April. All the deputies were expecting him to explain its composition and set out its programme in the usual manner. Instead, he caused a sensation by announcing the forthcoming marriage of the duc d'Orléans with Princess Helena of Mecklenburg-Schwerin. Since he would ask the Chamber to vote the couple an annual income of two million francs, he continued, the question of giving Nemours his establishment was being indefinitely postponed, but the proposal for Louise's dowry was maintained. This was an

extremely cunning manoeuvre; surprised by the happy news of the
engagement of the heir to the throne, the deputies could hardly refuse
the marriage settlement demanded, nor the dowry for Louise that
was so artfully tacked on to it.

The duc d'Orléans, whose marriage was designed to guarantee
the dynasty's future, was now twenty-six. Tall, elegant, blond and
blue-eyed, he cut an impressive figure. Although not as intellectually
gifted as his younger brothers d'Aumale and Montpensier, like them
he had received an excellent education at the Lycée Henri IV.
Unsurprisingly, the punishing schedule that Louis-Philippe, inspired
by Mme de Genlis, imposed on him had touched off an adolescent
rebellion at the age of fourteen, which reached its peak when he
deliberately farted in front of his tutor during a Greek exam.[21] He
could sometimes appear cold and reserved, but this was simply a
façade, as he revealed when his eight-year-old brother the duc de
Penthièvre, nicknamed 'Pinpin', was dying in 1828. Writing to
Adélaïde to tell her the end was imminent, he added:

> I know I have the misfortune to appear insensitive; I think that
> this mostly comes from not being able to express my emotions,
> and not liking to show others what I feel, which makes me seem
> cold, but if people could see how depressed I am when I see
> mother and Pinpin together, they'd change their minds about
> me.[22]

Orléans had strong political views, which were by no means all
to his father's taste. Devoted to the army, he was convinced that a
forward foreign policy, pursued if necessary beyond the brink of war,
was the only way for the July monarchy to keep the loyalty of 'that
moderate patriotic opinion which placed my father on the throne,
and which alone keeps him on it today'. Determined to correct 'the
hostile and anti-French settlement of 1815', he had ambitious plans
to expand France's frontiers beyond the limits prescribed by the
Congress of Vienna. He later modified this stance, but in August
1837 Louis-Philippe was sufficiently concerned by his views to write
him an extraordinarily frank warning:

> ... you are accused, or at the least suspected, of a bellicose
> disposition which is less inclined than mine to place prudence

17. *Entente Cordiale*: at Eu, in 1845. Louis-Philippe (centre)
points towards Adélaïde on his right. Queen Victoria sits beneath him,
while Prince Albert stands to his left, pointing towards Victoria.
Marie-Amélie wears a turquoise bonnet.

18. Horace Sébastiani:
an official portrait,
by Winterhalter.

19. Horace Sébastiani:
an unofficial portrait,
by Daumier.

20. *Right.*
The great survivor:
Talleyrand in old age,
by Ary Scheffer.

21. *Below.*
'Apoplexy Replacing
Paralysis at London',
by Daumier.
Sébastiani, after a
mild stroke, succeeds
the crippled Talleyrand
as French ambassdor
to London, 1835.

POLITICIANS (*left to right*).
22. Louis-Mathieu, comte Molé: Louis-Philippe's shrewdest prime minister, engraving from a portrait by Ingres.
23. Francois Guizot, the dominant French politician of the 1840s, by Daumier.
24. Jean de Dieu Soult, Marshal of France, Duke of Dalmatia, in London for Queen Victoria's wedding, 1838, by George Campion.
25. Adolphe Thiers: 'You need perils . . . they are titles to the crown.'

26. Power behind the throne:
Adélaïde pulling Louis-Philippe's strings, a cartoon of 1833.

27. 'The unmarried mother at Longchamps.' Adélaïde taking her supposed
brood of bastards to the races. The child on the left has Louis-Philippe's
pear-shaped head – a clear allusion to incest.

28. Fieschi's infernal machine: twenty-five musket-barrels with the
triggers wired together mounted on a frame. But it failed
to kill Louis-Philippe.

29. A precursor of *The Day of the Jackal*: the musket disguised as a
walking-stick used by Alibaud to fire at Louis-Philippe.

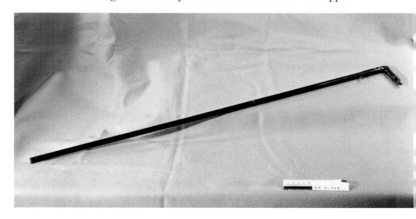

30. The infernal machine at work: the bloodbath on the Boulevard du Temple
of 28 July 1835, painted from memory by one of its intended victims,
Louis-Philippe's son the prince de Joinville.

31. The head of
Joseph Fieschi, the
morning after his execution,
20 February 1836, by
Jacques-Raymond
Brascasset.

THE 1848 REVOLUTION.

32. *Left.* The corpse of a demonstrator carried around the Paris streets as a call to insurrection, 23 February.

33. *Below.* Fighting at the Chateau d'Eau on the place du Palais-royal, 24 February.

and the needs of peace before the glory of the battlefield and the dangerous glamour of victory. This is what our enemies are trying to insinuate; this is the thrust of the attack, and this is how they are trying to demonstrate that peace and prudence will be buried with me, and that when you succeed me the warlike spirit and *bellomania* of Louis XIV will once more mount the throne.[23]

Intellectual Orléans may not have been, but he did have an instinctive feel for the main ideas and movements of the age. Well before his father, he realized that the major issues of the 1840s would be domestic and social ones, placing war and diplomacy in the shade. In October 1841, he discussed these in a long letter to his younger brother Joinville. Although his proposed remedies were repressive and his tone apocalyptic, unlike many of his contemporaries he at least recognized there was a problem:

> ... to cure the malady, one must first face up to it, and it is serious: the insurrection is at our gates; the lower classes prefer to tear from the rich by force of arms the bread they could so easily obtain by work; this social war (to which, I fear, we are fatally condemned) is given a political appearance which makes it even more dangerous by concealing its real aim which would otherwise frighten many of those taking part ... the domestic question is everything today, and would be even if all foreign policy matters were resolved and settled for the whole of the king's reign.[24]

Alongside his military and official duties, before his marriage Orléans also found time for a crowded private life. His first mistress, at the age of nineteen, was a Polish countess, swiftly followed by the actress Léontine Fay, and these were succeeded by many others. By 1835, Louis-Philippe was becoming concerned that excessive womanizing might be undermining his heir's precious health. Confiding to Marie-Amélie his worries about Orléans' latest mistress, whom he did not name, he wrote: 'There is no time to lose, in view of some confidences he let slip to me about the state of exhaustion he is in. That wretched woman is tiring him out, a fact that she's flaunting everywhere, and he doesn't have the courage to break with her. Each day more of his vital forces are being drained away.'[25]

It was this state of affairs that Helena of Mecklenburg was called
on to remedy, and she was well equipped for the task. Tall and
blonde, she had style, dignity and intelligence. She was also ambitious. Brought up in an obscure North German principality, she
was happy to exchange it for the prospective throne of France. The
doubts about the stability of the July monarchy that had prevented
other suitable brides from accepting Orléans' hand mattered little to
her. A Protestant, she refused to convert to Catholicism, but
accepted that any future children would be raised as Catholics. On
30 May 1837, in a splendid ceremony at Fontainebleau, she married
Orléans and assumed a new identity and title as Hélène, duchesse
d'Orléans. It was the beginning of a genuinely happy marriage.[26]

The wedding gave Molé the chance to introduce the most
important – and courageous – measure of his ministry. On 8 May
he announced in the Chamber that, to celebrate the happy event, an
amnesty to all political prisoners was being granted. This was the
project that Gérard had first formed in the autumn of 1834, but which
had successfully been opposed both by the *doctrinaires* in the ministry
and by the king himself. Now, however, the situation had changed.
Louis-Philippe was won over by the idea that his eldest son's
marriage should be an occasion for national reconciliation, and was
keen for the amnesty to be seen as his personal initiative. Crucially,
to avoid the charge from conservatives that it was an act of weakness,
the amnesty was presented as a gesture of confidence in the stability
and popularity of the regime. As its preamble put it: 'Order having
been reinforced, the vanquished factions can now attribute their
reprieve only to the generosity of the king.'[27]

The amnesty was not a hasty piece of opportunism, but the first
move of a carefully thought out policy. Now that the methods of
resistance had for the moment conquered the forces of disorder, it
was time, in Molé's words, 'to stretch out a hand to all who return
sincerely to the fold'. But timing was of the essence. As Molé put it
in a letter of 6 June 1837: 'I had had a plan since 6 September [when
the Molé–Guizot ministry took office]. All I needed was the marriage,
so that I could group around it all the measures on which I was
relying to reconcile the king with France and France with the king.
Once the marriage was certain, I never lost confidence and, as I took
everything one step at a time, the heavens helped me.'[28]

Over the previous year, Molé had also taken care to buttress his position by cultivating Orléans. He had consulted him over the formation of his ministry – and particularly over the choice of a minister of war. He also sounded him out before issuing the amnesty, and received an enthusiastic response. Of all the measures at the government's disposal, Orléans wrote, 'this one is the most powerful, and gives more advantage to our side than any security measure'. It also helped that Orléans' marriage worked out so well; when his second son was baptized, the duke invited Molé to the ceremony, describing the boy as 'a child born under your ministry, to which his parents owe their happy union'.[29]

In general, the amnesty had an excellent effect on public opinion. After years in which successive governments had talked only the language of struggle and emergency, Molé's action was greeted with relief as a return to normalcy. As the nineteenth-century historian Paul Thureau-Dangin observed: 'Many felt that joy that the news of peace brings after a long and hard war.'[30] Louis-Philippe, carefully monitoring reactions to the announcement from the Tuileries, was delighted. Reporting to Adélaïde on 12 May, he wrote:

> I think that the amnesty is having an excellent effect. I have seen women from [the working-class area of] the Faubourg St Marceau applauding from their windows. In the council of ministers, we have heard details of what the prisoners who have been pardoned have been saying. It's a mixed bag. None reacted with abuse, many said nothing at all, some declared that it doesn't make any difference and wouldn't stop them in future, and quite a few have said positive things. A small number have displayed gratitude.[31]

Having stretched out his hand to the left, Molé now did the same with the right. Since its sacking by the Paris crowd in February 1831, the Church of St Germain l'Auxerrois had stood gutted and empty. On 12 May, the government recommended to the king that it be restored and reopened for public worship. Catholic opinion reacted with delight; the Archbishop of Paris, Mgr de Quélen, who until now had kept himself aloof from the July monarchy, made his first visit to the Tuileries since the fall of Charles X to thank Louis-Philippe for his action.[32]

The next initiative in the process of reconciliation was conceived and implemented by the king himself. Its focus was an abandoned monument even more controversial than St Germain l'Auxerrois – Versailles. Partially sacked and its remaining contents sold at auction during the Revolution, by the 1830s the palace was falling into ruin. Louis-Philippe, who remembered its glory from his youth, was determined to save it from destruction. In a spectacular application of cultural politics, he aimed to reconcile this symbol of the old regime with post-revolutionary France by transforming it into a museum of national history. His goal was very clearly stated by the dedication that is still inscribed on the restored façade: 'To all the glories of France'. To underline just how completely the project was his own, Louis-Philippe paid for it all out of his own income from the civil list, spending in total twenty-three and a half million livres.[33]

Not only was the king's rebuilding of Versailles an exceptional achievement, it also offers a revealing glimpse of his views of the old regime under which he had been raised. To create the museum, the eighteenth-century warren of courtiers' apartments and their connecting staircases was ripped out. This was partly to make room for picture galleries, but it also had an ideological aspect – to destroy for ever the setting of those court intrigues that, in Louis-Philippe's opinion, had paralysed the absolute monarchy and paved the way for the Revolution. As he put it to his friend Dupin: 'Before Versailles could be restored, these partitions had to be knocked down, these rats' nests destroyed, and the usurped space reconquered.'[34] On the one hand, this means that it is now impossible to visualize the palace as it really was before 1789. On the other, without Louis-Philippe's amazing energy and dedication, there would probably be no Versailles left to visit at all.

By the summer of 1837, enough work had been done for the museum to be officially inaugurated. Once again, the occasion was timed as a celebration of the duc d'Orléans' marriage. One thousand five hundred people were invited to a ceremony and festivities that lasted a day and a night. They were shown round the restored palace and given a banquet. A performance of Molière's *Le Misanthrope* was then put on in the theatre, with an entr'acte devised by Eugène Scribe in which all the great men of the seventeenth century paid homage to the glory of Louis XIV. The proceedings concluded with a torchlit promenade. The occasion made an unforgettable impression on the participants. Guizot, who attended, found it splendid. However, he could not resist using it to illustrate one of his favourite themes, the triumph of the middle classes:

> I still remember how struck I was by that eager, curious crowd, and how, in some confusion, it followed the king and his suite from room to room: it was the new France, diverse, bourgeois, democratic, invading the palace of Louis XIV; peers, deputies, magistrates, administrators, scientists, writers, artists; a peaceful invasion, but an unstoppable one; conquerors looking slightly astonished in the midst of their conquest, and not quite ready to enjoy it, but confident and resolved to retain it. The representatives of the former ruling class, the heirs to its great names and their splendid memories, were not lacking in the crowd, and circulated happily in the familiar setting; but the ease they displayed was no longer matched by their importance; a people that had become great by and for itself, and was now trying to become free, dominated the palace of the great king and had taken the place of his court.[35]

The bold and imaginative actions of the summer of 1837 created a genuine surge in popular support for the Crown. In many ways, they marked the high point of the reign. Louis-Philippe was delighted; at last he had a prime minister whose policies mirrored his own, and which were enjoying striking success. As Adélaïde put it to Sébastiani on 12 June: 'Enthusiasm for our dear king is once again what it was in 1830, and affection for him has reached the level which he deserves; I've never seen him looking so well, he is rejuvenated.' Talleyrand's niece, mistress and Egeria the duchesse de Dino, usually just as hard-headed as Adélaïde and considerably more detached, came to an even more lyrical conclusion:

> The daring measure of the amnesty, the reopening of St Germain l'Auxerrois, the marriage of the duc d'Orléans, the admirable inauguration of Versailles, have all transformed the scene to everybody's benefit, enabling the postponement of difficulties which have not, however, been removed. But at present we are

enjoying the sweetest, most brilliant, most magical honeymoon
between king and people that can be imagined.[36]

*

APPROPRIATELY FOR A prime minister who had come to power
because his predecessor was too bellicose, Molé pursued a prudent
foreign policy. In this, as in domestic affairs, he was at one with
Louis-Philippe. However, this caution did not preclude firmness
where necessary. Although Molé's parliamentary opponents consistently accused him of excessive deference to the other Powers, these
charges were much exaggerated. Molé was quite prepared to take an
aggressive stand if he thought France's essential interests were
threatened, once even going so far as to threaten Austria with war.
His ministry was also notable for some hard-fought military campaigns in Algeria and even Mexico, which offered greater scope for
action than the crowded European chessboard.

Molé's entry to office was viewed with dismay in London, where
he was regarded as anti-English and more inclined to the continental
Powers, particularly Austria and Prussia. This was unfair, and said
more about Palmerston's exaggerated suspicions where anything
French was concerned than about his counterpart's true sentiments.
There is no reason to doubt Molé's sincerity when, on 7 January
1837, he declared to the Chamber of Peers: 'My personal opinion is
that the English alliance should form the basis of our foreign policy,
and that the present peace of Europe would be undermined, if this
understanding were to be broken.'[37]

On first entering office with Guizot in September 1836, Molé
inherited a situation in Algeria that quickly became disastrous. Since
the capture of Algiers in 1830, France had faced the choice, soon to
become a commonplace of nineteenth-century imperialism, of limiting
herself to her coastal conquests or extending them into the interior.
Thiers as prime minister, unsurprisingly, had been an enthusiastic
partisan of further expansion, and had approved an ambitious offensive plan submitted by the governor-general of Algeria, Marshal
Clauzel. By the time Molé had replaced Thiers in power, it was too
late to countermand the first part of Clauzel's strategy, an expedition
against the hostile town of Constantine.[38]

Setting off on 9 November 1836, too late in the campaigning

season, in too much haste and poorly supplied, Clauzel's little army of ten thousand men soon ran into difficulties. By the time they reached Constantine, the freezing cold had lowered the troops' morale and effectiveness, and torrential rain had made the roads impassable and forced the abandonment of much of the supplies and siege equipment. Without the latter, the chances of taking Constantine, sheltering behind strong walls and protected by a ravine on three sides, were drastically reduced. After the failure of a night attack on 23/24 November, withdrawal became inevitable. Despite the remarkable courage of officers and men, including Louis-Philippe's second son Nemours, this only just avoided turning into a rout; three thousand soldiers were either killed or died of disease afterwards. For all those with Napoleonic experience, the return from Constantine, in icy conditions and harassed at every step by the enemy's light cavalry and partisan bands, made comparisons with the retreat from Moscow inescapable. For Sébastiani, writing to Adélaïde from London, 'the most deplorable aspect of the affair' was the similarity of the telegraphic dispatch announcing the setback to the bulletin issued in 1812 by the defeated Napoleon at Smolensk![39]

Clearly, such a painful defeat could not go unavenged. In a wider context, however, Molé was determined to repudiate Clauzel's forward policy, and pull back the French presence to within defensible limits. Clauzel was recalled, and replaced as governor-general by the more methodical General Damrémont. At the beginning of October 1837 the second expedition to Constantine set out, with roughly the same number of troops as before but this time with adequate siege artillery. It was led by Damrémont, with Nemours, who had insisted on accompanying him, at the head of one of the brigades. Constantine was reached in six days, and after exhausting efforts in the mountainous terrain, the gun batteries were manhandled into place. The bombardment began on 11 October but the following day, while inspecting an advanced outpost, Damrémont, walking next to Nemours, was killed by an enemy cannonball. Nonetheless a breach was opened up in the city walls, and on the morning of the 13th, after a bitterly contested assault whose issue was several times in doubt, Constantine was taken.[40]

With a disaster effaced, the glorious death of the commander and a royal prince present at the moment of triumph, the capture of

Constantine was a propaganda as well as a military victory for the
July monarchy. It also stabilized the situation in Algeria, and made
possible a period of consolidation. It did not put an end to intermittent warfare – which was often savage, with atrocities committed on
both sides – but the French presence acquired a new permanence.

Elsewhere in the world, Molé proved himself an effective prac-
titioner of the gunboat diplomacy pioneered by his enemy Palmerston. In early 1838, he sent a naval squadron to Haiti, independent
from France since 1825, to enforce payment of long-promised, but
never delivered, compensation to expropriated French colonists. A
blockade of Buenos Aires was also mounted to intimidate the
Argentinian dictator Juan Manuel de Rosas, who had menaced French
interests in the country. Most spectacularly, another squadron was
dispatched in October 1838 to Mexico, where again French subjects
had been threatened. The supposedly impregnable fort of San Juan
d'Ulloa was bombarded into submission and the port of Vera Cruz
taken by assault. The expedition also gave Louis-Philippe's third son,
the prince de Joinville, who commanded one of its ships, the chance
to prove his courage and increase his popularity.[41]

Nearer home, after seven years of stalemate the Belgian question
was finally resolved. Having obstinately refused to recognize the
independence of Belgium, in March 1838 William I of Holland
unexpectedly decided to do so. Having waited this long, however,
the Belgians now felt they were entitled to some territorial and
financial revisions in their favour. They were alone in this view, and
had France taken their side she would have found herself isolated in
the face of all the major Powers, including Britain. Through astute
personal diplomacy, including considerable pressure exerted on his
son-in-law Leopold of the Belgians, Louis-Philippe in collaboration
with Molé was able to broker a compromise. Belgium's territorial
demands were rejected, but the payments she was required to make
on the state debt from the days of her union with Holland were
halved. On this basis the Treaty of London, giving Belgium international recognition as an independent and neutral state, was signed
on 19 April 1839.[42]

Almost exactly a year earlier, on 17 May 1838, Talleyrand, who
had done so much to found not only Belgium but also the July
monarchy, had died aged eighty-four at his Paris house on the Rue

St Florentin. A week earlier he had been taken ill at dinner, and found to have a tumour in one of his thighs and an infection at the base of his spine. His heart was also failing, and it was clear that he had not long to live. One of the great deathbed scenes of the nineteenth century then ensued. The duchesse de Dino, Talleyrand's niece and mistress, was determined that he should be reconciled with the church, as was her daughter Pauline, who may well have been his daughter also. In Catholic eyes, Talleyrand had much to atone for: bishop of Autun until 1791, during the Revolution he had proposed the decree nationalizing church lands, accepted the Civil Constitution of the Clergy that the Pope had rejected, and later married. Yet the old man had no intention of signing anything that would compromise his dignity or negate his life's actions. Eventually, after negotiations worthy of the Congress of Vienna, he and the priest attending him found a mutually acceptable form of words.[43]

With consummate diplomatic timing, Talleyrand put off signing the statement until the actual morning of his death. He did so at 6 a.m. on 17 May, in a bedroom packed with family and friends, before four official witnesses including Molé. At 8.30, in a remarkable departure from etiquette, Louis-Philippe and Adélaïde arrived to say goodbye. Talleyrand retained enough presence of mind to give the necessary instructions for receiving the king, and formally to thank Louis-Philippe for the honour he was doing the house of Talleyrand-Périgord. After Louis-Philippe left, Adélaïde, who had already paid a visit the previous day, stayed on. As she got up to leave, Talleyrand took her hand and murmured: 'Je vous aime bien.' At 3.30 p.m., having made his confession and received extreme unction, he died.[44]

*

IN DOMESTIC POLICY, Molé's unexpected boldness continued well beyond the summer of 1837. The following autumn, he decided to capitalize on the success of the amnesty and the marriage of the duc d'Orléans, and asked the king to call a general election. Louis-Philippe thought the course risky, but agreed, and the Chamber was dissolved on 3 October. Yet the results did not give Molé the convincing majority for which he had hoped. His own support remained unchanged at 163 deputies; the *doctrinaires* lost about twenty seats, but the main beneficiary was not the ministry but the centre-left led by Thiers. It is puzzling why Molé's generally impressive record did not translate into electoral success. He had difficulty putting across his central message – the need for conciliation as well as resistance – clearly and simply during the campaign. Perhaps it was too sophisticated for the rough-and-tumble of the hustings. It is also probable that Molé, the former servant of Napoleon who once described himself simply as 'an old servant of his country', was ill at ease in the new age of party politics.[45]

Without a stable majority, all the government's legislation had to be fought for. Despite this, some significant laws were passed providing for more humane treatment of the insane, regulating bankruptcy and enlarging the jurisdiction of justices of the peace. An ambitious plan to lay the foundations of a French railway system, however, was rejected. On a wider level, in 1838, for the first time during the July monarchy, the budget was not only balanced but went into surplus to the tune of 80 million francs. Parliamentary politics may have remained a battleground, but France as a whole was enjoying peace and prosperity.[46]

Coordinated opposition to the ministry began to emerge in the Chamber in the winter of 1837. Its prime mover was Thiers, bolstered by his grouping's gains in the recent elections yet frustrated of what he saw as his rightful place in office. He was also angry that Molé's 'ministry of lackeys', as he termed it, had managed to survive for so long without basing itself on the major parties – and party leaders – in the Chamber, and was concerned that this might mark a precedent for the future. In the debate on the king's speech in December 1837, he launched a strong attack on the government, but was heavily defeated in the subsequent vote. Undaunted, Thiers then made overtures to the younger, more impetuous *doctrinaires*, proposing that they combine with the centre-left to defeat the ministry in the forthcoming vote on secret service funding, and managed to convince them. Guizot, however, was much more hesitant, and when he did finally intervene on Thiers' side on the second day of the debate, 14 March 1838, for the first time in his parliamentary career his speech fell flat. The secret service funds were voted to the government by a convincing majority, and Molé's adversaries retired to lick their wounds for the rest of the session.[47]

Throughout the summer recess, Thiers and Guizot pondered their next moves. For Guizot in particular, this was the moment of decision. He was uncomfortably aware that for a leader of the right to turn on a prime minister with whom he had recently served, in partnership with the left, and particularly with Thiers of whose bellicose foreign policy views he strongly disapproved, smacked of the rankest opportunism. He decided the risk was worth taking, but that he would have to commit himself totally to the attack or not at all. In his view, the alliance against Molé would have to be made as broad as possible, without regard to political differences, and postponing the question of what would succeed the existing ministry until after it was overthrown. At some point in the winter of 1838, he paid an unannounced visit to Odilon Barrot, leader of the most left-wing elements in the loyal 'dynastic' opposition, and told him bluntly: 'You're surprised to see me; I've come to join you in fighting this personal government [of Louis-Philippe]; it's time to finish with these minister-favourites.'[48]

To tone down the appearance of naked self-interest, the Coalition, as it was soon dubbed, needed a principle to champion. It found it in Thiers' old rallying-cry: 'The king should reign but not govern.' Throughout their campaign, Guizot, Thiers and Barrot all charged that Molé was simply a mouthpiece for Louis-Philippe, through whom the royal power was being dangerously extended to control foreign policy, the army, and the Chamber by the use of patronage and placemen. To counter this, they argued, ministries should be cohesive, based on a strong united party in the Chamber, and headed by an effective and independent prime minister. As Thiers had maintained to Louis-Philippe's face during his own tenure of office, the king should be relegated to the position of neutral arbiter.

Much of this reasoning was logical and natural, a sign of the evolution of Louis-Philippe's regime from a 'limited' to a fully parliamentary monarchy. However, the leaders of the Coalition wildly exaggerated their case. Wrapping themselves in the colours of the July revolution, they accused Louis-Philippe of trying to do by stealth what Charles X had by force, and subverting the Chamber by corruption and 'personal government'. This was a travesty of the truth. The central difference between Louis-Philippe and Charles was that the former never attempted to sustain in office a government that had clearly lost the confidence of the Chamber, and certainly never contemplated using emergency measures to do so. For him, that was the essential lesson of 1830, and the key to his understanding of his constitutional role.[49] Even the king's opponents, in their more honest moments, admitted that, eight years on, the struggle of 1830 between Crown and Chambers had been resolved. As Guizot, in an unguarded moment, wrote in the *Revue Française*:

> In theory, the quarrel [between Crown and Chambers] goes on, as both advance their opposing pretensions. In fact, beneath the sound and fury, whether through wisdom or weakness, both powers wish to live in peace. The constitutional struggle is not serious.[50]

Even Thiers concurred, although he could not resist a back-handed comparison between the July monarchy and its restoration predecessor: 'I repeat, if one did not know there are limits beyond which the government of July would never go, there would be reason for alarm in seeing repeated, after only eight years, such serious faults which have been so cruelly punished.'[51]

By the time the new session of the Chambers opened on 17 December 1838, Louis-Philippe's spirits had been buoyed by another important and happy event. On 24 August the duchesse d'Orléans gave birth to a son, who was christened Louis-Philippe Albert, and created comte de Paris. Already a success in emotional terms, the duc d'Orléans' marriage had now produced that vital requirement, an heir. (Two years later, in November 1840, it provided a second, in the person of Robert, duc de Chartres.) The ministry may have been facing attack, but the dynasty had never seemed more secure.

The king's speech from the throne at the opening of the session was anodyne. It made some uncontroversial comments about foreign policy, thanked the Chamber for contributing to France's current prosperous state through its cooperation with the Crown, and expressed the wish that this would continue. The Coalition, however, had its grand attack planned. The means would be the Chamber's reply to Louis-Philippe's speech, the address, which was equivalent to a vote of confidence. If a hostile address was passed, the ministry would be doomed. On 22 December, the Coalition scored a first success when it gained a two-thirds majority on the commission elected to draft the address, including Guizot and Thiers. The text that emerged threw down the gauntlet both to Molé and to Louis-Philippe. Its assertion that the main powers in the state should keep within their constitutional limits was essentially an attack on the crown, and it also claimed that the present ministry did not enjoy the confidence of the deputies. It was read out in the Chamber to acclaim from one side, and fury from the other.

The Coalition made one major miscalculation. It thought that its numbers and audacity would intimidate Molé's supporters and encourage them to abandon him. In fact, the opposite effect was achieved. The ministerial party, outraged by the alliance of circumstance between Thiers, Guizot and Barrot, closed its ranks and acquired a cohesion it had never previously known. The fact that it contained few orators forced Molé to confront his adversaries in the Chamber virtually alone, but he was not deterred. The valetudinarian prime minister was galvanized by the attacks launched against him, and displayed remarkable energy. 'If I was not convinced that I am neither worthy nor important enough to be given a mission by Providence,' he wrote to a friend, 'I would see the hand of God in the health and strength He has sent me.'[52] Molé was also strongly buttressed by the constant help and encouragement of the king. Louis-Philippe saw him regularly and wrote to him daily assuring him of his confidence. On 19 December 1838, he commiserated with Molé on the opposition he faced, but continued:

> What consoles me is the determination which with so much satisfaction I see in you to fight to the death against this detestable coalition. If I were not so interested in your success, I would not be giving you, with all my heart, all the support and reinforcement that I can ... you would be doing me an injustice if you were not convinced that I have never had any other thought or wish than to keep you [as prime minister], and to sustain you with all my force and means.[53]

The debate on the address opened on 7 January. To survive, the ministry had to carry its own amendments to each hostile section of the text; if this proved impossible, it would fall. Its first opponent to show himself was Guizot, anxious to prove to his own followers that he had shaken off his previous hesitations. He launched into a vehement attack on the government, decked out with Latin quotations:

'Gentlemen, Tacitus says of courtiers that they act basely, the better to become masters, *omnia serviliter pro dominatione*.' Unfortunately for Guizot, he had got his Tacitus wrong. When he had finished, one of Molé's more erudite colleagues was seen whispering furiously in his ear, and the prime minister got to his feet. 'Gentlemen,' he began, 'Tacitus does not use the words just cited about courtiers, but about ambitious men.' He then gave a spirited defence of his ministry, and sat down to an ovation.[54]

Molé had put his finger on the Coalition's central weakness. Tellingly, when beginning their speeches Guizot, Thiers and their colleagues felt bound to preface their attacks on the government by denying precisely the charge levelled by the prime minister at them, that they were motivated solely by ambition. This blunted their effectiveness, and did not convince the Chamber. In addition, they were discomfited rather than bolstered by the support they received from the most extreme deputies of the right and left, both legitimists and republicans. In the first vote, on the beginning of the address, the ministry's amendment was carried by seven votes; a tiny majority, but a majority nonetheless.

By this time, five days into the debate, the atmosphere in the Chamber was tumultuous. The heat and violence of the parliamentary battle, observers agreed, were unprecedented. At one point, when Molé let slip in a speech that the struggle was exhausting him, Guizot shouted at him: 'Die, dog!' In his memoirs, Molé vividly evoked his opponent 'grinding his teeth, letting fall from his lips a wish for my death, and setting out to conquer power with all the enemies of the monarchy'.[55] Against this stormy setting, the ministry managed to pass its next three amendments, all on different aspects of foreign policy, with majorities ranging from four to twenty-nine. In an indication of the Chamber's dislike of the extent of royal power in this area, an amendment expressing general approval of the government's handling of diplomacy was rejected by nine votes. However, this was neutralized the next day by the defeat of an opposition amendment that condemned it.[56]

The final debate, on 19 January, concerned the most crucial passage of the address — its call for the royal authority to be circumscribed and its threat to withdraw support from the government until this had been accomplished. As the deputies were all

exhausted by now, the session was short, and the ministry won
by nine votes. The amended address as a whole was then carried by
thirteen votes. Ironically, 221 deputies supported the revised address,
exactly the same number as had passed the address of 1830 that had
led to the July revolution. Unlike their predecessors, though, the new
221 were defending the royal prerogative rather than attacking it.[57]

Louis-Philippe had followed each vote with minute attention and
growing delight. On 12 January he had told Molé: 'My dear count,
I'm delighted that your successes are still mounting in crescendo.'
Three days later, he was writing: 'My dear count! Another victory!
I congratulate you with all my heart.' The passage of the revised
address brought forth a string of superlatives:

> My dear count, I do not think that the parliamentary annals of
> any country can boast of such a struggle as that which you have
> sustained with so much honour and success, nor of any victory
> so complete and brilliant as your conversion of the draft address
> into its present form. All thanks be rendered to you. This is
> what I say from the bottom of my heart, while making the most
> ardent wishes that this triumph is followed by many others.[58]

Molé had won a remarkable personal victory, beating off the
most ferocious attacks that the Coalition's leading orators could
throw at him. Yet he was painfully aware that small majorities of the
sort he had received in the debate on the address would not allow
him to govern effectively. The boldest course was to dissolve the
Chamber and call fresh elections, in the hope that these would give
the ministry the mandate it desired. More than ever determined to
keep his prime minister, Louis-Philippe was happy to take this path.

The problem with this strategy was that Molé's supporters were
unwilling to risk their seats once more, barely fifteen months after
the last election. They would only be convinced of its necessity if
all other options were shown to have been tried and failed. Louis-
Philippe thus made a half-hearted attempt to form a new ministry
under Marshal Soult, but with broadly similar policies to Molé's.
Soult was equally unenthusiastic, and was probably relieved when an
abscess on one of his teeth forced him to take to his bed. He did,
however, take careful measures to demonstrate to Louis-Philippe that
he was not malingering. On 28 January he summoned the king's

valet, who had been sent to him with a message, into his bedroom so the man could report back how swollen his face was. The next morning, he repeated the exercise. As Louis-Philippe related to Molé: 'The Marshal had my valet brought into his bedroom, told him that the inflammation had almost reached his ear and was worse than yesterday, that there was no question of his being able to come and see me today, that he was quite distraught, et cetera.'[59]

The comedy served its purpose, and persuaded the ministerial deputies that there was now no option but to go to the country. On 2 February 1839, the Chamber was dissolved and a general election announced. The subsequent campaign was the most furiously contested of the entire reign. Throughout France, both sides organized and mobilized. Molé's camp set up a central committee in Paris, which directed its local branches through assiduous correspondence. True to its diverse origins, the Coalition needed three separate committees, representing the parties of Thiers, Guizot and Barrot, but they were kept together by regular meetings of the leaders. Both the government and the opposition press attacked their enemies ferociously. The former, especially the *Journal des Débats* and *La Presse*, pilloried the Coalition as hypocritical and opportunist. The latter, more numerous and including the *Courrier Français*, the *Constitutionnel* and *Le Temps*, mounted a sustained polemic against the court, which they saw as Molé's principal bulwark. As was widely and correctly assumed, their real target was the crown itself. In a dangerous development that recalled 1830, the king himself was being drawn into the political fray.[60]

If Louis-Philippe hoped fervently for Molé's victory, so too did Adélaïde. Although Molé had initially taken offence at her private correspondence with Sébastiani, a modus vivendi had been reached on this issue,[61] and Adélaïde had stayed a firm supporter of the prime minister. Her letters to Sébastiani, which form a running commentary on the political situation in 1838 and early 1839, regularly express hopes for Molé's political survival: 'I am ... confident that our ministry here will survive because I'm convinced that this will be the best and happiest outcome for our dear king and for our good and beautiful France ... I hope very much that things will stay as they are, and that we will keep the present ministry, which I am sure is the only possible one, and the best we could have.'[62] Predictably, she loathed Molé's enemies, particularly Guizot whom she found deeply hypocritical. On Christmas Eve 1838, just before the parliamentary battle over the address, she wrote:

> We are greatly agitated about what's going on in the Chamber, and indignant at the monstrous coalition, which in my view is the crowning shame for those who have formed it . . . in truth no honest soul could be other than revolted by such conduct and such infamous intrigues, and all for the sake of ambition, egoism and gaining <u>portfolios</u> with no thought that they might ruin everything; so this is the fine <u>Puritanism</u> of the *doctrinaires* who ally themselves to all factions, all parties, to achieve their ends; it's dreadfully disgusting and very sad.[63]

Adélaïde had good reason to dislike the Coalition, since she probably attained the peak of her power during Molé's ministry. While she never sat in the council of ministers, the king had no hesitation in transmitting her views and encouragement to it. In September 1838, while Adélaïde was at Randan, Louis-Philippe wrote to her: 'I have already told the ministers, and will tell them again, what you say to me in all your letters about the improvement in public opinion, and the approval that the ministry has gained.' If she actually had a correspondence with Molé, this has been either lost or destroyed, so in its absence one must assume that her main channel of communication with him was through her brother. She did, however, meet with the prime minister to coordinate policy when the king was elsewhere. In early March 1839, Louis-Philippe informed Molé that he was making an excursion to St Cloud. He wrote that there was no change in the political situation, but added: 'My sister, who is staying here so she can see you, will tell you where I stand.'[64]

In a further sign of Adélaïde's growing influence in 1838 and 1839, the press attacks on her reached their height. They were led by the legitimist journal *La Mode*, which in the spring of 1838 published a detailed denunciation of Adélaïde's hold on Molé's government. It was dramatically entitled 'The Hidden Power Visible to the Naked Eye':

> Open all the newspapers that have not sold themselves to the ministry; for some time they have written about nothing else but a hidden force, an elusive influence, a mysterious power that

hampers all government business and throws a multitude of unconstitutional spokes in the wheels of the machinery of the state.

Nobody dares call this secret power by its real name, and we know very well the reason why; because it is generally supposed to be where it never has been. But we ... know exactly where it lies, and see it not on the throne, but next to it ... let us give credit to Madame Adélaïde for the marvels of government that are currently astounding all our eyes. Yes, Madame Adélaïde, that is the name of the mysterious influence which holds sway above the head of M. Molé and which pulls the strings of the puppets Barthe [the minister of justice], Montalivet and company.

Read this week's court circular; Madame Adélaïde has not left the side of her august brother Louis-Philippe for an instant: she arrives with him at the Tuileries, she leaves with him. See the royal carriage driving down the Champs-Elysées; Madame Adélaïde always has papers in her hand, she is examining reports, consulting memoranda and taking notes with a pencil. Nothing is decided, nothing is done, without taking Madame Adélaïde's advice: she is the nymph Egeria of the Tuileries ... when the council of ministers assembles, Madame Adélaïde sits in an adjoining room with the door ajar, and does not miss a word of what is said ... Such is the power that hovers over the system of 15 April [the formation date of Molé's ministry] and which for some unknown reason is dubbed *secret*, since it seems quite visible to us.[65]

With shrewd irony, the article concluded by adapting Thiers' famous dictum on the royal authority: 'Madame Adélaïde does not reign, but she governs.'

La Mode may have exaggerated, but it was sharp and well informed, and as a royalist publication it had a better grasp of traditional high politics than the republican newspapers. It was the only major journal to analyse and criticize Adélaïde's political role in substantial articles. It did not, however, stop there. Scattered throughout its columns were regular hints that Adélaïde was having an affair with, or was secretly even married to, baron Atthalin, her brother's handsome aide-de-camp whom she had first met in 1814 on the voyage from Palermo to Marseille. As with most allegations of this sort, the story is impossible to disprove completely, but it remains very unlikely. There is no whiff of it in Adélaïde's surviving letters. These could conceivably have been weeded of compromising material, but there are no references to it, either, in the correspondence of those close to her. The memoirist best placed to know the truth, Mme de Boigne, flatly denies any liaison. It certainly seems inconceivable that Adélaïde could have been Atthalin's wife in any form, since from December 1836 the position was occupied by Thérèse Lelandais.[66]

One suspects that the real reason *La Mode* returned to the story so often was the scope it gave for cutting political puns on Adélaïde's putative married name. From 'Mme Atthalin' she was swiftly dubbed 'Athalie', the French name for the biblical villainess Athaliah. The epithet had a very special significance. It was the title of Racine's great tragedy, adapted from the Bible story, which was a staple of French drama and regularly performed throughout the early nineteenth century. In the play Athalie, having usurped the throne of Judah by destroying the house of David, overlooks its last surviving member, the young Joas, who eventually overthrows and kills her in turn. *La Mode* gleefully underlined the parallels between the house of David and the dethroned Bourbons, Athalie and Adélaïde, and Joas and the duc de Bordeaux. In 1838, it published an engraving of the crowning of Joas, with a commentary comparing Athalie's crimes with those of the Orléans family. The government reacted with ferocity. *La Mode* was condemned under the September laws to a huge fine of 20,000 francs and its editor to a year in prison – proof of the political charge contained in these cultural references.[67]

Where *La Mode* led, many other newspapers followed. If 'Athalie' remained Adélaïde's most common nickname, it was supplemented by several others, all reflecting unfavourably on her alleged sexual debauchery, lust for power and physical appearance – Mme Messalina, La Camarilla and, most cruelly, Mme Laide (Mrs Ugly).[68] Since Adélaïde's rough skin and reddish complexion, in fact an inheritance from her father, was assumed to be the product of a fondness for drink, she was regularly pilloried as an alcoholic. In May 1833, the author of a slanderous pamphlet about Adélaïde's private life was brought to trial, in closed session to protect her honour. As a result, it is unclear what the allegations against her were.[69]

All these themes were taken up in cartoons as well as in words. Before the September laws imposed preliminary censorship on them, Adélaïde was a regular target of caricaturists. In several, she was portrayed as an alcoholic, swigging from a bottle or clutching it to her bosom. In others, she was shown surrounded by a brood of illegitimate children, including, in a broad hint at incest, some with Louis-Philippe's features. Another of the children was depicted as black, in a cruel example of one of Adélaïde's acts of charity being turned against her.[70] During the 1820s she had adopted a young Turkish boy, the son of the Pasha of Athens, whose parents had been massacred during the Greek revolt against the Ottoman Empire. Christened Gottlieb Saly by the German officer who had originally rescued him, the boy was brought up with Louis-Philippe's family, went into the French navy and ended as captain of a frigate. In her will, Adélaïde left him an annuity of 3,000 francs.[71] For the opposition press, however, he was simply one of her bastards.

The most remarkable cartoon of Adélaïde, although circulated in France, was published in Brussels in 1833. While the others only indirectly stressed her political importance by showing her always at Louis-Philippe's side, this one portrayed her literally as the power behind the throne. The seated king is represented addressing a crowd of deputies while Adélaïde, crouching behind, manipulates him by a system of hidden pulleys. Out of the side of his mouth Louis-Philippe whispers to her: 'Don't pull the wrong string, Madame!'[72] The image is striking, and further evidence that, to the better-informed newspapers and caricaturists, Adélaïde's extensive role in policy-making was an open secret.

The press onslaught on Adélaïde was brutal, but she lived in an age in which journalists and cartoonists did not spare their victims. To what extent these attacks were inspired by the fact that she was a woman is an important and complicated issue. Gender history is a relatively new field, but an important and still rapidly developing one, and has yielded a variety of interpretations of the role of women in past society. A standard view of the attacks on Adélaïde would see them as fuelled by a perception that she had transgressed the limits of the domestic 'private sphere' reserved for women into the 'public sphere' of politics, an exclusively male preserve. For her detractors, it was natural that this perversion of the traditions of her sex should be mirrored in a debauched private life – hence their insistence on her alcoholism, incest and illicit progeny.[73]

There is undoubtedly some truth in this analysis. However, as the pioneering collections of essays edited by Clarissa Campbell Orr, *Queenship in Britain, 1660–1837* and *Queenship in Europe, 1660–1815* argue, in reality the dividing line, at least for well-born women, between the 'public' and 'private' spheres was more porous than has up until now been supposed. Charitable works and patronage of the arts are two obvious examples. At court, women actually held salaried public office, especially as ladies-in-waiting. As such, they formed part of, and sometimes helped to influence, the political world. At the highest level, a queen consort had an important say in public appointments, often extending beyond her household or the court. In countries where a reigning queen was permitted, of course, she had all the normal powers of a head of state.[74]

Problems arose, however, when a woman who was not actually a reigning queen became heavily involved in policy-making. This clearly was the case with Adélaïde. Trespassing on this masculine domain, particularly in the open and direct way she did, exposed her to a line of attack summed up with withering sarcasm by *La Mode*: 'As for us, who know that Mme Adélaïde is one of the most enlightened women of her century, second to no statesman in the science of government, we regret only that our laws and usages do not permit the King of the French to appoint her prime minister.' The contrast with Marie-Amélie, who kept well out of politics and was rarely lampooned either in cartoons or in print, is striking.[75]

Adélaïde was pilloried partly, but not solely, because she was a woman. The opposition press preyed on her because, regardless of her sex, they disliked her political views. Sometimes, they attacked them openly. At others, they used a method that, then as now, has always proved effective in discrediting a foe – sexual slander. It is significant that the most sustained assault on Adélaïde came from the legitimist *La Mode*, which clearly knew of her profound hatred for the elder Bourbons, as well as her specific role in July 1830. For the republican press, which did not have this particular political reason to detest her, she was generally far less of a target.

Comparison between Adélaïde and her near-contemporary, Marie Antoinette, reveals a similar picture. As a particularly high-profile and powerful queen, Marie Antoinette became the object of an exceptionally violent campaign of pornographic pamphlets and cartoons, accusing her of rampant sexual promiscuity, especially incest and lesbianism. The most common conclusion is that she was vilified because the increasing influence she acquired went well beyond traditional gender boundaries.[76] Yet as Vivian Gruder has recently and convincingly argued, the scurrilous attacks on Marie Antoinette became a flood only after 1789, when she took up an unpopular political position against the Revolution. In the struggle that ensued, the queen's opponents turned on her with every weapon they could, including the stock repertory of sexual smears. As Gruder comments, pornography was merely 'a handmaiden to politics, following in its path, an instrument in a preceding and larger political combat'. Adélaïde was attacked in the same way, less because she was a woman per se, than because her political choices made her enemies.[77]

It is unclear what impact the press denigration of Adélaïde had on the general election itself. The broader onslaught on royal power of which it formed a part, however, did achieve success. The polls opened on 2 March 1839, and over the next few days it became clear that the ministry had been narrowly, but decisively, defeated. Its supporters in the Chamber had been reduced from the iconic number of 221 to between 190 and 200, while the combined opposition could muster roughly 240 deputies. Despite its political incoherence, the sheer breadth of the Coalition had given it victory. On 8 March, Molé handed his resignation to Louis-Philippe.[78]

As could have been predicted, the Coalition now began to break apart. Within eight days, unsurprisingly, Thiers, Guizot and Barrot found that they disagreed too much to form a government together, and ushered in the longest ministerial crisis of the July monarchy. Louis-Philippe's enemies accused him of prolonging this so as to increase his own power, but the charge is unfair. In a clear demonstration of his credentials as a constitutional monarch, the king accepted the verdict of the electorate, let go of Molé, and did his best to form a ministry drawn from the Coalition, unpalatable though he found this. Once this attempt failed, he turned to Soult, who was acceptable to all parties, to act as his go-between in constructing a replacement government.

Having recently recovered from his abscess, the marshal soon suffered an equally unpleasant experience. By 21 March, he thought he had been successful in organizing a ministry based on Thiers and the centre-left, with himself as prime minister. But just as the ordinances inaugurating this were about to be signed in the king's presence, Thiers demanded that the section of the new government's programme dealing with policy towards Spain be altered to make it tantamount to intervention. Why he did this remains unclear. He may have felt at the last minute that the ministry was unviable in the long run, or he may have wished publicly to avenge himself on Louis-Philippe for his dismissal over the Spanish question three years earlier. Either way, Thiers infuriated his colleagues and damaged his reputation; Soult burst out that from now on 'there is an abyss between me and that little man'.[79]

With the prospect of the new session of the Chambers, scheduled for 4 April, opening with no government in place, Louis-Philippe was forced to an unprecedented expedient. He appointed a caretaker ministry, composed of politicians and public servants with no firm party affiliations, until a more permanent one could be found. By now, the political uncertainty was having dangerous repercussions. A financial downturn, apparent since the beginning of the year, worsened, unemployment rose, and there was rioting on the day the Chambers opened. As April gave way to May, there was no sign of an end to the crisis.

The impasse was broken by a threat from the streets. On 12 May a group of roughly six hundred republicans led by Armand Barbès, a veteran of the Society of the Rights of Man, and the professional revolutionary Auguste Blanqui, attempted a coup d'état in the capital. They mowed down a detachment of soldiers outside the Palais de Justice, read a proclamation at the Hôtel de Ville, and tried to raise the workers of the central quarters of St Denis and St Martin. By the end of the day, however, they had been dispersed by troops, Barbès had been captured and Blanqui had fled. Twenty-eight soldiers and between fifteen and forty insurgents were killed.[80]

The insurrection of 12 May never seriously menaced the regime.

Like the assassination attempts on Louis-Philippe, what it did do was shock its supporters into closing ranks and suspending their in-fighting. The king was quick to exploit this. 'Marshal, I think this is the moment to go fishing,' he remarked to Soult. 'In troubled waters,' replied the Marshal.[81] Just hours after the rising had been defeated, a new, broadly centrist, ministry was formed, with Soult as prime minister and foreign minister. Barbès and Blanqui had proved more effective cabinet-makers than any of the politicians.

The Soult ministry survived for several months, but since it contained none of the leading figures in the Chamber, its situation was always weak. It won a large majority in the debate on the address at the opening of the 1840 session, but immediately afterwards ran into difficulties. Guizot, wishing to rebuild his position after the discredit the Coalition had brought on it, decided to retire temporarily from the Chamber, but not from politics. His eye fell on the London embassy. The ministry had two reasons for granting him the post. First, it would remove a potential parliamentary rival, and second, several of the ministers were friends and former colleagues of Guizot's and felt obliged to him.[82] Both in private and at meetings of the council, they began to exert pressure for Sébastiani's recall.

For Louis-Philippe and Adélaïde, this was an especially bitter pill to swallow. They had already been forced to part with Molé; now it was the turn of Sébastiani, who was not only a trusted ally but a personal friend. As perhaps intended, it was a particular blow to Adélaïde. The recall of Sébastiani and his replacement by Guizot, whom she detested, would block one of the principal sources of her power, her private correspondence with France's ambassador to England. Since she wrote in her brother's name, it would also weaken Louis-Philippe's hold on foreign policy in general. All these implications were clear to the distressed and furious Adélaïde. As she put it to Sébastiani in January 1840:

I feel more than ever, my dear good general, how much I am your friend, because I am suffering for you, for our dear king, for our poor country and its service, and am filled with profound indignation at these abominable intrigues and manoeuvres which are directed above all against our poor dear king and the royal power; they want to strip him and deprive him of all his true friends, he has said this himself to the whole council, and that they are forcing his hand, by compelling him to choose between an <u>immediate</u> dissolution of the ministry (for that is what has been said in the most formal and positive manner) and your recall.[83]

Louis-Philippe resisted as long as he could, but knew he could not risk losing the ministry and returning to the crisis of the previous months. He did, however, extract the promise that Sébastiani would be rewarded with a marshal's baton.[84] Mortified but bowing to the inevitable, Sébastiani prepared to leave London, and Guizot's nomination was announced on 5 February.

The ministry survived its victim by less than a month. On 20 February, the Chamber debated a government bill granting an annual income of 500,000 francs to the duc de Nemours on his forthcoming marriage. The bride was Victoria of Saxe-Coburg, whose uncle Leopold had already married Nemours' sister Louise. Nemours had suffered at the hands of the deputies in 1837, when the first project to provide him with a suitable establishment had had to be withdrawn, but this time his chances were felt to be better. However, a press campaign was mounted against the bill, and this gave the ministry's enemies, especially Thiers, an opportunity to overthrow it. By six votes, they threw out the bill, and Soult and his colleagues resigned. Having proved his importance by making government impossible for the past year, Thiers was now the inevitable choice for prime minister. On 1 March 1840, he took office at the head of a centre-left ministry.[85]

The upheavals of 1838 to 1840 were decisive for the July monarchy. The Molé ministry, which for two years had managed to combine royal approval with majorities in the Chamber, had been toppled by a parliamentary coalition that saw it as too subservient to Louis-Philippe. In fact, the real beneficiary of Molé's fall was not Thiers but his coalition partner Guizot. Thiers' ministry of March 1840 swiftly collapsed, whereas Guizot succeeded him and stayed in power for seven years. Yet the triumph of Guizot, which outwardly brought political stability at last, ultimately proved fatal to the regime. As leading minister, Guizot consistently refused all compromise with the opposition inside and outside the Chamber, and ended by dangerously isolating the Crown from the rest of the country. Ironically Molé, vilified as a man of the old order and a lackey of the king, proved in office significantly more pragmatic and flexible than his *doctrinaire* rival. He would be called on once more, but by then it was too late.

Chapter Ten

RECOURSE TO GUIZOT

THIERS' SECOND MINISTRY lasted only seven months. From the start, it embodied the paradoxes of the Coalition that had given birth to it. Its members, and most of its parliamentary supporters, were a strange hybrid of *doctrinaires* and the centre-left. As a result, its position was hesitant and contradictory. Ironically, its first instinct was to follow the path set out by Molé, announcing a 'policy of transaction' that exactly echoed Molé's of national reconciliation. To this end, to celebrate the duc de Nemours' marriage in April 1840 Molé's amnesty was extended, but this did not have the same success as in 1837. A few conservative prefects were also removed and replaced by more moderate ones. But when the first significant proposal for parliamentary reform, a very moderate bill forbidding deputies from holding public office, was tabled at the end of March 1840, Thiers first postponed it and then ensured it was buried in committee. He could hardly do otherwise, with his *doctrinaire* colleagues fulminating against any concessions to the left, and his rival Guizot stiffening their resistance from London.[1]

Partly to distract attention from the government's domestic weakness, but also as a genuine homage to France's recent glories, Thiers conjured up a grand symbolic gesture. Guizot was ordered to ask Palmerston for British permission for Napoleon's remains to be transported from St Helena back to France. Palmerston could hardly refuse, but found the whole idea slightly comic. 'This is a thoroughly French request,' he wrote wryly.[2] On 12 May the 'return of the ashes', as the project was dubbed, was announced in the Chamber. It was greeted with all the enthusiasm Thiers had hoped for. In the country at large, however, the effect was more disturbing, and nostalgia for the emperor reached alarming proportions. This gave the Bonapartist and radical press an opportunity to exalt the Napoleonic legend to the detriment of the petty political intrigues of the July monarchy. But there was no going back, and on 7 July Louis-Philippe's third son Joinville, protesting that he was being used as 'an undertaker's mute', was dispatched to bring back Napoleon's body from the South Atlantic.[3]

One unwelcome result of this wave of sentimental Bonapartism was to encourage Prince Louis-Napoleon to attempt another coup d'état. Having stayed only briefly in America, the emperor's nephew was now living in London, and judged the moment ripe for a second expedition to France. This time his destination was Boulogne, where he had contacts with the 42nd regiment of the line which he was convinced would rally to his cause. Revealing the extent of the false hopes raised by the 'return of the ashes', he planned to name Thiers his prime minister if he succeeded.

Louis-Napoleon's invasion began on 3 August 1840, and like the first at Strasbourg, quickly turned into farce. It involved fifty-six people, packed on to a London pleasure-steamer inappropriately named the *Edinburgh Castle*. They were accompanied by a small eagle (some sources say a vulture) picked up on the way at a Thames-side bird-fancier's, to be released at the landing on French soil as a symbol of the emperor's return. After a stormy voyage, the *Edinburgh Castle* landed off Boulogne early in the morning of 6 August. The conspirators marched into the town and tried to rally the 42nd regiment to their cause, but were rebuffed and forced to retreat. They fled back to the beach and began to row to their ship in a lifeboat, but were fired on by the local National Guard and quickly surrendered. The eagle was impounded by the customs authorities.[4]

After this second attempt to overthrow the regime, it was impossible to avoid trying Louis-Napoleon. This task was entrusted to the Chamber of Peers, which on 6 October that year sentenced him to life imprisonment. He was immediately transported to the fortress of Ham, where Charles X's ministers had been detained. To the government's relief, there had been little opposition agitation; even newspapers normally sympathetic to Bonapartism had condemned Louis-Napoleon's enterprise. In fact, the proceedings of the Chamber of Peers had been eclipsed by another trial, far away at Tulle in the Massif Central, that of the beautiful Mme Lafarge, a lady of the upper bourgeoisie accused of poisoning her husband. By a bizarre coincidence, Mme Lafarge was the granddaughter of Hermine Crompton, the English girl who, along with Pamela Syms, had been Louis-Philippe's and Adélaïde's childhood companion. She was found guilty with extenuating circumstances, and given a life sentence. Unlike Louis-Napoleon, she served the full term.[5]

By the time Napoleon's remains returned to France, his nephew had been ensconced at Ham for over a month and Thiers had been out of power for two. Joinville's frigate docked at Cherbourg on 30 November. The emperor's coffin was transported up the Seine on a black-painted barge, while crowds of peasants on both banks sank to their knees in homage. At Courbevoie it was lifted on to a huge funeral car draped in purple velvet and captured enemy battle-flags. On the morning of 15 December it trundled down the Champs-Elysées to its destination, the Invalides military hospital, where the king, the royal family, the peers and deputies were waiting. Despite the freezing cold, roughly half a million Parisians turned out to watch the procession. The government had feared that such a huge crowd could lead to political disturbances, even a Bonapartist uprising, but in the event it was almost wholly peaceful – a further sign of the growing political stability.

When the coffin was brought into the Invalides, Joinville, who commanded the escort, announced to his father: 'Sire, I present to you the body of the Emperor Napoleon.' – 'I receive it in the name of France,' replied Louis-Philippe. Beside him Marshal Soult was weeping, but his own feelings must have been closer to satisfaction. For sixteen years he had been a proscribed refugee, while Napoleon had been ruler of France. Yet it was Napoleon who had died in exile, and now he himself, as King of the French, was burying his rival.[6]

If Thiers' domestic policy produced few concrete results, his foreign policy proved disastrous. It centred on the Eastern question raised by the decline of the Ottoman empire and its implications for the equilibrium of Europe. Admittedly, Thiers inherited two incompatible sets of priorities from his predecessors, but he proceeded to make the situation very much worse. On the one hand, France had historically close ties with Turkey and was determined to protect her from the expansionism of her most powerful neighbour, Russia. On the other, for almost a century France had dreamed of controlling Egypt, which although virtually independent was still technically under Ottoman suzerainty.[7] Since 1805 the Pasha of Egypt had been the formidable ex-soldier of fortune Mehmet Ali, who had considerably expanded its economy and territory. He had also equipped it with a westernized army, trained largely on French principles by French instructors. In 1831 he had rebelled against the sultan with the aim of adding Syria to his dominions, and although the revolt had ended in a compromise it was clear that this would not last.[8]

The response of most French politicians to this problem was fundamentally contradictory: to keep Mehmet Ali as a client while at the same time upholding the integrity of the Ottoman empire. Interestingly, the only major exception was Molé, who saw Mehmet Ali's rising star as more of a danger than an opportunity. When the Pasha increased the stakes in 1838 by announcing his intention to become the hereditary ruler of an independent Egypt and Syria, Molé anticipated even Palmerston in threatening to use force if he did so.[9] However, these warnings delayed for only a year the outbreak of renewed war between the Egyptians and the Turks, with disastrous results for the latter. In June 1839 the sultan's army was routed at Nezib, and a few weeks later his navy deserted to the enemy. There was nothing now between Mehmet Ali and Constantinople.

Coming to power in the wake of these Egyptian victories, all Thiers' inclinations were to support Mehmet Ali. In this, he did no more than reflect prevailing opinion, but he added to it a dangerous edge of bellicosity and brinkmanship. The battle of Nezib convinced him that Mehmet Ali was invincible, and that his claims could safely be backed to the hilt. Beyond this, he saw the alluring prospect of a grateful Pasha substantially reinforcing France's great power status by according her the dominant influence in the eastern Mediterranean. He failed to realize that this was an outcome the other Powers, especially Britain, would not stomach. To avoid this, even Russia was prepared to pose as the defender of the Ottoman empire. This course of action offered Russia one further crucial benefit: it put her on the same side as Britain, and excellently placed to break up the latter's understanding with France.[10]

It was particularly unfortunate that at this moment of crisis, Louis-Philippe's well-established system for managing France's pivotal relationship with Britain was no longer functioning. Through Adélaïde's correspondence with Talleyrand, and then with Sébastiani, he had kept daily watch on it, and had ensured that it had survived intact for a decade. Now, just as it faced a dangerous new threat, his trusted ambassador Sébastiani had been forced to quit his post, the vital stream of letters and instructions channelled through Adélaïde had come to an end, and Sébastiani had been replaced by Guizot, a powerful politician but a complete novice in diplomacy. Since Adélaïde hated Guizot, there was no prospect of her correspondence with the London embassy being continued. Finally, Thiers as prime minister never enjoyed the full confidence of Louis-Philippe, and as the diplomatic situation worsened, Guizot too lost faith in him.[11] In many ways, the Eastern crisis was one further consequence of the Coalition; one cannot imagine Louis-Philippe, Adélaïde, Molé and Sébastiani making the mistakes that Thiers and Guizot did.

Secure in his illusions about the strength of his position, Thiers rejected a final compromise proposal, tabled by Austria and Prussia, that Mehmet Ali be granted control of south Syria and Palestine for life in addition to hereditary possession of Egypt. In London, Guizot failed to grasp how swiftly the other Powers were drawing together to counter Mehmet Ali and isolate France. On 15 July 1840, Palmerston and the ambassadors of Russia, Prussia and Austria signed a treaty committing their countries to defend the Ottoman empire and issuing an ultimatum to Mehmet Ali. Egypt was conceded to the Pasha on a hereditary basis, as well as the Pashalik of Acre for life, if he agreed to these terms within ten days. If he did not, the offer of Acre would be withdrawn; if he delayed for a further ten days, he would lose the hereditary title to Egypt as well. France was not made a party to the agreement, which was simply read to a horrified Guizot by Palmerston at the Foreign Office two days later.[12]

This public humiliation, and the coercion of her client, infuriated French public opinion. Louis-Philippe was no exception; when the news of the treaty was brought to him, he began shouting so loudly that Marie-Amélie had to shut the door of his study so that the sound could not be heard in the gallery outside. In his view, the Powers had pushed France into a corner from which war was the only exit – a poor recompense for all the efforts he had made to preserve peace since 1830. 'This time,' he bellowed at the Austrian and Prussian ambassadors, 'don't think that I will distance myself from my ministry and my country; you want war, and you shall have it, and, if necessary, I shall unmuzzle the tiger.'[13]

This display of anger, however, was not entirely sincere. Up until the treaty of 15 July, Louis-Philippe had shared Thiers' confidence that Mehmet Ali was unstoppable, and that his territorial demands could safely be backed. Unlike his prime minister, however, he was determined not to let these drag France into a general European war. Once the Powers had made it clear that this would be the result if the French government encouraged Egypt to defy their ultimatum, the king began privately preparing a diplomatic retreat, and he had no compunction about sacrificing Thiers to this end if necessary. As he put it in late July to the comte de Ste Aulaire, his ambassador to Austria who was currently on leave in Paris: 'I shan't let myself be carried along too far by my little minister. At bottom, he wants a war, and I don't want one; and if he leaves me no option, I'll break him rather than confront the whole of Europe.'[14]

This was easier said than done. In defying the Powers, Thiers had patriotic opinion on his side, infuriated at the humiliation of the treaty of 15 July. If Louis-Philippe sacked him at this point, he risked once again being attacked as a partisan of peace at any price, which in the heated atmosphere could have dangerous consequences. For the moment, the king had to retain Thiers, while covering himself by rattling his sabre even more menacingly than his prime minister. As he later explained to Pasquier: 'If, straight after the treaty, I had declared for peace, M. Thiers would have resigned, and I would today be the most unpopular of men. Instead of that, I shouted even louder than him, and left him to cope with all the difficulties.'[15] After 15 July, it was no longer a question of whether Thiers would go, but when. All now depended on the timing.

In August and September 1840, France's house of cards in the Middle East swiftly collapsed. On 16 August Mehmet Ali backed down and accepted the Powers' ultimatum, calculating that this would at least leave him as hereditary ruler of Egypt. The sultan, however, emboldened by the international support he was receiving, proclaimed his deposition anyway. To add insult to injury, on 11 September a British naval squadron bombarded Beirut, which Mehmet Ali's forces had occupied. When the news of this reached Paris on 2 October, the capital was gripped by war fever. Army recruitment offices were swamped by volunteers, and the 'Marseillaise' was played before all theatre performances.

With so many enemies arrayed against her, it was unclear which one France should concentrate her efforts on. Following in his hero Napoleon's footsteps, Thiers favoured attacking Austria in Italy. The press, however, almost unanimous in demanding war, championed an offensive against the German states with the aim of reconquering the Rhine frontier for France. What it failed to predict was the wave of patriotic fury this provoked among the Germans themselves; all sections of society united in a common Francophobia, and emergency military planning was begun. It is no coincidence that this forgotten confrontation gave birth to the two great hymns of German nationalism, 'Die Wacht am Rhein' and 'Deutschland über Alles'.[16]

In the autumn of 1840, a general European war, which France was bound to lose, was very close. But Louis-Philippe needed Thiers for just a little longer. After several weeks of wrangling over the terms of France's response to the Powers' actions, king and prime minister finally agreed on a compromise Note, dated 8 October and delivered to Britain, Russia, Austria and Prussia. This accepted that Mehmet Ali would lose Syria, but stated that France would oppose his deposition in Egypt by force. In London, Palmerston smoothly assured Guizot that Britain and the other Powers had no intention of carrying out the threat of deposition, and this effectively ended the Eastern crisis.[17]

Despite the easing of the tension, Thiers continued with a military build-up. He planned to call up 150,000 conscripts of the class of 1841 straight away, and to use the National Guard as a front-line force. This was strikingly similar to his actions in 1836, when despite agreeing with Louis-Philippe to postpone intervention in Spain, behind his back he had increased the troops on the border. It is difficult to know whether Thiers was still genuinely planning for war, or simply seeking to create a patriotic issue on which to resign.[18]

Whatever they were, Thiers' calculations were disrupted by a bolt from the blue. At 6 p.m. on 15 October Louis-Philippe was passing in his carriage along the Quai des Tuileries, when there was a loud explosion followed by a thick cloud of smoke. He had been fired on by an unemployed forty-three-year-old domestic servant called Marius Darmès, but his assailant had overcharged his carbine and it had blown up in his hands and wounded him. Like the king's other would-be assassins, Darmès was both a fanatic and a misfit; he lived in a tiny, squalid room in the Faubourg St Denis, having been evicted from his previous lodgings for exposing himself to his female neighbours. He had clearly been driven to attempt regicide by the patriotic fervour engendered by the Eastern crisis. If he had succeeded, he told his interrogators, France 'would have broken the treaty of 15 July . . . and given liberty to all people'. Tried by the Chamber of Peers and condemned to death, Darmès was guillotined on 31 May 1841.[19]

Darmès' act may have endangered Louis-Philippe's life, but it considerably strengthened his political position. By his own admissions, Darmès had linked his action to the febrile public mood created by Thiers' foreign policy, and no more damaging connection could be imagined. Louis-Philippe now had sufficient public backing to rid himself of his prime minister. The new session of the Chambers was due to open on 28 October, and on the 20th the speech from the throne drafted by the ministry was submitted to him. He found the language it used over the Eastern crisis too bellicose, took from his pocket a far more conciliatory version that he himself had written, and read it aloud to the assembled ministers. This time no compromise was possible; Louis-Philippe was determined to remove Thiers, and Thiers was probably equally keen to go. After a brief discussion, the ministers offered their resignations, and the king, with effusive expressions of regret, accepted them.[20]

Louis-Philippe wasted no time over his next moves. He called Marshal Soult to the Tuileries, and sent for Guizot from London. Within a very short time, by 29 October, the new government was in place. Soult became prime minister, but the real power was held by Guizot as foreign minister. Grouped around them was a homogenous cabinet of the centre-right, with two of Guizot's key allies, Duchâtel and Humann, at the interior and finance respectively. Guizot saw the new ministry as a continuation of the broadly based conservative administration of 11 October 1832 and its successors.[21] Yet it was to last far longer than these — until the last days of the reign.

*

THE KING ACCEPTED Guizot's entry into office as inevitable, but initially viewed his new foreign minister with suspicion. He had worked with Guizot in several governments since 1830, but had never established cordial relations with him. Guizot's subsequent role in the Coalition and the fall of Molé had turned Louis-Philippe's coolness into active dislike. Remarkably, within a few months the two men had established an effective and durable working relationship.

The reason for this transformation was that Guizot the foreign minister proved to be very different from the Guizot who had campaigned with Thiers under the slogan 'The king reigns but does not govern'. This confirms the charge of hypocrisy against him, but the change was essential to the smooth running of government. While always insisting on his own independence, Guizot now recognized that the monarch was not simply a cipher, but had an active role to play in policy-making. As he put it in a famous speech to the Chamber in May 1846:

> ... the throne is not an empty chair that has been padlocked so that nobody can sit on it, simply to prevent usurpation. A free and intelligent person, who has his own ideas, feelings, desires and wishes, sits in this chair. The duty of this person ... is to govern only in accord with the other great public institutions created by the Charter, with their consent, their adhesion and their support. The duty of the crown's counsellors is to convince it to accept the same ideas, measures and policy that they are able to make the Chambers accept. This is true constitutional government: not just the only real, legal and constitutional, but the only worthy one.[22]

Like George III with Pitt the younger, Louis-Philippe had at last
found a leading minister with whom he could work, and who could
also, unlike Molé, deliver solid majorities in the Chamber. On the
essentials of policy both men were in complete agreement: conservatism and stability at home, and peace abroad. Parliamentary support
for this strategy was ensured by Guizot's healing of the split caused
by the Coalition and reuniting all the conservative deputies under his
own leadership, apart from a small irreconcilable group that stayed
loyal to Molé.

It was also crucial that Guizot was a great orator, in an age when
parliamentary votes could be swayed one way or another by a single
speech in the Chamber. Louis-Philippe was well aware of the
importance of having his policies presented by a prestigious speaker.
A few years before Guizot came to power, the king had once
lamented to Montalivet: 'Why can't I find a tongue? If I had one in
the Chamber, I'd have everything.' In Guizot he finally found what
he was looking for. The immediate results were excellent, but they
ended by blinding him to his minister's weaknesses. When in the
mid-1840s Montalivet pointed out the dangers of the latter's growing
inflexibility, Louis-Philippe burst out: 'You want to take M. Guizot
from me! You want to rip my tongue from my palate!'[23]

It is noticeable that the king's attitude to Guizot only began to
thaw when the latter's silver tongue started to reap dividends. It is
no coincidence that Louis-Philippe's first cordial letter to his foreign
minister, of January 1841, is a note of congratulations on a particularly brilliant speech that had ensured the passage of an important
bill for modernizing the fortifications of Paris. Once Guizot's usefulness became clear, Louis-Philippe was even ready to sacrifice some
of his prerogative in the interests of a smooth working relationship.
He bowed to Guizot's condition that he should not see the instructions and dispatches to France's ambassadors abroad before they were
sent. If he wanted to see them afterwards, he would have to ask for
them afterwards. If these restrictions irked him, he never let it show.[24]

There was one clear loser from this new arrangement – Adélaïde.
Having taken such pains to ensure personal control of official
diplomatic correspondence, it is hardly likely that Guizot would have
tolerated the continuation of her unofficial diplomatic role. Though
this is nowhere stated in the sources, it is probable that he extracted

a promise from Louis-Philippe that this would end. There is no
evidence that she ever corresponded with the new ambassador to
London, the comte de Ste Aulaire, as she had with Talleyrand and
Sébastiani. For the moment, she remained her brother's closest
adviser, wielding her influence from her armchair in his study, but as
the years wore on even this function was increasingly filled by
Guizot. Adélaïde remained Louis-Philippe's trusted confidante, but
her power was waning.

If Adélaïde had had to give way, her protégés could only follow
her and accept the inevitable. In the autumn of 1841, Sébastiani wrote
Louis-Philippe a letter intimating that he had made his peace with
the new ministry. The king passed it on to Guizot with a coldly
calculating comment: 'It's one of those acts of submission that it's
good to record, and whose value can be determined later.'[25] Dupin,
pillar of the centre-left and long-standing adviser of Adélaïde's,
recognized that power had now shifted away from him, but was
less philosophical. Writing to Thiers on 27 July 1845, the anniversary of the 1830 revolution, he let drop a barbed aside: 'It is fifteen
years to the day since we both fought to achieve quite another result
than the triumph of the *doctrinaires*.'[26]

A major factor in the length and stability of the Soult–Guizot
ministry was economic prosperity. Whereas Molé had had to cope
with a slump from 1837 to 1839, from then until the autumn of 1846
boom conditions prevailed. Crucially, between 1841 and 1845 bread
prices reached their lowest level under the July monarchy. During
this period, France's first moves towards industrialization were also
gathering pace. In 1841 alone, French industrial production leaped
to 16 per cent above the average annual rate for the century, and
between 1839 and 1846 production in the most dynamic and innova-
tory sectors of industry – cotton and silk textiles, mining, metals and
chemistry – rose by 61 per cent. Statistics such as these have led one
distinguished historian of the period, David Pinkney, to argue that
the years 1840–47 were decisive in the development of modern
France.[27]

It is not surprising that the government's attitude to these changes
was cautious, based on the widely diffused economic principles of
free trade and laissez-faire. It admitted very few exceptions to this
rule. The important law of 11 June 1842 laid the foundations of

France's railway system by using a combination of state, local and private resources to finance a network radiating from Paris to Belgium, the Channel coast, Strasbourg, Marseille, Nantes and Bordeaux. Also, child labour in factories employing over twenty workers was limited by the law of 22 March 1841. It was forbidden for children under eight, restricted to eight hours per day for those under twelve, and to twelve for those under sixteen. Compulsory schooling was introduced for the under-twelves. However, in the absence of a central inspectorate, the law was only patchily enforced.[28]

It was against this background that Guizot's famous phrase 'Enrichissez-vous!', an exhortation to the French to advance themselves by their own efforts, became notorious. In the popular imagination, it has come to stand for the materialism of the July monarchy, just as Marie Antoinette's 'Let them eat cake!' encapsulates the frivolity of the old regime. Like Marie Antoinette, Guizot probably never uttered these words, or if he did, they were taken out of context by his enemies. But they so accurately reflected his rigidly elitist outlook that they were easy to believe.[29]

Words like these underlined Guizot's glaring failure to address the 'social question' – the working-class impoverishment and dislocation that, as in Britain, often accompanied France's industrial expansion in these years. Was the same true of Louis-Philippe? In the king's correspondence with his ministers there is very little mention of economic or social issues, or of the condition of the working classes. This may not have been indifference so much as a simple failure to comprehend the newly emerging world of manufacturing capitalism. As Guy Antonetti has pointed out, Louis-Philippe's own fortune was pre-industrial, that of a *grand seigneur* with vast landed estates. His experience as an employer never encompassed mines or textile mills, and they remained foreign territory to him.[30]

Yet in one area Louis-Philippe did break free of the economic strictures of laissez-faire. In times of severe crisis, he strongly supported state-sponsored public works to relieve unemployment and alleviate suffering. Partly this was simple pragmatism; the French Revolution had graphically shown him the link between hardship and political upheaval. Yet this limited interventionism was also based on a moral insistence that work was the only way to escape poverty. When in March 1835 Marie-Amélie praised a sermon on charity she had just heard, Louis-Philippe replied: 'The best charity is to provide work; it gives useful results, and combats idleness and in some cases hypocrisy.'[31]

For the moment, prosperity relegated the social question to the background. After a year of relative stability, Guizot felt it was time to consolidate his parliamentary majority with new elections. Born of the chaos of the Coalition, the present Chamber was unpredictable and prone to factionalism. Guizot wished to simplify the options and offer the electorate a clear political choice between right and left. Above all, he aimed to weld his own following into a unified and disciplined body, which he revealingly dubbed *le parti conservateur*, resembling the Conservative party that Sir Robert Peel had just launched in England.[32]

The results, which were announced in the second week in July after a lacklustre campaign, did not fulfil these hopes. In theory, they gave Guizot a majority of seventy, but much of this was made up of small individual groupings of the centre-right which remained stubbornly independent. Paris also gave cause for concern; of the twelve seats in the capital, the opposition gained ten, and two of these were won by open republicans. Guizot was disappointed but, as usual, undaunted. He girded his loins for the struggle, and set out 'to regain in the Chamber what we should have won in the electoral colleges'. He was to do this, with considerable success, for the next four years.[33]

Just as the political world returned to normality, Louis-Philippe, his family and the entire July monarchy were struck by calamity. At 11 a.m. on 13 July 1842, the duc d'Orléans set out from the Tuileries for Neuilly to say goodbye to his parents and sisters before leaving to inspect a military camp at St Omer. Since he was pressed for time, he had ordered a fast carriage from the stables. The only one available was a light open cabriolet, driven by a postilion and with room for only one passenger and a groom behind. Foolishly, the two horses assigned to it were young and only recently trained. Halfway along the route, just beyond the Barrière de l'Etoile, they began to give trouble. At the Porte Maillot, the postilion lost control of them. Orléans prepared to jump, but at that moment he was thrown unexpectedly, probably by a sudden jolt of the frail vehicle. He fell backwards heavily, fracturing his skull on the edge of the pavement, and sprawled unconscious in the roadway. Meanwhile the postilion, not realizing what had happened behind him, had managed to rein in the horses; looking back and seeing that his passenger had disappeared, he quickly doubled back to the scene of the accident.[34]

Orléans was carried into the nearest building, a run-down shack with a grocer's stall outside, and laid out inside. The family were immediately informed; his wife and children were taking the waters at Plombières, but Louis-Philippe, Marie-Amélie and Adélaïde rushed out from Neuilly on foot and had reached the park gates before their carriage caught up with them. From there they were driven to the grocer's shop, and were shortly afterwards joined by their daughter Clémentine, their daughter-in-law the duchesse de Nemours, Aumale and Montpensier. As the news spread, ministers, members of the royal household and old friends like Gérard began to arrive, while a large silent crowd gathered outside. The tiny, packed room, with the distraught parents, siblings and officials surrounding the body on the mattress on the floor, bore a ghastly resemblance to the duc de Berry's deathbed twenty-two years before.[35]

It was soon clear that there was no hope. The fracture of the skull was obviously fatal, and the only palliative the doctors could try was cupping. Orléans never regained consciousness, except for a brief moment when he struggled up on his mattress and demanded, in German, for the door to be closed. Sentimental commentators have assumed that these words were addressed to his absent wife, the former Princess of Mecklenburg. It is more likely, however, that they were meant for his valet, who was also German. Finally, at 4.30 p.m., Orléans made a last movement and died. Marie-Amélie, on her knees by the mattress, gave a piercing cry that echoed round the crowd outside.[36]

The death of Orléans, aged only thirty-one, shattered the royal family, which in many ways never recovered. 'It should have been me!' burst out Louis-Philippe as he embraced his eldest son for the last time. Marie-Amélie could not be separated from the body for almost three weeks, and throughout that time kept vigil over it in the chapel at Neuilly. Louis-Philippe's second son, Nemours, who was particularly close to his elder brother, refused to believe the news when he was told. Normally cold and reserved, he lost all control, and tried to batter down the door behind which the doctors were carrying out Orléans' autopsy, shouting that his brother could not be dead, and that he had to see him. The duchesse d'Orléans, who had rushed back from Plombières, immediately went into mourning, and stayed in it for the rest of her life. When the time came for the body to be taken to Notre-Dame to lie in state, there were unbearably painful scenes. Louis-Philippe refused to give up the urn containing Orléans' heart, and it had to be removed from his grip by the Archbishop of Paris, while the Bishop of Evreux had to prise Marie-Amélie off her son's coffin.[37]

With her brother and sister-in-law distraught and sequestered for long periods, it was Adélaïde who held the family together. Her nephews and nieces gathered round her and accepted her authority. She rose to the challenge, but the personal cost was immense. She had survived emigration, bombardment and attempted assassination, but the death of her eldest nephew left her permanently diminished. As Mme de Boigne observed, she 'lost in Monsieur le duc d'Orléans the object of her most tender affections, her dearest hopes and . . . never [got over] this cruel event'.[38]

On a wider level, the duc d'Orléans' death was a tremendous blow to the regime itself. Dashing, charismatic and often politically astute, Orléans had embodied the future of the July monarchy. Enormously popular with the army, he was also respected by the public. Striking evidence of this was provided by the crowds who filed past his body from 6 a.m. to nightfall during the two days it lay in state in Notre-Dame.[39] One can only speculate on whether Orléans could have saved the dynasty, had he survived. It is difficult, though, to imagine him sinking into the fatalistic indecision that the rest of his family displayed in 1848, much of which can be traced back to his death.

On 5 August 1842, Orléans' remains were taken from Notre-Dame to the family chapel at Dreux along roads lined with mourners, and buried there. His immediate legacy was an urgent constitutional question. The heir to the throne was now his three-year-old son, the comte de Paris. Since it was very likely that Louis-Philippe, now sixty-nine, would die before his grandson legally came of age at eighteen, provision had to be made for a regency. Feeling that France's still-volatile state required the regent to be a man, Orléans had in his will expressed the wish that this should be Nemours.

Louis-Philippe concurred, and the ministry swiftly framed a bill to guarantee this, stipulating that the regent should always be the royal prince closest to the throne in the order of succession established by the Charter. But at this stage politics intervened. Stiff and aloof – 'a born archduke', in his father's words – Nemours had nothing of his dead brother's common touch. He was also a conservative inclined to the politics of *résistance*. The opposition therefore put forward the candidacy of the duchesse d'Orléans, who had a more liberal reputation, even though she had no desire to be regent.[40]

On 26 July Louis-Philippe had opened the new session of the Chambers with a tearful speech in which he spoke of his loss, and of the need for a workable regency law. This was presented to the deputies on 9 August, and the debate began on the 18th. A victory for the ministry was never seriously in doubt, but for such a vital measure the greatest possible degree of unanimity was needed. The most striking speech was made by Thiers, who out of loyalty to the regime he had helped to found broke ranks with the opposition and spoke in favour of the government's proposal. On 20 August, the regency bill passed the Chamber by 310 votes to 94. It was an impressive display of support for the monarchy, but it did not make good the loss that had occasioned it.[41]

One important result of Orléans' death was to remove the only figure apart from Adélaïde who could rival Guizot in Louis-Philippe's confidence. Now, weighed down by age and loss, the old king drew increasingly close to his leading minister. This was most obvious in foreign policy. There was good reason for this; diplomacy had always been Louis-Philippe's central preoccupation, and Guizot, although he had had little experience of foreign affairs before 1840, swiftly became absorbed in them. Though he was virtually the head of government as well as foreign minister during these years, nine of the fourteen chapters of his memoirs dealing with this period are devoted to foreign policy.[42]

The main focus of Louis-Philippe's and Guizot's efforts, which brought them both rewards and disappointment, was the relationship with Britain. They shared the same perspective on this. Louis-Philippe passionately believed that close links between the two countries would both ensure that France was never again isolated in Europe, and, more grandly, guarantee world peace. Guizot, whose political model was Britain and whose life's work as a scholar was a multivolume history of the British revolution of the seventeenth century, strongly agreed.[43]

Ironically this policy, far ahead of its time, owed much of its success to old-fashioned family diplomacy. The careful links built up by Louis-Philippe with the house of Saxe-Coburg proved extremely fruitful. The marriage of his daughter Louise to Leopold of Saxe-Coburg made her the aunt by marriage of both the new Queen of England, Victoria, and of Victoria's husband Prince Albert. Two further Coburg marriages, in 1840 and 1843 respectively, of Louis-Philippe's children the duc de Nemours and Princess Clémentine, made both cousins of Victoria and Albert. Through these connections, Victoria had become particularly fond of Louise and Clémentine, and had not forgotten that Louis-Philippe had been a close friend of her dead father the Duke of Kent.[44]

It was hardly surprising, therefore, that the most spectacular demonstration of the new-found Anglo-French friendship should have been Victoria's personal initiative, and first broached through her Orléans cousins. At some point in the course of 1843, she casually let slip to Clémentine: 'I'm thinking of making a visit to meet your parents ... leave it to me to arrange and keep it a secret.'[45] Such a plan had immense significance: it would be the first time a British sovereign had set foot on French soil since Henry VIII had met François I on the Field of the Cloth of Gold in 1520. More practically, it would resoundingly break the quarantine in which the July monarchy had been kept since 1830 by the other European rulers, none of whom had accepted invitations to visit France, and substantially improve Louis-Philippe's status among his fellow-monarchs.

It helped considerably that by this time Palmerston was no longer foreign minister. He had now been replaced by Lord Aberdeen, after the elections of 1841 had removed the Whigs and brought in a Conservative government led by Sir Robert Peel. Fifty-seven at the time, sensitive, courteous and high-minded, Aberdeen had the advantage of being genuinely concerned with European affairs and with building European peace. As a young ambassador to Austria during the Napoleonic wars, he had been present at the battle of Leipzig and been horrified by the suffering he had witnessed. He was therefore receptive to policies designed to avoid such scenes in the future, and when in June 1843 Victoria told him and Peel about her plan to visit Louis-Philippe, he readily agreed.[46]

To emphasize the purely personal and family nature of the meeting, it was decided that Victoria should not go to Paris, but stay with Louis-Philippe at his country residence, the Château d'Eu, on the Norman coast near Le Tréport. At 5.15 p.m. on 2 September 1843, the royal yacht was sighted from the French coast. Louis-Philippe immediately set off in his own royal barge to escort his guests on shore. He was so impatient to greet them that when the vessels drew alongside he had to be restrained from climbing aboard the yacht too soon and falling into the water. Once on land, Victoria, Albert and Aberdeen were welcomed by Marie-Amélie, Adélaïde, the duchesse d'Orléans and the princesse de Joinville, amid the novel spectacle of a large crowd shouting: 'Long live the Queen of England!' Louis-Philippe, delighted, kept repeating to Victoria how happy her visit made him, and what a great friend of his her father had been.[47]

Victoria and Albert stayed at Eu for five days, which passed in a whirl of picnics, excursions and concerts. On a personal level, the meeting achieved everything that could have been desired. Victoria was delighted by her reception. Louis-Philippe's 'gaiety and vivacity charmed and amused' her, and she was deeply impressed by Marie-Amélie, for whom she conceived 'a filial tenderness'. Of Adélaïde, who gave her an ornamental box of blue enamel set with diamonds, she commented in her diary: 'With all her little faults and fads, she is a very good, agreeable and intelligent old lady.' With some shrewdness, however, Victoria added that Adélaïde must make Marie-Amélie's position difficult, 'because nobody does anything without consulting her, and, truth be told, she usurps the queen's place'.[48]

By the time Louis-Philippe had bidden his guests goodbye, standing on the deck of a small steamboat, waving his hand and crying 'Adieu! Adieu!' to them, it was clear he had scored a notable diplomatic coup. France's relations with Britain, and his own standing in Europe, had been boosted in the most striking manner.[49]

The most significant result of the visit to Eu came in the next few months. In October 1843, Aberdeen invited the French chargé d'affaires in London, the comte de Jarnac, to come and stay with him at his own country seat, Haddo House in Scotland. In the course of long and friendly conversations, Aberdeen showed Jarnac a letter he was writing to his brother, Sir Robert Gordon, the British ambassador to Vienna. In it, he described the aim of his policy towards France as the achievement of 'a cordial good understanding'. Whether Jarnac passed this phrase directly back to his government is unclear, but just two months later it appeared in the mouth of Louis-Philippe himself. In his speech from the throne to the Chambers on 27 December, the king spoke of 'the sincere friendship that unites me to the queen of England and the *cordiale entente* that exists between her government and my own'. The *entente cordiale* between Britain and France may have been cemented by Edward VII and Lord Lansdowne in 1904, but it was first launched by Louis-Philippe and Lord Aberdeen in 1843.[50]

Underlining the importance of royal 'summit diplomacy' to the creation of the *entente*, the visits continued; indeed, at one point Louis-Philippe expressed the wish that they should become an annual event. On 8 October 1844, he himself landed at Portsmouth and travelled to Windsor to stay there with Victoria. Slightly ominously, it was the first time a French king had arrived in England since Jean II had been brought there as a prisoner after the battle of Poitiers in 1356. This time the atmosphere was very different. Louis-Philippe was warmly received everywhere; Victoria invested him with the Order of the Garter, and a delegation from the City of London came to Windsor to present him with an address, to which he replied in English. He also paid a visit to his old home in Twickenham, which must have prompted reflections on the difference between his situation then and now.[51] Yet as he later told Victor Hugo, what moved him most was a much humbler incident:

Near Windsor, at an inn, a man who had run after my carriage stopped just by me at the door and cried: 'Long live the king! Long live the king! Long live the king!' in French. Then he added, still in French: 'Sire, you are very welcome among this ancient people of England; you are in a country that knows how to appreciate you.' This man had never seen me before and will never see me again. He wanted nothing from me. It seemed to me that this was the voice of the people. It touched me more than all the official compliments.[52]

The last in this series of meetings between Victoria and Louis-Philippe took place at Eu in September 1845. It was not originally scheduled to take place at all, since Victoria had planned to spend the summer in Germany. However, after a violently anti-French toast to commemorate the battle of Waterloo was given in her honour at a banquet there by the King of Prussia, she decided to stop off at Eu on her return journey to soothe French sensibilities. Once again, the visit was a great success, and the *entente* was reaffirmed.[53]

Yet beneath the grandeur and glamour of these royal occasions, several problems remained. In themselves these did not amount to a great deal; in no area of the globe did essential British and French interests clash during the 1840s. More worrying was the flood of hostility that engulfed public opinion in both countries against the other when even a minor diplomatic clash occurred. In France, still smarting from her humiliation over the Eastern crisis, the smallest dispute with Britain was seized on as proof of her neighbour's insupportable arrogance and deep-seated malevolence towards France. In Britain, where the Duke of Wellington remained the greatest living national hero, the legacy of the Napoleonic wars was an irreducible suspicion of French bad faith and latent expansionism. With the exception of Palmerston, the contrast between the goodwill shown by British and French politicians and heads of state, who did everything possible to resolve the conflicts that arose, and the strident and nationalist press and public opinion that made their task infinitely more perilous, is striking. In launching the *entente cordiale* and attempting to apply it in a sincere and generous spirit, the leaders of Britain and France were far ahead of the public on both sides of the Channel.

One major humanitarian cause suffered from this persistent rivalry – the abolition of the slave trade. In 1831, Britain and France had agreed that their navies should have a mutual right to search ships from both their countries suspected of carrying slaves. This collaboration was broken off as a result of the Eastern crisis. Guizot attempted to revive it, and proposed a bill to this effect. In January 1842, however, the bill was wrecked by a hostile amendment passed almost unanimously by a Chamber that saw it only as a surrender to British domination of the seas. It was only after intensive diplomatic efforts, beginning with a long discussion between Guizot and

Aberdeen during Victoria's first visit to Eu, that a replacement treaty was signed and ratified in 1845.[54]

The next confrontation, which could have been invented to satirize the absurdities of misplaced patriotism, took place against the exotic setting of Tahiti. In November 1843 Admiral Dupetit-Thouars, acting beyond his instructions, annexed the island to France. However, he soon found himself faced by a group of outraged British Methodist missionaries, led by the Revd George Pritchard, who was also the British consul. Pritchard refused to recognize the annexation, was accused by the French of fomenting rebellion, and imprisoned for four days in an insanitary cellar by an over-zealous French naval captain. He was finally sent away on board a British ship. The British press erupted in predictable fury, and there was a similar reaction in France. After several months, Guizot and Aberdeen reached a settlement: Tahiti became not a French possession, but a protectorate, and the French government awarded Pritchard an indemnity for his ill-treatment (which was never paid). It was an entirely sensible compromise, but the fact that Guizot had appeared to make concessions fuelled a damaging perception in France that he was entirely subservient to Britain.[55]

The reef on which this first *entente cordiale* broke, however, lay in European waters. Despite the defeat of the followers of Don Carlos, Spain remained unstable, and a focus of rivalry between Britain and France. Guizot's not unreasonable solution was for Spain to be recognized as falling within France's sphere of influence, and Portugal within Britain's. Aberdeen was prepared to acquiesce in this. Yet this arrangement was soon sorely tested. The young Queen of Spain, Isabella, was now eleven, and a husband would soon have to be found for her. Louis-Philippe had no desire to involve France yet further in Spanish affairs by marrying one of his own sons to Isabella, but he was nonetheless determined that her spouse should be a Bourbon, from either the Spanish or the Neapolitan branch. The most unacceptable candidate was King Leopold of the Belgians' nephew, also – confusingly – called Leopold of Saxe-Coburg. Although this young man had multiple family links with the Orléans, he was just as closely related to Victoria and Albert, and as such was strongly favoured by Britain.[56]

Throughout 1843 and 1844, considerable efforts were made to

resolve the Spanish question through collaboration. Aberdeen appeared to accept that henceforth only a Bourbon should be allowed to marry Isabella. Yet Guizot still felt it necessary to emphasize to Aberdeen, during the meeting at Eu in September 1843, how strongly France would reject the Saxe-Coburg candidacy. If it were ever resurrected, he warned, Louis-Philippe would have no hesitation in offering one of his own sons as a husband for Isabella's younger sister, the Infanta Luisa.[57]

From now on, French diplomacy concentrated on finding a suitable Bourbon marriage for Isabella. By 1845 her cousin, Don Francisco, Duke of Cadiz, had emerged as the leading contender. Unfortunately, he posed problems, acknowledged in the fact that his family nickname was not the masculine diminutive of Francisco, Paquito, but the feminine, Paquita. To Isabella and her mother, the redoubtable regent Cristina, he was an uninspiring match. To sweeten the bitter pill, France offered to compensate Cristina by promising Louis-Philippe's youngest son, the duc de Montpensier, as a husband to the Infanta Luisa.[58]

It remained to calm British fears that if, as seemed likely, Isabella and Don Francisco produced no children, the next Spanish king might be Montpensier's son and thus closely tied to France. During Victoria's second visit to Eu in September 1845, Guizot therefore promised Aberdeen that if the Montpensier marriage did take place, it would not do so until Isabella and Don Francisco had produced children. However, to ensure that this news did not further discourage his Spanish counterparts, he thoughtfully kept it from them.[59]

This increasingly rickety house of cards did not take long to collapse. In June 1846 Peel's ministry resigned over the Corn Law crisis, the Whigs returned to power, and Aberdeen left the Foreign Office. His replacement was the Francophobic Palmerston,[60] who was determined not to allow Louis-Philippe a free hand in Spain and swiftly reactivated the candidacy of Leopold of Saxe-Coburg for Isabella's hand. Guizot considered that this freed him from his promise given to Aberdeen nine months before, and he boldly proceeded to negotiate simultaneous marriages between Isabella and Don Francisco, and Luisa with Montpensier. He was probably justified in doing so; whether he was wise is another matter. Louis-

Philippe was much more reluctant to take the risk, and only agreed under considerable pressure from Guizot.[61]

The double marriage took place in Madrid on 10 October 1846, but France's diplomatic triumph was short-lived. The price she paid for it was the first *entente cordiale*. Palmerston, the press and public opinion were unsurprisingly outraged, but so too were Aberdeen, now in opposition, and Victoria herself, who wrote to Leopold of the Belgians that Louis-Philippe had 'behaved dishonestly'. For the remainder of the July monarchy, relations with the Power that Louis-Philippe, Adélaïde and their collaborators had made the cornerstone of their foreign policy plunged to their lowest ebb since 1830. With no realistic substitute for Britain as a potential partner in view, France was now diplomatically isolated.[62] It was little consolation that, against all expectations, the Spanish marriages fulfilled their primary purpose with surprising success. Isabella and Don Francisco eventually had eleven children – the last survivor died, aged ninety-four, in 1958 – and Luisa and Montpensier ten.

*

THE LAST GENERAL ELECTIONS of the July monarchy were held in July 1846. The circumstances were propitious for the government. The Spanish marriages had not yet developed into a crisis, the economy was booming, and the opposition's rhetoric failed to galvanize the voters. Guizot finally got the majority he had sought in 1842; it rose by twenty-five to thirty seats to approximately one hundred.[63] Guizot had achieved that vital political combination that had eluded all of Louis-Philippe's previous prime ministers – unquestioned control of the Chamber and the confidence of the king. The furious battles between crown and parliament that had dogged the constitutional monarchy since 1814 seemed finally resolved, and political stability attained.

Yet the very success of Guizot's system opened it to powerful criticism. Through careful electoral organization and uninhibited use of government pressure in the localities, he had turned a large proportion of France's smaller constituencies into government preserves, securely in the pocket of the ministry. This created an impressive majority, but also handed the opposition the potent – and often justified – charge of corruption to throw at him. On a wider level, this development accentuated a growing political cleavage between the docile rural and small-town seats and the cities where the opposition was strong, culminating in Paris where out of the twelve seats available only one ministerial deputy was elected in 1846.[64]

These problems were signs of more structural flaws. Since 1830, France had undergone significant industrial and social change, but the electoral system had failed to keep up with this reality. Major population centres were now seriously under-represented – again, Paris contained one-tenth of the electorate, but returned only three per cent of the deputies. Above all, the electorate itself was startlingly unrepresentative of the general population. The 200 francs tax qualification had enfranchised a mere 0.5 per cent of French people in 1831; with the rise in incomes this figure had risen by 1846, but only to 0.7 per cent.[65] Guizot's success may finally have stabilized the constitutional monarchy at one level, but its roots in the country at large were beginning to look dangerously shallow.

This tiny parliamentary electorate was isolated not only from the population as a whole, but from two other major pillars of the regime: the municipal electorate and the National Guard. Since 1831, under a rather complicated system, in communes of less than a thousand inhabitants the top 10 per cent of taxpayers could vote in local elections, rising to 14 per cent if the population was over one thousand, and 19 per cent if it was over fifteen thousand. This meant that out of a total French population of 35,400,000 in 1846, perhaps three million had the municipal vote, whereas fewer than 300,000 exercised it at national level.[66] As for the National Guard, the law of March 1831 which allowed membership only to those who could afford the necessary time and equipment effectively limited this to the middle classes, but was still broad enough to include many Frenchmen who were unable to vote in general elections. This restrictive parliamentary franchise formed a bottleneck in civil society; hundreds of thousands of Frenchmen could elect their country's local representatives and were expected to defend it as National Guardsmen at moments of crisis, but were denied the most important vote of all.

The situation bore a striking resemblance to that in Britain at the beginning of the previous decade. Before the reform bill of 1832, the British electoral system had presented many of the same key features as that of Louis-Philippe's France. The famous 'rotten boroughs', totalling roughly one-third of the seats in the House of Commons, exactly mirrored those smaller French constituencies tied by patronage to Guizot's ministry. The electorate was also tiny. However, even before 1832 the electorate of England and Wales was still proportionately larger than that of France after 1830 – 3.2 per cent of the population as opposed to 0.5 per cent.[67]

In both France and Britain, these comparable inequalities generated similar movements for reform. In Britain, after a lull in the 1820s the movement for electoral reform gathered momentum after 1829, until the Whig party inside parliament and popular mobilization outside forced the measure through in 1832.[68] In France, electoral reform was proposed in the Chamber in 1840, as well as a bill for parliamentary reform which sought to ban deputies from holding paid public positions. Both efforts failed, but were renewed early in 1842, when a bill to add to the electoral roll those inscribed on the jury list was debated, followed by a further one to curb ministerial patronage in the Chamber. These attempts too were defeated, but created enough of an echo in the political nation for Thiers and Barrot, as leaders of the opposition, to make electoral and parliamentary reform a major theme of their common programme in the 1846 elections.[69]

The effect of the 1830 revolution in France in encouraging the British movement for reform in 1832 has been noted by British historians.[70] Yet the parallels between 1832 in Britain and the fall of the July monarchy in France in 1848 have rarely if ever been discussed, and they are illuminating. Britain before the reform bill had a well established constitutional monarchy, but an antiquated and unrepresentative electoral system. In Britain, the latter eventually grew so unpopular that fear of revolution induced the party in office to amend it. Whether or not Britain would actually have been plunged into revolution if the reform bill had been rejected is an imponderable, but it can certainly be strongly argued that it would have, and that this imminent peril was only averted by the bill's passage.[71] In France, on the other hand, Louis-Philippe, Guizot and Guizot's party stubbornly refused to concede even the smallest measure of reform until it was far too late, and as a result were swept away by a Parisian uprising. The fall of the July monarchy was thus no more inevitable than that of the British constitution in 1832. One was saved by a fortunate combination of events and individuals; the other was lost by an unfortunate series of events, but especially by the short-term mistakes and failures of individuals.

It is particularly bizarre that Guizot, the historian and political admirer of Britain, did not perceive these parallels himself and act on them. The answer probably lies in his psychology rather than his intellect. The revolution of 1789 had bereaved and traumatized him, and he saw reform as the beginning of a slippery slope that would lead inevitably to a repetition of its horrors. More generally, he had always seen life as a struggle; he accepted and even gloried in this, and was confident of his ability to meet this latest challenge. The ultimate roots of this attitude were religious. As he grew older, Guizot's native Calvinism assumed an increasingly important place in his thought. In both his contemporary writings and his memoirs, there is a strong sense that he came to see the reform question in theological terms, a metaphysical conflict between good and evil, with the existing electors as the elect and the multitude outside as the damned. This was certainly his interpretation of the latter's victory in the 1848 revolution. Writing to a friend a few months afterwards, he concluded: 'I didn't think that the Devil would win the battle against us as he has done.'[72]

Despite being the leading minister, Guizot was still only a minister. If the king had opposed him on such a central issue, he would have had to resign. Yet on this, as on virtually everything else, Louis-Philippe supported him to the hilt. Why he did so at first seems baffling. Although his experience of the Revolution had been quite as traumatic as Guizot's, he did not have the latter's doctrinal rigidity, and prided himself on his political astuteness. Yet in one area, constitutional propriety, he was dogmatic. The one important difference between Britain in 1832 and France just before 1848 was that in Britain a ministry with a parliamentary majority supported reform; in France it did not. For Louis-Philippe, to replace a functioning government simply because its views on reform were unpopular outside the Chambers was not only unconstitutional – it was a dangerous concession that could lead to revolution. When

Guizot openly discussed with him at the end of 1847 whether he should make way for a ministry prepared to pass reform, the king was categoric:

> I am quite resolved not to act outside the constitution and to accept its necessities, even if they are unpleasant; but at this moment there is no constitutional necessity; you have always had a majority; to whom would I be ceding in changing my ministers now? Not to the Chambers, nor to the clear and regularly expressed wish of the country, but to demonstrations with no other authority than the pleasure of those who participate in them, and to a clamour which at bottom clearly has evil intentions. No, my dear minister, if the constitution dictates that we should separate, I will do my constitutional duty; but I won't make this sacrifice in advance and to appease ideas of which I don't approve.[73]

A further reason for Louis-Philippe's stance emerged at the beginning of 1848, when Montalivet, worried by Guizot's growing isolation in the country, saw the king and begged him to change his ministry. In reply, Louis-Philippe raised a wider issue than reform, or even respect for the Charter. If Guizot went, his probable successor would be Thiers, and Thiers would menace the European peace for which the king had laboured for eighteen years:

> I don't have any absolute, and therefore stupid, hostility to electoral reform in itself, but it can only be judged at any given moment by what its results may be. In the short term, the consequence will be a Molé ministry, but that will always end in giving way to Thiers; now Thiers means war even more certainly than in 1840, and that is the overthrow of my policy – it means adventure and ruin; that's what your reform will lead to! I repeat, you're not having it.[74]

Both the constitutional case and the concern for European peace were solid rational arguments in favour of Louis-Philippe keeping Guizot. However, by late 1847 the ministry itself was becoming increasingly divided over support for the unreformed French electoral system, and several members of Guizot's own party had come to favour some measure of reform.[75] Had Guizot resigned, it might not

even have been necessary for the king to find an entirely new
government; a little *replâtrage* might have been enough. The possibility that a more left-wing ministry, especially one led by Thiers,
might be dangerously bellicose was a more serious consideration.
However, Thiers was nothing if not unpredictable, and there is no
way of knowing whether his aggressive foreign policy views would
have remained the same, particularly if he had had to carry out a
major programme of domestic reform. It is significant that the
republic that succeeded the July monarchy, which contained all those
radical tendencies Louis-Philippe feared most, scrupulously avoided
provoking a European war.

However plausible his reasoning, there was also an element of
obstinacy in Louis-Philippe's clinging to Guizot. He was now in his
mid-seventies, and age had made him more inflexible. Towards his
family in particular, he was becoming increasingly autocratic. When
his younger sons Joinville and Aumale became concerned at Guizot's
immobilism and ventured to criticize him in private, they were swiftly
moved away from the centre of power. Aumale was made Governor
of Algeria in September 1847, and Joinville was sent to join him the
following January. The duchesse d'Orléans, who increasingly held a
court of her own in the Pavillon de Marsan in the Tuileries and
cultivated links with the opposition, stayed in Paris, but the political
distance between her and her parents-in-law was obvious.[76]

Outside the family, a number of friends and ex-ministers of the
king also became alarmed that a gap was developing between the
monarchy and the country. It is significant that they were all also
close to Adélaïde – Gérard, Sébastiani, Molé, Pasquier. In the last
years of the reign, the first two often discussed their fears with
Adélaïde. Only Sébastiani, however, brought them up directly with
Louis-Philippe. 'Sire, a great emptiness surrounds the throne,' he
began – 'I can see you're getting old,' the king snapped back.
Sébastiani left in a fury, and relations between the two men were
never the same again.[77]

While she listened to the concerns of her circle, Adélaïde
studiously avoided taking sides. Part of the reason was her increasingly poor health, which robbed her of the necessary energy to
sustain a serious argument either with her friends or with her brother.
When Montalivet, immobilized by gout, sent his wife to broach his

concerns with Adélaïde, she simply replied: 'Tell Montalivet that I am grateful for the thought that has made him send you to me, but I'm exhausted and no longer in any state to undertake the smallest conflict with my dear king.'[78] In addition, her devotion to Louis-Philippe increased, if anything, with age. One sign of this was that, in order to be physically closer to him, she no longer worked in her study. Instead, as Mme de Boigne recalled:

> she stayed in the salon that opened on to it, with her hat on, and her shawl and gloves nearby, ready at any moment to go into the study, which the king might enter by the back way, or to go to him at the first signal, either to stay with him in his apartments or to go for a drive in his carriage, or to walk with him on the terrace [of the Tuileries] or through the galleries of the Louvre, when he was tired of working and felt the need of some air.[79]

Adélaïde's relations with Guizot had thawed, too. Her personal feelings towards him never became warm, but she appreciated how important he was to her brother and how much he helped him in his task. She was delighted by Guizot's election victory in August 1846, writing to her nephew Nemours: '... we should thank God for the superb result of our elections ... the Chamber has renewed itself satisfactorily in every way [and] there are new conservative deputies of excellent quality'. When Pasquier warned her towards the middle of 1847 that retaining Guizot was becoming dangerous, she simply replied: 'What can you expect? ... it's partly the others' fault; no minister has ever understood the king like M. Guizot, or managed him so tactfully.'[80]

As 1847 wore on, Guizot appeared unassailable. Relations between crown and parliament, so critical in any constitutional monarchy, were more fully resolved than at any time since 1814, and much of the credit for this belonged to him. However, the focus of politics was shifting towards electoral reform, and the opposition and a section of public opinion were beginning to stir. Louis-Philippe, his family and his circle may have been divided on how to respond to this, but on one thing they were agreed: dangerous times lay ahead.

Chapter Eleven

THE LAST FRENCH KING

IN THE MIDDLE OF 1846, the boom of the previous five years had come sharply to an end. That summer, the harvest failed over most of France. The effects were swiftly felt in the price of bread, still the staple food of most of the population: from 34 centimes for a weight of four livres, it rose to 49 centimes. This sparked violent disturbances all over rural France. Bands of peasants forcibly prevented the export of grain to other regions, or organized its compulsory sale at a 'just price'. Riots broke out, and in the worst case, at Buzançais in the Indre, a wealthy landowner was murdered. Louis-Philippe followed all these incidents carefully, and grew increasingly frustrated by the weak response of the local authorities. In January 1847 he wrote to Guizot: 'I am concerned by the inadequacy of the forces available to us. It is starting to allow disorder to triumph at various points, and since we still have four or five months of scarcity to get through, I think a substantial and immediate increase in the *gendarmerie* is indispensable.' He suggested transferring ten thousand soldiers from the regular army for this purpose.[1]

Inevitably, the agricultural crisis rebounded on industry and commerce. With most consumer spending now limited simply to subsistence, demand for manufactured goods slumped. Textiles – as in England, at the vanguard of industrial development – were particularly hard-hit. In one major centre of production, Roubaix, by May 1847 eight thousand out of a total workforce of thirteen thousand were unemployed, while in another, Rouen, even for those still in work there were drastic wage cuts of 30 per cent.[2]

The agricultural and manufacturing slump coincided with a financial crisis of confidence. The need to import grain to avoid famine had taken its toll on France's gold reserves and reduced the amount of capital available for investment. Then, in the summer of 1846, the railway boom of the 1840s suddenly collapsed. Constructing railway lines had proved much more expensive than initially anticipated, and several of the companies involved ran out of funds, leading to spectacular bankruptcies. This time the middle as well as the working classes suffered, as their savings were swallowed up. All nine of the departmental banks, set up from 1818 onwards on the model of the Bank of France, had failed by the beginning of 1848.[3]

The crash was particularly disturbing because so many of its features were unfamiliar. On one level, it was a subsistence crisis of the 'old' type, caused by harvest failure. But this was combined with a financial and manufacturing crisis of a 'new' type, as the speculative bubble created by France's first major shift to industrial capitalism burst.[4] In a further portent of the future, the slump was also international, as other industrializing countries, particularly Britain, slid into recession. Louis-Philippe dimly grasped this international dimension, but typically viewed it in diplomatic, rather than economic, terms. For him, it was the breakdown in France's *entente* with Britain caused by the Spanish marriages that had destroyed the confidence of French investors: 'the general, and even rapid, fall in the public funds of every country is a fact that requires the most serious reflection. Without in any way discounting various contributory factors such as the railways, harvest failure etc . . . the principal cause seems to be the internal state of England, that of her government, and perhaps most of all that of her relations with ourselves.'[5]

By the end of 1847 the worst of the crisis was over, a fact symbolized by the Bank of France lowering the interest rate from 5 to 4 per cent on 27 December. Substantial grain imports, and a good harvest for 1847, brought bread prices down and removed the spectre of dearth. Yet the after-effects of the downturn – worker unemployment in the cities, fearful peasants in the countryside and bourgeois worried about their investments – remained acute. The result was a loss of confidence not only in the economy but in the regime as well. Baffled by the scope and complexity of the slump, an angry public instead sought scapegoats, and the ageing king and his inflexible leading minister were the obvious candidates.[6]

As always, the situation in Paris was the most dangerous. The economic crisis was more severe in the capital than in the provinces, and its intensity is revealed by the statistics gathered by an inquiry later conducted by the Parisian Chamber of Commerce. According to these, fully 56 per cent of the Paris workforce was unemployed in the spring of 1848. The figures varied by industry, from 19 per cent in the food trades to a catastrophic 88 per cent among gilders of wood. Ominously high, also, were the unemployment rates among the stalwarts of insurrection: the metalworkers (58 per cent), furniture-makers (72.5 per cent), and those indispensable makers of barricades, the building-workers (64 per cent).[7]

In these ominous circumstances, the government was not idle. In this case at least, the usual picture of Guizot's ministry sticking rigidly to its laissez-faire principles in the face of popular distress is inaccurate. On the contrary, it intervened on a substantial scale. Having averaged 10 million francs per annum over the previous nine years, welfare spending in 1847 doubled to 20 million. In particular, the government was acutely aware of the link between high bread prices and disorder in the capital, of which July 1789 was only the most frightening example. Three hundred thousand Parisians were given coupons to help them buy bread in the course of 1847. To modern eyes, given the scale of the crisis of 1846–7, these measures may well seem inadequate, but by the standards of the time they were significant, and no other European government during the slump did more. If Guizot's ministry had shown as much flexibility in the political as in the social domain in 1847, its fate might well have been different.[8]

Instead of buckling under these pressures, Guizot's power only grew. On 29 September 1847, the seventy-seven-year-old Soult finally decided he was too old to continue in government, and went into retirement. Guizot replaced him, becoming prime minister in title as well as fact. For the parliamentary opposition, this was the last straw. Frustration with Guizot's dominance, and with his political immobilism, led certain key members of the 'dynastic left' down a perilous path. Its leader Odilon Barrot and his associate Duvergier de Hauranne, who had been one of the most radical leaders of the Coalition of 1838–9, opened negotiations with the Parisian republicans to mount a campaign to achieve electoral reform and, once more, to curb the royal prerogative. By doing so, in alliance with figures whose goals went well beyond loyal opposition, they were lending themselves to a potential mass movement that they could not ultimately control.[9]

The main method of mobilizing support was a series of popular banquets, at which the dynastic left and the republican leaders made speeches propagating their joint programme. The idea, however, was less radical than it sounded. The cost of the banquets put them far beyond the pockets of most ordinary workers, they were held on private premises to avoid infringing the official ban on public meetings, and only existing electors were to be allowed to attend. The proposals aired by the dynastic left at these banquets were also hardly revolutionary. Its main demand, a reduction of the tax-paying qualification for the vote from 200 to 100 francs, would only have increased the electorate by two hundred thousand. Yet as the campaign wore on – roughly seventy banquets were held in the course of 1847 – its tone became increasingly republican. Barrot and Duvergier were often uncomfortably surrounded at gatherings where no toast to the king was drunk and inflammatory sentiments were voiced. Their isolation was compounded by the fact that their former allies of the centre-left, especially Thiers, studiously avoided any association with the movement.[10]

To Adélaïde, the outlook was worrying, but not alarming. Her main concern was that the agricultural crisis should end, and with it the sufferings of the poor which she was convinced the opposition was exploiting for its own ends. As she wrote to her nephew Nemours on 21 July 1847:

Thank God, the harvest is excellent everywhere, which was absolutely essential, and I flatter myself that bit by bit this will calm this sort of agitation whose existence cannot be denied, and which our good friends are fanning as much as they can. There has certainly been a succession of unfortunate incidents

for some time now, and in the current state of public opinion
I'll be glad when we've got through July; not that I have the
slightest serious concern.[11]

As winter and its attendant hardships approached, Adélaïde
repeated these sentiments to Joinville, currently stationed with his
naval squadron at La Spezia. 'We must attend to [the common
people],' she insisted, 'to win them back to our side.' In no sense,
however, was she speaking of political concessions, but simply the
provision of charity and work where necessary.[12] In view of what
happened four months later, this may seem complacent, but only with
hindsight. From Adélaïde's standpoint in October 1847, the harvest
had been good, the forces of law and order remained loyal, and the
banqueting campaign had revealed as much division as unity in
the ranks of the opposition. The situation was not good, but it was
under control.

More immediately damaging to the government was a series of
scandals – those 'unfortunate incidents', as Adélaïde delicately termed
them – which rocked the upper levels of society throughout 1847.
The first cases revealed greed and corruption in the government and
administration. There were several serious incidents of embezzlement
by civil servants. In May, the journalist and deputy Emile de Girardin
claimed in his newspaper *La Presse* that a member of the government
had offered one individual a peerage in exchange for a bribe of
80,000 francs. Although Girardin refused to name either party, the
Chamber of Peers formally charged him with insulting its dignity;
damagingly, it then acquitted him.[13]

A few months later, two much bigger fish swam into the nets of
justice. It emerged that in 1843 the minister of public works, Jean-
Baptiste Teste, a close friend of Soult, had received a bribe of 100,000
francs from a former minister, General Cubières, in exchange for
renewing a concession for a salt-mining company. In July 1847, both
men and their associates were tried before the Chamber of Peers.
On the evening of the day on which his guilt became plain, Teste
tried to commit suicide. For good measure, he shot himself with
two pistols, in the mouth and the chest; amazingly, he survived. On
17 July, the defendants were found guilty and sentenced to civic
degradation and heavy fines, to which three years' imprisonment was

added in Teste's case. Although the ministry had acted honourably throughout the trial, and made no effort to cover up the scandal, it was inevitably tainted by the misdeeds of a former colleague. As Victor Hugo memorably put it: 'M. Guizot is personally incorruptible, yet he governs by corruption. He reminds me of an honest woman who keeps a brothel.'[14]

The next crime was far darker. At 4.30 a.m. on 18 August, the servants at the Hôtel Sébastiani at no. 55 Rue du Faubourg St Honoré were woken by seven piercing screams, followed by the ringing of an internal bell. The sounds came from the apartment of Marshal Sébastiani's daughter, the duchesse de Praslin, who lived with her husband, the duc de Praslin, in her father's house. A maid and a valet immediately rushed there, but found to their horror that the door was locked from the inside. Beyond, they could hear the noise of a terrible struggle.

When the servants finally found an unlocked door and entered their mistress's bedroom, silence had descended. The room was a shambles, with blood spattered everywhere. The duchesse de Praslin lay dying by a sofa. She had multiple stab wounds, her throat had been cut, and she had been finished off by two blows to the head with a candlestick. When she was lifted up, a fashionable novel was found lying under her body, ironically titled *The Best Sort of People*.[15]

Suspicion soon focused on the duc de Praslin. It was memorably summed up by the shrewd police chief Allard when he first viewed the scene of the crime: 'This is not the work of a professional. . . . It is a vile business clumsily done. It is the work of a gentleman.'[16] Although the duc lived in separate rooms from his wife, he had access to her apartment, and it is unlikely that an assailant from outside would have had time to escape before the alarm was raised.

The full truth of what happened that night will never be known, because on the afternoon of 18 August the duc swallowed arsenic and died six days later, having admitted nothing. However, it is probable that he killed his wife. After twenty-three years of marriage, he had come to loathe her. He had also become close to the governess of his nine children, Henriette Deluzy, though she seems not to have been his mistress. The duchesse, obsessively jealous of her husband, was not convinced, and was threatening divorce proceedings that would both have ruined the duc's reputation and separated him from his

children, to whom he was devoted. With this motivation, it is likely
that he entered his wife's bedroom in the early hours, attempted to
collapse the canopy of her bed over her to make her death look like
an accident, tried to cut her throat when this failed, and then battered
her to death when she resisted.[17]

The crime was shocking in itself, but particularly so for Louis-
Philippe and Adélaïde. The duchesse de Praslin was not only
Sébastiani's daughter, but a close friend and confidante of Adélaïde,
who often referred to her in her correspondence. The royal family's
reaction is graphically depicted by Louis-Philippe, who was writing
to Guizot from Eu when the news arrived at midnight on 18 August.
The king broke off, then resumed: 'I had got this far in my letter
when a courier brought me a letter from Duchâtel [the interior
minister] informing me of the crime, the horror committed upon the
unfortunate duchesse de Praslin whom we loved so much, and I can't
continue my letter!!' Adélaïde and Marie-Amélie were shattered when
told the news. As Louis-Philippe wrote to Guizot two days later:
'What a horrible and frightful affair! We have all received a cruel
shock, and my poor sister has been deeply shaken ... The queen
had such a strong nervous convulsion that I had to restrain her.'[18]

The murder irrevocably changed what was left of Sébastiani's
life. The duchesse de Praslin had been his only child, and he had
been very close to her. Now, at seventy-one, he found himself
responsible for nine grandchildren who had been orphaned in the
most atrocious circumstances. He retired increasingly into private life,
and devoted himself to their upbringing. He died suddenly, while
eating lunch, on 20 July 1851.[19]

The scandal caused a sensation in public opinion, and dealt real
damage to the July monarchy. The duc de Praslin had been a pillar
of the establishment; a peer of France, and an equerry to the duchesse
d'Orléans. That such an eminent figure should be capable of such an
appalling act seemed to reveal something rotten in the regime itself.
Anti-aristocratic sentiment became marked, fanned by the radical
press; crowds formed outside the Hôtel Sébastiani, not to sympathize
with the bereaved but to hiss the wicked duke. Fury was intense
when Praslin's suicide became known, and rumours spread that
he had been spirited out of France on Louis-Philippe's orders so as
to spare him from paying for his crime. As Tocqueville put it on

27 August: 'The horrible event which has fixed everyone's attention for the last eight days is calculated to inspire a vague terror and profound unease in all hearts.'[20]

The butchery of the duchesse de Praslin was the second major shock Adélaïde had received in just over a year. On 16 April 1846, the royal family had been driving through the park of Fontainebleau in its specially adapted charabanc when two shots rang out from just four metres away. The charabanc was riddled with buckshot, but miraculously no one was hurt. The would-be assassin was a forty-eight-year-old ex-soldier and forester called Pierre Lecomte, who had retired from royal service two years before, conceived a quite irrational grudge against Louis-Philippe after unsuccessfully trying to have his pension converted into a lump sum, and decided to kill him. He had lain in wait for his prey since four that morning on a makeshift shooting platform concealed behind a wall, and had missed only because the platform had shifted under his feet at the last moment.[21] Adélaïde, who had been sitting near her brother when Lecomte fired, was badly upset by the experience, and took some time to recover. Mme de Boigne, who took care of her when she returned to the Tuileries, thought that the long-term effect would even be fatal:

> Her complexion, always dark, was usually ruddy; it was now grey and leaden; her eyes were dull and her lips pale. Although the eighteen pellets of buckshot fired by Lecomte hit a vehicle containing fourteen people without harming any of them, it is nonetheless true that he struck Mme Adélaïde her death-blow.[22]

For some time Adélaïde's health had been declining; the asthma that had always afflicted her was getting worse, and her mobility was now extremely restricted. She seems to have sensed that she did not have much longer to live, and accepted the fact with calm, resignation and perhaps even relief. These feelings are evident in a letter she wrote to the duchesse de Nemours, to whom she was close, on 28 August 1846:

> ... today is my birthday, and a serious one for me, because I'm now sixty-nine, and that's no longer a joke; I'm entering my seventieth year, and I certainly feel it, though I definitely

wouldn't want to begin my life all over again; I put myself in
God's hands as to the manner of my leaving it, without upsetting
myself at the sight of the approaching end; in fact I often find
the thought comforting.[23]

For a while Adélaïde's symptoms were relieved by a new and
painful-sounding treatment perfected by Dr Ducrocq of Manosque,
which involved injecting ammonia into her throat, but by the end of
1847 she had grown increasingly frail. Sitting at the round table after
dinner with her sister-in-law and nieces, she would sometimes fall
into an alarmingly heavy sleep. These signs were noted with concern
by her family. They were also observed by the anonymous author of
an account of Adélaïde's last days, who clearly knew her very well
and may possibly have been her legal adviser and confidant, the
influential centre-left deputy André Dupin. The writer recalled how
on the afternoon of Christmas Day 1847 he went to see Louis-
Philippe: 'I asked the king for news of his sister; he replied that
things were going steadily, but the duc de Nemours who was present
pulled a face which revealed that Madame was in a worse state than
the king seemed to think.'[24]

A few days earlier, Louis-Philippe had caught a heavy cold which
he passed on to Adélaïde. She took to her bed, but even now her
thoughts remained fixed on political matters. In particular, she was
concerned about the new session of the Chambers, due to reopen on
28 December, and about how her brother's speech from the throne
'would be received in the wake of the reformist banquets whose
effects preoccupied her' – perhaps she had been more alarmed by
them than she showed. On the day itself, she insisted on being
carried from her bedroom to the window of her private gallery which
overlooked the route the king was to take. The old fear of assassination was also present: 'Equally, she wished to see him return, as if
she was still possessed by those anxieties that had especially tor-
mented her since Lecomte's attempt at Fontainebleau.' As it was,
everything went smoothly, and Louis-Philippe and his sons paid
Adélaïde a visit immediately on arriving back at the Tuileries to tell
her what an excellent reception they had had.[25]

Adélaïde had two disturbed nights following this agitation, but
appeared to have stabilized by 30 December. Watched over by her

maid Joséphine, she installed herself in an armchair in her gallery. At
six that evening, Louis-Philippe came to see her, and found her alert
and in good spirits. 'I feel better,' she told him, 'I hope I'll have a
good night; go and rest, my friend, you need it.'[26] These were the
last words she spoke to her brother. Typically, she was thinking of
him rather than herself.

At 10.30 p.m., after dining and holding his salon, the king
returned to his sister's apartments and found her asleep in her
armchair and breathing easily. Not wishing to disturb her, he left. In
fact, Adélaïde was slipping into a coma. Towards eleven Joséphine
noticed that she had gone pale and that her hands were cold. She
rushed next door to warn Pigache, the doctor on duty, and Adélaïde's
secretary Lamy. Pigache ran to warn Louis-Philippe, who hurried
over immediately, followed by Marie-Amélie and all of their children
currently in the Tuileries. Two priests were sent for, who 'extended
to the unfortunate princess, speechless and insensible, the last com-
forts of religion. All the royal family gathered in the gallery were on
their knees, and mingled their prayers and tears with the entreaties
of the ministers of God.' At 3.40 a.m. on 31 December 1847,
unconscious but surrounded by the brother, sister-in-law, nephews
and nieces to whom she had devoted her life, Adélaïde died.[27]

At ten the next morning, some of Adélaïde's closest friends were
allowed to pay their respects to her. Perhaps significantly, they
included Raoul de Montmorency. There is no mention of Atthalin
being present. At twelve Dupin was summoned to the Tuileries, as
Adélaïde's legal adviser, for the reading of her will. The document
was found in her study, and the official witnesses assembled to hear
it: Nemours, Joinville and Montpensier for the family and Guizot
and the justice minister Hébert for the government, but also old
confidants like Gérard and Sébastiani.[28] Louis-Philippe was not
present, but his emotions on later reading the opening paragraphs
can only be imagined:

It is to you, dear and beloved brother, the object of my most
cherished affections, that I address my last wishes. You know
that I clung to life only for you, that I had no other interest in
it than your own, that it meant nothing to me apart from you!
You were always perfect towards me, you have been the pride,

the honour of our family, you have been my consolation in every respect. I bless you for it, and when you read this, in the first moments of the cruel pain of my death ... if, as I hope ... God in his infinite mercy takes pity on me, reflect that I am happy in a better world than this one! ... I shall ask God to aid you, to give you the strength you need to continue, for as long as he thinks proper, the hard, but so useful and glorious, task of securing the happiness of our family and of our dear country, and then to prepare you for, and ease for you, the rough passage from life to death, so that we shall all be reunited in that happy and eternal life ... where there shall be no more separation. Oh! Let it be thus!'[29]

Not only the testament, but also the provisions of the will, centred on Louis-Philippe. All of Adélaïde's enormous estate, worth approximately thirty-nine million francs, went to him during his lifetime. Only after his death was it to be divided. Half was assigned to the dead duc d'Orléans' younger son the duc de Chartres, to Nemours' and Clémentine's mother-in-law the Duchess of Saxe-Coburg, to Louise and her son the comte de Flandre, and to Marie's husband the Duke of Württemberg. The other half was bequeathed to Nemours, Joinville and Montpensier, with the last, as the youngest child, getting twice as much as the other two. None of these three, who had hoped that their aunt's will would finally make them independent of their father, was pleased by these dispositions, increasing the political tensions already present in the royal family.[30]

Louis-Philippe was distraught by his sister's death. At three in the afternoon of 31 December, the Chamber of Peers presented itself at the Tuileries to offer their condolences. Among them was Victor Hugo. 'The king came up to me,' he recalled, 'and said: "I thank M. Victor Hugo; he always supports us on sad occasions." His voice was then cut off by tears ... What an emptiness for an old man! Emptiness in the heart, in the home, in the daily routine. It was painful to see him cry. One felt that his sobs were coming from the bottom of his soul.'[31]

On 5 January, Adélaïde was buried in the Orléans family chapel at Dreux. Two kilometres outside the town the funeral procession formed up, escorted by several bishops, one squadron of cuirassiers and another of dragoons, an infantry regiment and the local National Guard. Nemours, Joinville and Montpensier walked behind the coffin, accompanied by numerous aides-de-camp, and Marshal Gérard, who was sobbing. Just outside the royal chapel the king joined the procession and led it inside, where Marie-Amélie and her daughters were waiting. A mass was then said and absolution given. At the close of the *De Profundis*, as Adélaïde's body was carried into the vault, Louis-Philippe collapsed in tears and had to be supported by his sons.[32]

The king's devastation at the loss of his sister, which was still fresh when the 1848 revolution broke out just six weeks later, raises the question of whether Adélaïde's death contributed to the fall of the July monarchy. Mme de Boigne, convinced of the impotence of individuals in the face of great events, responded firmly in the negative in her memoirs:

> I have often heard it said: 'If Mme Adélaïde had lived, the revolution of 1848 would never have happened.' This is a mistake. First of all, in the period of transition in which we are living, from time to time tempests arise that trouble all minds. Nothing can stop them until they have accomplished their task.[33]

More specifically, even if Adélaïde had survived into 1848, the state of her health might well have made her a cause of worry to Louis-Philippe rather than a source of strength. Tellingly, the tone of her relatives' references to her after the revolution is less one of regret that she had not been present to give advice, than of relief that she had been spared the collapse of everything for which she had worked for eighteen years. This was Louis-Philippe's own view. Responding to a letter of condolence from Dupin on the first anniversary of Adélaïde's death, he commented:

> When I lost my excellent sister, who was so loved, and who appreciated you so much, I was far from expecting that I would shortly almost have to thank God for calling her to Him before the explosion of disasters that the year 1848 rained down on France and on ourselves. That is the general feeling of all those who, like you, were attached to her; though her courage was unshakeable, what would have happened to her, in the enfeebled

state to which her illness had reduced her, during the nine long days of that almost miraculous odyssey that my excellent and beloved queen so nobly and painfully endured with me?[34]

Yet this is not the whole picture. It is impossible to know what Adélaïde would have recommended to her brother had she been alive in February 1848. Even so, it is difficult to imagine her sinking into the paralysis that gripped him as the revolution progressed; she was a decisive person, and knew that in crisis situations firm action of almost any sort is preferable to none. Louis-Philippe wavered both in July 1830 and in February 1848. Their different outcomes probably owed much to her presence on the first occasion and her absence on the second.

The last word on Adélaïde should go to Victor Hugo, who enjoyed the two great advantages of literary genius and access to Louis-Philippe and his family. These gave him a clearer insight than most contemporaries, and subsequent historians, into Adélaïde's remarkable qualities and the importance of her political role. On hearing of her death, he recalled a visit that his favourite daughter Léopoldine (Didine) had made to her some years before:

> My dear little Didine went to see her one day with her mother; Mme Adélaïde gave her a doll. My daughter, who was then seven, returned enraptured. A few days later, she heard a great argument in my salon between *Philippistes* and *Carlistes* [supporters of Louis-Philippe and Charles X]. Still playing with her doll, she said in a low voice: 'As for me, I'm an *Adélaïdiste*.'
> This made me an *Adélaïdiste* as well. The death of this brave old princess has caused me great sorrow.[35]

*

THE OPENING OF THE CHAMBERS which had so worried Adélaïde on her sickbed marked the first step towards revolution. The tone of Louis-Philippe's speech from the throne, intended as a riposte to the banqueting campaign, was uncompromising. Worse, like Louis XVI on 23 June 1789 and Charles X on 2 March 1830, he used its last paragraph to throw down a challenge to his audience: 'In the midst of the agitation that blind or enemy passions are fomenting, one conviction animates and sustains me: that we possess in our constitutional monarchy, in the union of the great powers of the state, the sure means of surmounting all these obstacles and satisfying all the moral and material interests of our beloved country.'[36]

Unlike the words of Louis XVI and Charles X, this last phrase contained no threat of emergency action — that would have undermined the whole basis and justification of Louis-Philippe's reign. However, the opposition were infuriated to have 'blind or enemy passions' ascribed to them. On the evidence available, the responsibility for this hard line was essentially the king's. A few days before the opening session, Guizot had told Louis-Philippe that some measure of electoral and parliamentary reform might become inevitable, in which case he himself should perhaps leave the field to a new ministry that could carry it out successfully. It was at this meeting that the king had replied that this would be unconstitutional, since Guizot still had a parliamentary majority. Obviously Guizot is the only source for this exchange, but, aware of its importance, he emphasized in his memoirs that 'every idea, movement and word' of the interview was engraved on his memory, and that he had reproduced them 'with scrupulous fidelity'.[37]

The debate on the address to the speech from the throne, begun in the Chamber of Deputies on 22 January, was long and turbulent. The most notable contribution was made on the 27th by Alexis de Tocqueville, who had already completed his first great work, *Democracy in America*, before being elected as a progressive conservative deputy in 1839. Outwardly, Tocqueville admitted, the situation was calm, but he warned that these appearances were deceptive. Alive to the growing influence of early socialists like Etienne Cabet, Louis Blanc, Charles Fourier and Pierre-Joseph Proudhon, he predicted that the next wave of popular demands would not be political, but social.

Do you not feel [he declaimed to his colleagues], by a sort of instinctive intuition that defies analysis, but which is certain, that the earth is trembling again in Europe? Do you not feel . . . a whiff of revolution in the air? . . . Can you be sure what will happen in France, a year, a month, perhaps a day from now? You cannot; but what you do know is that there is a tempest on the horizon, and that it is bearing down on you.[38]

Tocqueville's answer to these rhetorical questions was practical
and limited: electoral reform, and the replacement of Guizot by
Thiers.[39] Given the government's majority, the latter was clearly
impossible, but increasing numbers even of the ministry's supporters
were coming to feel that the former might be necessary. Their
concerns were given voice by the wealthy carpet-manufacturer and
recently elected deputy, Charles-Jean Sallandrouze, who tabled an
amendment to the address which, while endorsing the government,
expressed the wish that it should introduce 'wise and moderate
reforms'. When the proposal was discussed on 12 February, it proved
sufficiently popular to make even Guizot flinch. His majority had
just been slashed in the voting on a previous amendment, and this
pressure extracted from him, against Louis-Philippe's wishes, a half-
promise of concessions. His words, however, were roundabout and
elliptical:

> On such a matter, Messieurs, to promise is to do more than act;
> because in promising one destroys what exists without replacing
> it. A sensible government can and sometimes should make
> reforms, but it does not announce them in advance; when it
> judges the moment ripe, it acts; until that moment, it keeps
> silent. I could say more; I could say, basing myself on the most
> illustrious examples, that up to that juncture it actually opposes
> them; several of the great reforms that have been achieved in
> England have been accomplished by men who had fought them
> right up until the moment when they felt it was their duty to
> carry them out.[40]

This was the only time that Guizot the great Anglophile publicly
cited Britain's recent history to illuminate his attitude to reform in
France. Yet the point he made was bad history. The Whigs had been
openly committed to parliamentary reform before implementing it in
1832. Even Peel had been privately convinced of the need to repeal
the Corn Laws for some time before doing so, against the wishes of
most of his Conservative party, two years previously in 1846.[41] It
was hardly surprising that Guizot's parallel should be strained and
inaccurate; the central theme of British politics since 1831 had been
judicious concession to avert a major upheaval, which up to now he
had resolutely refused to imitate in France.

Guizot's speech ensured the rejection of the Sallandrouze amendment, but by a majority of only thirty-three. The opposition then refused to vote on the text of the address as a whole, which was favourable to the government, and this move was passed almost unanimously. On paper, the ministry was victorious, but deep unease had been revealed within its own ranks, and its authority on the crucial questions of electoral and parliamentary reform had been seriously eroded. Guizot had hinted that such measures might be introduced in the current legislative session, but his sibylline phrases were quite inadequate to stem the growing demand for change.

Even as the debate on the address was continuing, the reform campaign was planning its next move. An organizing committee of radical deputies, and some republicans, announced their intention of holding another banquet in the 12th *arrondissement* of Paris on 19 January. By this time, however, the authorities' attitude to these gatherings had hardened, and on the 14th the Prefect of Police refused permission for the event to take place. Reformist banquets had been banned before, though this could hardly be called a liberal action, but in the current atmosphere the decision was unwise. At this perceived, and perhaps intended, provocation, the opposition closed ranks; Barrot, Duvergier and the centre-left deputies, who had originally decided not to attend the banquet, now declared that they would do so.[42]

Once again, while citing the example of Britain, the government was failing to apply it. By passing the 1832 reform bill, the Whig ministry had neutralized its most dangerous enemy, the mass cross-class organizations such as the Birmingham Political Union which had been set up to demand constitutional change, and which if systematically resisted could conceivably have become revolutionary. The reform bill had driven a wedge through this movement, pacifying the middle-class elements, rallying them to the side of authority, and isolating the radical and working-class activists.[43] In contrast, in France in 1848 aggressive actions like banning the projected banquet united the opposition instead of dividing it, and made it considerably more dangerous.

Proof of this was soon apparent. The only concession Odilon Barrot demanded for taking part in the banquet was that it should be postponed until after the debates on the address, and this was readily granted. Even Thiers, who up until now had held himself aloof from the banqueting campaign, fiercely defended the proposed gathering in the Chamber. The only sign of unease the organizers betrayed was a decision to raise the price of attending from three to six francs, to hold the banquet on a weekday rather than on a Sunday, and to move it from the 12th *arrondissement* to the much wealthier Champs-Elysées. Having inflamed public opinion, they now wished to keep the workers at arm's length.[44] The central fact was, however, that the opposition was now committed to staging a demonstration that had been forbidden by the authorities. The government and its opponents had manoeuvred themselves into a confrontation.

On 19 February, at a meeting at the restaurant Durand on the Place de la Madeleine, the decision was taken to hold the banquet on Tuesday the 22nd, and that this would be preceded by a mass popular procession in which ninety-two opposition deputies would take part. Thiers' opportunism was more than usually transparent on this occasion. Clearly hoping that the protests would bring him to power but unwilling to be compromised by them, he said nothing, but stood throughout at the door of the meeting room, nodding his head vigorously or gesticulating in support of the speeches he approved.[45]

Yet almost as soon as the decision to proceed was taken, many of the participants began to get cold feet. On the same day that they fixed the date of the banquet, three representatives of the organizing committee met with emissaries of the government and drew up a secret agreement designed to ensure the demonstration was contained. It was agreed that the ninety-two deputies would go to the banquet and take their seats, at which point a commissioner of police would notify them that the gathering was illegal. Odilon Barrot would then make a brief reply upholding the right of assembly, but agreeing to leave with his colleagues. The matter would then be placed before the appeal court, and until it had reached its decision no deputy would attend any other banquets, and each side would do everything possible to prevent the newspapers allied with them from publishing inflammatory articles.[46]

This slightly absurd compromise, which would not have been necessary if Louis-Philippe and his ministry had not adopted such an uncompromising stance on reform in the first place, did initially appear to have resolved the crisis. Yet it was a very delicate arrangement, and as such vulnerable to sabotage by extremists on both sides. The fatal blow was not long in coming. On the morning of 21 February, the main opposition newspapers, the *National*, the *Réforme* and the *Démocratie pacifique*, published the official programme of the next day's banquet. Drawn up by the republican Armand Marrast, who was both editor of the *National* and one of the banquet's organizers, it was an obvious challenge to the government. In this plan, the banquet took second place to a huge popular procession, marshalled down to the last detail. Most provocative of all, it appealed to the National Guard to take part in the march, in uniform and in their individual legions under their officers.[47]

The entry of the National Guard on to the scene was an ominous development. As the symbol both of the 1830 revolution and of organized popular support for the July monarchy, it had an almost talismanic status. By appealing for its backing, Marrast and the opposition press were not only breaking the 1831 law placing it exclusively in the hands of the civil power and forbidding it to play an independent political role, they were also attempting to appropriate a key component of the regime's legitimacy. No government could have ignored this action and kept its authority. The ministers therefore swiftly decided on three measures. The National Guard was reminded that it was forbidden to assemble except by a formal order from its commander-in-chief, the existing law against disturbances of the peace was reissued, and the banquet was unequivocally banned. Arrangements were made to post up these resolutions, justified by a preliminary proclamation, throughout Paris by the next morning.[48]

This turn of events caused consternation among the opposition deputies and the banquet's organizers. They realized immediately how gravely Marrast's plans for the procession damaged their position, and how close it brought a confrontation that, at bottom, few of them desired. In the course of two successive meetings held that afternoon at Odilon Barrot's house, they capitulated completely. At the first, the deputies voted by eighty to seventeen not to attend the banquet. This time Thiers abandoned his silence and spoke forcefully in favour of climbing down. At the second, the organizing committee decided that, for the time being, the banquet should be cancelled. Even Marrast, having let the genie out of the bottle, now tried to put it back in. 'For the sake of humanity, for the love of the people,' he exclaimed, 'give up the banquet . . . If a conflict takes place, the population will be crushed. Do you wish to sacrifice it to the hatred of Louis-Philippe and M. Guizot?'[49]

In fact, Louis-Philippe was filled with glee rather than hatred. He was delighted when he heard that the opposition had backed down, and felt that his decision to take a hard line had been completely vindicated. He crowed his satisfaction to Salvandy, the minister of education, who in 1830 had remarked that Charles X's government was dancing on a volcano and had recently repeated the warning to his own colleagues. 'Well, Salvandy! You told us yesterday we were sitting on a volcano; it really is something, your volcano! They've given up the banquet, dear man! I told you it would be no more than a puff of smoke!'[50]

Yet Louis-Philippe was being overconfident. His parliamentary opponents may have been routed, but however quickly the government's proclamation was published across the capital it would not reach enough Parisians in time to prevent large numbers of them assembling the next morning. A fateful combination of royal intransigence, opposition provocation, and blunders caused by fear and panic, had made a trial of strength on the streets inevitable.

*

THE KEY TO THE SITUATION now lay with the forces of order, and with the plans at their disposal to contain the expected disturbances. On paper, the government had solid grounds for confidence. There were 31,000 regular troops concentrated in and around Paris, well armed and provisioned, supplemented by 3,900 municipal guards, a military police force under the orders of the Prefect of Paris.[51] The army staff also had a detailed strategy for repressing disorder, prepared by Marshal Gérard after the last attempted Parisian rising in May 1839.

The 'Gérard plan' aimed to ensure government control of the centre of Paris, conceived as a semicircle based on the Seine stretching from the Place de la Bastille in the east to the Place de la Concorde in the west. This would be achieved by the occupation of key positions, to be linked at all times by regular patrols of between twenty-five and ninety men, thus not only containing any potential insurrection but also allowing it no time to develop. As Gérard wrote in the introduction to his plan: 'To comb through Paris in every direction via strong patrols; to protect these patrols with reserves established at points that can be used as local centres of operation, which I term strategic points; to connect these points to each other by simple lines of communication – this is the goal that I have set myself.'[52]

With the example of the July revolution and the subsequent riots of the 1830s in mind, Gérard was well aware of the problems the warren of streets on the central right bank posed for the movement of troops: 'The field of operations is simply a series of defiles without any order.' Fortunately, he continued, it could be controlled via seven main streets, which he termed 'strategic lines', radiating out from the central *quais* of the right bank and including the Rues Montmartre, St Denis, St Martin, Filles du Calvaire and Richelieu. These lines in turn dictated the 'strategic points' to be occupied: the Places des Victoires, de la Concorde, de la Bastille, de l'Hôtel de Ville and de la Pointe Ste Eustache, the Boulevard St Denis, and the centre of operations, the Place du Carrousel next to the Tuileries.[53]

Methodical and minutely detailed, the 'Gérard plan' was shrewdly calculated both to give insurrection no chance to develop on the ground and to preserve what had so signally collapsed in July 1830, the lines of communication between the government forces. Yet in the context of February 1848, it had dangerous flaws. The most central one was that it was designed to contain a revolt, not a revolution. This was reflected in the relatively small number of troops Gérard deemed necessary, and put very precisely at 5,965 men, 530 horses and 10 cannon.[54] It is true that nobody in command foresaw that the events of February 1848 would develop into a revolution, and indeed it was not inevitable that they would. Yet it remains remarkable that at no point during Louis-Philippe's reign was any wider plan ever drawn up to prepare for this eventuality, despite the grim precedents of 1789 and 1830.

The answer to this mystery went back to the origins of the July monarchy. Despite its increasing conservatism, its defenders could not conceive that there could be a genuine mass rising against a political system that had itself been born of a revolution. This – their – revolution, they were convinced, had ended the series of upheavals in France since 1789. It defied logic that the people would overthrow a regime they had themselves created. Yet history often defies logic, and the intellectual certainty of Guizot and his colleagues left them dangerously exposed to the unpredictability of events.

Louis-Philippe's attitude was rather different from that of his ministers. A realist to his fingertips, he shared their hope but not their confidence that France's revolutionary cycle had really been broken. But despite his record of energetically suppressing Parisian insurrections in the 1830s, he was far more pessimistic about the prospects of resisting a full-scale revolution. This view was probably rooted in his early experiences of 1789 and the indelible impression it had made on him. As Guizot commented perceptively in his memoirs:

> While realizing the errors of the Revolution, Louis-Philippe never completely freed himself from its spell; he had seen it at the beginning in such brilliance and strength. . . . that it seemed to him to possess irresistible and fatal power. He saw it as both necessary and infinitely difficult to fight against its passions and its demands; and though convinced that these were irreconcilable with a free and ordered government, he was not convinced that such a government could successfully oppose them.[55]

Louis-Philippe had always had a streak of fatalism, and this can only have reinforced the attitude Guizot describes. Taken together, these factors made him vulnerable to a collapse of will in the face of a further instalment of the upheavals that had dominated his life.

A further flaw in the 'Gérard plan' was its reliance on the Paris National Guard as well as on the regular army. At first sight, this seemed entirely sensible; with 85,000 men in its ranks, the National Guard was a major component of the forces of order. Throughout the 1830s its loyalty had never wavered, and it had played a crucial part in repressing the disturbances of those years. Yet since then its dispositions had become far less certain, to the extent that Louis-Philippe, fearing a repeat of the review in 1827 at which Charles X had been insulted, had not inspected it since 1840. Unsurprisingly, given the fact that many of the National Guardsmen who were expected to defend the regime did not qualify to vote for its deputies, large numbers of them had been won over by the movement for electoral reform.[56] The National Guardsmen chose their own officers, and in the course of 1847 the effect of the banqueting campaign had been shown in the number of politically radical ones they elected.

Under these circumstances, the most sensible course would have been to alter the 'Gérard plan' to exclude the National Guard from its operations. Louis-Philippe had been warned of its unreliability, in particular by Montalivet, himself a colonel of the National Guard cavalry, in January. Yet the king and his ministers stubbornly refused to alter their opinions or their actions. Part of the responsibility lies with General Jacqueminot, the incompetent and frequently ill commander-in-chief of the Paris National Guard, who consistently misinformed his superiors about his troops' state of mind. Louis-Philippe questioned him twice on the matter, once in January after speaking to Montalivet, and again on 22 February, the day the banquet was to have been held. On the second occasion, Jacqueminot answered that of 384 companies, only six or seven were ill-disposed, a claim that even the king seems to have disbelieved.[57]

At a deeper level, the government's reluctance to doubt the National Guard's loyalty was as much psychological as practical. For a regime that owed its existence to a popular revolution, yet obstinately refused to extend the vote to more than a tiny elite, the National Guard offered its most important democratic credentials. Standing proxy for the people in a very real sense, the Guard formed a critical part of the July monarchy's legitimacy. For Louis-Philippe and his ministers, the possibility of its defection was thus so alarming that they preferred not to contemplate it. Given the situation, this was the worst possible course of action. An armed confrontation could have been avoided by conceding electoral reform, or in all probability won by using the army alone. Instead, the government opted for the latter path, but using the unreliable National Guard. In its fear of an expanded electorate, the July monarchy delivered itself into the hands of a far less predictable and more dangerous body.

This combination of a hard-line policy towards popular protest, and complacent confidence in the National Guard, comes across clearly in the correspondence of Louis-Philippe's eldest surviving son Nemours, who played an important military role in February 1848. Writing to his brother Joinville, currently serving in Algeria, he

recognized that the opposition would attempt to subvert the National
Guard, but was sublimely confident that this would have no effect.
The rioters, he predicted, would avoid

> any appearance of radicalism or communism, the fear of which
> would rally most of the National Guard to the side of the
> authorities. On the contrary, they will use against us a certain
> number of National Guardsmen who have been won over to the
> side of sedition, which could badly affect the morale of many of
> their comrades. Nevertheless, should the occasion arise, every-
> body agrees that we will have with us a sufficient number of
> National Guards who oppose all disorder to lend us the moral
> force we need.[58]

The need for the 'moral force' that only the National Guard
could provide seems to have blinded Nemours to the dangers of its
deployment. His arguments are unlikely to have convinced Joinville,
who with his younger brother Aumale had been sent to Algeria
precisely because he had become alarmed that his father's increasing
conservatism was leading to a revolutionary situation. Indeed, a
subtext of Nemours' letters at this time is his determination to
prevent Joinville and Aumale returning to France to challenge the
government's intransigent stance. 'In this situation, my dear friend,'
he concluded, 'I'm not thinking of advising you to return . . . If there
is an upheaval, [even] if you left the moment you got this letter
you'd arrive too late. It's also by no means certain there will be one
. . . Pass this letter on to Aumale, who should also know the way
things stand.'[59]

The final mistake made in these days was not to create a unified
command. The National Guard was headed by General Jacqueminot,
and the regular troops, grouped in the 1st military division, by
General Tiburce Sébastiani. The latter was more competent than the
former, but both owed their positions to their connections rather than
to their talents. Jacqueminot was the father-in-law of Duchâtel, the
interior minister, and Tiburce Sébastiani the brother of Marshal
Sébastiani. For these reasons, as well as their exemplary political
loyalty, they were kept in place, although their shortcomings were
plain. There was a tacit understanding, but no more than that,
between the king and his ministers that if the situation became

dangerous the leadership of both army and National Guard would be entrusted to the prestigious Algerian veteran Marshal Bugeaud. In the meantime, Nemours attempted to play a coordinating role between Sébastiani and Jacqueminot, but he had neither the necessary institutional nor the personal authority to make himself obeyed. To Bugeaud, who was ambitious for overall command, this situation and the delays it imposed were deeply frustrating. 'Time is pressing,' he told one of the ministers. 'I'm a good doctor, but not so good that I can save the dying.'[60]

For a brief moment on the evening of 21 February, it was decided to implement the Gérard plan for the following morning. However, after the news that the banquet had been cancelled, coupled with a report that even the leaders of the republican secret societies had renounced any attempt at insurrection the next day, the order was countermanded as being both unnecessary and provocative. Thus when the first crowds began to gather on the morning of the 22nd, under a persistent drizzle from a grey sky, they were unopposed by the forces of order. Leaderless, they milled about along the route that the pre-banquet procession was to have taken, but posed no serious threat. During the afternoon, however, a large crowd gathered in the Place de la Concorde, and began to build a first barricade on the corner of the Rue de Rivoli and the Rue St Florentin. Eventually pushed out of the square by the municipal guards, it then began to loot gun shops along the Rue St Honoré.[61]

At their command post, the National Guard headquarters in the wing of the Tuileries fronting on to the Rue de Rivoli, Tiburce Sébastiani and Jacqueminot had been following the day's events closely. When they received the news of these latest developments, at around 5 p.m., they finally decided to apply the Gérard plan. Ominously, when the drums beat the summons to arms for the National Guard throughout the city, the response was poor, and even those who did turn out were often ill-disposed. There was, however, no such problem with the army; by 9 p.m. it had occupied all the prescribed 'strategic points', encountering little resistance. At 1 a.m. on 23 February, calm having returned to the city with the night, the troops were ordered back to barracks, leaving behind only a few detachments. Six hours later, they began to move into position again, dispersing the crowds which this time had gathered in the central right-bank areas around the Rue Montmartre and the Rue du Temple. For several hours, their mastery of this 'heartland of revolt', as Gérard termed it, was unchallenged.[62]

The turning-point came in mid-morning, when the National Guard was called out once more. It would have been much better if it had stayed at home. Only one legion, the 1st, was solidly loyal. The 2nd and 3rd went to their posts shouting: 'Long live reform!' and 'Down with the system! Down with Guizot!' Assigned to protect the Bank of France, the 3rd legion then interposed itself between the municipal guard and the crowd, forcing the former to return to barracks, and finally used their bayonets to prevent the cuirassiers of the regular cavalry from clearing the Place des Victoires. The 4th legion somehow found time to draw up a petition demanding the ministry's impeachment. The effect on the line regiments stationed next to the National Guard can be imagined. Just off the Rue St Denis, a passer-by asked an army officer: 'Is the riot serious?' – 'It's not the rioters I'm worried about,' replied the officer, shrugging his shoulders – 'So what are you worried about?' – 'The National Guard, who if things carry on like this will have their fun by shooting us in the back.'[63]

It was at the news of the Guard's defection, significantly, that Louis-Philippe began to crumble. Up until that moment, he had been breezily confident that having wrong-footed his political opponents, he would have no trouble dispersing the Parisians. The morning's events destroyed all these certainties at one blow. If the king wished to maintain his hard-line policy, it was now clear that he must order the regular troops, if necessary, to fire on the National Guard, and at the end of this path gaped the abyss of civil war. Like Louis XVI in 1789, this was a step Louis-Philippe refused to take.[64] To turn on the National Guard would be symbolically to turn on his own people, and this he was psychologically incapable of doing. For the moment, he simply sank back in his chair, muttering over and over again: 'I've seen enough blood!' After the event, he explained his thinking in more detail:

> Could I have defended myself? With what? The army? Oh! I know it would have done its duty bravely ... But only the army was willing, and that wasn't enough for me. The National

Guard, that force on which I was so happy to base my rule, the National Guard of Paris, the city which before all the rest had said to me in 1830: 'Take the crown and save us from the republic!' The National Guard of Paris, which I'd always treated so well, either stood aside, or declared against me. Defend myself? No, I couldn't![65]

Louis-Philippe's paralysis in the face of the National Guard was shared by almost all his advisers. Even Guizot and his colleagues, those staunch partisans of *résistance*, felt no differently. In manuscript notes he wrote later, in the third person, about the February revolution, the king took pains to emphasize this fact:

Indeed, one could not, and above all should not have, undertaken to give the order to the troops of the line to fire on the National Guard. The ministers ... had all declared that they would not take upon themselves the responsibility of such a measure, and undoubtedly Louis-Philippe would have rejected it had the council advised him to do so.[66]

From this point on, concessions became inevitable. The first was the dismissal of Guizot. That morning, horrified by the tidings about the National Guard, Marie-Amélie had made one of her rare political interventions and begged her husband to replace his prime minister. She had been supported in this by her youngest son Montpensier. Finally yielding, Louis-Philippe called Guizot and Duchâtel to the Tuileries at 2.30 p.m. The two ministers found him in his study, flanked by Marie-Amélie, Nemours and Montpensier. The king told them of his decision, stressing how reluctantly he had taken it: 'It is with bitter regret that I am parting with you; but necessity and the safety of the monarchy demand this sacrifice. My own wishes must come second; I'm going to lose a lot of ground; I shall need time to win it back.' With these words, nineteenth-century France's longest ministry came to an end.[67]

Having failed to make concessions from a position of strength, Louis-Philippe now found out how difficult this is to do successfully from one of weakness. His first move was to send for Molé, who had consistently warned of the dangers of Guizot's political intransigence and accepted the necessity of extending the franchise. As Molé put it later: 'My opinion that reform was advisable was known to the king, and he was well aware that in calling me to form a ministry, he was giving his consent to this measure.'[68]

Whatever pleasure Molé must have felt at finally triumphing over his enemy Guizot was surely tempered by the circumstances of his victory. The monarchy's situation was dangerous, perhaps fatal. It could only be saved, he advised the king, by the two most popular politicians still loyal to the crown, Thiers and Odilon Barrot; they, rather than himself, should be asked to form a government. Louis-Philippe was horrified: 'Call Thiers! What would Europe say?' – 'It's not Europe we should be thinking about at this moment,' replied Molé. 'The house is on fire.' Eventually he agreed to see if his political allies would be willing to serve under him, and whether Thiers' support could be expected. His conviction that he was not the man for the job, however, was shown in his lack of energy over the next few hours.[69]

Meanwhile, as the news of Guizot's dismissal spread, confrontation between the soldiers and the people gradually ceased. This was a positive development, but it left the crowd very much in the ascendant. Groups of Parisians marched through the streets, compelling the householders along their route to illuminate their windows in celebration. The largest procession gathered on the Place de la Bastille and headed west along the boulevards. At around 9.30 in the evening, it arrived in front of the foreign ministry on the Boulevard des Capucines, occupied until that afternoon by Guizot and now guarded by the 14th regiment of the line. The pressure of the front ranks on the troops became intense, as they were pushed by those behind, and the soldiers had to cross bayonets to prevent themselves being forced back. At that moment an isolated shot rang out – it has never been established from which side. Almost certainly without orders, the nervous soldiers hastily fired two volleys into the mass of people facing them. The effect was lethal: over sixty demonstrators were killed, and over eighty wounded.[70]

The 'fusillade of the Boulevard des Capucines' has sometimes been seen as the catalyst that transformed a riot into a revolution. It was certainly a windfall for those who did wish to overthrow the monarchy. Sixteen of the bodies left lying on the pavement were placed on a passing cart and carried in a symbolic cortège first to the offices of the *National* and the *Réforme*, where inflammatory harangues were delivered, and then on a three-hour circuit of the eastern right bank. The republican leaders swiftly met and decided to mount a full-scale insurrection. Soon afterwards the tocsin rang out from the city churches, summoning the Parisians to arms, and the building of barricades began. It has been estimated that 1,512 barricades, comprising 1,277,640 paving-stones pulled up from the streets, went up in Paris during the February revolution, mostly on this single night.[71]

Yet even if the catastrophe of the Boulevard des Capucines could have been averted, this would probably not have prevented some other incident having the same effect. The mistakes of Louis-Philippe and his ministers in handling the crisis created such an unstable situation that any ceasefire was vulnerable to the smallest act of sabotage or, as most likely in this case, a simple accident. The real turning-point was not the Boulevard des Capucines affair, but the miscalculation over the National Guard: from that moment on, the king and his advisers were on a slippery slope.

The history of the next few hours is complex and frequently unclear. Events succeeded each other so rapidly that even the participants often had difficulty remembering them exactly. In addition, much of the testimony of those on the government side was given to a commission of inquiry set up by the succeeding regime to establish whether they had committed any criminal acts during the February revolution. Reading their words now, one gets the impression that they were understandably trying to present their actions in as moderate and pacific a light as possible. But although some mysteries remain, a broad outline of what occurred can be established.

The Boulevard des Capucines fusillade convinced Molé, who heard the news on his way back from an unsatisfactory meeting with Thiers, that it was no longer possible for him to form a government. As the dominant figure of the parliamentary left, with useful links to the banqueting movement, Thiers now seemed the only politician who could defuse the crisis, and by midnight Louis-Philippe had accepted the fact. At the same time, having hesitated all day, he finally took the decision to entrust overall command of the troops and the National Guard to Bugeaud. Probably he hoped that the conservative marshal would counterbalance Thiers' tendency to populism. He was wrong, and this action was the last fatal mistake of his reign. Although personal friends, Thiers and Bugeaud differed significantly on how to deal with the situation, and these differences dealt the final blow to the regime.[72]

Arriving at the Tuileries in the early hours of the morning, Thiers had a detailed, and at times difficult, conversation with the king. Thiers was prepared to form a ministry on three conditions: that Odilon Barrot should be his principal collaborator, that a scheme of electoral and parliamentary reform be introduced that added seventy to eighty seats to the Chamber and made the holding of certain public offices incompatible with the function of deputy, and that a general election be held. Even at this critical stage, Louis-Philippe made strenuous objections to these demands. He finally agreed to authorize an official announcement that Thiers had been charged, with Barrot, to form a government, and to allow Thiers to retire the next day if a compromise could not be found on the two other issues.[73]

At the mention of Bugeaud's appointment Thiers became uncomfortable, and complained that the decision had been taken without consulting him. Aware of the unfair odium Bugeaud had incurred during the Paris rising of 1834 as the 'butcher of the Rue Transnonain', he no doubt feared that the marshal's reputation would compromise the ministry's attempts at pacification. Nonetheless, he accepted the fait accompli with which the king had presented him, and left to concert his strategy with Bugeaud.[74]

Arriving at his headquarters at around two in the morning, Bugeaud had immediately set about restoring his officers' battered morale. He was a confident and charismatic commander, and his words and actions soon had the desired effect. A veteran of the bloody siege of Saragossa during the Peninsular War, he had the added advantage of knowledge of urban warfare. He swiftly drew up a plan of attack to wrest the centre of Paris from the insurgents. Like Marmont in 1830, he ordered three columns east to crush the uprising – in two cases, with the same destinations, the Hôtel de Ville and the Place de la Bastille. Unlike Marmont, however, he made his columns substantial ones. The first, commanded by General Bedeau and aimed at the Place de la Bastille, was 2,000 strong; the second, led by

Tiburce Sébastiani and ordered to march on the Hôtel de Ville, had fully 3,500 men. A smaller force under Colonel Brunet was dispatched across the left bank to reinforce a detachment already in position at the Panthéon. Bugeaud had learned a further lesson from 1830: to prevent the Parisians isolating his forces by building barricades behind them after they had passed, he assigned a further column to follow in the wake of the two first columns to keep their lines of communication open. Significantly, he excluded the National Guard from any role in his operations.[75]

Bugeaud's swift adoption of an offensive policy sits uneasily with Louis-Philippe's professed desire to avoid the shedding of blood. It even raises the question whether the king's insistence – after the event – that he had been determined not to fire on the National Guard was not a disingenuous attempt to disguise a moment of simple panic as a principled stand. This is, however, unlikely, since many witnesses testified to the king's reluctance to shed blood throughout the revolution. Louis-Philippe probably hoped that Bugeaud's offensive, coupled with the spreading news of a Thiers–Barrot reforming ministry, would rally the National Guard and pacify the crowds. The alternative, a pitched battle in the streets, was too awful to contemplate, so he did not. This impression is confirmed by Bugeaud's testimony to the later commission of inquiry into the events of these days. When he left the king's study to take charge of his headquarters, the marshal recalled, he had received 'not one order, not one instruction'.[76]

Despite his sanguinary reputation, Bugeaud's own attitude towards the use of force on 24 February was ambiguous. On the surface, he was pugnacious. According to an authoritative account, when Thiers arrived at his headquarters the marshal confidently outlined his plan of attack, and added: 'I'll have the pleasure of killing a lot of this rabble.' His views on the National Guard were equally robust: 'It would no doubt be very unfortunate if it refused to march with us, or tried to march against us . . . that would be no reason to throw in my hand.'[77]

Bugeaud's orders to his commanders, however, belied his words. In his testimony to the commission of inquiry, he insisted that the main aim of his columns was to 'rally' the National Guard to the side of the authorities. He also claimed that the troops 'received

instructions not to take the initiative in hostilities, to act by persuasion, and only to use their weapons if attacked'. These words must
be treated with caution, since Bugeaud had every reason to minimize
his bellicosity in front of the commission; but that is equally no
reason to rule them totally out of court. They are also confirmed by
General Bedeau at his own appearance before the commission.
Bedeau recalled that he was ordered 'to act in concert with the
National Guard that I would find on my route in order to open up
communications with the Place de la Bastille, to announce the
formation of the Thiers–Barrot ministry, to restore order and public
tranquillity, and only to use force if these efforts proved futile'.[78]

The columns set off at 5.30 in the morning of 24 February. Their
cautious instructions did not prevent those of Sébastiani and Brunet
reaching the Hôtel de Ville and the Panthéon respectively with little
difficulty and few casualties. It was a different matter, however, for
Bedeau. Advancing north and then turning east along the boulevards,
he encountered little resistance until the corner of the Boulevard
Bonne-Nouvelle and the Rue St Denis, where a substantial barricade
blocked his path. At this moment, critically, a group of National
Guardsmen interposed themselves, claiming that the news of the
appeal to Thiers and Barrot was not yet widely known in the area,
and begging Bedeau not to open fire but to send to headquarters for
proclamations announcing the new ministry.[79]

In a further demonstration of the authority the Guard enjoyed
even in the eyes of the regular army, Bedeau did not brush this
intervention aside and summon the barricade's defenders to disperse,
but agreed to the request.[80] Why he did so is unclear: his action fell
just within the cautious remit Bugeaud had given him, but the delay
while he waited for further orders gave the crowd gathering around
him time to expand and made his task even more difficult. It is most
probable that he sensed Bugeaud's unease that if he opened fire he
might not be supported by Thiers and Barrot. Disavowal by a
superior civilian authority was a soldier's worst nightmare, and fear
of this is the likeliest reason for Bedeau's hesitation.

At approximately 8 a.m. a wealthy local merchant, M. Fauvelle-
Delebarre, offered to go himself to Bugeaud's headquarters, acquaint
him with the situation, and bring back instructions. He returned at
nine with an extraordinary document: a command to cease all hostil-

ities, pull back to the Tuileries, and leave the maintenance of calm in Paris to the National Guard.[81]

The genesis of this order is the greatest mystery of the February revolution. None of those in a position to issue it — Bugeaud, Thiers, Barrot and Louis-Philippe himself — afterwards accepted responsibility. Since the ceasefire was the second decisive event that doomed the July monarchy, this is perhaps not surprising. Bugeaud later claimed that the order came specifically from the king, while Louis-Philippe, Thiers and Barrot never directly addressed the issue. On balance, it seems unlikely that Bugeaud would have given the command on his own. Retreat was not in his character, and in any case his strategy had by no means failed: Bedeau may have been in difficulties, but Sébastiani and Brunet had reached their positions and were holding them successfully.

It is far more probable that Thiers and Barrot had a hand in the order; the real question is whether Louis-Philippe did too. In his evidence to the commission of inquiry, Bugeaud's answer was unequivocally yes. At about 8 a.m. on 24 February, he stated, 'MM. Thiers and Barrot brought me an order from the king to pull the troops back at every point and to concentrate them around the Tuileries and the Tuileries gardens, wishing, they said, to leave to the National Guard alone the task of restoring order.' Yet Louis-Philippe himself, in an hour-by-hour analysis of the events of the 23rd and 24th that he later set down, strongly implied that Thiers and Barrot called the ceasefire first and only informed him afterwards. 'At 9.30 or 10 a.m.,' he wrote, in the present tense and once again in the third person, 'Thiers and O. Barrot notify the king that they have given the order to cease firing.' The ultimate responsibility for this fateful decision will probably never be settled. More important than who took the decision was the crucial factor that made it possible — the general lack of political will to resolve the crisis by force.[82]

General Bedeau's retreat, hemmed in by the crowds along the Boulevard Bonne-Nouvelle, soon degenerated into a rout. The Parisians jostled the soldiers, whose new orders forbade them to respond, broke up their ranks, and even forced them to reverse arms. When they reached the Place de la Concorde, inextricably mixed with the people, the municipal guards stationed there took them for insurgents and fired on them. When Bedeau finally managed to reform them, they were completely demoralized. A similar fate befell Sébastiani's troops drawn up in front of the Hôtel de Ville. Ordered in turn to cease hostilities, they stood by impotent while the situation around them grew increasingly chaotic, until a captain of the National Guard entered the Hôtel de Ville unopposed. This enterprising officer told Tiburce Sébastiani and the Prefect of Paris, whom he found there, that he was taking over the building in the name of the people, whereupon both men simply left. Now leaderless, the soldiers outside disbanded, many giving up their arms to the people, and drifted back to their barracks.[83]

The news of Bedeau's disaster was brought to the king at the Tuileries at around 10.30 a.m. After briefly considering Thiers' advice to retire with the army to St Cloud and regroup there, he decided to hold his ground. Something then happened that awoke eerie echoes of that earlier ill-fated defence of the palace on 10 August 1792, and definitively broke Louis-Philippe's will to resist. Like Louis XVI, he went outside to review the regular troops and the remaining National Guards massed in the Place du Carrousel. At first there were shouts of 'Long live the king!', but when Louis-Philippe came to the National Guards his reception grew much more mixed. The 4th legion in particular cried: 'Long live reform! Down with the ministers!', broke ranks, and advanced menacingly towards him. As Louis XVI had done fifty-five years earlier, Louis-Philippe turned around, went back into the Tuileries, sank into an armchair and put his head in his hands.[84]

The ground-floor study where the king sat slumped swiftly became a scene of pandemonium. Members of the royal family, ministers and generals crowded into the room, and were continually joined by officers, politicians and even spectators who simply walked in from the Tuileries courtyard. Thiers, in the grip of a temporary breakdown, kept repeating: 'The sea is rising! The sea is rising!' In these circumstances, it was easy to take the decision to replace him as prime minister with Barrot. Bugeaud, attacked by several of those present as an obstacle to pacification, was similarly sacrificed, and Marshal Gérard was sent for to succeed him.[85]

By this time messengers were arriving to report that a cry for the king's abdication had gone up from the ever-growing crowds outside. This news was given added urgency by a sudden outbreak of firing just to the west. The Château d'Eau guard post on the Place du Palais-royal, held by a detachment of the 14th regiment of the line that the previous day had delivered the 'fusillade of the Boulevard des Capucines', had been attacked. Convinced that the regiment had deliberately fired on the people, the Parisians were determined to punish them, as their ancestors had the Swiss Guard on 10 August 1792. Eventually they forced the soldiers back inside the guardhouse and set it on fire. The soldiers were eventually allowed to surrender, but their commanding officer was murdered.[86]

With the sound of musketry coming closer, shouts of 'Abdication!' rose from the back of the packed study in the Tuileries. They were repeated by several of those around the king's armchair. Finally, overwhelmed, the old man muttered the fateful words: 'I abdicate.' He then got up, walked to the door of the salon where the queen was waiting, and repeated more loudly: 'I abdicate!' If Louis-Philippe's actions that day echoed those of Louis XVI, Marie-Amélie's recalled those of Marie Antoinette. She was, after all, her niece. Like her aunt on 10 August 1792, she urged her husband to stay and fight to the last. 'Better to die here than leave by that door!' she sobbed. 'Get on your horse, the army will follow you!' Then, turning to everyone in the room: 'You'll regret this! . . . You didn't deserve such a good king!'[87]

At this moment Marshal Gérard entered the study. Although he was seventy-five (the same age as Louis-Philippe), lame and blind in one eye, he had immediately obeyed the royal summons. Even though he was not in uniform, he was put on a horse and sent out into the streets to announce the abdication and try to calm the tumult. For good measure, Nemours thrust an olive branch into his hand as a sign of peace. As he was approaching the Place du Palais-royal, however, Gérard realized that he had no written proof of the abdication to show the crowds. He immediately sent an aide-de-camp back to the Tuileries to request this, and the king complied.[88]

Louis-Philippe is one of the few monarchs in modern history to have left an account of his own abdication. 'I sat at my desk,' he recalled, 'writing out my abdication in a few lines, in the midst of a crowd of people, some of them unknown to me, but whose greedy eyes followed each word I formed, and shouting all together: "Hurry up, get it over with, you don't have a moment to lose, don't make it

so long." ' While passing the crown to his grandson the comte de
Paris, the king omitted to make the boy's mother, the duchesse
d'Orléans, regent. There was an altercation when this was spotted,
since the duchesse was a political ally of many in the room, but
Louis-Philippe insisted that this would be illegal, and those around
him grudgingly gave way:

> 'All right! All right! Just give us the paper straight away,
> because any defence is out of the question, and if you delay,
> you'll expose yourself and all your family to the greatest peril.'
> — 'But I must take a copy.' — 'That's impossible,' they replied,
> grabbing hold of the paper, which was immediately whisked
> away, I have no idea where, without my being able to keep any
> copy.[89]

If Adélaïde had been alive, could she have averted such a
humiliating catastrophe? It would have been extremely difficult for
her to urge a confrontational course. She had always stressed the
July monarchy's popular origins more than Louis-Philippe, and a
Parisian revolution against it would have embarrassed her even more
than him. It is suggestive, however, that February 1848 was the first
insurrection Louis-Philippe had faced without her at his side — the
last occasion had been in May 1839, when she was still fit and well.
Had Adélaïde been present and in good health in 1848, it is difficult to think this would have made no difference. Whichever choice
she had made between a hard-line policy and one of concession, she
would not have allowed herself to become disastrously caught
between the two, as her brother did. Discouragement and indecision
were not in her nature, and she would surely have fortified him
against both.

It was now just after midday. Louis-Philippe's plan was to leave
the capital and retire to Eu, where he hoped at least to be left in
peace. The duchesse d'Orléans and Nemours were to stay behind to
protect the young king and his brother. Carriages were ordered, and
the king hurriedly changed from his uniform into a frock-coat. By
this time, however, the crowd had penetrated into the Place du
Carrousel. Seeing the carriages lumbering out of the stables, they
fired on them, killing a groom and two horses, then seized and burnt
them. Fortunately for the royal family, Nemours, who witnessed the

attack, immediately ordered three light vehicles that happened to be standing in the courtyard of the Tuileries to whip up, drive along the *quai*, and wait in the Place de la Concorde.

The little procession left the palace and began to walk across the Tuileries gardens: at its head the exhausted Louis-Philippe, supported by Marie-Amélie, then his daughter Clémentine and her husband the Duke of Saxe-Coburg, the duchesse de Nemours and her children, the duc and duchesse de Montpensier, and a few retainers. The faithful Montalivet and a squadron of National Guard cavalry provided the escort.[90]

At the Place de la Concorde, there was a moment of acute anxiety: the carriages were nowhere to be seen. As he stood on the site where Louis XVI, Marie Antoinette and his own father had been guillotined, terrible pictures rose up in Louis-Philippe's mind. Writing later to Guizot, he recalled 'the frightful magic lantern of everything the Place [de la Concorde] had witnessed, and which flashed through my memory during those short, yet at the time extremely long, moments I spent on 24 February on that very spot!'[91]

Shortly afterwards, the carriages were seen approaching. They pulled up, and the fugitives – fifteen in all – squeezed in. The soldiers, National Guardsmen and onlookers still on the Place did not at first realize what was happening; when they did, there were a few cries of 'Long live the king!' Surrounded by Montalivet's National Guard cavalry and two squadrons of cuirassiers, the convoy moved off towards the west.[92]

*

THE LAST ACT OF the July monarchy was played out not by Louis-Philippe, but by his daughter-in-law. After the king's departure, the duchesse d'Orléans returned with her children to her apartments in the Pavillon de Marsan. She was found there soon afterwards by Adélaïde's old friend Dupin, who had been walking to the Chamber of Deputies when he had heard the news of Louis-Philippe's abdication, and had rushed over to the Tuileries to see for himself what was going on.[93]

The two principal accounts of what happened next, those of Dupin and of the duc de Nemours, do not agree. Dupin claims that a messenger arrived from Louis-Philippe, telling his daughter-in-law to meet him with her children by the Place de la Concorde, where Odilon Barrot, the new prime minister, would take charge of her. According to Nemours, he himself urged the duchesse to make her way to the Place, where he was gathering the remaining loyal troops, who could then escort her in an orderly withdrawal either to St Cloud or to the fort of Mont-Valérien to the west of the city.[94]

Which version is correct, or why they differ, is of secondary importance. The result was that the duchesse set off in turn across the Tuileries gardens on Dupin's arm. With her free hand she led the little comte de Paris, whose other hand was taken by a colleague of Dupin's, the marquis de Grammont. The duc de Chartres, who was slightly unwell, was carried by his doctor, and a few officers who had stayed on at the palace brought up the rear.[95]

Whatever plan the little group may have had at the beginning, it had changed by the time they approached the Place de la Concorde. This may have been because they learned that Louis-Philippe had already left and that Barrot had not yet arrived (the latter, having vainly tried to pacify the crowds on the boulevards, had installed himself in the ministry of the interior on the Rue de Grenelle and, inexplicably, did not leave it until the early afternoon). It may also be that the duchesse d'Orléans, fired by the idea of a grand gesture to rally support for her son, had a moment of inspiration. Either way, as the party entered the Place de la Concorde, Dupin took off his hat and cried: 'Long live the comte de Paris, King of the French! Long live Mme la duchesse d'Orléans, the regent!' Dupin seems to have been hoping for a 'popular coronation' similar to that of Louis-Philippe on 31 July 1830. He claimed in his memoirs to have advised the duchesse to 'entrust herself to the National Guard' and to exchange his own arm for that of a Guard officer, which she did. The gamble worked; the crowd on the Place took up Dupin's cry, and opened up a path for the duchesse to the nearby Chamber of Deputies.[96]

To ratify the succession by the acclamation of the people's representatives was a bold stroke, but a risky one. A number of deputies, meeting at midday, had declared for the republic, and were already preparing their moves in the Chamber. They had also just secured the support of the greatest parliamentary orator of the day, the poet Alphonse de Lamartine, who from his original legitimist stance had over the years moved steadily to the left. The radical republicans had decided on insurrection after the fusillade of the Boulevard des Capucines the previous day.[97]

The duchesse d'Orléans entered the Chamber at 1.30 p.m., holding each of her sons by the hand. She was greeted by a standing ovation and cries of: 'Long live the king!' 'Long live the regent!' Barrot was still absent, but Dupin mounted the tribune in his place, announcing the abdication of Louis-Philippe and the accession of the comte de Paris, and demanding that the enthusiasm with which the deputies had just greeted him be formally recorded. But this initial triumph was swiftly undermined by the republicans' delaying tactics. Lamartine moved that the session should be suspended because of the presence of 'the august princess'. The moderate president of the Chamber, Jean Sauzet, perhaps believing Lamartine well disposed, agreed, and asked the duchesse and her children to leave. Amid mounting chaos the duchesse, who had been joined by Nemours, refused. As the press of bodies around the tribune grew intolerable, she and her family retreated slowly up through the ranked benches. Symbolically, they finally installed themselves among the deputies of the centre-left, the party of Dupin, Molé and Sébastiani, which had always furnished the July monarchy's best friends and shrewdest advisers.[98]

As the tumult subsided, the republican Alexandre Marie came to the tribune to question the validity of the duchesse d'Orléans' regency and to call for the formation of a provisional government – clearly intended as the first step towards a republic. Marie was interrupted by Barrot, arriving at the eleventh hour at the scene of the action, who was immediately called to speak. He began well, appealing to the deputies' honour to protect the young king and his mother. This was received with enthusiasm, which the duchesse and the little comte de Paris rose to acknowledge. The duchesse then indicated that she wished to address the assembly, and launched into an emotional appeal: 'Messieurs, I have come here with everything in the world I hold most dear . . .'[99]

This could have been an electrifying moment, swinging the deputies conclusively to the duchesse's side in a burst of sentiment. However, her voice was drowned out in the hubbub that arose as republicans tried to prevent her speaking, while monarchists insisted that she be allowed to continue. Instead of calming the situation and enabling the duchesse to proceed, Barrot simply ploughed on with his own speech, and the slim chance was lost. His peroration went on too long, and had little effect on his listeners. It also provided the necessary time for a final, and decisive, intervention. Hardly had Barrot sat down than rifle-butts were heard hammering on the doors, and a crowd of armed National Guardsmen, workers and students surged in, waving tricolour flags and shouting: 'Down with the regency! Down with the regime!' In the face of this invasion, flooding over the tribune and the centre of the Chamber, the deputies fled to the high ground of the upper benches.[100]

Clapping his hat on his head, Sauzet declared the session closed, but Lamartine nonetheless began to make a speech calling for a provisional government. He was cut off by a second irruption of insurgents, bellowing: 'Down with the Chamber! Long live the republic!' Sauzet's hat was knocked off, and he was chased from the president's chair. Muskets were levelled at the duchesse d'Orléans and her party, who were hustled off down a nearby corridor. Carried along by the flood, the duchesse lost sight of her children. The comte de Paris, passed from hand to hand above the press, was eventually pushed to safety through an open window; the duc de Chartres was briefly trampled underfoot, then rescued and sheltered in the apartment of an usher to the Chamber, one M. Lipmann. The duchesse was only reunited with her sons two days later.[101]

'Thus was accomplished, with a terrifying rapidity without example in the history of any country, the overthrow of the constitutional monarchy.' Writing these words a year later, Louis-Philippe still seemed stunned by the speed with which his rule had collapsed. A regime that had lasted eighteen years and appeared to have vanquished all its opponents had been toppled in just three days. Its formidable army − admittedly in obedience to orders − had retreated almost without firing a shot. In a few areas of Paris there had been fierce fighting, but the death toll had been remarkably light: 72 soldiers and 289 Parisians. As 24 February drew to a close, the king had abdicated, his ministers were in flight, and his grandson and heir was in hiding.[102]

With Louis-Philippe and his family swept from the stage, those who had opposed them since 1830 had finally come into their own.

In the Chamber the elderly Dupont de l'Eure, who had replaced Sauzet in the president's chair, and Lamartine, who was still standing at the tribune, between them improvised a list of five members of the provisional government, which they read out to the crowd and the dozen republican deputies who had remained. Naturally, Lamartine's name was at its head. At four in the afternoon, the two men left to install themselves in the Hôtel de Ville, that bastion of revolutionary Paris.[103] Though they did not know it at the time, they had changed history permanently. Over the next hundred and sixty years France would see four republics, one empire, and one regime born of occupation. She would never be a monarchy again.

EPILOGUE

ON LEAVING PARIS, Louis-Philippe's plan had been to retire to Eu while his grandson's rule was established, and then live out his days there. His route took him first to St Cloud and then to the Trianon, from where his daughter Clémentine and her husband the Duke of Saxe-Coburg struck out on their own. By the evening of 24 February the royal party had reached Dreux. Early the next morning, however, Louis-Philippe was woken to be told that the attempt to secure his grandson's succession under a regency had failed, and that the republic had been proclaimed.[1] There was no way of knowing what the new regime's attitude would be to Louis-Philippe and his family — it might be content to see them exiled to a comfortable location, or it might decide to arrest them. With the 'magic lantern' of the Place de la Concorde fresh in his mind from the previous day, Louis-Philippe was not prepared to wait and find out.

It was now imperative to get out of France as quickly as possible. The fugitives agreed to head for the Norman coast, and then find a ship that would take them to England. Their first destination was a small property near Honfleur belonging to M. de Perthuis, a former aide-de-camp of Louis-Philippe's. This was little more than a gardener's cottage, but it was close to the sea and conveniently hidden from the road by a high hedge. Louis-Philippe, Marie-Amélie, Montpensier, the duchesse de Nemours and her children arrived there on the evening of the 26th.[2]

From this refuge, the party secretly contacted the captain of the *Express*, an English steamer of the Southampton–Le Havre service, and asked him to take them aboard. The captain, however, refused, feeling that he would be going beyond his authority in doing so. Increasingly desperate, Louis-Philippe next travelled to Trouville to try and hire a fishing-boat to make the crossing, but with no success. Worse, he was recognized and had to leave the town precipitately.

The authorities still did not know the fugitives' precise hideout, but the net was closing around them.[3]

Just as the danger was mounting, the family's luck suddenly turned. The captain of the *Express* had informed the Admiralty of their plight, and the British government had immediately ordered him to concert plans for a rescue with its consul in Le Havre, George W. Featherstonhaugh. On 2 March the British vice-consul, William Jones, presented himself at the Perthuis cottage and informed the delighted inhabitants of the plan. It was decided to act straight away; Louis-Philippe, posing as Featherstonhaugh's uncle under the name of William Smith, would lead the party on to the quay at Le Havre, where the consul would be waiting to escort them on to the *Express*.[4]

That same evening Louis-Philippe, disguised in glasses, a muffler and a bulky jacket, shepherded his wife, daughter-in-law and grandchildren on to the Honfleur–Le Havre ferry. At Le Havre Featherstonhaugh was waiting on the quayside. As had been arranged, he stepped forward, shook Louis-Philippe's hand and exclaimed in English: 'Well, uncle! How are you?' – 'Quite well, I thank you, George,' replied Louis-Philippe, also in English, and continued the conversation as the group moved towards the *Express*. It is remarkable, and oddly heartening, that the perils of the situation made no impression on Louis-Philippe's customary loquacity. As Featherstonhaugh afterwards wryly remarked: 'My dear Uncle talked so loud and so much that I had the greatest difficulty to make him keep silent.'[5]

Having taken his charges on board, Featherstonhaugh then went on to the bridge, and was absent some while. Though he did not tell them at the time, this was because Louis-Philippe had in fact been recognized on the quayside, perhaps as a result of his performance as William Smith, and the commander of the fort of Le Havre had come aboard demanding to inspect the cabins. The captain of the *Express*, however, refused to allow this, insisting that he had to leave immediately; the commander grudgingly left, and the boat finally weighed anchor.[6]

This close call underlines what a perilous business Louis-Philippe's escape was, and how nearly it ended in capture. And if it had, what would his fate have been then? Despite the violence in some areas of Paris on 23 and 24 February, it has become commonplace to contrast the relatively peaceful change of regime in February 1848 with the bloodletting of the first Revolution and the Terror. Yet it is very unlikely that the chief motor of both upheavals, the Paris crowd, was any less violent in 1848 than in 1789 or 1792; the fate of the 14th regiment of the line at the Château d'Eau was little different from that of the Swiss Guard fifty-five years earlier. Both the Tuileries and Neuilly were sacked in 1848, and Neuilly for good measure was burned to the ground. If apprehended, Louis-Philippe could quite conceivably have been lynched — as would certainly have happened with Charles X's ministers in 1830 if the Parisians had got their hands on them. If, on the other hand, he had been taken into regular custody, it would have been difficult to avoid putting him on trial. In that eventuality, would the provisional government have shown the courage he himself had displayed with Polignac and his colleagues, and spared his life?

At dawn on 3 March, the *Express* landed at Newhaven. Louis-Philippe and his family put up at the Bridge Inn, which swiftly became packed with well-wishers, including Sir Robert Peel's brother and sister-in-law. That same day, a messenger arrived from Queen Victoria offering the refugees Claremont House in Surrey as a place of residence. Claremont had been the home of Louis-Philippe's son-in-law Leopold of the Belgians during his first marriage to George IV's daughter Charlotte, and had remained in his possession. The next day, Louis-Philippe, Marie-Amélie, Montpensier, the duchesse de Nemours and her children travelled there from Lewes by railway. They were reunited with Nemours, Clémentine and the Duke of Saxe-Coburg at Croydon station.[7]

*

SLOWLY THE REST OF the family and their close friends made their way to England, some with more difficulty than others. As Louis-Philippe was fleeing the Tuileries on 24 February, Adélaïde's devoted companion Mme de Montjoie had retired to her apartment with a crippling migraine. Shortly afterwards a complete stranger walked in, warned her that the crowd was coming up the main staircase, told her to sweep what valuables she could into her handbag, and gallantly escorted her out of the building. Her sister Mme de Dolomieu and a friend escaped separately from the Tuileries, and were given a lift to

St Cloud on a milk-cart whose driver refused any payment for his services.[8]

In Algiers, the prince de Joinville and the duc d'Aumale received the news of the revolution on 27 February. With a powerful and loyal army at their disposal, they could have carried on the struggle from North Africa or even invaded the mainland, but with remarkable selflessness they declined to do so. On 3 March, they left Algiers with their wives by sea, and landed in England eighteen days later. By now the duchesse d'Orléans and her children were the only absent family members. They had escaped from Paris to Germany, and had taken up residence in Eisenach. They did not visit England until the following year; the duchesse wished to remain independent of her father-in-law, while Louis-Philippe on his side was unhappy that she had allowed herself to be proclaimed regent, against his wishes, in the Chamber of Deputies on 24 February.[9]

At the end of the year a final tragedy struck, no less cruel for its banality. Many of the inhabitants of Claremont, in particular Marie-Amélie, Mmes de Montjoie and de Dolomieu, and Louis-Philippe's long-serving librarian Vatout, were struck down with digestive disorders. It took some time for the cause to be discovered. The lead piping in the house, which had been uninhabited since Princess Charlotte's death in 1817, had become defective, and had contaminated the water supply. The household packed up and moved to the Star and Garter inn at Richmond while the Claremont plumbing was made safe. Marie-Amélie recovered, but the two ladies-in-waiting and the librarian did not. Mme de Montjoie and Mme de Dolomieu, who for forty years had shared all the Orléans' vicissitudes and had recently survived the sack of the Tuileries, ended as victims of lead poisoning in Surrey.[10]

Although outwardly Louis-Philippe was as clear-sighted – and as voluble – as ever, in reality he was becoming increasingly frail. It is quite possible that the decline in his health was accelerated by the lead in the Claremont pipes, which at one point had turned his teeth black. Nonetheless, he followed every detail of the stormy progress of the Second Republic in France, and discussed with Guizot, Thiers and Broglie, who all visited him in the course of 1849 and 1850, the project of 'fusion' – an agreement over the succession between the two branches of the house of Bourbon as the first step to a restoration of the monarchy. He also made two extended visits to St Leonards, to take the sea air, from March to October 1849, and once more in the spring of 1850.[11]

By his return to Claremont from this second trip, Louis-Philippe was clearly very ill. Though it is uncertain what his ailment was, its symptoms were an alarming loss of weight and growing weakness. On 25 August, the doctors warned Marie-Amélie that the end was imminent, and she told her husband the same day. Louis-Philippe's response was typically brave and imperturbable: 'That means I'm going to have to take my leave.' Then he confessed and took the sacraments. He died, surrounded by his family, at 8 a.m. on 26 August. A week later, he was buried in a small Catholic chapel in Weybridge.[12]

Marie-Amélie survived Louis-Philippe by sixteen years. She stayed on at Claremont, living a life of exemplary piety, and died there on 24 March 1866, aged eighty-four. She outlived her eldest daughter Louise, Queen of the Belgians, who died in the same year as Louis-Philippe, aged only thirty-eight. All her other children lived on until the end of the century, and some of them beyond. Three of her four surviving sons eventually returned to France. After Louis-Philippe's death, the duc de Nemours acted as head of the family for many years, and died at Versailles in 1896. Encouraged by Thiers, the prince de Joinville considered standing for the presidency of the Second Republic in 1851, but – in an echo of the Hundred Days – the project was nipped in the bud by Louis-Napoleon's coup d'état. Joinville joined the French army in September 1870 to fight the Prussians, and died in Paris in 1900.[13]

In 1870 the duc d'Aumale also went back to France, established himself on his estate at Chantilly, and devoted himself to restoring and embellishing the château and its grounds. He was elected to the Académie Française in 1871, and died in Sicily twenty-six years later. The duc de Montpensier settled in Spain, his wife's native country, and became a significant figure in Spanish politics. He died at his home in Sanlucar de Barrameda near Seville in 1890.[14] Princess Clémentine, who had married the Duke of Saxe-Coburg in 1843, had the satisfaction of seeing her son Ferdinand become King of Bulgaria in 1887. She died in Vienna in 1907. The inscription on her tomb reads: 'King's daughter, no queen herself, yet king's mother'.

On Louis-Philippe's death his grandson, the twelve-year-old comte de Paris, became, in the eyes of Orléanists, King of the French. Yet the allegiances of French royalists continued to be divided, between himself and the representative of the elder Bourbon branch, Charles X's grandson the duc de Bordeaux – or the comte de Chambord, as he preferred to style himself from the mid-1830s. Thus the damaging split between Orléanists and legitimists that had bedevilled Louis-Philippe's reign continued after his fall and deeply compromised the prospects for a restoration. The rivalry sometimes surfaced in unexpected places. While the comte de Paris joined the Union army in the American Civil War for a time, one of Polignac's sons became a Confederate general.

Faced with the historic opportunity presented by the fall of Napoleon III in 1870, the two Bourbon branches finally settled their differences. The result was the policy of 'fusion': since the comte de Chambord was conveniently childless, it was agreed that the comte de Paris would recognize him as king in exchange for his own recognition as heir apparent. In 1873, a restoration on these terms seemed imminent. Chambord, however, proved unwilling to make the wider political compromises necessary to take the throne, culminating in his symbolic refusal to accept the tricolour flag. The comte de Paris, whose grandfather Louis-Philippe had actually reintroduced the tricolour in 1830, could only look on in despair as his best hope of one day wearing the crown was dashed. After 1873, it became clear that France would not return to a monarchy, but embark instead on a third republic.

The comte de Chambord remained in exile in Austria, dying there in 1883. The comte de Paris, on the other hand, returned to France as soon as he could. However, the semi-royal status he soon acquired in his home country alarmed the new republican regime, which exiled him and all future heads of the Orléans family in 1886. This law was not repealed until 1950. The comte died in England, at Stowe House, Buckinghamshire, on 8 September 1894. His great-great-nephew – and Louis-Philippe's great-great-great-great-grandson – Henri, comte de Paris, is the present pretender to the French throne.[15]

In 1876 the bodies of Louis-Philippe and Marie-Amélie were exhumed from their resting-place in Weybridge and brought back to lie in French soil. On 9 June, they were interred in the royal chapel at Dreux.[16] Louis-Philippe had always liked the medieval practice of placing sculpted effigies of the deceased over their graves, and a splendid marble statue of himself standing, a protective hand on the shoulder of a kneeling and praying Marie-Amélie, now dominates the tombs of the successive generations of his family that fill the circular vault. In a small apse discreetly behind lie those closest to him: his mother, his eldest son — and Adélaïde.

*

THE FATES OF the other major figures of Louis-Philippe's reign reflected the continuing instability of French politics over the next thirty years. After the February revolution, Molé kept a low profile for a few months. As the Chamber of Peers had been abolished, he no longer had a political platform, but in August 1848 he was returned at a by-election to the new National Assembly. He concentrated his efforts on helping to rebuild relations between the Orléans and the elder Bourbon branch, and to this end was even reconciled with Guizot. He protested strongly when Louis-Napoleon Bonaparte — third time lucky — mounted a successful coup d'état on 2 December 1851, paving the way for the Second Empire. He died suddenly at Champlâtreux, his country home, on 23 November 1855, aged seventy-four.[17]

Guizot was to outlive his old rival by nineteen years. On 24 February he had had to flee from the ministry of the interior, where he had taken refuge, by the back garden. He was then hidden by friends for a week before escaping to Brussels posing as the valet of the minister of Württemberg to Paris. From there he went to England and took up residence at no. 21 Pelham Crescent in Brompton, then a village just outside London. In July 1848 he was offered the chair in French language and literature at Oxford, but turned it down. When the threat of prosecution was lifted, he returned to France and stood, unsuccessfully, as a candidate in the elections of May 1849. With Molé, he worked strenuously for 'fusion' between the Orléans and the elder branch of the family, but his efforts did not bear fruit until after his death. In his old age he wrote his memoirs, and became increasingly involved in the affairs of the French Protestant church.

His relationship with Mme de Lieven continued intermittently until
the latter's death in 1857. He died at his house in Normandy, Val-
Richer, on 12 September 1874, at the ripe old age of eighty-seven.[18]

Unlike his two older colleagues, Thiers had in 1848 still not
reached the summit of his career. After his collapse on 24 February,
he briefly went to ground at the home of a friend, the bibulously
named contessa Taverna-Martini. He soon re-emerged, however, and
in June that year was returned in a by-election to the National
Assembly. He swiftly became a leader of the right-wing 'party of
order' under the Second Republic. When Louis-Napoleon mounted
his coup d'état he was briefly imprisoned, then exiled to England for
eighteen months. He was out of politics until 1863, and spent his time
completing his twenty-volume *History of the Consulate and Empire*.
When the Second Empire of Napoleon III, as Louis-Napoleon had
now become, began to liberalize, Thiers returned to parliament and
emerged as one of the regime's most powerful critics.[19]

When the catastrophic war of 1870 toppled the Second Empire
and left France facing a German invasion, Thiers' hour finally
arrived. The Third Republic was swiftly proclaimed, and in February
1871 his colleagues almost unanimously elected him Chief of the
Executive Power. Thiers ended the war, though at the cost of ceding
Alsace and Lorraine to Germany. Hardly had he done this than he
was confronted by the last, and biggest, Parisian insurrection of the
century, the Commune. Fuelled in equal measure by disgust at the
peace terms, distrust of the new French regime and utopian idealism,
the Parisian workers and the National Guard set up an independent
radical government, to which they hoped the rest of France would
rally. In a definitive act of revenge for February 1848, Thiers sent in
the troops. In the 'bloody week' of 21–28 May after the city was
taken, they killed roughly twenty thousand people. The repression
fulfilled its aim: there would never again be a successful Parisian
revolution.[20]

Although he had helped to found the July monarchy, Thiers was
convinced that France's future stability would now best be ensured
by a republic. He devoted his last years in office to realizing this
goal. By the time he resigned his post, undermined by growing right-
wing opposition in the Assembly, on 24 May 1873, this aim had been

substantially achieved. Politically active to the very end, Thiers died at St Germain-en-Laye on 3 September 1877, aged eighty.[21]

The rest of Louis-Philippe's friends and collaborators generally made their peace with his successors. Gérard became a senator under the Second Empire shortly before his death in 1852. Dupin was elected to the Second Republic's National Assembly in 1849, and during the Second Empire accepted the office of attorney-general. He died, at the age of eighty-two, in 1865. Barrot briefly became prime minister under the Second Republic, protested at Louis-Napoleon's coup d'état, and stayed out of politics for a decade. However, he rallied to the Second Empire in its last year, when it appeared to be evolving in a genuinely constitutional direction. Barrot settled comfortably into the Third Republic, and in 1872 was appointed president of the Council of State by his old ally under the July monarchy, Thiers. He died on 6 August 1873.[22]

For the last two years of his life, Louis-Philippe remained in close touch with Montalivet, and named him as his executor. After Louis-Philippe's death, Montalivet remained fiercely loyal to his memory, and when in 1862 Napoleon III publicly attacked the July monarchy's record, he sprang to its defence in print. In the 1870s, he accepted Thiers' conservative republic, and in 1879 was appointed a senator for life. He died the next year, aged seventy-nine.[23] Of the great literary chroniclers of Louis-Philippe's reign, Mme de Boigne died in 1866. She ended her memoirs, however, at the revolution of 1848. Victor Hugo, whose pages on the king in his journal are the most penetrating about him ever written, became internationally famous with the publication of *Les Misérables* in 1862, and ended his days as the Third Republic's greatest cultural monument. He died in 1885, was given a lavish state funeral and was buried in the Panthéon.

*

'WHEN ONE THINKS that his reward for eighteen years of peace and prosperity is a little burial vault in some obscure English village, that gives long pause for some sad reflections.' Thus King Leopold of the Belgians to Dupin, just after Louis-Philippe's death.[24] Leopold's verdict was clearly not unbiased; he was the dead man's son-in-law, and owed him his throne. Yet his comment contains much truth.

Louis-Philippe did give France considerable peace and prosperity for almost two decades. His reward was even more meagre than Leopold foresaw: not only a sad death in exile, but the neglect of history.

Compared with that devoted to his contemporary and rival Napoleon, the literature on Louis-Philippe and his reign is tiny. Yet the achievements of the King of the French, though more modest, were in many ways more admirable than those of the Emperor of the French. Above all, Louis-Philippe succeeded where his cousins of the elder branch had ultimately failed, and established a viable constitutional monarchy in France. He guided the institution through the upheaval of 1830, which could well have destroyed it, resolved the tensions between executive and legislature that had defeated Louis XVIII and Charles X, and laid the foundations for a parliamentary system. The latter was neutralized under the Second Empire, but re-emerged under the Third Republic, whose constitution, significantly, was shaped by former Orléanists. 'I am one of those who would rather see France great than France free,' the nationalist deputy Léon Faucher proclaimed in 1840.[25] To those who share this sentiment, Napoleon will always be a hero; but those who think the opposite should always be grateful to Louis-Philippe.

In theory Louis-Philippe ruled alone, but in practice his reign was a collaboration between himself and Adélaïde. This is one of the most remarkable — and certainly least known — aspects of the July monarchy. Adélaïde's first and fundamental achievement was her acceptance in July 1830, on her absent brother's behalf, of the lieutenant-generalcy of the kingdom, which led swiftly to the throne. Thereafter, her discussions with Louis-Philippe in his study each evening made her, if not a co-author of his policy, then something very close to it. The fact that Adélaïde's power was combined with no official or elected position did at times jeopardize those relations between Crown and parliament that Louis-Philippe had done so much to restore. But on balance her influence was far more positive than destructive. She played a critical part in her brother's pacific diplomacy, particularly in France's relations with Britain, and her political instincts were often sounder than his. Whether her death contributed to the July monarchy's fall in February 1848 is an open question.

The circumstances of that fall remain controversial. To those who wish to dismiss the French constitutional monarchy as doomed from its inception, it was inevitable. This verdict, however, is open to doubt. Taken as a whole, from 1814 through to 1848, the system showed considerable resilience. It weathered a major storm in 1830, and then continued into its most successful phase under Louis-Philippe. Its final collapse owed at least as much to short-term mistakes – poor civil–military coordination, the calling-out of the National Guard, and above all the failure to concede electoral reform – as to any deep-seated structural flaws.

Yet in one area, the fall of the July monarchy cannot entirely be explained by short-term causes. The paralysis of Louis-Philippe and his ministers when faced by revolution in 1848 revealed an insecurity at the very heart of the regime. Divine right, so eroded in the course of the previous century, no longer conferred the moral authority necessary for drastic repressive action. Democracy, which was to provide it in the future, had not yet been established. The fragile legitimacy of the July monarchy, based on membership of the Bourbon family, a restricted franchise and the volatile National Guard, was not a sufficient substitute. Things might have been different if electoral reform had been accorded in time, but it was not. The contrast between Louis-Philippe's collapse of confidence on 24 February 1848 and the ruthlessness of the Second Republic, reinforced by universal male suffrage, in suppressing the mass rising of the Parisian workers in the June Days four months later, is striking.[26] As Louis-Philippe wryly remarked on hearing of the June Days: 'Republics are lucky: they can shoot people.'

Combined with this factor, and sometimes indistinguishable from it, was a genuinely honourable motive. Louis-Philippe was profoundly imbued with the traditional maxim that a king must never make war on his own people. 'I didn't want the crown at the price of civil war!' he once exclaimed in exile.[27] This scruple was also shared by his predecessors. Louis XVI had refused to flee to the provinces in July and again in October 1789 because he feared this would unleash a civil war. Even Charles X, once he had lost Paris in July 1830, never seriously contemplated carrying on the struggle from the Loire. Reluctance to shed blood may have helped doom the last French kings; if so, like many political failings, this was at least a moral virtue.

The French constitutional monarchy made many mistakes. Its initial errors prompted the disastrous upheaval of the Hundred Days, and made its task thereafter much more difficult. Between 1819 and 1830, it became a force for division rather than for national unity. Above all, throughout its life it relied on a grossly restrictive electoral system that prevented it from taking firm root in all sections of the population. Yet it did make a major effort to heal the wounds of the previous twenty-five years, particularly under Louis XVIII and Louis-Philippe. It also gave the French more genuine liberty than any previous order had given them, and more than several subsequent ones. Finally, it did its utmost to 'end the Revolution', and to set France on an evolutionary path to stable constitutional government. If in the short term it failed, it left a substantial – and unfairly neglected – legacy to modern France.

NOTES

Abbreviations

AN – Archives Nationales, Paris

BN – Bibliothèque Nationale, Paris

AP – Archives Privées, Archives Nationales, Paris

INTRODUCTION

1. Comte de Mirabeau, speech to the National Assembly of 18 Sept. 1789, reproduced in G. Chaussinand-Nogaret, *Les grands discours parlementaires de la Révolution, de Mirabeau à Robespierre 1789–1795* (Paris 2005), pp. 48–9.
2. Victor Hugo, *Journal 1830–1848*, ed. H. Guillemin (Paris 1954), p. 16.
3. One should, however, mention two exceptions: A. Jardin and A. J. Tudesq, *La France des notables, 1815–1848* (2 vols, Paris 1973), and I. Backouche, *La monarchie parlementaire, 1815–1848* (Paris 2000).
4. F. Furet, *La Révolution, de Turgot à Jules Ferry: 1770–1880* (Paris 1988), p. 381.
5. P. Rosanvallon, *La monarchie impossible: les chartes de 1814 et de 1830* (Paris 1994), p. 179.
6. D. H. Pinkney, *Decisive Years in France, 1840–1847* (Princeton, NJ, 1986), pp. 30–1); H. A. C. Collingham, *The July Monarchy: A Political History, 1830–1848* (London 1988), pp. 348, 355.
7. R. Magraw, *France 1815–1914: The Bourgeois Century* (London 1983), p. 94, and *A History of the French Working Class* (2 vols, Oxford 1992), vol. 1, pp. 121–2.
8. H. Heine, *Lutèce*, in *Samtliche Werke*, ed. M. Windfuhr (16 vols, Hamburg 1975–97), vol. 13, p. 238, letter of 6 Nov. 1840.
9. R. Arnaud, *Adélaïde d'Orléans (1777–1847)* (Paris 1908).
10. There has been more recent work on the restoration – P. Mansel, *Louis XVIII* (London 1981); E. de Waresquiel and B. Yvert, *Histoire de la restauration 1814–1830: naissance de la France moderne* (Paris 1996); R. S.

Alexander, *Rewriting the French Revolutionary Tradition* (Cambridge 2003)
– than on the July monarchy: P. Pilbeam, *The 1830 Revolution in France*
(London 1991); H. A. C. Collingham, *The July Monarchy, 1830–1848: A
Political History* (London 1988).

PROLOGUE: SPRING 1814

1. P. Mansel, *Louis XVIII* (London 1981, Stroud 1999), 1999 edn, pp. 176–7.
2. T. C. W. Blanning ed., *The Short Oxford History of Europe: Eighteenth-
   century Europe 1688–1815* Oxford 2000), p. 248.
3. C. Greville, *Memoirs* (8 vols, London 1938), vol. 1, p. 10; C. Hibbert,
   George IV (London 1976 edn), p. 406; Mansel, *Louis XVIII*, p. 147.
4. Henri, marquis Dugon, *Au service du roi en exil: épisodes de la contre-
   révolution d'après le journal et la correspondance du président de Vezet* (Lyon
   1968), p. 324.
5. The standard biography of the king is Mansel, *Louis XVIII*. Some of
   Louis' writings and correspondence has also been published: see G.
   Pallain ed., *Correspondance inédite du prince de Talleyrand et du roi Louis
   XVIII pendant le congrès de Vienne* (Paris 1881); E. Daudet, 'A travers
   les papiers de Louis XVIII. Ses notes de lecture', *Le Correspondant*,
   vol. 238 (Jan.–Mar. 1910), pp. 24–47; 'Quelques lettres de Louis XVIII',
   Nouvelle Revue, vol. 116 (Jan. 1899), pp. 26–45; 'Louis XVIII et le comte
   d'Artois', *Revue des Deux Mondes*, 1 Feb. 1906, pp. 559–95, and 15 Feb.,
   pp. 824–60.
6. Marshal Macdonald, *Souvenirs* (Paris 1892), p. 319.
7. Charles X still awaits his definitive biographer. In the meantime, the
   most recent studies are V. W. Beach, *Charles X of France* (Boulder,
   Colorado, 1971), and J. Cabanis, *Charles X, roi ultra* (Paris 1972). For a
   sense of Charles' political views before he became king, see L. Pingaud
   ed., *Correspondance intime du comte de Vaudreuil et du comte d'Artois
   pendant l'émigration, 1789–1815* (2 vols, Paris 1889). For Charles' journey
   to Paris in 1814, see comte Lefebvre de Behaine, *Le comte d'Artois sur la
   route de Paris* (Paris 1921).
8. There is an immense literature on Talleyrand, beginning with his own
   Mémoires (5 vols, Paris 1891–2). The best recent biography is E. de
   Waresquiel, *Talleyrand: le prince immobile* (Paris 2003). Also important
   are G. Lacour-Gayet, *Talleyrand, 1754–1838* (4 vols, Paris 1928–34), M.
   Poniatowski, *Talleyrand* (4 vols, Paris 1982–95), L. Madelin, *Talleyrand*
   (Paris 1944) and, in English, D. Cooper, *Talleyrand* (London 1932) and
   P. G. Dwyer, *Talleyrand* (London 2002). For Talleyrand's role in the

first restoration, see C. Dupuis, *Le ministère Talleyrand en 1814* (2 vols, Paris 1919–20).

9. Sir Denis Brogan, *The French Nation from Napoleon to Pétain* (London 1957), p. 11.

10. E. de Waresquiel and B. Yvert, *La restauration, 1814–1830: naissance de la France moderne* (Paris 1996), p. 50. For the contribution of royalist conspiracy to the restoration, see F. de Bertier, *Souvenirs inédits d'un conspirateur* (Paris 1990), and G. de Bertier de Sauvigny, *Le comte Ferdinand de Bertier et l'énigme de la Congrégation* (Paris 1948).

11. *Mémoires du chancelier Pasquier* (6 vols, Paris 1893–5), vol. 6, p. 10.

12. G. de Bertier de Sauvigny, *La restauration* (Paris 1955), p. 78.

13. Ibid.

One THE ORLÉANS: FATHER AND SON

1. G. Antonetti, *Louis-Philippe* (Paris 1994), p. 431.

2. Louis-Philippe, '1814. Souvenirs; manuscrit autographe. Claremont, le 25 novembre 1849', pp. 14–15, Archives Nationales, Paris, Archives de la Maison de France, 300 AP(III) 13. Louis-Philippe later regretted that he had not boarded the *Undaunted* and met Napoleon incognito: 'This encounter could have been very piquant for me, if I had managed to get a warning in time to Captain Usher, the commander, who knew me well, to conceal my name, and allow me to engage in conversation with Napoleon without him knowing who I was.' Ibid., pp. 15–16.

3. On the Orléans family in the eighteenth century, see A. Britsch, *La jeunesse de Philippe-Egalité* (Paris 1926), and 'Philippe-Egalité avant la Révolution', *Revue d'Etudes Historiques*, vol. 70 (1904), pp. 337–63, 478–504; B. F. Hyslop, *L'apanage de Philippe-Egalité, duc d'Orléans, 1785–1791* (Paris 1965); A. Lanne, *La fortune des d'Orléans: origine et accroissement* (Paris 1905); G. de Broglie, *L'Orléanisme, ressource libérale de la France* (Paris 1981); G. Poisson, *Les Orléans. Une famille en quête d'un trône* (Paris 1999). For the wider political and constitutional aspects of their actions in this period, see J. Egret, *Louis XV et l'opposition parlementaire* (Paris 1970).

4. The best modern biography of Louis-Philippe-Joseph is E. Lever, *Philippe-Egalité* (Paris 1996). See also A. Castelot, *Philippe-Egalité: le prince rouge* (Paris 1950), and H. la Marle, *Philippe-Egalité: 'Grand Maître' de la Révolution* (Paris 1989). Part of Louis-Philippe-Joseph's correspondence was published shortly after his death: *Correspondance de Louis-Philippe-Joseph, duc d'Orléans, avec Louis XVI, la reine, Montmorin,*

Liancourt, Biron, Lafayette etc. (Paris 1800). On Louis-Philippe-Joseph's
rebuilding of the Palais-royal, see H. Morand, 'Philippe-Egalité et la
construction du Palais-royal', *Le Correspondant*, vol. 304 (1926),
pp. 290–3; R. Héron de Villefosse, *L'anti-Versailles ou le Palais-royal de
Philippe-Egalité* (Paris 1974); V. Champier and G.R. Sandoz, *Le Palais-
royal d'après des documents inédits* (2 vols, Paris 1900).

5. For a full account, see Lever, *Philippe-Egalité*, pp. 162–83. For a
   contemporary view, more sympathetic to Louis-Philippe-Joseph, see
   Mémoires du duc des Cars (2 vols, Paris 1890), vol. i, pp. 179–85.

6. On Louis-Philippe-Joseph's Anglomania see A. Britsch, 'L'Anglomanie
   de Philippe-Egalité d'après sa correspondance autographe (1778–1785)',
   Le Correspondant, vol. 303 (1926), pp. 280–95. On Anglomania and
   Anglophobia in eighteenth-century France see J. Grieder, *Anglomania in
   France, 1740–1789: Fact, Fiction and Political Discourse* (Geneva 1985);
   N. Hampson, *The Perfidy of Albion: French Perceptions of England during
   the French Revolution* (London 1998); and F. Acomb, *Anglophobia in
   France, 1763–1789: An Essay in the History of Constitutionalism and
   Nationalism* (Durham, North Carolina, 1950). For an important recent
   analysis of modern Anglo-French relations, see R. and I. Tombs, *That
   Sweet Enemy: The French and the British from the Sun King to the Present*
   (London 2006). For a stimulating overview of Anglomania in modern
   Europe, see I. Buruma, *Voltaire's Coconuts, or Anglomania in Europe*
   (London 1999).

7. Voltaire's views on England are discussed in A. M. Rousseau,
   L'Angleterre et Voltaire (Oxford 1976), and P. Gay, *Voltaire's Politics:
   The Poet as Realist* (Princeton 1959), pp. 39–65. Like Voltaire, Montes-
   quieu also spent some time in England, from Nov. 1729 to Apr. 1731; his
   'Notes sur l'Angleterre', although less famous than the *Lettres philosop-
   hiques*, are published in his *Oeuvres complètes*, ed. R. Caillois (2 vols,
   Paris 1949–51), vol. i, pp. 875–84. For the influence of England on
   Montesquieu's thought, see C. Dédéyan, *Montesquieu ou les lumières
   d'Albion* (Paris 1990). There is an interesting recent analysis of the
   'Notes sur l'Angleterre' in I. Stewart, 'Montesquieu in England: his
   "Notes on England", with commentary and translation' (2002), Oxford
   University Comparative Law Forum 6 at ouclf.iuscomp.org. On Orléans
   Anglophilia and its effect on diplomacy in this period, see J. Black,
   *Natural and Necessary Enemies: Anglo-French Relations in the Eighteenth
   Century* (London 1986), pp. 8–16, and *From Louis XIV to Napoleon. The
   Fate of a Great Power* (London 1999), pp. 70–4.

8. See Britsch, 'L'Anglomanie de Philippe-Egalité', pp. 294–5.

9. Ibid., p. 286. See also Lever, *Philippe-Egalité*, pp. 210–15.

10. For Mme de Genlis' own version of her life, see her *Mémoires inédits de*

Mme la comtesse de Genlis pour servir à l'histoire des 18ème et 19ème siècles (8 vols, Paris and London 1825). Her most important work on education, a didactic novel whose hero and heroine are clearly modelled on Louis-Philippe and Adélaïde, is *Adèle et Théodore* (3 vols, Paris 1782). There is also a good modern biography: G. de Broglie, *Mme de Genlis* (Paris 1985).

11. Antonetti, *Louis-Philippe*, pp. 79–92.

12. On Fénelon and *Télémaque* the best recent study is C. Dédéyan, *Télémaque ou la liberté de l'esprit* (Paris 1991). On the use of *Télémaque* in Louis XVI's education, see P. Girault de Coursac, *L'éducation d'un roi* (Paris 1972), pp. 89–94.

13. For the influence of Rousseau's educational theories in the eighteenth century, see W. Boyd, *The Educational Theory of Jean-Jacques Rousseau* (New York 1963), and, more recently, J. Bloch, *Rousseauism and Education in Eighteenth-century France* (Oxford, Voltaire Foundation, 1995).

14. Antonetti, *Louis-Philippe*, pp. 109–10.

15. Louis-Philippe, *Mémoires* (2 vols, Paris 1973–4), vol. 1, pp. 15–16; R. Arnaud, *Adélaïde d'Orléans* (Paris 1908), pp. 41–2.

16. Louis-Philippe to Adélaïde, 31 Jan. 1807, cited in Antonetti, *Louis-Philippe*, p. 102. For evidence of Adélaïde's careful education by Mme de Genlis during the Revolution, see AN 300 AP(III) 6, 'Mme Adélaïde (1777–1847): journaux, carnets, correspondance, 1789–1817', dossiers 1–10.

17. The mystery of Pamela's origins will probably never be resolved. Stella Tillyard, in her recent biography of Pamela's husband, Lord Edward Fitzgerald, inclines to the view that she was indeed the illegitimate child of Mme de Genlis and Louis-Philippe-Joseph (S. Tillyard, *Citizen Lord: Edward Fitzgerald, 1763–1798* (London 1997), pp. 305–6.) This involves questioning the reliability of the correspondence between Forth and Louis-Philippe-Joseph relating to Pamela's adoption, cited by Amédée Britsch (Britsch, *La jeunesse de Philippe-Egalité*, pp. 375–8). My instinct is to take this correspondence at face value, and to conclude that Pamela was, as claimed, an abandoned English child.

18. For Pamela's success in this, see Louis-Philippe and Marie-Amélie to Adélaïde, 30 Nov. (no year given), AN 300 AP(IV) 8, pièce 128. See also Adélaïde's reference in Oct. 1824 to reading Susan E. Ferrier's *The Inheritance* (3 vols, Edinburgh 1824) – one of the few British novels with a heroine called Gertrude. AN 300 AP(III) 6, Archives de la Maison de France, Mme Adélaïde (1777–1847), dossiers 37, 38, journal entry for 10 October 1824.

19. Victor Hugo, *Journal, 1830–1848*, ed. H. Guillemin (Paris 1954), pp. 313–14.

20. On the two-year crisis that preceded the Revolution, and Orléans' part in it, see J. Egret, *La pré-Révolution française, 1787–1788* (Paris 1962), pp. 150–92.

21. Antonetti, *Louis-Philippe*, pp. 146–7.

22. Lafayette's role in the French Revolution is dealt with in detail in L. Gottschalk, *Lafayette in the French Revolution: Through the October Days* (Chicago 1969), and *Lafayette in the French Revolution: From the October Days through the Federation* (Chicago 1973), and in B. M. Shapiro, *Revolutionary Justice in Paris, 1789–1790* (Cambridge 1993). There is a good modern French biography: E. Taillemite, *La Fayette* (Paris 1989).

23. Louis-Philippe, *Mémoires*, vol. 1, pp. 101–2.

24. This inquiry, whose voluminous proceedings are published as *Procédure criminelle instruite au Châtelet de Paris sur la dénonciation des faits arrivés à Versailles dans la journée du 6 octobre 1789* (Paris 1790), is best followed in Shapiro, *Revolutionary Justice*, pp. 84–120.

25. Lever, *Philippe-Egalité*, pp. 348–50, 415–19.

26. Antonetti, *Louis-Philippe*, pp. 162–3.

27. Lever, *Philippe-Egalité*, p. 403.

28. The best accounts of this process are A. Sorel, *L'Europe et la Révolution française* (8 vols, Paris 1885–1905), vol. 2, *La chute de la royauté*, pp. 299–342, and T. C. W. Blanning, *The Origins of the French Revolutionary Wars* (London 1986), pp. 99–113.

29. Sorel, *La chute de la royauté*, pp. 305–6.

30. Antonetti, *Louis-Philippe*, pp. 213–14.

31. The fullest and most up-to-date treatment of the *journée* of 10 August is R. Allen, *Threshold of Terror: The Last Hours of the Monarchy in the French Revolution* (Stroud 1999).

32. For these campaigns and Louis-Philippe's role in them, see A. Chuquet, *Les guerres de la Révolution* (11 vols, Paris 1886–96), vol. 2, *Valmy* (Paris 1887), pp. 194, 211, and vol. 4, *Jemmapes et la conquête de la Belgique (1792–1793)* (Paris 1890), pp. 80, 95–6.

33. Louis-Philippe, *Mémoires*, vol. 2, p. 301. For Mme de Genlis' account of these events, see her *Mémoires*, vol. 4, pp. 113–18. For that of Louis-Philippe, see his *Mémoires*, vol. 2, pp. 287–303.

34. Ibid., p. 303.

Two THE ORLÉANS: BROTHER AND SISTER

1. Cited in H. A. C. Collingham with R. S. Alexander, *The July Monarchy: A Political History of France, 1830–1848* (London 1988), p. 103;

R. Arnaud, *Adélaïde d'Orléans* (Paris 1908), p. 295; G. Antonetti, *Louis-Philippe* (Paris 1994), p. 742.

2. Louis-Philippe, *Mémoires* (2 vols, Paris 1973–4), vol. 2, p. 303.

3. S. Tillyard, *Citizen Lord: Edward Fitzgerald, 1763–1798* (London 1997), pp. 141, 148–53; Arnaud, *Adélaïde d'Orléans*, p. 86 n. 2; Mme de Genlis, *Mémoires inédits de Mme la comtesse de Genlis pour servir à l'histoire des 18ème et 19ème siècles* (8 vols, Paris and London 1825), vol. 4, pp. 115, 120–2.

4. E. Lever, *Philippe-Egalité* (Paris 1996), p. 472.

5. A. Chuquet, *Les guerres de la Révolution* (11 vols, Paris 1886–96), vol. 5, *La trahison de Dumouriez* (Paris 1891), pp. 137, 212, 218, 231.

6. Arnaud, *Adélaïde d'Orléans*, pp. 90–2.

7. Louis-Philippe, *Mémoires*, vol. 2, p. 404.

8. This account of Philippe-Egalité's death is taken from Lever, *Philippe-Egalité*, pp. 491–2.

9. Antonetti, *Louis-Philippe*, p. 245.

10. Ibid., pp. 246–7.

11. Arnaud, *Adélaïde d'Orléans*, p. 101.

12. AN 300 AP(III) 6, Archives de la Maison de France, 'Mme Adélaïde (1777–1847): journaux, carnets, correspondance, 1789–1817', dossier 4, 'Compositions littéraires et extraits historiques', Bremgarten 1794.

13. Ibid., dossier 7, 'Mme Adélaïde: extraits et notes de littérature et d'histoire d'Angleterre', p. 62; ibid., dossier 8, p. 1.

14. Ibid., dossier 6, 'Mme Adélaïde: extraits et notes de littérature et d'histoire d'Angleterre', unnumbered but p. 8.

15. Arnaud, *Adélaïde d'Orléans*, pp. 112–29.

16. The tribulations of the duchesse d'Orléans during the Revolution can be followed in E. Delille, *Journal de la vie de SAS Mme la duchesse d'Orléans douairière* (Paris 1822), and G. du Bosq de Beaumont and M. Bernos eds, *La famille d'Orléans pendant la Révolution d'après sa correspondance inédite* (Paris 1913).

17. Arnaud, *Adélaïde d'Orléans*, pp. 144–5.

18. Antonetti, *Louis-Philippe*, pp. 257–8.

19. Ibid., pp. 287–90.

20. Ibid., p. 296, T. E. B. Howarth, *Citizen King: The Life of Louis-Philippe, King of the French* (London 1961), pp. 101–2.

21. To take just two examples, Louis-Philippe to Adélaïde, 28 Sept. 1810, AN 300 AP(IV) 8, pièce 110, and Louis-Philippe to Adélaïde, 6 May 1814, AN 300 AP(IV) 9, pièce 2.

22. Cited in M. Poniatowski, *Louis-Philippe et Louis XVIII; autour du journal de Louis-Philippe en mars 1815* (Paris 1980), pp. 390, 403.

23. For Louis-Philippe's relations with Princess Elizabeth, see F. Fraser,

Princesses: The Six Daughters of George III (London 2005, paperback edn), pp. 226–7, 300. There is much evidence of Louis-Philippe's closeness to the Duke of Kent in his correspondence with Adélaïde; for example, in his letter to her of 31 Jan. 1807: 'C'est vraiment un excellent homme et je ne puis assez me louer de ses procédés' (AN 300 AP(IV) 8, pièce 72).

24. G. de Diesbach, *Histoire de l'émigration, 1789–1814* (Paris 1975, 1984), 1984 edn, pp. 563–4.

25. Antonetti, *Louis-Philippe*, p. 427. See also AN 300 AP(III) 13, 'Souvenirs, manuscrit autographe, Claremont, le 25 novembre 1849', pp. 29–34.

26. Arnaud, *Adélaïde d'Orléans*, pp. 148–9.

27. Louis-Philippe to Adélaïde, 31 Jan. 1806, AN 300 AP(IV) 8, pièce 62.

28. For Marie-Amélie's biography, see the life written shortly after her death by the historian and Orléans family retainer Auguste Trognon, *Vie de Marie-Amélie, reine des Français* (Paris 1872). For Talleyrand's remark, see ibid., p. 2.

29. Louis-Philippe to Adélaïde, 28 Sept. 1810, AN 300 AP(III) 8, pièce 110.

30. See, for example, Louis-Philippe to Adélaïde, 'outside Genoa', 6 May 1814, giving her news of his safe arrival there on his journey to Paris: 'Tu verras le récit de notre voyage dans ma lettre à Amélie', and eight extracts from letters of Louis-Philippe to Marie-Amélie during the summer of 1815 in Adélaïde's papers, AN 300 AP(IV) 9, pièces 2, 16.

31. *Journal de Marie-Amélie, reine des français, 1800–1866*, ed. S. d'Huart (Paris 1981).

32. S. Kale, *French Salons: High Society and Political Sociability from the Old Régime to the Revolution of 1848* (Baltimore and London 2004), p. 146.

33. For the princesse de Lieven, see *Lettres de François Guizot et de la princesse de Lieven, 1836–1846*, ed. J. Naville (3 vols, Paris 1963), and J. Charmley, *The Princess and the Politicians: Sex, Intrigue and Diplomacy, 1812–1840* (London 2005); and for the duchesse de Duras, A. Bardoux, *La duchesse de Duras* (Paris 1898). For a wider view of the urban society in which these Egerias operated, see A. Corbin, J. Lalouette and M. Riot-Sarcey eds, *Femmes dans la cité, 1815–1871* (Grane 1997), esp. pp. 237–50; C.-I. Brelot, 'De la tutelle à la collaboration: une femme de noblesse dans la vie politique (1814–1830)', and pp. 251–9; N. Dauphin, 'Les salons de la restauration. Une influence spécifique sur les milieux dirigeants'. Not all Egerias were actually the mistresses of the men they influenced, as Thiers' biographers argue in the case of his confidante Mme Dosne; J. P. T. Bury and R. P. Tombs, *Thiers, 1797–1877: A Political Life* (London 1986), pp. 49–52.

34. Arnaud, *Adélaïde d'Orléans*, pp. 51–2.

35. See, for example, her letter of 19–20 Sept. 1834 from her château of Randan in the Auvergne to Louis-Philippe in Paris: 'You are my first thought, dear beloved friend, and getting up just now, opening my window and seeing this glorious view and breathing in the good pure air, it wrung my heart to think how much you would enjoy it if you were here, and that instead I am ninety-two leagues away from you.' AN 300 AP(III) 51, p. 5.

36. AN 300 AP(III) 6, 'Mme Adélaïde (1777–1847): journaux, carnets, correspondance, 1789–1817', dossiers 37, 38, journal, entry for 13 Aug. 1817. In fact, Adélaïde's journal is not, as at first appears, simply for the year 1817, but goes well beyond it, to 17 Oct. 1841. This fact has been overlooked until now because the journal is intermittent, and not written on consecutive pages.

37. The best recent biographies of Mme de Staël are S. Balayé, *Madame de Staël: lumières et liberté* (Paris 1979), and in English, M. Fairweather, *Madame de Staël* (London 2005). For George Sand, see her own *Histoire de ma vie* (20 vols, Paris 1854–5), and C. Cate, *George Sand: A Biography* (London 1975). For Marie d'Agoult, see *Mémoires, souvenirs et journaux de la comtesse d'Agoult*, ed. C. Dupechez (Paris 1990), and J. Vier, *La comtesse d'Agoult et son temps* (2 vols, Paris 1955–9). The position of women in French society in this period is a vast subject, but see C. G. Moses, *French Feminism in the Nineteenth Century* (New York 1984); J. Rendall, *The Origins of Modern Feminism: Women in Britain, France and the United States* (London 1985); H. D. Lewis, 'The legal status of women in nineteenth-century France', *Journal of European Studies*, vol. 10 (1980), pp. 178–88.

38. AN 300 AP(III) 6, dossiers 14–26: 'Règlements de vie et de retraite, copies de textes, pensées sur la religion, litanie'.

39. AN 300 AP(I) 14, pièce 10: 'Notice sur Louis-Philippe-Joseph, duc d'Orléans, et sur ses enfants', p. 99.

40. AN 300 AP(III) 6, dossier 36: 'Mme Adélaïde: journal, 23 Apr.–4 Sept. 1814', pp. 2, 12.

41. Antonetti, *Louis-Philippe*, pp. 432–5.

42. Louis-Philippe to Marie-Amélie, 19 May 1814, copy of letter in Adélaïde's papers: 'Lettres de mon frère', AN 300 AP(IV) 9, pièce 5.

43. Ibid.

Three TEN MONTHS AND A HUNDRED DAYS

1. *Mémoires de la comtesse de Boigne, née d'Osmond: récits d'une tante* (2 vols, *Mercure de France* edn, Paris 1999), vol. 1, pp. 377–80; P. Mansel, *Louis XVIII* (Sutton edn, Stroud 1999), p. 271.

2. On the structure of the Napoleonic regime and the limited possibilities for opposition available, see J. Godechot, *Les institutions de la France sous la Révolution et l'Empire* (Paris 1951); I. Collins, *Napoleon and his Parliaments, 1800–1815* (London 1979); L. Bergeron, *L'épisode Napoléonien. Aspects intérieurs, 1799–1815* (Paris 1972); and L. de Villefosse and J. Bouissonouse, *L'opposition à Napoléon* (Paris 1969).

3. D. M. G. Sutherland, *France 1789–1815: Revolution and Counter-revolution* (London 1985), p. 387.

4. The best overall treatment of this crucial area is N. Aston, *Religion and Revolution in France, 1780–1804* (Basingstoke and London 2000): for Protestants and Jews in particular see ibid., pp. 244–58.

5. Mansel, *Louis XVIII*, pp. 118–19.

6. The senatorial constitution is published in full in P. Rosanvallon, *La monarchie impossible: les chartes de 1814 et de 1830* (Paris 1994), pp. 193–6.

7. For the text of the declaration of St Ouen, see ibid., pp. 209–10.

8. For the text of the Charter, see also ibid., pp. 250–7, and (for Louis XVIII's and Ferrand's speeches), 246–9.

9. R. Magraw, *France 1815–1914: The Bourgeois Century* (London 1983), p. 33.

10. F. O'Gorman, *The Long Eighteenth Century: British Political and Social History 1688–1832* (London and New York 1997), p. 369.

11. For the preamble to the Charter, see Rosanvallon, *La monarchie impossible*, pp. 250–1.

12. For the full text of the declaration of 23 June 1789, see G. Lefebvre and A. Terroine, *Recueil de documents relatifs aux séances des états-généraux de 1789*, vol. 1(ii): *la séance du 23 juin* (Paris 1962), pp. 273–86. There is an English translation of its most important articles in J. Hardman, *The French Revolution Sourcebook* (London 1999), pp. 101–3.

13. See Rosanvallon, *La monarchie impossible*, p. 251.

14. See, for example, J. Godechot, *La contre-révolution: doctrine et action, 1789–1804* (Paris 1961), pp. 109–12; J. Roberts, *The Counter-revolution in France, 1789–1830* (Basingstoke 1990), pp. 80–4; J.-J. Oechslin, *Le mouvement ultra-royaliste sous la restauration: son idéologie et son action politique (1814–1830)* (Paris 1960), pp. 40–1; B. Valade, 'Les théocrates', in J. Tulard ed., *La contre-révolution* (Paris 1990), pp. 286–309; R. S.

Alexander, *Rewriting the French Revolutionary Tradition* (Cambridge 2003), p. 6; F. Baldensperger, *Le mouvement des idées dans l'émigration française, 1789–1815* (2 vols, Paris 1924), vol. 2, pp. 111–246, esp. pp. 133–48.

15. See Artois' important letter to his sister-in-law Marie Antoinette of 6 Apr. 1791: '. . . je ne crains pas de répéter ce que je regarde comme ma profession de foi. Je vivrai et mourrai, s'il le faut, pour défendre les droits de l'autel et du trône . . . La déclaration du 23 juin ou la teneur des cahiers [the lists of grievances brought by the deputies to the Estates General of 1789] sont des bases dont je ne m'écarterai jamais.' F. Feuillet de Conches ed., *Louis XVI, Marie Antoinette et Mme Elisabeth: lettres et documents inédits* (6 vols, Paris 1864–73), vol. 2, p. 34. Artois did not waver from these essential views for the rest of his life.

16. For the *monarchiens*, see J. Egret, *La révolution des notables: Mounier et les monarchiens* (Paris 1950); R. Griffiths, *Le centre perdu: Malouet et les 'monarchiens' dans la Révolution française* (Grenoble 1988); comte de Montlosier, *Souvenirs d'un émigré*, ed. comte de Larouzière-Montlosier and E. d'Hauterive (Paris 1951); F. Furet and M. Ozouf eds., *Terminer la Révolution* (Grenoble 1990), pp. 25–111.

17. On this form of monarchy as embodied in the constitution of 1791, see F. Furet and R. Halévi, *La monarchie républicaine: la constitution de 1791* (Paris 1996).

18. The standard biography of Lafayette is the multivolume work by Louis Gottschalk: *Lafayette Comes to America* (Chicago: Chicago University Press 1935); *Lafayette Joins the American Army* (Chicago: Chicago University Press, 1937); *Lafayette and the Close of the American Revolution* (Chicago: Chicago University Press, 1942); *Lafayette between the American and the French Revolutions* (Chicago: Chicago University Press, 1950); with M. Maddox, *Lafayette in the French Revolution, through the October Days* (Chicago and London: Chicago University Press, 1969); with M. Maddox, *Lafayette in the French Revolution: From the October Days through the Federation* (Chicago and London: Chicago University Press, 1973). There is also a good recent French biography: E. Taillemite, *La Fayette* (Paris: Fayard, 1989). On Lafayette during the restoration see S. Neely, *Lafayette and the Liberal Ideal, 1814–1824* (Carbondale, Ill., 1991).

19. Articles 13, 14 and 15 of the Charter: Rosanvallon, *La monarchie impossible*, pp. 252–3, 255.

20. S. Rials, 'Essai sur le concept de monarchie limitée (autour de la charte de 1814)', in S. Rials, *Révolution et contre-révolution au 19ème siècle* (Paris 1987), pp. 119–25.

21. Of the two major nineteenth-century histories of the restoration, A. de Vaulabelle, *Histoire des deux restaurations jusqu'à l'avènement de Louis-*

Philippe (de janvier 1813 à octobre 1830) (8 vols, Paris 1847–57) took a pessimistic (see vol. 8 pp. 447–52), and L. de Viel-Castel, *Histoire de la restauration* (20 vols, Paris 1860–78), an optimistic view of the restoration's ultimate prospects (see vol. 1, pp.I–III). In more recent times, G. de Bertier de Sauvigny, in *La restauration* (Paris 1955) and P. Mansel in *Louis XVIII*, have continued the 'optimistic' school. E. de Waresquiel and B. Yvert, *Histoire de la restauration, 1814–1830: naissance de la France moderne* (Paris 1996), while not denying the political ambiguities of the restoration, stress its contribution to the development of modern France (p. 10). The best recent statement of the 'pessimistic' viewpoint is Alexander, *Rewriting the French Revolutionary Tradition*.

22. There is some disagreement among historians over the nature of this consensus, but much more agreement on the fact that it did exist: see G. Holmes, 'The achievement of stability: the social context of politics from the 1680s to the age of Walpole', in J. Cannon ed., *The Whig Ascendancy: Colloquies on Hanoverian England* (London 1981), pp. 1–23, esp. pp. 3–4, 21–2; J. C. D. Clark, *Revolution and Rebellion: State and Society in England in the Seventeenth and Eighteenth Centuries* (Cambridge 1986), pp. 74–7; F. O'Gorman, *The Long Eighteenth Century: British Social and Political History 1688–1832* (London and New York 1997), pp. 42–3, 160–3, 172–3; J. H. Plumb, *The Growth of Political Stability in England, 1675–1725* (London 1982 edn), pp. xvi–xviii, 176–87.

23. See Rosanvallon, *La monarchie impossible*, pp. 252–3, and Rials, 'Essai sur le concept de monarchie limitée', pp. 110–12.

24. *la monarchie impossible*, pp. 274–8. Though an extract is reproduced in Rosanuallon, pp. 274–8, the 'Souvenirs' are only briefly discussed in the body of the work, and the most recent biography of Louis-Philippe, G. Antonetti, *Louis-Philippe* (Paris 1994), cites only the section dealing with the Charter's denial to Louis-Philippe of membership by birth of the Chamber of Peers (ibid., pp. 443–4).

25. '1814. Souvenirs; manuscrit autographe. Claremont, le 25 novembre 1849.' Archives Nationales, Paris, Archives de la Maison de France, 300 AP(III) 13, p. 93.

26. Ibid., pp. 77–8.

27. Ibid., pp. 80–1.

28. The speeches of Louis XVIII and of Ferrand are reproduced in Rosanvallon, *La monarchie impossible*, pp. 246–9.

29. Louis-Philippe to Adélaïde, 6 May 1814, AN 300 AP(IV) 9, pièce 2.

30. Louis-Philippe to Adélaïde, 9 May 1814, AN 300 AP(IV) 9, pièce 3.

31. '1814. Souvenirs', AN 300 AP(III) 13, pp. 19–20.

32. Cited in Antonetti, *Louis-Philippe*, p. 427.

33. '1814. Souvenirs', AN 300 AP(III) 13, pp. 29–32.

34. Antonetti, *Louis-Philippe*, p. 445; R. Arnaud, *Adélaïde d'Orléans (1777–1847)* (Paris 1908), p. 297.

35. Cited in A. Martin-Fugier, *La vie quotidienne de Louis-Philippe et de sa famille* (Paris 1992), pp. 65–6.

36. 'Mme Adélaïde. Journal, 23 avril–14 septembre 1814.' AN 300 AP(III) 6, dossier 36, entry for 29 July.

37. Ibid., entries for 2 Aug. and 2 Sept. 1814.

38. Ibid., entry for 18 Aug. 1814.

39. Ibid., entry for 20 Aug. 1814.

40. Ibid.

41. Ibid., entry for 2 Sept. 1814.

42. Bertier de Sauvigny, *La restauration*, p. 104.

43. Ibid., p. 103.

44. Mansel, *Louis XVIII*, pp. 204–5; Bertier de Sauvigny, *La restauration*, pp. 105–6.

45. Ibid., p. 103.

46. Boigne, *Mémoires*, vol. 1, pp. 404–5.

47. 'Mme Adélaïde. Journal.' AN 300 AP(III) 6, dossier 36, entry for 14 Sept. 1814.

48. Waresquiel and Yvert, *Histoire de la restauration*, pp. 63–4.

49. Bertier de Sauvigny, *La restauration*, p. 91.

50. Mansel, *Louis XVIII*, pp. 191, 208; Bertier de Sauvigny, *La restauration*, pp. 110–12.

51. Ibid., pp. 107–8.

52. Alexander, *Bonapartism and Revolutionary Tradition in France: The Fédérés of 1815* (Cambridge 1991), pp. 156–7; and Alexander, *Rewriting the French Revolutionary Tradition*, p. 31.

53. 'Relation de ce qui m'a concerné dans les événements qui ont eu lieu après le débarquement de Buonaparte en France, suivie de ma correspondance après que j'en suis sorti', AN 300 AP(III) 13, p. 6.

54. Ibid., pp. 7–8.

55. Ibid., p. 8.

56. Louis-Philippe to Marie-Amélie, 30 May 1814, AN AP 300(IV) 9, pièce 6; and '1814. Souvenirs', AN AP 300(III) 13, pp. 101–2.

57. L. Madelin, *Fouché 1759–1820* (2 vols, Paris 1930), p. 316.

58. Cited in M. Poniatowski, *Louis-Philippe et Louis XVIII: autour du journal de Louis-Philippe en mars 1815* (Paris 1980), p. 221.

59. There is an immense literature on the Hundred Days; three established classics are H. Houssaye, *1815: la première restauration, le retour de l'Ile d'Elbe, les cent-jours* (Paris 1893), and J. Thiry, *Le vol de l'aigle: le retour*

de Napoléon de l'Ile d'Elbe aux Tuileries (Paris 1942) and *Les cent-jours* (Paris 1943). For two stimulating recent treatments see D. de Villepin, *Les cent-jours ou l'esprit de sacrifice* (Paris 2001), and A. Roberts, *Waterloo: Napoleon's Last Gamble* (London 2005). On the specific question of Napoleon's motivation, see A. Chuquet, 'Le départ de l'Ile d'Elbe', *Revue de Paris*, 1 Feb. 1920, and *Correspondance inédite du prince de Talleyrand et du roi Louis XVIII pendant le congrès de Vienne* ôed. G. Pallain (Paris 1881): Talleyrand to Louis, 13 Oct. 1814, p. 43 and n. 2; Louis to Talleyrand, 21 Oct. 1814, pp. 71–2; and Talleyrand to Louis, 7 Dec. 1814, pp. 170–1.

60. Houssaye, *1815*, pp. 282–8; Bertier de Sauvigny, *La restauration*, pp. 116–17.

61. Houssaye, *1815*, pp. 114–20; Madelin, *Fouché*, vol. 2, pp. 324–5. Madelin argues that Fouché's real aim was a regency for Napoleon's son (though the fact that the boy was in the custody of his Habsburg relatives in Vienna was surely an insuperable obstacle to this plan). If this had failed, Madelin continues, Fouché would simply have gained control of Paris using d'Erlon's troops, and negotiated with the returning Napoleon from a position of strength. Houssaye, however, thinks Fouché was strongly tempted to put Louis-Philippe on the throne. Poniatowski, *Louis-Philippe et Louis XVIII*, pp. 213–24, supports the view that the 'conspiracy of the North' was an attempted Orléanist coup.

62. 'Relation', AN AP 300(III) 13, pp. 77–8 n. 1.

63. Cited in Antonetti, *Louis-Philippe*, p. 471.

64. 'Relation', AN 300 AP(III) 13, pp. 13–14.

65. Ibid., p. 14.

66. *Souvenirs du maréchal Macdonald, duc de Tarente* (Paris 1892), pp. 337–8.

67. Louis-Philippe, 'Extrait de mon journal du mois de mars 1815' (Twickenham 1816), in Poniatowski, *Louis-Philippe et Louis XVIII*, p. 250. These published extracts, however, form only a heavily expurgated version of the original manuscript 'Relation' in AN 300 AP(III) 13.

68. Vaulabelle, *Histoire des deux restaurations*, vol. 2, pp. 229–30; Viel-Castel, *Histoire de la restauration*, vol. 2, p. 362.

69. 'Relation', AN 300 AP(III) 13, p. 109.

70. Ibid., pp. 109–10.

71. For Mortier's biography, see J. C. E. Frignet-Despréaux, *Le maréchal Mortier, duc de Trévise* (3 vols, Paris and Nancy 1913–20).

72. 'Relation', AN 300 AP(III) 13, p. 152.

73. Ibid., p. 59.

74. Ibid., pp. 172–4.

75. Ibid., p. 208.

76. See J. Hardman, *Louis XVI* (New Haven and London 1993), p. 188; M. Price, *The Fall of the French Monarchy: Louis XVI, Marie Antoinette and the Baron de Breteuil* (London 2002), p. 158.

77. 'Relation', AN 300 AP(III) 13, pp. 211–18.
78. Ibid., pp. 226–7.
79. Antonetti, *Louis-Philippe*, p. 459.
80. 'Relation', AN 300 AP(III) 13, pp. 91–2.
81. Antonetti, *Louis-Philippe*, p. 463.
82. Ibid., pp. 465–6.
83. See the extraordinary scenes in the Chamber of Deputies on 26 Jan. 1844, when Guizot, then prime minister, was attacked for having accompanied Louis XVIII to Ghent; P. Thureau-Dangin, *Histoire de la monarchie de juillet* (7 vols, Paris 1884–92), vol. 5, pp. 238–43.
84. Lord Acton, *Lectures on the French Revolution* (London 1920 edn), p. 223; J.-P. Bois, *Dumouriez: héros et proscrit* (Paris 2005), p. 367.
85. Antonetti, *Louis-Philippe*, p. 468; E. de Waresquiel, in *Talleyrand: le prince immobile* (Paris 2003), p. 434, attributes the phrase to Talleyrand.
86. Louis-Philippe to Adélaïde, 1 Aug. 1815, AN 300 AP(IV) 9, pièce 11.
87. On the 'White Terror' see the study by D. Resnick, *The White Terror and the Political Reaction after Waterloo* (Cambridge, Mass., 1966).
88. Louis-Philippe to Adélaïde, 10 Aug. 1815, AN 300 AP(IV) 9, pièce 14.
89. Mansel, *Louis XVIII*, p. 246.
90. Louis-Philippe to Marie-Amélie, 10 Aug. 1815, AN 300 AP(IV) 9, pièce 16, p. 29 (pièce 16 comprises extracts of Louis-Philippe's letters to Marie-Amélie that he sent to Adélaïde to avoid giving the same information twice to his wife and sister).
91. Ibid.
92. Ibid., p. 24.
93. Ibid., pp. 26–8.
94. *Vieux souvenirs de Mgr le prince de Joinville, 1818–1848*, ed. D. Meyer (Mercure de France edn, Paris 1986), p. 31.
95. Victor Hugo, *Journal, 1830–1848*, ed. H. Guillemin (Paris 1954), entry for 15 Aug. 1844, p. 106.

Four CROWN AND PARLIAMENT, 1815–29

1. Quoted in G. Antonetti, *Louis-Philippe* (Paris 1994), p. 471.
2. G. de Bertier de Sauvigny, *La restauration* (Paris 1955), p. 174.
3. E. de Waresquiel, *Le duc de Richelieu 1766–1822: un sentimental en politique* (Paris 1990), p. 258.
4. Antonetti, *Louis-Philippe*, p. 476.
5. Quoted in E. de Waresquiel and B. Yvert, *Histoire de la restauration, 1814–1830: naissance de la France moderne* (Paris 1996), p. 202.

6. T. Zeldin, *The Political System of Napoleon III* (London 1958), pp. 142–53.

7. For an overall study of ultra-royalism see J.-J. Oechslin, *Le mouvement ultra-royaliste sous la restauration. Son idéologie et son action politique (1814–1830)* (Paris 1960). For its principal leaders see *Mémoires et correspondance du comte de Villèle* (5 vols, Paris 1888–90) and J. Fourcassié, *Villèle* (Paris 1954); P. Robin-Harmel, *Le prince Jules de Polignac, ministre de Charles X* (2 vols, Paris and Avignon 1941–50); E. Beau de Loménie, *La carrière politique de Chateaubriand, 1814–1830* (2 vols, Paris 1929); M. Fumaroli, *Chateaubriand: poésie et terreur* (Paris 2004); G. de Diesbach, *Chateaubriand* (Paris 1995), and Chateaubriand's own classic *Mémoires d'outre-tombe* (Livre de Poche edn, 3 vols, Paris 1973); G. de Bertier de Sauvigny, *Le comte Ferdinand de Bertier (1782–1864) et l'énigme de la Congrégation* (Paris 1948). For an excellent regional study of the ultras, see D. Higgs, *Ultraroyalism in Toulouse* (Baltimore 1973). The comte d'Artois' close links with the ultras are suggested by the title of J. Cabanis' biography: *Charles X, roi ultra* (Paris 1972).

8. In addition to Oechslin, *Le mouvement ultra-royaliste*, pp. 24–41, for an introduction to Bonald and de Maistre see J. Godechot, *La contre-révolution: doctrine et action, 1789–1804* (Paris 1961), pp. 93–112, and B. Valade, 'Les théocrates', in J. Tulard ed., *La contre-révolution* (Paris 1990), pp. 286–309. For Chateaubriand and the Charter, see Beau de Loménie, *La carrière politique*, vol. 1, pp. 12–33, 82–121. For Louis-Philippe's view of Polignac's reservations about taking the oath to the Charter, see his letters to Adélaïde of 7 and 9 Oct. 1815: AN 300 AP(IV) 12, pp. 283–92.

9. For Richelieu's political views at this juncture, see Waresquiel, *Le duc de Richelieu*, pp. 213–15, 275–81, 306–7, and *Lettres du duc de Richelieu au marquis d'Osmond, 1816–1818*, ed. S. Charléty (Paris 1939).

10. For Decazes and Louis XVIII, see E. Daudet's important *Louis XVIII et le duc Decazes, 1815–1820* (Paris 1899). For Decazes' biography, see R. Langeron, *Decazes, ministre du roi* (Paris 1960).

11. For the *doctrinaires*, see D. Johnson, *Guizot: Aspects of French History, 1787–1874* (London 1963) pp. 32–42, 161–2, and P. Rosanvallon, *Le moment Guizot* (Paris 1985). Rémusat has left important memoirs: *Mémoires de ma vie*, ed. C. Pouthas (5 vols, Paris 1958–67).

12. An exception to the scholarly neglect of the period 1814–48 has been the number of recent works on French liberalism: S. Holmes, *Benjamin Constant and the Making of Modern Liberalism* (London 1984); C. B. Welch, *Liberty and Utility: The Ideologues and the Transformation of Liberalism* (New York 1984); L. Girard, *Les libéraux français, 1814–1875*

(Paris 1985); A. Jardin, *Histoire du libéralisme politique: de la crise de l'absolutisme à la constitution de 1875* (Paris 1985); G. A. Kelly, *The Humane Comedy: Constant, Tocqueville and French Liberalism* (London 1992). For Lafayette's career in these years see S. Neely, *Lafayette and the Liberal Ideal, 1814–1824: Politics and Conspiracy in an Age of Reaction* (Carbondale, Ill., 1991).

13. For Périer's biography see M. Bourset, *Casimir Périer: un prince financier au temps du romantisme* (Paris 1994), and J. Wolff, *Les Périer: la fortune et les pouvoirs* (Paris 1993). Laffitte wrote his memoirs: *Souvenirs de Jacques Laffitte racontés par lui-même* (3 vols, Paris 1844–5).

14. For the Carbonari, see A. B. Spitzer, *Old Hatreds and Young Hopes: The French Carbonari against the Bourbon Restoration* (Cambridge, Mass., 1971); for Lafayette's role within it see Neely, *Lafayette*, pp. 166–210, 219–22, 231–8.

15. Waresquiel and Yvert, *Histoire de la restauration*, p. 229; Bertier de Sauvigny, *La restauration*, p. 201.

16. Ibid.

17. P. Mansel, *Louis XVIII* (Sutton edn, Stroud 1999), pp. 28–31.

18. *Souvenirs-portraits de Gaston de Lévis (1764–1830), suivis de lettres intimes de Monsieur comte de Provence au duc de Lévis*, ed. J. Dupâquier (Mercure de France edn, Paris 1993), p. 355.

19. Bertier de Sauvigny, *La restauration*, pp. 171–2; Mansel, *Louis XVIII*, pp. 330–1; Daudet, *Louis XVIII et le duc Decazes*, pp. 234–9, 301.

20. Waresquiel and Yvert, *Histoire de la restauration*, pp. 205–8; Marquis de Noailles, *Le comte Molé (1781–1855): sa vie, ses mémoires* (6 vols, Paris 1922–30), vol. 6, pp. 262–3.

21. Bertier de Sauvigny, *La restauration*, pp. 205–11; Waresquiel and Yvert, *Histoire de la restauration*, pp. 166–7; P. W. Schroeder, *The Transformation of European Politics, 1763–1848* (Oxford, 1996 paperback edn), pp. 591–3.

22. De Serre's correspondence has been published: comte de Serre, *Correspondance* (7 vols, Paris 1876–82). There is also a biography: B. Combes de Patris, *Un homme d'état sous la restauration: le comte de Serre (1776–1824), d'après sa correspondance et des documents inédits* (Paris 1932).

23. Antonetti, *Louis-Philippe*, p. 488.

24. *Mémoires de la comtesse de Boigne, née d'Osmond: récits d'une tante* (Mercure de France edn, 2 vols, Paris 1999), vol. 1, pp. 664–5; Antonetti, *Louis-Philippe*, pp. 491–2.

25. AN 300 AP(IV) 18, 'Mme Adélaïde. Lettres reçues de Marie-Amélie et de ses enfants, 1815–1829', dossier 19, p. 167.

26. Louise to Adélaïde, 14 July 1827, ibid., p. 174.

27. *Vieux souvenirs de Mgr le prince de Joinville, 1818–1848*, ed. D. Meyer, (Mercure de France edn, Paris 1986), pp. 24–5; A. Martin-Fugier, *La vie quotidienne de Louis-Philippe et de sa famille, 1830–1848* (Paris 1992), pp. 176, 183.

28. Antonetti, *Louis-Philippe*, pp. 490–1; Martin-Fugier, *La vie quotidienne*, pp. 176–9, 185–90.

29. Ibid., pp. 195–9, and p. 175 for Trognon and Cuvillier-Fleury. Trognon published a life of Marie-Amélie after her death: A. Trognon, *Vie de Marie-Amélie, reine des Français* (Paris 1872); both Cuvillier-Fleury's journals and his correspondence with the duc d'Aumale have been published: *Journal intime de Cuvillier-Fleury*, ed. E. Bertin (2 vols, Paris 1903); *Correspondance du duc d'Aumale et de Cuvillier-Fleury*, ed. F. H. G. Limbourg (4 vols, Paris 1910–14).

30. Martin-Fugier, *La vie quotidienne*, pp. 176–8.

31. Joinville, *Vieux souvenirs*, pp. 32–4; Antonetti, *Louis-Philippe*, p. 500.

32. Ibid., pp. 501–2.

33. AN 300 AP(IV) 18, dossier 19, 'A ma bonne et chère tante', p. 63.

34. R. Arnaud, *Adélaïde d'Orléans (1777–1847)* (Paris 1908), pp. 234–5.

35. Joinville, *Vieux souvenirs*, p. 37.

36. Louise to Adélaïde, 9 Aug. 1826, AN 300 AP(IV) 18, dossier 19, p. 137.

37. Marie-Amélie to Adélaïde, 20 Mar. 1829, ibid., p. 316.

38. AN 300 AP(IV) 9, 'Roi Louis-Philippe. Lettres à sa soeur Mme Adélaïde, 1814–1828', pièce 27.

39. AN 300 AP(III) 6, 'Mme Adélaïde (1777–1847): journaux, carnets, correspondance, 1789–1817', dossiers 37, 38.

40. Louis-Philippe to Raoul de Montmorency, 26 May 1820, AN 300 AP(III) 73, 'Familiers de Louis-Philippe: Atthalin, Dupin, d'Elchingen, Heymès, Montmorency, Vatout', dossier 'Papiers de Raoul de Montmorency', pièce 187.

41. AN 300 AP(III) 6, dossiers 37, 38.

42. Bertier de Sauvigny, *La restauration*, pp. 218–19.

43. Pasquier left important memoirs: *Mémoires du chancelier Pasquier* (6 vols, Paris 1893–5).

44. R. S. Alexander, *Rewriting the French Revolutionary Tradition* (Cambridge 2003), pp. 88–92.

45. Waresquiel and Yvert, *Histoire de la restauration*, pp. 276–87.

46. J. Lucas-Dubreton, *Louvel le régicide* (Paris 1925), p. 86.

47. Ibid., p. 93.

48. Ibid., pp. 93–6, 98–105.

49. P. Mansel, *Paris between Empires, 1814–1852* (London 2001), p. 168.

50. Lucas-Dubreton, *Louvel*, pp. 66–7.

51. Antonetti, *Louis-Philippe*, p. 492.

52. Lucas-Dubreton, *Louvel*, pp. 114–15.

53. Ibid., p. 100, and Antonetti, *Louis-Philippe*, p. 493.

54. Bertier de Sauvigny, *La restauration*, p. 222; Mansel, *Louis XVIII*, pp. 371–2; Daudet, *Louis XVIII et le duc Decazes*, pp. 419–41.

55. Bertier de Sauvigny, *La restauration*, p. 229.

56. Mansel, *Paris between Empires*, p. 179.

57. Antonetti, *Louis-Philippe*, p. 493.

58. On Mme du Cayla, see E. Perret, *La dernière favorite des rois de France. La comtesse du Cayla* (Paris 1937); C. Decours, *La dernière favorite: Zoé du Cayla, le grand amour de Louis XVIII* (Paris 1993); and Mansel, *Paris between Empires*, p. 191.

59. Ibid.

60. Sosthènes de la Rochefoucauld left extensive memoirs, modelled on the writings of his famous ancestor, the seventeenth-century duc de la Rochefoucauld: *Mémoires de M. de la Rochefoucauld, duc de Doudeauville* (10 vols, Paris 1861–3).

61. For example, Mansel, *Louis XVIII*, pp. 401, 408–13.

62. Alexander, *Rewriting the French Revolutionary Tradition*, pp. 140, 187–91.

63. *Mémoires du baron d'Haussez, dernier ministre de la marine sous la restauration* (2 vols, Paris 1896–7), vol. 1, p. 44 n. 1.

64. Waresquiel and Yvert, *Histoire de la restauration*, pp. 370–1; Mansel, *Louis XVIII*, p. 404.

65. AN 300 AP(III) 6, dossiers 37, 38, entry for 13 Sept. 1824.

66. Ibid.

67. Ibid., entry for 14 Sept. 1824.

68. Ibid.

69. Ibid., entry for 15 Sept. 1824.

70. Ibid.

71. Ibid., entry for 16 Sept. 1824.

72. Ibid., entry for 17 Sept. 1824.

73. Antonetti, *Louis-Philippe*, pp. 495, 516–17.

74. AN 300 AP(III) 6, dossiers 37, 38, 'Conversation de mon frère avec le roi Charles X. Neuilly ce mardi 21 septembre 1824.'

75. Alexander, *Rewriting the French Revolutionary Tradition*, p. 193.

76. Ibid., pp. 188–9; Mansel, *Louis XVIII*, p. 405.

77. Antonetti, *Louis-Philippe*, p. 519.

78. Waresquiel and Yvert, *Histoire de la restauration*, pp. 381–2.

79. Bertier de Sauvigny, *La restauration*, pp. 510–11. For religion and anti-clericalism during the restoration, see G. Bertier de Sauvigny, *Le comte Ferdinand de Bertier et l'énigme de la Congrégation* (Paris 1948); G. Cholvy and Y.-M. Hilaire, *Histoire religieuse de la France contemporaine* (2 vols, Toulouse 1985); R. Gibson, *A Social History of French*

Catholicism, 1789–1914 (London 1989); G. Cubitt, *The Jesuit Myth: Conspiracy Theory and Politics in Nineteenth-century France* (Oxford 1993).

80. Waresquiel and Yvert, *Histoire de la restauration*, p. 378.

81. See R. A. Jackson, *Vive le roi! The French Coronation from Charles V to Charles X* (Chapel Hill, North Carolina, 1984), p. 193.

82. Given its importance for the history of France between 1789 and 1871, there are surprisingly few studies of the National Guard; the only general scholarly survey for the nintenth century is L. Girard, *La garde nationale, 1814–1871* (Paris 1964).

83. Louis-Philippe, cited in Antonetti, *Louis-Philippe*, pp. 527–8; Girard, *La garde nationale*, pp. 142–4.

84. Waresquiel and Yvert, *Histoire de la restauration*, pp. 390–3; Bertier de Sauvigny, *La restauration*, p. 532; Girard, *La garde nationale*, pp. 145–6.

85. On the jury bill and its importance, see S. Kent, *The Election of 1827 in France* (Cambridge, Mass., and London 1975), pp. 19–30, though Kent's conclusions are qualified in Alexander, *Rewriting the French revolutionary tradition*, pp. 214–15.

86. Kent, *The Election of 1827*, pp. 82–96; C. Pouthas, *Guizot pendant la restauration: préparation de l'homme d'état, 1814–1830* (Paris 1923), pp. 369–86, 423–39.

87. Kent, *The Election of 1827*, pp. 158–61.

88. E. Daudet, *Le ministère de M. de Martignac, sa vie politique et les dernières années de la restauration* (Paris 1875), pp. 171–9, 194–212. There is also a recent biography of Martignac: F. Boyer, *Martignac (1778–1832): l'itinéraire politique d'un avocat bordelais* (Paris 2002).

89. Robin-Harmel, *Le prince Jules de Polignac*, vol. 2, pp. 107–8.

90. Ibid., vol. 1, pp. 157–8, 194–9.

91. D. H. Pinkney, *The French Revolution of 1830* (Princeton, NJ, 1972), pp. 8–10.

92. Bertier de Sauvigny, *La restauration*, pp. 578–9.

Five CRISIS AND CONFRONTION

1. On the crisis of July 1789 see J. Godechot, *La prise de la Bastille* (Paris 1965); M. Price, *The Fall of the French Monarchy: Louis XVI, Marie Antoinette, and the Baron de Breteuil* (London 2002), pp. 71–100; P. Caron, 'La tentative de contre-révolution de juin–juillet 1789', *Revue d'histoire moderne et contemporaine*, vol. 8 (1906–7), pp. 5–34, 649–78. On the 1830 revolution the most important works in any language are D. H. Pinkney, *The French Revolution of 1830* (Princeton, NJ, 1972) and

P. Pilbeam, *The 1830 Revolution in France* (London 1991). See also J.-L. Bory, *La révolution de juillet* (Paris 1972); J. M. Merriman ed., *1830 in France* (New York and London 1975) and G. de Bertier de Sauvigny ed., *La révolution de 1830 en France* (Paris 1970).

2. E. Beau de Loménie, *La carrière politique de Chateaubriand de 1814 à 1836* (2 vols, Paris 1929), vol. 2, pp. 329–36.

3. E. de Waresquiel and B. Yvert, *Histoire de la restauration, 1814–1830: naissance de la France moderne* (Paris 1996), pp. 437–40.

4. G. de Bertier de Sauvigny, *La restauration* (Paris 1955), p. 596.

5. P. W. Schroeder, *The Transformation of European Politics, 1763–1848* (Oxford 1996 paperback edn), pp. 668–9; Pinkney, *The French Revolution*, pp. 14–18.

6. Waresquiel and Yvert, *Histoire de la restauration*, p. 442; *Mémoires du chancelier Pasquier* (6 vols, Paris 1893–5), vol. 6, p. 461; comte de Guernon-Ranville, *Journal d'un ministre* (Caen 1873).

7. Waresquiel and Yvert, *Histoire de la restauration*, pp. 437–8.

8. R. S. Alexander, *Rewriting the French Revolutionary Tradition* (Cambridge 2003), pp. 244–7.

9. For George III's political role see J. Brooke, *George III* (London 1972), esp. pp. 85–92, 125–61, 183–99, 223–59, and the classic R. Pares, *King George III and the Politicians* (Oxford 1953); K. W. Schweizer, *Lord Bute: Essays in Reinterpretation* (Leicester 1988); J. Cannon, *The Fox–North Coalition: Crisis of the Constitution, 1782–1784* (Cambridge 1969), esp. pp. 233–6. For Queen Victoria's relations with Melbourne and Peel, see C. Woodham-Smith, *Queen Victoria: Her Life and Times*, vol. 1, *1819–1861* (London 1972), pp. 143–82, 249–50, and E. Longford, *Victoria RI* (London 2000 edn), pp. 71–5, 117–18, 237.

10. For Charles' role in the crisis of July 1789, see Price, *The Fall of the French Monarchy*, pp. 71–2, 84–7, 93–6.

11. Guernon-Ranville, *Journal*, pp. 142–3.

12. For Charles' words see Pinkney, *The French Revolution*, pp. 18–19; for those of Louis XVI see G. Lefebvre and A. Terroine, *Recueil des documents relatifs aux états-généraux de 1789*, vol. 1 (ii), *La séance du 23 juin* (Paris 1962), p. 284.

13. G. Antonetti, *Louis-Philippe* (Paris 1994), pp. 148–9.

14. Ibid., p. 550.

15. Guernon-Ranville, *Journal*, pp. 35–51.

16. Ibid., pp. 40–51.

17. Ibid., pp. 69–71.

18. Ibid., p. 73.

19. *Mémoires du baron d'Haussez, dernier ministre de la marine sous la*

restauration (2 vols, Paris 1896–7), vol. 2, pp. 231, 239; Guernon-Ranville, *Journal*, pp. 72–4.

20. Guernon-Ranville, *Journal*, pp. 92–3.

21. Cited in Antonetti, *Louis-Philippe*, pp. 558–9.

22. AN 300 AP(III) 13, dossier '1814. Souvenirs; manuscrit autographe. Claremont, le 25 novembre 1849', p. 80.

23. AN 300 AP(III) 73, 'Familiers de Louis-Philippe: Atthalin, Dupin, d'Elchingen, Heymès, Montmorency, Vatout.' Journal de Vatout, pièces 1–171, 1830, pièce 63, entry for 19 June 1830.

24. Pinkney, *The French Revolution*, p. 37; Pilbeam, *The 1830 Revolution*, pp. 34–5.

25. Guernon-Ranville, *Journal*, pp. 123–7.

26. Ibid., p. 142.

27. Pinkney, *The French Revolution*, pp. 42–3; Pilbeam, *The 1830 Revolution*, pp. 60–1.

28. R. Magraw, *France, 1815–1914: The Bourgeois Century* (London 1983), p. 42; Bertier de Sauvigny, *La restauration*, pp. 608–9.

29. H. d'Estre, *Bourmont: la chouannerie, les cent-jours, la conquête d'Alger (1773–1846)* (Paris 1934), p. 250.

30. *Mémoires du baron d'Haussez*, vol. 2, p. 242.

31. Guernon-Ranville, *Journal*, p. 155.

32. Comte d'Artois to Marie Antoinette, 6 Apr. 1791, in *Louis XVI, Marie Antoinette et Mme Elisabeth: lettres et documents inédits*, ed. F. Feuillet de Conches (6 vols, Paris 1864–73), vol. 2, p. 34.

33. P. Robin-Harmel, *Le prince Jules de Polignac, ministre de Charles X* (2 vols, Paris and Avignon 1941–50), vol. 1, pp. 196–8.

34. Pinkney, *The French Revolution*, pp. 81–2.

35. On the role of journalists in July 1830, see D. L. Rader, *The Journalists and the July Revolution in France* (The Hague 1973). See also I. Collins, *The Government and the Newspaper Press in France, 1814–1881* (Oxford 1959), pp. 55–63, and C. Ledré, *La presse à l'assaut de la monarchie, 1815–1848* (Paris 1960), pp. 87–123.

36. For Thiers, see the excellent biography by J. P. T. Bury and R. P. Tombs, *Thiers 1797–1877: A Political Life* (London 1986).

37. E. de Waresquiel, *Talleyrand: le prince immobile* (Paris 2003), p. 561; Bury and Tombs, *Thiers*, pp. 20–2.

38. Pinkney, *The French Revolution*, pp. 85–8.

39. Bury and Tombs, *Thiers*, pp. 7–16.

40. Pinkney, *The French Revolution*, pp. 90–2.

41. L. G. Michaud, *Biographie universelle* (45 vols, Paris and Leipzig, 1843–65), vol. 27, p. 18. Marmont left voluminous memoirs: *Mémoires du maréchal Marmont, duc de Raguse, de 1792 à 1841* (9 vols, Paris 1857).

42. Bertier de Sauvigny, *La restauration*, pp. 51–4; Waresquiel, *Talleyrand*, pp. 440–7.

43. *Mémoires de la comtesse de Boigne, née d'Osmond: récits d'une tante* (Mercure de France edn, 2 vols, Paris 1999), vol. 2, pp. 161–3.

44. *Mémoires du maréchal Marmont*, vol. 8, pp. 231, 238.

45. Ibid., pp. 236–7.

46. Ibid., p. 238.

47. Service Historique de l'Armée de Terre, Château de Vincennes, D³ 131, Correspondance militaire générale, juillet–août 1830, dossier juillet 1830.

48. Price, *The Fall of the French Monarchy*, pp. 185–6.

49. *Mémoires du maréchal Marmont*, vol. 8, p. 287.

50. Guernon-Ranville, *Journal*, p. 154.

51. *Mémoires du chancelier Pasquier* (6 vols, Paris 1893–95), vol. 6, pp. 262–3.

52. Robin-Harmel, *Le prince Jules de Polignac*, vol. 2, pp. 104–10.

53. Guernon-Ranville, *Journal*, p. 72.

54. A. Trognon, *Vie de Marie-Amélie, reine des Français* (Paris 1872), pp. 179–80.

55. *Journal intime de Cuvillier-Fleury*, ed. E. Bertin (2 vols, Paris 1903), vol. 1, p. 205; *Vieux souvenirs de Mgr le prince de Joinville, 1818–1848*, ed. D. Meyer (Mercure de France edn, Paris 1986), p. 43.

56. *Journal intime de Cuvillier-Fleury*, vol. 1, p. 205.

57. R. Arnaud, *Adélaïde d'Orléans (1777–1847)* (Paris 1908), p. 257.

58. Antonetti, *Louis-Philippe*, p. 560.

59. *Journal intime de Cuvillier-Fleury*, vol. 1, p. 36, entry for 7 Jan. 1829.

60. Waresquiel, *Talleyrand*, p. 553.

61. AN 300 AP(III) 73. Journal de Vatout, 1830, pièce 63, p. 31, 'Juin 1830'.

62. Waresquiel, *Talleyrand*, p. 558.

63. BN, nouvelles acquisitions françaises 20601. Papiers A. Thiers, vol. 1, Correspondance 1830–4. 'Notes sur les événements de 1830. Visite de M. Thiers à Neuilly pour offrir la couronne au duc d'Orléans. Note dictée par lui', fos 83–4.

Six THE JULY REVOLUTION

1. D. H. Pinkney, *The French Revolution of 1830* (Princeton, NJ, 1972), pp. 93–5.

2. G. de Broglie, *Guizot* (Paris 2002 edn), p. 110.

3. Pinkney, *The French Revolution*, pp. 98–100.

4. *Mémoires du maréchal Marmont, duc de Raguse* (9 vols, Paris 1857), vol. 8, p. 238.

5. Pinkney, *The French Revolution*, pp. 104–7.

6. *Mémoires du maréchal Marmont*, vol. 8, p. 243 n. 1.

7. Ibid., pp. 242–3. For a modern review of the military situation, see R. Price, 'The French army and the revolution of 1830', *European Studies Review*, vol. 3 (1973).

8. *Mémoires du maréchal Marmont*, vol. 8, p. 274.

9. For the attitude of the army in July 1789, see S. F. Scott, *The Response of the Royal Army to the French Revolution* (Oxford 1978), pp. 51–70.

10. *Mémoires du maréchal Marmont*, vol. 8, pp. 245–6.

11. P. Pilbeam, *The 1830 Revolution in France* (London 1991), pp. 61–2; J. Harsin, *Barricades: The War of the Streets in Revolutionary Paris, 1830–1848* (London 2002).

12. E. de Waresquiel and B. Yvert, *Histoire de la restauration, 1814–1830: naissance de la France moderne* (Paris 1996), p. 460; *Souvenirs d'Abraham Rösselet*, ed. R. de Steiger (Neuchâtel 1857), p. 304.

13. Pinkney, *The French Revolution*, p. 271.

14. Ibid., pp. 114–19.

15. *Mémoires du général comte de St Chamans* (Paris 1896), pp. 491–503.

16. *Mémoires du maréchal Marmont*, vol. 8, p. 285.

17. Ibid., p. 261; *Mémoires du général comte de St Chamans*, p. 491.

18. *Mémoires du maréchal Marmont*, vol. 8, p. 250.

19. Pinkney, *The French Revolution*, p. 126.

20. Comte de Guernon-Ranville, *Journal d'un ministre* (Caen 1873), p. 179.

21. See R. Allen, *Threshold of Terror: The Last Hours of the Monarchy in the French Revolution* (Stroud 1999), pp. 101–24, 139–66.

22. L. G. Michaud, *Biographie universelle* (45 vols, Paris and Leipzig 1843–65), vol. 37, p. 505; P. Caron, *Les massacres de septembre* (Paris 1935), pp. 500–1; A. Maag, *Geschichte der Schweizertruppen in französischen Diensten während der Restauration und Julirevolution (1816–1830)* (Biel 1899), p. 87.

23. *Mémoires du maréchal Marmont*, vol. 8, pp. 259–60.

24. Ibid., p. 262.

25. P. Mantoux, 'Talleyrand en 1830 d'après des mémoires contemporaines', *Revue Historique*, vol. 78 (1902), p. 273.

26. Pinkney, *The French Revolution*, p. 121; Pamela Pilbeam puts the figure somewhat higher, at 1,800 insurgents and 200 soldiers killed, and 4,500 insurgents and 800 soldiers injured. Pilbeam, *The 1830 Revolution*, p. 62.

27. Pinkney, *The French Revolution*, pp. 138–40.

28. *Mémoires du chancelier Pasquier* (6 vols, Paris 1893–5), vol. 6, pp. 273–4. Mortemart left his account of his experiences in July 1830, which has been published: duc de Mortemart, 'Un manuscrit sur les journées de juillet', *Le Correspondant*, vol. 321 (Dec. 1930), pp. 641–58, 801–23.

29. For Sébastiani's biography, see General J.-T. de Mesmay, *Horace Sébastiani: soldat, diplomate, homme d'état, maréchal de France (1772–1851)* (Paris 1948).
30. Cited in Pinkney, *The French Revolution*, p. 150.
31. BN, nouvelles acquisitions françaises 20601. Papiers A. Thiers, vol. 1, Correspondance 1830–4. 'Notes sur les événements de 1830. Visite de M. Thiers à Neuilly pour offrir la couronne au duc d'Orléans. Note dictée par lui' vol. 1, fos 84–5.
32. Cited in G. Antonetti, *Louis-Philippe* (Paris 1994), p. 568; *Mémoires de la comtesse de Boigne, née d'Osmond: récits d'une tante* (Mercure de France edn, 2 vols, Paris 1999), vol. 2, pp. 263–4.
33. AN 300 AP(III) 73, 'Familiers de Louis-Philippe: Atthalin, Dupin, d'Elchingen, Heymès, Montmorency, Vatout.' Dossiers 1–171, Journal de Vatout, pièce 63, p. 29, entry for 28 July 1830.
34. B. Appert, *Dix ans à la cour du roi Louis-Philippe et souvenirs du temps de l'Empire et de la Restauration* (3 vols, Berlin and Paris 1846), vol. 1, pp. 255–6; Antonetti, *Louis-Philippe*, p. 575.
35. R. Arnaud, *Adélaïde d'Orléans (1777–1847)* (Paris 1908), pp. 263–4.
36. BN, nouvelles acquisitions françaises 20601, vol. 1, fos 86–7.
37. Ibid., fos 88–9.
38. Ibid., fos 89–90.
39. M. Price, *The Fall of the French Monarchy: Louis XVI, Marie Antoinette and the Baron de Breteuil* (London 2002), pp. 148–9.
40. BN, nouvelles acquisitions françaises 20601, vol. 1, fos. 90–91; Pinkney, *The French Revolution*, pp. 151–2.
41. Antonetti, *Louis-Philippe*, pp. 582–3.
42. Ibid., pp. 580–1.
43. AN 300 AP(III) 73. Dossiers 1–171, Journal de Vatout, pièce 35, pp. 38–9, entry for 30 July 1830.
44. BN, nouvelles acquisitions françaises 20601, vol. 1, fo. 87.
45. AN 300 AP(IV) 199. 'Lettres de Mme Adélaïde, 1814–1847, et biographie et notes.'
46. Antonetti, *Louis-Philippe*, p. 583.
47. *Mémoires du chancelier Pasquier*, vol. 6, pp. 285–8; Mortemart, 'Un manuscrit', pp. 803–8.
48. *Mémoires du maréchal Marmont*, vol. 8, pp. 293–4, 296.
49. Ibid., pp. 295–7.
50. Pinkney, *The French Revolution*, pp. 154–6, 165–7; *Mémoires du baron d'Haussez, dernier ministre de la marine sous la restauration* (2 vols, Paris 1896–7), vol. 2, pp. 291–301.
51. Mortemart, 'Un manuscrit', p. 814; *Mémoires du chancelier Pasquier*, vol. 6, p. 301.

52. Mantoux, 'Talleyrand en 1830', p. 283.

53. Pinkney, *The French Revolution*, pp. 158–60.

54. Antonetti, *Louis-Philippe*, p. 590; *Mémoires de Cuvillier-Fleury*, ed. E. Bertin (2 vols, Paris 1903), vol. 1, p. 235.

55. *Mémoires, correspondance et manuscrits du général Lafayette* (6 vols, Paris 1837–8), vol. 6, pp. 409–10; O. Barrot, *Mémoires posthumes* (3 vols, Paris 1875–6) vol. 1, pp. 124–5.

56. For Lafayette's first balcony scene, see L. Gottschalk and M. Maddox, *Lafayette in the French Revolution: Through the October Days* (Chicago and London 1969), pp. 377–8.

57. Antonetti, *Louis-Philippe*, pp. 592–4; J. P. T. Bury and R. P. Tombs, *Thiers, 1797–1877: A Political Life* (London 1986), p. 37; *Mémoires . . . du général Lafayette*, vol. 6, p. 411.

58. A summary of what the 'programme de l'Hôtel de Ville' was generally thought by the radicals to contain is published in P. Rosanvallon, *La monarchie impossible: les chartes de 1814 et de 1830* (Paris 1994), pp. 305–6.

59. Antonetti, *Louis-Philippe*, p. 190.

60. On the republican movement and its opposition to the July monarchy the best works are P. Pilbeam, *Republicanism in Nineteenth-century France, 1814–1871* (Basingstoke and London 1995), pp. 95–154, and J. Harsin, *Barricades: The War of the Streets in Revolutionary Paris, 1830–1848* (New York and Basingstoke 2002).

61. *Mémoires de la comtesse de Boigne, née d'Osmond: récits d'une tante* (Mercure de France edn, 2 vols, Paris 1999), vol. 2, pp. 310–11.

62. Ibid., pp. 314–22.

63. *Vieux souvenirs de Mgr le prince de Joinville*, ed. D. Meyer (Mercure de France edn, Paris 1986), pp. 45–6.

64. *Mémoires de la comtesse de Boigne*, vol. 2, pp. 333–6.

65. Ibid., p. 338.

66. Ibid., pp. 339–41.

67. Ibid., pp. 261, 329–30, 341–2.

68. Antonetti, *Louis-Philippe*, pp. 595–6.

69. *Mémoires du maréchal Marmont*, vol. 8, p. 308; *Souvenirs d'Abraham Rösselet*, p. 302.

70. Antonetti, *Louis-Philippe*, pp. 596–7.

71. Ibid., pp. 597–600.

72. Pinkney, *The French Revolution*, pp. 172–3; Antonetti, *Louis-Philippe*, p. 600. On the march to Rambouillet (and the considerable devastation it wrought on its way) see Archives Nationales, Paris, F[1]c 121, 'Révolution de juillet: mouvement de la colonne parisienne sur Rambouillet'. Dossier: 'Etat des objets divers pris dans l'intérieur du parc de Versailles, côté de Trianon, lors des événements des 27 août et jours suivants.' For

example, the marchers robbed Neuville, one of the gatekeepers of the park of Versailles, of sheets, a feather mattress, five copper pots, a pair of blue trousers, 130 bottles of wine and 100 bottles of beer. I am grateful to Steven Clay for drawing my attention to the F¹c series.

73. For Philippe-Egalité's alleged role in the October days, see E. Lever, *Philippe-Egalité* (Paris 1996), pp. 349–61; J. Hardman, *Louis XVI* (New Haven and London 1993), p. 173.

74. Pinkney, *The French Revolution*, pp. 174–5; Antonetti, *Louis-Philippe*, p. 601; *Mémoires du chancelier Pasquier*, vol. 6, p. 326.

75. Pinkney, *The French Revolution*, p. 176.

76. For contemporary accounts of Charles X's journey to Cherbourg by three participants, see *Mémoires du maréchal Marmont*, vol. 8, pp. 317–32; baron de Damas, *Mémoires, 1785–1862* (2 vols, Paris 1922–3), vol. 2, pp. 180–200; Barrot, *Mémoires posthumes*, vol. 1, pp. 131–87.

77. Rosanvallon, *La monarchie impossible*, p. 307.

78. For the revision of the Charter see P. Thureau-Dangin, *Histoire de la monarchie de juillet* (7 vols, Paris 1884–92), pp. 28–42, and the best modern account, Rosanvallon, *La monarchie impossible*, pp. 93–121, which also prints the revised text in full, pp. 350–5.

79. H. A. C. Collingham with R. S. Alexander, *The July Monarchy: A Political History of France 1830–1848* (London 1988), pp. 70–1.

80. Antonetti, *Louis-Philippe*, pp. 610–11; Rosanvallon, *La monarchie impossible*, pp. 348–50.

81. Antonetti, *Louis-Philippe*, pp. 611–12.

82. Arnaud, *Adélaïde d'Orléans*, p. 283 n. 3.

83. The Grande Mademoiselle left important memoirs, which have been regularly reprinted since the eighteenth century. For a nineteenth-century edition see *Mémoires de Mlle de Montpensier*, ed. M. A. L. de Boissi (10 vols, Paris 1823); for the most recent edition see *Mémoires de la Grande Mademoiselle*, ed. B. Quilliet (Mercure de France edn, Paris 2005). For a modern French biography, see C. Bouyer, *La Grande Mademoiselle: la turbulente cousine de Louis XIV* (Paris 2004). There are also two biographies in English: Vita Sackville-West, *Daughter of France: The Life of Anne Marie Louise d'Orléans, Duchesse de Montpensier (1627–1693)* (London 1959), and V. J. Pitts, *La Grande Mademoiselle at the Court of France, 1627–1688* (Baltimore, Md., 2000).

Seven THE KING AND HIS SISTER

1. G. Antonetti, *Louis-Philippe* (Paris 1994), pp. 624–5.
2. A. de Vigny, *Mémoires inédits, fragments et projets*, ed. J. Sangnier (Paris 1958), p. 100.
3. R. Arnaud, *Adélaïde d'Orléans (1777–1847)*, pp. 290, 292–3.
4. P. Rosanvallon, *Le moment Guizot* (Paris 1985), pp. 273–9; D. Johnson, *Guizot: Aspects of French History 1787–1874* (London 1963), pp. 321, 352–66; J. R. Jennings, 'Conceptions of England and its constitution in nineteenth-century French political thought', *Historical Journal*, vol. 29 (1986), pp. 65–86.
5. C. de Rémusat, *Mémoires de ma vie*, ed. C. Pouthas (5 vols, Paris 1958–67), vol. 2, p. 287.
6. D. H. Pinkney, *The French Revolution of 1830* (Princeton, NJ, 1972), p. 128.
7. P. Rosanvallon, *La monarchie impossible: les chartes de 1814 et de 1830* (Paris 1994), p. 351 (article 13 of the revised Charter).
8. Ibid., pp. 356–8; P. Thureau-Dangin, *Histoire de la monarchie de juillet* (7 vols, Paris 1884–92), vol. 2, pp. 56–62; Antonetti, *Louis-Philippe*, pp. 669–72.
9. P. Bastid, *Les institutions politiques de la monarchie constitutionnelle (1814–1848)* (Paris 1954), pp. 121, 317–42.
10. Adélaïde to General Sébastiani, 8 Mar. 1839, Archives Nationales, Paris, 300 AP(III) 959, pièce 372.
11. Louis-Philippe to Adélaïde, 26 Sept. 1838, AN 300 AP(IV), pièce 170.
12. Antonetti, *Louis-Philippe*, p. 690.
13. Comte de Montalivet, *Fragments et souvenirs* (2 vols, Paris 1899–1900), vol. 2, pp. 70–1.
14. Adélaïde to Sébastiani, 6 Feb. 1836, AN 300 AP(III) 959, pièce 234.
15. See below, pp. 211–2,
16. J. P. T. Bury and R. P. Tombs, *Thiers, 1787–1877: A Political Life* (London 1986), p. 20; *Mémoires de Cuvillier-Fleury*, ed. E. Bertin (2 vols, Paris 1903), vol. 2, p. 129, entry for 18 Feb. 1835.
17. For an overview of the ministries of Louis-Philippe's reign, see C. Pouthas, 'Les ministères de Louis-Philippe', *Revue d'Histoire Moderne et Contemporaine*, vol. 1 (Apr.–June 1954), pp. 102–30.
18. AN 300 AP(III) 73, 'Familiers de Louis-Philippe: Atthalin, Dupin, d'Elchingen, Heymès, Montmorency, Vatout.' Dossiers 1–171, Journal de Vatout, pièce 65, 'Souvenirs de 1830', p. 77.
19. Montalivet, *Fragments et souvenirs*, vol. 1, pp. 3–6, 13–29.

20. Louis-Philippe to Raoul de Montmorency from Twickenham, 13 Aug. 1816: 'Je désire, mon cher Raoul, que vous me rapportiez deux faux toupets au moins, car les miens sont rétrécis d'une manière affligeante.' AN 300 AP(III) 73, dossier 'Papiers de Raoul de Montmorency', pièce 179.

21. *Souvenirs de Alexis de Tocqueville publiés par le comte de Tocqueville* (Paris 1893), pp. 7–9. The most vivid rendition of Louis-Philippe's conversational style, however, is that of Victor Hugo in his *Journal, 1830–1848* (Paris 1954), esp. pp. 98–112.

22. Vigny, *Mémoires inédits*, p. 106.

23. Adélaïde to Louis-Philippe, 19 Sept. 1834, AN 300 AP(III) 51, dossier 2, 'Lettres de Mme Adélaïde', pièce 83, p. 5; Louis-Philippe to Adélaïde, 19 Mar. 1835, AN 300 AP(IV) 10, 'Lettres de mon frère', fo. 130.

24. Arnaud, *Adélaïde d'Orléans*, p. 287 n. 2.

25. Louis-Philippe to Adélaïde, 24 and 25 Mar. 1835, AN 300 AP(IV) pièces 135, 136.

26. The only biography of Adélaïde is Arnaud, *Adélaïde d'Orléans*; this gives a readable account of her life, but is based entirely on secondary sources, and is ultimately hostile.

27. Hugo, *Journal*, p. 312.

28. Montalivet, *Fragments et souvenirs*, vol. 1, pp. 16–18.

29. Ibid., pp. 29–30.

30. Hugo, *Journal*, p. 313.

31. *La Mode*, vols 34–5 (Jan.–June 1838), 9ème livraison, p. 237.

32. Duchesse de Dino, *Chronique de 1831 à 1862, publiée par la princesse de Castellane* (4 vols, Paris 1909–11), vol. 2, p. 16.

33. Letters from Adélaïde to Talleyrand are published in *Le prince de Talleyrand et la maison d'Orléans*, ed. comtesse de Mirabeau (Paris 1890), and from Talleyrand to Adélaïde in F. Masson, 'Lettres du prince de Talleyrand et de Mme de Dino à Mme Adélaïde', *Nouvelle Revue Rétrospective*, vol. 15 (1901), pp. 145–68, 217–40, 337–60, 385–408, and vol. 16 (1902), pp. 49–65. Given that this published total comprises 55 letters from Adélaïde and 53 from Talleyrand, that many of the replies are missing, and that there are substantial chronological gaps, it is clear that a significant amount of the correspondence must have been lost or destroyed. The letters of Adélaïde to Sébastiani, bought by the comte de Paris at a sale in 1889 and which centre on the period of Sébastiani's embassy to England from 1835 to 1840, are much more complete, though there are fewer letters from Sébastiani. This correspondence is now in AN 300 AP(III) 959, pièces 197–437.

34. Adélaïde to Sébastiani, 2 June 1835, ibid., pièce 206.

35. *Mémoires de la comtesse de Boigne, née d'Osmond: récits d'une tante* (Mercure de France edn, 2 vols, Paris 1999), vol. 2, p. 328.

36. Arnaud, *Adélaïde d'Orléans*, pp. 314–15.

37. B. Appert, *Dix ans à la cour du roi Louis-Philippe et souvenirs du temps de l'empire et de la restauration* (3 vols, Berlin and Paris 1846), vol. 2, pp. 299–301.

38. For Flahaut's biography see F. de Bernardy, *Flahaut, fils de Talleyrand, père de Morny* (Paris 1974).

39. See G. de Broglie, *Madame de Genlis* (Paris 1985), pp. 415–16.

40. André Dupin left important memoirs: *Mémoires de M. Dupin* (4 vols, Paris 1855–61).

41. Adélaïde to Sébastiani, 25 Apr. 1836, AN 300 AP(III) 959, pièce 251.

42. AN 300 AP(III) 73, dossiers 1–171, Journal de Vatout, 'Evénements de la révolution de 1830', pièce 35.

43. Adélaïde to Sébastiani, 5 Apr. 1838, AN 300 AP(III) 959, pièce 332.

44. Adélaïde to the ducs de Chartres and de Nemours, 24 Dec. 1832, AN 300 AP(IV) 199, 'Duc de Nemours: lettres de Mme Adélaïde'.

45. E. Cabet, *Révolution de 1830 et situation présente (novembre 1833)* (Paris 1833), p. 137.

46. For a comprehensive treatment in English of republicanism in these years see P. Pilbeam, *Republicanism in Nineteenth-century France, 1814–1871* (Basingstoke 1995), pp. 99–140. For a thorough study of the Parisian republicanism in the same period see J. Harsin, *Barricades: The War of the Streets in Revolutionary Paris, 1830–1848* (New York and Basingstoke 2002), pp. 43–52, 65–79. See also H. A. C. Collingham with R. S. Alexander, *The July Monarchy: A Political History of France 1830–1848* (London 1988), pp. 137–8.

47. Harsin, *Barricades*, p. 50; Pilbeam, *Republicanism*, pp. 99–103.

48. On the National Guard, see L. Girard, *La Garde Nationale, 1814–1871* (Paris 1964).

49. See above, p. 119–21.

50. The most recent biography of Périer is M. Bourcet, *Casimir Périer: un prince financier au temps du romantisme* (Paris 1994). For examples of what Périer's policy of *résistance* meant in practice, see C. Breunig, 'Casimir Périer and the troubles of Grenoble, Mar. 11th–13th, 1832', *French Historical Studies*, vol. 2 no. 4 (1962), pp. 469–89, and P. Pilbeam, 'The emergence of opposition to the Orléanist monarchy, August 1830–April 1831', *English Historical Review*, vol. 85, no. 334 (Jan. 1970), pp. 12–28.

51. For Thiers' divided loyalties between the *mouvement* and the *résistance*, see Bury and Tombs, *Thiers*, pp. 43–6; Thureau-Dangin, *Histoire de la monarchie de juillet*, vol. 2, pp. 33–43.

52. For examples of historians' use of these terms, from the nineteenth century on, to analyse the July monarchy's politics, see Thureau-Dangin,

Histoire de la monarchie de juillet, vol. 1, pp. 76–83, and Collingham, *The July Monarchy*, pp. 24–5.

53. BN, nouvelles acquisitions françaises 20601, Papiers A. Thiers, vol. 1, Correspondance 1830–4, fo. 93: '30 septembre 1830 – appréciation du caractère de M. Casimir Périer. Note dictée par M. Thiers'.

54. Sébastiani to Thiers, 5 Mar. 1836, BN, nouvelles acquisitions françaises 20606, vol. 6, Correspondance 1836, M-S, fo. 191.

55. Montalivet, *Fragments et souvenirs*, vol. 1, pp. 15–16; *Mémoires de la comtesse de Boigne*, vol. 2, pp. 325–6.

56. See above, pp. 36–7

57. Adélaïde to maréchal Gérard, 28 Nov. 1832, Archives Bryas, Château de Mauvières. Lettres de Mme Adélaïde d'Orléans au maréchal Gérard.

58. P. Robin-Harmel, *Le prince Jules de Polignac, ministre de Charles X* (2 vols, Paris and Avignon 1941–50), vol. 2, pp. 117–28.

59. Ibid., p. 134.

60. Pinkney, *The French Revolution*, pp. 319–20.

61. Robin-Harmel, *Le prince Jules de Polignac*, vol. 2, 134–5.

62. Montalivet's memoirs, *Fragments et souvenirs*, are a crucial source for the reign of Louis-Philippe. They are strongly biased in favour of the king, but the privileged access to him that Montalivet enjoyed gave him insights into Louis-Philippe's character and policies that most contemporaries lacked.

63. *Mémoires du chancelier Pasquier* (6 vols, Paris 1893–5), vol. 6, p. 439 n. 1; Robin-Harmel, *Le prince Jules de Polignac*, vol. 2, p. 152.

64. *Mémoires de la comtesse de Boigne*, vol. 2, p. 329.

65. Montalivet, *Fragments et souvenirs*, vol. 1, pp. 165–8.

66. Antonetti, *Louis-Philippe*, p. 637; Montalivet, *Fragments et souvenirs*, vol. 1, pp. 176–80.

67. Montalivet, *Fragments et souvenirs*, vol. 1 pp. 191–9.

68. Pinkney, *The French Revolution*, pp. 356–7.

69. Robin-Harmel, *Le prince Jules de Polignac*, vol. 2, p. 162.

70. Pinkney, *The French Revolution*, pp. 357–8.

71. Antonetti, *Louis-Philippe*, p. 638.

72. Pinkney, *The French Revolution*, pp. 359–61.

73. Montalivet, *Fragments et souvenirs*, vol. 1, pp. 258–9, 264–76.

74. Antonetti, *Louis-Philippe*, p. 639.

75. Girard, *La garde nationale*, pp. 187–95; Antonetti, *Louis-Philippe*, pp. 646–7.

76. Girard, *La garde nationale*, pp. 211–12. Girard estimates that of the overall national total of 3,573,475 National Guardsmen, 623,291 were actually armed.

77. Thureau-Dangin, *Histoire de la monarchie de juillet*, vol. 1, pp. 80–3, 210–27; P. W. Schroeder, *The Transformation of European Politics, 1763–1848* (Oxford 1996 paperback edn), pp. 677–8; Collingham, *The July Monarchy*, pp. 186–90.

78. Schroeder, *The Transformation of European Politics*, pp. 557–70, 592–3.

79. Thureau-Dangin, *Histoire de la monarchie de juillet*, vol. 1, pp. 57–67; Antonetti, *Louis-Philippe*, pp. 618–20.

80. Louis-Philippe to Sébastiani, 27 Dec. 1834, AN 300 AP(III) 42. Dossier 7: Sébastiani, pièce 213.

81. Cited in E. de Waresquiel, *Talleyrand, le prince immobile* (Paris 2003), p. 158.

82. Ibid., pp. 173–4, 586–8.

83. Louis-Philippe to count Molé, 28 Sept. 1830, AN 300 AP(III) 34. Dossier 1: Lettres du roi Louis-Philippe au comte Molé 1830, pièce 25; duchesse de Dino to Adélaïde, 2 Nov. 1830, in F. Masson, 'Lettres du prince de Talleyrand', *Nouvelle Revue Rétrospective*, vol. 15, p. 166.

84. Cited in Waresquiel, *Talleyrand*, p. 400.

85. Ibid., p. 577.

86. Adélaïde to Talleyrand, 22 Jan. 1834, in *Le prince de Talleyrand*, p. 42; Adélaïde to Sébastiani, 11 Dec. 1835, AN 300 AP(III) 959, pièce 225.

87. Arnaud, *Adélaïde d'Orléans*, pp. 324–5; Waresquiel, *Talleyrand*, p. 575.

88. Talleyrand to Adélaïde, 9 Feb. 1831, in Masson, 'Lettres de Talleyrand', *Nouvelle Revue Rétrospective*, vol. 15, p. 357.

89. Talleyrand to Adélaïde, 27 June 1831, ibid., vol. 16, p. 52, and 2 Oct. 1830, ibid., vol. 15, p. 146.

90. Marquis de Noailles, *Le comte Molé (1781–1855): sa vie, ses mémoires* (6 vols, Paris 1922–30), vol. 5, pp. 129–31.

91. P. Mansel, *Paris between Empires, 1814–1852* (London 2001), pp. 271–2.

92. Thureau-Dangin, *Histoire de la monarchie de juillet*, vol. 1, pp. 67–75; Antonetti, *Louis-Philippe*, pp. 615–24. Schroeder is less convinced that the Belgian crisis could have triggered a major war: *The Transformation of European Politics*, pp. 670–80.

93. Louis-Philippe to the duc d'Orléans, 31 Aug. 1837, AN 300 AP(III) 172, pièce 118; Louis-Philippe to Molé, 28 Oct. 1836, ibid., 34, pièce 148.

94. Schroeder, *The Transformation of European Politics*, pp. 680–1; Thureau-Dangin, *Histoire de la monarchie de juillet*, vol. 1, pp. 152–9.

95. Collingham, *The July Monarchy*, p. 187; Thureau-Dangin, *Histoire de la monarchie de juillet*, vol. 1, p. 70.

96. Ibid., pp. 159–60, 170–80.

97. Talleyrand to Adélaïde, 15 Dec. 1830, in Masson, 'Lettres de Talleyrand', *Nouvelle Revue Rétrospective*, vol. 15, p. 234.

98. A. Martin-Fugier, *La vie quotidienne de Louis-Philippe et de sa famille*,

1830–1848 (Paris 1992), pp. 211–14. For Louise, see M. Kerckvoorde, *Louise d'Orléans, la reine oubliée 1812–1850* (Paris 1991).

99. Schroeder, *The Transformation of European Politics*, p. 684.

100. Victor Hugo, *Les Misérables*, in *Oeuvres complètes* (48 vols, Paris 1880–9), *Roman*, vol. 8, p. 24.

Eight THE YEARS OF DANGER

1. See C. Pouthas, 'Les ministères de Louis-Philippe', *Revue d'Histoire Moderne et Contemporaine*, vol. 1 (1954), pp. 111–12.

2. For *replâtrage* under the Third Republic see A. Soulier, *L'instabilité ministérielle sous la troisième république (1871–1938)* (Paris 1939), p. 479, and J. Ollé-Laprune, *La stabilité des ministres sous la troisième république (1879–1940)* (Paris 1962), pp. 13, 21–2.

3. P. Rosanvallon, *Le moment Guizot* (Paris 1986), pp. 277–9; G. de Broglie, *Guizot* (Paris 2002 edn), p. 265.

4. P. Thureau-Dangin, *Histoire de la monarchie de juillet* (7 vols, Paris 1884–92), vol. 1, pp. 188–94; H. A. C. Collingham with R. S. Alexander, *The July Monarchy: A Political History, 1830–1848* (London 1988), pp. 42–3; J. P. T. Bury and R. P. Tombs, *Thiers 1797–1877: A Political Life* (London 1986), p. 44.

5. G. Antonetti, *Louis-Philippe* (Paris 1994), p. 652.

6. Comte de Montalivet, *Fragments et souvenirs* (2 vols, Paris 1899–1900), vol. 1, pp. 318–20.

7. F. Guizot, *Mémoires pour servir à l'histoire de mon temps* (8 vols, Paris 1858–67), vol. 2, pp. 180–8; Thureau-Dangin, *Histoire de la monarchie de juillet*, vol. 1, pp. 410–14.

8. Collingham, *The July Monarchy*, pp. 60–1.

9. Ibid., p. 62; I. Collins, *The Government and the Newspaper Press in France, 1814–1881* (Oxford 1959), p. 77. On the July monarchy and the press, see also C. Ledré, *La presse à l'assaut de la monarchie, 1815–1848* (Paris 1960), pp. 125–259; C. Charle, *Le siècle de la presse, 1830–1939* (Paris 2004), pp. 37–71; J. Popkin, *Press, Revolution and Social Identities in France 1830–1835* (University Park, Pennsylvania, 2002).

10. Ledré, *La presse*, pp. 139–42.

11. *Journal intime de Cuvillier-Fleury*, ed. E. Bertin (2 vols, Paris 1903), vol. 1, p. 303, entry for 13 Mar. 1831; Victor Hugo, *Journal 1830–1848*, ed. H. Guillemin (Paris 1954), p. 53, entry for 15 Dec. 1840.

12. AN 300 AP(III) 6. Archives de la Maison de France. Mme Adélaïde (1777–1847). Dossiers 37, 38, entry for 25 Feb. 1832.

13. On Lyon in the wake of the July revolution, see R. J. Bezucha, 'The revolution of 1830 and the city of Lyon', in J. M. Merriman ed., *1830 in France* (New York and London 1975), pp. 119–38. On the revolt of 1831, see F. Rudé, *Les révoltes des canuts, novembre 1831 à avril 1834* (Paris 1982), and G. J. Sheridan, 'The political economy of artisan industry: government and the people in the silk trade of Lyon, 1830–1870', *French Historical Studies*, vol. 11 (1979), pp. 215–38.

14. Collingham, *The July Monarchy*, p. 65. For the role of the radical press in the 1831 revolt, see J. Popkin, *Press, Revolution and Social Identities in France, 1830–1835* (University Park, Pennsylvania, 2002).

15. P. W. Schroeder, *The Transformation of European Politics, 1763–1848* (Oxford 1996 paperback edn), pp. 685–6.

16. Antonetti, *Louis-Philippe*, p. 688; P. Mansel, *Paris between Empires, 1814–1852* (London 2001), pp. 283–4.

17. R. Arnaud, *Adélaïde d'Orléans (1777–1847)* (Paris 1908), p. 304; Antonetti, *Louis-Philippe*, p. 689; Thureau-Dangin, *Histoire de la monarchie de juillet*, vol. 2, pp. 100–9.

18. Cited in Antonetti, *Louis-Philippe*, p. 689.

19. J. Harsin, *Barricades: The War of the Streets in Revolutionary Paris, 1830–1848* (New York and Basingstoke 2002), pp. 58–9.

20. Victor Hugo, *Les Misérables*, in *Oeuvres complètes* (48 vols, Paris 1880–9), *Roman*, vol. 8, p. 426.

21. There is an excellent modern biography of Hugo in English: G. Robb, *Victor Hugo* (London 1997).

22. Harsin, *Barricades*, p. 59.

23. *Mémoires de la comtesse de Boigne, née d'Osmond: récits d'une tante* (Mercure de France edn, 2 vols, Paris 1999), vol. 2, pp. 389–90.

24. Victor Hugo, *Les Misérables*, *Roman*, vol. 8, p. 494.

25. Antonetti, *Louis-Philippe*, pp. 393–4.

26. Harsin, *Barricades*, pp. 60–1.

27. Thureau-Dangin, *Histoire de la monarchie de juillet*, vol. 2, p. 149. For two important recent studies of the duchesse de Berry and the 1832 rising, see H. de Changy, *Le soulèvement de la duchesse de Berry, 1830–1832: les royalistes dans la tourmente* (Paris 1986), and Jo Burr Margadant, 'The duchesse de Berry and royalist political culture in post-revolutionary France', *History Workshop Journal*, issue 43 (spring 1997), pp. 23–52.

28. François-René, vicomte de Chateaubriand, *Mémoires d'outre-tombe* (Livre de poche edn, 3 vols, Paris 1973), vol. 3, pp. 314–49; Collingham, *The July Monarchy*, pp. 126–7.

29. Antonetti, *Louis-Philippe*, pp. 702–3; Arnaud, *Adélaïde d'Orléans*, pp. 329–30.

30. Collingham, *The July Monarchy*, pp. 128–9; Antonetti, *Louis-Philippe*, p. 704.

31. For legitimist–republican electoral alliances, see marquis de Noailles, *Le comte Molé (1781–1855): sa vie, ses mémoires* (6 vols, Paris 1922–30), vol. 5, p. 289; A. Jardin and A. J. Tudesq, *La France des notables, 1815–1848* (2 vols, Paris 1973), vol. 1, pp. 167–8.

32. Louis-Philippe to Adélaïde, 24 June 1831, AN 300 AP(IV) 10, pièce 77.

33. *Mémoires de M. de la Rochefoucauld, duc de Doudeauville* (10 vols, Paris 1861–3), vol. 10, p. 196.

34. Adélaïde to Marshal Gérard, 28 Nov. 1832, Archives Bryas, Château de Mauvières. Lettres de Mme Adélaïde d'Orléans au Maréchal Gérard.

35. *Mémoires de la comtesse de Boigne*, vol. 2, p. 327; Adélaïde even made Barrot, along with Dupin, her executor: Victor Hugo, *Journal 1830–1848*, ed. H. Guillemin (Paris 1954), p. 312.

36. Louis-Philippe, *Mémoires* (2 vols, Paris 1973–4), vol. 2, p. 223; comte de Montalivet, *Fragments et souvenirs* (2 vols, Paris 1899–1900), vol. 1, p. 16.

37. AN 300 AP(III) 6. Archives de la Maison de France. Mme Adélaïde (1777–1847). Dossiers 37, 38, entry for 26 Apr. 1833.

38. The duc de Broglie left memoirs: *Souvenirs (1775–1870) de feu le duc de Broglie* (4 vols, Paris 1886). His friend Guizot also wrote a biography of him: *Le duc de Broglie* (Paris 1872). For Humann, see F. Ponteil, *Un type de grand bourgeois sous la monarchie de juillet: Georges Humann, 1780–1842* (Paris 1977).

39. For a modern biography of Soult, see N. Gotteri, *Le maréchal Soult* (Paris 2000). Soult's correspondence with Louis-Philippe and his family has been published in Maréchal Soult, *Correspondance politique et familière avec Louis-Philippe et la famille royale*, ed. L. and A. de Saint-Pierre (Paris 1959).

40. Hugo, *Journal*, pp. 99–100, entry for July 1844.

41. Thureau-Dangin, *Histoire de la monarchie de juillet*, vol. 2, pp. 223–33, 336–41.

42. Schroeder, *The Transformation of European Politics*, pp. 689–90.

43. Collingham, *The July Monarchy*, pp. 192–3.

44. Archives Bryas. Lettres de Mme Adélaïde d'Orléans au maréchal Gérard.

45. *Le prince de Talleyrand et la maison d'Orléans*, ed. comtesse de Mirabeau (Paris 1890), pp. 201–67.

46. Schroeder, *The Transformation of European Politics*, pp. 716–18; Thureau-Dangin, *Histoire de la monarchie de juillet*, vol. 3, pp. 304–5.

47. Antonetti, *Louis-Philippe*, p. 717; Collingham, *The July Monarchy*, p. 151.

48. R. J. Bezucha, *The Lyon Uprising of 1834* (Cambridge 1974), pp. 149–74; P. Pilbeam, *Republicanism in Nineteenth-century France, 1814–1871* (Basingstoke and London 1995), pp. 121–3.

49. Harsin, *Barricades*, pp. 80–9; Pilbeam, *Republicanism*, p. 125.

50. *Hanin Burricades*, pp. 84, 90–101, and fig. 7.

51. Antonetti, *Louis-Philippe*, p. 723; Harsin, *Barricades*, p. 103.

52. Collingham, *The July Monarchy*, p. 164.

53. Thureau-Dangin, *Histoire de la monarchie de juillet*, vol. 2, pp. 252–6.

54. *Mémoires de M. Dupin* (4 vols, Paris 1855–61), vol. 3, pp. 106–19; Thureau-Dangin, *Histoire de la monarchie de juillet*, vol. 2, pp. 264–7.

55. Antonetti, *Louis-Philippe*, pp. 726–7; AN 300 AP(III) 33, dossier 5, pièces 75, 76; Adélaïde to Sébastiani, 20 May 1835, ibid., 959. Adélaïde d'Orléans, soeur de Louis-Philippe, pièce 205.

56. Antonetti, *Louis-Philippe*, pp. 728–9; Collingham, *The July Monarchy*, p. 153.

57. Thureau-Dangin, *Histoire de la monarchie de juillet*, vol. 2, pp. 277–80, esp. p. 277 n. 2.

58. Collingham, *The July Monarchy*, p. 154; Pouthas, 'Les ministères de Louis-Philippe', p. 115.

59. *Adresse d'un constitutionnel aux constitutionnels* (Paris, Feb. 1835).

60. Ibid., pp. 10–15, 43–5.

61. Ibid., p. 23.

62. Thureau-Dangin, *Histoire de la monarchie de juillet*, vol. 2, pp. 301–5; Collingham, *The July Monarchy*, pp. 154–5, 163.

63. Harsin, *Barricades*, p. 105.

64. AN 300 AP(III) 959. Adélaïde d'Orléans, soeur de Louis-Philippe, pièce 205.

65. Ibid., pièce 211; J. Lucas-Dubreton, *Louis-Philippe et la machine infernale, 1830–1835* (Paris 1951) pp. 274–5; *Vieux souvenirs de Mgr le prince de Joinville, 1818–1848*, ed. D. Meyer (Mercure de France edn, 1986), p. 71 n. 1.

66. Ibid., p. 71

67. Ibid., pp. 71–2; *Souvenirs du général comte de Rumigny, aide-de-camp du roi Louis-Philippe (1789–1860)*, ed. R.-M. Gouraud d'Ablancourt (Paris 1921), p. 267; Harsin, *Barricades*, p. 148; Lucas-Dubreton, *Louis-Philippe*, p. 280 n. 1.

68. Ibid., pp. 239–46, 282–3, 328 n. 1.

69. *Vieux souvenirs*, pp. 72–3.

70. Adélaïde to Sébastiani, 31 July 1835, AN 300 AP(III) 959. Adélaïde d'Orléans, soeur de Louis-Philippe, pièce 215.

71. Lucas-Dubreton, *Louis-Philippe*, pp. 237–9, 247–50, 258–62; Harsin, *Barricades*, pp. 155–6.

72. B. Appert, *Dix ans à la cour du roi Louis-Philippe et souvenirs du temps de l'empire et de la restauration* (3 vols, Berlin and Paris 1846), vol. 3, p. 313.

73. Collingham, *The July Monarchy*, pp. 165–6.

74. Collins, *The Government and the Newspaper Press*, pp. 82–3; Ledré, *La presse*, pp. 167–76.

75. Lucas-Dubreton, *Louis-Philippe*, pp. 329, 347–9. For the painting of Fieschi's head, see fig.31.

76. Thureau-Dangin, *Histoire de la monarchie de juillet*, vol. 2, pp. 420–5.

77. T. Silvestre, *La conspiration des quarante* (Paris 1864), p. 21.

78. Antonetti, *Louis-Philippe*, p. 751; J. P. T. Bury and R. P. Tombs, *Thiers 1787–1877: A Political Life* (London 1986), p. 248; Collingham, *The July Monarchy*, p. 203.

79. Bury and Tombs, *Thiers*, p. 56; Thureau-Dangin, *Histoire de la monarchie de juillet*, vol. 3, pp. 28–30.

80. Antonetti, *Louis-Philippe*, pp. 755–8.

81. R. Bullen, *Palmerston, Guizot and the Collapse of the Entente Cordiale* (London 1974), pp. 10–15.

82. Ibid., pp. 11, 194–6, 201–3; Schroeder, *The Transformation of European Politics*, pp. 724, 751–2, 755–6.

83. Adélaïde to Sébastiani, 20 May 1835, AN 300 AP(III) 959. Adélaïde d'Orléans, soeur de Louis-Philippe, pièce 205.

84. Adélaïde to Sébastiani, 23 Mar. 1836, ibid., pièce 243.

85. D. Porch, *The French Foreign Legion* (London 1991), pp. 1–2, 23–5, 41.

86. Thureau-Dangin, *Histoire de la monarchie de juillet*, vol. 3, pp. 99–109; Collingham, *The July Monarchy*, p. 207; Antonetti, *Louis-Philippe*, pp. 763–5.

87. Porch, *The French Foreign Legion*, pp. 41, 49–50.

88. Montalivet, *Fragments et souvenirs* vol. 2, p. 47.

89. Ibid., pp. 48–50.

90. Adélaïde to Sébastiani, 26 June 1836, AN 300 AP(III) 959. Adélaïde d'Orléans, soeur de Louis-Philippe, pièce 262.

91. On Alibaud, see Harsin, *Barricades*, pp. 168–72; Adélaïde to Sébastiani, 28 Oct. 1836, AN 300 AP(III) 959. Adélaïde d'Orléans, soeur de Louis-Philippe, pièce 278.

Nine VICTORY AND DEFEAT

1. Molé to Louis-Philippe, 24 July 1837, Archives du comte Molé, Château de Champlâtreux, registre G, fo. 77bis; Louis-Philippe to Molé, 6 Nov. 1836, AN 300 AP(III) 34. Dossier 1, roi Louis-Philippe au comte Molé, pièce 154; Louis-Philippe to Molé, 24 Oct. 1830, ibid., pièce 59; Louis-Philippe to Molé, 18 Jan. 1839, ibid., pièce 38. Lettres du roi Louis-Philippe au comte Molé, année 1839, dossier 1, janvier 1839, pièce 33.

2. For Molé's biography see his memoirs: marquis de Noailles, *Le Comte*

Molé (1781–1855): sa vie, ses mémoires (6 vols, Paris 1922–30), and J.-A. de Sédouy, *Le Comte Molé ou la séduction du pouvoir* (Paris 1994).

3. For Guizot's biography, see his own *Mémoires pour servir à l'histoire de mon temps* (8 vols, Paris 1858–67); D. Johnson, *Guizot: Aspects of French History, 1787–1874* (London 1963); G. de Broglie, *Guizot* (Paris 2002 edn). For a recent study of Guizot's ideas, see P. Rosanvallon, *Le moment Guizot* (Paris 1985).

4. For Molé's deeply hostile attitude to the *doctrinaires*, see his 'Notice manuscrite' on Guizot in Noailles, *Le Comte Molé*, vol. 6, pp. 242–62.

5. Broglie, *Guizot*, p. 16; Comte Molé, *Souvenirs de jeunesse*, ed. marquise de Noailles (Mercure de France edn, Paris 1991), p. 44–5.

6. Rosanvallon, *Le moment Guizot*, p. 20.

7. Molé's speech at the opening session of the Chambers, 2 Mar. 1837, cited in Noailles, *Le Comte Molé*, vol. 5, p. 264; for 'flexible resistance' see above, p. 206; Molé's speech in the Chamber of Peers, 6 Apr. 1838, Noailles, *Le Comte Molé*, vol. 5, p. 314.

8. P. Thureau-Dangin, *Histoire de la monarchie de juillet* (7 vols, Paris 1884–92), vol. 4, p. 392 n. 1.

9. On the princesse de Lieven see J. Charmley, *The Princess and the Politicians: Sex, Intrigue and Diplomacy 1812–1840* (London 2005); on Molé and Mme de Castellane see Sédouy, *Le Comte Molé*, pp. 128–32, 154–8, 179–82; on their use of Adélaïde as an intermediary with Louis-Philippe, see comte de Montalivet, *Fragments et souvenirs* (2 vols, Paris 1899–1900), vol. 1, pp. 17–18.

10. Thureau-Dangin, *Histoire de la monarchie de juillet*, vol. 3, p. 122.

11. There is an immense literature on Louis-Napoleon, but see A. Dansette, *Le second empire* (3 vols, Paris 1972–6), esp. vol. 1, *Louis-Napoléon à la conquête du pouvoir*; L. Girard, *Napoléon III* (Paris 1986); J. F. McMillan, *Napoleon III* (London 1991); W. H. C. Smith, *Napoleon III* (London 1972).

12. Thureau-Dangin, *Histoire de la monarchie de juillet*, vol. 3, p. 128.

13. McMillan, *Napoleon III*, p. 12; D. Porch, *Army and Revolution: France 1815–1848* (London 1974), pp. 129–30.

14. Thureau-Dangin, *Histoire de la monarchie de juillet*, vol. 3, p. 133.

15. Adélaïde to Adèle de Ste Aldegonde, 21 Nov. 1836, AN 300 AP(III) 31. Louis-Philippe: papiers Ste Aldegonde, 1815–65, pièce 307.

16. G. Antonetti, *Louis-Philippe* (Paris 1994), pp. 772–4; Adélaïde to Sébastiani, 19 Nov. 1836, AN 300 AP(III) 959, Adélaïde d'Orléans, soeur de Louis-Philippe, pièce 280.

17. J. Harsin, *Barricades: The War of the Streets in Revolutionary Paris, 1830–1848* (New York and Basingstoke 2002), pp. 173–81.

18. Antonetti, *Louis-Philippe*, pp. 772–8.

19. Thureau-Dangin, *Histoire de la monarchie de juillet*, vol. 3, pp. 154, 159–61.

20. Antonetti, *Louis-Philippe*, p. 780.

21. A. Martin-Fugier, *La vie quotidienne de Louis-Philippe et de sa famille, 1830–1848* (Paris 1992), pp. 185–95.

22. Duc d'Orléans to Adélaïde, 7 July 1828, AN 300 AP(IV) 18, Mme Adélaïde. Lettres reçues de Marie-Amélie et de ses enfants, 1815–1829, dossier 19, pp. 246–7.

23. Duc d'Orléans to maréchal Gérard, Oct. 1832, Archives Bryas, Château de Mauvières. Lettres de Ferdinand-Philippe, duc d'Orléans; duc d'Orléans to prince de Joinville, 26 July 1839, AN 300 AP(III) 111. Lettres reçues du roi et de la famille royale. Dossier: duc 'Orléans au prince de Joinville, 1835–41, pièce 509; Louis-Philippe to duc d'Orléans, 31 Aug. 1837, AN 300 AP(III) 172, pièce 18.

24. Duc d'Orléans to prince de Joinville, 14 Oct. 1841, AN 300 AP(III). Lettres reçues du roi et de la famille royale. Dossier: duc d'Orléans au prince de Joinville, 1835–41, pièce 510.

25. Martin-Fugier, *La vie quotidienne*, pp. 241–2.

26. Ibid., pp. 268–71; Antonetti, *Louis-Philippe*, pp. 781–6.

27. Thureau-Dangin, *Histoire de la monarchie de juillet*, vol. 3, pp. 195–6.

28. Ibid., pp. 207–8.

29. Duc d'Orléons to Comte Molé, 26th Sept. 1840, Archives du Comte Mdé, Regostre A, fo. 69.

30. Thureau-Dangin, *Histoire de la monarchie de juillet*, vol. 3, p. 197.

31. AN 300 AP(IV) 10. Lettres de mon frère, pièce 162.

32. H. A. C. Collingham with R. S. Alexander, *The July Monarchy: A Political History of France 1830–1848* (London 1988), p. 211.

33. Martin-Fugier, *La vie quotidienne*, pp. 130–4.

34. *Mémoires de M. Dupin* (4 vols, Paris 1855–61), vol. 3, p. 158.

35. Thureau-Dangin, *Histoire de la monarchie de juillet*, vol. 3, pp. 203–4; Guizot, *Mémoires*, vol. 4, p. 240.

36. AN 300 AP(III) 959. Adélaïde d'Orléans, soeur de Louis-Philippe, pièce 293; duchesse de Dino to baron de Barante, 13 June 1837, cited in Thureau-Dangin, *Histoire de la monarchie de juillet*, vol. 3, p. 206.

37. Ibid., p. 278.

38. Collingham, *The July Monarchy*, pp. 246–9.

39. Thureau-Dangin, *Histoire de la monarchie de juillet*, vol. 3, pp. 509–16; Sébastiani to Adélaïde, 16 Dec. 1836, AN 300 AP(III) 7. Archives de la Maison de France. Adélaïde d'Orléans (1777–1847). Dossier: Lettres d'Horace Sébastiani, 1836–41 et sans dates, pièce 133.

40. Thureau-Dangin, *Histoire de la monarchie de juillet*, vol. 3, pp. 524–35.

41. Ibid., pp. 306–8.

42. P. W. Schroeder, *The Transformation of European Politics, 1753–1848* (Oxford 1996 paperback edn), pp. 716–17; Antonetti, *Louis-Philippe*, p. 794.

43. E. de Waresquiel, *Talleyrand: le prince immobile* (Paris 2003), pp. 610–13.

44. Ibid., p. 612; *Mémoires de la comtesse de Boigne, née d'Osmond: récits d'une tante* (Mercure de France edn, 2 vols, Paris 1999), vol. 2, p. 529.

45. Thureau-Dangin, *Histoire de la monarchie de juillet*, vol. 3, pp. 210–17, 327.

46. Collingham, *The July Monarchy*, p. 213; Sédouy, *Le Comte Molé*, p. 202.

47. Thureau-Dangin, *Histoire de la monarchie de juillet*, vol. 3, pp. 218–24, 228–9.

48. O. Barrot, *Mémoires posthumes* (4 vols, Paris 1875–6), vol. 1, p. 321.

49. See, for example, Adélaïde to Sébastiani, 8 Mar. 1839, commenting on the unfavourable result for the Crown of the March 1839 elections: '. . . dans la loyauté et les principes constitutionnels de notre bien-aimé roi, il subira et se conformera à ce qui est le voeu du pays', AN 300 AP(III) 959, Adélaïde d'Orléans, soeur de Louis-Philippe, pièce 372.

50. Cited in Thureau-Dangin, *Histoire de la monarchie de juillet*, vol. 3, p. 264.

51. Ibid., p. 350.

52. Molé to Barante, 24 Feb. 1839, cited in ibid., p. 346 n. 1.

53. AN 300 AP(III) 37. Dossier 7, Lettres de Louis-Philippe à M. le Comte Molé, année 1838. Décembre. Pièce 212.

54. Sédouy, *Le Comte Molé*, pp. 206–8.

55. Noailles, *Le Comte Molé*, vol. 6, p. 244.

56. Thureau-Dangin, *Histoire de la monarchie de juillet*, vol. 3, pp. 332–8.

57. Sédouy, *Le Comte Molé*, pp. 208–9.

58. Louis-Philippe to Molé, 12, 15 and 19 Jan. 1839, Archives du Comte Molé, registre A, fos 28, 29, 31.

59. Louis-Philippe to Molé, 28 and 29 Jan. 1839, AN 300 AP(III) 38. Lettres de Louis-Philippe à M. le Comte Molé, année 1839. Dossier 1. Janvier. Pièces 44, 45.

60. Collingham, *The July Monarchy*, pp. 215–17; Thureau-Dangin, *Histoire de la monarchie de juillet*, vol. 3, pp. 346–56.

61. See, for example, Sébastiani to Molé, 20 Sept. 1837: 'N'oubliez pas que vous avez à l'ambassade de Londres un ami sur lequel vous pouvez compter et un ami reconnaissant.' Archives du Comte Molé, registre F, fo. 134.

62. Adélaïde to Sébastiani, 15 Feb. and 2 Mar. 1838, AN 300 AP(III) 959. Adélaïde d'Orléans, soeur de Louis-Philippe, pièces 321, 323.

63. Ibid., pièce 364.

64. Louis-Philippe to Adélaïde, 25 Sept. 1838, AN 300 AP(IV) 10, Lettres

de mon frère, pièce 168; Louis-Philippe to Molé, 14 Mar. 1839, ibid., (III) 38. Lettres du roi Louis-Philippe au Comte Molé. Année 1839. Dossier 3, mars, pièce 94.

65. *La Mode*, 34–35, 9ème année, janvier–juin 1838, 9ème livraison, pp. 237–8.

66. R. Arnaud, *Adélaïde d'Orléans (1777–1847)* (Paris 1908), p. 298 n. 2; *Mémoires de la comtesse de Boigne*, vol. 1, p. 647; M. Laurent-Atthalin, *Vie du général baron Atthalin, 1784–1856* (Colmar 1978), p. 128.

67. *La Mode*, 34–35, 9ème année, janvier–juin 1838, 9ème livraison, pp. 213–16; ibid., 10ème livraison, pp. 241–3; C. Ledré, *La presse à l'assaut de la monarchie, 1815–1848* (Paris 1960), p. 170.

68. See, for example, *Le Charivari*, 31 Jan. 1839, 8ème année, no. 31; *La Mode*, 29 Feb. 1840, 38–39, 11ème année, janvier–juin 1840, p. 261.

69. Arnaud, *Adélaïde d'Orléans*, pp. 295–6.

70. BN, Cabinet des Estampes.

71. *Vieux souvenirs de Mgr le prince de Joinville, 1818–1848*, ed. D. Meyer (Mercure de France edn, 1986), pp. 172–3; AN 300 AP(IV) 18. Dossier 21, Testament et codicilles de SAR Mme la Princesse Adélaïde, Eu, 28 Aug. and 15 Sept. 1842.

72. BN, Cabinet des Estampes.

73. See L. Hunt, 'Introduction', in L. Hunt ed., *Eroticism and the Body Politic* (Baltimore, Md., 1991), p. 5. For an overview of the main themes in gender history, see J. Scott, 'Gender: a useful category of historical analysis', *American Historical Review*, vol. 91, no. 5 (1986), pp. 1053–75. For women and the public and private spheres in the French revolutionary era, see J. Landes, *Women and the Public Sphere in the Age of the French Revolution* (Ithaca, NY, 1988).

74. C. Campbell Orr ed., *Queenship in Britain, 1660–1837: Royal Patronage, Court Culture and Dynastic Politics* (Manchester and New York 2002), pp. 34–6, and *Queenship in Europe, 1660–1815: The Role of the Consort* (Cambridge 2004).

75. *La Mode*, 34–35, 9ème année, janvier–juin 1838, 9ème livraison, pp. 237–8. For two important gender-based analyses of Louis-Philippe's reign and of representations of his family, see J. Burr Margadant, 'Gender, vice and the political imaginary: reinterpreting the failure of the July monarchy, 1830–1848', *American Historical Review*, vol. 104, no. 5 (Dec. 1999), pp. 1461–96, and 'Representing Queen Marie-Amélie in a "bourgeois" monarchy', *Historical Reflections* (summer 2006), vol. 32, no. 2, pp. 421–51.

76. L. Hunt, 'The many bodies of Marie Antoinette: political pornography and the problem of the feminine in the French Revolution', in Hunt ed., *Eroticism and the Body Politic*, pp. 108–30, and L. Hunt, *The Family*

Romance of the French Revolution (Berkeley, Ca. 1992), pp. 97–114; S. Maza, *Private Lives and Public Affairs: The Causes Célèbres of Prerevolutionary France* (Berkeley, Los Angeles, and London 1993), pp. 207–10.

77. V. Gruder, 'The question of Marie Antoinette: the queen and public opinion before the Revolution', *French History*, vol. 16, no. 3 (Sept. 2002), p. 298.

78. Thureau-Dangin, *Histoire de la monarchie de juillet*, vol. 3, p. 359.

79. *Mémoires de M. Dupin* (4 vols, Paris 1855–61), vol. 4, p. 15.

80. Harsin, *Barricades*, pp. 124–38.

81. Collingham, *The July Monarchy*, p. 218.

82. Broglie, *Guizot*, pp. 229–30.

83. Adélaïde to Sébastiani, 29 Jan. 1840, AN 300 AP(III) 959. Adélaide d'Orléans, soeur de Louis-Philippe, pièce 407.

84. Ibid.

85. Thureau-Dangin, *Histoire de la monarchie de juillet*, vol. 4, pp. 95–111; Antonetti, *Louis-Philippe*, pp. 808–11.

Ten RECOURSE TO GUIZOT

1. J. P. T. Bury and R. P. Tombs, *Thiers 1787–1877: A Political Life* (London 1986), pp. 63–6; H. A. C. Collingham with R. S. Alexander, *The July Monarchy: A Political History of France, 1830–1848* (London 1988), pp. 224–6.

2. P. Thureau-Dangin, *Histoire de la monarchie de juillet* (7 vols, Paris 1884–92), vol. 4, p. 160.

3. G. Antonetti, *Louis-Philippe* (Paris 1994), p. 816.

4. J. F. McMillan, *Napoleon III* (London 1991), pp. 13–14; Thureau-Dangin, *Histoire de la monarchie de juillet*, vol. 4, pp. 265–9; A. Dansette, *Histoire du second empire* (3 vols, Paris 1961–76), vol. 1, *Louis-Napoléon à la conquête du pouvoir*, pp. 160–1.

5. McMillan, *Napoleon III*, pp. 14–15; E. Saunders, *The Mystery of Marie Lafarge* (London 1951), pp. 233–52.

6. P. Mansel, *Paris between Empires, 1814–1852* (London 2001), pp. 369–72; Thureau-Dangin, *Histoire de la monarchie de juillet*, vol. 4, pp. 406–12.

7. On the origins of this French foreign-policy tradition, see F. Charles-Roux, *Le projet français de conquête de l'Egypte sous Louis XVI* (Cairo 1929), and J. Hardman and M. Price eds., *Louis XVI and the comte de Vergennes: correspondance, 1774–1787* (Oxford 1998), pp. 135–44.

8. P. W. Schroeder, *The Transformation of European Politics, 1763–1848* (Oxford 1996 paperback edn), pp. 726–7.

9. Collingham, *The July Monarchy*, pp. 221–2.

10. Thureau-Dangin, *Histoire de la monarchie de juillet*, vol. 4, pp. 5–10; Bury and Tombs, *Thiers*, pp. 67–8; Collingham, *The July Monarchy*, pp. 223–4.

11. See, for example, Adélaïde writing from Eu to Sébastiani, 15 Aug. 1840: 'M Guizot est parti hier matin, vous jugez que sa présence ne me manque pas.' Archives Nationales, Paris, 300 AP(III) 959. Adélaïde d'Orléans, soeur de Louis-Philippe, pièce 419; G. de Broglie, *Guizot* (Paris 2002 edn), pp. 252–3.

12. Schroeder, *The Transformation of European Politics*, pp. 743–4; Collingham, *The July Monarchy*, pp. 228–9.

13. Thureau-Dangin, *Histoire de la monarchie de juillet*, vol. 4, pp. 242–3.

14. Ibid., pp. 243–6.

15. Ibid., p. 243 n. 2.

16. Ibid., pp. 300–7, 311–26; Antonetti, *Louis-Philippe*, p. 823. For Franco-German relations during the July monarchy as a whole, see R. Poidevin and K. G. Faber, *Les relations franco-allemandes, 1830–1848* (Metz 1977).

17. Collingham, *The July Monarchy*, pp. 233–4.

18. Ibid., p. 234.

19. J. Harsin, *Barricades: The War of the Streets in Revolutionary Paris, 1830–1848* (New York and Basingstoke 2002), pp. 189–98.

20. Thureau-Dangin, *Histoire de la monarchie de juillet*, vol. 4, p. 347.

21. F. Guizot, *Mémoires pour servir à l'histoire de mon temps* (8 vols, Paris 1858–67), vol. 3, p. 2, vol. 8, pp. 97–9.

22. Ibid., vol. 8, p. 84.

23. Comte de Montalivet, *Fragments et souvenirs* (2 vols, Paris 1899–1900), vol. 2, pp. 73–4.

24. Louis-Philippe to Guizot, 30 Jan. 1841, AN 42 AP 286. Dossier 2, janvier–juin 1841, pièce 131; Guizot, *Mémoires*, vol. 8, pp. 75–7.

25. Louis-Philippe to Guizot, 21 Nov. 1841, AN 42 AP 286. Dossier 3, juillet–décembre 1841, pièce 307.

26. BN, nouvelles acquisitions françaises 20616. Papiers A. Thiers, vol. 16, correspondance 1841–5, fo. 282.

27. D. H. Pinkney, *Decisive Years in France, 1840–1847* (Princeton, NJ, 1986), pp. 30–1, 148–54.

28. Ibid., pp. 36–40; Collingham, *The July Monarchy*, p. 355.

29. Broglie, *Guizot*, pp. 333–6.

30. Antonetti, *Louis-Philippe*, pp. 846–7.

31. Louis-Philippe to Adélaïde, 25 Mar. 1835, AN 300 AP(IV) 10, fo. 136.

32. P. Rosanvallon, *Le moment Guizot* (Paris 1985), pp. 277–9, 279 n. 2. Johnson, *Guizot*, pp. 69–70, urges caution about the Guizot–Peel comparison.

33. Thureau-Dangin, *Histoire de la monarchie de juillet*, vol. 5, pp. 75–8.

34. Ibid., pp. 79–80; *Mémoires de la comtesse de Boigne, née d'Osmond: récits d'une tante* (Mercure de France edn, 2 vols, Paris 1999), vol. 2, pp. 567–9.

35. Thureau-Dangin, *Histoire de la monarchie de juillet*, vol. 5, pp. 80–1; Victor Hugo, *Journal, 1830–1848*, ed. H. Guillemin (Paris 1954), pp. 76–9; *Mémoires de la comtesse de Boigne*, vol. 2, pp. 571–2.

36. Thureau-Dangin, *Histoire de la monarchie de juillet*, vol. 5, p. 81; *Mémoires de la comtesse de Boigne*, vol. 2, pp. 571–2.

37. Ibid., pp. 594–5.

38. Ibid., pp. 572–3, 585–6, 591–2.

39. Mansel, *Paris between Empires*, pp. 379–80.

40. Thureau-Dangin, *Histoire de la monarchie de juillet*, vol. 5, pp. 91–9. For Louis-Philippe on Nemours, see Daniel Stern (comtesse Marie d'Agoult), *Histoire de la révolution de 1848* (2 vols, Paris 1862), vol. 1, p. 98 n. 3. For Victor Hugo on Nemours, see Hugo, *Journal*, p. 218, entry for 24 Feb. 1847: 'M de Nemours is embarrassed and embarrassing. When he approaches you, with his blond whiskers, his blue eyes, his red sash [of the *Légion d'Honneur*], his white waistcoat and his sad air, he throws you into consternation. He never looks you in the eye. He is always searching for the right word and never knows what he is saying.'

41. Antonetti, *Louis-Philippe*, pp. 839–40.

42. Guizot, *Mémoires*, vols 6–8.

43. See Louis-Philippe's speech from the throne of 26 Dec. 1844, referring to friendship between France and England as 'that happy accord which guarantees the peace of the world'. Cited in Antonetti, *Louis-Philippe*, p. 854. Guizot's history of the English revolution appeared at intervals between 1826 and 1856: *Histoire de la révolution d'Angleterre depuis l'avènement de Charles I jusqu'à la restauration de Charles II* (2 vols, Paris 1826–7); *Histoire de la république d'Angleterre et de Cromwell (1649–1658)* (2 vols, Paris 1854); *Histoire du protectorat de Richard Cromwell et du rétablissement des Stuarts (1658–1660)* (2 vols, Paris 1856).

44. Thureau-Dangin, *Histoire de la monarchie de juillet*, vol. 5, pp. 191–2.

45. Ibid., p. 192.

46. The best biography of Aberdeen is M. E. Chamberlain, *Lord Aberdeen: A Political Biography* (London 1983). For Aberdeen at Leipzig, see ibid., pp. 134–5, and L. Iremonger, *Lord Aberdeen: A Biography of the Fourth Earl of Aberdeen* (London 1978), pp. 63–5. Aberdeen also corresponded with the princesse de Lieven: see *Correspondence of Lord Aberdeen and Princess Lieven, 1832–1854*, ed. E. J. Parry (2 vols, London 1938–9).

47. J. Duhamel, *Louis-Philippe et la première entente cordiale* (Paris 1951), pp. 64–5.

48. Thureau-Dangin, *Histoire de la monarchie de juillet*, vol. 5, pp. 194–5; Duhamel, *Louis-Philippe*, pp. 94, 97.

49. Ibid., p. 101.

50. Thureau-Dangin, *Histoire de la monarchie de juillet*, vol. 5, pp. 206–10; Antonetti, *Louis-Philippe*, p. 860.

51. Duhamel, *Louis-Philippe*, pp. 144–67.

52. Hugo, *Journal*, p. 112.

53. Duhamel, *Louis-Philippe*, pp. 191–222.

54. Thureau-Dangin, *Histoire de la monarchie de juillet*, vol. 5, pp. 444–53; Collingham, *The July Monarchy*, pp. 296–7.

55. For a full account of the Pritchard affair, see Thureau-Dangin, *Histoire de la monarchie de juillet*, vol. 5, pp. 364–74, 389–96, 407–10.

56. Schroeder, *The Transformation of European Politics*, pp. 768–71.

57. Thureau-Dangin, *Histoire de la monarchie de juillet*, vol. 5, pp. 197–200.

58. Antonetti, *Louis-Philippe*, p. 866; R. Bullen, *Palmerston, Guizot and the Collapse of the Entente Cordiale* (London 1974), p. 86.

59. Ibid., Schroeder, *The Transformation of European Politics*, pp. 770–1.

60. For Palmerston's policy towards France during his ministries of the 1830s and 1840s, see Bullen, *Palmerston*. For biographies of Palmerston see K. Bourne, *Palmerston: The Early Years, 1784–1841* (London 1982); J. Ridley, *Palmerston* (London 1970); and most recently J. Chambers, *Palmerston: the People's Darling* (London 2004).

61. Collingham, *The July Monarchy*, pp. 323–4.

62. Bullen, *Palmerston*, pp. 144–5; Collingham, *The July Monarchy*, pp. 324–5.

63. Thureau-Dangin, *Histoire de la monarchie de juillet*, vol. 6, pp. 23–30.

64. Collingham, *The July Monarchy*, p. 388.

65. Ibid., pp. 71–2.

66. Ibid., p. 80; Antonetti, *Louis-Philippe*, pp. 645–6.

67. F. O'Gorman, *Voters, Patrons and Parties: The Unreformed Electorate of Hanoverian England, 1734–1832* (Oxford 1989), p. 179, table 4.3.

68. M. Brock, *The Great Reform Act* (London 1973); J. Cannon, *Parliamentary Reform, 1640–1832* (Cambridge 1973), pp. 165–241.

69. Thureau-Dangin, *Histoire de la monarchie de juillet*, vol. 4, pp. 146–53, 184; ibid., vol. 5, pp. 50–8; Collingham, *The July Monarchy*, pp. 388–9; J. P. T. Bury and R. P. Tombs, *Thiers 1797–1877: A Political Life* (London 1986), pp. 88–90.

70. Brock, *The Great Reform Act*, pp. 109–10; R. Quinault, 'The French revolution of 1830 and parliamentary reform', *History*, vol. 257 (Oct. 1994), pp. 377–93.

71. See M. I. Thomis and P. Holt, *Threats of Revolution in Britain, 1789–1848* (London and Basingstoke 1977), pp. 89–91, 97–8; Brock, *The Great*

Reform Act, pp. 307–9; G. Rudé, *The Crowd in History 1730–1848: A Study of Popular Disturbances in France and England* (New York 1964), p. 267.

72. Johnson, *Guizot*, pp. 403–4; Rosanvallon, *Le moment Guizot*, pp. 308, 309 n. 3, 310, 326 n. 3, 327.
73. Guizot, *Mémoires*, vol. 8, pp. 544–5.
74. Montalivet, *Fragments et souvenirs*, vol. 2, p. 96.
75. Thureau-Dangin, *Histoire de la monarchie de juillet*, vol. 7, pp. 2–12.
76. A. Martin-Fugier, *La vie quotidienne de Louis-Philippe et de sa famille, 1830–1848* (Paris 1992), pp. 295–301; Antonetti, *Louis-Philippe*, p. 904.
77. Montalivet, *Fragments et souvenirs*, vol. 2, pp. 85–6; General J.-T. de Mesmay, *Horace Sébastiani: soldat, diplomate, homme d'état, maréchal de France (1772–1851)* (Paris 1948), pp. 220–1.
78. *Fragments et souvenirs*, vol. 2 pp. 86–7.
79. *Mémoires de la comtesse de Boigne*, vol. 2, p. 618.
80. Adélaïde to Nemours, 22 Aug. 1846, AN 300 AP(IV) 199. Dossier: Lettres de Mme Adélaïde, 1814–47; Montalivet, *Fragments et souvenirs*, vol. 2, p. 87.

Eleven THE LAST FRENCH KING

1. H. A. C. Collingham with R. S. Alexander, *The July Monarchy: A Political History, 1830–1848* (London 1988), p. 361; A. Jardin and A. J. Tudesq, *La France des notables*, vol. 1, *L'évolution générale, 1815–1848* (Paris 1973), pp. 234–7; Louis-Philippe to Guizot, 19 Jan. 1847, Archives Nationales, Paris, 42 AP, Fonds Guizot, 286. Dossier 14, janvier–juin 1847, pièce 1668. The most thorough work on contemporary methods of dealing with popular discontent, especially in the countryside, is R. Price, 'Techniques of repression: the control of popular protest in mid-nineteenth-century France', *Historical Journal*, vol. 25, no. 4 (1982), pp. 859–87.
2. Jardin and Tudesq, *La France des notables*, vol. 1, p. 237.
3. G. Antonetti, *Louis-Philippe* (Paris 1994), p. 883.
4. E. Labrousse, 'Panoramas de la crise', in E. Labrousse ed., *Aspects de la crise et de la dépression de l'économie française au milieu du 19ème siècle* (La Roche-sur-Yon 1956), pp.III–XXIV.
5. Louis-Philippe to Guizot, 19 Jan. 1847, AN 42 AP 286, dossier 14, janvier–juin 1847, pièce 1668.
6. Jardin and Tudesq, *La France des notables*, vol. 1, p. 240.
7. T. J. Markovitch, 'La crise de 1847–1848 dans les industries parisiennes', *Revue d'Histoire Economique et Sociale*, vol. 43 (1965), p. 257.

8. R. Magraw, *A History of the French Working Class* (2 vols, Oxford 1992), vol. 1, p. 121.

9. N. Gotteri, *Le maréchal Soult* (Paris 2000), pp. 722–3; G. de Broglie, *Guizot* (Paris 2002 edn), pp. 350–1; P. Thureau-Dangin, *Histoire de la monarchie de juillet* (7 vols, Paris 1884–92), vol. 7, pp. 78–87, 100–14.

10. Collingham, *The July Monarchy*, p. 397; Thureau-Dangin, *Histoire de la monarchie de juillet*, vol. 7, pp. 83–7, 100–14; Antonetti, *Louis-Philippe*, p. 900. Collingham puts the number of banquets held during 1847 much higher than Thureau-Dangin and Antonetti, at 180. Collingham, *The July Monarchy*, p. 398.

11. AN 300 AP(IV) 199. Dossier: Lettres de Mme Adélaïde, 1814–47.

12. Adélaïde to prince de Joinville, 28 Oct. 1847, AN 300 AP(III). Prince de Joinville (1818–1900). Lettres reçues du roi et de la famille royale, Lettres de Mme Adélaïde au prince de Joinville, pièce 317.

13. Collingham, *The July Monarchy*, p. 393.

14. Victor Hugo, *Journal, 1830–1848*, ed. H. Guillemin (Paris 1954), p. 245, entry for 20 June 1847. For Hugo's minutely observed description of the Teste–Cubières trial, in which he participated as a peer of France, see ibid., pp. 239–40, 246–7, 253–78.

15. S. Loomis, *A Crime of Passion* (London 1968), pp. 215–24; Hugo, *Journal*, p. 290, entry for 27 Aug. 1847. Loomis' book, based on careful study of the documents relating to the Praslin case in the Archives Nationales, is the best account.

16. Cited in Loomis, *A Crime of Passion*, p. 220.

17. Ibid., pp. 124–6, 161–9, 216–17, 238–49.

18. AN 42 AP 286. Dossier 15: juillet–décembre 1847, pièce 1839; Louis-Philippe to Guizot, 20 Aug. 1847, ibid., pièce 1841.

19. L. G. Michaud, *Biographie universelle* (45 vols, Paris and Leipzig 1843–65), vol. 38, p. 612.

20. Loomis, *A Crime of Passion*, p. 242; Collingham, *The July Monarchy*, p. 394; Thureau-Dangin, *Histoire de la monarchie de juillet*, vol. 7, p. 95.

21. J. Harsin, *Barricades: The War of the Streets in Revolutionary Paris, 1830–1848* (New York and Basingstoke 2002), pp. 32–3.

22. *Mémoires de la comtesse de Boigne, née d'Osmond: récits d'une tante* (Mercure de France edn, 2 vols, Paris 1999), vol. 2, p. 622.

23. AN 300 AP(IV) 199. Dossier: Lettres de Mme Adélaïde, 1814–47.

24. Ibid. (III) 7. Archives de la Maison de France. Adélaïde d'Orléans (1777–1847). Dossier: Mort de Mme Adélaïde, 1847, pièce 150, pp. 1–2.

25. Ibid., pp. 2–3.

26. Ibid., p. 4.

27. Ibid., pp. 4–5.

28. Ibid., p. 5; *Mémoires de M. Dupin* (4 vols, Paris 1855–61), vol. 1, pp. 383–4.

29. AN 300 AP (IV) 18. Dossier 21: Testament et codicilles de Mme la Princesse Adélaïde, Eu, 28 Aug. 1842.

30. AN 300 AP(I) 949. Liquidation de la succession de feue SAR Mme la Princesse Adélaïde. Pièce 19, Etat de liquidation et partage de succession de SAR Mme la Princesse Adélaïde d'Orléans, fos 3–49; A. Martin-Fugier, *La vie quotidienne de Louis-Philippe et de sa famille, 1830–1848* (Paris 1992), pp. 283–4.

31. Hugo, *Journal*, p. 312.

32. R. Arnaud, *Adélaïde d'Orléans (1777–1847)* (Paris 1908), pp. 350–2.

33. *Mémoires de la comtesse de Boigne*, vol. 2, p. 607.

34. *Mémoires de M. Dupin*, vol. 4, p. 394.

35. Hugo, *Journal*, p. 312.

36. Thureau-Dangin, *Histoire de la monarchie de juillet*, vol. 7, pp. 342–3.

37. F. Guizot, *Mémoires pour servir à l'histoire de mon temps* (8 vols, Paris 1858–67), vol. 8, p. 545.

38. Cited in Thureau-Dangin, *Histoire de la monarchie de juillet*, vol. 7, p. 366. For Tocqueville's life and career see A. Jardin, *Alexis de Tocqueville, 1805–1859* (Paris 1984), and H. Brogan's important new study, *Alexis de Tocqueville: Prophet of Democracy in the Age of Revolution* (London 2006).

39. Thureau-Dangin, *Histoire de la monarchie de juillet*, vol. 7, p. 367.

40. Ibid., pp. 387–90.

41. N. Gash, *Sir Robert Peel: The Life of Sir Robert Peel after 1830* (London 1972), pp. 480–1, 564, and *Aristocracy and People: Britain 1815–1865* (London 1979), p. 238.

42. Thureau-Dangin, *Histoire de la monarchie de juillet*, vol. 7, pp. 380–2.

43. F. O'Gorman, *The Long Eighteenth Century: British Political and Social History, 1688–1832* (London and New York 1997), pp. 365–6, 373–4; N. D. LoPatin, *Political Unions, Popular Politics and the Great Reform Act of 1832* (Basingstoke and London 1999), pp. 172–3.

44. Thureau-Dangin, *Histoire de la monarchie de juillet*, vol. 7, pp. 381–2, 386, 399.

45. Ibid., p. 403.

46. Antonetti, *Louis-Philippe*, pp. 912–13.

47. Thureau-Dangin, *Histoire de la monarchie de juillet*, vol. 7, pp. 411–12.

48. Antonetti, *Louis-Philippe*, pp. 646, 658–9, 913.

49. Thureau-Dangin, *Histoire de la monarchie de juillet*, vol. 7, pp. 416–17.

50. Ibid., p. 420.

51. Harsin, *Barricades*, p. 255.

52. Service Historique de l'Armée de Terre, Château de Vincennes, IM

(Mémoires et Reconnaissances) 2001, 'Instruction explicative des diverses dispositions du système de défense établi pour la ville de Paris, rive droite de la Seine', p. 1.

53. Ibid., p. 2.
54. Ibid., p. 4.
55. Guizot, *Mémoires*, vol. 2, p. 48.
56. Thureau-Dangin, *Histoire de la monarchie de juillet*, vol. 7, pp. 401–2; Antonetti, *Louis-Philippe*, pp. 911–12; L. Girard, *La garde nationale, 1814–1871* (Paris 1964), pp. 281–2.
57. Comte de Montalivet, *Fragments et souvenirs* (2 vols, Paris 1899–1900), vol. 2, pp. 90–2; Thureau-Dangin, *Histoire de la monarchie de juillet*, vol. 7, pp. 433–4.
58. Duc de Nemours to prince de Joinville, 12 Feb. 1848, AN 300 AP(III) 111. Prince de Joinville (1818–1900). Lettres reçues du roi et de la famille royale. Duc de Nemours au prince de Joinville, 1847–85, pièce 630.
59. Ibid.
60. Thureau-Dangin, *Histoire de la monarchie de juillet*, vol. 7, pp. 428–30, 452–3.
61. Ibid., p. 428; Harsin, *Barricades*, p. 257.
62. Thureau-Dangin, *Histoire de la monarchie de juillet*, vol. 7, pp. 430–1; Service Historique de l'Armée de Terre, IM (Mémoires et Reconnaissances) 2001, 'Instruction explicative', p. 5.
63. Thureau-Dangin, *Histoire de la monarchie de juillet*, vol. 7, pp. 435–7; Girard, *La garde nationale*, pp. 283–5.
64. J. Hardman, *Louis XVI* (New Haven and London 1993), pp. 160, 171.
65. Thureau-Dangin, *Histoire de la monarchie de juillet*, vol. 7, p. 441 n. 1.
66. AN 300 AP(III) 13. Dossier: 1848, Notes du roi, fo. 64.
67. Broglie, *Guizot*, pp. 356–8.
68. AN BB30 297, pièce 449: Molé's deposition to Cour d'Appel of Paris, 31 Mar. 1848.
69. Thureau-Dangin, *Histoire de la monarchie de juillet*, vol. 7, pp. 449–50.
70. Harsin, *Barricades*, pp. 258–61.
71. Ibid., pp. 261, 252.
72. Antonetti, *Louis-Philippe*, pp. 918–19.
73. Thureau-Dangin, *Histoire de la monarchie de juillet*, vol. 7, pp. 462–4.
74. Bury and Tombs, *Thiers*, pp. 94–5.
75. Thureau-Dangin, *Histoire de la monarchie de juillet*, vol. 7, pp. 460–2; Harsin, *Barricades*, p. 263. After the Feb. 1848 revolution, between Feb. and May 1849, Bugeaud actually wrote a short treatise on urban warfare which was lost for many years and then discovered and published in 1997: Maréchal Bugeaud, *La guerre des rues et des maisons*, ed. M. Bouyssy (Paris 1997) – see p. 8 for its provenance.

76. AN BB30 297, pièce 561, Marshal Bugeaud's deposition made at Périgueux to representatives of the Cour d'Appel of Paris, 3 Apr. 1848.

77. Thureau-Dangin, *Histoire de la monarchie de juillet*, vol. 7, p. 465.

78. AN BB30 297, pièce 561, Marshal Bugeaud's deposition; and ibid., pièce 564, deposition of General Bedeau to Cour d'Appel of Paris, 21 Mar. 1848.

79. Ibid.

80. Thureau-Dangin, *Histoire de la monarchie de juillet*, vol. 7, p. 467.

81. AN BB30 297 pièce 564, deposition of General Bedeau.

82. AN BB30 297 pièce 561, deposition of Marshal Bugeaud; ibid., 300 AP(III) 13. Dossier: 1848, Notes du roi, fo. 61.

83. Thureau-Dangin, *Histoire de la monarchie de juillet*, vol. 7, pp. 475–7, 482–3.

84. Antonetti, *Louis-Philippe*, p. 921; R. Allen, *Threshold of Terror: The Last Hours of the Monarchy in the French Revolution* (Stroud 1999), pp. 65–71, 87–91.

85. Thureau-Dangin, *Histoire de la monarchie de juillet*, vol. 7, pp. 486–8.

86. Collingham, *The July Monarchy*, p. 411; M. du Camp, *Souvenirs de l'année 1848* (Paris 1876), pp. 85–92.

87. Thureau-Dangin, *Histoire de la monarchie de juillet*, vol. 7, pp. 490–2.

88. AN BB30, pièce 451, deposition of Marshal Gérard to Cour d'Appel of Paris, 3 Apr. 1848.

89. AN 300 AP(III) 13. 'Récit du départ des Tuileries le jeudi 24 février jusqu'à l'arrivée à Claremont, le samedi 4 mars 1848', pp. 4–5.

90. *Mémoires de M. Dupin*, vol. 4, pp. 457–8; Montalivet, *Fragments et souvenirs*, vol. 2, pp. 172–4.

91. Louis-Philippe to Guizot, 14 Apr. 1850, AN 42 AP Fonds Guizot, 193, pièce 20.

92. Antonetti, *Louis-Philippe*, p. 923.

93. *Mémoires de M. Dupin*, vol. 4, pp. 465–6.

94. Ibid., pp. 467–8; Thureau-Dangin, *Histoire de la monarchie de juillet*, vol. 7, p. 499.

95. *Mémoires de M. Dupin*, vol. 4, p. 468.

96. Ibid., pp. 469–70; Thureau-Dangin, *Histoire de la monarchie de juillet*, vol. 7, pp. 499–501, 503–4.

97. Collingham, *The July Monarchy*, p. 412.

98. *Mémoires de M. Dupin*, vol. 4, pp. 471–81.

99. Thureau-Dangin, *Histoire de la monarchie de juillet*, vol. 7, p. 509.

100. *Mémoires de M. Dupin*, vol. 4, pp. 493–5.

101. Ibid., pp. 493–8; Thureau-Dangin, *Histoire de la monarchie de juillet*, vol. 7, pp. 510–13, 520–1.

102. AN 300 AP(III) 13. Dossier 1848: notes du roi, fo. 63; Harsin, *Barricades*, p. 252.

103. Thureau-Dangin, *Histoire de la monarchie de juillet*, vol. 7, pp. 513–14.

Epilogue

1. Guy Antonetti, *Louis-Philippe* (Paris 1994), pp. 925–6.

2. Archives Nationales, Paris, 300 AP(III) 13. 'Récit du départ des Tuileries le jeudi 24 février jusqu'à l'arrivée à Claremont, le samedi 4 mars 1848', pp. 26, 47, 53.

3. P. Thureau-Dangin, *Histoire de la monarchie de juillet* (7 vols, Paris 1884–92), vol. 7, p. 523.

4. AN 300 AP(III) 13, 'Récit', pp. 99–107.

5. Ibid., pp. 108–11; R. and I. Tombs, *That Sweet Enemy: The French and the British from the Sun King to the Present* (London 2006), p. 346.

6. AN 300 AP(III) 13, 'Récit', p. 115.

7. Ibid., pp. 118–23.

8. *Mémoires de la comtesse de Boigne, née d'Osmond: récits d'une tante* (Mercure de France edn, 2 vols, Paris 1999), vol. 2, pp. 680–1; AN 300 AP(III) 13, 'Récit', p. 16.

9. Thureau-Dangin, *Histoire de la monarchie de juillet*, vol. 7, pp. 523–5; Antonetti, *Louis-Philippe*, p. 925.

10. *Mémoires de la comtesse de Boigne*, vol. 2, p. 688.

11. Antonetti, *Louis-Philippe*, pp. 930–4; *Louis-Philippe: l'homme et le roi, 1773–1850* (catalogue of exhibition at Archives Nationales, Paris, Oct. 1974–Feb. 1975), p. 150.

12. Ibid., p. 153; Antonetti, *Louis-Philippe*, p. 937.

13. *Louis-Philippe: l'homme et le roi*, p. 154; J. P. T. Bury and R. P. Tombs, *Thiers 1797–1877: A Political Life* (London 1986), pp. 129–35; D. Paoli, *Fortunes et infortunes des princes d'Orléans, 1848–1918* (Paris 2006), p. 327.

14. Ibid., pp. 198–203, 249, 292.

15. Ibid., pp. 117–19, 133–40, 205–9, 271–5, 313.

16. Antonetti, *Louis-Philippe*, p. 937.

17. Marquis de Noailles, *Le Comte Molé (1781–1855): sa vie, ses mémoires* (6 vols, Paris 1922–30), vol. 6, pp. 315–16; J.-A. de Sédouy, *Le Comte Molé, ou la séduction du pouvoir* (Paris 1994), pp. 229–41.

18. G. de Broglie, *Guizot* (Paris 2002 edn), pp. 361–72, 382–3, 389–99, 427–44, 450–89.

19. Bury and Tombs, *Thiers*, pp. 101–8, 135–6, 148, 161–9.

20. Ibid., pp. 196–209. The literature on the Commune is vast; for two

important studies see J. Rougerie, *Paris libre 1871* (Paris 1971), and R. Tombs, *The Paris Commune 1871* (London and New York 1999).

21. Bury and Tombs, *Thiers*, pp. 219–29, 239–40.

22. O. Barrot, *Mémoires posthumes* (4 vols, Paris 1875–6), vol. 1, pp. XXI–XXVII (biographical notice by P.-L. Duvergier de Hauranne).

23. Comte de Montalivet, *Fragments et souvenir* (2 vols, Paris 1899–1900), vol. 1, pp. LXXXI–CXXV (biographical notice by G. Picot).

24. Cited in H. A. C. Collingham with R. S. Alexander, *The July Monarchy: A Political History of France, 1830–1848* (London and New York 1988), p. 414.

25. L. Faucher, *Biographie et correspondance* (2 vols, Paris 1875), vol. 1, p. 101, Léon Faucher to Henry Reeve, 17 Nov. 1840.

26. For the June Days, see J. Harsin, *Barricades: The War of the Streets in Revolutionary Paris, 1830–1848* (New York and Basingstoke 2002), pp. 294–318; P. Amann, *Revolution and Mass Democracy: The Parisian Club Movement in 1848* (Princeton, NJ, 1975), pp. 248–323; M. Traugott, *Armies of the Poor: Determinants of Working-class Participation in the Parisian Insurrection of June 1848* (Princeton, NJ, 1985); C. Tilly and L. H. Lees, 'The people of June 1848', in R. Price ed., *Revolution and Reaction: 1848 and the Second French Republic* (London and New York 1975), pp. 170–209. For Louis-Philippe's verdict on the June Days, see Antonetti, *Louis-Philippe*, p. 919. For the problem of legitimacy posed by a small electorate, see R. Tombs, *France 1814–1914* (London and New York 1996), p. 191.

27. Thureau-Dangin, *Histoire de la monarchie de juillet*, vol. 7, p. 440 n. 1.

BIBLIOGRAPHY

PRIMARY SOURCES

PUBLIC HOLDINGS

ARCHIVES NATIONALES, PARIS

Archives de la Maison de France (300 AP)
— 300 AP (I): 948, 949
— 300 AP (III): 6, 7, 13, 14, 31, 33, 34, 37, 38, 39, 40, 42, 51, 54, 73, 111, 172, 959
— 300 AP (IV): 8, 9, 10, 14, 18, 199

Fonds Guizot (42 AP)
— 42 AP: 66, 165, 193, 286

Série BB (Ministère de la Justice)
— BB30 297

Série F¹C (Esprit public, élections, conseils généraux, conseils d'arrondissement)
— F¹C I 121

BIBLIOTHÈQUE NATIONALE, PARIS

Papiers A. Thiers
— Nouvelles acquisitions françaises: 20601, 20606, 20608, 20616

SERVICE HISTORIQUE DE L'ARMÉE DE TERRE, VINCENNES

Série D³ 131: Correspondance militaire générale, juillet–août 1830; dossier: Révolution de 1830
Série E⁵ 132 ter: Correspondance générale militaire. Cahiers d'enregistrement, 1 janvier 1839–31 décembre 1848
Série F¹ I: Correspondance générale militaire, janvier–23 février 1848
Fi I: Correspondance générale militaire, 24 février–4 mars 1848
Série Mémoires et Reconnaissances: IM 2001, 2002, 2151

PRIVATE HOLDINGS

ARCHIVES BRYAS, CHÂTEAU DE MAUVIÈRES

Lettres de Louis-Philippe au Maréchal Gérard, 1833–4
Lettres de Mme Adélaïde d'Orléans au Maréchal Gérard
Lettres de Ferdinand-Philippe, duc d'Orléans
Lettres du Roi des Belges Léopold, 1831–2

ARCHIVES DU COMTE MOLÉ, CHÂTEAU DE CHAMPLÂTREUX

Registre A: letters of Louis-Philippe, Mme Adélaïde, Ferdinand-Philippe, duc
   d'Orléans to comte Molé
Registre F: letters of Maréchal Sébastiani to comte Molé
Registre G: letters of comte Molé to Louis-Philippe

PUBLISHED PRIMARY SOURCES

Mémoires, souvenirs et journaux de la comtesse d'Agoult ed. C. Dupechez (Paris
   1990)
Comtesse d'Agoult (as Daniel Stern), *Histoire de la révolution de 1848* (2 vols,
   Paris 1862)
B. Appert, *Dix ans à la cour du roi Louis-Philippe et souvenirs du temps de
   l'Empire et de la Restauration* (3 vols, Berlin and Paris 1846)
Correspondance du duc d'Aumale et de Cuvillier-Fleury ed. F. H. G. Limbourg
   (4 vols, Paris 1910–14)
O. Barrot, *Mémoires posthumes* (3 vols, Paris 1875–6)
F. de Bertier, *Souvenirs inédits d'un conspirateur* (Paris 1990)
Mémoires de la comtesse de Boigne, née d'Osmond: récits d'une tante (2 vols,
   Mercure de France edn, Paris 1999)
G. du Bosq de Beaumont and M. Bernos eds, *La famille d'Orléans pendant la
   Révolution d'après sa correspondance inédite* (Paris 1913)
Souvenirs (1775–1870) de feu le duc de Broglie (4 vols, Paris, 1886)
Marshal Bugeaud, *La guerre des rues et des maisons* ed. M. Bouyssy (Paris
   1997)
E. Cabet, *Révolution de 1830 et situation présente (novembre 1833)* (Paris 1833)
Mémoires du duc des Cars (2 vols, Paris 1890)
François-René, vicomte de Chateaubriand, *Mémoires d'outre-tombe* (Livre de
   poche edn, 3 vols, Paris 1973)
Journal intime de Cuvillier-Fleury ed. E. Bertin (2 vols, Paris 1903)
Baron de Damas, *Mémoires, 1785–1862* (2 vols, Paris 1922–3)

E. Daudet, 'Quelques lettres de Louis XVIII', *Nouvelle Revue*, vol. 116 (Jan. 1899), pp. 26–45

———, 'Louis XVIII et le comte d'Artois', *Revue des Deux Mondes*, 1 Feb. 1906, pp. 559–95, and 15 Feb., pp. 824–60

———, 'A travers les papiers de Louis XVIII. Ses notes de lecture'. *Le Correspondant*, vol. 238 (Jan.–Mar. 1910), pp. 24–47

E. Delille, *Journal de la vie de SAS Mme la duchesse d'Orléans douairière* (Paris 1822)

Duchesse de Dino, *Chronique de 1831 à 1862, publiée par la princesse de Castellane* (4 vols, Paris 1909–11)

Henri, marquis Dugon, *Au service du roi en exil: épisodes de la contre-révolution d'après le journal et la correspondance du président de Vézet* (Lyon 1968)

Mémoires de M. Dupin (4 vols, Paris 1855–61)

L. Faucher, *Biographie et correspondance* (2 vols, Paris 1899–1900)

Susan E. Ferrier, *The Inheritance* (3 vols, Edinburgh 1824)

Félicité, comtesse de Genlis, *Adèle et Théodore* (3 vols, Paris 1782)

———, *Mémoires inédits de Mme la comtesse de Genlis pour servir à l'histoire des 18ème et 19ème siècles* (8 vols, Paris and London 1825)

The Greville Memoirs, 1814–1860 eds L. Strachey and R. Fulford (8 vols, London 1938)

Comte de Guernon-Ranville, *Journal d'un ministre* (Caen 1873)

Lettres de François Guizot et de la princesse de Lieven, 1836–1846 ed. J. Naville (3 vols, Paris 1963)

F. Guizot, *Mémoires pour servir à l'histoire de mon temps* (8 vols, Paris 1858–67)

———, *Le duc de Broglie* (Paris 1872)

J. Hardman, *The French Revolution Sourcebook* (London 1999)

——— and M. Price eds, *Louis XVI and the Comte de Vergennes: Correspondence, 1774–1787* (Oxford, Voltaire Foundation, 1998)

Mémoires du baron d'Haussez, dernier ministre de la marine sous la restauration (2 vols, Paris 1896–7)

Heinrich Heine, *Lutèce*, in *Samtliche Werke* ed. M. Windfuhr (16 vols, Hamburg 1975–97)

Victor Hugo, *Journal 1830–1848* ed. H. Guillemin (Paris 1954)

———, *Les Misérables: Oeuvres complètes* (48 vols, Paris 1880–89), *Roman* vol. 8

Vieux souvenirs de Mgr le prince de Joinville ed. D. Meyer (Mercure de France edn, Paris 1986)

Mémoires, correspondance et manuscrits du général Lafayette (6 vols, Paris 1837–8)

Souvenirs de Jacques Laffitte racontés par lui-même (3 vols, Paris 1844–5)

G. Lefebvre and A. Terroine, *Recueil de documents relatifs aux séances des états-généraux de 1789*, vol. 1(ii), *La séance du 23 juin* (Paris 1962)

Souvenirs-portraits de Gaston de Lévis (1764–1830), suivis de lettres intimes de Monsieur comte de Provence au duc de Lévis ed. J. Dupâquier (Mercure de France edn, Paris 1993)

Louis XVI, Marie Antoinette et Mme Elisabeth: lettres et documents inédits ed. F. Feuillet de Conches (6 vols, Paris 1864–73)

Louis-Philippe, *Mémoires* (2 vols, Paris 1973–4)

Marshal Macdonald, *Souvenirs* (Paris 1892)

Journal de Marie-Amélie, reine des Français, 1800–1866 ed. S. d'Huart (Paris 1981)

Mémoires du maréchal Marmont, duc de Raguse, de 1792 à 1841 (9 vols, Paris 1857)

F. Masson, 'Lettres du prince de Talleyrand et de Mme de Dino à Mme Adélaïde', *Nouvelle Revue Rétrospective*, vol. 15 (1901), pp. 145–68, 217–40, 337–60, 385–408, and vol. 16 (1902), pp. 49–65

L. G. Michaud, *Biographie universelle* (45 vols, Paris and Leipzig 1843–65)

Comte Molé, *Souvenirs de jeunesse* ed. marquise de Noailles (Mercure de France edn, Paris 1991)

Comte de Montalivet, *Fragments et souvenirs* (2 vols, Paris 1899–1900)

Baron de Montesquieu, *Oeuvres complètes* ed. R. Caillois (2 vols, Paris 1949–51)

Comte de Montlosier, *Souvenirs d'un émigré* ed. Comte de Larouzière-Montlosier and E. d'Hauterive (Paris 1951)

Mémoires de Mlle de Montpensier ed. M. A. L. de Boissi (10 vols, Paris 1823)

Duc de Mortemart, 'Un manuscrit sur les journées de juillet', *Le Correspondant*, vol. 321 (Dec. 1930), pp. 641–58, 801–23

Marquis de Noailles, *Le Comte Molé (1781–1855): sa vie, ses mémoires* (6 vols, Paris 1922–30)

Correspondance de Louis-Philippe-Joseph, duc d'Orléans, avec Louis XVI, la reine, Montmorin, Liancourt, Biron, Lafayette etc . . . (Paris 1800)

G. Pallain ed., *Correspondance inédite du prince de Talleyrand et du roi Louis XVIII pendant le congrès de Vienne* (Paris 1881)

Mémoires du Chancelier Pasquier (6 vols, Paris 1893–5)

E. J. Parry ed., *Correspondence of Lord Aberdeen and Princess Lieven, 1832–1854* (2 vols, London 1938–9)

L. Pingaud ed., *Correspondance intime du comte de Vaudreuil et du comte d'Artois pendant l'émigration, 1789–1815* (2 vols, Paris 1889)

Procédure criminelle instruite au Châtelet de Paris sur la dénonciation des faits arrivés à Versailles dans la journée du 6 octobre 1789 (Paris 1790)

Charles, comte de Rémusat, *Mémoires de ma vie* ed. C. Pouthas (5 vols, Paris 1958–67)

Lettres du duc de Richelieu au marquis d'Osmond, 1816–1818 ed. S. Charléty (Paris 1939)

Mémoires de M. de la Rochefoucauld, duc de Doudeauville (10 vols, Paris 1861–3)

P.-L. Roederer, *Adresse d'un constitutionnel aux constitutionnels* (Paris 1835)

Souvenirs d'Abraham Rösselet ed. R. de Steiger (Neuchâtel 1857)

Souvenirs du général comte de Rumigny, aide-de-camp du roi Louis-Philippe (1789–1860) ed. R.-M. Gouraud d'Ablancourt (Paris 1921)

Mémoires du général comte de St Chamans (Paris 1896)

George Sand, *Histoire de ma vie* (20 vols, Paris 1854–5)

Comte de Serre, *Correspondance* (7 vols, Paris 1876–82)

T. Silvestre, *La conspiration des quarante* (Paris 1864)

Marshal Soult, *Correspondance politique et familière avec Louis-Philippe et la famille royale* ed. L. and A. de Saint-Pierre (Paris 1959)

Prince de Talleyrand, *Mémoires* (5 vols, Paris 1891–2)

Le prince de Talleyrand et la maison d'Orléans ed. comtesse de Mirabeau (Paris 1890)

Souvenirs de Alexis de Tocqueville publiés par le comte de Tocqueville (Paris 1893)

A. Trognon, *Vie de Marie-Amélie, reine des Français* (Paris 1872)

A. de Vigny, *Mémoires inédits, fragments et projets* ed. J. Sangnier (Paris 1958)

Mémoires et correspondance du comte de Villèle (5 vols, Paris 1888–90)

SECONDARY SOURCES

F. Acomb, *Anglophobia in France, 1763–1789: An Essay in the History of Constitutionalism and Nationalism* (Durham, NC, 1950)

Lord Acton, *Lectures on the French Revolution* (London 1920 edn)

R. S. Alexander, *Bonapartism and Revolutionary Tradition in France: The Fédérés of 1815* (Cambridge 1991)

———, *Rewriting the French Revolutionary Tradition* (Cambridge 2003)

R. Allen, *Threshold of Terror: The Last Hours of the Monarchy in the French Revolution* (Stroud 1999)

P. Amann, *Revolution and Mass Democracy: The Parisian Club Movement in 1848* (Princeton, NJ, 1975)

G. Antonetti, *Louis-Philippe* (Paris 1994)

R. Arnaud, *Adélaïde d'Orléans (1777–1847)* (Paris 1908)

N. Aston, *Religion and Revolution in France, 1780–1804* (Basingstoke and London 2000)

I. Backouche, *La monarchie parlementaire, 1815–1848* (Paris 2000)

S. Balayé, *Madame de Staël: lumières et liberté* (Paris 1979)

F. Baldensperger, *Le mouvement des idées dans l'émigration française, 1789–1815* (2 vols, Paris 1924)

A. Bardoux, *La duchesse de Duras* (Paris 1898)

P. Bastid, *Les institutions politiques de la monarchie constitutionnelle (1814–1848)* (Paris 1954)

V. W. Beach, *Charles X of France* (Boulder, Colo., 1971)

E. Beau de Loménie, *La carrière politique de Chateaubriand, 1814–1830* (2 vols, Paris 1929)

L. Bergeron, *L'épisode napoléonien. Aspects intérieurs, 1799–1815* (Paris 1972)

F. de Bernardy, *Flahaut, fils de Talleyrand, père de Morny* (Paris 1974)

G. de Bertier de Sauvigny, *Le comte Ferdinand de Bertier et l'énigme de la Congrégation* (Paris 1948)

——— , *La restauration* (Paris 1955)

——— , ed., *La révolution de 1830 en France* (Paris 1970)

R. J. Bezucha, 'The revolution of 1830 and the city of Lyon', in J. M. Merriman ed., *1830 in France*, pp. 119–38

——— , *The Lyon Uprising of 1834* (Cambridge 1974)

J. Black, *Natural and Necessary Enemies: Anglo-French Relations in the Eighteenth Century* (London 1986)

——— , *From Louis XIV to Napoleon. The Fate of a Great Power* (London 1999)

T. C. W. Blanning ed., *The Origins of the French Revolutionary Wars* (London 1986)

——— , *The Short Oxford History of Europe: Eighteenth-century Europe 1688–1815* (Oxford 2000)

J. Bloch, *Rousseauism and Education in Eighteenth-century France* (Oxford, Voltaire Foundation, 1995)

J.-P. Bois, *Dumouriez: héros et proscrit* (Paris 2005)

J.-L. Bory, *La révolution de juillet* (Paris 1972)

M. Bourcet, *Casimir Périer: un prince financier au temps du romantisme* (Paris 1994)

K. Bourne, *Palmerston: The Early Years, 1784–1841* (London 1982)

C. Bouyer, *La Grande Mademoiselle: la turbulente cousine de Louis XIV* (Paris 2004)

W. Boyd, *The Educational Theory of Jean-Jacques Rousseau* (New York 1963)

F. Boyer, *Martignac (1778–1832): l'itinéraire politique d'un avocat bordelais* (Paris 2002)

C. Breunig, 'Casimir Périer et les troubles de Grenoble, March 11th-13th, 1832', *French Historical Studies*, vol. 2, no. 4 (1962), pp. 469–89

A. Britsch, 'Philippe-Egalité avant la Révolution', *Revue d'Etudes Historiques*, vol. 70 (1904), pp. 337–63, 478–504

——— , *La jeunesse de Philippe-Egalité* (Paris 1926)

——, 'L'anglomanie de Philippe-Egalité d'après sa correspondance autographe (1778–1785)', *Le Correspondant*, vol. 303 (1926), pp. 280–95

M. Brock, *The Great Reform Act* (London 1973)

Sir Denis Brogan, *The French Nation from Napoleon to Pétain* (London 1957)

H. Brogan, *Alexis de Tocqueville: Prophet of Democracy in the Age of Revolution* (London 2006)

G. de Broglie, *L'Orléanisme, ressource libérale de la France* (Paris 1981)

——, *Mme de Genlis* (Paris 1985)

——, *Guizot* (Paris 2002 edn)

J. Brooke, *George III* (London 1972)

R. Bullen, *Palmerston, Guizot and the Collapse of the Entente Cordiale* (London 1974)

I. Buruma, *Voltaire's Coconuts, or Anglomania in Europe* (London 1999)

J. P. T. Bury and R. P. Tombs, *Thiers, 1797–1877: A Political Life* (London 1986)

J. Cabanis, *Charles X, roi ultra* (Paris 1972)

C. Campbell Orr ed., *Queenship in Britain, 1660–1837: Royal Patronage, Court Culture and Dynastic Politics* (Manchester and New York 2002)

——, ed., *Queenship in Europe, 1660–1815: The Role of the Consort* (Cambridge 2004)

J. Cannon, *The Fox–North Coalition: Crisis of the Constitution, 1782–1784* (Cambridge 1969)

——, *Parliamentary Reform, 1640–1832* (Cambridge 1973)

——, ed., *The Whig Ascendancy: Colloquies on Hanoverian England* (London 1981)

P. Caron, 'La tentative de contre-révolution de juin–juillet 1789', *Revue d'histoire moderne et contemporaine*, vol. 8 (1906–7), pp. 5–34, 649–78

——, *Les massacres de septembre* (Paris 1935)

A. Castelot, *Philippe-Egalité: le prince rouge* (Paris 1950)

M. Chamberlain, *Lord Aberdeen: A Political Biography* (London 1983)

J. Chambers, *Palmerston: The People's Darling* (London 2004)

V. Champier and G. R. Sandoz, *Le palais-royal d'après des documents inédits* (2 vols, Paris 1900)

H. de Changy, *Le soulèvement de la duchesse de Berry, 1830–1832: les royalistes dans la tourmente* (Paris 1986)

C. Charle, *Le siècle de la presse, 1830–1939* (Paris 2004)

F. Charles-Roux, *Le projet français de conquête de l'Egypte sous Louis XVI* (Cairo 1929)

J. Charmley, *The Princess and the Politicians: Sex, Intrigue and Diplomacy, 1812–1840* (London 2005)

G. Chaussinand-Nogaret ed., *Les grands discours parlementaires de la Révolution, de Mirabeau à Robespierre* (Paris 2005)

G. Cholvy and Y.-M. Hilaire, *Histoire religieuse de la France contemporaine* (2 vols, Toulouse 1985)

A. Chuquet, *Les guerres de la Révolution* (11 vols, Paris 1886–96)

——— , 'Le départ de l'Ile d'Elbe', *Revue de Paris*, 1 Feb. 1920

J. C. D. Clark, *Revolution and Rebellion: State and Society in England in the Seventeenth and Eighteenth Centuries* (Cambridge 1986)

H. A. C. Collingham with R. S. Alexander, *The July Monarchy, 1830–1848: A Political History* (London 1988)

I. Collins, *The Government and the Newspaper Press in France, 1814–1881* (Oxford 1959)

——— , *Napoleon and his Parliaments, 1800–1815* (London 1979)

B. Combes de Patris, *Un homme d'état sous la restauration: le comte de Serre (1776–1824), d'après sa correspondance et des documents inédits* (Paris 1932)

A. Corbin, J. Lalouette and M. Riot-Sarcey eds, *Femmes dans la cité, 1815–1871* (Grane 1997)

G. Cubitt, *The Jesuit Myth: Conspiracy Theory and Politics in Nineteenth-century France* (Oxford 1993)

A. Dansette, *Le second empire* (3 vols, Paris 1972–6)

E. Daudet, *Le ministère de M. de Martignac, sa vie politique et les dernières années de la restauration* (Paris 1875)

——— , *Louis XVIII et le duc Decazes, 1815–1820* (Paris 1899)

C. Decours, *La dernière favorite: Zoé du Cayla, le grand amour de Louis XVIII* (Paris 1993)

C. Dédéyan, *Montesquieu ou les lumières d'Albion* (Paris 1990)

——— , *Télémaque ou la liberté de l'esprit* (Paris 1991)

G. de Diesbach, *Histoire de l'émigration, 1789–1814* (Paris 1984)

——— , *Chateaubriand* (Paris 1995)

J. Duhamel, *Louis-Philippe et la première entente cordiale* (Paris 1951)

C. Dupuis, *Le ministère Talleyrand en 1814* (2 vols, Paris 1919–20)

P. G. Dwyer, *Talleyrand* (London 2002)

J. Egret, *La révolution des notables: Mounier et les monarchiens* (Paris 1950)

——— , *La pré-révolution française, 1787–1788* (Paris 1962)

——— , *Louis XV et l'opposition parlementaire* (Paris 1970)

H. d'Estre, *Bourmont: la chouannerie, les cent-jours, la conquête d'Alger (1773–1846)* (Paris 1934)

M. Fairweather, *Madame de Staël* (London 2005)

J. Fourcassié, *Villèle* (Paris 1954)

F. Fraser, *Princesses: The Six Daughters of George III* (London 2005 paperback edn)

J. C. E. Frignet-Despréaux, *Le maréchal Mortier, duc de Trévise* (3 vols, Paris and Nancy 1913–20)

M. Fumaroli, *Chateaubriand: poésie et terreur* (Paris 2004)

F. Furet, *La Révolution, de Turgot à Jules Ferry* (Paris 1988)

——, and M. Ozouf eds, *Terminer la Révolution* (Grenoble 1990)

N. Gash, *Sir Robert Peel: The Life of Sir Robert Peel after 1830* (London 1972)

——, *Aristocracy and People: Britain 1815–1865* (London 1979)

P. Gay, *Voltaire's Politics: The Poet as Realist* (Princeton, NJ, 1959)

L. Girard, *La garde nationale, 1814–1871* (Paris 1964)

——, *Les libéraux français, 1814–1875* (Paris 1985)

P. Girault de Coursac, *L'éducation d'un roi* (Paris 1972)

J. Godechot, *Les institutions de la France sous la Révolution et l'Empire* (Paris 1951)

——, *La contre-révolution: doctrine et action, 1789–1804* (Paris 1961)

——, *La prise de la Bastille* (Paris 1965)

N. Gotteri, *Le maréchal Soult* (Paris 2000)

L. Gottschalk and M. Maddox, *Lafayette in the French Revolution: Through the October Days* (Chicago 1969)

——, *Lafayette in the French Revolution: From the October days through the Federation* (Chicago 1973)

J. Grieder, *Anglomania in France, 1740–1789: Fact, Fiction and Political Discourse* (Geneva 1985)

R. Griffiths, *Le centre perdu: Malouet et les 'monarchiens' dans la Révolution française* (Grenoble 1988)

V. Gruder, 'The question of Marie Antoinette: the queen and public opinion before the Revolution', *French History*, vol. 16, no. 3 (Sept. 2002), pp. 269–98

J. Hardman, *Louis XVI* (New Haven and London 1993)

N. Hampson, *The Perfidy of Albion: French Perceptions of England during the French Revolution* (London 1998)

R. Héron de Villefosse, *L'anti-Versailles ou le Palais-royal de Philippe-Egalité* (Paris 1974)

C. Hibbert, *George IV* (London 1976)

D. Higgs, *Ultraroyalism in Toulouse* (Baltimore, Md. 1973)

S. Holmes, *Benjamin Constant and the Making of Modern Liberalism* (London 1984)

H. Houssaye, *1815: la première restauration, le retour de l'Ile d'Elbe, les cent-jours* (Paris 1893)

T. E. B. Howarth, *Citizen King: The Life of Louis-Philippe, King of the French* (London 1961)

L. Hunt, ed., *Eroticism and the Body Politic* (Baltimore, Md. 1991)

——, *The Family Romance of the French Revolution* (Berkeley, Calif., 1992)

B. F. Hyslop, *L'apanage de Philippe-Egalité, duc d'Orléans, 1785–1791* (Paris 1965)

Bibliography

L. Iremonger, *Lord Aberdeen: A Biography of the Fourth Earl of Aberdeen* (London 1978)

R. A. Jackson, *Vive le roi! The French Coronation from Charles V to Charles X* (Chapel Hill, NC, 1984)

A. Jardin, *Alexis de Tocqueville, 1805–1859* (Paris 1984)

———, *Histoire du libéralisme politique: de la crise de l'absolutisme à la constitution de 1875* (Paris 1985)

———, and A.-J. Tudesq, *La France des notables, 1815–1848* (2 vols, Paris 1973)

J. R. Jennings, 'Conceptions of England and its constitution in nineteenth-century French political thought', *Historical Journal*, vol. 29 (1986), pp. 65–86

D. Johnson, *Guizot: Aspects of French History, 1787–1874* (London 1963)

S. Kale, *French Salons: High Society and Political Sociability from the Old Régime to the Revolution of 1848* (Baltimore and London 2004)

G. A. Kelly, *The Humane Comedy: Constant, Tocqueville and French Liberalism* (London 1992)

S. Kent, *The Election of 1827 in France* (Cambridge, Mass., and London 1975)

M. Kerckvoorde, *Louise d'Orléans, la reine oubliée 1812–1850* (Paris 1991)

H. La Marle, *Philippe-Egalité: 'Grand Maître' de la Révolution* (Paris 1989)

E. Labrousse ed., *Aspects de la crise et de la dépression de l'économie française au milieu du 19ème siècle* (La Roche-sur-Yon 1956)

G. Lacour-Gayet, *Talleyrand, 1754–1838* (4 vols, Paris 1928–34)

J. Landes, *Women and the Public Sphere in the Age of the French Revolution* (Ithaca, NY, 1988)

R. Langeron, *Decazes, ministre du roi* (Paris 1960)

A. Lanne, *La fortune des d'Orléans: origine et accroissement* (Paris 1905)

M. Laurent-Atthalin, *Vie du général baron Atthalin, 1784–1848* (Colmar 1978)

C. Ledré, *La presse à l'assaut de la monarchie, 1815–1848* (Paris 1960)

Comte Lefebvre de Behaine, *Le comte d'Artois sur la route de Paris* (Paris 1921)

E. Lever, *Philippe-Egalité* (Paris 1996)

H. D. Lewis, 'The legal status of women in nineteenth-century France', *Journal of European Studies*, vol. 10 (1980), pp. 178–88

E. Longford, *Victoria RI* (London 2000 edn)

S. Loomis, *A Crime of Passion* (London 1968)

N. D. LoPatin, *Political Unions, Popular Politics and the Great Reform Act of 1832* (Basingstoke and London 1999)

Louis-Philippe, l'homme et le roi, 1773–1850 (catalogue of exhibition at Archives Nationales, Paris, Oct. 1974–Feb. 1975)

J. Lucas-Dubreton, *Louvel le régicide* (Paris 1925)

———, *Louis-Philippe et la machine infernale, 1830–1835* (Paris 1951)

A. Maag, *Geschichte der Schweizertruppen in französischen Diensten während der Restauration und Julirevolution (1816–1830)* (Biel 1899)

J. F. McMillan, *Napoleon III* (London 1991)

L. Madelin, *Fouché* (2 vols, Paris 1930)

R. Magraw, *France 1815–1914: The Bourgeois Century* (London 1983)

P. Mansel, *Louis XVIII* (London 1981)

――――, *Paris between Empires, 1814–1852* (London 2001)

P. Mantoux, 'Talleyrand en 1830 d'après des mémoires contemporains', *Revue historique*, vol. 78 (1902), p. 273

J. Burr Margadant, 'The duchesse de Berry and royalist political culture in postrevolutionary France', *History Workshop Journal*, issue 43 (spring 1997), pp. 23–52

――――, 'Gender, vice and the political imaginary in postrevolutionary France: reinterpreting the failure of the July monarchy, 1830–1848', *American Historical Review*, vol. 104, no. 5 (Dec. 1999), pp. 1461–96

――――, 'Representing Queen Marie-Amélie in a "bourgeois" monarchy', *Historical Reflections/Réflexions Historiques*, vol. 32, no. 2 (summer 2006), pp. 421–51

T. J. Markovitch, 'La crise de 1847–48 dans les industries parisiennes', *Revue d'histoire économique et sociale*, vol. 43 (1965)

A. Martin-Fugier, *La vie quotidienne de Louis-Philippe et de sa famille* (Paris 1992)

S. Maza, *Private Lives and Public Affairs: The Causes Célèbres of Prerevolutionary France* (Berkeley, Los Angeles, and London 1993)

J. M. Merriman ed., *1830 in France* (New York and London 1975)

General J.-T. de Mesmay, *Horace Sébastiani: soldat, diplomate, homme d'état, maréchal de France (1772–1851)* (Paris 1948)

H. Morand, 'Philippe-Egalité et la construction du Palais-royal', *Le Correspondant*, vol. 304 (1926), pp. 290–3

C. G. Moses, *French Feminism in the Nineteenth Century* (New York 1984)

S. Neely, *Lafayette and the Liberal Ideal, 1814–1824* (Carbondale, Ill., 1991)

J.-J. Oechslin, *Le mouvement ultra-royaliste sous la restauration: son idéologie et son action politique (1814–1830)* (Paris 1960)

F. O'Gorman, *Voters, Patrons and Parties: The Unreformed Electorate of Hanoverian England, 1734–1832* (Oxford 1989)

――――, *The Long Eighteenth Century: British Political and Social History 1688–1832* (London and New York 1997)

J. Ollé-Laprune, *La stabilité des ministres sous la Troisième République (1879–1940)* (Paris 1962)

D. Paoli, *Fortunes et infortunes des princes d'Orléans, 1848–1918* (Paris 2006)

R. Pares, *George III and the Politicians* (Oxford 1953)

E. Perret, *La dernière favorite des rois de France. La comtesse du Cayla* (Paris 1937)

P. Pilbeam, 'The emergence of opposition to the Orléanist monarchy, August 1830–April 1831', *English Historical Review*, vol. 85, no. 334 (Jan. 1970), pp. 12–28

———, *The 1830 Revolution in France* (London 1991)

———, *Republicanism in Nineteenth-century France, 1814–1871* (Basingstoke and London 1995)

———, *The Constitutional Monarchy in France, 1814–48* (London 2000)

D. H. Pinkney, *The French Revolution of 1830* (Princeton, NJ, 1972)

———, *Decisive Years in France, 1840–1847* (Princeton, NJ, 1986)

V. J. Pitts, *La Grande Mademoiselle at the Court of France, 1627–1688* (Baltimore, Md., 2000)

J. H. Plumb, *The Growth of Political Stability in England, 1675–1725* (London 1982 edn)

R. Poidevin and K. G. Faber, *Les relations franco-allemandes, 1830–1848* (Metz 1977)

G. Poisson, *Les Orléans. Une famille en quête d'un trône* (Paris 1999)

M. Poniatowski, *Louis-Philippe et Louis XVIII: autour du journal de Louis-Philippe en mars 1815* (Paris 1980)

———, *Talleyrand* (4 vols, Paris 1982–95)

F. Ponteil, *Un type de grand bourgeois sous la monarchie de juillet: Georges Humann, 1780–1842* (Paris 1977)

J. Popkin, *Press, Revolution and Social Identities in France, 1830–1835* (University Park, Pennsylvania, 2002)

D. Porch, *Army and Revolution: France 1815–1848* (London 1974)

———, *The French Foreign Legion* (London 1991)

C. Pouthas, *Guizot pendant la restauration: préparation de l'homme d'état, 1814–1830* (Paris 1923)

———, 'Les ministères de Louis-Philippe', *Revue d'histoire moderne et contemporaine*, vol. 1, (Apr.–June 1954), pp. 102–30

M. Price, *The Fall of the French Monarchy: Louis XVI, Marie Antoinette and the Baron de Breteuil* (London 2002)

R. Price, 'The French army and the revolution of 1830', *European Studies Review*, vol. 3 (1973)

———, ed., *Revolution and Reaction: 1848 and the Second French Republic* (London and New York 1975)

———, 'Techniques of repression: the control of popular protest in mid-nineteenth-century France', *Historical Journal*, vol. 25, no. 4 (1982), pp. 859–87

D. L. Rader, *The Journalists and the July Revolution in France* (The Hague 1973)

J. Rendall, *The Origins of Modern Feminism: Women in Britain, France and the United States* (London 1985)

D. Resnick, *The White Terror and the Political Reaction after Waterloo* (Cambridge, Mass., 1966)

S. Rials, *Révolution et contre-révolution au 19ème siècle* (Paris 1987)

J. Ridley, *Palmerston* (London 1970)

G. Robb, *Victor Hugo* (London 1997)

A. Roberts, *Waterloo: Napoleon's Last Gamble* (London 2005)

J. Roberts, *The Counter-Revolution in France, 1789–1830* (Basingstoke 1990)

P. Robin-Harmel, *Le prince Jules de Polignac, ministre de Charles X* (2 vols, Paris and Avignon 1941–50)

P. Rosanvallon, *Le moment Guizot* (Paris 1985)

———, *La monarchie impossible: les chartes de 1814 et de 1830* (Paris 1994)

J. Rougerie, *Paris libre 1871* (Paris 1971)

A. M. Rousseau, *L'Angleterre et Voltaire* (Oxford 1976)

F. Rude, *Les révoltes des canuts, novembre 1831 à avril 1834* (Paris 1982)

G. Rudé, *The Crowd in History, 1730–1848: A Study of Popular Disturbances in France and England* (New York 1964)

V. Sackville-West, *Daughter of France: The Life of Anne-Marie-Louise d'Orléans, Duchesse de Montpensier (1627–1693)* (London 1959)

E. Saunders, *The Mystery of Marie Lafarge* (London 1951)

P. W. Schroeder, *The Transformation of European Politics, 1763–1848* (Oxford 1996 paperback edn)

K. W. Schweizer, *Lord Bute: Essays in Reinterpretation* (Leicester 1988)

J. Scott, 'Gender: a useful category of historical analysis', *American Historical Review*, vol. 91, no. 5 (1986), pp. 1053–75

S. F. Scott, *The Response of the Royal Army to the French Revolution* (Oxford 1978)

J.-A. de Sédouy, *Le Comte Molé ou la séduction du pouvoir* (Paris 1994)

B. M. Shapiro, *Revolutionary Justice in Paris, 1789–1790* (Cambridge 1993)

G. J. Sheridan, 'The political economy of artisan industry: government and the people in the silk trade of Lyon, 1830–1870', *French Historical Studies*, vol. 11 (1979), pp. 215–38

W. H. C. Smith, *Napoleon III* (London 1972)

A. Sorel, *L'Europe et la Révolution française* (8 vols, Paris 1885–1905)

A. Soulier, *L'instabilité ministérielle sous la Troisième République (1871–1938)* (Paris 1939)

A. Spitzer, *Old Hatreds and Young Hopes: The French Carbonari against the Bourbon Restoration* (Cambridge, Mass., 1971)

I. Stewart, 'Montesquieu in England: his "Notes on England", with commentary and translation', Oxford University Comparative Law Forum 6 (2002) at ouclf.iuscomp.org

D. M. G. Sutherland, *France 1789–1815: Revolution and Counter-revolution* (London 1985)

E. Taillemite, *La Fayette* (Paris 1989)

J. Thiry, *Le vol de l'aigle: le retour de Napoléon de l'Ile d'Elbe aux Tuileries* (Paris 1942)

——, *Les cent-jours* (Paris 1943)

M. Thomis and P. Holt, *Threats of Revolution in Britain, 1789–1848* (London and Basingstoke 1977)

P. Thureau-Dangin, *Histoire de la monarchie de juillet* (7 vols, Paris 1884–92)

S. Tillyard, *Citizen Lord: Edward Fitzgerald, 1763–1798* (London 1997)

R. Tombs, *France 1814–1914* (London and New York 1996)

——, *The Paris Commune, 1871* (London and New York 1999)

R. and I. Tombs, *That Sweet Enemy: the French and the British from the Sun King to the Present* (London 2006)

M. Traugott, *Armies of the Poor: Determinants of Working-class Participation in the Parisian Insurrection of June 1848* (Princeton, NJ, 1985)

J. Tulard ed., *La contre-révolution* (Paris 1990)

A. de Vaulabelle, *Histoire des deux restaurations jusqu'à l'avènement de Louis-Philippe (de janvier 1813 à octobre 1830)* (8 vols, Paris 1847–57)

L. de Viel-Castel, *Histoire de la restauration* (20 vols, Paris 1860–78)

J. Vier, *La comtesse d'Agoult et son temps* (2 vols, Paris 1955–9)

L. de Villefosse and J. Bouissonouse, *L'opposition à Napoléon* (Paris 1969)

D. de Villepin, *Les cents-jours ou l'esprit de sacrifice* (Paris 2001)

E. de Waresquiel, *Le duc de Richelieu: un sentimental en politique* (Paris 1990)

——, *Talleyrand: le prince immobile* (Paris 2003)

——, and B. Yvert, *Histoire de la restauration 1814–1830: naissance de la France moderne* (Paris 1996)

C. B. Welch, *Liberty and Utility: The Ideologues and the Transformation of Liberalism* (New York 1984)

J. Wolff, *Les Périer: la fortune et les pouvoirs* (Paris 1993)

C. Woodham-Smith, *Queen Victoria: Her Life and Times*, vol. 1, *1819–1861* (London 1972)

T. Zeldin, *The Political System of Napoleon III* (London 1958)

PERIODICALS

Le Charivari, 18, 28 and 31 January 1839

La Mode, 7 July 1832, 12 January and 1 June 1833; 9ème, 10ème et 12ème livraisons, January–June 1838; 30 March, 4 May, 13 July and 21 December 1839; 29 February and 14 March 1840; 21 August, 13 and 27 November, 4 and 18 December 1841; 27 November 1842; 6 January 1848

INDEX

450

Index

  land 52
entente cordiale 315, 316, 317, 319
Erlon, Jean-Baptiste Drouet d' 73, 74
Estates General 23, 52, 55, 56, 129–31,
  139–40
European states system 95
expansionism, French 214–15, 316

family diplomacy 313
Faucher, Léon 376
Fauvelle-Delebarre, M. 356–7
Fay, Léontine 271
Featherstonhaugh, George W. 368
Fénelon, abbé 19
Ferdinand IV, King of Naples and the Two
  Sicilies 44
Ferdinand, King of Bulgaria 371
Ferdinand VII, King of Spain 110
Ferrand, Antoine, comte 53, 62
Fieschi, Joseph 250–1, 252–4, 261
Figueras 40, 42, 43
first estate 51, 56, 57
Fitzgerald, Lord Edward 33–4
FitzJames, duc de 124
Flahaut, Charles de 202
Flahaut, Mme de 200, 203
Flandre, comte de 336
Foreign Legion 258
Forth, Nathaniel Parker 21
Fouché, Joseph 72, 74, 82, 83–4
four ordinances (July 1830) 108, 137, 138–9,
  158, 162, 172, 192, 194, 203, 207
Fourier, Charles 339
Francis I, Emperor of Austria 26, 86–7
Frederick William III, King of Prussia 11
Frederick William IV, King of Prussia 316
free trade 307
Freiburg 39
French Revolution (1789)
  legacy of 1, 3, 207
  militaristic traditions of 215
  Orléanist plot to seize throne 24–5
  political parties' view of 92–3
  storming of the Bastille 23
Friedland, Battle of 65
Friedrichstadt 40
Friends of the People (club) 204
Fronde 188
Furet, François 3

Gasparin, Adrien de 268–9
Genlis, Félicité, comtesse de 18–22, 24, 25,
  26, 29–30, 32, 33, 35, 37–9, 45, 99
George I, King of Great Britain 59
George III, King of Great Britain 129, 306
George IV, King of Great Britain 18, 222,
  369
Gérard, Etienne-Maurice, comte, Marshal of
  France 205, 310, 375
  and abdication of Louis-Philippe 359
  and Adélaïde 202, 206, 210, 324, 335, 337
  and Belgium 231, 241
  correspondence 7, 207, 237, 241
  Gérard plan for repressing disorder 344–5,
    346, 347, 349
  as minister of war 208, 209
  opposition to four ordinances 158, 162, 203
  as prime minister 245, 248, 272
German states 303
Ghent 80, 82
Girardin, Emile de 330
Gisquet, Henry Joseph 227
La Glaneuse (socialist newspaper) 230
Gontaut, duchesse de 109
Gordon, Major 15
Gordon, Sir Robert 315
Gouvion St Cyr, Marshal 95, 104
Grammont, marquis de 362
Grandvaux affair 255
'green cabinet' 12
Grégoire, abbé 104
Grenoble 71, 104, 244
Greville, Robert Fulke 10
Guernon-Ranville, comte de 128, 132, 136–7,
  138, 146, 147, 208, 210, 265
Guibourg, Achille 236
Guizot, François 92, 95, 100, 121, 148, 275,
  361, 370
  and accession of Louis-Philippe 174
  after 1848 revolution 373–4
  alliance with Thiers 244–5, 254, 259
  character and background 263–5, 322
  charges of corruption against 320, 331
  and Coalition 280–1, 282, 283–4, 286,
    287, 288, 305
  dismissal 351–2
  and *doctrinaires* 205, 207, 260
  as education minister 225, 226, 239, 240,
    247
  and electoral reform 319–25, 339–41